CLARENDON ANCIENT HISTORY SERIES

General Editors

BRIAN BOSWORTH   MIRIAM GRIFFIN

DAVID WHITEHEAD   SUSAN TREGGIARI

The aim of the CLARENDON ANCIENT HISTORY SERIES is to provide authoritative translations, introductions, and commentaries to a wide range of Greek and Latin texts studied by ancient historians. The books will be of interest to scholars, graduate students, and advanced undergraduates.

MARCUS TULLIUS CICERO

Speech on Behalf of Publius Sestius

Translated with Introduction and Commentary

by

ROBERT A. KASTER

CLARENDON PRESS·OXFORD

OXFORD
UNIVERSITY PRESS

Great Clarendon Street, Oxford OX2 6DP

Oxford University Press is a department of the University of Oxford.
It furthers the University's objective of excellence in research, scholarship,
and education by publishing worldwide in

Oxford New York

Auckland Cape Town Dar es Salaam Hong Kong Karachi
Kuala Lumpur Madrid Melbourn Mexico City Nairobi
New Delhi Shanghai Taipei Toronto

With offices in

Argentina Austria Brazil Chile Czech Republic France Greece
Guatemala Hungary Italy Japan Poland Portugal Singapore
South Korea Switzerland Thailand Turkey Ukraine Vietnam

Oxford is a registered trade mark of Oxford University Press
in the UK and in certain other countries

Published in the United States
by Oxford University Press Inc., New York

British Library Cataloguing in Publication Data
Data available

Library of Congress Cataloging in Publication Data
Cicero, Marcus Tullius.
[Pro Sestio. English & Latin]
Speech on behalf of Publius Sestius / Marcus Tullius Cicero;
translated with introduction and commentary by Robert A. Kaster.
p. cm.
Includes bibliographical references and index.
ISBN-13: 978-0-19-928302-6 (alk. paper)
ISBN-10: 0-19-928302-8 (alk. paper)
ISBN: 13-978-0-19-928303-3 (alk. paper)
ISBN-10: 0-19-928303-6 (alk. paper)
1. Cicero, Marcus Tullius. Pro Sestio. 2. Cicero, Marcus Tullius–
Criticism and interpretation. 3. Sestius, Publius. I. Kaster, Robert
A. II. Sestius, Publius. III. Title.
PA6281. S5 2006
875'. 01–dc22   2006008891

Typeset by SPI Publisher Services, Pondicherry, India
Printed in Great Britain
on acid-free paper by Biddles Ltd., King's Lynn, Norfolk

ISBN 0–19–928303–6   978–0–19–928303–3
ISBN 0–19–928302–8 (Pbk.)   978–0–19–928302–6 (Pbk.)

1 3 5 7 9 10 8 6 4 2

collegis carissimis

PREFACE

CICERO defended Publius Sestius against a charge of public violence in early March of 56 BCE, intending to discharge the obligation he owed for Sestius's efforts as tribune the previous year to win his restoration from exile. Because he based his defence on an ample account of recent Roman political history and a 'survey' of the commonwealth's current condition, it is among the longest of his extant speeches. It is also arguably the most important of his political speeches that survive from the nearly two decades separating the *Speeches against Catiline* and the *Second Philippic*.

Though Cicero of course did not know it at the time, it was to be his last significant public performance as an independent political agent before the upheaval that followed Caesar's murder; in little more than a month Caesar and Pompey would meet at Luca, and Cicero would be kept on a short leash until the outbreak of civil war. The speech's account of recent history and of the men who made it, though plainly tendentious and self-serving, provides any student of Rome with a full and fascinating way into the period. Because so much of the account concerns public meetings, demonstrations, and outbursts of violence, it is highly pertinent to the current debate on the place of 'the crowd in Rome in the late Republic'; more generally, the speech—with its energy, drama, and broad scope—is among the best introductions we have to traditional Republican values and ethics in action. Yet though elements of the speech—especially the notorious discussion of *populares* and *optimates* (96–143)—have attracted significant scholarly attention, it is fair to say that the work as a whole has been neglected. Most important, it has received no commentary in any language since H. A. Holden's edition, first published in 1883.

In the translation and commentary that follow I have attempted to meet the needs of two quite different audiences: the readers with little or no Latin whom the Clarendon Ancient History series addresses, especially students who might be coming to Roman forensic oratory for the first time, and more advanced scholars of late Republican history and culture. Inevitably, it has not been possible to serve both audiences at every turn: some readers will surely find parts of the commentary too elementary, while others will find some notes too technical or detailed. But given that another 120 years might pass before the speech receives another commentary, I thought it best to cast my net as widely as possible, and to trust readers to ignore—as readers of commentaries always do—material that does not address their interests.

It is a pleasure now to thank, once again, the people and institutions responsible for fostering my work in 2003–4, when the basic research for this project and most of a first draft were completed: Princeton University and the National Endowment for the Humanities supported a leave of absence for that academic year, while the Institute for Advanced Study's School of Historical Studies—and more personally, Glen Bowersock and Heinrich von Staden—provided the ideal setting and company for a visitor's happy delvings. Susan Treggiari and Miriam Griffin, the Clarendon Ancient History series' Roman editors, first invited my participation and thereafter offered a marvellously helpful combination of encouragement and criticism: my thanks to them especially, and to Hilary O'Shea, whose editorial touch is always impeccable, and to Tom Chandler, whose copy-editing was a marvel of efficiency. I owe thanks also to Cynthia Damon, Denis Feeney, Michael Gagarin, Leofranc Holford-Strevens, John Morgan, and Katharina Volk for consultation and advice on individual points; to Gordon Kelly, for sharing some of his work in advance of publication; and to Margaret Laird for advice on the software used in creating the maps. Harriet Flower, Chris Kraus, and Andrew Riggsby all helped refine the introduction; Ted Champlin, Andy Dyck, Elaine Fantham, John Ramsey, Brent Shaw, Peter White, and Jim Zetzel all variously pushed, prodded, and improved the whole manuscript or large parts of it. I know that none of these readers follows me every step of the way, and where I failed to take their good advice the usual acknowledgements of responsibility apply; Peter requests that I also accept responsibility for any advice from him that I wrongheadedly adopted.

The thanks offered to four of my Princeton friends in the paragraph above are a fraction of the gratitude all my colleagues in the Department of Classics inspire. Their intellectual openness and

mutual respect, their companionship, and their concern for community provide the best sort of setting for teaching and scholarship. It is
a great gift for which I am daily grateful: I hope that by dedicating
this book to them I can make a small return.

R. A. K.

Princeton, New Jersey
31 October 2005

CONTENTS

LIST OF MAPS

ABBREVIATIONS

Reference works and editions cited by abbreviated title are listed below; for works cited by author's surname and date of publication, see 'References'. Titles of ancient Greek and Latin texts are abbreviated according to *OCD*[3]. Cicero's correspondence is cited according to the vulgate system (e.g. *Att.* 3. 4. 5), with the numbering of D. R. Shackleton Bailey's edition added in parentheses after the vulgate book- and letter-numbers (e.g. *Att.* 3. 4(49). 5).

CIL	*Corpus Inscriptionum Latinarum.* 17 vols. Berlin: G. Reimerum. 1863–
CLA	D. R. Shackleton Bailey, *Cicero's Letters to Atticus.* Cambridge Classical Texts and Commentaries, 3–9 (Cambridge: Cambridge University Press, 1965–70)
D-G	W. Drumann, *Geschichte Roms in seinem Übergange von der republikanischen zur monarchischen Verfassung.* 2nd edn. P. Groebe. 6 vols. (Berlin: Gebrüder Bortraeger. 1899–1929)
FS	J. W. Crawford, *M. Tullius Cicero: The Fragmentary Speeches.* 2nd edn. American Philological Association: American Classical Studies, 37 (Atlanta: Scholars Press, 1994)
LTUR	E. M. Steinby (ed.), *Lexicon Topographicum Urbis Romae.* 6 vols. Rome: Quasar. 1993–2000
LUO	J. W. Crawford, *M. Tullius Cicero: The Lost and Unpublished Orations.* Hypomnemata, 84 (Göttingen: Vandenhoeck & Ruprecht, 1984)
MAR	L. Haselberger, et al., *Mapping Augustan Rome.* Journal of Roman Archaeology Supplementary series, 50 (Portsmouth, RI: Journal of Roman Archaeology, 2002)
MRR	T. R. S. Broughton, *The Magistrates of the Roman Republic.* 3 vols. (Cleveland and Atlanta: American Philological Association, 1951–86)
NTDAR	L. Richardson, *A New Topographical Dictionary of Ancient Rome* (Baltimore: The Johns Hopkins University Press, 1992)

*OCD*³	S. Hornblower and A. Spawforth (eds.), *The Oxford Classical Dictionary*. 3rd edn. (Oxford: Oxford University Press, 1996)
OLD	P. G. W. Glare (ed.), *The Oxford Latin Dictionary* (Oxford: Oxford University Press, 1968–82)
*PIR*²	E. Groag, et al. (eds.), *Prosopographia Imperii Romani saec. I. II. III.* 2nd edn. (Berlin: Walter de Gruyter, 1933–)
RE	A. F. von Pauly, et al. (eds.), *Paulys Real-Encyclopädie der classischen Altertumswissenschaft.* (Stuttgart: J.B. Metzler, 1894–1972)
RE Suppl.	G. Wissowa, et al. (eds.), *Paulys Real-Encyclopädie der classischen Altertumswissenschaft*, Supplementbände. 15 vols. (Stuttgart: J.B. Metzler, 1903–78)
RRC	M. H. Crawford, *Roman Republican Coinage*. 2 vols. (Cambridge: Cambridge University Press, 1974)
RS	M. H. Crawford (ed.), *Roman Statutes*. 2 vols. Bulletin of the Institute of Classical Studies Supplement, 64 (London: Institute of Classical Studies, 1996)
Syme *RP*	R. Syme, *Roman Papers*. 7 vols. (Oxford: Oxford University Press, 1979–91)
TLRR	M. C. Alexander, *Trials in the Late Roman Republic*. Phoenix Supplementary volume, 26 (Toronto: University of Toronto Press, 1990)

Introduction

For we know... that Cicero was habitually led by anger or grief to heap up comment on his own feelings in a way that almost exceeds the demands of relevance; still, that he here takes up a lot of papyrus with a rather lengthy account of a very turbulent period seems to bear on the matter at hand in no small way.

The Bobbio Scholiast

Indeed, the year-by-year sequence of events itself grips the mind only moderately...; but an extraordinary man's suspenseful and varied experiences often rouse wonder, anticipation, gladness, distress, hope, fear; if, furthermore, they are rounded off by a noteworthy denouement, the mind draws a full and delightful pleasure from the text.

Cicero, on himself

1. 'THIS DRAMA... OF MY ACTIONS AND THEIR OUTCOMES': CICERO, EXILE, AND THE 'STANDARD VERSION'

As the finest day in the life of Marcus Tullius Cicero came to a close, the scene looked something like this:

It was already evening as he walked through the Forum and up (the Carinae) to his house, his fellow citizens escorting him, no longer orderly and silent but greeting him with shouts and applause wherever he went, calling him the fatherland's saviour and founder. Many a light shone in the narrow streets as people put lamps and torches in the doorways, and women set up lights on the rooftops, too, honouring the man and hoping to catch a glimpse of him as he went up in great ceremony, attended by the noblest men. Most of these had fought great wars and returned home to triumph after extending Rome's dominion over land and sea, but now they walked along murmuring their agreement on this point: though the Roman people owed thanks to many of its leaders and generals for wealth and spoils and power, it had

Cicero alone to thank for its safety and salvation, seeing that he had rescued it from such extraordinary peril.[1]

The day was 5 December 63; the peril, Catiline's attempt to overthrow Rome's civil regime; and the thought 'but not for long' must occur to anyone who imagines that scene with knowledge of the sequel.

That knowledge can lend a sense of inevitability to the chain of events that turned Cicero's happy glory to the despair and disgrace that he experienced as an exile little more than four years later. Certainly, the larger sequence that ran from the triumph of 5 December 63 to the echoing triumph of his return from exile on 4 September 57 had in Cicero's own mind the shapeliness of a necessary, dramatic unity, complete with its distinct acts.[2] But there was nothing inevitable about the congeries of choices, made by many different actors, that led first to Cicero's exile, then to his return, and thereafter to the trial that occasioned his defence of Publius Sestius.

To survey those choices we can begin with the signal date of 5 December, when Cicero brought about the execution, without trial, of the five chief conspirators whom Catiline had left behind in Rome when he set out for his army in Etruria on the night of 8 November. Cicero no doubt believed that he was responding properly both to the 'ultimate decree of the senate' that had been passed already on 21 October, directing the consuls to 'see that the commonwealth receive no harm', and to the senatorial debate held before the executions on 5 December, when the senate put its authority behind the view that the conspirators should die. His action, however, was

---

[1] Plut. *Cic.* 22. 3–4: unlike much in Plutarch's account of Cicero, the picture is surely drawn from a source favourable to the subject; the concluding comparison of victorious generals with a civilian leader, in the latter's favour, resumes a theme famously sounded at *Cat.* 4. 20–2. Unless indicated otherwise, all translations are my own, and all dates are BCE; citations given in the text as numbers enclosed in parentheses refer to sections of the *pro Sestio*.

[2] Thus the letter to Lucius Lucceius, *Fam.* 5. 12(22), from which the epigraph and section-heading above are taken: '(4) It seems to me that a monograph of moderate length could be assembled, from the beginnings of the conspiracy to my return,... (6) this drama, so to speak, of my actions and their outcomes (which) has various "acts" and many changes of both plans and circumstances.' There are many accounts of the period and of Cicero's role in it: for an excellent overview see Wiseman 1994*a*, 346–67, 1994*b*, 368–81; for accounts with a biographical focus, see Gelzer 1969*b*, 97–152, Rawson 1975, 89–121, and Mitchell 1991, 63–168 (Cicero), Tatum 1999, 62–208 (Clodius), Seager 2002, 75–109 (Pompey), Gelzer 1968, 50–101 (Caesar).

plainly contrary to Roman legal tradition. Unlike Catiline and his supporters who had taken the field under arms, these men could not be held to have simply forfeited their rights as citizens, which included the right not to be deprived of life without trial. Those rights had been won with the expulsion of the kings and the establishment of the Republic, and protection from summary execution was guaranteed by the *lex Sempronia* of 123. Cicero was soon, and predictably, attacked for behaviour both illegal and 'regal'.[3]

But actions that were illegal *de iure* did not at all guarantee trouble for Cicero *de facto*. The consul Lucius Opimius, in 121, and again Gaius Marius, as consul in 100, had previously followed out the senate's 'ultimate decree' by using force to suppress citizens deemed 'seditious', and neither had paid a price at law.[4] These were precedents to which Cicero was swift to point, and there was little reason to think he would be called to account as long as the consensus of leading men stood behind him and his action.

Not even the emergence of a fierce enemy, in the person of Publius Clodius Pulcher, need have changed that state of affairs. Differences of character and temperament aside—and it would be difficult to imagine a person less like Cicero than the louche, fashionable, and patrician Clodius—their enmity was rooted in events that Cicero did not initiate and probably could not honourably have avoided. In early December 62 Clodius profaned the rites of the Good Goddess (*Bona Dea*) that were performed annually 'for the well-being of the Roman people': dressed as a woman (the rites were barred to men),

---

[3] On the legal status of the executions, see 11 **domestic enemies** n.; on the criticisms of Cicero, 25 **brought ruin**, 38 **The things**, 109 **'tyrant'** nn. (these and further references in bold type are to items discussed in the Commentary).

[4] Cicero cites both of these precedents already at *Cat.* 1. 4; he refers to Opimius' suppression of Gaius Gracchus and Marcus Fulvius Flaccus (*MRR* 1. 520) in this speech at 140 (n.), alluding also to the fact that Opimius, though prosecuted in 120 for his actions, was acquitted (*TLRR* no. 27); for Marius' action, which led to the death of Lucius Appuleius Saturninus (37 n.) and his followers, see *MRR* 1. 574; Cicero alludes to another possible precedent—the consul Quintus Lutatius Catulus' use of the 'ultimate decree' against his colleague, Lepidus, in 78—only glancingly, at *Cat.* 3. 24. The rioting of 100 did lead—thirty-seven years later—to the trial before the people of Gaius Rabirius for *perduellio* (roughly, 'treason'), in which he was defended by Cicero (see Cicero's extant *Rab. Perd.* with *TLRR* no. 220); at the time of the riots Rabirius was not a magistrate but a private citizen of equestrian status answering the consul's summons to 'protect the commonwealth'.

Clodius stole into Caesar's home, where the rites were being performed by Caesar's wife, who was also allegedly Clodius' lover; his discovery and capture produced a scandal.[5] After a certain amount of dithering and debate the senate decided in the spring of 61 that Clodius should be tried for sacrilege before a specially constituted court, and after a substantial amount of bribery Clodius was narrowly acquitted—but not before Cicero was called as a witness and gave testimony that exploded Clodius' alibi.

Though Cicero and Clodius had clashed before, Cicero had not sought this particular challenge; it is also true, however, that he did not throw the bit once he had it between his teeth. In the months following the trial he repeatedly denounced Clodius as a threat to the commonwealth on a par with Catiline. He affronted Clodius' honour, too, and that of his older sister, by amusing an audience, in public, with a witticism implying that sister and brother were lovers.[6] By the summer of 60, and probably well before, they were enemies of the sort that—in another time and a different culture—might well have settled their differences in a duel. But Roman vengeance generally took less direct, physical forms and preferred to work through communal institutions. So Clodius had to bide his time.[7]

That he found his opportunity at all had less to do with his own devices than with the needs and decisions of much greater men. The greatest of these was Pompey, who landed at Brundisium, after

[5] Sources for the incident and subsequent trial (= *TLRR* no. 236) are reviewed in Moreau 1982, Tatum 1999, 62–86; the phrase 'for the well-being of the Roman people' occurs at *Har. resp.* 12. On the cult and rites see Scullard 1981, 116–17, 199–201, Brouwer 1989.

[6] For Cicero's attacks on Clodius in the late 60s, see 42 **old forces** n. The sexual slur is reported at *Att.* 2. 1(21). 5, from mid-60; on the allegation see 16 **what sort of muscle** n. and App. 2.

[7] If Clodius' interest in seeking plebeian status, and hence the tribunate, was motivated from the start by a desire to take vengeance on Cicero, the enmity on his side was fixed no later than the spring of 61; but that view of his motives is perhaps more simple than secure, see n. 12. The conspicuous laws Clodius passed as tribune in 58 with Cicero as their target tend to obscure the fact that it would have been open to him—or to any other Roman citizen—to prosecute Cicero on any one of several charges any time after 5 Dec. 63: that no such attempt was made, and indeed that Cicero faced no greater consequences than the occasional insult, shows how intricately interwoven political consensus was with what we call criminal law at Rome (see Riggsby 1999), and how fundamentally secure Cicero's position was, until it was too late.

vanquishing Mithradates and settling Rome's expanded holdings in the East, at about the same time Clodius outraged the Good Goddess. For all his prestige as a general of world-historical stature, Pompey cannot have been Rome's happiest man on his return. Earlier in 62, while still away, he had received a long letter in which Cicero, apparently spurred to tactless presumption by the elation of December's glory, boasted of his role as the commonwealth's saviour, probably going so far as to compare his domestic triumph with Pompey's conquests abroad: the letter, which Cicero had not kept private, rankled the general and cast a chill over the two men's relations for some time.[8] But the effrontery of an exultant ex-consul was as nothing compared with the reception Pompey received from the 'Best Sort' (*optimates*), the conservative leaders of the Senate, who had long viewed his rise to prominence—largely outside the path of a conventional senatorial career—with the zesty blend of principled outrage and personal envy that flavoured much of Roman politics.

Having dismissed his army on his return—thereby demonstrating that he was not another Sulla—Pompey had several straightforward needs, chief among them land for his veterans and ratification of his disposition of the eastern territories. None of this was unprecedented, but the 'Best Sort', led by the Metelli, Lucius Lucullus, the orator Hortensius, the younger Cato, and others, would not hear of it: finding the distribution of public land distasteful as a matter of ideology and the satisfaction of Pompey distasteful as a matter of political rivalry, they blocked him at every turn. After the frustrations of a year and more, Pompey was ready to form a political alliance with Caesar, who intended to stand for the consulship in 60, and with his longtime rival, the amazingly wealthy Crassus. The coalition of these three men, informal and (at first) unpublicized, is known inaccurately, but usefully, as the 'First Triumvirate'.[9] Relying on Pompey's

---

[8] The letter is characterized as long and boastful at *Schol. Bob.* 167. 23–9 St. (on *Planc.* 85); its circulation no later than fall 62, and probably earlier, is implied by *Sull.* 67. For Pompey's snub and Cicero's response, *Fam.* 5.7(3). 2–3 (April 62); for Cicero's comparison of his own achievements with generals' conquests, including Pompey's, see n. 1 above. For the relations of the two men more generally, see Johannemann 1935.

[9] The coalition of Caesar, Pompey, and Crassus was distinguished from the later coalition of Octavian, Antony, and Lepidus in that the latter, though also an informal agreement at its inception, received legal sanction through the *lex Titia* of Nov. 43,

veterans and the wealth and clients of Pompey and Crassus both, Caesar was certain to gain the consulship for 59; Pompey for his part could then anticipate the legislation that would bring him what he wanted.

Despite the chill in their relations, Cicero too had a connection with Pompey that went back to their youthful military service together under Pompey's father, and as praetor in 66 Cicero had supported, against optimate opposition, the bill that gave Pompey supreme command against Mithradates. But though he found at least some of the *optimates'* obstructionism wrong-headed, he was too much the senatorial conservative himself simply to part ways with the obstructionists: when Caesar, by then consul-designate, invited him to join the combination with Pompey and Crassus near the end of 60, Cicero pondered, then declined.[10]

As for the sequel, it is easier to state what appears to have happened than to explain precisely why. At least since spring of 61 Clodius had been seeking to gain status as a plebeian with the aim of winning election as a tribune of the plebs, an office from which his patrician birth barred him.[11] Though hindsight has, since antiquity, encouraged belief that Clodius aimed from the outset to use the office as a weapon against Cicero, his motives are likely to have been more complex and shifting;[12] in any case, his bid for the transfer had for some time come to nothing. Then, in April 59, Clodius got his wish: Caesar as consul convened the appropriate assembly, Pompey provided his support as augur, and Clodius' adoption by the young plebeian Publius Fonteius was accomplished, a sham, but a lawful one.[13] Caesar's decision to oblige Clodius—who had after all

establishing 'the Board of Three to set the commonwealth on a sound footing' (*triumviri rei publicae constituendae*). Provided the distinction is kept in mind, there is no harm in speaking of the 'First Triumvirate' or the 'triumvirs', and those terms will be used throughout this book.

[10] The overture from Caesar is mentioned in *Att.* 2. 3(23). 3–4 (Dec. 60); for other positions offered by Caesar in the course of 59, which Cicero declined—and later repented of declining—see *Att.* 2. 4(24). 2, 2. 5(25). 1–2, 2. 18(38). 3, 2. 19(39). 5, *Fam.* 14.3(9). 1, and cf. *Prov. cons.* 41, *Att.* 9. 2a(169). 1 (March 49).

[11] See 15 **transfer** n.

[12] See the judicious review of the evidence in Tatum 1999, 87 ff., esp. 97–8.

[13] On the assembly (*comitia curiata*), convened only for religious purposes, and the procedure (*adrogatio*), see 16 **one of the consuls** n.

violated the Good Goddess's rites in Caesar's house while in pursuit of Caesar's wife—remains a puzzle of the period: Cicero's contemporary correspondence says nothing of Caesar's motives, while in their subsequent writings Caesar has no occasion to comment and Cicero offers different explanations at different times, now blaming Caesar, now partly—but not quite completely—exculpating him.[14] The consequences, in any case, were clear: sometime in the summer Clodius won election as tribune; the promises Pompey reportedly exacted as the price of his support, to the effect that Clodius would do nothing to harm Cicero, came to seem ever less reliable as the year went on; and Cicero grew progressively more apprehensive, first thinking that Pompey was deceived in reporting Clodius' promises, then coming to believe that he himself was the one being deceived.[15] Writing to his brother in late fall 59, Cicero foresaw trouble but expressed hope (*QFr.* 1. 2(2). 16):

Still, it seems that people will not be lacking on my side—they're making pronouncements, offers, promises in quite a marvelous way. As for myself, I have very high hopes and even higher spirits.... But here's how the matter stands: if (Clodius) brings a charge against me, all Italy will gather in my support, so I'll come away with glory heaped on glory; but if he tries force, I expect that I'll be able to meet him with force, thanks to the eager support not just of friends but even of strangers.... Our old band of patriots is on fire with zeal and affection for me, and any who previously stood apart or lacked gumption now find themselves allied with the patriots out of hatred for these kings.

[14] At *Dom.* 41 Cicero says that Caesar's decision was made suddenly and out of pique at certain statements, construed as criticism, that Cicero made while defending Gaius Antonius (n. 37 below). In the present speech Cicero equivocates, saying (16) that 'one of the consuls (viz., Caesar, unnamed) suddenly freed (Clodius) ... either (as I believe) because he had been prevailed upon or (as some thought) because he bore a grudge against me': he at least superficially distances himself from an explanation based on Caesar's hostility and leaves unspecified the cause of the alleged 'grudge'. In *Prov. cons.* 41–2—by which time Cicero's footing has again shifted (see sect. 5 below)—he still equivocates ('he transferred my enemy to the plebs, whether out of anger at me ... or because he had been prevailed upon'), but the reason for Caesar's possible anger is now Cicero's own refusal of the overtures and honors Caesar had extended (n. 10 above). Cf. 16 **either (as I believe)** n.

[15] See *Att.* 2. 19(39). 4 (July 59), 2. 20(40). 1 (mid-July 59), 2. 21(41). 6 (late July 59); cf. *Att.* 2. 42(42). 2, 2. 23(43). 3, 2. 24(44). 5 (all Aug.? 59).

Thus he was confident that—the triumvirs ('kings') notwithstanding—he would meet the threat whatever form it took.

He did not, though again it is easier to summarize what happened than to explain in all particulars why. Among the chief sources of our difficulty is the fact that Cicero's contemporary correspondence gives out with the letter to Quintus just quoted, not to resume until after his departure from Rome in March 58. By the time we learn anything further he is either engaged in retrospective blame-pinning in the correspondence from exile (cf. 46 **some felt** n.) or presenting in the speeches after his return some form of the 'standard version' he had plainly settled on while still away from Rome.[16] The most elaborate of these performances is the one on offer in the present speech. The story unfolds as follows.

After entering his tribunate on 10 Dec. 59 Clodius first promulgated and passed some legislation that—while noxious in Cicero's view—had nothing to do with Cicero himself; then, three and a half months into his term, Clodius promulgated another law, 'on the life (*caput*) of a citizen', intended to punish with exile—retroactively as well as prospectively—anyone who put a Roman citizen to death without trial.[17] The measure's promulgation was greeted (Cicero says) by a great public outcry, massive demonstrations, and demands that the consuls—Aulus Gabinius, a devoted follower of Pompey, and Lucius Calpurnius Piso Caesoninus, Caesar's father-in-law—take action to protect Cicero and thwart Clodius. But Clodius (Cicero alleges) had already purchased the consuls' connivance with a promise of rich provincial assignments, secured by a law promulgated simultaneously with the law aimed at Cicero, and Pompey's impulse

---

[16] Like the versions previously presented in *Red. pop.* (7 Sept. 57) and *Dom.* (29 Sept. 57; cf. also *Pis.*, nearly a year and a half after the present speech), the version offered in *Sest.* comprises the same essential elements as the one Cicero delivered to the senate on 5 Sept. 57, the day after his return to Rome, when he 'spoke from a prepared statement because of the magnitude of the occasion' (*Planc.* 74). Unless we suppose that he drafted the latter during his stately progress from Brundisium to Rome, it should be dated to the latter part of his exile, when his recall was already securely in prospect; in any case, he had by that time surely fixed in his mind the basic version of events served up in these speeches.

[17] On the promulgation and passage of this law, see 25 **public notice was given**, 53 **assembly was asked** nn. For the chronology of all events mentioned in this summary see App. 1; for a good account of Cicero's exile, differing in some details from those in this book, see Kelly 2006, ch. 4.4.

to help was (as Cicero delicately puts it in this speech: 67) slowed. Cicero was left defenceless. After first contemplating armed resistance or even suicide, Cicero resolved—in deliberations prominently elaborated in this speech (36–50)—that it would be the most patriotic course for him to withdraw and thereby spare his fellow-citizens the bloodshed that resistance would bring.

So he went out from Rome on the day Clodius' law was passed (18(?) March 58), leaving behind his wife and children and heading south after a day or two spent at his suburban properties. Within those first few days, as Cicero learned while on his journey, Clodius promulgated a second law, declaring that Cicero had been exiled: once the law was passed, his property would be confiscated, his family rights would be lost, and he could be executed on sight if found within 400 miles of Italy.[18] Making his way ultimately to Brundisium, he sailed for Dyrrachium (mod. Durrës) on 29 April and travelled thence by the *via Egnatia* to Thessalonica in Macedonia. There he was sheltered by Gnaeus Plancius, quaestor of the province, until mid-November 58; then the expected arrival of his enemy Lucius Piso, who would soon take up the province's governorship after his term as consul, caused him to return to Dyrrachium, where he remained for the balance of his time away.

While in Thessalonica and Dyrrachium Cicero relied on his correspondents to track the chief milestones in the effort to secure his recall. These included the first stirrings of senatorial discussion favouring his return, on 1 June 58 (68); on 29 October, the promulgation of a bill for his recall by eight of the ten tribunes of the year—a positive sign, though the bill was not brought to a vote (69); the election of new tribunes for 57, including Publius Sestius and Titus Annius Milo, all said to be loyal to Cicero, and of two new consuls, one of them—Publius Cornelius Lentulus—reliably favourable, the other—Quintus Caecilius Metellus Nepos—a known enemy who had already attacked Cicero for his actions in 63 (70); in fall, further drafts of legislation for his recall (most of which Cicero found

---

[18] On this law see 65 **proposal** n. and App. 3. Cicero first thought of going to Sicily, where he still had friends and clients from his term as quaestor there in 75, but under the law of exile it was too close to home, and the governor of the province warned him off (*Planc.* 95–6, Plut. *Cic.* 32. 2); hence, too, his statement that he could not stay in Malta (*Att.* 3. 4(49)).

deficient) and the good news that Nepos (who also happened to be Clodius' kinsman) had dropped his resistance to Cicero's return; the promulgation of legislation for his recall by the new tribunes after they entered office on 10 December 58, followed soon by strong expression of support for such legislation in the senate's first meeting of the new year, on 1 January 57 (72–4); and the convening of an assembly to vote on the tribunes' law on 23 January (75).[19] But before that vote could be held the assembly was violently disrupted by Clodius' thugs: as Cicero paints the scene, 'the Tiber was filled then with the bodies of citizens, the sewers stuffed, the blood had to be cleared from the forum with sponges' (77). Informed of the outcome, Cicero wrote, in the last of the extant letters from exile, 'I see that I am utterly destroyed' (*Att.* 3. 27(72)).

He was not destroyed, but for his rescue we have no evidence or account until the 'standard version' found in the orations delivered after his return.[20] According to these accounts, the mayhem of 23 January brought the public life of Rome to a standstill, through February and beyond, partly under the oppressive influence of Clodius' lawless gangs, partly as an expression of outraged protest and sympathy on the part of Cicero's allies in the senate. By late spring, however, Cicero's chief ally, the consul Lentulus, was able to mobilize the forces of good order and set in motion the events leading to Cicero's recall. In late May or early June the senate met in the temple of Honos and Virtus, built by Marius, Cicero's fellow native of Arpinum, whose generalship had saved Rome from German hordes just as (the symbolism was not subtle) Cicero's statesmanship had saved Rome from Catiline. There the senate passed a decree directing all provincial governors to insure Cicero's safety (this included not least Cicero's enemy Piso, then governing Macedonia) and bidding the consuls to send letters to the towns of Italy directing 'all who wished the commonwealth's safety' to gather in Cicero's support. During the games in honour of Apollo (*ludi Apollinares*) in July those crowds did gather in vast numbers, to show their favour while

---

[19] For the events mentioned in this speech, see the notes to the relevant sections; on the legislation drafted in the fall of 58, and Cicero's response to it, see 72 **tribunes** n.; on Nepos and the vicissitudes of his relations with Cicero, 72 **his colleague** n.

[20] For the events that follow see 71–92, 116, 128–31 nn. and App. 1, and cf. esp. *Red. sen.* 6–8, 24–8.

the senate, following Pompey's lead, met to pass further supportive decrees. The law restoring Cicero was promulgated, and on 4 August, as the centuriate assembly (*comitia centuriata*) was convened for the vote, Cicero—having been informed that the vote would be held and evidently confident of the outcome—set sail from Dyrrachium and touched Italian soil again at Brundisium the next day. A stately, triumphant procession the length of the *via Appia* brought him to Rome on 4 September, the first day of the Roman games (*ludi Romani*), and to a reception that must have recalled—in a way that suitably rounded off the drama—the glorious scene of his homecoming on the evening of 5 December 63. In the days immediately following, in addresses to the senate and people, Cicero told much the same edifying story (with some variations in nuance suitable for the different audiences), and promised to act in the public interest with the same manly independence he had displayed in the past.[21]

But all was not yet safe by any means. Though he gained restoration of his prized house on the Palatine and compensation for other property that had been confiscated or looted after his departure, Cicero, his brother, and the tribune Milo, his ally, continued to be assailed by Clodius' thugs. Worse, Clodius himself had regained a role in formal public life, not without the support of some senatorial conservatives who still wished to see Pompey thwarted and were ready to use Clodius for that purpose. Although Milo, while still tribune in 57, had managed to obstruct and postpone the elections for curule aedile in which Clodius was a candidate, the elections had finally been held, and Clodius gained office, on 20 January 56. Almost immediately Clodius used Rome's legal institutions to attack the two ex-tribunes who had done most to support Cicero the previous year, bringing Milo to face charges in a trial before the people, and instigating the charges against Sestius that we will examine in the next section.

Now, many of the events just described surely happened much as I have recounted them; but certainly not all. The narrative of events

---

[21] For more or less subtle variations between *Red. sen.* and *Red. pop.* see e.g. 15 **transfer**, 29 **banished**, 34 **alleged purpose**, 50 **boded no good**, 107 **Gnaeus Pompeius** nn., and on the speeches more generally Mack 1937, 18–48, Nicholson 1992; for the assertion of undiminished *libertas*—political independence—that caps both, see *Red. sen.* 36 and *Red. pop.* 25. The latter assertion was made on the same day C. proposed that Pompey be given an extraordinary command to set the grain supply in order, an act that C.'s enemies soon mocked as a betrayal of his principles (e.g. *Dom.* 4).

to the time of Cicero's return to Italy, especially, reflects what I have called the 'standard version', which he crafted to put matters in a way most creditable to himself and most useful in his circumstances after his return. But that version relies significantly on silence, misdirection, and occasionally outright falsehood to achieve its effects, not least in the present speech. These deceptions, and the ways in which they serve the speech's larger strategic aims, are treated thoroughly in the commentary; here I can note several major elements that find suppression of the truth and subtle misdirection working in tandem.

The first of these elements is the role played by the consuls of 58, Piso and Gabinius, who were still off governing their provinces at the time of this speech. Cicero depicts the pair as villains on a par with Clodius:[22] vicious themselves in contrasting but complementary ways—Gabinius patently corrupt in matters both financial and sexual, Piso hypocritically concealing an array of hedonist impulses behind a façade of old-fashioned austerity—the two work, consistently and in unison, to damage both Cicero's interests and the commonwealth's by sins of omission and commission, failing to oppose Clodius once their connivance has been bought by rich provincial assignments and abusing their powers in stifling the protests of Cicero's supporters. The caricatures are very broadly drawn—the career of Piso, in particular, offers nothing to support and not a little to contradict Cicero's portrait[23]—with the aim of taking revenge on two men Cicero counted as enemies, by defaming and humiliating them in their absence.

Yet broad though they are, the caricatures do not lack their more subtle aspects. By stressing the 'pact' for the provincial assignments that the consuls struck with Clodius—a matter that it was properly the senate's to arrange—and their refusal to act on the senate's wishes—despite their proper role (as the 'Best Sort' saw it) as the senate's 'servants'[24]—the portraits line up with and reinforce the

[22] On the caricatures Cicero draws and the elements of invective they comprise, see 18–23 nn.; on Ciceronian invective more generally, Corbeill 1996 and 2002; Craig 2004.

[23] Though in this speech Cicero gleefully anticipates that Piso would be prosecuted for extortion after returning from his governorship (33), he was to be disappointed; subsequently, Piso was elected censor for 50 and exerted a sane and moderating influence in the time just before the civil war: see 19 **The other one** n., ad fin.

[24] On this conception of the magistrates' role, see 137 **magistrates rely** n.

ideology of senatorial supremacy that animates the speech and informs Cicero's political position more generally. Further, the consuls' refusal to follow the senate's lead is linked to the stress Cicero places on their general passivity, as time and again they are described as just 'sitting and watching' while Clodius commits one outrage after another.[25] This emphasis serves another purpose, that of misdirection. For though as a matter of law and precedent there was really very little that a consul in the late Republic *could* do directly to thwart a tribune, constantly recurring to the consuls' passivity tends to deflect attention from the inactivity of others: most notably, Clodius' nine fellow tribunes, all allegedly Cicero's allies, who certainly could have obstructed Clodius' attacks—had those attacks been even nearly as unpopular as Cicero claims.[26] Similarly, by speaking simply of 'the consuls' and describing them as acting in unison from one end of their term to the other, Cicero suppresses the fact that at least one of them—Gabinius—had openly broken with Clodius by the middle of the year.[27] But acknowledging this break would not only disrupt the neat, schematized scenario Cicero had created, it would also, and more importantly, tend to raise uncomfortable questions about the role of another, greater man— Pompey—whose protégé Gabinius was.

For Pompey too had broken with Clodius not long before Gabi-nius;[28] but acknowledging that break would require Cicero to be more forthcoming than he wished to be about Pompey's earlier toleration (at very least) of Clodius' actions and his role in the events leading to Cicero's exile. Not only had Pompey given his support as augur to Clodius' transfer to the plebs; not only had his guarantees of Clodius' good behaviour come to seem to Cicero plainly deceitful; but in the weeks just before Clodius passed the first law aimed at Cicero, Pompey had equivocated with a senatorial delegation seeking his support for Cicero, had rejected Cicero's son-in-law when he came on a similar mission, and had literally turned his back on Cicero

---

[25] For Cicero's attacks on the consuls' alleged passivity, see 33 **consuls sat and watched** n., with *Red. sen.* 11, *Pis.* 9, 10, cf. *Vat.* 18.

[26] On the consuls' position see esp. 25 **all citizens . . .** n.; on the effective limits on tribunician vetoes in this period, Morstein-Marx 2004, 124–8, with further refs.

[27] See *Dom.* 66, 124, *Pis.* 27–8, Cass. Dio 38. 30. 2, and on the date (prob. June), App. 1 at n. 13.

[28] Cf. 56 **Great Mother**, 58 **Gnaeus Pompeius**, 67 **Here at last** nn., with App. 1 at n. 12.

himself, not even bidding him to rise after he had thrown himself at Pompey's feet in abject supplication.[29] When, a few weeks before Sestius' trial, a speaker on the senate floor described Pompey's behaviour in 58 as 'perfidy' (*QFr.* 2. 3(7). 3), he was saying no more than the truth. But to none of this does the 'standard version' refer in any way. To the extent that Cicero acknowledges it at all in this speech, it is only by implication, suggesting that Pompey had been made cautious in his dealings with Cicero by a false tale that Cicero plotted against his life (41); instead of a reference to Pompey's break with Clodius, there is the vague and euphemistic description (67) of Pompey's 'reawaken(ing) his habit of constructive engagement in the people's business after that habit had been . . . slowed by some suspicion'.

Euphemism and deception play a part, too, in characterizing the actions of Cicero's supporters, Milo and Sestius, who unquestionably met the paramilitary forces of Clodius by gathering similar forces of their own.[30] Or to put it in the terms Cicero uses: Clodius relied exclusively on 'brigands' and 'desperadoes' who were 'hired' to 'afflict' the commonwealth and 'drain its blood';[31] Sestius merely 'fortif(ied) himself with supporters in order to conduct his magistracy safely' (79); and both he and Milo did so only when they had been left no other choice (86, 89–90, 92). Here, however, we come squarely to the charge and trial that occasioned this speech, and to the governing strategy that Cicero chose, in which the sorts of deception, misdirection, and euphemism just noted are merely tactics. To these topics we can now turn.

2. THE DEFENDANT, THE CHARGE, AND THE TRIAL

Had Cicero's speech not survived, we would scarcely know less of what Sestius actually did as tribune in 57, because Cicero by design says almost nothing on that subject. He does, however, say a fair

---

[29] On these events, belonging to (prob.) the first half of March 58, see App. 1 n. 6.

[30] Perhaps in part with money supplied by Cicero himself: cf. *Att.* 4. 2(74). 7 with 2 **hired brigands**, 127 *I should not have chosen* nn.

[31] On the terms 'brigands' and 'desperadoes' see the Glossary; on the physical metaphors that Cicero uses to depict the commonwealth as an embodied entity, the better to identify it with himself, see esp. 17 **branded** n.

amount about Sestius' earlier life and career (all cast in terms that support his larger argument), so that he becomes something more than a shadowy figure glimpsed a handful of times in Cicero's other writings.[32] Thus we know that his father, Lucius Sestius, had himself been tribune of the plebs 'at a very favourable time for our community' (6), which is to say, the 90s, the decade in which Sestius must have been born, sometime before 93. When Cicero adds that after his tribunate the elder Sestius 'was less keen to enjoy further office than to be seen worthy of it' (6), he means that the man either was rejected by the voters or chose to withdraw from public service. Either outcome left him free to tend to the family's holdings in Cosa, on the coast of Etruria, where their very substantial shipping enterprise was based.[33] The family's wealth would have assisted the younger Sestius not only when he began his public career but also, earlier, in attracting marriages with two senatorial families: his first wife came from an obscure but respectable family (the *gens Albania*) and gave Sestius a daughter and a son before dying; his second wife belonged to a family of great notability, the Cornelii Scipiones, albeit from a branch that happened at the time to be in disgrace.[34]

Sestius married Cornelia around 68 and not long after gained his first elective office, as a military tribune attached to one of the four consular legions that in this period constituted Rome's standing army. Military tribunes had once been the chief staff officers of a legion's commander, and though by the late Republic the actual military significance of the position had largely been eclipsed by the commander's legates (*legati*), the military tribunate remained an attractive way for a member of a lesser senatorial family like Sestius to gain a foothold in public service from which he could then proceed to further office.[35] And that is what Sestius appears to

[32] On Sestius' earlier life and career, see 6–13 with nn. Cicero thanked Sestius for his public efforts on behalf of his recall immediately on his return, *Red. sen.* 15, 20, 30; on Sestius' efforts behind the scenes, see 71 **Publius Sestius traveled** n. and *Att.* 3. 20(65). 3 with 72 **tribunes...** n. On his activities after this trial, see nn. 38, 78.

[33] See esp. D'Arms 1981, 55–61, with Manacorda 1978 and Will 1979; Richardson 2001 offers nothing new. On the likelihood that the family's shipping interests were tied to wine production, D'Arms 1981, 58.

[34] On the two marriages, 6–7 nn.; on the daughter and son born from the first marriage, 6 **this boy here** n.

[35] On the military tribunate see the Glossary and 7 **military tribune** n.

have done, winning a place as a quaestor for 63 in the elections held in 64 (8–12).

The quaestors were the 'detail men' of Republican administration, assigned by lot to supervise the treasury or grain supply or water supply, or to serve as seconds to the consuls in Rome or to the former magistrates who governed the various provinces. Sestius was assigned to Cicero's colleague as consul in 63, Gaius Antonius. We would like to know whether Sestius by this point had already established relations with Cicero himself. If he had not, he must soon have demonstrated his willingness to provide useful and reliable service, for Cicero in effect set him as a spy upon Antonius, whose involvement with Catiline was strongly suspected. Sestius was present in the senate and received an extraordinary and highly complimentary notice when Cicero first denounced Catiline on 8 November (*Cat.* 1. 21 'this excellent young man here, Publius Sestius'). Then, instead of accompanying Antonius as he marched north to face Catiline in Etruria, Sestius was first sent by Cicero on a military mission to secure Capua (9), only later catching up with Antonius before the final battle with Catiline at Pistoria (12). Cicero exploits these activities early in the speech, to support his tactical linking of Catiline and Clodius, on the one hand, and all efforts to resist them both, on the other.[36]

When Antonius went off to govern Macedonia after Catiline's defeat, Sestius went with him as proquaestor and (it appears) continued to serve as Cicero's confidential informant; yet he evidently found the duty more to his liking than anticipated—indeed, in December 62 Cicero registered surprise that Sestius was now as keen to remain in province as he previously had been keen to return. He remained there, so far as we know, until late 60, when Antonius returned to Rome, and to a prosecution for (probably) *maiestas* ('treason') in which Cicero defended him, reluctantly and unsuccessfully, in spring of 59.[37] But we know nothing of any other activity on Sestius' part until the early fall of 58, when he re-enters the record as a tribune-designate, drafting legislation for Cicero's restoration with the intent of introducing it after he entered office on 10 December. In

---

[36] On the linking of Clodius and Catiline, see 42 **old forces of conspiracy** n.

[37] Confidential informant: see 8 **noticed and reported** n. Cicero's surprise: *Fam.* 5.6.(4). 1. Antonius' trial: *TLRR* no. 241.

the event, it was an initiative that Cicero quickly forestalled, for he found Sestius' draftsmanship woefully inadequate, and that not for the last time.[38] Perhaps Sestius, in Cicero's view, was more a man of action than of words.

It was certainly his actions as tribune in 57 that earned him the repeated thanks he receives as one of Cicero's chief saviors, along with Milo and the consul Lentulus; and it was his actions as tribune that inspired his prosecution, when on 10 February 56 'a certain Marcus Tullius' charged him with *vis*, or 'public violence'.[39] As already noted, we know almost no specific acts that Sestius committed as tribune, and in this speech Cicero designedly and energetically will avoid mentioning any overt act that might have been an object of the charge. Though he spends 6,600 words (in the Latin text) on the events leading up to and following his own departure in 58, and another 2,100 words on the events of 57, when Sestius was tribune, he uses exactly 125 words to describe a single act of Sestius as tribune (79)—and that happens to concern an episode in which Sestius himself was the victim, not the perpetrator, of a violent attack. As we shall see (below and sect. 3), Cicero had a good strategic reason

---

[38] Cicero's critique of Sestius' draft: *Att.* 3. 20(65). 3, *Att.* 3. 23(68). 4; we know that Sestius was in communication with Cicero, advising him to remain in Thessalonica, already in summer 58 (*QFr.* 1. 4(4). 2). Cicero later criticized Pompey's choice of Sestius to draft a sensitive letter to Caesar, *Att.* 7. 17(141). 2 (Feb. 49); cf. also Cicero's mock outrage that some witticisms 'even' of Sestius' (*dicta . . . etiam Sestiana*) were being circulated under his own name, *Fam.* 7. 32(113). 1 (Feb./March 50), and Catullus' complaint (44. 10–21) of the 'chill' he received from reading a speech by Sestius, a 'bad book' that was 'full of poison and plague'.

[39] *QFr.* 2. 3(7). 5: 'a certain Marcus Tullius' reflects Cicero's turn of phrase (*a quodam M. Tullio*) in referring to a man who had the same *praenomen* and *nomen* as he but was certainly no close kin; the 'charge' was, strictly, a 'demand' (*postulatio*) that Sestius appear before the presiding officer, at which point the prosecutor would 'denounce his name' (*nominis delatio*). As the same letter shows, Sestius was also charged on the same day with *ambitus*, or electoral corruption, obviously in connection with his candidacy for the tribunate in 58 (= *TLRR* no. 270): if the trial went forward at all, Sestius must have been acquitted, for the penalties included expulsion from the senate and banishment for ten years (cf. 133 **that law of mine** n.), neither of which Sestius suffered. That the accuser in one case was a member of the *gens Tullia*, the relevant law in the other Cicero's own *lex Tullia de ambitu*, suggests that the knife was being twisted as it was inserted. The interval—33 days by Roman (inclusive) reckoning—between Tullius' initial *postulatio* (10 Feb.) and the trial's end (14 March: *QFr.* 2. 4(8). 1) is comparable to the interval attested for Gabinius' trial for treason (*maiestas*) in 54 (*TLRR* no. 296: *postulatio* no later than 20 Sept., verdict on 23 Oct.).

for proceeding as he did. Yet his strategy does fairly well obscure what the charge took as its target—fairly well, but not completely, for we know the *sorts* of acts that the charge was meant to cover, and we can plausibly draw a few inferences.[40]

Sestius was charged under a law governing acts of 'public violence' (*lex Plautia de vi*). Such legislation came fairly late to Roman public law. The first attested prosecution under the *lex Plautia*, that of Catiline, dates to 63 (Sall. *Cat.* 31. 4). The law itself probably dates to 70, and in any case succeeded and extended the law of 78 passed by the consul Quintus Lutatius Catulus (*lex Lutatia*) in response to the insurrection of his colleague, Marcus Aemilius Lepidus. The legislation was intended to control 'public violence'—violence 'against the public interest' (*contra rem publicam*)—not in the broad sense that any violence among fellow-citizens is 'against the public interest' (as Cicero later found it useful to argue, tendentiously: *Mil.* 14) but as the phrase would reasonably describe a blow aimed intentionally at the community as a whole, a threat to the civil order amounting to, or potentially leading to, sedition or insurrection. A range of acts were covered by the law: engaging in conspiracy to take up arms against the civil regime, as obviously in the case of the Catilinarians; possessing or stockpiling weapons (cf. 34 **temple of Castor** n.) or occupying (strategic) public places (Ascon. 55. 12–13 Cl., cf. 28 **equestrians ...** n.) or forming an armed gang with the intent of committing a bad act (cf. the statement ascribed to the prosecutor at 84); assaulting a magistrate or his house (as Clodius did twice to Milo in 57: 85 **another tribune**, 95 **has assailed** nn.); or attacking even a private citizen or his house, if that citizen's well-being was deemed to be in the public interest (e.g. *Har. resp.* 15). A violent act could be decreed to be 'against the public interest' by the senate; absent that decree—as, clearly, in Sestius' case—it was up to a prosecutor to establish the grounds by plausible argument.

Now, the prosecutor did assert that Sestius assembled an armed posse (84), and because doing so was not per se grounds for a charge,

---

[40] With the following paragraph, on the prosecution's possible case, cf. Alexander 2002, 213–17; the account of legislation on *vis* is based primarily on Lintott 1999*a*, 110–24, Riggsby 1999, 79–84. For actual prosecutions under the *lex Plautia de vi*, see the index in *TLRR* 220; for prosecutions of Catiline's followers that reached a verdict, *TLRR* nos. 226, 228–34, and for the prosecution of Catiline himself, no. 223.

Cicero did not need to deny it:[41] the crucial question was whether the gang had been used to perform acts that could plausibly be described as 'against the public interest', or had been assembled with the intention of performing such acts. About specific acts that Sestius allegedly performed with his gang we know nothing whatever; but two facts we happen to know about the prosecution's case throw light on the imputation of intent. First, one of the witnesses, Publius Vatinius, not only testified against Sestius but also gave the prosecutor transcripts of certain harangues (*contiones*) that Sestius delivered to the assembled people, to be read out in court: presumably the prosecution thought these gave evidence of intent.[42] Second, the prosecutor drew a contrast between Sestius and Milo. The latter had first attempted to prosecute Clodius for 'public violence' before assembling his own posse; if Sestius did not make the same attempt (we can imagine the prosecutor reasoning), he must have had bad motives from the outset. In this light, too, we can appreciate why the only specific episode from Sestius' tribunate that Cicero describes was a violent attack that Sestius himself suffered, for that attack accounts for his motives and establishes a plea of 'self-defence'. As for the comparison of Sestius with Milo, Cicero turns it against his opponents so handily (86–90) that the prosecutor must in retrospect have regretted drawing it: indeed, if Vatinius had been muttering 'from the beginning' that the prosecutor was engaged in 'collusive prosecution' (*praevaricatio*)—mounting his case in such a way as to assist the defence—the way the comparison played out could not have diminished his suspicion.[43]

As was already noted, the charge was lodged, and the process leading to the trial set in motion, on 10 February 56, when 'a certain Marcus Tullius' sought leave to prosecute Sestius. Because Rome lacked the institutions of police and public prosecutor that are

[41] For the possibility that Cicero borrowed money to finance such a posse, see n. 30.

[42] *Vat.* 3, specifying that the transcripts were produced in the course of the prosecutor's speech (*in iudicio*): cf. the analogous documents—the laudatory decree of the Capuan senate and a letter of Cicero's own written during the crisis of 63—read out during Cicero's speech (10–11), though place-holding rubrics stand in for these in the extant text.

[43] *Vat.* 3, referring to the prosecutor, Albinovanus, 'whom you (Vatinius) had judged from the beginning to be a *praevaricator*', sim. *Vat.* 41.

taken for granted in a modern state, all prosecutions were brought at the initiative of individual citizens; by the time of the trial, Tullius' place as accuser had been taken by another man, Publius Albinovanus, supported by one Titus Claudius (*Vat.* 3), who evidently added his name to the charge as a 'subscriber' (*subscriptor*).[44] Unlike some of Rome's 'standing courts of inquiry' (*quaestiones perpetuae*) that had a specific 'inquisitor' (*quaesitor*, usually a praetor) assigned as presiding officer for a full year, the court for 'public violence' had its president chosen by lot as each case was brought: in this case the presiding officer was the praetor Marcus Aemilius Scaurus.[45] For the defence, Cicero offered Sestius his services immediately on learning that the charge had been lodged—even though (as he twice says) he was rather irritated with the man at the time—and indeed on the next day, 11 February, he included a lavish encomium of Sestius in his defence of Lucius Calpurnius Bestia, in the process establishing one premise of his eventual argument.[46] As he makes plain in writing to his brother, Cicero made his offer with the protocols of Roman reciprocity very much in his mind. Because Sestius had assisted him in a time of need, and because Cicero himself had prominently publicized that assistance, he was expected to return the favour when the opportunity arose, and he would be rightly criticized if he did not: appearing in court as the other's 'patron' (*patronus*) or 'advocate' (*advocatus*) was among the most honourable ways to discharge that responsibility. By the time of the trial in early March, the defence had been filled out by Quintus Hortensius and

[44] For these and other details of the trial's personnel see *TLRR* no. 271; Tullius either ceded his role voluntarily to Albinovanus or lost it in the procedure called *divinatio*, in which each would-be prosecutor argued before the court's presding officer why he should be chosen to go forward. For the procedures of the standing courts (*quaestiones perpetuae*), Greenidge 1901, 456 ff., Lintott 2004, 68 ff.; see also at n. 53 below.

[45] On Scaurus, see 101 **your father** n.; at the trial for *vis* at which Cicero defended Caelius a few weeks later (= *TLRR* no. 275), the presiding officer was a certain Gnaeus Domitius (Calvinus?).

[46] Irritation: *QFr.* 2. 3(7). 5, 2. 4(8). 1; we do not know the cause, though it conceivably has to do with an equally mysterious debt of Sestius' mentioned in a letter of 17 Jan. (*QFr.* 2. 2(6). 1). Trial of Bestia on 11 Feb.: *QFr.* 2. 3(7). 6, *TLRR* no. 268, *LUO* no. 49; Cicero alleged that Bestia saved Sestius' life when he was attacked, in the episode that figures in *Sest.* 79 ff. In the present speech too we find Cicero defending one man while praising another who was also facing prosecution: the encomium of Milo at 85 ff. is very much developed with an eye to his defence, which Cicero was assisting, see esp. 71–92 (introd.) n.

Marcus Licinius Crassus—a leader of the 'Best Sort' and one of the 'triumvirs', respectively—and the young orator and poet Gaius Licinius Calvus.[47]

The trial began with the selection of the panel of 'judges' (*iudices*) who rendered the verdict. Since 70, when the *lex Aurelia* replaced the law of Sulla that had entrusted the standing criminal courts entirely to senators, the panels were drawn from pools representing the three wealthiest and most influential categories of the citizenry: senators (largely, the body of current and former magistrates, at this time numbering 600); equestrians (*equites*), men enrolled by the censors in the 18 equestrian centuries of the 'centuriate assembly' (*comitia centuriata*); and 'treasury tribunes' (*tribuni aerarii*).[48] The *lex Plautia* under which Sestius was tried called for the accuser to select a set of judges from each of the three pools, which the defence could then review, rejecting those it wished.[49] The number of *iudices* who heard cases of 'public violence' is not attested before 52, when Pompey's law on public violence (*lex Pompeia de vi*) altered procedures to check corruption; evidence from the other standing criminal courts in the period 70–52 suggests a panel on the order of 75 members, with 25 drawn from each of the three orders.[50] Once the judges had publicly sworn their oath (2 **authority** n.), the participants took their seats in the open air of the forum, the presiding officer and his assistants on the tribunal, the judges facing the benches where the interested parties sat, with the speakers for the prosecution and their witnesses on one side of the court, the defendant, his advocates, witnesses, and

[47] The advocates are named at *Schol. Bob.* 125. 25 St.; on Hortenius and Crassus see 3 **Quintus Hortensius** and 39 **Marcus Crassus** nn.; on use of multiple advocates, 3 **summed up the case** n. Acc. to Plut. *Cic.* 26. 5, Sestius insisted on speaking in his own defence during a trial in which he was represented 'by Cicero and others': if the anecdote—which has Sestius 'wanting to say everything himself and giving no one else a chance to speak'—is not hopelessly garbled or a fiction, the present trial is ruled out, and it must refer to the trial in 52, prob. for electoral corruption (*ambitus*), in which Cicero again defended Sestius (*TLRR* no. 323, *LUO* no. 75).

[48] On the 'treasury tribunes' and their relation to the 'equestrians' strictly so called, see the Glossary.

[49] On the process, called *editio* and *reiectio*, see Berry 1996, 316–17.

[50] Discussion and refs. in e.g. Jones 1972, 69, Marshall 1985, 157, Robinson 1995, 4; on the procedures set by the *lex Pompeia*, under which only 51 of 360 originally empanelled members actually voted, see Jones 1972, 70, and on the extension of those new procedures to all courts, Gruen 1974, 237–9.

family on the other; a *corona* ('garland') of onlookers wreathed this
central tableau and extended as far as the public's interest warranted,
or the speakers' voices could carry. The speaker or speakers for the
prosecution presented their case first, then the defendant's advocates,
followed by any witnesses called to give testimony: we know that
Pompey was present to offer a testimonial on Sestius' behalf;[51] the
prosecution called at least three witnesses, the senator Lucius Aemilius Lepidus Paullus (perhaps curule aedile at the time), an equestrian named Gellius, and Publius Vatinius, who had been tribune of
the plebs in 59 and was now playing an important role in the legal
attack on Sestius.[52] On the day following the witnesses' appearances,
a special session was held in which Vatinius was allowed to make a
statement before being subjected to a fierce interrogation by Cicero,
the invective (with oblique criticism of Caesar) that survives as the
'speech against Vatinius' (*in Vatinium*).[53] Cicero's was thus the last
voice on the defendant's side the judges heard before the case was
entrusted to their verdict, as his speech had been the last delivered for
the defence on the previous day.

3. CICERO'S SPEECH: STRUCTURE, PREMISES, STRATEGY

By the middle of the first century BCE the basic structure of a forensic
speech, as defined by the canons of Hellenistic rhetoric, was thoroughly familiar at Rome.[54] In a fairly brief opening (*exordium*) the

---

[51] *Fam.* 1. 9(20). 7. A decree of the Capuan senate (*decuria*), praising his actions
there in 63, was also read out during Cicero's speech: 10 COUNCILORS' DECREE n.

[52] Anticipating the appearances of Gellius and Vatinius, Cicero included vicious
attacks on both of them in his speech: see 110–11 and 132–5, respectively, with
Schmitz 1985, 100–11. C. says nothing of Lepidus, whose role as a witness is
mentioned only in *QFr.* 2. 4(8). 1, where he is called 'our friend' (*Paullus noster*).

[53] On the procedure, which perhaps grew out of Vatinius' allegation of 'collusive
prosecution' (n. 43 above), see esp. Alexander 2002, 209–12; for the speech see the
still-important commentary by Pocock (1926).

[54] For the rhetorical doctrine on the parts of a forensic speech see Lausberg 1998,
§§263–442. The term 'forensic' (<Lat. *forensis*/'pertaining to the forum') concerns
the public setting in which trials were held, in the civic center of the city (cf. the
rhetorical label *genus iudiciale*, 'the sort (of speech) pertaining to a *iudicium*', the

counsel established the general framework in which the judges were to see the case's most salient features; more importantly, he introduced himself to the judges by beginning to create for himself a character (*ethos*) that would incline the judges to approve him and listen sympathetically. This opening was commonly followed by a prelude to the main argument, a *praemunitio* or 'advance fortification': because the settled disposition of character was thought especially important in judging the likelihood that a given person had committed a given act, the speaker here commonly surveyed the defendant's earlier life and career and established that they were blameless; in so doing he tried to set aside any doubts the prosecutor had raised under that heading, and any other doubts or side issues that might hinder him from presenting the relevant facts of the case in the most useful way. For that was the speaker's job in the speech's central section: to give a statement of the facts (*narratio*) that highlighted the elements most favourable to his side, suppressing or spinning those that were less favourable and generally laying the groundwork for the segment of the speech in which he presented the arguments he thought his version of the facts sustained (*argumentatio*), both to corroborate his own preferred view of the matter (*confirmatio*) and to contradict the prosecution's allegations (*refutatio*). With those ends accomplished the speaker wrapped up his case in a final section, the *peroratio*, summarizing the chief substantive points and, especially, appealing to the judges' emotions, to stir their pity (*misericordia*) for his client's guiltless suffering and often, complementarily, to arouse their righteous indignation (*invidia*) at those responsible for that suffering.

latter term embracing the setting, 'court', the process, 'trial', and the outcome, 'judgement'); the corresponding label derived from Greek, 'dikanic' (<*dikanikos/* 'pertaining to justice (*dikē*)'), concerns the speech's goal. The summary that follows in the text presumes a speech of defence, Cicero's most common forensic mode. On the relation between the expectations of Roman advocacy and Cicero's habits, the essays in Powell and Paterson 2004 provide a helpful survey and further refs.; the essays in May 2002, though organized differently and concerned with Cicero's oratory more generally, are also helpful. For the relation between rhetorical theory and oratorical practice in antiquity more generally, see the essays in Wooten 2001, including Craig 2001, on *Sest.* Other important treatments of the speech as a work of forensic oratory in its context are May 1988, 90–105, and esp. Riggsby 1999, 89–97.

This structure was always more a flexible guide than a straitjacket and as such could be adjusted according to the needs of any given case. In some speeches Cicero uses the form much as it is outlined here.[55] More often he deviates significantly from the 'textbook case': thus, when he defends Marcus Caelius Rufus, also on a charge of 'public violence', several weeks after this speech, the expected 'parts' are all present, but not at all in the expected proportions; rather, the 'advance fortification', which aims to clear Caelius' character while blackening that of Clodius' sister, Clodia, accounts for forty-eight of the speech's eighty sections (*Cael.* 3–50)—no doubt in part because most of the substantive charges had been addressed by Marcus Crassus (*Cael.* 23; Caelius had already spoken on his own behalf, too), but also because Cicero found it easier to speak to Caelius' character than address the remaining charges, and because blackening the character of Clodia, as an anticipated prosecution witness, was a chief goal in the speech. The present speech's deviation from the norm is more striking still.

There is indeed an introduction in which Cicero frames the chief issues of the case (1–2) and starts to create for himself an appropriate character, that of a loyal friend and patriot aggrieved by the persecution of another patriot who has also done him great personal service (3–5). There is a preliminary survey of Sestius' earlier career, which establishes his character in a way useful to his defence (6–13). Cicero does narrate an episode from Sestius' tribunate that (as noted in section 2 above) addresses by implication a substantive aspect of the charge—his intent in gathering an armed force—in a way that combines a positive argument (of self-defence) with refutation of the prosecution (71–92). And there comes the moment when Cicero's 'speech is suddenly checked in its course' (144) by the moving sight of the distraught defendant, his family, and his supporters, and he turns to rouse the judges to pity for them all in a peroration (144–7).

[55] So e.g. the speech on behalf of Sextus Roscius of Ameria that first made his name: 1–14 *exordium* (with a touch of *praemunitio*); 15–29 *narratio*; 37–142, *argumentatio*, including *refutatio* (37–81: arguments based on motive, means, and opportunity) and *confirmatio* (83–142: shifting suspicion to plausible others); 143–54 *peroratio*. The transition between narration and argument comprises a passage of indignation and outraged lament (*conquestio*, 29–34) and a statement of the propositions that the argument will address (*partitio*, 35–6, cf. Lausberg 1998, §347).

But those more conventional segments of the speech account for fewer than forty of its one hundred forty-seven sections. A complete outline of the speech looks like this:[56]

1–5	Introduction
6–13	Review of Sestius' Character and Career
14–92	An Account of the Relevant Events
	15–35 The Events of 59-58: The Attack of Clodius, Gabinius, and Piso
	36–50 A Consular *apologia*
	51–2 A Transition Back to the Narrative
	53–66 The Account of 58 Resumed: Other Acts of 'Criminal Frenzy'
	67–71 The Balance of 58: The Tide Turns
	71–92 The Events of Early 57 and the Defence of Sestius
93–6	A Conclusion, and a Transition
96–135	*optimates*, *populares*, and the Political Condition of Rome
136–47	Conclusion
	136–43 Exhortation
	144–7 Commiseration

Clearly, Cicero is engaged in a defence of an uncommon sort, based on a singular understanding of the phrase 'relevant events'. That understanding determines both the character of the speech's longest section (14–92), from most of which the defendant is entirely absent (Sestius appears only once between sections 15 and 71), and the presence of the excursus (as it is commonly called) on '*optimates*' and '*populares*'. In the balance of this section we will consider the criterion by which Cicero defines relevance, then take up the so-called excursus in section 4.

As in the defence of Caelius, Cicero no doubt gained a certain freedom by speaking last, in this case after three others had preceded him. Cicero's characterization of the speech of Hortensius, who spoke immediately before him, suggests that already in that speech Hortensius had offered a broad summary of the case (3 n.), which in turn suggests that any allegations about specific acts would have been addressed by the first two speakers, Calvus and (as in Caelius' trial)

---

[56] For somewhat different formal analyses of the speech, see May 1988, 90–105, MacKendrick 1995, 198–204; for more detailed analysis of 96–135, the 'excursus' on *optimates* and *populares*, see sect. 4 below.

Crassus. But merely having freedom does not determine how one uses it; on that point it seems clear that Cicero had decided to use his freedom to develop a unified, comprehensive, and bold strategy that can be seen to account for every element of the speech. The strategy simply takes at face value the premise of the charge of 'public violence'. If the violence in question was 'against the public interest' (*contra rem publicam*: sect. 2), then perpetrating it was by definition a blow against the body politic, a political crime in the deepest and broadest sense of the phrase. The charge was thus a political charge justifying a political defence in what was fundamentally a political trial.[57]

This is the reason that the 'standard version' of Cicero's travails becomes the backbone of the speech, putting those travails before our eyes in the most complete surviving form.[58] Because the charge against Sestius alleged acts of public violence detrimental to the common-wealth that he performed as tribune, Cicero must give an account of his tribunate; because Sestius' '*entire* tribunate sought *only* to support' Cicero's welfare (a point he could not have put more emphatically: 14), he must give an account of how his own welfare came to be imperiled; and because Sestius could not be convicted of public violence for supporting Cicero's welfare if his welfare could be shown to be indistinguishable from the commonwealth's, the account of how Cicero's welfare came to be imperilled must be indistinguishable from an account of how the commonwealth's welfare was imperilled.

This imperative controls the selection and treatment of all the most salient details in the speech. If in the survey of Sestius' earlier life Cicero stresses his loyal attachment to older, authoritative men and his vigorous actions in suppressing the Catilinarians (6–12), he does so not just because such attitudes and actions are praiseworthy in themselves but because they anticipate Sestius' loyal attachment to another older, authoritative man—Cicero—in circumstances where (as we are repeatedly told) the crimes of Clodius and his 'henchmen' merely continue the crimes of Catiline (see esp. 42 **old forces** n.). If the narrative of the events of 58 stresses that outrageous laws were passed on every front (33, 55–7) or that the consuls abused their

---

[57] See above all Riggsby 1999, 79–84, and 2002*a*, 189 ff.

[58] *On His Times*, the poem in three books begun later in 56, must have been more detailed still, but the general shape and orientation would have been the same: cf. 70 **Publius Lentulus**, 71 **bad omens** nn.

powers in punishing individual citizens while abdicating their proper role as the 'ministers' of the senate (25 **all citizens**, 29 **banished**, 137 **magistrates** nn.), it does so not just because the laws passed or the consuls' failings were deplorable in themselves, but because they cumulatively demonstrated that the institutions and mechanisms crucial to the civil community's proper functioning had been smashed. And if Cicero himself is ever to the fore, it is not just because he is ever his own favourite subject: rather, if the attacks upon himself undermined the commonwealth, if his expulsion laid it low, if his restoration revived it, if in fact the commonwealth's interests differed in no important way from his own—all propositions repeatedly advanced in this speech—then virtually no action on Sestius' part to secure his return could be 'against the public interest'.[59] Instead, as Cicero will nearly propose (83), the people should raise a statue of Sestius in the forum.

Cicero surely did not find it an alien or unpleasant chore to equate his welfare with the commonwealth's, for it is something he does repeatedly in public statements after his return.[60] Yet Cicero's predilections should not obscure the fact that this approach was the most effective blanket defence he could offer Sestius. Nor should they distract attention from an aspect of his argument that both shows it to be something more than self-aggrandizement raised pathologically to the level of principle and at the same time underscores several important ideological points.[61] That aspect is made plain, for example, by the following passages:[62]

[59] For the propositions noted, see e.g. 5, 12, 24, 27, 31–3, 49–50, 53–4, 60, 71, 73, 83–4, 87, 112, 128–9, 144–5, 147, and cf. *Schol. Bob.* 125. 31–126. 3, 128. 24–8 St., Alexander 2002, 214.

[60] e.g. *Red. sen.* 4, 25, 32, 36, *Red. pop.* 25, *Dom.* 1–2, 87, 99, 137, 141, *Vat.* 8, *Har. resp.* 15, 45, 47. Stressing the importance of this identification in *Sest.* is the signal contribution of May 1988, 90–105; cf. also Graff 1963, 34–5, Habicht 1990, 50; the importance is well appreciated at Craig 2001, 116–17.

[61] On 'Cicero's conceit' the fundamental discussion is Allen 1954, who shows that Cicero was not generally regarded as exceeding the very generous limits placed on self-praise in Roman elite culture; that he often displays sensitivity to the generally accepted norms; and that when self-praise cannot be avoided, he justifies it by the well-established aristocratic principle of having to maintain his 'worthy standing' (*dignitas*); cf. also Graff 1963, 77–80. On 'self-reference in Cicero's forensic speeches' more generally, see the helpful survey in Paterson 2004.

[62] Cf. also 31–3, 38, 74, 120–3; on the chronology of the passages cited, see the notes ad loc. and App. 1.

27 'what greater distinction could anyone find in all history than this, that all patriots, on their own and in concert, and the entire senate, as a matter of public policy, took on the dress of mourning for one of their fellow-citizens?' (referring to the intercalary month in 58, before his departure);

50 'the commonwealth had a crucial stake in my staying alive (as many men said in the senate while I was away (cf. 129)), and I was for that reason commended to the protection of foreign peoples by letters sent by the consuls in accord with the senate's resolution' (May/June 57);

73 'Accordingly ((Lucius Cotta) went on), because by my absence I had rescued the commonwealth from perils no less great than on a certain occasion when I had been present, it was appropriate that I be not just restored by the senate but also honored' (1 Jan. 57);

121 '... I whom Quintus Catulus and many others in the senate had called 'father of the fatherland'';

128 'For did the senate ever commend any citizen, save me, to the protection of foreign nations... ever express formal thanks to the Roman people's allies for any citizen's well-being, save mine? In my case alone did the conscript fathers decree that provincial governors with the power of command, together with their quaestors and legates, safeguard my life and well-being. In my case alone, since the founding of the city, did the consuls send letters, in accordance with the senate's decree, to call together from the length and breadth of Italy all who desired the commonwealth's safety: what the senate never decreed when the commonwealth as a whole faced danger it thought it must decree to preserve my well-being alone' (May/June 57);

129 'the hero (viz., Pompey)... bore witness, in a prepared statement of his views, to the fact that I alone had saved the fatherland... Why note that a packed meeting of the senate so fully aligned itself with his statement that only a single enemy of the people dissented, and that very fact was entrusted to the public records, so that generations to come would ever remember it... the senate decreed that no one was to watch the heavens for omens, that no one was to bring to bear any cause for delay, and that if anyone did otherwise, he would patently be seeking to overturn the commonwealth: his act would be regarded most

gravely by the senate and be made the subject of discussion in that body. ...' (July 57).

We should note first that there is no reason to doubt that these statements are true as matters of fact. We know, for example, that copies of the senate's decrees were not only stored in the treasury (*aerarium*) but also posted in bronze, allowing them in principle to be confirmed 'by generations to come', as Cicero says; we also know that the senate and people had previously assumed mourning dress to mark a public catastrophe, and we know they would do so in the future, but it appears that they had in fact never done so in response to an individual's misfortune—and by doing so they did indeed signal that the individual's misfortune was tantamount to a public catastrophe.[63] Second, such passages show that Cicero's premise in the speech, identifying himself and his interests with the commonwealth and the public interest, did not involve self-aggrandizement at all, if by that is meant inflating one's worth beyond some generally recognized assessment: the generally recognized assessment was exactly that his well-being was identical with the commonwealth's. Nor did his premise involve boasting, if that means engaging in self-praise and making proud claims about one's abilities or status. Cicero was neither praising himself nor making claims of his own; he was *reporting* what others had said of him in praise, for the most part as matters of the formal public record; and what others had said of him in praise quite clearly provided him with the basis for his defence. Viewed in terms of Republican ideology, the acts of praise he records were no more or less than the patriot's just reward, the good opinion that good men spread abroad about him (*bona fama bonorum*: 139 n.): by recalling that praise, Cicero was merely wearing the public character he was entitled to wear, and he was wearing it in a cause that stood very near the top of the Roman hierarchy of moral imperatives, 'warding off the perils' that had been launched against one 'who had most earned (his) gratitude' (2).[64]

---

[63] On the assumption of mourning dress see 26 n. Cicero in fact seems rather scrupulous in reporting such testimony: see 121 n., on the title *pater patriae*, which he conspicuously, and with good reason, does not claim was first bestowed on him, or bestowed by senatorial decree.

[64] On this imperative see 2 **thanking** n.

Now, it is certainly true that the praise Cicero reports cannot have been the simple, transparent, unanimous, and spontaneous thing that he represents it as being. He neglects to mention, for example, that when the people and the senate adopted mourning to show their support in 58, they were following his own lead, for he had assumed mourning after Clodius promulgated the first law aimed against him—a move that Cicero himself later came to regard as a tactical error, as his correspondence from exile shows.[65] And whatever was going through Pompey's mind on the day in July 57 when he read from a prepared statement to declare Cicero the commonwealth's unique saviour, it surely cannot have been simple; for that declaration was very much like the claim that, when communicated to Pompey by Cicero himself early in 62, had put a frost on their relations, and Pompey himself was the man who had most flagrantly betrayed Cicero during his crisis. But such considerations did not matter in the Roman economy of praise. In this economy, praise was a commodity, a thing of value traded back and forth. Like a piece of currency put into circulation, it became fungible, and the recipient was free to spend it as he thought best suited his needs. In this instance those happen to be the rhetorical needs created by Cicero's chosen strategy.

Far more important than their spontaneity or authenticity is the fact that the acts of praise Cicero records—the quasi-ritual gestures of public mourning, the decrees and letters—were *acts*: visible, public, and memorable performances of consensus.[66] In that respect the evidence that Cicero presents throughout the speech not only corroborates the premise on which his main strategy rests but also puts before us, as it put before the judges at the trial, images of Roman public life as it should be, when the civil community is unified in agreement and acts out that agreement as one body in dramatic and

[65] *Att.* 3. 15(60) (17 August 58) 'I was blind—blind, I say—in assuming mourning dress and in calling upon the people'; cf. 53 **assembly was asked** n.

[66] On the performative aspects of Roman public life in the Republic, including forensic oratory itself, with different readings of their political significance, see e.g. Nicolet 1980, 343–81, Axer 1989, Vasaly 1993, Flower 1996 and 2004, Leach 2000, Gunderson 2000, Flaig 2003, Bell 2004, 199 ff., Steel 2005; on assemblies of the people (*contiones*), see 28 n.

unambiguous terms.[67] Just such consensus is Cicero's theme in the least expected and most notorious segment of the speech, the so-called excursus on *optimates* and *populares* that dominates the last third of his defence. To that segment we can now turn.

4. 'TRANQUILLITY JOINED WITH WORTHY STANDING'

As we have already seen, both the prosecutor and Cicero invoked Milo as an example in their speeches, the former evidently to draw a contrast with Sestius, the latter to establish a parallel. In the process, the prosecutor had remarked the fact that Milo's attempt to prosecute Clodius late in 57 had been frustrated by none other than the 'breed of the Best Sort' (*natio optimatium*: 96)—the senatorial conservatives— with whom Cicero was most closely aligned.[68] Seizing dramatically upon the phrase, Cicero takes the opportunity to present 'an excellent lesson for the younger generation... and one that it is... not inconsistent with our listeners' advantage, (the judges') duty, and the case of Publius Sestius itself'.[69] The excursus that he then develops has commonly been read as a freestanding political 'manifesto' (96–143).[70] Its argument can be summarized along these lines:

[67] Cf. 118 the people as a body n., on the phrase *populus* (*Romanus*) *universus* that Cicero uses repeatedly when describing the demonstrations in his favour in the spring and summer of 57.

[68] On the two sides' invocation of Milo, see above in the text at n. 43. That the prosecutor used the phrase *natio optimatium* with ref. to Milo's frustrated prosecution is clear in the context (95 by the senate's authority n.; differently Alexander 2002, 214, though his general view of the 'excursus' is substantially in harmony with that developed here). The exact tack the prosecutor took is of course unknown, but a plausible form of words is not difficult to imagine (96 No doubt n.), and there is in fact good reason to think that Hortensius himself—optimate leader and member of Sestius' own defence team—had aided in that frustration at a meeting of the senate on 14 Nov. 57 (95 by the senate's authority n.). The sting of the prosecutor's phrase lay in the noun *natio*, 'breed' or 'tribe': see 96 'breed of the Best Sort' n.

[69] *Sest.* 96; concern to provide a 'lesson for the youth' appears first expressly at 51, cf. also 14 for our youth n.

[70] See e.g. Meyer 1919, 135 n. 2 ('politische Broschüre'), Wood 1988, 63 ('platform for the *optimates*'), Christes 1988, 303 ('programmatischer Teil'), Wiseman 2002, 292–3 ('manifesto'). On the segment's 'political thought', esp. the phrase 'tranquillity joined with worthy standing' (*cum dignitate otium*): Boyancé 1941, Wirszubski 1954,

Public affairs at Rome have always been contested by men of two sorts (96): 'men of the people' (*populares*), who sought to please the many, and 'men of the best sort', who sought the approval of 'all the best sort of men'. The latter category, properly understood (and despite the label's aristocratic overtones), is 'beyond counting', including all 'who do no harm, are not wicked or rabid in their nature, and are not hobbled by embarrassments in their domestic affairs (i.e. bankruptcy)' (97). These good people are guided by their leaders (i.e. the senate: 137) toward the common goal of 'tranquillity joined with worthy standing' (*cum dignitate otium*: 98), a personal and communal state in which the best men serve the public interest and enjoy the appropriate reward of personal prestige.

True, the opponents of the best men—the 'desperadoes' and their leaders (i.e. Clodius)—act with great energy in setting snares for patriots (100); yet there are examples for patriots to follow (101–2: those named chiefly include two of the presiding praetor's ancestors). More important, though there have been times when patriots and the people were at odds (103–5, referring to the period from the 130s on), those times are evidently, blessedly, behind us. *Now* the whole civil community is united, as it should be, and the wicked have only the 'hired henchmen' on whom they can rely (104–6): the wicked thus are isolated, a small though pestilential force distinct from the unified and healthy body politic.

Indeed, to gauge their isolation, to appreciate the fact that the 'Best Sort' (*optimates*) now are truly 'popular' (*populares*), one need only consider the 'three places where the Roman people's judgement and desires touching the commonwealth can be expressed' (106): the assemblies of the people (*contiones*), where the representatives of the Best Sort are heard with great approval and rapt attention while their opponents are received coldly (106–7); the voting assemblies (*comitia*), where patriots receive the favour of election they have earned while the supposedly 'popular' candidates go down to equally deserved, and humiliating, defeat (108–14); and the theatrical shows (*ludi*) and gladiatorial contests where 'the Roman people as a body' repeatedly shower the Best Sort with admiration, and show their

Fuhrmann 1960, Balsdon 1960 (with Lacey 1962), André 1966, 295 ff., Weische 1970, Adomeit 1980 (with Lübtow 1984–5), Christes 1988, Takahata 1999, Dalfen 2000.

support for Cicero's recall, while the others, when they venture to appear at all, barely escape alive (115–27).

With his central contentions thus established, Cicero concludes (127–32) with a defence of himself and the Best Sort. He then returns to his point of departure by exhorting the youth with a profoundly conservative defence of the status quo (136–43): let them follow the 'one path...approved by patriots...(which) lies in understanding that the civil community was organized in the wisest possible way by (their) ancestors', with the senate placed at its head, the people's elected magistrates as the senate's 'ministers', the whole edifice supported by the equestrian order and all the other categories of the citizen body in harmonious cooperation.

This 'lesson for the younger generation' has commonly been read, independent of the rest of the speech, as a serious exercise in political thought; and read as such, it is has been condemned as barren.[71] This is not unfair; indeed, if the argument truly aimed to offer a serious lesson in political thought—or even a politically serious 'programme'—it would be a good deal worse than merely barren. Quite apart from the doubtful proposition that more of the status quo was all the commonwealth needed to ease the strains under which its political system was plainly labouring, Cicero's account suffers from several obvious formal flaws. It is grossly tendentious on matters general and specific: on the one hand, its definition of the 'Best Sort'—so broad as to include all who are not actually criminal, insane, or bankrupt—bears no relation to the denotation and connotation of *optimates* in the contemporary political culture; on the other hand, the 'survey' of the voting assemblies it offers is so intent on contrasting the assembly of the plebs (*concilium plebis*), which voted the law for his exile, with the timocratic centuriate assembly (*comitia centuriata*), which voted the law for his recall, that it completely ignores the tribal assembly of the people as a whole (*comitia tributa*) that was the usual site of consular legislation, including not only his own legislation of 63 but also—rather embarrassingly for his argument—Caesar's agrarian legislation of 59, still the target of optimate loathing. It is also far from lucid in its explanatory moves, or seamless in its construction. If the contrast between 'popular' and 'optimate'

---

[71] See esp. Balsdon 1960.

politicians that has 'always' existed at Rome (96) has 'now' been replaced by a state of affairs in which the *optimates* are truly popular and everyone—apart from the 'hired henchmen'—agrees enthusiastically on matters of public interest (106), we should very much like to know why, beyond the bland and incredible assertion that the people 'have no reason to dissent' (104, cf. 106 **our civil community** n.); and if the present unanimity is all that Cicero assures us it is, then the old contrast between 'popular' and 'optimate' paths that reasserts itself to give his exhortation of the young a rousing finale (138–9) is at best beside the point, if not actually contradictory. But such contrasts and other clichés, old and new, are the bone and sinew of this segment as a whole. The 'harmony of the orders' (*concordia ordinum*) and 'consensus of all patriots' (*consensio omnium bonorum*) to which the finale alludes are among the most familiar of Ciceronian shibboleths, here mirrored at the outset by the relatively new coinage, 'tranquillity joined with worthy standing'.[72] The very move with which he begins—presenting the distinction between 'popular' and 'optimate', only to collapse it almost immediately—is among the more conspicuous recurrent gestures in the 'post-return' speeches more generally, and a variation on a basic premise of many speeches before the assembled people in the late Republic: that the important distinction lay not between *optimates* and *populares* but between 'true' and 'false' *populares*—those who really had the people's interests at heart (oneself and one's allies) and those who claimed to do so out of self-seeking motives (the other side).[73]

---

[72] For an ideal 'harmony' binding together members of all classes—even contented slaves—under the senate's benevolent leadership, see esp. *Cat.* 4. 15–16, with Wood 1988, 193–4, and cf. 97 **even freedmen**, 106 **our civil community** nn.; Cicero is more typically concerned with the *concordia* of the two most prestigious orders, senators and equestrians (cf. *Att.* 1. 14(14). 4, 17(17). 9, 18(18). 3, with Mitchell 1979, 197–205). The phrase 'tranquillity with worthy standing' (*cum dignitate otium*: cf. n. 70) appears as such for the first time here in Cicero's extant works, and thereafter in the same form (or as *otium cum dignitate*) at *De or.* 1. 1, *Fam.* 1. 9(20). 21. But already at *Red. pop.* 16 *otium* and *dignitas* stand together, joined with *salus* ('well-being'), as the gifts Pompey has bestowed on Cicero individually and on the commonwealth as whole (cf. also *Leg. agr.* 2. 9); and that is in complete accord with Cicero's conception in this speech (98), where *cum dignitate otium* is expressly the goal *not* of statesmen only (*optimates* in the normal, narrow sense of the term) but of all who are not 'desperadoes' (*optimates* in the broad sense Cicero develops in 97–8).

[73] On 'popular' vs. 'optimate' in the post-return speeches, see Riggsby 2002*a*, 183; on the basic premise and its 'ideological monotony', see the important discussion of

All of which is to say that this segment looks much less like a serious exercise in political thought than what it is in fact: a tendentious and deceptive part of a tendentious and deceptive speech, aiming to achieve a practical goal. Whatever Cicero hoped that 'the youth' would collectively take away from this lesson, they were not its primary audience. That audience was the wealthy and conservative panel of judges, to whom it told a story they would have wanted to hear, and one that was of a piece with the strategy that shapes the rest of the speech. It is a fundamentally optimistic story: the old ways are the wisest and the status quo is the best; the 'desperadoes' and 'hired henchmen', though neither few nor weak, have no legitimate role in the civil community and should be removed; and the cause for optimism is confirmed by the 'survey' demonstrating the popularity of the *optimates*. To be sure there is still work to be done to make the civil community fully whole (specifically, getting rid of the 'hired henchmen': see 106 n.). But the judges are to understand that much progress has been made, both in isolating the 'desperadoes'—as a group apart from the far larger group that enjoys consensus—and in restoring a commonwealth that had been battered and overthrown by Cicero's departure. In this respect the 'excursus' simply extends and reinforces Cicero's basic argument: all of Sestius' acts on his behalf, like the acts of all his supporters, were intended, at the same time and indistinguishably, to restore the commonwealth. In this respect, too, it is fitting both that Sestius should appear prominently, near the end of the survey, as a recipient of thunderous popular favour (124), and that the events leading to Cicero's return should be incorporated, not as linear narrative like the narrative leading to his departure (15–50), but in episodic fragments that support his story of a consensual community restored (see esp. 107–8, 127–31). To the extent that Sestius' acquittal meant that the judges accepted Cicero's argument, we can understand why, in reporting the verdict to his brother, Cicero

Morstein-Marx 2004, 203–40; the premise's distinction between 'true' and 'false' *populares* is further reflected in this speech by the distinction Cicero draws (106–7) between 'true' and 'false' assemblies of the people (*contiones*). This segment is of course not the only part of the speech in which Cicero relies on clichés for persuasion's sake: see esp. 91 **who among us** n., on the commonplace account of the origins of human civilization capping his argument on the matter of self-defence.

said, 'Our friend Sestius was acquitted...and—*a point that was crucial for the commonwealth, to make clear that there is no disagreement in a case like this*—he was acquitted by the judgement of all' (*QFr.* 2. 4(8). 1). The unanimous verdict enacted the consensus of patriots that Cicero in this segment of the speech does his brilliant best to construct.

The foregoing remarks also imply a position on one other question that must be addressed: was this segment already included in the speech Cicero delivered, or is it a 'manifesto' written and 'stitched into' the speech after he had delivered it? The latter view is understandable (I once assumed as much myself).[74] As a glance at the outline of the speech makes plain (p. 25), it would be possible to move directly from the end of section 92, where Cicero concludes his remarks strictly pertinent to Sestius, to a peroration something like the one we find in 143–7: if we had a text in that form, no critic would posit a lacuna where the present discussion now stands, because nothing necessary would appear to be lacking. It does happen, of course, that Cicero introduces the discussion as a response to the prosecutor's use of the phrase 'breed of the Best Sort' and apparently responds to other remarks from that quarter (127)—though such touches do not strictly guarantee that the discussion was originally part of the speech: they could have been inserted to lend verisimilitude to the charade, as Cicero went about his work in a later period of leisure;[75] and one could similarly explain the fact that the discussion continues the basic strategy of Cicero's defence. Yet such argumentative continuity seems to pose a larger problem for the 'stitching' hypothesis than performance gestures like the response to the prosecution; for if the remarks in substance and strategy are not just 'consistent with' the earlier defence (as Cicero promises: 96) but continue and extend it in different form, there seems less reason to regard that form as alien to the original

---

[74] So e.g. Wiseman (cited n. 70), and many before (see the refs. at Stroh 1975, 51 n. 89).

[75] Compare e.g. the scores of occasions on which Cicero puts questions to the judges, or asks them to listen (recall, look, consider, etc.), in the five speeches of the second *actio* against Verres—speeches written after the trial was over, and never delivered.

structure. Further, the extended attacks on two witnesses who tes- tified against Sestius—Gellius (110–11) and Vatinius (132–5)—also more likely originated in the immediate circumstances of the trial than in a later supplement.[76]

But a different consideration should persuade us, finally, that something very much like this 'lesson' was originally included as part of the speech. It is psychologically incredible that Cicero— having described at length the outrages and humiliations attending his departure—would forgo the opportunity to celebrate the tri- umph of his recall, a celebration found in every other recitation of the 'standard version'; at the same time, it is rhetorically incredible that he would elide that triumph in a speech where his recall is strategically equated with the restoration of the commonwealth. And as already noted, that triumph is deeply embedded, as argu- mentative support, in the analysis of 106–31. One could of course posit that the recall originally received a different treatment, later replaced by the excursus; but what would be the gain?[77]

5. EPILOGUE: AFTERMATH

After his unanimous acquittal on 14 March, Sestius slipped from history's centre stage, reappearing as an actor only episodically there- after. He remained in the senate and in public life, winning a term as

[76] At *Vat.* 1, delivered the day after this speech, Cicero says (disingenuously) that he was 'perhaps less restrained than (he) should have been a little before now' (*paulo ante*): if he refers to the attack in 133–5, as the most economical inference suggests, it guarantees that that segment, at least, was part of the original speech. Note also that C.'s remarks at *Clu.* 139 do not encourage belief that he would insert a purely personal 'manifesto' in a forensic speech.

[77] As a formal consideration of secondary importance, note that one transition in this section is a miracle of clumsiness (127 **Do *you* try** n.): had Cicero worked up the excursus at leisure, he could surely have done better. Note also that any supposed 'stitching' would have to have been done very quickly, since the barely concealed hostility to Caesar running through the speech (see esp. 16 **either (as I believe)**, 132 **a gentle person** nn.) shows that it must have been in circulation before Cicero's public stance toward Caesar shifted after the meeting at Luca (next sect.). *Dom.*, another speech Cicero thought a boon to 'the youth', went into circulation soon after it was delivered (*Att.* 4. 2(74). 2).

praetor (probably) no later than 54 and incurring in the process a charge of electoral corruption against which Cicero would defend him, once again, in 52. After the effective beginning of the civil war in January 49 he was assigned a command in Cilicia by the senate but went over to Caesar after the defeat of the Pompeians at Pharsalus; the connection with Caesar allowed him occasionally to serve as mediator between the dictator and Cicero, with whom he remained in close touch and who, for his part, is still found expressing loyal gratitude for Sestius' old services when seeking a favour on his behalf a decade after this trial. He was active in the senate at least until 39; if he lived into his seventies, he could have seen his son, Lucius, who still wore the bordered toga of a child in March 56, take on the bordered toga of a consul in 23, after being named to succeed Augustus in that office.[78]

Cicero, though he hardly guessed it at the time, was barely a month removed from the political marginalization that would last for more than a dozen years.[79] It was a busy month. The satisfaction that he registered when reporting Sestius' verdict to Quintus cannot have been diminished by his successful defences, late in March and at the very beginning of April, of Publius Asicius and Marcus Caelius Rufus, both on charges emerging from the murder of the Alexandrian ambassador Dio; in the latter case he also extended his campaign to humiliate Clodius, by slandering his sister famously and

[78] Praetorship: *MRR* 2. 222; Badian 1984*b*, 106. Trial in 52: see n. 47 above. Cilician command: *MRR* 2. 264. Relations with Cicero: see e.g. *Att.* 5. 17(110). 4 (mid-Aug.? 51), *Fam.* 5. 20(128). 5 (Jan. 49), 6. 10a(223). 1 (Sept.(?) 46), *Att.* 13. 7(314) (June 45), 14. 1(355). 2 (April 44), 15. 27(406). 1, 29(408). 1 (July 44), 13a(417). 1 (Oct. 44), *MBr.* 2.5(5). 4 (April 43); for Cicero's favour, *Fam.* 13. 8(321). 3 (Nov. 46 / Sept. 45?). Time in senate: Reynolds 1982, 63–4 (on the date), 69–71. On young Lucius: 6 **this boy here** n.

[79] For the chronology of the following events, with full references, see App. 1. The story of Cicero's reining in has often been told: for a standard account, see e.g. Gelzer 1969*b*, 157–68, Rawson 1975, 127–30, Wiseman 1994*b*, 393–4; for a different view, Mitchell 1969 and 1991, 168 ff. It must be acknowledged that several crucial events in this month (Cicero's participation in the senate discussion of 5 April, the interview between Pompey and Quintus in Sardinia), together with Cicero's own rationale for his actions, are not attested before *Fam.* 1. 9(20), a long *apologia* written two and a half years later, to justify his shift in political behavior to Lentulus, who as consul in 57 had championed his recall. Like the present speech (esp. 36–50), any document that finds Cicero in self-justifying mode is likely to offer a version of the truth that has been improved in ways, and to an extent, that cannot fully be controlled.

with impunity. Perhaps, too, the exhilaration of that victory still buoyed him up when on 5 April, the day after Caelius' trial ended, he proposed at a meeting of the senate that the distribution of land in Campania be taken up when the senate met again on 15 May.

This part of Caesar's programme had been a special target of optimate hostility since 59.[80] Caesar, who must have been informed with all speed of Cicero's proposal, was going to do what needed to be done to blunt that hostility. He had already met with Crassus at Ravenna, in Cisalpine Gaul, to discuss their understanding, and probably had arranged to meet for the same purpose with Pompey at Luca, when Pompey left Rome to attend to his supervision of the grain supply:[81] Cicero's proposal could be added to the agenda. The conference followed the senate meeting of 5 April by two weeks, give or take a day or two. The outcome was a renewed agreement among the triumvirs: most importantly, Pompey and Crassus would win election as consuls for 55 and be given five-year provincial commands to follow, and Caesar's own command in the Gauls and Illyricum would be extended for five more years. Cicero would be kept on a short leash. Pompey conveyed the latter point to Quintus Cicero, who was in Sardinia as his legate on the grain commission: Quintus had won Pompey's approval for Cicero's recall by promising that his political behaviour would be unproblematic, and on that ground Pompey had made his own promises to Caesar; now was the time for Cicero to make those promises good, and stop opposing Caesar.[82]

The message was soon conveyed to Cicero by Quintus and by another emissary of Pompey, and Cicero capitulated. When the senate discussed the matter of Campanian land on 15–16 May, Cicero stayed away from the meeting, remarking to Quintus that he was in a tight

---

[80] The praetors Lucius Domitius Ahenobarbus and Gaius Memmius had attacked it, and Caesar's other consular measures, early in 58, before Caesar left for his command in Gaul (Suet. *Iul.* 23. 1), and the tribune Publius Rutilius Rufus had raised the question in the senate in Dec. 57 (*QFr.* 2. 1(5). 1).

[81] That special command, approved on Cicero's motion in Sept. 57 (*Att.* 4. 1(73). 6), was voted funding at the same meeting of the senate on 5 April: *QFr.* 2. 6(10). 1.

[82] This issue, one of trustworthiness (*fides*) and honour, is the chief reason Cicero gives for his subsequent behaviour at *Fam.* 1. 9(20). 9 (cf. n. 79 above); secondary reasons include (ibid. 10) the malice and jealousy with which certain optimate leaders treated him, a recurrent theme of this period, cf. 46. **some felt** n.

spot on the issue, and nothing came of the discussion (*QFr.* 2. 7(11). 1–2). Before long he had occasion to compose what he describes, in writing to Atticus, as a 'rather shameful little recantation' (*sub-turpicula . . . παλινῳδία*). It is not quite clear whether this was a lost speech delivered in the senate supporting certain requests by Caesar that Cicero had previously opposed, or the extant speech 'On the consular provinces', delivered in early July, when the senate deliberated on the provinces to be assigned to the consuls of 55, in anticipation of the consular elections expected later that month. For the point at hand it does not much matter.[83] In the latter speech Cicero spoke strongly in favour of Caesar and his Gallic command, acknowledging that he had shifted his ground while arguing, in a passage of great agility and rhetorical brilliance (*Prov. cons.* 18–25), that it was only an act of patriotism for him to do so. But no amount of agility and brilliance could conceal the immense and very public humiliation that the shift entailed. That it very possibly came a year to the day after another brilliant scene—the senate meeting in July 57 at which Pompey, reading from a prepared statement, had declared Cicero Rome's unique saviour—was a further, unexpected twist in 'the drama' of his 'actions and their outcomes'.[84] It was not a twist that Cicero took any pleasure in contemplating.

6. A NOTE ON THE TRANSLATION

The translation is based on Tadeusz Maslowski's excellent Teubner edition of 1986; the relatively few places where I depart from his text are tabulated in Appendix 4 and discussed in the relevant notes of the commentary. In turning Cicero's Latin into English, I have had two main aims. First, I have tried to make the translation maximally

[83] The relation between the 'recantation' and *Prov. cons.* turns in part on the relative dating of the speech and the letter that speaks of the recantation (*Att.* 4. 5(80). 1): see App. 1 nn. 41–2, with e.g. Balsdon 1962, 137–9, *CLA* 2. 233, *LUO* no. 54, Marinone 2004, 119 (B 13). On the senate's practice of determining provincial commands before the election of the consuls who would hold them, see 24 **their pick of the provinces** n.

[84] On the most likely dating of the senate meetings in 57 (8–9 July) and 56 (1–9 July), see App. 1.

readable—by which I mean, able to be read *aloud* in a comprehensible and even pleasing way—while still retaining Cicero's sentence structure as much as possible. In the latter regard I have set a goal different from that of Shackleton Bailey's fine translation (1991), which often breaks Cicero's long sentences down into smaller, more easily digestible units: that is a perfectly reasonable approach, but because the architecture of Cicero's sentences is important to his effect—is what makes him Cicero, in no small part—I thought it worth the attempt to be faithful in this respect.[85] Second, I have translated recurrent key terms of Roman political life (institutions, values) by using the same English word or phrase for the corresponding Roman term as consistently as English and Latin usage allow, and by trying to choose English terms that are both idiomatic enough to fall within a reader's comfort zone and yet sufficiently distinctive to be noticeable when the terms reappear: e.g. *dignitas* is always 'worthy standing', *civitas* is always 'civil community' (save for the one instance when it refers to membership in the 'civil community', i.e. 'citizenship'). An asterisk precedes each of these terms the first time that it appears in a given note in the commentary, and each is explained in the Glossary.

[85] On the other hand, I have taken liberties within clauses, for example in replacing some passive constructions with active, where that aided clarity and momentum, or in rendering some of Cicero's beloved doublets (*furor ac scelus*), when they verge on hendiadys, as adjective + noun phrases ('criminal frenzy').

Translation

(1) If anyone used to wonder before, judges, why brave and large-spirited citizens could not be found, in numbers befitting the commonwealth's great resources and our dominion's worthy standing, to put themselves and their well-being boldly on the line for the sake of our civil regime and the freedom that we share, let him now marvel to see *any* citizen who is patriotic and brave, rather than fearful or given to thinking of himself instead of the commonwealth. For without recalling and pondering individuals' misfortunes case by case, you can (on the one hand) see at a glance that those who joined the senate and all patriots in reviving the commonwealth when it was battered and rescuing it from the assault of domestic brigands are now defendants, distraught and clad in mourning, waging desperate struggles in which their lives as citizens, their reputations, their role in the community, their fortunes, and their children are at stake. And you can see (on the other hand) that the sort of people who did sharp and repeated violence to all things divine and human, bringing upheaval and destruction upon them, not only dart about with an energized delight but even devise perils for the best and bravest citizens while entertaining no fear for themselves. (2) Many aspects of this situation are deplorable, but nothing is less tolerable than this: it is not through their own brigands, not through impoverished and criminal desperadoes, but through *you* that they try to imperil *us*— the most patriotic through the most patriotic—judging that those whom they have failed to destroy with stones, swords, and torches, with their violence, their battery, and their material resources, they will be able to crush using your authority, your sense of religious obligation, and your verdicts. I once thought, judges, that I would be obliged to use my voice in thanking those who have most earned my gratitude and publicizing their acts of beneficence; but <since> I am now forced to use it in warding off the perils launched against them, let this voice of mine chiefly serve those whose efforts have restored its use to me and to you and to the Roman people.

(3) Now, though Quintus Hortensius, a most distinguished and eloquent gentleman, has summed up the case for Publius Sestius and has left out nothing that called for lament on the commonwealth's behalf, or for argument on the defendant's, I shall nonetheless undertake to speak, lest my efforts for the defence appear to have been withheld from that man—of all people!—who guaranteed they would not be withheld from all my other fellow-citizens. Accordingly, I affirm, judges, that in speaking last in this case I have taken on a role that owes its character more to a display of devotion than to the conduct of a formal defence, more to an expression of grievance than to a display of eloquence, more to my distress of mind than to my intellect. (4) So if I speak more sharply or with less restraint than those who spoke before, I ask that you make such allowances as you think ought to be granted to distress born of devotion and to righteous anger: for no distress can be more closely bound to a sense of duty than the distress I feel at the peril of one who has most earned my gratitude, and no anger is more praiseworthy than that kindled by the outrageous conduct of men who have decided they must wage war against all who toiled on behalf of my well-being. (5) But seeing that the other speakers have addressed the individual charges, I shall speak about Publius Sestius' overall condition—about the kind of life he has lived, his nature and character, his unbelievably warm esteem for patriots, his zeal for preserving the tranquillity and well-being that we share—and I shall strive to bring it about (may I only succeed!) that in this unmethodical and general speech of defence I appear to have omitted nothing that is pertinent to your inquiry, to the defendant, and to the public interest. And because Fortune herself set Publius Sestius' tribunate at the very point at which the civil community's crisis was gravest, when the commonwealth, overturned and battered, lay in ruins, I shall not address those themes of greatest scope and importance before I give you to understand the foundation and first stages from which has risen his great distinction, won in affairs of highest importance.

(6) Publius Sestius' father, judges, was (as most of you recall) a wise, pure, and strict man who came in first in the elections for tribune of the plebs—in a field that included some of the most notable men at a very favourable time for our community—but was thereafter less keen to enjoy further office than to be seen worthy

of it. With his father's sponsorship Sestius married the daughter of Gaius Albanius, a most honourable and respected man, and from her had this boy here and a daughter now married: he thus won such favour from two very serious men of old-fashioned strictness that neither could have held him dearer or found him more agreeable. Though with his daughter's death Albanius ceased to be called Sestius' father-in-law, he did not cease to feel the affection and goodwill proper to that tie: he continues to esteem him today, as you can judge from his constant attendance at this trial and from his anxious concern. (7) While his own father was still alive Sestius took to wife the daughter of that most excellent and unfortunate man, Lucius Scipio, toward whom he displayed a conspicuous devotion that won general approval. Setting off at once for Massilia, to console by his visit the father-in-law who had been cast out when the commonwealth was tossed on turbulent seas—a man then prostrate in a foreign land who would rightly have followed in the footsteps of his ancestors—he brought Scipio's daughter to him, so that man, by seeing and embracing her beyond all expectation, might put aside, if not all his grief, at least some part of it; and by his own very substantial, attentive, and dutiful acts besides, he helped the father to bear his misery, while he lived, and the daughter to bear her loneliness. I could go on at length about his generosity, his dutiful behavior in private life, his term as military tribune, and his temperate behavior in the duties of that office; but I have before my eyes the commonwealth's worthy standing, which draws me forcefully to itself and urges me to leave these lesser matters behind.

(8) Though as quaestor he was assigned by lot to my colleague, Gaius Antonius, his sharing in my thoughts and plans made him my own. Scruple over an aspect of dutiful behavior (as I judge these things) prevents me from describing in detail how much Publius Sestius noticed and reported when he was with my colleague, and how farsighted he was; and about Antonius I say only this, that at no point in our community's time of fear and peril did he have the will either to remove (by denial) or to palliate (by dissimulation) the general terror of us all and the suspicion that some entertained about him in particular. If you were rightly inclined to praise my indulgence toward my colleague, when it came to propping him up and keeping him in line, together with my most careful guardianship of

the commonwealth, you ought to praise Publius Sestius almost equally, for so attending to the consul to whom he was assigned that he was a good quaestor in the consul's eyes and the best sort of citizen in the eyes of all of you.

(9) When that conspiracy burst forth from its shadowy lair and was dashing about energetically and openly under arms, it was Publius Sestius, too, who came with an army to Capua, which we thought that band of impious criminals would target because of its numerous strategic advantages, and he hurled headlong from the town Gaius Mevulanus, Antonius' military tribune, a desperado who had plainly been involved in the conspiracy at Pisaurum and in other parts of coastal Umbria. More than that: when Gaius Marcellus not only came to Capua but even infiltrated a massive gladiatorial school, as though from an enthusiasm for armed combat, Publius Sestius saw to it that he was expelled from the city. That is why the distinguished association of Capua then expressed their thanks to Publius Sestius in my presence (because their city was saved in and by my consulship, they adopted me as their sole patron), and on the present occasion the same people (now as 'settlers') and their town councillors, men of the greatest bravery and excellence, make plain in a written testimonial the good that Publius Sestius did for them, and with their decree they pray that he escape his present peril. (10) Please, Lucius Sestius, read out what the councillors of Capua have decreed, so that your voice—though now the voice of a child—can let your family's enemies glimpse the effect it clearly will have when it has grown strong with age. (THE COUNCILORS' DECREE.) The decree that I've had read is not a forced expression of duty, offered because the Capuans are neighbours or clients or enjoy a formal relation as guest-friends, nor is it offered out of self-interest or as a conventional compliment. No, this decree recalls real danger that was endured and survived, it acknowledges a benefaction of greatest scope, it gives voice to a manifest sense of obligation, it bears solemn witness to times gone by. (11) And at that same time—when Sestius had already freed Capua from its terror, and the senate, joined by all patriots, had caught and crushed our domestic enemies under my leadership and had freed this city from the gravest dangers—I wrote a letter to summon Publius Sestius, and the army with him, back from Capua: when he read the letter he hastened to fly back to Rome

with quite unbelievable speed. So that you can call to mind the horror of those days, listen to the letter and stir your memory to reflect on past fears. (THE LETTER OF CICERO AS CONSUL.)

On Publius Sestius' arrival, momentum was drained from the onslaughts and machinations of the conspiracy's remnant and of the new tribunes of the plebs, who in the final days of my consulship wished to overthrow what I had accomplished. (12) After it became clear that—with Marcus Cato, then tribune of the plebs and an extraordinarily brave patriot, defending the <common>wealth— the senate and people of Rome could, without a military garrison and through its own majesty, easily protect the worthy standing of those who had guarded the well-being of all at the cost of their own peril, Sestius sped off with his forces and caught up with Antonius. What am I to say here of the deeds by which the quaestor roused the consul to do what needed doing, of the goads that he applied to a man who was perhaps eager for victory but nonetheless too fearful of 'the impartial god of war' and war's random chances? It is a long tale to tell, but this I shall say briefly: had it not been for Marcus Petreius' exceptionally patriotic spirit, the surpassing manliness he displayed in the public interest, his supreme authority with the soldiers, and his marvellous experience on campaign, and had Publius Sestius not been there to assist him in rousing Antonius with exhortations, accusations, and sheer compulsion, the war would have been suspended for the winter: then once Catiline had emerged from the Apennines' frosts and great snows and, with a whole summer ahead of him, had begun to plunder Italy's mountain pasturages and sheepfolds, he would never have fallen before much blood was shed and all Italy was utterly laid waste. (13) This, then, is the spirit that Publius Sestius brought to his term as tribune of the plebs—to leave to one side his quaestorship in Macedonia and to come at last to more recent events. Yet I must not fail to mention the truly singular uprightness he showed in the duties of that office, the traces of which I myself recently saw in Macedonia—traces not lightly impressed, to be spoken of for a short time only, but set deep and eternal in the province's memory. Yet let us pass by this stage in his career, albeit casting a respectful backward glance as we leave it behind, and set the swiftest course for his tribunate, which has now for some time been summoning and, as it were, drawing my discourse irresistibly to itself.

(14) Now, Quintus Hortensius has already spoken of this tribunate, and indeed has spoken of it in terms that seemed to offer not
only a defence against the charge brought but also a memorable
lesson for our youth on the orderly and authoritative way to engage
in politics. Nonetheless, because Publius Sestius' entire tribunate
sought only to support my reputation and my interests, I believe
that I must treat the subject too, if not to offer a discussion of greater
finesse, then at least to decry the circumstances with greater passion—and if in doing so I were to choose to attack some people with
more than usual asperity, who would not grant me the freedom to
bruise with my speech those whose frenzied crimes did me violence?
Still, I shall proceed with restraint and have thought for the circumstances of the defendant here rather than my own grievances: if some
tacitly disapprove the restoration of my well-being, then let their
dissent remain hidden; if others worked to harm me at some point in
the past but are behaving with discretion now, then let bygones be
bygones; and if others openly oppose and attack me, I will put up
with it to the extent that I can, nor will what I say offend anyone save
a person who has so put himself in my path that I will be seen not to
have attacked him but to have collided with him.

(15) But before I begin to speak about Publius Sestius' tribunate,
I must set out in detail the shipwreck that the commonwealth
suffered in the previous year: for you will find that everything Sestius
later said, did, and intended was aimed at picking up the pieces and
restoring the well-being of us all. There had already passed that
infamous year when, amid great tumult and widespread fear, a bow
was bent against me alone (as the uninformed commonly said), but
in truth against the entire commonwealth, thanks to the transfer to
the plebs of a frenzied desperado who, though he bore a grudge
against me, was far more sharply hostile to the tranquillity and
well-being of us all. Gnaeus Pompeius, a most distinguished man
and (despite the best efforts of many) a most devoted friend to me,
had through every sort of pledge, agreement, and oath bound this
fellow to a solemn promise that he would do nothing against me if he
became tribune. That utterly wicked man, sprung from the foul
welter of every form of crime, judged that he would not violate his
oath grossly enough if he did not make the man who had acted to
ward off another's perils fear perils of his own. (16) Though this foul

and monstrous beast had been constrained by the auspices, bound by the ways of our ancestors, and held fast by the chains of sacrosanct legislation, one of the consuls suddenly freed him by using a law passed in the curiate assembly, either (as I believe) because he had been prevailed upon or (as some thought) because he bore a grudge against me—in any case, he was plainly ignorant and careless of the vast and ruinous crimes that loomed. That tribune of the plebs enjoyed great success in setting the commonwealth on its head, not through his own muscle—for what sort of muscle could a man have whose way of life had left him enervated from debauching his brother, having sex with his sister, and engaging in every unprecedented form of lust?—(17) but assuredly because the commonwealth suffered a kind of deadly bad luck: that blind and mad tribune of the plebs had stumbled upon—what's the word I want? 'consuls'? Am I to use *this* title of men who turned our dominion upside down and betrayed your worthy standing, men who are the enemies of all patriots and who thought they had been provided with the fasces and all the other tokens of highest office and dominion so they could destroy the senate, afflict the equestrian order, and eradicate all the laws and customs of our ancestors? By the immortal gods, if you do not yet wish to recall the wounding crimes with which they branded the commonwealth, picture in your minds the expressions on their faces and how they strode about: what they did will more readily come to mind if you imagine the way they looked.

(18) One of them—dripping with perfumed oils, his hair crimped and curled, despising his accomplices in lust and the old despoilers of his oh-so-delicate boyhood, puffed up with conceit in the face of the usurers who hang about the Well-Head (they had forced him to seek the tribunate as a safe haven, lest in that monstrous Scylla's strait of debt he become affixed to the column)—this one was showing his contempt for the equestrian order, threatening the senate, peddling himself to his henchmen, declaring that they had saved him from having to face a charge of electoral bribery, and affirming that he expected to gain a province through their efforts whatever the senate's will in the matter; indeed, he believed that if he did not gain a province, there was no way that he'd retain his civic well-being. (19) The other one—good gods!—how he strode about, so foul and fierce in appearance, so formidable to look upon! You would swear that

you were looking at one of the old longbeards, a model of the ancient
dominion, the very image of antiquity, a pillar of the commonwealth,
dressed—no refinement here!—in our plebeian purple (almost
brown, really) and with hair so unkempt that he seemed bent on
eradicating the Seplasia from Capua, where he was then holding the
duumvirate for the adornment it would add to his image. And—my
word!—what shall I say about that lofty brow of his, which struck
people as not so much a brow but a guarantee of the commonwealth:
such seriousness was in his look, so furrowed in concentration was
his brow—like a surety on deposit, it seemed to underwrite the full
burden of his year as consul. (20) He was on everyone's lips: 'Still, the
commonwealth has a great and sturdy support; he gives me someone
to set against that slimy blot; 'pon my word, his glance alone will cure
his colleague's lust and irresponsibility; the senate will have someone
to follow for the year, and patriots won't lack for an authoritative
leader.' People were congratulating me in particular, because I would
be able to set against the frenzied and reckless tribune of the plebs a
man who was not only a friend and relation by marriage but also a
brave and steadfast consul.

And in fact one of the two deceived no one's expectations. For who
would think that the tiller of so great a dominion could be held
steady, the commonwealth safely piloted amid the currents and
swells of so vast a sea, by a person who suddenly emerged from
shadowy brothel orgies, undone by drink, gambling, whoring, and
adultery after being raised to the highest rank—against all expectation and thanks to others' resources—when in his drunken state not
only could he not face the threatening storm, he could not even stand
the unaccustomed sight of daylight? (21) The other one, clearly,
deceived many in every aspect of his behavior, for the very notability
of his lineage—that charming little match-maker—had commended
him to people's consideration. All of us who are patriots always give
our backing to notable men, both because it serves the commonwealth's interests that notable men be worthy of their ancestors and
because the memory of distinguished men who have earned the
commonwealth's gratitude counts for a lot with us, even after they
have died. Because people saw that he was always solemn, always
reserved, always a bit shaggy and unkempt, and because his name
suggested that sober soundness was innate in his household, they

were pleased to back him and in their hopes summoned him to match the uprightness of his ancestors—forgetting his mother's lineage the while. (22) For my part—I'll speak the truth, judges— I never reckoned that the fellow harboured the degree of criminality, recklessness, and cruelty that I, along with the rest of the commonwealth, came to perceive, though I was long aware that he was at base good for nothing and irresponsible, commended from his youth by the mistaken judgement that people had formed of him; and indeed the set of his expression masked the cast of his mind, as the walls of his house masked his disgraceful behavior. But that sort of concealment could not last long, nor be so impenetrable that observant eyes could not see through it. We saw the way he lived, his slothful and supine behavior; those who had approached a bit closer got a good view of his pent-up lusts; his conversation, too, gave us a handle on his hidden disposition. (23) A learned fellow, he used to praise this or that philosopher—he couldn't say their names, but still he praised them—especially those who are said, beyond all others, to praise pleasure and urge its pursuit. What sort of pleasure and when and how it should be pursued—those questions he did not ask, he had simply devoured the very name of 'pleasure' with every <particle> of his being, and he used to say that the same philosophers were brilliantly right in claiming that the wise act entirely for their own sakes, that any person who's right in the head should not get involved in administering the commonwealth, that nothing is preferable to a tranquil life stuffed full of pleasures; and he used to declare that the contrasting principles of others—that we should toil in the service of our worthy standing, give thought to the commonwealth, take account of duty, not advantage, in every aspect of life, undergo dangers, receive wounds, face death on behalf of the fatherland—well, those were just the ravings of madmen. (24) This was the consistent tenor of his daily conversation: from it—as from the sort of people I observed keeping him company in his private quarters, and the fact that his very home was so smoky that it exuded the heavy odor <of gluttony>—I concluded that while not a jot of good could be expected to come from that non-entity, there was certainly no reason to fear any harm. But this is the way things stand, judges: if you gave a sword to a little boy or a weak old man or a cripple, he could harm no one by making a frontal attack but could wound even the bravest man with the weapon's powerful blade if he came upon him unarmed; just so, when the consulship was given like a sword to people without strength and vigour, who on their own could never have stabbed anyone, they found the commonwealth exposed, and they cut it to pieces, armed with the title of supreme power. They openly made a pact with the tribune of the plebs that they could have their pick of the provinces and as large an army and budget as they might like, provided that they first handed over the commonwealth, battered and bound, to the tribune; moreover, they said that the deal, once struck, could be sealed with my blood. (25) And when the affair was exposed—for neither dissimulation nor concealment could keep such an enormity secret—public notice was given, at one and the same time, of the tribune's proposals that brought ruin to me and the provinces to the consuls, by name.

At this the senate grew concerned; you, gentlemen of the equestrian order, were aroused; all Italy together was thrown into a tumult. In short, all citizens of every sort and rank thought that in this matter, where the public interest was critically at stake, aid should be sought from the consuls and their high office—though the pair of them alone, apart from the frenzied tribune, were the tornadoes bearing down on the commonwealth: so far from coming to our fatherland's aid as it plunged to its ruin, they grieved that it was taking so long to collapse. Daily they were called upon, by the laments of all patriots and especially the senate's entreaties, to look after my interests, to do something, finally, to refer the matter to the senate. They took the offensive, not just refusing these requests but even laughing in the face of all the most substantial men of the senatorial order. (26) Hereupon, when a crowd of unbelievable size had gathered on the Capitol from every part of the city and all of Italy, a unanimous decision was taken to put on mourning-dress and to defend me in every way possible, as a matter of individual initiative, seeing that public leadership had failed the public interest. At the same time, the senate met in the temple of Concord—the very precinct that called to mind the memory of my consulship—and there the entire senatorial order, in tears, made its appeal to the curly-headed consul; for the other consul—the shaggy and austere one— was intentionally keeping to his house. Oh, the arrogance with which that slimy blot spurned the prayers of that most substantial body and the tears of our most distinguished citizens! What contempt he heaped on me, that wastrel of the entire fatherland's wealth! (For why should I call him merely 'wastrel of his ancestral wealth,' which he lost entirely though he was plying his trade?) You came to the senate—I mean you, gentlemen of the equestrian order, and all patriots with you—dressed in mourning, and for the sake of my life as a citizen you prostrated yourselves at the feet of that utterly filthy pimp; and when your entreaties had been spurned by the brigand, Lucius Ninnius, a man of unbelievable loyalty, largeness of spirit, and firm resolve, brought the issue before the senate as a matter touching the public interest, and a packed meeting of the senate voted to assume mourning dress for the sake of my well-being.

(27) What a day that was, judges, mournful for the senate and all patriots, a source of woe to the commonwealth, a grievous one for me in the sorrow it brought my household—but for the memory that posterity will have of me, glorious! For what greater distinction could anyone find in all history than this, that all patriots, on their own and in concert, and the entire senate, as a matter of public policy, took on the dress of mourning for one of their fellow-citizens? And yet this was done not as a formal gesture of entreaty but as an expression of genuine grief: indeed, whom could you entreat when all others had taken on the trappings of grief, and it was a sufficient sign of a man's wickedness that he had not? I leave to one side what the tribune did when, amid the general grief, the community had changed to the dress of mourning—that violent predator of all things divine and human summoned the most notable of the youth and the most honourable members of the equestrian order, who had made entreaties for my salvation, and exposed them to his henchmen's swords and stones. It's the consuls who are my subject, the men on whose trustworthiness the commonwealth ought to depend. (28) One consul flew from the senate meeting quite beside himself—his thoughts and expression no less upset than they would have been a few years ago if he had chanced upon a gathering of his creditors—and then, calling an assembly of the people, delivered a speech the likes of which a victorious Catiline would never have delivered: people were mistaken (he said) if they supposed that the senate was still of any consequence in the commonwealth, while the equestrians who had been on the Capitoline under arms when I was consul were

going to pay the penalty for what they did that day; the time had come for those who had lived in fear—he was referring, of course, to the conspirators—to avenge themselves. Now if he had merely said these things he would have deserved any and every sort of punishment, for the very speech of a consul, if pernicious, can undermine the commonwealth; but consider what he *did*. (**29**) In the people's assembly he banished Lucius Lamia, who not only held me in singularly high esteem because of my very close friendship with his father but was also eager even to meet death on behalf of the commonwealth: in an assembly of the people the consul gave notice that Lamia should put 200 miles between himself and the city, because he had dared make an entreaty on behalf of a citizen, on behalf of a citizen who had given good service, on behalf of a friend, on behalf of the commonwealth.

What would you do with such a person, to what fate would you reserve so perverse a member of the community, or rather an enemy of the community so steeped in crime? To say nothing of all the other enormities that he shares with his monstrously polluted colleague and that bind them together, he has this one all to himself: he expelled from the city, he banished—I do not say a Roman knight, a most honored and virtuous man, a superb citizen and patriot who together with the senate and all other patriots was then mourning the misfortune of a friend and of the commonwealth—no, I say only a Roman citizen, whom a consul expelled from his fatherland as though by decree, without trial. (**30**) Our allies and the Latins used to resent nothing more bitterly than this: to be ordered by our consuls (as happened very rarely) to leave Rome. And in *their* case they could still return to their own civil communities, to their own household gods, and no disgrace adhered to any particular person by name, since the disadvantage was shared by all of the same status. But now what have we? Will a consul send Rome's citizens beyond her boundaries and away from their household gods, expel them from their fatherland, pick out whom he pleases, condemn and cast them out individually and by name? If this man had ever supposed that you would be playing the role you now play in the commonwealth, if he believed that even a phantom likeness of courts and judges would remain in our community, would he ever have dared to exclude the senate from the people's business, spurn the entreaties of the equestrian order, and in short overturn the rights and freedom of all citizens with his untoward and unprecedented decrees?

(31) Although you are listening very alertly and very kindly, judges, I am still concerned lest someone among you might wonder at the purpose of so long a speech that reaches back so far into the past, or how the misdeeds of those who manhandled the commonwealth before Publius Sestius' tribunate are relevant to his case. It is, however, my aim to show that all of Publius Sestius' policies, and the guiding thought of his whole term in office, had this end in view, to bring as much healing as he could to the commonwealth when it was battered beyond hope. And if in placing those terrible wounds before your eyes I shall seem to say rather a lot about myself, please do forgive me. For you and all patriots have judged that disaster of mine to be the most grievous wound to the commonwealth, and Publius Sestius is now a defendant not on his own account, but on mine: since this man spent all the vigour of his tribunate to secure my well-being, my cause of a bygone time is inextricably linked to his defence right now.

(32) The senate, then, was plunged in grief, the civil community—having taken on the dress of mourning as a matter of public policy—was the picture of shabby disarray, there was not a town, not a colony, not a prefecture in Italy, not a corporation of public revenue-collection at Rome, not a club, not a council or any public body whatever that had not then passed a decree in the most honorific terms concerning my well-being: when suddenly the two consuls decreed that senators must return to their normal dress. What consul ever prohibited the senate from obeying its own decrees? What tyrant ever forbade the distressed to grieve? Is it not enough, Piso (to say nothing of Gabinius), that you so grossly deceived men's expectations of you, discounted the senate's authority, despised the views of all the most patriotic men, betrayed the commonwealth, and did violence to the name of consul? Did you also dare to issue a decree forbidding people to mourn my catastrophe, their own catastrophe, the catastrophe of the commonwealth, and to make this grief of theirs plain in their dress? Whether the adoption of mourning was intended to express their grief or to register an appeal, who ever was so cruel as to keep anyone from grieving on his own account or making a supplication for others? (33) Do you mean to say that

people do not commonly dress in mourning of their own accord when their friends are in distress? Will no one do the like for you, Piso? Not even that lot you appointed to your staff, not only without the senate's advice and consent, but even in the face of its resistance? Perhaps, then, some will be motivated to mourn the misfortune of a desperado who has betrayed the commonwealth: will the senate not be allowed to mourn the distress of a citizen who abounds in the affection of patriots for the excellent service he has done the fatherland, when that distress is joined by the distress of the civil community at large? The same consuls—if we ought to call 'consuls' men whom everyone would prefer not just to forget but even to eliminate from the calendar—these consuls, when their provincial assignments were a done deal, were brought by that demon, that plague upon the fatherland into an assembly of the people in the circus Flaminius, where—to the accompaniment of your loud lamentation, judges—they voiced their approval of all the measures being taken against me and against the commonwealth.

And while the same consuls sat and looked on a law was proposed with these clauses: 'Let the auspices have no force...,' 'Let no one bring word of portents...,' 'Let no one veto a law...,' 'Let it be permitted to bring a law to a vote on all days when public business can be conducted...,' 'Let the *lex Aelia* and *lex Fufia* have no force...' Does anyone fail to see that by this one proposal the entire commonwealth was undone? (34) And while the same consuls looked on, a levy of slaves was conducted at the Aurelian tribunal for the alleged purpose of forming clubs, as street by street people were enlisted, formed up into squads, and incited to violent assault, murder, and plunder. And when the same men were consuls, weapons were openly stockpiled in the temple of Castor, the steps leading to the temple were removed, armed men controlled the forum and assemblies of the people, murders were committed, people were stoned, the senate was null, and the rest of the magistrates counted for nothing. One man usurped all their power with his armed brigands—not that he raised a finger in violence himself, but once his deal over the provinces had removed the two consuls from the people's business, he rode rampant: threatening some, making pledges to others, he controlled many people with terror and fear and a still larger number with hopes and promises.

(35) With matters standing this way, judges—the senate having no leaders but, in place of leaders, traitors or rather outright enemies, with the whole equestrian order arraigned by the consuls, the authority of all Italy cast back in its face, some men banished by name, others terrorized by threats, with arms stored in temples, armed men in the forum, and the consuls not just silently turning a blind eye but stating their express approval—when we all saw the city, if not yet utterly razed and overturned, then already held captive and oppressed, still, judges, I would have stood fast against this vast wickedness thanks to the zeal of patriots. But other fears and other anxious suspicions moved me.

(36) Indeed, judges, I will today give you a full accounting of my actions and intentions, and I will disappoint neither you, eager as you are to hear, nor the crowd—greater than I can ever recall—that attends this trial. For if I—in so righteous a cause, when the senate was so zealous, all patriots so magnificently united, <the equestrian order> so poised at the ready, in short, all Italy prepared for any sort of conflict—if in such circumstances I withdrew before the frenzy of an utterly despicable tribune of the plebs, if I shrank in fear before the irresponsibility and recklessness of the thoroughly contemptible consuls, then I grant that I was too cowardly, devoid of spirit and strategy. (37) For what parallel can the case of Quintus Metellus provide? Though all patriots favoured his cause, it had not been officially taken up by the senate, nor by any category of the citizenry acting on their own initiative, nor by all Italy, through its decrees. Indeed, Metellus had had his eye more on some notion of personal glory than on the commonwealth's manifest well-being when he stood alone in refusing to swear allegiance to a law passed by violence: in short, his great bravery seemed to be based on the stipulation that he would gain a glorious reputation for resolve in exchange for his loving attachment to the fatherland. Moreover, he had to deal with Gaius Marius' unconquered army, and he had as his personal enemy the saviour of the fatherland, Marius, then holding his sixth consulship; he had to deal with Lucius Saturninus, then tribune of the plebs for a second time, an alert fellow and a popular champion of the people's cause who was at least personally if not politically temperate: Metellus withdrew, lest he either lose with disgrace when beaten by real men or gain a victory that cost the commonwealth

many brave citizens. (38) *My* side had been taken up by the senate openly, by the equestrian order most keenly, by all Italy as a public matter, by all patriots strenuously as their own. The things I had done I did not as one acting on his own authority but as a leader who had the general will behind me, with a view not only to my glory as an individual but to the shared well-being of all citizens and—it is scarcely too much to say—of all nations; and I had done them with the provision that all men would ever be obliged to vouch for and defend my action.

I, however, was locked in conflict not with a victorious army but with hired thugs incited to plunder the city; my enemy was not Gaius Marius, who struck fear in the enemy while giving hope and support to the fatherland, but two perverse monsters whom poverty, huge debt, irresponsibility, and wickedness had consigned to the tribune of the plebs as chattel bound hand and foot. (39) Nor was I dealing with Saturninus, who—knowing that an insult was intended when the grain supply at Ostia was transferred from himself, as quaestor, to Marcus Scaurus, then the foremost man of the senate and the civil community—single-mindedly sought satisfaction for his anger, but with some rich idlers' whore, with the adulterer of his own sister and the high-priest of debauchery, with a poisoner, a will-forger, an assassin, a brigand. If I defeated these people by force of arms— something it would have been easy and right to do, and what our bravest patriots were demanding that I do—I had no worry that anyone would criticize my use of violence to ward off violence or grieve over the death of citizen-desperadoes, or rather homegrown public enemies. But the following considerations moved me: in all assemblies of the people that demon was shouting that his actions against my well-being had the support of Gnaeus Pompeius, a most distinguished man and most amicably disposed to me now, as he was (to the extent possible) then; Marcus Crassus, the bravest of men, with whom I enjoyed every degree of friendship, was declared by that pestilence to be very hostile to my interests; and Gaius Caesar, who was not obliged to be estranged from me through any fault of my own, was declared by the same man, in the assemblies of the people that he convened daily, to be most hostile to my well-being. (40) His line was that he would enjoy the support of these three men as advisers in making his plans and as helpers in carrying them out;

and he remarked that one of them had a very large army in Italy, while the other two, though then holding no office, could if they wanted to raise and command their own armies—and were going to do just that. And he put me on notice that there would be no trial before the people nor any contest covered by law, no debate, no chance to argue my case—just force of arms, commanders and their armies, war.

You might ask: did an enemy's speech, especially one so void of substance, move me when it was aimed so wickedly at men of the greatest distinction? No, of course, I was moved not by what *he* said, but rather by what was *not* said by the men against whom that wicked talk was aimed: for though they had other reasons for their persistent silence then, people who saw cause for fear everywhere nonetheless came to think their silence eloquent, the absence of denial a kind of acknowledgement. The three, however, were not a little anxious for another reason: they thought that all they had accomplished the previous year was being undermined by the praetors and weakened by the senate and the foremost men of the community, they didn't want to alienate a popular tribune, and they said their own dangers touched them more nearly than mine. (41) But still, Crassus was saying that the consuls ought to undertake my defence, while Pompeius appealed to their good faith and said that though he held no magistracy he would not fail them if they took up my cause as a matter of the public interest. The latter gentleman, though keenly attached to me and eager to preserve the commonwealth, was warned by agents posted at my house specifically for that purpose that he should take care because a plot had been laid against his life in my home, and the same suspicion was fed by letters some other people wrote, by messengers dispatched by still others, and by comments made in person by others again. The upshot was that while he certainly feared nothing from me, he thought that he should beware of *them*, lest they set some mischief in motion and blame it on me. Caesar himself, however, who some very badly misinformed people supposed was angry with me, was at the city gates, and was there with supreme power of command; his army was in Italy, and in that army he had appointed a brother of my enemy the tribune to a command.

(42) So when I took all this in (and none of it was hidden)—the senate, without which the civil community could not survive, entirely

destroyed; the consuls, who ought to lead the way in establishing public policy, responsible by their own acts for utterly eradicating such policy; the most powerful men represented (falsely, but still terrifyingly) in all the people's assemblies as advising my destruction; harangues delivered daily against me with not a voice raised on my behalf or the commonwealth's; the legionary standards thought to be poised to strike against your lives and property (falsely, but still it was thought); the old forces of conspiracy and Catiline's perverse band, once put to rout and defeated, now renewed and under a new leader following an unexpected reversal of fortune: when I took all this in, judges, what was I to do? At the time, I know, your earnest support did not fail me, though I almost failed to match it with my own. (43) Was I, a man with no public office, to engage in a passage at arms with a tribune of the plebs? The patriots would have vanquished the wicked, the brave men the supine; death would have come to the man who by this medicine alone could be stopped from bringing a plague to the commonwealth. What then? Who could take responsibility for the sequel? Who, in short, doubted that the tribune's blood— especially if spilled with no public authority—would be avenged and defended by the consuls? When one of them said in an assembly of the people that I had two choices—to die once or prevail twice—what did 'prevail twice' mean? Obviously, that if I had a fight to the finish with the utterly mad tribune, I would have to contend with the consuls and the rest of his 'avengers'. (44) For my part, even if it had been necessary that I die, and not receive a wound that was curable for myself but deadly for the one who dealt it, then, judges, I would have chosen to die rather than prevail twice: for the second conflict would have meant that we could not maintain the common- wealth as either winners or losers. But if in the first conflict I and many patriots had fallen in the forum, laid low by the tribune's violence, the consuls, I suppose, would have summoned the senate—which they had wholly erased from our civil community; they would have issued a call to arms—the men who had forbidden that the commonwealth be defended even by a call to mourning; after my death they would have distanced themselves from the tribune—the men who had willed that the same moment bring my destruction and their own reward.

(45) Now, I did have remaining one option, which some fierce and large-spirited hero might remark: 'You could have resisted, you could

have fought back, you could have met death in battle.' On this point I call you to witness—yes, you, our fatherland—and you, gods of our hearths and our ancestors: it was for the sake of your shrines and precincts, it was for the well-being of my fellow citizens, which has ever been dearer to me than my life, that I avoided that conflict and its bloodshed. And indeed, if I happened to be on a voyage with some friends, judges, and hordes of pirates, bearing down on us from all directions with their fleet, threatened to destroy the ship unless I alone were surrendered to them, should the passengers refuse and prefer to die with me rather than hand me over to the enemy, I would hurl myself into the depths, to save the rest, sooner than bring people so attached to me into harm's way, much less to certain death. (46) Surely, then, given that this ship of state was bobbing on the deep amid storms of civil division and dissension, its helm wrested from the senate's grasp, with so many armed vessels apparently poised to attack unless I alone were surrendered; and given that proscription, murder, and plunder were being bruited about, that some failed to defend me out of concern for their own peril, that others were being whipped up by a longstanding hatred of patriots, that some felt mere malice while others thought I stood in their way, that some wanted to avenge some hurt and others just hated the very idea of the commonwealth and the tranquil stability that patriots enjoy and were for these many and varied reasons calling for my head, and mine alone: given all this, was I to fight to the finish—thereby bringing, if not destruction, then assuredly gravest peril to you and your children—rather than meet and undergo, myself alone on the behalf of all, the doom that hung over everyone's head?

(47) 'The wicked would have been beaten.' Yes, but they were fellow-citizens who would have been beaten, by resort to arms, by a person without public standing who even as consul had preserved the commonwealth without resort to arms. But if the patriots had been beaten, who would remain? Don't you see that the commonwealth would have passed into the control of slaves? Or, as some people think, ought I have calmly met my death? What—did I do what I did to *escape* death? Was there anything that I could think more desirable? When I was engaged in matters of such great moment amid so vast a horde of wicked men, do you suppose that death, that exile were not constantly before my eyes? Did I not foretell all this, clear as

prophesy, when I was in the very midst of the engagement? Or was I to think life worth embracing, when I was first immersed in my family's great grief, then torn from their side—*that* was a bitter stroke—while everything that was mine by nature or by fortune was stripped from me? Was I so ignorant, so naïve, so devoid of practical intelligence or native wit? Had I heard, seen, learned *nothing* from my reading and inquiry? Was I unaware that the course of life is short, that of glory eternal? that since death is a certainty fixed for all, each man should wish that his life, which must yield to death's necessity, be seen as a gift offered up to the fatherland, not a thing hoarded until nature makes its claim? Did I not know that the very wisest men have disagreed on just this point, some saying that human awareness and feelings are extinguished at death, others contending that it is precisely when they have passed from the body that wise and brave men's minds truly perceive and come alive—the former alternative, to be without sensation, not being a thing worth fleeing, the latter, to perceive more acutely, being actually desirable? (**48**) Finally, given that I had always gauged all my actions according to the standing of which I was held worthy, given that I thought no human pursuit should be divorced from the goal of worthy standing, was I—a consular with such a record of achievement—to fear death, which even Athenian maidens (the daughters of king Erechtheus, I believe) are said to have faced with contempt on the fatherland's behalf? Especially when I belong to the same civil community whence Gaius Mucius came into Porsenna's camp and tried to kill him, though death stared him in the face; whence first the elder Publius Decius, then some years later his son, endowed with his father's manliness, vowed to give themselves and their lives to death, when battle lines were already drawn, in return for victory and the well-being of the Roman people; whence countless others have met death with utter calm in various wars, partly to win glory, partly to avoid disgrace; and where, within living memory, the father of Marcus Crassus here, a man of extraordinary bravery, took his own life with the same hand that had often dealt death to Rome's enemies, so that he would not have to see his personal enemy's victory.

(**49**) As I turned these and many similar thoughts over in my mind, I came to this understanding: if my death had the effect of ending the people's cause, then no one would ever again dare to champion the commonwealth's well-being against wicked citizens. And so I thought that if I perished—not just by an act of violence, but even by disease—the model for acting to preserve the commonwealth would perish with me: for were I not restored by the senate and people of Rome with the eager support of all patriots—which obviously could not have happened had I been killed—who would ever again set his hand to any aspect of public affairs that threatened to rouse the slightest ill-will against him? Accordingly, judges, I saved the commonwealth by my departure: at the cost of my own pain and grieving I protected you and your children from slaughter, devastation, arson, and plunder; one man alone, I twice saved the commonwealth, once to my glory, once to my grief.

And indeed, in this regard I shall never deny that I am human, so as to boast that I felt no grief at being deprived of my excellent brother, my dearly beloved children, my exceptionally loyal wife, the sight of you, the fatherland, this rank of honor that I enjoy. If I had been unmoved, what sort of favour would I have done you, in abandoning for your sake things I held cheap? In fact, to my mind this ought to be the surest sign of my supreme affection for the fatherland, that though I could not but suffer utter misery when parted from it, I preferred to suffer than to have it undermined by wicked men. (50) I remember, judges, that the great and godlike man who was sprung from the same roots as I to be the salvation of our dominion, Gaius Marius, in deep old age had to flee the force of arms raised almost justly against him: he first hid his aged body submerged in the marshes, then found refuge with the destitute and humble folk of Minturnae, who pitied him, and thereafter came in a tiny boat to the most desolate shores of Africa, since he was avoiding all ports and inhabited lands. *He* kept himself alive so he could gain vengeance—a very doubtful hope, and one that boded no good for the commonwealth—whereas the commonwealth had a crucial stake in my staying alive (as many men said in the senate while I was away), and I was for that reason commended to the protection of foreign peoples by letters sent by the consuls in accord with the senate's resolution: had I given up my life, would I not have betrayed the commonwealth? And now that I have been restored, the model of loyalty to the commonwealth lives on in it with me: if that model is maintained, imperishable, is it not obvious that this civil community of ours will live forever too?

(51) For wars with foreign kings, peoples, tribes have long since been tamped down, so that we now have splendid relations with those whom we allow to be at peace; furthermore, virtually no one has gained the ill-will of the citizens at home from wars won abroad. By contrast, we often must stand up against the baneful plans of reckless citizens at home, and the commonwealth must keep in store a remedy for those perils: that, judges, is what you would have lost entirely, had the senate and people of Rome been robbed by my death of the power to express their grief for me. I therefore advise you young men who aim at worthy standing, at involvement in the people's business, and at glory—this is a lesson I have a right to teach—if ever a crisis summons you to defend the commonwealth against wicked citizens, do not go slack and shrink from planning brave responses because you remember my misfortune. (52) First of all, there is no danger that anyone will ever encounter consuls of this sort, especially if these get what is coming to them. In the second place, I expect that never again will any wicked man claim that he is assailing the commonwealth with the advice and support of patriots, while they remain silent, nor terrorize civilians with threat of armed military force, nor will a general encamped by the city gates have just cause for allowing the fear he inspires to be falsely bandied and bruited about. Moreover, the senate will never be so stifled that it lacks even the power to entreat and to grieve, or the equestrian order so oppressed that its members are banished by a consul. Although all these things came to pass—and other, much more serious things that I intentionally set aside—you see that the commonwealth has nonetheless called me back, after a brief interval of grief, to the worthy standing that I previously enjoyed.

(53) To return, then, to my main thesis in this speech, that in that year the commonwealth was overcome by all these forms of woe thanks to the consuls' crime: first on the very day—deathly to me, grievous to all patriots—when I tore myself from the fatherland's embrace and left your sight, yielding to the tribune's criminal frenzy and treacherous missiles out of fear for your danger, not my own, leaving behind the fatherland, which I hold the dearest thing, because of that very dearness, when not only my fellow humans but even the city's dwellings and holy precincts mourned my misfortune—so dreadful, so grievous, so sudden—and when no one among you

could bear to look upon the forum, the senate-house, the light of day: on that day, I say—or rather, not 'day', at the very hour, at the very second that the assembly was asked to approve my destruction, and the commonwealth's, it was also asked to approve the assignment of provinces to Gabinius and Piso. By the immortal gods who protect and preserve this city and its dominion, what prodigies, what crimes you saw in the public realm! A citizen who, together with all patriots, had defended the commonwealth on the authority of the senate was expelled from the city, not on some other charge but on those very grounds, and he was expelled, moreover, without a hearing, with violence, stones, cold steel, and with the slave population roused against him; the law was passed with the forum laid waste, deserted, abandoned to cut-throats and slaves, and it was passed despite the senate's having taken on the dress of mourning to oppose it. (54) Amid the great upheaval of our community the consuls did not suffer even a night to separate my <misfortune> and their reward: immediately upon the blow that was dealt me they swooped in to drain my blood and—though the commonwealth was still breathing—to drag off its spoils. As for the expressions of gratitude and felicitations, the feasting, the sharing out of the treasury, the favours done, hoped for, promised, the booty, the expansive joy of a few amid the grief of all the rest—of these things I say nothing. My wife was roughly treated, my children were sought out for slaughter, my son-in-law—a Piso at that—was repulsed as a suppliant at the feet of the consul Piso, my property was plundered and handed over to the consuls, my home on the Palatine was set ablaze: the consuls feasted. But even if they rejoiced at my downfall, they nonetheless should have been moved by the city's peril.

(55) But to step back now from my own concerns: call to mind the other plagues of that year—for thus you will most readily see how strong a dose of medicine, of every sort, the commonwealth needed last year's magistrates to administer—namely, the vast number of laws, not only those that were put to a vote but also those that were posted as pending. For with those fine consuls—keeping mum, shall I say? not a bit of it, even expressing their approval—laws were voted on under whose terms the review of the censors, that most weighty judgement of the most reverend magistracy, was to be uprooted from the commonwealth; the clubs were not only to be restored, in the case

of the old ones, contrary to the senate's decree, but countless new ones were to be enrolled by that gladiator alone; nearly a fifth of the public income was to be lost by lowering the price of grain by $6\frac{1}{3}$ *asses* per measure; that instead of Cilicia, which he'd settled on as his price for betraying the commonwealth, Gabinius would be given Syria—the one wastrel thus given <the chance> to decide twice on the same matter and (though <the law on the first deal> had already been voted) to change his province <thanks to a new> law.

(56) I leave to one side the law that on a single motion destroyed all regulations attaching to matters of religious scruple, the auspices, and magistrates' powers, all laws governing the right to put legislation to a vote and the proper time for doing so, I omit to mention every blot on the record of our domestic affairs: even foreign nations, as we saw, were shaken by the frenzy of that year. By a tribunician law the distinguished priest of the Great Mother at Pessinus was ejected from and robbed of his priesthood, and the shrine belonging to the most holy and ancient cult was sold at a staggering price to Brogitarus, a filthy fellow unworthy of that religion, especially since he wanted it not for the sake of practising the cult but to violate it; the people bestowed the title 'king' on men who had never even requested it of the senate; condemned exiles were restored to Byzantium at the very time that citizens who had not been condemned were being exiled. (57) King Ptolemy, though he had not yet himself received the title 'ally' from the senate, was still the brother of a king who, having the same standing, had already attained that honor from the senate: he was of the same lineage, with the same ancestors, the same longstanding association with us; in short, as king he was, if not yet an 'ally', then certainly not an enemy. Placidly and calmly relying on the dominion of the Roman people, he was enjoying to the full his father's and grandfather's kingdom in regal tranquillity, with nary a thought or hint that anything was afoot, when it was voted by the tribune's same hired hands that—seated on his throne with his royal purple and sceptre and the tokens of kingly rule—he be put up for public auction: at the command of the Roman people, who have customarily restored their kingdoms even to kings conquered in war, a king who was our friend was seized and all his property was confiscated, though no wrongdoing had been alleged, no claim made for restoration of property wrongly taken.

(58) That year saw many painful, disgraceful, and riotous events; still, I think it probably would be right to say that this treatment of Ptolemy was—next to the crime those monsters wrought against me—the worst. When our ancestors defeated Antiochus the Great in a massive conflict over land and sea, they bade him rule south of the Taurus Mountains and took Asia Minor from him as a penalty, giving it to Attalus to rule. We ourselves have recently waged a long and hard war with the Armenian king Tigranes, because he had virtually challenged us to war by injuring our allies. Not only was Tigranes a violent person in his own right, but when Mithradates, that most bitter enemy of our dominion, was driven from Pontus, Tigranes defended him with the resources of his realm; though he was dealt a good blow by <Lucius> Lucullus, a man and general of the highest calibre, Tigranes kept his remaining forces and his original hostile intentions. Yet when Gnaeus Pompeius saw him as an abject suppliant in his own camp, he made him rise, and he set back on his head the emblem of kingship that Tigranes had cast off: after giving him certain specific injunctions, he bade him rule, judging that being seen to set a king upon his throne brought no less glory to himself and our dominion than holding him in bondage. (59) <This man, then, who> made <war on us,> who both was himself an enemy of the Roman people and received into his kingdom our most bitter foe, who clashed with us directly, closed with us in battle, and almost put our dominion at stake, rules today and has gained by his entreaty the title 'friend and ally' that he had violated by his aggression. By contrast, that wretched Cypriot, who was ever our friend, ever our ally, about whom no really serious suspicion ever reached either the senate or our commanders in the field, was put on the auction block 'alive and aware' (as the saying goes), with all his worldly goods. Look—why should other kings think their crowns secure, when they see the precedent that this deadly year provided and recognize that they could be stripped of all their regal good fortune by some tribune and his countless henchmen?

(60) But in that affair they even sought to blot the splendid distinction of Marcus Cato, ignorant as they are of the real vigour that inheres in seriousness of character, uprightness, largeness of spirit—in a word, manliness—which remains calm when the storm is raging, provides a beacon in the gloom, abides and cleaves to its

homeland even after it has been dislodged, shines always with its own light and never is soiled by others' dirty doings. Marcus Cato ought to be banished, not honored, and that affair ought to be laid upon him as a burden, not offered as a trust—or so *those* men supposed, saying openly in an assembly of the people that they had torn from Marcus Cato's head the tongue that had always spoken freely against extraordinary commands. They will soon, I hope, come to feel the abiding presence of that well-known freedom, now made even more vigorous (if that is possible): for even when Marcus Cato had given up hope that his personal authority could have any effect, he gave voice to his grief in a verbal brawl with the despicable consuls and, while lamenting my and the commonwealth's misfortune after my departure, attacked Piso in such terms that that utterly shameless desperado almost came to regret the province he got in the bargain. 'Why then did Cato obey the measure?', one might ask. (61) As if he has not before now sworn allegiance to other laws that he thought had been passed illegally. He does not expose himself by making the sort of flamboyant gesture that would deprive the <common> wealth of a citizen like himself when the commonwealth derives no advantage. In my consulship, when he was tribune of the plebs-elect, he put his life on the line by expressing an opinion that he knew would arouse ill-will and bring danger upon his own head; he spoke forcefully, he acted energetically, he made no secret of what he thought, and he was a leader, a moral force, an active participant in the affair, not because he failed to see the risk he ran but because he thought that when the commonwealth was engulfed in such a tempest he should heed nothing but the fatherland's perils.

(62) His term as tribune then followed. What am I to say about his unique greatness of spirit, his unbelievable manliness? You remember the day when the temple was seized by one of his colleagues and we all feared for the life of this heroic citizen: he went himself into the temple, rock-steady in his purpose, he quelled people's shouts with his authority and an attack by the wicked with his manliness. He faced danger then, but he faced it in a cause whose gravity there is no need for me to describe now. If, by contrast, he had not obeyed that utterly atrocious measure concerning Cyprus, the commonwealth would in no way have been spared the disgrace: for the kingdom had already been confiscated when the measure designating Cato by

name was brought forward—and if he rejected the legitimacy of *that* measure, do you doubt that he would have become the target of violence, when he alone seemed to be undermining all that they were up to that year? (63) He understood this too: since the blot of having auctioned off the kingdom was going to stain the commonwealth beyond anyone's ability to cleanse it, it was more expedient that any good the commonwealth could gain from the disaster be salvaged by himself than that it <be wasted> by others. And even if he were forced from the city by some other violent act in those circumstances, he would easily have borne it; indeed, inasmuch as he had kept away from the senate the whole previous year—where yet (had he come) he could have seen that I allied myself with all his public policies— could he calmly remain in the city when I had been expelled and when, though the attack was nominally launched against me, the whole senate and his opinion in particular were in effect condemned? In fact he yielded to the same circumstances as did I, the same frenzied tribune, the same consuls, the same threats, treachery, and terror. I drained a larger draught of grief, but he drank no smaller cup of anguish.

(64) When allies, kings, and free communities were being wronged in so many and such grievous ways, the consuls should have complained: kings and foreign tribes have always been under the protection of that magistracy. Were the consuls ever heard to utter a sound? (Come to that, who would pay attention, however loudly they wished to complain?) When I, a citizen, was beset for the fatherland's sake through no bad act of my own, these consuls failed to protect me not only while I was still standing but even after I had been laid low: were they about to complain about the king of Cyprus? I had yielded to the plebs' ill-will, if you claim that they were estranged from me (which was not in fact the case); to the general circumstances, if there seemed to be disturbance on every side; to force, if violence was in store; to the deal that had been made, if the magistrates were in cahoots; to the public interest, if my fellow-citizens were in danger. (65) Why, when a proposal was being made on the life and standing of a citizen—what sort of citizen is beside the point—and his goods were being posted for auction as forfeit, why, when the Twelve Tables and the laws that it is a sacrilege to disobey hallow the principle that no measure can be introduced to the disadvantage of a specific individual and no

measure concerning a person's life as a citizen can be voted save in the centuriate assembly—why were the consuls not heard to utter a sound, why did it become established in that year—so far as it lay in the power of those two plagues upon our dominion—that *any* citizen could justly be driven from the civil community by a measure brought against him by name through the efforts of thugs whipped up at an assembly presided over by the tribune of the plebs?

(66) As for the measures that were published that year, the promises that many received, the plans that were drafted, the hopes formed, the plots hatched—what am I to say? Was there any spot on earth that was not promised to someone, any conduct of public business capable of being planned, desired, imagined that was not dealt out? Any kind of command or public charge, any plan for minting money or raking it in that was not devised? Was there any tract of land of any extent, inland or coastal, where some client-kingdom was not established? Any king that year who did not judge he either ought to buy something that was not his or ransom back something that was? Did anyone look to the senate for a province, a budget, a staff appointment? Return from exile was made ready for people condemned for crimes of public violence while that 'priest of the people' prepared a bid for the consulship: as the tribune of the plebs set all this in motion with the consuls' help, patriots groaned and the wicked took heart.

(67) Here at last—later than he would have liked, and very much against the wishes of those who had deflected this most excellent and heroic man from defending my well-being through their plots and concocted terrors—Gnaeus Pompeius reawakened his habit of constructive engagement in the people's business after that habit had been, not lulled to sleep, but slowed by some suspicion. This is the man who had mastered with a victor's manliness citizens utterly steeped in crime, the fiercest enemies, vast tribes, kings, peoples strange and wild, innumerable pirates, even slaves, who ended all wars on land and sea and extended the bounds of the Roman people's dominion to the ends of the earth: *he* did not allow a few criminals to overturn the commonwealth that he had often saved as much with his blood as with his policies. He stepped up to act in the public interest, he blocked with his authority the measures still awaiting execution, he expressed his indignation at what had already been

done: people began to see a glimmer of hope. (**68**) On 1 June a packed meeting of the senate passed a decree concerning my return on the motion of Lucius Ninnius, whose loyalty and manliness never wavered on my behalf. Some good-for-nothing named Ligus, an appendage of my enemies, interposed a veto. My situation had now reached the point where it seemed to perk up and take life. Whoever had added to my grief by joining in Clodius' criminal doings, wherever he came, whatever trial at law he underwent, was condemned; no one could be found to admit that he had voted against me. My brother had left his governorship of Asia with a great show of mourning and with still greater genuine grief: as he approached the city the whole community had come out to meet him with tears and lamentation. Discussion was held in the senate more freely, and members of the equestrian order hurriedly gathered; the noble Piso, my son-in-law, who was not allowed to enjoy the reward for his devotion either from me or from the Roman people, demanded of his kinsman his father-in-law's return; the senate kept refusing to take up any business if the consuls did not first move my restoration.

(**69**) Success now seemed within our grasp, and the consuls had lost all freedom of action because of their bargain over the provincial assignments: whenever senators who then held no public office demanded the opportunity to state their opinion about me, the consuls said they were deterred by Clodius' law. When at length they found this position untenable, a plan was formed to murder Gnaeus Pompeius: after the plan was uncovered and a weapon seized, he shut himself up in his house for the balance of my enemy's tribunate. Eight tribunes promulgated a bill for my return: this showed, not that I had gained friends in my absence (quite the opposite: in my misfortune some whom I had taken to be friends proved otherwise), but that they had always had the same desire though not the same freedom to act on it. Of the nine tribunes whom I had had on my side, one defected in my absence—a fellow who had stolen his cognomen from the ancestral masks of the Aelii, only to appear to be one of the tribe, not one of the clan. (**70**) In this year, then, when the magistrates for the next year had already been elected and their good faith gave all patriots grounds to hope for a better political situation, the leader of the senate, Publius Lentulus, became my champion, pitting his authority and express judgement against the resistance of Piso and Gabinius, and on the motion of the eight tribunes made a truly excellent statement on my case: though he saw that he would gain greater glory and more gratitude for a most substantial favour were the matter held over without action to his own consulship, he nonetheless preferred that so important a matter be completed sooner by others than later by himself. (71) Meanwhile, at about this time, judges, Publius Sestius travelled to see Gaius Caesar for the sake of my well-being: he thought that it would contribute to the citizens' harmony if Caesar was not ill-disposed to the case, and make it easier to bring the affair to a good end. What he did, how much he accomplished, has no bearing on the matter at hand; for my part, I judge that if Caesar was inclined to be well-disposed to me (as I believe was the case), Sestius gained no further ground; if Caesar was rather hostile, Sestius gained not much. But still, you see the man's punctiliousness and uprightness.

Now I enter on the topic of Sestius' tribunate; for he made that journey before, for the commonwealth's sake, as tribune-elect. When the year came to an end and people seemed to be reviving—if not yet because the commonwealth had been regained then at least in the hope of regaining it—those two vultures clad in commanders' cloaks left the city, with bad omens and people's curses—I only wish that they indeed had suffered what people were praying for! For then we would not have lost the province of Macedonia, with a whole army, nor our cavalry and best infantry units in Syria. (72) The tribunes of the plebs entered office, having unanimously affirmed that they would publish a measure concerning my recall. For starters, my enemies bought one of these—the one whom people, in mockery and grief, called 'Gracchus', because it was the community's fate that that little field mouse, when plucked from the thorn-bushes, would try to nibble away at the commonwealth. Then another—not the famous Serranus summoned from his plough, but the one from the barren estate of Gavius Olelus, grafted onto the Atilii of Calatia from the Gavii of Gaul—suddenly removed his name from the posted notice after the posting of some entries in account books. The first of the year arrives, and you know what comes next better than I, who for my part only repeat what I heard: the senate with its full throng, the people on tenterhooks, the gathering of delegations from all of Italy, the grave and manly performance of the consul Publius

Lentulus, even the restraint shown concerning me by his colleague, who said that though he and I were personal enemies because of our political disagreements, he would overlook that enmity for the sake of the conscript fathers and the commonwealth's crisis.

(73) Then, when Lucius Cotta was called on to give his opinion first, he gave a statement completely worthy of our commonwealth, to the effect that no action taken concerning me had been in accord with justice, the ways of our ancestors, or the laws; no one could be removed from the civil community without a trial; where a person's life as a citizen is at stake, not only can no legislative measure be proposed but no judicial decision can be made save in the centuriate assembly; what was done amounted to an act of violence, a conflagration of the commonwealth, shaken to its foundation in unsettled times; once justice and the courts had been uprooted, with a great revolution threatening, I had swerved a bit from my course and, in the hope of finding peace for the future, had escaped the storm-tossed seas that lay before my eyes. Accordingly (he went on), because by my absence I had rescued the commonwealth from perils no less great than on a certain occasion when I had been present, it was appropriate that I be not just restored by the senate but also honored. He also made a number of shrewd points, including this: the measure concerning me, which that utterly mad and debauched enemy of proper shame and chastity had written, was such—in its language, substance, and resolutions—that even had it been properly brought to a vote it could not have the force of law; accordingly, since I was not absent under the terms of any law, I did not need to be restored by passage of a law but could properly be recalled by the authority of the senate. (74) Everyone thought that this was plainest truth; but when Gnaeus Pompeius was called upon for his opinion after Cotta, he said that though he could approve and praise Cotta's view, he himself judged that for the sake of my tranquillity, to be certain that I would be rid of harassment from 'popular' quarters, the Roman people's beneficence toward me ought to be joined to the senate's authority. When all had spoken for my restoration, with each speaker trying to outbid the last in terms of solemn honor, and unanimous support had been expressed in a vote, Atilius Gavianus then got to his feet, as you know: though he had been bought, even he did not dare to veto the proposal, but he asked that he be given the

night to ponder the matter. The senate erupted in a clamour of lamentation and entreaty; Atilius' father-in-law threw himself at his feet in supplication; Atilius gave his word that he would cause no delay the next day, and was believed. The meeting was adjourned. In the course of the long night that followed, the 'ponderer' had his fee doubled. In the days that followed during the month of January there were very few on which the senate was permitted to meet; but when it did meet, it conducted no business save that touching my case.

(75) Though the senate's authority was being blocked by every kind of delay, insulting deception, and crooked dealing, there came at last a day on which the assembly of the plebs could take up my case, 23 January. The person proposing the bill, Quintus Fabricius, a gentleman most devoted to me, occupied the sacred precinct a little before dawn. Sestius—the man arraigned here on a charge of public violence—spent the day quietly: the alleged chief agent and defender of my interests did not set foot in public but waited to see what my enemies had planned. And what about those who plotted to bring Publius Sestius to trial—how did they conduct themselves? Since they had seized the forum, the Comitium, and the senate house in the dead of night with armed men and many slaves, they launched a violent attack on Fabricius, killing a number of people and wounding many. (76) They violently drove off Marcus Cispius, a tribune of the plebs and a man of greatest excellence and resolve, as he was entering the forum: there they caused a horrendous massacre and went about in a body, with swords drawn and bloodied, calling out and looking for my brother, a man of extraordinary excellence and bravery, and most devoted to me. He for his part would gladly have offered up his body to their weapons, not in resistance but to end his life in his great grief and yearning for me, save that he had kept himself alive to work for the hope of my return. Be that as it may, when he faced the monstrous violence of those brigands steeped in crime and was driven from the Rostra, whither he had come to plead with the Roman people for his brother's well-being, he hid in the Comitium, where his slaves and freedmen shielded him with their bodies: thus he warded off death under the protection afforded, not by law and legal procedure, but by flight and the cover of night. (77) You recall, judges, how the Tiber was filled then with the bodies of citizens, the sewers stuffed, and how the blood had to be cleared from the

forum with sponges—surely (everyone thought) such massive armed force and such lavish logistical support was not private or plebeian but patrician and praetorian.

You charge Sestius with no involvement at all, either on that most tumultuous of days or before. 'But yet there was violence done in the forum.' Of course—when was there ever greater? We have very often seen rock-throwing, less often—but still too often—drawn swords; but who ever saw such slaughter in the forum, such great heaps of bodies, save perhaps on that awful day when Cinna and Octavius clashed? What stirred feelings to such a pitch? For civil unrest often arises from the obstinacy or resolve of a tribune's veto, when the person bringing the bill has culpably and wickedly promised some advantage or boon to the ignorant; it arises when magistrates clash, but it arises gradually, first when voices are raised, then when an assembly of the people is breaking up, and only later, and rarely, does it come to actual violence: who ever heard of such unrest stirred up at night, when not a word had been uttered, no assembly of the people had been called, no law had been put to the vote? (78) Is it really likely that a Roman citizen, or any free person, would come down to the forum armed with a sword before dawn, to prevent passage of a motion concerning me, save those who for a long time now have been battening on the life's blood of the commonwealth thanks to that pestilentially desperate citizen? Here now I ask the prosecutor himself, who complains that Publius Sestius, as a tribune, had an armed guard of massive proportions: he didn't that day, did he? Certainly not. And for that reason the commonwealth's interests were undone, and they were undone not by appeal to auspices, not by a veto, not by ballots, but by violence, by the fist, by the sword. For if that praetor who declared that he had watched the heavens for omens had announced a sighting to Fabricius, the commonwealth would have been dealt a blow, but one that, once received, it could bear. If one of Fabricius' fellow-tribunes had entered a veto with him, the commonwealth would have been harmed, but constitutionally. Would you spring assassins from prison, join them with the rookie gladiators brought in surreptitiously to grace the aedileship you planned, and let them loose before dawn, would you eject magistrates from a sacred precinct, produce the grossest sort of massacre, and clear the forum—and then, when you have done all this with force of arms, accuse of public violence a man who protected himself with a bodyguard, not to attack you but to save his own life?

(79) And yet not even from that point on did Sestius fortify himself with supporters in order to conduct his magistracy safely in the forum and serve the needs of the commonwealth. Thus, relying on the sacrosanct status of tribunes and reckoning that he was protected by laws it is a sacrilege to break—not only against violence and the sword but even against verbal attack and interruption—he came into the temple of Castor and announced to the consul that he had observed an unfavourable omen: thereupon that gang of Clodius' thugs, already victorious in the massacre of citizens, suddenly raised a clamour, became inflamed, and moved to the attack, setting upon the unarmed and unprepared tribune, some with swords, some with clubs and chunks torn from the barriers. Sestius here, already wounded numerous times, his body weakened and lacerated, lost consciousness and collapsed. Only the general belief that he was already dead kept him from being killed: when they saw him lying torn by many wounds and breathing his last, pale as death and done for, they finally stopped hacking at him, more out of exhaustion and misapprehension than from pity and the sense that enough was enough. (80) And *Sestius* is the one arraigned for public violence? Why—because he's still alive? Well, that's through no fault of his own: had one final blow landed, it would have drained the breath of life for good. Accuse Lentidius: he didn't hit the right spot. Abuse Titius, the Sabine from Reate, for rashly crying out 'He's dead!' But why accuse Sestius himself? He didn't fail to offer himself to his enemy's weapons, did he ? He didn't fight back, did he? He didn't fail—as the order commonly given to gladiators puts it—to 'receive the sword', did he?

Is this very thing—that he could not die—a case of public violence? or that a tribune of the plebs bled on the temple? or that when he'd been carried off and first came to himself, he didn't give the order to be carried back? Where is the crime here? What do you criticize him for doing? (81) I ask you this question, judges: if on that day Clodius' no-good clan had achieved what they wanted, if Publius Sestius, who was left for dead, had actually been killed, would you have taken up arms, roused yourselves to match the spirit of our fathers, the manliness of our ancestors? Would you at long last have

demanded that that deadly brigand give you back the commonwealth? Or would you still keep mum, still delay, still be afraid, though
you saw the commonwealth crushed and trampled by utterly criminal
assassins and by slaves? If, therefore, you would avenge this man's
death—if in fact you had it in mind to be free men living in a
commonwealth—do you reckon that you should hesitate over what
you ought to say, to feel, to think, to judge about his manliness while
he is still alive? (82) But those very men—the sort to murder their
own kin, whose unbridled frenzy is nurtured by their longstanding
impunity—were so horrified by the violence of their own crime that
if the belief in Sestius' death had persisted a bit longer, they considered killing their own Gracchus, to pin the crime on us. That little
bumpkin—not an incautious fellow, and anyway the good-for-
nothings couldn't keep quiet about it—perceived that Clodius' thugs
were after his blood, to quench the ill will their crime had caused. He
snatched up the mule-driver's cowl he had worn when he first came
to Rome to vote and held up a harvester's basket to cover his features:
when they went around, some looking for Numerius, other for
Quintus, he was saved by the mistake due to his two first names.
You all know that the fellow was at risk the whole time until Sestius
was known to be alive; and if that fact had not been revealed—sooner
than I would have liked—that lot's murder of their own hireling
would have succeeded, not in shifting the ill-will to their intended
targets, but in lessening the disgrace of their utterly atrocious crime
by, as it were, an agreeable crime. (83) And if, judges, Publius Sestius
had given up the ghost in the temple of Castor, as he nearly did, I am
quite certain that—if only the senate had its proper role in the commonwealth, if the majesty of the Roman people were reinvigorated—
a statue would at some point be raised in the forum to honor Sestius
as one who died for the commonwealth. Indeed, none of those you
see, whose statues our ancestors set in the forum and on the Rostra
after they died, would deservedly be given precedence over Publius
Sestius in respect of either the atrociousness of his death or the zeal
displayed for the commonwealth: for when he had championed the
cause of a citizen stricken by catastrophe—a friend, a man who had
earned the commonwealth's gratitude—and the cause of the senate,
Italy, and the commonwealth, when he upheld the sacred auspices
and announced what he had perceived, those wicked plagues on the

community cut him down in broad daylight, in the sight of gods and men, in the most sanctified precinct, as he was acting in the most sanctified cause and in the most sanctified office. Will anyone say, then, that his life ought to be stripped of its honors, when you would think his death worthy of an eternal monument's honor?

(84) 'You hired henchmen,' the prosecutor says to Sestius, 'you placed them under constraint and got them ready.' To do what? To lay siege to the senate, send citizens into exile without a trial, steal their goods, burn their houses, overturn their dwellings, set the temples of the immortal gods on fire, dislodge tribunes of the plebs from the Rostra by force of arms, sell whatever provinces he wants to whomever he wants, recognize foreign kings, use our legates to restore to free communities people convicted on charges that make their lives as citizens forfeit, detain the foremost man of the community under siege at sword-point? It was to do these things, I suppose—which could never have been done if the commonwealth had not been crushed by armed force—that Publius Sestius assembled his band and the resources he needed. 'But the time was not yet ripe, the actual state of affairs did not yet force patriots to these sorts of protection.' I had been expelled, not entirely by that criminal's band, but still not without it: you mourned in silence. (85) The forum had been seized the preceding year, the temple of Castor occupied by fugitives as though it were some city's citadel: silence reigned. Men made desperate by need and recklessness were running everything with uproar, tumult, violence: you put up with it. <Some> magistrates were being driven from sacred precincts, others were being entirely forbidden to enter the forum: no one resisted. Gladiators from the praetor's entourage were seized and brought into the senate, they confessed, they were thrown into prison by Milo, then released by Serranus: not a peep. The forum was strewn with the bodies of Roman citizens massacred at night: not only was no special court of inquiry established, but even the existing venues for trial were uprooted. You saw a tribune of the plebs lie dying after receiving more than twenty wounds, another tribune of the plebs—a godlike man (yes, I shall say what I think, and what all agree with me in thinking), godlike and endowed with a remarkable, an unprecedented largeness of spirit, gravity, and loyalty—had his house attacked by Clodius' army wielding flame and the sword.

(86) On this topic even you praise Milo, and rightly: for have we ever seen his like for immortal manliness? Seeking no other reward than the good opinion of patriots—a thing nowadays thought passé, and despised—he faced every form of danger, the most demanding toil, the most consequential conflicts and enmities, and alone among all our fellow-citizens has, I think, demonstrated in deed, not words, what it is ever right for outstanding men to do in the commonwealth, and what they are constrained to do: it is ever right to resist by law and the courts the crimes of reckless men who seek to overturn the commonwealth; but if the laws are not in force, if the courts have been suspended, if the commonwealth has been overwhelmed by arms and is held fast by a violent and reckless cabal, then life and liberty must of necessity be defended with a bulwark of force. To perceive this is the role of practical intelligence; to act on it, of bravery; to perceive and to act, of complete and compounded manliness. (87) Milo began his involvement in the commonwealth's affairs as tribune of the plebs—and I shall speak at some length in his praise, not because he himself prefers this to be a subject of talk rather than sincere judgement, or because I delight in bestowing these fruits of praise on him when he is here present, especially when my words could not do the subject justice, but because I believe that if I can commend Milo's case as praised by the prosecutor's own words, you will judge that the case of Sestius, under the current charge, is on an equal footing: so then, Titus Annius began his involvement in the commonwealth's cause as one wishing to restore a citizen to the fatherland after he had been snatched away. The cause was straightforward, his plan resolved, and it met with agreement and concord on all sides. He had the assistance of his colleagues, one of the consuls was highly enthusiastic, the other's sentiments were almost pacific, only one of the praetors was opposed, the senate's will was unbelievably supportive, the equestrian order had rallied spiritedly to the cause, Italy was alert. Only two men had been bribed to throw up a roadblock, and Milo saw that if those two despicable and contemptible characters were unable to manage so large a task, he would complete his undertaking with scarcely an effort. He acted with authority, with careful planning, working with the most august category of the citizenry, conducting himself according to the example set by brave patriots: he gave the most scrupulous thought to

the course of action worthy of the commonwealth and of himself, to who he was, to the goals he ought to have, and to the compensation he owed his ancestors.

(88) Now, that gladiator saw that if it became a contest of character he could not match this man's ethical seriousness, and so he along with his army had resort to flame and sword, to daily murder, arson, and plunder: he began to attack Milo's house, to waylay him when he travelled, to provoke and terrorize him with violence. He did not budge this man of utmost seriousness and utmost resolve, and though his anguish, his innate spirit of freedom, his eager and pre-eminent manliness all urged this bravest of men to turn back and break violence with violence—especially when violence had been offered so often—his restraint and his capacity for careful thought were such that he held his anguish in check: he did not take vengeance in the same way he had been provoked but sought to bind his opponent, if he could, in the coils of the law even as he did his exultant war dance over the destruction he had wrought in the commonwealth. (89) He came to the forum to lodge an accusation. Who has ever done that in a way so appropriate to the commonwealth's cause, provoked by no personal enmity, with no reward in prospect, with no others demanding that he do it—or even thinking he would? The other fellow's spirit was broken, for with Milo prosecuting he despaired of managing the disgraceful miscarriage that had marked his earlier trial. Lo and behold, one consul, one praetor, one tribune of the plebs produced new and unprecedented edicts, forbidding his arraignment, forbidding his summoning, forbidding his being sought out, forbidding any mention whatever of judges or judgements! What could that man do—born as he was for manliness, for worthy standing, for glory—when the violence of criminals was supported while law and the courts were uprooted? Was he, a tribune of the plebs and an exceptional man, to offer his neck to a private citizen and utter wastrel? Was he to cast off the cause he had taken on, or just shut himself up in his house? Reckoning it equally disgraceful to lose or to be frightened off or to hide, he made sure that since he could not use legal measures against the man, neither he nor the commonwealth would have reason to fear peril from his violence.

(90) How then can you accuse Sestius out of one side of your mouth while praising Milo out of the other for arranging the same

sort of armed protection? Or do you suppose that the man who defends his domicile, keeps fire and sword away from his hearth and home, seeks leave to be safe—in the forum, in a sacred precinct, in the senate chamber—do you suppose that man rightly arranges for armed protection, while you ought to prosecute for public violence a man whose wounds remind him, when he sees them daily all over his body, that he needs some sort of armed guard to protect his head and neck and throat and flanks? (91) For who among us does not know, judges, how in the state of nature, before the time when either natural or civil law had been codified, human beings once wandered at random, dispersed over the earth, and possessed only the goods that murder and bloodshed enabled them to seize or retain through physical force? When, therefore, the first people of true manliness and practical intelligence arose and came to understand that human-kind was by nature teachable, they gathered the scattered people into one place and led them from their bestial state to practise justice and mildness. Then the possessions and activities that bear on the common advantage, which we call 'public,' then the human gatherings that later were labelled 'civil communities,' then the assemblages of dwellings that we call 'cities' were marked off by walls, when the principles of divine and human law had been discovered. (92) Nothing more clearly marks the difference between this way of life, refined by our distinctively human qualities, and that monstrous way of life than the difference between law and violence. If we do not wish to use the first of these, we are obliged to use the other: if we want violence to be eradicated, then law must prevail—which is to say, the courts that embody the whole concept of law; but if the courts fall out of favour or cease to exist, then violence inevitably holds sway. Everyone sees this; Milo both saw it and took steps to avail himself of the law and ward off violence. He wanted to have recourse to the law, so that real manliness might vanquish recklessness; he found it necessary to use violence, lest manliness be vanquished by recklessness. Sestius' position was the same, if not in bringing a formal accusation under the law—nor indeed was there need for everyone to do the same thing—then surely in being compelled to defend his well-being and acquire armed protection against violent assault.

(93) O immortal gods, do you offer us *any* way out, do you give the commonwealth *any* grounds for hope? How few men of such

manliness will be found to embrace all the best interests of the commonwealth, to act in the service of patriots, to seek glory that is solid and real? Especially when they know the current circumstances of the pair who almost wrote 'The End' for the commonwealth, Gabinius and Piso. The former daily drains immeasurable quantities of gold from the incredibly ample riches of Syria, he declares war against peaceful peoples in order to pour their ancient, untapped wealth into the bottomless pit of his appetites, he ostentatiously builds a villa so vast that it makes a hovel of the villa that as tribune he used to describe in detail, from a painted representation, in one assembly after another, so that he—pure and unselfish fellow that he is—could bring ill-will upon an extraordinarily brave citizen of the highest calibre. (94) For his part, Piso first of all sold peace at a huge price to the peoples of Thrace and Dardania and then handed Macedonia over to them to harass and despoil, so they could make up the cost; he shared out with their Greek debtors the goods of creditors who were Roman citizens; he extorted huge sums from the people of Dyrrachium, he plundered Thessaly, ordered the people of mainland Greece to pay a fixed sum each year, and still did not leave standing in any public place or sacred precinct a single statue, painting, or adornment. Thus do those men, who fully and justly merit any and every sort of punishment, conduct themselves outrageously, while these two men stand here accused. I could mention Numerius, Serranus, Aelius, the flotsam of Clodius' seditious rabble, but I will not; still, you can see these characters engaging in nimble skullduggery even now, nor will they have a moment's fear for themselves as long as you have some reason to fear for yourselves.

(95) For why should I speak of the aedile himself who has even accused Milo on a charge of public violence and fixed a date for the trial? Still, no wrong done to him will ever lead Milo to regret that he has displayed such manly constancy for the commonwealth's sake— yet what will the younger generation think when they see these things? The man who has assailed, razed, burned public monuments and temples and his enemies' homes, who is always tightly guarded by his hired assassins, walled in by armed men, fortified by informants (of whom there is a surplus these days), who has summoned a band of foreign criminals and bought slaves skilled in murder, and during his tribunate emptied the prison into the forum—now as

aedile he darts busily about and launches an accusation against the man who to some degree checked his ecstatic frenzy. By contrast, the man who took safeguards so that he could defend his household gods in private life and the rights of a tribune and the auspices in the public sphere was not granted leave by the senate's authority to accuse in an appropriate way the man by whom he has been accused outrageously. (96) No doubt this is the point of the question that you addressed to me, in particular, in your speech of prosecution, when you asked what our 'breed of the Best Sort' is—for that's the phrase you used. The answer to your question provides an excellent lesson for the younger generation to learn, and one that it is not difficult for me to teach: I shall say a few words on the subject, judges, and what I have to say (I believe) will not be inconsistent with our listeners' advantage, your own duty, and the case of Publius Sestius itself.

In this civil community of ours there have always been two sorts of people eager to engage in the people's business and conduct themselves with more than ordinary distinction therein: one set of these have wanted to be considered, and to be, 'men of the people,' the other 'men of the best sort'. Those whose words and deeds were intended to please the many were considered 'men of the people,' whereas those who so conducted themselves that their policies were commended by all the best sort of men were considered 'men of the best sort'. (97) Who, then, are 'all the best sort of men'? If you mean how many of them there are, they are beyond counting, and indeed we could have no stability were that not the case: some take the lead in public policy, others follow, some are members of the grandest categories of the citizenry, to whom the senate chamber lies open, others are Roman citizens in the towns and countryside, some are businessmen, and there are even freedmen who are 'men of the best sort'. The full complement of men in this category is distributed geographically and by rank, as I have said; but the category as a whole (lest there be any mistake on this point) can be pinpointed and defined briefly. All men are 'men of the best sort' who do no harm, are not wicked or rabid in their nature, and are not hobbled by embarrassments in their domestic affairs. The fact of the matter, then, is that those whom you called a 'breed' are just those who are sound and sane and have their domestic affairs in good order. The men who, in piloting the commonwealth, serve the will, the interests, and the views of the latter folk are considered defenders of the 'men of the best sort' and are them-selves counted the most serious men of the best sort, the most distinguished citizens, and the foremost men of the civil community. (**98**) What, then, is the goal of these pilots of the commonwealth, what ought they keep in view to guide their course? The condition that is the most excellent and most desirable in the view of all who are sane, patriotic, and flourishing: tranquillity joined with worthy standing. All who desire this condition are 'men of the best sort', those who achieve it are reckoned the men of the highest calibre, the men who preserve the civil community: for it is not fitting that people either get so carried away by the worthy standing derived from public affairs that they do not provide for their own tranquillity, or embrace any form of tranquillity that is at odds with worthy standing.

Moreover, this tranquil worthiness has the following bases or components, which the civil community's foremost men must watch over and protect even at the risk of their own lives as citizens: the sources of religious scruple, the auspices, the magistrates' formal powers, the senate's authority, positive law, the ways of our ancestors, the law courts, the authority to pass judgement, the validity of one's word, the provinces, our allies, the glory of our dominion, the military, the treasury. (**99**) It requires a largeness of spirit, ample intelligence, and great resolve to defend and champion so many important spheres of activity, since in so large a citizen body there is a great mass of men who look for upheaval and revolution, fearing punishment for the wrongs that weigh on their consciences, or who feed on civil discord and unrest because of a certain ingrained distemper, or who, when their finances are in shambles, prefer to go up in the flames of a general conflagration than burn all on their own. When people of this sort have found protectors to lead their vicious faction, the commonwealth is tossed by turbulent seas: vigi-lance is then required of those who have claimed the helm for themselves, and they must strive with all possible cunning and diligence to save what I just now called the 'bases and components', to maintain their course, and to reach the haven of tranquillity and worthy standing. (**100**) I would be lying, judges, if I said that this path is not rough or steep or full of snares and perils, especially since I have not only always understood it to be such but have also experienced it more keenly than any one else.

The commonwealth is assailed with greater forces than it is defended, because reckless desperadoes need only a subtle signal to set them going and are even roused all on their own against the commonwealth, whereas patriots are somehow less energetic: they ignore the first signs of trouble and are in the end stirred only by dire necessity, with the consequence that while they sluggishly hesitate, wanting to maintain their tranquillity even absent worthy standing, they sometimes lose both. (101) Moreover, the people who have claimed to be the commonwealth's bulwarks defect, if they are too irresponsible, or fail to meet the challenge, if they are too fearful: only those abide, and endure the worst for the commonwealth's sake, who are like your father, Marcus Scaurus, who stood up to all trouble-makers from Gaius Gracchus to Quintus Varius and was never daunted by any show of force, any threats, any general ill-will; or like your maternal grandfather's brother, Quintus Metellus, who as censor placed a black mark beside the name of Lucius Saturninus, then flourishing in the people's regard, who in the face of a mob incited to violence kept an in-grafted Gracchus from being added to the citizen-rolls, who alone refused to swear allegiance to a law he thought had been illegally passed and preferred to be dislodged from the civil community rather than from his views; or—to leave aside ancient examples, which our dominion has in an abun-dance worthy of its glory, and to avoid naming any of the living—like the recently lamented Quintus Catulus, who could never be moved from his chosen course by fear of peril's tempest or hope of honor's breeze.

(102) By the immortal gods, *these* are the models to imitate, those of you who seek worthy standing, who seek honor and glory! These are the models that offer true scope and splendour, godlike and deathless; these are the models that are on everyone's lips, that are entrusted to the memory of Rome's annals, that are handed down from generation to generation. It is a toilsome task, I do not deny it; the risks are great, I admit;

> many snares are set for patriots,

truer words have never been spoken; but

> to demand for yourself what many envy and many seek is folly,

the poet says,

> unless you carry out the toilsome task to the end with keenest intensity.

I would prefer that he had not also said what wicked citizens pluck from another context,

> let them hate me, so long as they fear me,

for those others were brilliant precepts to give to the younger generation. (103) But still, this principled path in administering the commonwealth was once something rather to be feared, when the masses' enthusiasm for the people's advantage was at odds with the commonwealth's interests in many areas of public business. Lucius Cassius moved his law concerning the secret ballot: the people thought its liberty was at stake in its passage; the foremost men of the community disagreed, fearing that the masses' rashness, exercised in wanton use of the ballot, endangered the well-being of the best sort of men. Tiberius Gracchus moved his agrarian law: it found favour with the people because it seemed to set the fortunes of poorer citizens on a more stable footing; the best sort of men struggled against it, because they saw it as a way of stirring up discord and judged that the commonwealth would be stripped of its defenders if the rich were dislodged from their long-time holdings. Gaius Gracchus moved his grain law: a delightful business for the plebs, for it generously provided sustenance free of toil; patriots, by contrast, fought back, because they reckoned that the plebs would be seduced from the ways of hard work and become slothful, and they saw that the treasury would be drained dry.

(104) In living memory too there are have been many instances (I intentionally passed them by in silence) when the people's excessive desires and the policy of the foremost men were in conflict. Now, however, there is no cause for the people to dissent from the elite and the leading men: it makes no demands and has no desire for revolution but is delighted by its own tranquillity, by the worthy standing of all the best men, and by the glory of the commonwealth overall. Accordingly, those who wish to foment unrest and cause upheaval, finding themselves unable to use largesse to stir the Roman people into a tumult—the plebs having embraced tranquillity and put the most serious bouts of unrest behind it—call assemblies of the people

crowded with their hired henchmen: they do not aim at giving speeches or making motions that the people in the assembly really want to hear, but by spreading their money around they make the audience appear to want to hear whatever they say. (105) You do not suppose, do you, that the Gracchi or Saturninus or any of the ancients who were considered 'men of the people' ever had hired henchmen in an assembly of the people? Not one of them did, because the largesse itself roused the masses with hopes for the proposed advantage; hiring them with wages was unnecessary. Consequently, though the 'men of the people' in those days found no favour with serious and respectable persons, they enjoyed the people's favourable judgement, which was displayed in any number of ways: they were applauded in the theatre, they got the votes to achieve their aims, people cherished their names, their ways of speaking, their looks, their very gaits. The men who opposed that lot were considered serious people of great substance; but while they had much influence in the senate, and the most influence with real patriots, they were not to the masses' liking, their proposals often got voted down, and if ever any of them was applauded, he had to fear that he had done something wrong. And yet whenever any matter of more than ordinary importance arose, it was the authority of these men that most moved the people.

(106) Now unless I am mistaken, our civil community is in a state where—if you get rid of the hired henchmen—there would be unanimous agreement on matters of public interest. And indeed, there are three places where the Roman people's judgement and desires touching <the commonwealth> can be expressed: in the assemblies where they are addressed by a magistrate, in their voting assemblies, and when they gather for games or gladiator shows. To take the first of these: what assembly of the people has there been in recent years—I mean a real assembly, not a gathering of hired henchmen—in which the agreement of the Roman people has not been perfectly clear? That utterly criminal gladiator convened many assemblies to talk about me, but no one attended who had not been corrupted, no one who was sound: no patriot wanted to look on his disgusting countenance or hear his hellish voice. Those assemblies of desperadoes were inevitably riotous. (107) By contrast, when the consul Publius Lentulus likewise convened an assembly to talk

about me, the Roman people gathered in a mass, all the categories of the citizenry, all Italy stood together: his case, made with utmost seriousness and eloquence, was received with such silence and such unanimous approval that it seemed nothing so 'popular' had ever reached the Roman people's ears. He then introduced Gnaeus Pompeius, who not only put his moral weight behind my well-being but <presented> himself as a suppliant of the Roman people: though his speech was serious and pleasing, as it always is in such assemblies, I assert that his views have never carried greater authority or his eloquence met with greater delight. (108) With what silence were all the other foremost men of the civil community attended when they spoke about me! (I do not name them at this point in my speech, lest my remarks seem ungrateful, if I say too little about any individual, or endless, if I say enough about them all.) Consider now that enemy of mine addressing a real assembly of the people in the Campus Martius: was there anyone who did not merely disapprove but did not think it a gross miscarriage that he was alive and breathing, let alone speaking? Was there anyone who did not judge his utterances a blot on the commonwealth, making all who listened complicit in his crime?

(109) I now turn to the assemblies where people vote, whether for magistrates or on laws. We often see many laws put to a vote (I set to one side those voted on when scarcely five people in a tribe can be found to vote, and not all of those in their proper tribe). That catastrophe of the commonwealth says that he brought to a vote a law concerning me, who he said was a 'tyrant' responsible for 'the theft of freedom'. Is there anyone who will admit that he cast his ballot when the measure aimed against me was being put to the vote? But when a measure, concerning me again, was put before the centuriate assembly in accordance with the decree of the senate, is there anyone who will not declare that he was present and cast his ballot for my well-being? Which of these measures ought to be regarded as 'popular', then, one on which people of all degrees of honor in the community, of all ages, and of all the categories of the citizenry are in agreement, or one in which demons roused to a frenzy swoop down and converge as though on the commonwealth's funeral? (110) Or is it the case that whatever side Gellius happens to take—a person unworthy both of his brother, a most distinguished

man and excellent consul, and of the equestrian order, of which he retains the title, though he's squandered its trappings—will be 'popular'? 'Yes, for the fellow's devoted to the Roman people.' Oh yes, in a quite unprecedented way: though as a youth he could have prospered amid the most substantial offices of Lucius Philippus, his stepfather and a man of the highest calibre, he was so far from being 'a man of the people' that all by himself he wasted his entire estate in gluttony; then passing from his coarse and filthy youth, in which he had reduced his patrimony from a fortune (as laymen reckon such things) to a pittance worthy of philosophers, he wanted to be thought a proper Greekling of leisure and of a sudden devoted himself to literary studies. Of course, he derived no benefit from readers who spoke pure Attic, and he often even pawned his books for wine: his belly's appetite was infinite, but not his purse. And so while ever living with the hope of a revolution, he was withering away in a commonwealth that was tranquil and placid.

Has there ever been *any* civil unrest in which he was not a ringleader? *Any* troublemaker with whom he was not a close friend? *Any* riotous assembly of the people that he did not stir up? Has he ever commended any patriot? 'Commended,' did I say? Rather, is there any sturdy patriot whom he has not attacked in the coarsest terms? (No doubt it was to be seen cultivating the plebs, not for the sake of his lust, that he married a woman who was once a slave.) (111) *He* cast his ballot concerning me, *he* was there, *he* joined in the parricides' feasts and celebrations—though I have to say that he gave me a measure of revenge when he kissed my enemies with that mouth of his. He is my enemy because he has nothing—as though it's my fault that he lost everything: did I steal your patrimony, Gellius, or did you eat it up? Was I the one to pay the price for your living it up, you wastrel swill-pot, so that if I defended the commonwealth against you and your cronies, you'd want me sent into exile? Not one of your friends and family wants to look at you, they flee at your approach, they avoid stopping and talking with you: your sister's son Postumius, a serious young man, showed an old man's wisdom in stigmatizing you when he did not include you among the large number of potential guardians for his children. But I've been carried away by the hatred I feel, on my own account and the commonwealth's (nor can I say which *he* hates more), and so I've said more than I ought on the subject of this utterly frenzied and bankrupt glutton. (112) To return to the point: when the city was held captive and oppressed and the measure against me was passed, Gellius, Firmidius, Titius, and demons of the same sort were the leaders and instigators of those mercenary gangs, and the one who actually brought the motion was every bit their match for shame, recklessness, and disgrace. But when the motion concerning my worthy standing was brought, no one thought he could be excused from voting even on grounds of illness or old age, and there was no one who did not think that he was restoring not just me but the commonwealth to its rightful place at the same time.

(113) Let's turn now to the assemblies in which magistrates are elected. There was recently a cadre of tribunes in which three were thought to be not in the least 'popular', while two were emphatically so. Of the former, who were not able to make their case in those assemblies of the people where all the participants were hirelings, I see that two have been elected praetors by the Roman people; and as far as I could gather from the word on the street and the pattern of voting, the Roman people wore it as a badge of honor that Gnaeus Domitius' resolute and outstanding spirit in the tribunate and Quintus Ancharius' loyal bravery found favour in their eyes, for the good intentions they displayed, even if they could not accomplish anything. As for Gaius Fannius, we see the sort of esteem in which he is held, and no one ought to doubt what judgement the Roman people will pass on him when he stands for office. (114) Well then, what have those two 'popular' tribunes accomplished? One of them acted with restraint, brought no motions, and merely took a political line different from what people expected—a good and righteous man, approved on all counts by patriots—but because he evidently did not fully understand where the people's sentiments truly lay during his tribunate, and because he mistook for the Roman people the mob hired to hear a harangue, he has not achieved the place that he would have very easily have reached had he not wanted to be 'popular'. The other one, who so asserted himself in the popular cause that he thought the auspices, the *lex Aelia*, the senate's authority, the consul, his own colleagues, and the good opinion of patriots all to be worthless, stood for the aedileship against patriots and people who were of the first rank, though their resources and influence were not

overwhelming: he did not even carry his own tribe and on top of that lost the Palatine tribe, which all those pestilential characters were allegedly using to harass the commonwealth, achieving in the election nothing that patriots would want him to achieve save defeat. Obviously, then, the people itself is, so to speak, not now 'popular,' seeing that it so emphatically rejects those who are considered 'popular' and finds most worthy of office those who oppose that lot.

(115) Let's come now to the games—for your alert attention and your gaze, judges, make me think that I may be permitted to speak in a more informal way. Demonstrations of favour in assemblies where the people vote or hear a harangue are sometimes genuine, sometimes flawed and corrupt, but when the people gather for plays and gladiator shows it is said to be quite customary that the applause they give, when some irresponsible people have purchased it, is meager and sporadic; still, when that happens it is easy to see how it has been arranged, and who is behind it, and what the upright mass of people is doing. Why should I speak now of the sorts of men or the kinds of citizen who receive the most applause? You all know the truth. Let's stipulate that it is a trivial phenomenon (something I do not actually believe, seeing that it is granted to all the best people); but if it is trivial, it is so in the eyes of serious people, whereas the sort whose lives depend on utterly trivial things, who are gripped and led by the gossip and (as they themselves say) the people's favour, cannot help but equate applause with immortality and hissing with death. (116) So I ask you above all, Scaurus, seeing that you produced the most elaborate and expensive games, did *any* of those 'popular' types look at your games, did *any* of them entrust his reputation to the theatre and the Roman people? And that notorious performer—no mere spectator, but an actor and a feature on the bill—the one who knows all his sister's special numbers, who is admitted to a gathering of women dressed as a harp-girl: he did not set eyes on your games during that fiery tribunate of his, nor on any others, save those from which he barely escaped alive. Once and only once, I assert, did that 'man of the people' entrust himself to an audience at the games, when honor had been paid to manliness in the temple of Virtus and the monument of Gaius Marius, who saved this dominion of ours, provided sanctuary to Marius' fellow-townsman and defender of the commonwealth.

(117) And indeed on that occasion the Roman people's sentiments were made perfectly clear on both sides of the question. First, when news of the senate's decree was learned, unanimous applause arose both for the fact itself and for the senate, and again when the individual members returned from the senate to watch the games; then when the consul who was himself giving the games took his seat, the people all stood, holding out their upturned hands, expressing their thanks, and weeping for joy, and made brilliantly clear their goodwill and their pity for me. But when that maniac arrived, driven by the impulse of his own deranged mind, the Roman people scarcely restrained themselves from exercising their hatred on his unspeakably polluted body but erupted with cries, threatening gestures, and clamorous curses. (118) But why speak of the Roman people's manly spirit, as it at long last caught a glimpse of freedom after its long servitude, in the case of a person whose dignity not even the actors spared when he was already a candidate for the aedileship sitting there before them? For when a comedy in Roman dress—'The Pretender', I believe—was being staged, the whole company leaned over, right into the polluted fellow's face, and harangued him in ringing unison:

> This, Titus, is the sequel for you, the outcome
> of your vicious way of life!

He sat as though he'd been pole-axed: the man who used to pack the assemblies of the people over which he presided with choruses of orchestrated abuse was being driven from the orchestra by the chorus's abuse! And since I have mentioned games, I will not omit to point out this as well: amid the great variety of thoughts that get expressed in the theater, all poetic tags that seemed relevant to current circumstances have always caught the notice of the people as a body and been given pertinent expression by the actor on stage.

(119) And I beg you, judges, not to suppose that I've been led by some spirit of frivolity to adopt this unaccustomed way of speaking, if I talk about poets, actors, and games in a court of law. I am not so ignorant of legal procedures, nor so unpractised in public speaking, that I go hunting indiscriminately for my material and pluck and pick embellishments from any and every source. I know what your serious purpose, my own role as advocate, this gathering, the worthy

standing of Publius Sestius, the scope of his peril, my own stage and station in life—I know what all these demand. But I undertook the task of instructing the next generation on this topic—who the best sort of people are—and in making that plain I must show that not all who are thought to be 'men of the people' are that in fact. This I shall accomplish most easily if I depict the true and uncorrupted judgement of the people as a whole and the most deep-seated feelings of our civil community. (120) Wasn't that what was achieved when—as soon as word of the senate's decree passed in the temple of Virtus was relayed to the theatre, at the games where a vast crowd was gathered—that supreme craftsman, who has (by Hercules!) ever played the best role in our commonwealth no less than on the stage, pled my case before the Roman people, with tears of fresh joy mixed with grief and longing for me, and with much weightier words than I could have done myself? He gave expression to the foremost poet's talent not only through his craft but also through his grief: for when he forcefully delivered the lines on

> the one who with mind resolved aided the commonwealth,
> set it upright, and stood with the Achaeans,

he was saying that I stood with all of *you*, he was pointing at all the categories of the citizenry! Everyone called for a reprise—

> when the going was uncertain
> he scarce balked to put his life at risk, unsparing of his fortunes.

What a clamour greeted that performance! (121) The practised movements of the stage went by the boards, applause rained down for the poet's words, the actor's intensity, and the thought that I was going to return:

> greatest friend amid the greatest war—

then in the spirit of friendship he added, and people approved, perhaps from some yearning they felt:

> endowed with greatest talent.

And what a groan arose from the Roman people when soon in the same play he delivered this phrase:

> Oh father—

I, I in my absence should be mourned as a father, he thought—I whom Quintus Catulus and many others in the senate had called 'father of the fatherland'. What copious tears he shed in lamenting my fall in flames and ruin—the father expelled, his home set afire and razed to the ground, the fatherland beset—and what an effect he achieved: first gesturing toward my earlier good fortune, then whirling round to say,

> All this I saw in flames!

he roused to weeping even those hostile to my person and envious of my success! (122) By the immortal gods! What a performance then followed! Every word, every gesture such that I think even Quintus Catulus, were he to come back to life, could speak the lines with distinction—for he was often accustomed freely to criticize and indict the people for rashness or the senate for folly:

> Oh ungrateful Argives, thankless Greeks, unmindful of the favour done you!

Though that was not quite true: for those prevented from restoring well-being to the one from whom they had received it were not ungrateful but unhappy, nor was any individual ever more thankful to anyone than all the people together were to me. But still, the following line that the poet wrote, most eloquently, with reference to me, the actor—not just the best, but the bravest—delivered with reference to me, when he pointed to all the categories of the citizenry and indicted the senate, the equestrian order, the Roman people as a body:

> You leave him in exile, you left him to be driven out, and now he's driven
>   out
> you put up with it!

How they all joined then in a demonstration, how the Roman people as a body made plain its feelings for a man who is not 'popular'— well, I for my part only heard the report, those who were present can more readily judge.

(123) And since the course of my speech has carried me to this point, let me develop it a bit further. The actor wept over my misfortune time and again, pleading my case with such deep feeling that that brilliant voice of his was stopped by tears; nor did the poet, whose talents I have ever esteemed, fail me in my hour of need; and

the Roman people made plain their agreement not only with their applause but also with their groans. Tell me, then: should an Aesopus or an Accius have said all this on my behalf—were the Roman people truly free—or should the foremost men of our civil community? In the 'Brutus' I was mentioned by name—

Tullius, who set freedom on a firm footing for the citizens—

and the line got countless encores. Did the Roman people seem uncertain that I and the senate had set in place what those desperadoes accused us of destroying?

(124) But the Roman people as a body made its verdict plain most importantly at the gladiatorial contests put on by Scipio, an offering worthy both of Scipio himself and of the Metellus in whose honor it was made, the sort of spectacle that is attended by a great crowd of all kinds of people, and in which the masses take special pleasure. Publius Sestius came to this gathering during his tribunate, when his activities centred on me alone, and he showed himself to the people—not because he was eager for applause, but so that my enemies could see for themselves the wishes of the people as a whole. He came, as you all know, from Maenius' column: such great applause arose, from vantage points as far away as the Capitol and from the barriers in the forum, that the unanimity of the Roman people as a body was said to have been greater and more evident than in any case in history. (125) Where then were those men who hold the reins of the people's assemblies, who lord it over the laws, who expel members of the civil community? Do the wicked citizens have in their pockets some other 'people' that found me offensive and hateful?

For my part, I think that the populace on no occasion has gathered in greater numbers than at those gladiatorial shows—not at any assembly of the people nor indeed at any voting assembly. What then did this infinite mass of humanity, this unanimous demonstration of the whole Roman people's sentiments, when it was thought that my case would be taken up in those very days—what did it make plain save that the Roman people as a body holds dear the well-being, the worthy standing, of its best citizens. (126) By contrast that praetor, who used to ask an assembly of the people whether it wished me to return—putting the question not in the established way of his father, of his grandfather, of his great-grandfather, in short of all his ancestors, but in the way of petty Greeks—and, on the strength of his hirelings' lifeless response, used to declare that the Roman people did not so wish: *he* never showed himself when he came to watch the gladiators, though he came every day. No, he would pop up suddenly, when he had crept in under the temporary seating, looking as though he were about to say

Mother, I call on you!

And so the shadowy route he took to see the show was coming to be called 'the Appian way'. Still, whenever he was glimpsed, the hissing that suddenly arose scared not just the gladiators but even their very horses! (127) Do you see, then, how great a difference there is between the Roman people and an assembly gathered for a harangue? Do you see that the lords of these assemblies are stigmatized by all the people's hatred, while those who are not allowed a hearing in assemblies of hirelings are honored by the Roman people in every sort of demonstration?

Do *you* try to use against me the name of Marcus Atilius Regulus, who instead of remaining at Rome preferred to return of his own accord to face punishment in Carthage, without the captives who were the cause of his dispatch to the senate? Do you say that *I* should not have chosen to return to Rome by resorting to gangs of armed gladiators? (128) As though violence was something I was after, who got nowhere while violence reigned, and who would never have been undermined without violence. Was I to reject this restoration—an event so illustrious that I must worry lest some reckon I was led to depart by a hunger for glory in the first place, that I might enjoy such a return? For did the senate ever commend any citizen, save me, to the protection of foreign nations? Did the senate ever express formal thanks to the Roman people's allies for any citizen's well-being, save mine? In my case alone did the conscript fathers decree that provincial governors with the power of command, together with their quaestors and legates, safeguard my life and well-being. In my case alone, since the founding of the city, did the consuls send letters, in accordance with the senate's decree, to call together from the length and breadth of Italy all who desired the commonwealth's safety: what the senate never decreed when the commonwealth as a whole faced danger it thought it must decree to preserve my well-being alone. For whom did the senate chamber ever yearn more, the forum mourn, whom did the very tribunals miss as much? With my departure there was no place that was not deserted, grim, speechless, filled with grief and mourning. Is there any locale in Italy where an eagerness for my well being, a testimonial to my worthy standing, was not firmly planted in the public records?

(129) Why bring to mind those divinely worded decrees of the senate touching my case? Why mention what occurred in the temple of Jupiter Best and Greatest, when the hero who in three triumphs celebrated the joining of the three regions of the world to this our dominion bore witness, in a prepared statement of his views, to the fact that I alone had saved the fatherland? Why note that a packed meeting of the senate so fully aligned itself with his statement that only a single enemy of the people dissented, and that that very fact was entrusted to the public records, so that generations to come would ever remember it? Why add that on the next day, at the urging of the Roman people itself and of those who had gathered from the townships of Italy, the senate decreed that no one was to watch the heavens for omens, that no one was to bring to bear any cause for delay, and that if anyone did otherwise, he would patently be seeking to overturn the commonwealth: his act would be regarded most gravely by the senate and immediately be made the subject of discussion in that body. And though the full body of the senate, by the gravity of its decree, slowed the criminal recklessness of a handful of men, it still added that if action were not taken in my case within the first five days on which action could be taken, I was to return to the fatherland with all my worthy standing restored. At the same time the senate decreed that thanks be given to those who had gathered from all of Italy for sake of my well-being and that the same people be asked to reconvene when the matter was taken up again. (130) The enthusiasm for my well-being reached such a competitive pitch that the same men whom the senate asked to convene were pleading with the senate on my behalf. In all these proceedings only one man was found to dissent openly from the earnest desire of patriots, so that even the consul Quintus Metellus, who was especially hostile to me because of serious disagreements touching the commonwealth, made a motion for my well-being.

Stirred both by the supreme authority of <the senate and> Publius
Servilius' speech—endowed as it was with a stunning sort of gravity,
virtually summoning from beyond the grave all the past Metelli and
thereby turning his kinsman Metellus' intentions away from Clodius'
brigandage and back to the worthy standing of the clan that he and
Metellus had in common, reminding him of the models provided by
his own household and especially of the calamity (call it 'glorious' or
'grievous') of the great Metellus Numidicus—why, that extraordinary
gentleman, a true Metellus indeed, burst into tears and on the spot
totally surrendered to Publius Servilius as he spoke, being unable any
longer to withstand his kinsman's truly godlike gravity, which carried
the full weight of the great days of yore: he declared himself reconciled with me, as a gift freely given in my absence. (131) Surely, if
distinguished men retain any awareness after death, this gesture was
in full measure pleasing not just to all the other Metelli but especially
to one in particular, a most heroic man and foremost citizen, his own
brother, who had shared in my travails, my perils, and my policies.

As for my return—who does not know what an occasion it was,
how on my arrival the people of Brundisium extended the hand of
welcome as though on behalf of all Italy and the fatherland itself, how
that day, the fifth of August, gave birth to my arrival and return and
was at the same time the birthday of my dearly beloved daughter,
whom I then first glimpsed after a most grievous period of yearning
and grief, and of the colony of Brundisium itself and (as you know)
<of the temple of Well-being>, how the house of those most excel-
lent and cultivated men, the Laenii—Marcus Laenius Flaccus, his
father, and his brother—received me with greatest joy, the same
house that in its grief had given me refuge the previous year and
kept me safe at its own peril? Along the length of the route all the
towns of Italy seemed to observe my arrival as a holiday; the roads
were thronged with delegations sent from every direction; my approach to Rome was distinguished by an unbelievable crush of
people offering congratulations; and as I passed from the city gate,
climbed to the Capitol, and then returned home, the profound joy
I felt was mixed with grief that so fair a civil community had been so
wretchedly oppressed.

(132) So you have the answer to your question, who are the 'Best
Sort'. They are not a 'breed', as you put it, though I recognize the

word: it's a favourite of the person by whom Publius Sestius sees himself chiefly attacked, who has longed for the destruction and dissolution of this 'breed,' who has often assailed and slandered Gaius Caesar—a gentle person to whom bloodshed is alien—by asserting that Caesar will never draw an easy breath as long as this 'breed' remains alive. He's made no headway concerning the Best Sort as a body; but he has persisted in working against me and attacking me, first through Vettius the informer, whom he brought before an assembly of the people and questioned about me and men of the highest distinction—though by directing the same perilous accusations at those citizens he actually earned my gratitude, because he placed me in the same category as men of the greatest substance and fortitude—(133) and afterward by devising every form of criminal snare against me, though I gave him no grounds beyond my desire to win the favour of patriots. He is the one who daily spun some fiction about me for his audiences; he is the one who advised a person most amicably disposed to me, Gnaeus Pompeius, to fear my house and keep an eye on me; he is the one who formed such a close bond with my enemy that Sextus Cloelius—a person in every way worthy of his closest friends—said of my proscription (which Vatinius was working to secure) that the latter was the board on which he himself wrote; he is the only one from among our senatorial order who openly gloated over my departure and your grief. All the while that he made his daily attacks, judges, I never said a word about him, and when I was being assailed by all the machinery of war and military might, I did not think it appropriate to complain about a single bowman. He declared that he did not like what I had achieved as consul: is that a secret, given his disregard for that law of mine which in no uncertain terms forbids anyone from giving gladiatorial shows within two years of standing, or intending to stand, for office? (134) On this subject, judges, I cannot adequately express my amazement at his temerity: he breaks the law as blatantly as possible, and that despite the fact that he cannot rely on his charm to elude conviction, or on his influence to be sprung, or on his material resources and sheer power to smash the laws and the courts! What is it that drives the fellow, that he is so lacking in restraint? I suppose he came across a gang of gladiators that was attractive, noted, and a fit subject for boasting, he knew how the people's enthusiasm would be stirred, what clamorous crowds would gather; and so, borne along by this expectation and fairly on fire with his lust for glory, he could not keep himself from putting on a show with them—and with himself the fairest among them. If that were the reason for breaking the law—when he was carried away by enthusiasm for the Roman people in response to their recent beneficence toward him—everyone would still agree that it was culpable; but when he adorned with the name 'gladiator' fellows who were not even selected from slaves put up for auction, but were bought from the workhouses, and then made some of them 'Samnites' and others 'challengers' by drawing lots, does he show any fear for where such license, such contempt for the law is going to lead? (135) He has two pleas to offer in defence, however. First he will say 'I put on beast-fighters, whereas the law as written covers gladiators.' How clever! But then consider his other argument, which is even sharper: he will say that he is putting on, not gladiators, plural, but a single gladiator, and that he shifted his entire aedileship into this one offering. What a brilliant aedileship! One Lion, 200 beast fighters. But fine, let him use this defence, I want him to think his case is strong: he's in the habit of summoning the tribunes of the plebs and upsetting due process with violence when he thinks his case is weak. I am amazed, not so much that he despises the law that I—his personal enemy—drafted, but that he has made it a matter of principle to reckon at naught any and every law moved by a consul. He showed his contempt for the lex Caecilia Didia and lex Licinia Iunia, and the law on extortion brought by Gaius Caesar, who (he customarily boasts) was equipped, fortified, and armed thanks to his own law and his own favour—does he think even that law is not a law? And they say that there are others who would annul Caesar's consular acts, though this excellent law is disregarded both by Caesar's father-in-law and by this creature of his! Now, the prosecutor has dared to urge you, judges, to 'at long last be stern', to 'at long last apply a cure to the commonwealth'. It is not a cure when the scalpel is applied to a part of the body that is healthy and whole, it is cruel butchery: the people who cure the commonwealth are those who cut out a plague on the civil community as though it were scrofula.

(136) But to bring my speech to a close, and to make certain that I finish speaking before you finish listening so attentively, I shall conclude my remarks on the Best Sort of men and on those who

lead them and defend the commonwealth, and I shall stir those of you young men who are notables to imitate your ancestors and urge those who are capable of achieving notability through your manly talent to follow the course that has brought success adorned by public office and glory to many new men. (137) Believe me, there is only one path to praise, to worthy standing, to office. It lies in being praised and esteemed by patriots who are wise and sound by nature, and in understanding that the civil community was organized in the wisest possible way by our ancestors, who—because they had not been able to endure the power of kings—created the annual magistracies with this aim in view: the magistrates would ever set the senate's policy in authority over the commonwealth, but the members of that body would be chosen from the people as a whole, with access to that highest category of the citizenry open to the manly exertions of all. They put the senate in place as the commonwealth's guardian, bulwark, and defender; they intended that the magistrates rely upon the senate's authority and be the ministers, as it were, of its most weighty wisdom; moreover, they intended that the senate itself be supported by the splendid estate of the orders next in rank at the same time that it preserved and increased the plebs' liberty and material advantages.

(138) The people who do what a man can do to protect this disposition are the Best Sort, whatever category of the citizenry they belong to; moreover, the people who most conspicuously take onto their own backs the burden of service to the commonwealth have always been considered the leaders among the Best Sort, the civil community's guarantors and protectors. I acknowledge that, as I said before, this category of people has many opponents, many enemies, many who wish them ill; many perils are put in their way, many wrongs are done them, they must face and undergo great travail. But all that I have been saying is concerned with manly behavior—not sloth—with worthy standing—not pleasure—with those who believe that they were born to serve the cause of the fatherland, their fellow citizens, and glorious praise—not for sleep and banquets and self-indulgence. For if there be any who follow the lead of pleasure and have surrendered to vices' snares and the allurements of sensual desires, let them forget about public office, let them not set a hand to matters of the public interest, let them passively savour their own

tranquillity, bought at the cost of brave men's toil. (139) By contrast, those who seek the good report of patriots—the only thing that can truly be called glory—ought to have as their goal the tranquillity and pleasure of others, not their own. They must sweat for the sake of our common advantages, they must confront the enmity of others, they must often face tempests for the commonwealth's sake, they must engage in desperate struggles with many who are reckless, wicked and, sometimes, even powerful. This is what we have heard, what has been handed down to us, what we have read about the intentions and the deeds of the most distinguished men; and we see that they have no share in praise who have at one time or another whipped up the people's minds to unrest or blinded the thoughts of the ignorant with largesse or brought any ill will upon brave and distinguished men who have earned the commonwealth's gratitude: our kind of people have always reckoned such citizens irresponsible and reckless and wicked and harmful, whereas those who checked their onslaughts, who stood up against the plots of the reckless with their own authority, good faith, resolve, and largeness of spirit have ever been considered the serious men, the foremost men, the leading men, the guarantors of our worthy standing and of our dominion.

(140) And lest any come to fear this way of life after seeing my misfortune or that of any others besides, there has been in this civil community only one man whom I (at any rate) can name, L. Opimius, who brilliantly earned the commonwealth's gratitude but came to a most unworthy end: his monument is the centre of greatest attention here in the forum, though his tomb lies in utter neglect on the coast at Dyrrachium. And yet the Roman people itself rescued him from peril at a time when he was engulfed in a blaze of ill-will because of Gaius Gracchus' death; it was a different gust of misfortune, blown his way by an unfair trial, that overthrew this excellent citizen. Of all the other men who followed this way of life, some were stricken by a sudden violent storm of popular displeasure but were nonetheless recalled and given a new lease on life by the people itself; the rest lived on entirely unscathed and untouched. By contrast, those who disregarded the senate's policies and the authority of patriots, who turned their back on the established ways of our ancestors and preferred to ingratiate themselves with the ignorant and impassioned masses have practically to a man given

the commonwealth the compensation of their immediate death or disgraceful exile. (141) But if among the Athenians—a Greek race very different from ourselves and our serious ways—there were men found to defend the commonwealth against the people's rashness, even though all who did so were expelled from the civil community, if the great Themistocles, the saviour of his fatherland, was not deterred from defending the commonwealth by either the catastrophe of Miltiades (who had saved the community a little before) or the exile of Aristides (who is said to have been the most just of all men), if afterward the same community's greatest men (whom there is no need to name), though confronted with so many examples of the people's irresponsible wrath, still defended that great commonwealth of theirs—what in the world ought *we* to do, who (first of all) have been born in the civil community that I consider the very seedbed of serious purpose and largeness of spirit, who (in the second place) have so glorious a place to stand that all human pursuits should appear trivial by comparison, and who (finally) have undertaken to watch over a commonwealth endowed with such worthy standing that dying in its defence is <more desirable> than gaining political mastery by assailing it?

(142) The Greeks whom I mentioned just before were unjustly condemned and expelled by the their fellow citizens; yet because of their service to their communities they are nonetheless held in such high regard today—not just in Greece but among us and in all other lands—that no one mentions their oppressors while all would prefer their catastrophe to those others' lordly power. Who among the Carthaginians was worth more—for planning and manly achievement—than Hannibal, who all by himself contended for so many years with so many of our generals, with dominion and glory as the stakes? Yet his own fellow-citizens cast him out of their community, while we see that he is celebrated, even though an enemy, in our literature and traditions. (143) Accordingly, let us imitate our own exemplars, men like Brutus, Camillus, Ahala, the Decii, Curius, Fabricius, Maximus, the Scipios, Lentulus, Aemilius, and countless others who set this commonwealth on a firm foundation and whom I at any rate set among the company of the immortal gods. Let us love the fatherland, let us follow the senate's lead, let us take thought for the interests of patriots; let us disregard the profits of the moment

while serving the cause of the glory we will enjoy with posterity, let us reckon as best that which is most right, let us hope for what we want but endure whatever happens, let us, finally, ponder the fact that though the bodies of great and brave men are mortal, their minds' movements and the glory of their manliness are eternal—and if we see this belief raised to the status of a holy principle in the case of the most sanctified Hercules, whose mortal life and manliness (it is said) immortality embraced after his body was cremated, let us be equally confident that those who through their policies and travails increased or defended or preserved this great commonwealth have attained immortal glory.

(144) But, judges, as I speak—and make ready to speak yet more—about worthy standing and the glory of the bravest and most distinguished citizens, my speech is suddenly checked in its course at the sight of the men sitting here. I see Publius Sestius, the defender, bulwark, agent of my well-being, of your authority, of the public interest—now a defendant. I see his son, still dressed in the bordered toga, looking at me with tears in his eyes. I see Milo, the champion of your liberty, the guardian of my well-being, the bulwark of our battered commonwealth, the deadly foe of our domestic brigands, who has put a stop to daily carnage, defended our homes and holy precincts, protected the senate chamber—himself dressed in mourning as a defendant. I see Publius Lentulus—whose father is in my eyes a god, and the source of the good fortune and repute that I, my brother, and our children enjoy—dressed in the wretched squalor of bereavement: where just last year he was deemed worthy of both the toga of manhood, by his father's judgement, and the bordered toga, by the people's, he now wears the toga of mourning, as a gesture of entreaty on behalf of his father, than whom there is no braver and more brilliant citizen, because of the sudden, bitter blow dealt by a most unjust proposal. (145) And I alone have inspired the disarray, the grief, the trappings of mourning of so many distinguished citizens, because they have defended me, because they have felt my misfortune and pain as their own, because they have restored me in response to the fatherland's grief, the senate's urgent demands, Italy's clamor, and the prayers of you all.

What did I do that was such a crime? Of what was I so terribly guilty on that day when I told you of the information that had been laid, the letters that had been intercepted, the confessions of men plotting our common destruction, when I followed your instructions? Even if it is a crime to love my fatherland, I have paid enough of a penalty: my home has been razed, my affairs have been scattered, my children have been harassed, my wife has been manhandled, my excellent brother, in a gesture of unbelievable devotion and unprecedented affection, has grovelled in utter disarray at the feet of our worst enemies; driven from the altars, the hearth, the gods of my ancestors, torn from family and friends, bereft of the fatherland that—to say the least—I had loved, I endured the cruelty of my enemies, the wrongdoing of the treacherous, the deceit of the malevolent. (146) If it is not enough that the sight of all this devastation greeted me on my return, then I much prefer, judges, I very much prefer to revisit that same misfortune rather than bring such catastrophe upon those who defended me and saved me. Could I live in this city when those whose actions permit me to enjoy it have been driven from it? I will not, I could not, judges; no, this child here, whose tears declare the depth of his filial devotion, will never see me enjoy my safety when he has lost his father because of me, nor will he have the chance to groan upon seeing me and to declare that he sees the man who destroyed his father and himself. I will indeed embrace these men, whatever fortune might come our way: no misfortune will ever tear me from the embrace of those whom you see in mourning because of me, nor will the foreign nations to which the senate entrusted my safety, and which it thanked on my account, see this man in exile because of me, without me at his side. (147) But the immortal gods—whose own sacred precincts received me on my arrival, escorted by these men here and the consul Publius Lentulus—and the commonwealth itself—the most sacred of all things—have entrusted these matters to the power vested in you, judges. It is yours to strengthen the resolve of patriots with your verdict and check the resolve of the wicked, yours to enjoy the services of these excellent citizens here, yours to restore me and make the commonwealth new. Accordingly, I call the gods to witness as I implore you: if you desired my restoration, save those who restored me to you.

Commentary

1–5. *Introduction (exordium)*[1]

Though C.'s defence will sometimes appear diffuse (cf. 5 'unmethodical and general'), its introduction shows a master of pointed compression at work. In the first segment (1–2), C. uses a favourite figure (1 **If anyone** n.) to frame the case in the terms he will develop throughout, as a crisis that finds the defenders of the Roman *civil community (*civitas*) beset by evildoers who are in but not of that community; the first sentence, especially, invokes a large number of highly valued and emotionally charged political and ethical concepts ('brave and large spirited . . . commonwealth . . . dominion . . . worthy standing . . . well-being . . . civil regime . . . freedom . . . patriotic': see Glossary). He then draws the judges into the conflict by stressing that they must choose sides (2 **nothing is less tolerable** n.). The reference to his own position that closes this segment (2 **I once thought** n.) is a bridge to the introduction's second part (3–5), which serves two interlocking purposes: to present his performance as the pious discharge of a personal obligation, and thereby to signal to the judges that—for reasons more germane to the defence than might first meet the eye—the speech will be at least as much about C. himself as it is about S.

1. If anyone used to wonder before C. often uses openings cast formally as conditions, and this figure is a particular favourite: see esp. *Div. Caec.* 1 'If anyone among you, judges, or among those present happens to *wonder*. . .', *Cael.* 1 'If anyone ignorant (of our legal institutions) chanced to be present, he would surely *wonder*. . .', *Rab. Post.* 1 'If anyone, judges, should *reckon* that . . .', and cf. the more direct (because not conditional) *Sex. Rosc.* 1 'I suppose, judges, that you are *wondering* why. . .' (cf. also *Prov. cons.* 1, and for other

---

[1] On the overall structure of this speech, and its relation to the conventional structure of forensic speeches, see Introd. §3. Words and phrases marked by an asterisk (*) are explained in the Glossary.

conditional openings *Caecin.* 1, *Arch.* 1, *Balb.* 1). The conceit of the anonymous observer allows C. to frame the opening in a tendentious yet seemingly objective way, by presenting not his own perspective but that of an impersonal, hypothetical other: the audience is invited, not to ask whether that perspective is valid or even reasonable (it is not a true condition, that is), but to accept it as the given framework of thought. Here the device allows C. to establish the broad canvas on which he will work, and esp. to place before his listeners two propositions that most Roman audiences—given the common view that other people are lamentably selfish, and that the present is always worse than the past—would be disposed to find unproblematic: individuals (oneself excepted, of course) have formerly been less devoted to the *public interest than they should be; and now things are in a truly perilous state.

With those propositions on the table, Cicero can explain the cause in the next sentence, introducing the contractualist premise that grounds this speech and Roman Republicanism more generally: any individual's devotion to the public interest—like his devotion to friends (2 **thanking**...and **publicizing**...nn.) or to the gods—entails a guarantee of reciprocity: *do ut des*, 'I give so that you give'. Under the terms of this contract such devotion should be requited, optimally by appropriate forms of honour (cf. 47 **glory eternal** n., 93–6 n., 143 **Accordingly** n.), minimally by appropriate protections; but not only has that contract broken down, its terms have been utterly reversed. (The patriot must still act for the *commonwealth's good even when the contract is broken, but that thought now remains only implied: see 95 **no wrong done him** n.; on C.'s later revision of honour's role in his political thought, esp. in *Off.*, see Long 1995.) The same premise of failed contractualism, offered here in the first extant forensic speech after his exile, rounded off his defence of Lucius Valerius Flaccus (pr. 63) in late summer (?) 59, the last extant forensic speech from before his exile (*Flac.* 105), when C. already knew that trouble was brewing.

judges   C. addresses a panel of male *iudices* between 30 and 60 years of age, each of whom would register his own vote on a wood tablet—marked 'A' (*absolvo*, 'I acquit') on one side and 'C' (*condemno*, 'I condemn') on the other—by obliterating the symbol of the rejected judgement; the verdict was determined by majority vote. Though the panel members individually decided questions of law and fact, they did not have the legal expertise or the procedural responsibilities of modern judges, nor did they deliberate together and speak with one voice in reaching their verdict, in the manner of a modern jury. On the composition and selection of the panel, see Introd. §2. Under the *lex Fufia* of 59, the vote was reported according to the three categories of judges (so many senators for acquittal or condemnation, so many equestrians, so many 'treasury tribunes'), allowing C. to record results in his correspondence (*QFr.* 2. 5(9). 4, 2. 16(20). 3, cf. Asc. 28. 25–7 Cl.); he will be able to report that these judges voted unanimously to acquit his client on 14 March 56 (*QFr.* 2. 4(8). 1).

brave and large-spirited As often when C. uses two modifiers (or nouns or verbs) where it seems one would suffice, he chooses terms that are complementary rather than synonymous, amplifying the thought and lending it weight: for these ethical terms, see the Glossary; on the stylistic gesture, Krostenko 2004.

dominion's On the basic sense of *dominion (*imperium*), see Glossary. Here parallel with *commonwealth, the term is used in an extended sense to suggest the dominance that Romans collectively enjoy and (prob.) the geographical space over which that dominance extends ('dominion' or 'empire' in the territorial sense: cf. Richardson 1991, 5–7).

worthy standing i.e. *dignitas*: more usually the attribute of persons (in this speech and Latin usage generally), see Glossary.

well-being On the physical and political sense of this term (*salus*), see Glossary; both senses are meant here.

civil regime Lit. 'set-up of the *civil community' (*status civitatis*): with *status rei publicae*, one of the two phrases C. uses when he wants to denote what we would call a constitution or what a Greek would call a *politeia*: see e.g. *Flac.* 3, *Red. sen.* 20, *Red. pop.* 16, 21, *Har. resp.* 41, 45, *Phil.* 7. 4, *Rep.* 1. 33–4, 70–1 (cf. *QFr.* 3. 5(25). 1), 2. 2, *Leg.* 2. 30, 3. 4, with Schofield 1995, 68. For the distinction between civil community and *commonwealth see the Glossary, and cf. 91, where both are in turn distinguished from *urbs*, the physical city.

freedom that we share   That is, in virtue of belonging to the same *civil community: on *freedom (*libertas*), see the Glossary.

patriotic   Lit. 'good': on the political connotation common in C.'s usage, see the Glossary.

those who joined … in reviving   He means his chief champions, S. and Milo, the former as the defendant in the present trial, the latter as the defendant on a charge, brought by Clodius (cf. 95), of having employed gladiators to force through a measure for C.'s recall: that trial before the people (*iudicium populi*) had begun on 2 Feb., was adjourned until 7 Feb., then adjourned again—after being disrupted by riotous demonstrations—until 17 Feb. (*QFr.* 2. 3(7). 1–2), when it was adjourned again until 7 May (*QFr.* 2. 6(10). 4); it appears to have been dropped (*TLRR* no. 266).

commonwealth when it was battered   The image of the battered *commonwealth (*res publica afflicta*), whether used alone or with a complementary metaphor (cf. 5 'overturned and battered'), is almost unique to C. and occurs with striking frequency in this speech, where it supports his strategy of identifying his own calamity with the commonwealth's (Introd. §3): see also 24, 31 (where the argumentative point is esp. clear), and 144, sim. *Dom.* 112, *Har. resp.* 40; elsewhere at *Att.* 1. 18(18). 3, 8. 11(161)d. 6 (to Pompey), *Fam.* 2. 5(49). 2 (otherwise only *Att.* 8. 11(161)c. 1, Pompey writing *to* C.; *Epist. ad Octav.* 4, a spurious letter, allegedly from C. to Octavian, whose author evidently studied C. closely; Sen. *Dial.* 9. 5. 3); cf. Reggiani 1991, Grilli 1994. On the metaphors of physical abuse applied to the personified commonwealth in this speech see also 17 **branded…**, 43 **medicine… nn.**

domestic brigands   The first of many references to Clodius and his supporters as *brigands (*latrones*) or to their behaviour as *brigandage (*latrocinium*: see 2, 26, 35, 39, 76, 81, 130, 144; cf. e.g. *Red. sen.* 10, 13, *Dom.* 107, 126, *Cael.* 78, *Pis.* 24, 30, *Att.* 4. 3(75). 3). C. had spoken similarly of Catiline (*Cat.* 1. 23, 27, 31, 2. 2, 16, 22, 24, 3. 17, *Mur.* 84; *Sull.* 70), whose work (C. regularly claims) Clodius was merely continuing (42 **old forces** n.); others turned the term against C. himself (see *Mil.* 47). Beyond being merely abusive, the term—like *public enemy (*hostis*) and *beast (*belua*)—aims to isolate the target by placing him beyond the bounds of the *civil community or (in the case of 'beast') all humanity, the better to suggest that he has no rights and deserves no consideration. By specifying '*domestic* brigands' here (cf. 11 '*domestic* enemies') C. further suggests that these forces of anarchic violence are in our very midst.

clad in mourning A defendant in a trial such as this, with his *life as a citizen (*caput*) at stake (next n.), would be expected to 'change garments' (*vestem mutare*) and put on mourning dress—a dark-dyed toga (*toga pulla*) or simply one that was unclean—and go about in an unkempt state—unwashed, unshaven, and with hair untrimmed—to signal the calamity he faced and to seek the pity of others, esp. the judges, and he would be joined in this by his family and friends: see e.g. *Clu.* 18, 192, *Mur.* 86, *Cael.* 4, *Planc.* 21, 29, *Scaur.* 49, *Lig.* 32–3, Plut. *Cic.* 9. 2, 19. 2, 30. 4, 35. 4. Attempts to deduce a single pattern from the rather general descriptive language (besides *vestem mutare,* common terms are *squalor/squalidus* and *sordes/ sordidatus,* the latter used here) are probably mistaken: the overall aim was to represent the suspension of life's normal concerns under the impact of overwhelming psychic pain, and the signs that could be used were no doubt fluid within a certain range. Senators like S. and Milo would probably also put off tokens of their rank—the gold ring, the tunic with the broad purple stripe (*latus clavus*)—as they did when mourning was declared for a public calamity (Livy 9. 7. 8, cf. *Red. sen.* 12 quoted at 26 **assume mourning dress** n. below; Cass. Dio 38. 14. 7 says that senators assumed the dress of equestrians, but no late Republican source points in that direction). C. remarks (*Red. sen.* 31) that there was a time within living memory when senators, at least, did not normally assume mourning when on trial, but by mid-1st century it appears to have been expected: Milo's failure to don mourning—read as arrogance—allegedly contributed to his conviction in 52 (Plut. *Cic.* 35. 4). On the forms of dress see *RE* 6A (1937), 2229–31 (G. Herzog-Hauser), Heskel 1994, 141–3; for other occasions on which the custom was observed, see 26 **put on mourning dress** n.

lives as citizens A charge of *public violence was a capital matter (*res capitalis*), with conviction entailing *deminutio capitis,* 'abridgement of the (convicted person's) head'. In late Republican practice this threatened not loss of life (one's physical head), in what we call capital punishment, but loss of *life as a citizen (see the Glossary): the consequences were exile—including status as an outlaw liable to be put to death on sight within a certain distance of the city—and loss of honour, property, and family rights. These potential losses are touched on in the phrases 'their reputations, their role in the community, their fortunes, and their children', and all were suffered by C. as a result of the second law Clodius passed against him in 58 (65 **proposal** n., Introd. §1).

role in the community   The one occasion in the speech where C. uses the term *civitas* to denote, not the *civil community itself, but membership in that community (citizenship).

the sort of people ... dart about with an energized delight   Above all, Clodius, who, having been elected aedile on 20 Jan. 56, was prosecuting Milo in a trial before the people (**those who joined** n., above) and was generally a disruptive presence in the *civil community (Introd. §1). When C. returns to the same thought in a passage capping the first major segment of the speech (93–6 n.), he will name several others whom he assigns to the same category.

all things divine and human   The phrase seems a cliché, a polar expression used merely to stress inclusiveness (cf. 'I searched high and low', 58 **over land and sea** n.), but it is not that. The expression occurs only here and in 27 in C.'s orations (cf. also *De or.* 1. 212, 3. 134, *Acad.* 1. 9), and it has specific point: throughout the 'post-return' speeches C. blames Clodius not only for assaulting Rome's human political institutions but also for his impiety, in the Bona Dea affair (39 'high-priest of debauchery', *Har. resp.* 8, 12, 33, 37–8, 44, 57, *Prov. cons.* 24, *Pis.* 87, 95, *Mil.* 13, 59, 72, 86–7; more allusively at *Dom.* 77, 80, 104–5, 110, cf. *Leg.* 2. 37), in the destruction of C.'s house (*Dom.* 106–9, 117–21, 127–32), and in his legislation over-turning (C. claims) the importance of *auspices (33 below); cf. 53 **By the immortal gods** n. A similar phrase, used of a person's overturning 'all laws (*iura*) divine and human', is reserved for the parricide (*Sex. Rosc.* 65, cf. 82 n.) and Julius Caesar (*Off.* 1. 26).

perils for the best and bravest citizens   He means the trials (*pericula*, 'perils') of S. and Milo; he will also speak e.g. of the plots laid against Pompey in 58 (see 69 **a plan** n.).

2. nothing is less tolerable than this   Rounding off his defence of Lucius Flaccus in 59, C. had charged that the prosecution aided the Catilinarian remnant by using the courts to take vengeance on patriots (esp. *Flac.* 96). In both cases the ploy seeks to force the judges to see themselves taking sides with either the righteous or the wicked; and in that broad sense the ploy was among C.'s oldest weapons, used at the end of the speech that first made his reputation, the defence of Sextus Roscius of Ameria in 80, when he offered the judges a choice between acquitting his client or aiding the forces of anarchic oppression in the person of Sulla's freedman Chrysogonus (see *Sex. Rosc.* 143–54, esp. 150, and cf. ibid. 8).

their own brigands   The phrase (*latrones suos*) implies that these brigands are 'their own' as their paid agents: the term *latro* here retains something of its original force (= mercenary fighter: Glossary), and the following appositive phrase ('impoverished . . desperadoes') conveys the sort of people recruited for this employment. Here and again in 38 C. refers to gangs that Clodius employed for purposes of *public violence; but C.'s own supporters, esp. Milo and S., adopted much the same means, perhaps in part financed by C. himself, if in speaking of the 'beneficence of friends' used to 'disgraceful' ends he means money borrowed to hire thugs (*Att.* 4. 2(74). 7, Oct. 57, with Shackleton Bailey ad loc., and cf. the prosecutor's taunt to which C. responds at 127, *I should not have chosen* n.). In the case of Milo and S., C. of course describes the measures as purely defensive: in this speech see esp. 79, 90; on the pervasive use of gangs and other sorts of orchestrated violence in this period, see Brunt 1966, Nowak 1973 (esp. 102 ff.), Nippel 1995 (esp. 70–8), Lintott 1999*a* (esp. 67–88). At 57 C. refers to Clodius' *hired hands more broadly, to include all who support him even in lawful assemblies, thus anticipating a major argument in the last third of the speech: see 57 **hired hands** n.

desperadoes   On the derivation of the term, see the Glossary. Catiline and his followers, acc. to C., had largely been such people (see 9, on Gaius Mevulanus, and cf. e.g. *Cat.* 1. 13, 23, 25, 27, 4. 5, 8, 22), as were Clodius and the consuls of 58 (15, 33). When C. defines the *Best Sort (*optimates*), broadly and tendentiously, as all those 'who do no harm, are not wicked or rabid in their nature, and are not hobbled by embarrassments in their domestic affairs' (97), he in effect means all who are not *desperadoes.

stones, swords, and torches   C. anticipates the attacks, on S.'s person and Milo's house (Feb. or March 57: App. 1), that play an important role in his argument at 79–92; Milo's house was again attacked on 12 Nov. 57 (95 **has assailed** n.). On violent demonstrations in late Republican Rome more generally, Nippel 1995, 47 ff., Lintott 1999*a*, 6 ff., 89 ff., Treggiari 2002, 99–100; C.'s rhetorical fondness for evoking 'fire and the sword' was familiar to his contemporaries, cf. 90 **fire and sword** n.

authority... sense of religious obligation... verdicts   Individual judges would have degrees of personal *authority that varied according to age, birth, rank, public service, and the like; but their formal role as *iudices* gave their verdicts (*sententiae*) uniformly authoritative weight (cf. *Sex. Rosc.* 154, *Verr.* 2. 3. 10, *Clu.* 6), because each member's sense of obligation (*religio*) to perform his duty conscientiously ('faith kept with one's word', *fides*, is often used in this connection) had been publicly affirmed when he took the oath that all *iudices* swore at the outset of a trial, placing themselves under religious sanction should they violate it (Mommsen 1899, 219 n. 2, Freyburger 1986, 213–17).

I once thought...   C. introduces the theme of his return from exile (a term he sedulously avoids, see 47 **exile** n.), soon joined to the theme of the misuse of political trials. As Riggsby points out (2002*a*, 189 ff.), seven of C.'s extant speeches from the period 57–52 were occasioned by criminal trials, and in four of them he prominently linked the case to the larger political context (*Balb.*, *Planc.*, *Mil.*, and *Sest.*, sim. the lost speech for Cispius = *LUO* no. 57, see *Planc.* 75–6). As Riggsby also remarks (ibid., and see Riggsby 1999, 79–84, corroborating Lintott 1999*a*, 107–24), the charge of *public violence virtually required a political defence, since that charge could be brought only when an act was alleged to be 'against the public interest' (*contra rem publicam*): it is for this reason that C. puts the tale of his own suffering at the speech's center and ties it to the suffering of the *commonwealth, see Introd. §3.

thanking... earned my gratitude   'Those who have earned my gratitude' (lit. 'those who have deserved well of me', *qui de me bene* *meriti sunt*), like its negative counterpart 'those who have earned my enmity' (*qui de me male meriti sunt*: e.g. *Red. pop.* 22, *Fam.* 7. 1(24). 4), was a fixed formula in the culture of gift-exchange and friendship (*amicitia*), denoting those who had done you a favour (*beneficium*: see text immediately following) and to whom you therefore owed an obligation (*officium*); the formula's negative counterpart implied an obligation to return ill for ill that was nearly as binding. C. is about to mention two of the most common ways of discharging that obligation, in publicizing the *beneficium* that the other has done you, and in serving him in his time of need (next nn.).

With the possible exception of personal *trustworthiness (*fides*), with which it was closely linked, no trait is more central to traditional Roman ethics than this sense of obligation based on gratitude (see e.g. *Planc.* 81, on gratitude as the defining human quality, and cf. *Off.* 1. 48); and since Roman politics was in good measure traditional Roman ethics writ large, the same sense of reciprocal obligation was central to the relations between individual and community on which Republicanism was based: see 1 **If anyone** n., and note the *decree of the senate describing C. as 'a citizen who has earned the common-wealth's gratitude' (quoted at *Dom.* 85; for the formula compare 21, 83, 139 below, *Red. sen.* 8, *Dom.* 9, Vell. 2. 45. 2 on Cicero as 'a man who earned the commonwealth's highest gratitude'; for the negative counterpart, Gell. *NA* 9. 2. 11).

Much thought was therefore given to gauging the strength of the obligation owed to friends, and to locating that obligation correctly in relation to other obligations, especially to the *civil community as a whole: see in general *Amic.* 36–43; *Off.* 3. 43–4. After returning from exile, C. declares that his concern for friends will be limited by his concern for the *public interest (e.g. *Red. pop.* 21, *Dom.* 27, *Planc.* 3); yet this could be a close call (*Planc.* 23), and in Feb. 55 he will say that his vast debt to Pompey prevents him from honourably opposing him, despite certain long-held principles he still believes valid (*Fam.* 1. 8(19). 2). He will also claim that concern for the common interest limits his hatred for his enemies and his desire to repay them (*Red. pop.* 23, an oddly academic passage on the payment of debts, repeated at *Planc.* 68, *Off.* 2. 69; cf. *Balb.* 61, *Amic.* 32, and esp. *Prov. cons.* 18–25). Indeed, proclaiming this sort of forbearance will cause him to be criticized for boasting (*Prov. cons.* 44), though of course there are also times when serving the common interest and satisfying his enmities happily coincide (*Prov. cons.* 1–2).

publicizing . . . beneficence The chief theme of *Red. sen.* and *Red. pop.*, immediately after his return: S. specifically is praised and thanked at *Red. sen.* 20 and 30, and see 15 **Gnaeus Pompeius**, 70 **Publius Lentulus**, 87 **Milo . . . affairs** nn. The theme is still prominent at *Balb.* 1 (late summer / early autumn 56) and reappears, in somewhat different form, at *Planc.* 1, 4 (July 54), cf. Paterson 2004, 93.

but since . . . The translation somewhat simplifies the arrangement of thought, since the Latin subordinates the preceding clause ('I once thought . . . acts of beneficence') to the present clause in a way not congenial to English idiom. (I follow most editors in regarding the main MSS' text as corrupt and in supplying a causal conjunction— Halm's *quoniam*, 'since'—to introduce this clause.)

serve those whose efforts . . . to the Roman people C. took satisfaction in discharging the obligation he owed S. through this defence despite feeling quite put out with a man he described as 'a peevish fellow' (*morosus homo*: *QFr.* 2. 3(7). 5, 2. 4(8). 1); despite the claim of deep emotion soon to come (3 **devotion** n.), the obligations of *pietas* could be satisfied independent of sentiment (cf. *Fam.* 1. 8(19). 3, on his subsequent relations with Pompey). With the note struck here, rounding off the first stage of the introduction, compare the very similar note on which C. closes the speech, at the end of 147.

3. Quintus Hortensius Eight years older than C., consul six years before him, and consistent spokesman of the **optimates*, Quintus Hortensius (*RE* 13) was already an established orator when he spoke against C. on the occasion of his first extant speech (*Quinct.*, in 81), and he was the undisputed master of the forum when C. returned from his studies in Athens and Rhodes in 77; C.'s victory over him in the prosecution of Verres (70) marked the beginning of C.'s ascendancy. Six more of C.'s extant orations were delivered in cases that found both men speaking for the defence (*Rab. Perd.* and *Mur.* in 63, *Sull.* in 62, *Flac.* in 59, *Planc.* and *Scaur.* in 54), with C. always speaking after Hortensius, as he did here. As the crisis built for C. in 58, Hortensius reportedly escorted a delegation from the **equestrian order to the senate on C.'s behalf (Cass. Dio 38. 16. 2–3, cf. 26 below), and

C. would later claim that Hortensius was nearly killed by Clodius' *henchmen ('slaves') for standing by him (*Mil.* 57, a memory perhaps coloured by C.'s gratitude for the augurate, see following). Yet C. surely counted him among the 'fishpond fanciers' (*piscinarii*)—wealthy *notables more interested in frivolous luxury than in the *commonwealth, and resentful (C. thought) of his own success—whom he criticized bitterly in 60–59 (*Att.* 1. 18(18). 6, 1. 19(19). 6, 1. 20(20). 3, 2. 1(21). 7, 2. 9(29). 1); C. at times also believed that Hortensius was among the *optimates* who had betrayed him in his crisis and let him down in exile (see 46 **some felt** n., and cf. 95 **by the senate's authority** n. with *Att.* 4. 3(75). 3, on Hortensius' probable role in obstructing Milo's prosecution of Clodius in Nov. 57). Still, C. manages graceful praise of his oratory at the end of *On the Orator* (3. 228–30), and he seems to have been genuinely grateful when in 53 Hortensius joined Pompey in nominating him for membership in the college of augurs, an honour C. dearly wanted. C. treated him handsomely after he died on the eve of the civil war, making him spokesman in a treatise urging the study of philosophy (the lost *Hortensius*), describing at the start of *Brutus* (1–6) how the news of Hortensius' death had shaken him, and giving an extended account of Hortensius' career and their work together at the end of the same treatise (317–30).

summed up the case   The technical term 'peroration' (*causa est... perorata*) could be used either of a speech's final section (so 136–47 below, combining exhortation and the stirring of pity) or, as here, of a speech that caps the case as a whole (cf. Suet. *Gramm.* 30. 3 with Kaster 1995 ad loc.). Hortensius spoke third, after Licinius Calvus (also known as Macer) and Crassus had addressed specific aspects of the charges (*Schol. Bob.* 125. 25 St. lists the advocates in the order Hortensius, Crassus, Calvus; for Calvus see also *QFr.* 2. 4(8). 1). In that position Hortensius must have done what C.—'summing up' the case for Murena in 63 when speaking third, after Hortensius and Crassus— described as 'not treating any particular part of the case but saying what seemed necessary about the matter as a whole' (*Mur.* 48); following Hortensius, C. could range still more widely, and does, cf. 5 below.

The four advocates sharing the defence in this trial is not the highest number known: on trial for extortion in 54, Marcus Scaurus (the presiding officer in this case) spoke for himself and was further represented by six advocates, including the unexpected pairing of C. and Clodius (*TLRR* no. 295). But the (admittedly very incomplete) record of trials for the period 70–50 shows no other case with as many as four advocates, and only three instances with as many as three (*TLRR* no. 177 (Verres), 224 (Murena), 276 (Balbus)): in all these cases the 'defence team' has the effect of demonstrating that the defendant is a person of social consequence who can call on the 'dutiful devotion' (*officium*) of *serious men (whatever the actual state of relations among the men themselves might be). Although C. participated in all but one of the defences just noted, and in a number of others in which two advocates spoke for the defence, he was later highly critical of such 'teams' (*Brut.* 207–8), on the ground that the practice (which had not been known when he was a lad) could produce fragmented cases in which a given speaker might make his appearance only to speak his own part, without having heard either the prosecution or the other advocates.

I shall nonetheless undertake . . . all my other fellow-citizens C. continues the theme of advocacy as friendship in action (1 **thanking** and **serve those whose efforts** nn.). The importance of the personal tie between advocate and defendant is a commonplace (e.g. *Mur.* 7–10, *Arch.* 1, 13, 28, and esp. *Sull.* 49, on the nearly absolute obligation to assist a friend in his defence, even against another friend), and C. will again present the defence of his client as inextricably linked to defence of himself at *Planc.* 3; Riggsby (2002*a*, 178) well remarks how C. takes pains at *Planc.* 77 to stress his personal ties to and feelings of gratitude for the defendant, to rebut the prosecutor's suggestion that the two had not been particularly close—'the reverse of modern claims of objectivity as the basis of the advocate's credibility'. On identification between advocate and client as the norm, cf. May 1981, and next n.

devotion . . . grievance . . . distress Here all felt by C. because of his relation to S., whose kindnesses (we are to understand) motivate C.'s devotion (*pietas*), which in turn prompts *querellae* (expressions of grievance) and *dolor*, a psychic pain symptomatic of several different emotions, including anger, grief, and indignation: just below C. will speak of distress born of devotion (*pius dolor*) and of righteous anger (*iusta iracundia*), forms of distress appropriate when someone close to you has been harmed. In due course C. will express considerable grievance and distress arising from his own travails (see 14 and the narrative that follows). All such affective expressions, so far from being irrelevant self-indulgence (as modern forensic canons would hold), serve two important ends in ancient rhetorical theory and practice: they aim to make the audience well disposed to the speaker and more receptive to his arguments by creating a certain character (*ethos*) for him (here and throughout the exordium, the character of the loyal friend); and they aim to arouse corresponding emotion (*pathos*) in the audience, so that they will feel pity (*misericordia*) for one wrongly harmed and righteous indignation (*invidia*) against those who have harmed him, esp. when—as C. will try to show in 15 ff.—the latter have used positions of power, trust, or privilege brutally or high-handedly (on *ethos* and *pathos* in Roman rhetoric, *Inv. rhet.* 1. 22, 100–9, *De or.* 2. 182–211, Quint. 6. 2. 8–36, May 1988, Wisse 1989). In his rhetorical works C. consistently holds that failure to display such passions, when appropriate, is damaging (esp. *Brut.* 278–9, on the dispasssionate Marcus Calidius), and he tends to the view that to display them convincingly the orator must actually feel them (esp. *De or.* 2. 188–96, cf. *Or.* 132 and more generally Wisse 1989, 257–69; contrast the Stoicizing line taken at *Tusc.* 4. 55). Accordingly, we often see the advocate in tears: e.g. *Rab. Post.* 47, *Planc.* 104, *Mil.* 105 ('I can no longer speak for weeping'—in a version of the speech, it is commonly thought, he did not deliver); cf. *Planc.* 76, C. mocked by an opponent for tears shed in a previous defence.

4. more sharply or with less restraint   C. anticipates the invective heaped upon enemies in the speech as the negative counterpart of the praise lavished on friends; and cf. 1 **thanking**, 14 **I shall proceed** nn.

for no distress ... my well-being   With these clauses C. rounds off the subjects of *pathos* (introduced in 3) and reciprocity (introduced in 2) before beginning the remarks that introduce his substantive exposition.

5. the other speakers ... individual charges   See 3 **summed up** n. We do not know how the other speakers divided the response to the charges, nor even specifically which of S.'s acts the prosecutors charged under the head of *public violence (see Alexander 2002, 212–17, and Introd. §2); when C. himself takes up a specific incident

(79–80), it is to offer by implication a plea of self-defence and, in the process, reduce the opposition's position to absurdity. But specific incidents aside, C.'s larger purpose is to undermine the entire premise of the charge (Introd. §3), and in that respect his speech is no less pertinent than those that preceded.

the kind of … character   C. often begins by reviewing the defendant's life, character, and early career: see *Arch.* 4 ff., *Flac.* (Milan frag.), *Cael.* 3 ff., *Planc.* 27 ff., *Rab. Post.* 4 (cf. *Sex. Rosc.* 15 ff., beginning with the defendant's father in the manner of 6 below). The practice is based on the belief that the pattern of a man's life before the alleged crime is more helpful in assessing culpability than the charges attached to a single action (so *Sull.* 69, where the usual pattern happens to be reversed, the section on life and character placed last rather than first); accordingly, it has its counterpart in invective also (e.g. *Har. resp.* 42–6, on Clodius, *Vat.* 11 ff., starting with Vatinius' alleged early activities as burglar and mother-beater, and cf. 18 below); on the 'rhetoric of character' in C.'s advocacy, see Riggsby 2004. C. takes up S.'s life story at a fairly late stage, when S. is already married, omitting the sorts of information about his youth that he had once recommended (*Inv.* 1. 35) and that he would retail in (e.g.) his defence of Caelius a few weeks later. Perhaps S.'s prosecutors (unlike Caelius') had not attacked his early life; in any case, the matters C. does stress in his review are traits or actions germane to C.'s positive defence (see 6–13 introd. n.).

tranquillity   Like *well-being (salus)*, invoked at the very outset (1 n.), *tranquillity (otium)* is among the most prominent concepts in the speech: C. will join it with *worthy standing (dignitas)* to form the foundation on which the last third of the speech is based, see 98 n. On the two aspects of the term, one evoking a state enjoyed by all citizens collectively ('domestic tranquillity'), the other a purely personal state ('leisure'), see the Glossary: here and (for the most part) throughout, C. means the former.

unmethodical and general   The speech is certainly highly general (*universa*), in the way (3 **summed up** n.) and for the reasons (Introd. §3) already remarked; it is unmethodical (*confusa*, lit. 'poured together', 'indiscriminate') in the related sense that C. does not proceed stepwise to pick out and respond to individual charges.

because The English reflects the slight looseness of the causal link in the Latin: C. will survey the foundation and first stages of S.'s career (5 **the kind of ... character** n.), not because his *tribunate occurred at a time of crisis, but because we can understand his tribunate's glorious success in meeting that crisis only if we understand its firm moral foundation.

Fortune herself Not 'fortune' as 'random chance' (cf. *QFr.* 1. 1(1). 4, contrasted with 'careful use of reason', *ratio et diligentia*), but the force, personified as the goddess Fortuna, that causes matters to turn out in ways humans cannot predict, both for good (as here and, e.g. *Fam.* 1. 5a(15). 4) and for ill (e.g. 17, the 'deadly bad luck' that accounts for the consulship of Piso and Gabinius, and *Fam.* 5. 17 (23). 3). At Rome Fortuna had temples (among other places) in the *forum Boarium* (with the temple of Mater Matuta: *NTDAR* 155, *LTUR* 2:281–5, *MAR* 127), on the Campus Martius (as 'Fortuna of this day', *Fortuna huiusce diei*: *NTDAR* 156, *LTUR* 2:269–70, *MAR* 128), and on the Quirinal (as 'Primordial Fortuna', *Fortuna Primigenia*, and 'Fortuna of the Roman people', *Fortuna Publica populi Romani Quiritium*: *NTDAR* 158, *LTUR* 2:285–7, *MAR* 248, cf. e.g. *Mil.* 83 vs. 87, dispensing good outcomes and bad). On Fortune in C., see Siani-Davies 2001, 113, and more generally Latte 1967, 176–83.

tribunate The first mention of this crucial office, on which see the Glossary; its holders (in successive years) included both C.'s main opponent, Publius Clodius Pulcher (15 **transfer ... desperado** and Introd. §1), and his main champions, S. and Milo; it is not one he sought himself (for speculation why, Wiseman 1971, 162 n.1).

overturned and battered On the metaphor see 1 **commonwealth ... battered** n.

the foundation and first stages See 5 **the kind of ... character** n.

6–13. *Anticipatory review of character and career (praemunitio)*

Set off from the *narratio*—C.'s version of events immediately germane to the case—by the transition clearly signalled at 14, these paragraphs provide a preliminary strengthening of his argument (*praemunitio* or *praeparatio*: Lausberg 1998, §§854–5), not by setting aside objections raised or anticipating difficulties in the argument to come, but by planting the seeds of two useful thoughts: that the admirable devotion S. earlier displayed to several authoritative men—his own father and his two fathers-in-law (6–7)—is of a piece with the devotion he displayed in supporting C. and working for his restoration; and that the admirable service S. offered as *quaestor in 63, protecting the *commonwealth when it was assailed by Catiline and his *henchmen (8–12), is of a piece with the service he offered as tribune, reviving the commonwealth when it was 'battered' by Clodius and his henchmen. The two points are also related, in so far as supporting C. is one and the same thing as supporting the commonwealth (Introd. §3) and in so far as Clodius and his henchmen merely continue the work of Catiline and his (42 **old forces** n.).

6. Publius Sestius' father   Lucius Sestius (*RE* 2, *MRR* 2. 22): his *praenomen* is known from the salutation of *Fam.* 5. 6(4) and two inscriptions identifying S. as 'son of Lucius'; the present passage is otherwise the only source of information. The year of his *tribunate, mentioned below, is not known: if it fell 'at a very favourable time for our community', yet not too late for him to be father of a man who was tribune in 57, then certainly in the 90s, after the suppression of Saturninus and before the outbreak of the Social War and the civil wars that followed, when C. was being educated in the home of Lucius Licinius Crassus (cos. 95) and public affairs were in the hands of 'sound' men like Crassus and his colleague Scaevola 'the Pontifex'; as *quaestor in 63 S. himself could not have been born after 93. The pattern of *praenomina* in the family ('Lucius' for this man and for S.'s only son (10 below), but 'Publius' for S.) suggests that the man's first son would also have been a Lucius: if S. had an older brother, then the tribunate would perhaps fall earlier in 90s rather than later. The elder Sestius was in any case obviously deceased by the time of this trial. On the family's commercial interests in Cosa, see Introd. §2.

as most of you recall   C.'s first 'prompting' gesture, telling the jury what is in their minds or how they are responding to his speech, cf. 25, 31, 33, 77, 115, and 9 **and . . . all of you** n. Beyond involving the judges in the speech, like the questions or requests he addresses to them (42, 81, 91, 119), these gestures insinuate useful thoughts, in this case that they 'of course' recall the worthy man C. sketches—even if he was an obscure figure whose public career had been of no consequence. In fact, if S.'s father had last been in the public eye 35 to 40 years earlier (previous n.), and if the process of 'selection and rejection' (Introd. §2) did not markedly skew the judges' average age toward the upper end of the eligible range (30–60 years), only a small minority of the panel would be able to recall what C. tells them they recall.

wise, pure, and strict   Fathers are proverbially strict (*severus*: e.g. *Dom.* 84, *Cael.* 37, *Phil.* 8. 13, *Tusc.* 4. 45), and defendants' fathers are commonly paragons of virtue and good repute (e.g. *Sex. Rosc.* 15, *Clu.* 11, *Cael.* 3), but the elder Sestius' cluster of excellences sets him apart: the only individuals C. elsewhere describes as both wise (*sapiens*) and morally pure (*sanctus*) are the elder Quintus Lutatius Catulus, cos. 102 (*Planc.* 12), and Socrates (*De or.* 1. 231).

came in first in the election   The order of the return had no bearing on magisterial competence, but being returned first was thought an honour: though C. tries to discount the criterion when it serves his argument (*Mur.* 18), he was himself quite proud of the fact that he had come in first when he stood for the praetorship (*Leg. Man.* 2: in fact, as he says, he was returned first three times, the polling having been suspended the first two times before the election was completed). See also *Pis.* 2 (mentioning his election as *quaestor and aedile), *Vat.* 11 (on S.'s election as quaestor), Mommsen 1887–8, 3. 414 n. 3.

thereafter less keen…worthy of it   C. toils to spin hay into gold. The elder Sestius either withdrew from further service to the *commonwealth or was defeated when he stood for further office: were he an opponent, C. could attack him for the former or demean him for the latter; cf. 114 below, on the subsequent defeats suffered by two men who had been tribune in 59.

With his father's sponsorship   Like any freeborn Roman, S. was subject to the 'paternal power' (*patria potestas*), and so not in possession of his own rights (*sui iuris*), while his father was still alive: beyond being expected to share his father's household, he had limited rights to own property and needed his father's permission to marry (on *patria potestas*, Saller 1986, 1994, 114–30, Lacey 1986; on its relation to marriage, Treggiari 1991, 15–16, 170–2). Plutarch notes, as an example of old Roman rectitude, that Crassus' two brothers, who married while their parents were still alive, continued to dine at the family table (*Crass.* 1. 1); in a few weeks C. will defend Caelius, taxed with a lack of filial piety for leaving his father's house while still in *patria potestas*, by saying that he acted 'not only with his father's permission but at his urging' (*Cael.* 18: not an unambiguous statement, given the sort of fellow Caelius was).

Gaius Albanius   On the name (vs. Albinius) see Shackleton Bailey 1989. From *Fam.* 13. 8(321). 1 it emerges that he was a senator and still alive in the mid-40s; though no magistracy is attested for him, he presumably was already a senator when he attended this trial (**constant ... concern** n., below). He is perhaps the Gaius Albanius whom C., writing from Tusculum in May 45, describes as a 'next-door neighbour' (*proximus ... vicinus*: *Att.* 13. 31(302). 4).

this boy here and a daughter   The daughter is not otherwise known; since already married, prob. (though not certainly) older than her brother, who still wore the *bordered toga (*toga praetexta*) of boyhood (144, and see following). The son is Lucius Sestius (*RE* 3) Alb. Quirinalis (*CIL* 15. 1445; 'L. Sestius' at *Fam.* 13. 8(321). 1; 'Alb'. is presumably based on his mother's family-name, i.e. 'Albanius'— giving him a double *nomen*—or 'Albanianus', Shackleton Bailey 1989). His birth is placed in or around 73 in standard accounts, presumably because of his service with Brutus (see below): that is too early if at this trial he was still wearing the *toga praetexta*, usually exchanged for the *toga virilis* at around 15 (ages ranging from 13 to 18 are known: Rawson 2003, 142); the ploy of having him read the Capuan decree (10), meant to stir the judges' compassion with his 'boyish voice', would be absurd if he were around 17 and of an age for military service. He was most likely born *c.*70 or 69, a few years before C.'s son, Marcus (b. 65), with whom he is mentioned as a comrade in arms on the side of Caesar's assassins at *MBrut.* 2. 5(5). 4 (April 43): he would then have been in his mid-20s when he served as Brutus' *proquaestor in 44–42 (*RRC* 1. 515 no. 502 and App. *BCiv.* 4. 51, where he is mistakenly called 'Publius', cf. Cass. Dio 53. 32. 4), in

circumstances when the age-criteria for service in various capacities
were prob. not very strictly applied. Though *proscribed as a result of
that service, he was pardoned and later flourished under Augustus,
who chose him as suffect consul when he himself laid down the
consulship in 23, the same year in which Lucius was honoured by
the dedication of a very prominently placed poem in Horace's collection of odes (1. 4).

very serious men of old-fashioned strictness   Commending S. by
commending the men who approved him, the expression extends to
Albanius the ethical aura already created for the elder Sestius, by
invoking two crucial traits besides 'strictness' (cf. **wise, pure, and
strict** n., above): the quality of being 'old-fashioned' (*antiquus*), a
trait always presumptively better than being contemporary or new-
fangled; and *seriousness (*gravitas*), on which see the Glossary. These
were the traits, for example, of the aged senator Publius Servilius,
who supported C. at a crucial juncture (130 **truly godlike gravity** n.);
by contrast, the consul Piso affected the appearance of this old-
fashioned seriousness but belied it by his behaviour (19 and nn.
below). (The main MSS offer an impossible text—one or another
version of *gravissimis antiquitatis viris*—for which most editors,
including Maslowski, prefer the reading 'men of most weighty an-
tiquity/old-fashioned ways', *gravissimae antiquitatis viris*, a form of
which is found in a late MS. But whereas it is not rare for the notion
'ancient/old-fashioned' to modify the idea of ethical gravity—see 130
below, with Vell. 2. 49. 3, Gell. 4. 14. 2, (Quint.) *DMai.* 4. 4—the idea
of being ethically 'weighty/grave' is never applied to 'antiquity' as a
modifier, presumably because it would be otiose. *Gravitas* is typically
an attribute of persons: I here translate Weidner's *gravissimis
antiqu<ae sever>itatis viris*; Mommsen's *gravissimis <summae>
antiquitatis viris* aims at a similar cure, as does, more clumsily,
Busche's *gravissimis <ac plenissimis> antiquitatis viris*, adopted by
Peterson.)

constant … concern   The usual practice for family and friends, not
only to lend the defendant moral support but as a show of strength
for the judges and the community: the more prominent and authoritative the friends, the more impressive the show, and Albanius'
standing as a senator (above) would have helped; cf. also 15 **Gnaeus**

Pompeius n. For his part S. was still dutifully supporting his former father-in-law a decade later: in *Fam.* 13. 8(321). 1 C. intercedes with a third party on behalf of S., who had requested the intercession on behalf of Albanius.

7. While his own father was still alive See 6 **With his father's sponsorship** n.; on the date of the marriage, next n.

Lucius Scipio Lucius Cornelius (*RE* 338, *MRR* 2. 555–6, 3:71) Scipio Asiagenes was an adherent of Marius and cos. 83 with Gaius Norbanus. After engaging Sulla at Teanum Sidicinum just N of Campania in 83, he was deserted by his army and captured with his son, but the two were released unharmed (*MRR* 2. 62). Scipio then broke the guarantees of good conduct he had given Sulla and raised another army with the intention of attacking Pompey (Appian *BCiv.* 1. 95, Plut. *Pomp.* 7. 3, cf. *Att.* 9. 15(183). 2); this army too deserted him, and he soon fled to Massilia (below), either before or after being *proscribed (Oros. 5. 21. 3, prob. from Livy). C.'s sketch, relying on euphemism and cliché ('commonwealth tossed on turbulent seas', see below), of course conveys none of this. That Scipio died soon after going into exile is often assumed, incorrectly. In view of the age of S.'s son by Albania (**this boy here** n.), S. cannot have married Cornelia, and Scipio cannot have died, before the early 60s; the sequence C. follows implies that the marriage preceded S.'s term as *military tribune, which itself probably did not long precede his election in 64 to the *quaestorship (see **military tribune** n. below): dating the marriage to *c*.68 will not be off by more than a year or two in either direction (*Fam.* 5. 6(4). 1 shows Cornelia pressing S.'s interests with C.'s wife, Terentia, in Dec. 62). Scipio himself could easily have lived until the late 60s: as cos. 83, he was born no later than 126; as one of Rome's moneyers (*tresviri monetales*) by 106 (*RRC* 1. 319 no. 311), a position usually held at the very start of a public career, he could have been born in the early 120s. Scipio's daughter must have been a mature bride in any case.

devotion . . . approval The praise C. heaps on S.'s devotion (*pietas*) and dutiful attention to his exiled father-in-law echoes the praise he heaped on the dutiful behaviour of his own son-in-law, Piso (54 n.), during his exile: e.g. *Fam.* 14. 1(8). 4 'Piso's humane feeling (*humanitas*), his manly behaviour (*virtus*), his affection (*amor*) for us all is so great that nothing could surpass it. I hope only that it might bring him some pleasure; I certainly see that it will bring him distinction in others' eyes (*gloria*)', sim. 14. 2(7). 1, 14. 3(9). 3. Unlike S., however, Piso was not able to bring the exile's beloved daughter to see him.

Setting off at once for Massilia 'At once' (*statim*), that is, upon marrying Cornelia, not upon Scipio's *proscription: on the chronology see above; the moving reunion C. is about to sketch implies some period of separation. Massilia (mod. Marseille), founded nearly six centuries earlier from the Ionian city of Phocaea in Asia Minor, was a Greek cultural center on the southern coast of Gaul. As an allied city independent of Roman control, it was a familiar destination for exiles from Rome: Verres fled there in 70, and Catiline put it about that he was heading there when he left Rome in Nov. 63 (*Cat.* 2. 14, 16, Sall. *Cat.* 34. 2; cf. also Sen. *Contr.* 2. 5. 13 for the rhetorician Moschus). Scipio could have had a comfortable existence: C.'s supporter Milo, anticipating conviction for the murder of Clodius when C. failed to mount an adequate defence, fled there in 52 and later had occasion to comment (sarcastically) on the excellence of the local mullets (Cass. Dio 40. 54. 3).

commonwealth was tossed on turbulent seas The first instance of the 'ship of state' metaphor that recurs frequently throughout the speech: see esp. 15, 20, 45–6, 97–9, with Fantham 1972, 126–8, May 1980. The metaphor's pedigree can be traced back to Alcaeus writing in the early 6th cent.; the figure, developed most elaborately in Latin by Horace (*Odes* 1. 14, with Nisbet and Hubbard 1970, 179–82), was used by C. in his youthful debut as a writer on rhetoric (*Inv.* 1. 4) and often elsewhere, e.g. *Dom.* 129, 137, *Pis.* 20–1, *Att.* 2. 7(27). 4.

footsteps of his ancestors Neither Scipio's father (who had no known public career) nor his grandfather (*RE* 324, *quaestor 167) was a distinguished man, but his great-grandfather was Lucius Cornelius (*RE* 337) Scipio Asiaticus, cos. 190 and brother of the great Scipio Africanus.

his own . . . dutiful acts besides For the corrupt text of the MSS I adopt Mommsen's solution (*maximis praeterea assiduisque officiis*), which seems slightly preferable to Maslowski's (*maximis praeterea suis studiis et officiis*): the choice does not bear on the 'very substantial dutiful acts' (*maximis officiis*: the phrase is secure in the MSS) but on the manner of their performance, with constancy (*assiduis*) or with zeal (*studiis*: Mueller's *maximis praeterea assiduisque studiis et officiis* combines both thoughts). We do not know what specific dutiful acts C. means.

generosity i.e. *liberalitas*: see the Glossary. The trait is plainly understood here to be a virtue; yet because it could be confused with a form of giving that was either spendthrift or self-interested— and because for one free man to receive (specifically) money from another was thought an unbecoming subordination—*generosity was not unproblematic. In this period it is most closely associated with Caesar (see Siani-Davies 2001, 206); it becomes an unequivocal ideal only in the imperial period, when the emperor's superordinate status is unambiguous and unquestioned (see Manning 1985).

military tribune On this elective military office, see the Glossary. At some point early in the 1st cent. BCE the requirement of 5–10 years' prior army service was dropped, and as commanders came to use more senior men as their immediates subordinates (*legate: see Glossary)—in part because they could not rely on a cadre of experienced *military tribunes—the prestige of the tribunate decreased. It still remained an attractive way for a young man from an equestrian or lesser senatorial family, like S., to begin his public career (Suolahti 1955, 103–4); and 'if the military tribunate … were the only pre-senatorial magistrac(y) the young Roman was going to hold, it was of course profitable for him to postpone (its) tenure as close as possible in time to his candidature for the quaestorship, for then the electorate would have fresh in memory all the merits he had gained' (ibid. 31), as S. indeed appears to have done (on the chronology, **Lucius Scipio** n. above).

temperate behaviour in … that office Lit. 'temperate behaviour associated with his province in that magistracy' (*provinciali in eo magistratu abstinentia*), where 'province' denotes not a geographical space but the magistrate's sphere of duty, the more general sense from which the geographical usage had emerged. On *temperance, see

the Glossary. C. praises a similar quality in S. when speaking of his
*proquaestorship in Macedonia (13).

8. quaestor... assigned by lot   On the office, see the Glossary. Like
the *military tribunes (above n.), *quaestors were elected in the tribal
assembly (*comitia tributa*): in the election for 63 S. was chosen by all
35 tribes (*Vat.* 11). The quaestor assigned to C. in 63, Titus Fadius
(*MRR* 2. 168, 3:89), supported C.'s recall as tribune in 57: for C.'s
thanks, see *Red. sen.* 21 and cf. 72 **tribunes** n.

Gaius Antonius   Gaius Antonius (*RE* 19, *MRR* 2. 531), son of the
Marcus Antonius (cos. 99) who plays a central role in C.'s dialogue *On
the Orator*, and uncle of the triumvir Mark Antony, who in 43 would
both arrange his uncle's censorship for the following year and secure
C.'s murder; the cognomen associated with him, 'Hybrida', was not
adopted by Antonius as part of his nomenclature but is a hostile
nickname ('Halfbreed') given him by others (Plin. *HN* 8. 213), presumably for reasons having to do with his mother's origins (cf. Quintus
Varius, tr. pl. 90, from Sucro in Spain, given the nicknames 'Hybrida'
and 'Hispanus', and 21 **his mother's lineage** n., on the background
of Piso's mother as a source of abuse). An unsavory character who
profited from Sulla's *proscriptions and was expelled from the senate
by the censors in 70, he prob. regained senatorial status as a *tribune of
the plebs in 68 (*MRR* 2. 141 n. 8); he became C.'s colleague as praetor in
66, with C.'s support (*MRR* 2. 151–2), and C.'s colleague as consul in 63,
after C. frustrated his political alliance with Catiline, who also stood for
the office (*MRR* 2. 166). Here and below (12), C. heavily hints at his
suspected involvement in Catiline's conspiracy (see also esp. Plut.
Cic. 12. 3–4, more equivocally *Cat.* 3. 14), from which he was allegedly
deflected when C. ceded to him the governorship of Macedonia
(Sall. *Cat.* 26. 4, cf. 13 below), originally allotted to C., in place of the
province (Cisalpine Gaul) that he had drawn; on his behaviour in the
field against Catiline at the end of 63 and early 62, see 12 below. After
governing Macedonia in 62–60 he was prosecuted in 59 by Marcus
Caelius Rufus (*TLRR* no. 241) and went into exile after C. defended
him unsuccessfully (*LUO* no. 37). As early as 1 Jan. 61 C. anticipated that
A. would be prosecuted, and showed no appetite for defending him
(*Att.* 1. 12(12). 1); he was later recalled by Caesar. C. shows him in a
somewhat more favourable light at *Flac.* 95, where it serves his ends to

present Antonius, after his trial, as a victim 'sacrificed' to Catiline's shade by his adherents; for C.'s version of his own treatment of Antonius, *Pis.* 5.

Scruple . . . prevents me   The relation between *quaestor and supervising magistrate was expected to be so close that it could be described in terms of filial attachment (e.g. *Red. sen.* 35, *Planc.* 28, see also *Div. Caec.* 45–6, 61, *Red. sen.* 21, Plut. *Caes.* 5. 3; cf. *Flac.* 77, on the sanctity of the bonds binding a magistrate's advisers, his *consilium*, to him): not least because the quaestor typically kept the magistrate's financial records, the two were supposed to remain in a relationship of confidentiality (*fides*) for life. S., in serving as C.'s spy, and C. himself, in setting a spy upon his colleague, would be expected to feel some scruple deriving from a sense of dutiful behaviour (*offici religio*); in this case the commonwealth's crisis outweighed the scruple, but C. must acknowledge the point, and treat the details discreetly, in speaking of the matter. That S. served C. in this way might suggest that—patriotism aside—the two already enjoyed some familiarity, certainly during and probably before C.'s consulship: this hint at a connection earlier than otherwise attested is perhaps the most interesting bit of information to emerge here.

noticed and reported   Any man in C.'s position would have a web of informants, ready to provide information out of friendship and in exchange for C.'s favour and influence, as C. makes plain in the cool letter sent to Antonius himself in Dec. 62 (*Fam.* 5. 5(5). 2): 'You yourself can attest that you have made no suitable return for (the favours I have done you), and I have heard from many people that you have even acted against my interests'—where the 'many' surely included S. himself, then on service with Antonius in Macedonia, with whom C. exchanged letters about the same time and remarked on Antonius' failings (*Fam.* 5. 6(4). 3). It was such sources that allowed C. to catch out the Catilinarians and avoid assassination (cf. Sall. *Cat.* 26. 3, 28. 2, the information laid by Fulvia) and that caused his enemies to mock his claims of having 'informed himself' on any given matter (see Shackleton Bailey on *Att.* 1. 14(14). 5); similarly, as the crisis built in 59 he clearly relied heavily on Atticus' contacts with Clodia to track her brother's doings (e.g. *Att.* 2. 12(30). 2, 2. 14(34). 1, 2. 22(42). 5) and felt badly underinformed when Atticus was not available (e.g. *Att.* 2. 22(42). 1, 4–5).

at no point . . . did he have the will . . . to palliate . . . One of the speech's more labored sentences: the translation coordinates 'denial' and 'dissimulation' with the relevant verbs more tidily than the Latin. Though C.'s scruple (cf. preceding) continues to blunt his point, the effect is still damning: C. avoids expressly aligning Antonius with the conspiracy, but the behaviour ascribed to him implies that he was at least wilfully careless of his position. When interrogating Vatinius soon after this speech (Introd. §2), C. speaks of Antonius more sympathetically, as the 'unfortunate consular' (*Vat.* 27–8).

attending to The verb C. uses, *observare*, can denote 'keep a watch over' and 'pay respectful attention to'; as the following clause shows, both senses are intended.

and . . . all of you I translate the reading found in some of the medieval MSS (*et vobis omnibus* P²BH: om. P¹GV), against Hertz's emendation (*et bonis omnibus*, 'all good men', i.e. 'patriots') adopted by (e.g.) Cousin 1965 and Maslowski. There is no decisive criterion for choosing: the latter is apt in a context that plays on 'good' (*patriotic) and 'best' ('most patriotic'); the former is apt as one of the gestures C. uses to tell the judges what they know or believe (cf. 6 **as most of you recall** n.) and suitably concludes a sentence governed in its first half by the judges' point of view ('you were rightly inclined').

9. conspiracy burst forth . . . openly under arms Though Catiline's lieutenant, Gaius Manlius, was reported to be in the field with an army in Etruria by 27 Oct. 63 (Sall. *Cat.* 30. 1, cf. next n.), C. must have in mind the effect of the *First Catilinarian*, delivered on 8 Nov., because of which Catiline famously 'left, departed, went out, *burst forth*' from Rome (*Cat.* 2. 1, culminating in the same verb used here), joining Manlius and bringing the conspiracy fully into the open. Since S. was still in Rome on 8 Nov. (*Cat.* 1. 21 'this excellent young man here (*huic*), Publius Sestius', where *huic* gestures to one present), his mission postdates that speech.

came with an army Given that S. aimed to dislodge one of Antonius' subordinate officers, and that it was C. who later summoned him back to Rome with his army (11 below), he was presumably dispatched by C., whom the senate had charged with safeguarding

Rome, while Antonius, nominally S.'s supervising magistrate, was sent with an army to pursue Catiline around the third week of Nov. (Sall. *Cat.* 36. 3). If Antonius himself sent S. to Capua, the chain of authority would be clarified (since S. was his *quaestor), but it would also be the only recorded anti-Catilinarian action on Antonius' part (on his behaviour in the field, see 12 below). In view of the chronology in the preceding n., this episode must postdate the senatorial decree of late Oct. that sent the praetor Quintus Pompeius Rufus to raise an army and secure Capua when news of Manlius' movements first reached Rome (Sall. *Cat.* 30. 5); on S.'s mission, targeted more specifically than the praetor's, see **Gaius Mevulanus** n. below.

Capua ... numerous strategic advantages   One of the chief cities of Campania and indeed all Italy, Capua was an Etruscan foundation that successively came under Oscan and Latin influence, and it was a loyal ally of Rome from the 4th cent. until it defected to Hannibal in 216. Set on the river Volturnus at the foot of Mt. Tifata and commanding both the *via Appia*, leading to Rome, and much of the most fertile land in Italy, it was in fact a strategic plum (for a fine aerial view, Frederiksen 1984, pl. VI): Pompey delegated (or tried to delegate) its protection to C. at the outbreak of the civil war in 49 (*Fam.* 16. 11(143). 3; on the question whether C. accepted the commission, *CLA* 4. 438–40). After the town was taken back from Hannibal in 211, it was reduced to the status of prefecture (Livy 26. 16. 9–10; Vell. 2. 44. 4, cf. 32 n., *Leg. agr.* 1. 18–19), stripped of its autonomy, and subjected to the jurisdiction of specially selected 'prefects' sent from Rome. A colony was established there by Caesar's agrarian legislation in 59, with an influx of new settlers joining the old: see **'settlers'** n. below, and Brunt 1971*a*, 313–19, 529–35 (its civic status); Frederiksen 1984, 285–311 (economic and social life under the Republic); and D'Isanto 1993, 15–24 (general survey). On C.'s earlier exploitation of Capua's strategic importance, and the fear it provoked, at *Leg. agr.* 2. 76–97, see Vasaly 1993, 231–43. With the sedition here compare that at Pompeii led by Publius Sulla (*Sull.* 60–2).

Gaius Mevulanus, Antonius' military tribune   On the office see 7 n. The MSS' 'Mevulanus', retained here hesitantly, is not otherwise known as a personal name: among possible alternatives much the most attactive is 'Mefulanus' (Hübner 1875, 41), which seems

attested epigraphically (*CIL* 1^2. 802 *Mefu*(*lanus*?)) and would probably be derived (as the suffix -*anus* hints) from the name of a place,
the *pagus Meflanus* in the Apennines NE of Beneventum, about
50 km from Capua. Since C. evidently dispatched S. after the senate
had sent the praetor Pompeius Rufus to Capua (**conspiracy burst
forth** and **came with an army** nn.), the move was probably aimed
specifically at this officer by C., based on his particular knowledge of
the tribune's leanings and activities, once Antonius was on his way
to Etruria.

Pisaurum and in other parts of coastal Umbria   Lit. '... other parts
of the *ager Gallicus*': Pisaurum, founded as a colony in 184, lay on the
via Flaminia within the *ager Gallicus* ('Gallic land', so called because
inhabited by the Senones, a Gallic tribe), the strip of land between
Ancona and Ariminum on the Adriatic coast in Umbria N of Picenum; on Catiline's following in the region see Harris 1971, 289–94.
As soon as Manlius' activities in Etruria became known at the end of
Oct. the senate sent the praetor Metellus Celer to levy troops in
Picenum and the *ager Gallicus* (*Cat.* 2. 5, Sall. *Cat.* 30. 5, 57. 2),
and C. elsewhere describes Camerinum (a town in Umbria), Picenum, and the *ager Gallicus* as being attacked by the 'sickness' of the
conspiracy's 'frenzy' (*Sull.* 53, cf. Sall. *Cat.* 27. 1, 42. 1).

Gaius Marcellus...an enthusiasm for armed combat   Not readily
identifiable with any other known Marcellus, unless he figures in a
story told by Orosius (6. 6. 7, prob. from Livy): 'An uprising fomen-
ted by the Marcelli, father and son, among the Paeligni (*c.*100 km
ENE of Rome) was betrayed by Lucius Vettius (cf. Cass. Dio 37. 41. 2)
and crushed after the conspiracy of Catiline was revealed, and punishment was exacted from both, by Bibulus among the Paeligni and
by Cicero among the Bruttii (far to the south).' Ref. to Marcus
Calpurnius Bibulus and C.'s brother, Quintus, as praetors puts the
episode in 62 (*MRR* 2. 173), thus after the incident at Capua here
described; earlier Catilinarian unrest in Bruttium is mentioned at
Sall. *Cat.* 42. 1. C.'s point is that—given Capua's standing as a major
center of gladiatorial schools (*familiae*), where Spartacus' rebellion
had begun 10 years earlier—the man intended to acquire gladiators
for use in the revolt: Publius Sulla was accused of doing the like (*Sull.*
54–5), and fear of a slave uprising in Capua bruited about at this time

might be linked to this incident (Sall. *Cat.* 30. 2, cf. 30. 7; for fear of gladiators, *Cat.* 2. 26); cf. the move briefly made to mobilize the gladiators Caesar kept at Capua at the start of the civil war in 49 (*BC* 1. 14. 4). With the disingenuous motive that (acc. to C.) Marcellus alleged—he merely wanted some instruction in close combat—Holden aptly compares the disingenuous explanation that (acc. to C.) the conspirator Cethegus gave to explain the cache of weapons found in his house: 'He said he had always been a connoisseur of good iron implements' (*Cat.* 3. 10).

association of Capua   Because C. refers to a time when Capua was still a subordinate prefecture with no civil structure of its own (see above and next nn.), he cannot properly refer to 'the people' (*populus*), using the collective term that usually denotes the individuals who share the rights and responsibilities of a self-governing community (e.g. 'the senate and people of Rome', *senatus populusque Romanus*). Instead C. uses the term *conventus* (lit. 'a coming together', 'gathering') in one of its technical senses, to refer to a local association of Roman citizens (*conventus civium Romanorum*: for the *conventus* at Capua see also Caes. *BCiv.* 1. 14. 5, and on the institution more generally *RE* 4 (1900), 1179–1200 (Kornemann)). Such a group would have formed the core of the colony established in 59 (see 'settlers' n.).

sole patron   Even in a not-yet-autonomous prefecture (above) an association of Roman citizens was competent to place itself in the clientship (*clientela*) of a patron (*patronus*). C. stresses that he was sole patron (sim. *Pis.* 25, also mentioning the gilded statue he received) because it was a special honour, most towns choosing more than one; Capua later chose Lucius Cornelius Balbus (*CIL* 10. 3854, referring also to his suffect consulship, therefore not before 40). In return for the honour, and for the support the town could provide when needed—much of the favour shown C. by Italian towns before, during, and after his exile (25–6, 32, 37–8, 72, 87, 128–9, 131) would have been due to his clients—the patron represented the town's interests at Rome by commending its citizens, interceding with third parties on their behalf, and esp. (in C.'s case) by his advocacy. Noted Romans could well be patrons of many towns: C. was also patron of, among others, Atella in Campania (*QFr.* 2. 13(17). 3, cf.

Fam. 13. 7(320). 1), Reate in Sabine territory (*Cat.* 3. 5, *Scaur.* 27, *Att.* 4. 15(90). 5), Volaterrae in Etruria (*Fam.* 13. 4(318). 1, cf. *Att.* 1. 19(19). 4), and of towns beyond Italy as well, esp. as a result of his *quaestorship in Sicily and later governorship of Cilicia: see Wiseman 1971, 45–7, Badian 1984*a*, Brunt 1988, 396–9, Deniaux 1993, 373–84, Lomas 2004.

'settlers'   Under the agrarian legislation passed by Caesar as consul in 59, a board of twenty commissioners, including Pompey, was established to distribute the land; the board was also responsible for establishing a colony at Capua (*MRR* 2. 191–2). Some of the settlers (*coloni*) would have been newcomers (cf. Caes. *BCiv.* 1. 14. 4), including veterans of Pompey's eastern campaigns, but C.'s phrasing here— 'the same people (now as "settlers")'—shows that some were the inhabitants of the former prefecture, enjoying a new label with their new status; on the likelihood that the latter had been members of a local 'association of Roman citizens', see **association of Capua** n. above. By this transformation the city regained a measure of self-rule (cf. Vell. 2. 44. 4), and with it a governing structure resembling the capital's, including a town council with members analogous to Rome's senators—the councillors (*decuriones*) whose decree is about to be read—and two chief magistrates (see 19 **duumvirate** n.) analogous to the consuls.

written testimonial   The advocate's laudatory review of the defendant's early life was important in establishing the sort of person he was (5 **the kind of ... character** n.), and testimonials of this sort, from individuals (cf. 15 **Gnaeus Pompeius** n.) and corporate entities, corroborated the sketch: esp. when provided by distant towns, such testimonials could be submitted in writing (e.g. *Sex. Rosc.* 25, *Sull.* 61, *Flac.* 36, *Cael.* 5, *Balb.* 39, *Planc.* 22, 28), as an alternative to a personal deputation (e.g. *Clu.* 195–7, *Flac.* 62–3, 100); see Greenidge 1901, 490–1. In 52, Pompey's judicial reforms abolished the appearance of these character witnesses (Plut. *Cat. min.* 48. 4, Cass. Dio 40. 52. 2).

10. Lucius Sestius   On S.'s son, see 6 **this boy here** n. Though C. is plainly addressing the boy, the MSS offer a comedy of errors: in an ancestor of the extant MSS a scribe, evidently thinking that C. was asking S. to read the decree, wrote 'P. Sesti', the only form of the name

given in the tradition here ('Lucius' is restored from *Fam.* 13. 8(321). 1);
a later scribe, concluding that C.'s reference to 'the voice of a child'
(*puerilis... vox*) was hardly consistent with the mature defendant,
changed the expression to 'the manly voice' (*virilis... vox*), the reading
that appears in half the medieval MSS. C. uses the boy to arouse the
judges' compassion (the unhappy child reappears for the same purpose
at the speech's end, 144); his implied premise—that the boy would
inherit his father's enemies and take vengeance when he was old enough
to prosecute them—justifies the comment that 'such expectations...
made (the children) good haters' (Rawson 2003, 224). On such inherited enmities see Hinard 1980, Epstein 1987, 43–6.

Councilors' Decree   Like the letter from Cicero referred to below
(11), and like documentary evidence and witnesses' testimony that is
more strictly germane to the charge in other cases (e.g. *Rosc. com.* 43,
Verr. 2. 1. 79, 94, 128, 2. 3. 87, 89, 99–100, *Cael.* 55), the decree is not
quoted in the text that C. released for circulation, but its introduction is marked by a place-holder phrase.

not a forced expression of duty... nor... out of self-interest   C. is
obliged to say this because such testimonials no doubt were commonly
just what he claims this one is not, expedient or superficial gestures for
a neighbor, a patron (9 n.), or a 'public guest-friend' (*hospes publicus*:
cf. *Balb.* 41–3, Wiseman 1971, 33–8), the last a distinguished Roman
who would perform for a town's citizens much the same services as a
patron, though the relationship would not have the same expressly
hierarchical cast as that between patron and client. For the contrast
between mere formality and real passion in such gestures, cf. 27 **not as
a formal gesture** n.; for a vivid narrative in which one such 'forced
expression' figures prominently, see *Verr.* 2. 4. 137–44.

11. the senate... had caught and crushed... under my leadership   As becomes clear immediately following, C. refers not to
the final defeat of Catiline (see 12, esp. **Marcus Petreius** n.) but to
the execution on 5 Dec. 63 of Lentulus Sura, Cethegus, and three
other leading conspirators whom Catiline had left behind in Rome—
the action that led to C.'s exile in 58 (Introd. §1 and 25 **brought ruin**
n.). C. thus presents for the first time, and in a characteristic way, a
theme that he will weave through the speech: on the one hand, the

action was a great victory, achieved under his leadership; on the other hand, responsibility for the action was not C.'s alone, or even primarily, but rested with the senate and was shared by all patriots (thus the real agents—the subjects—in the present sentence). The first thought is necessary because it allows the claim that C. alone saved the Republic (see esp. 129 **I alone** n.); the second thought is necessary because it relieves C. of responsibility for executing Roman citizens without trial (see esp. 38 **The things** n., and next n.). But beyond its rhetorical utility, the implied relationship between consul and senate—the former as the executive subordinate to the latter—is, in fact, central to his conception of Republicanism more generally: see esp. 137 **magistrates rely** n.

domestic enemies Because Lat. *hostis* refers to a *public enemy, and because such enemies were typically outsiders (Hannibal, etc.), C. adds the epithet 'domestic' (so *Cat.* 3. 14, 22, 28, *Sull.* 32, *Flac.* 95 on the Catilinarians; cf. *Red. pop.* 13 and 39 below on his tormentors in 58), to stress that the threat came, extraordinarily, from within: cf. Clodius' countercharge that C. himself was a *hostis Capitolinus, Dom.* 7, and 1 **domestic brigands** n. C. implies here, and made explicit elsewhere (e.g. *Cat.* 4. 10, 15), that one who was an enemy in this sense could not be regarded as a citizen and had no civic rights; thus when Catiline joined Manlius under arms in Nov. 63, the senate declared them both enemies (Sall. *Cat.* 36. 2). But though the men executed on 5 Dec., referred to here, were decreed by the senate to have acted 'against the commonwealth' (Sall. *Cat.* 50. 3), that decree was properly a prelude to a trial, not summary execution, and gave C. little cover in point of strict legality (Berry 1996, 178, on *Sull.* 21, is concise and helpful; more fully Ungern-Sternberg 1970, 86 ff., esp. 123–9; and Drummond 1995, esp. 95 ff., cf. 53 **assembly** n.). Even had the senate judged that one of the five, the praetor Lentulus, had 'lost the rights of a citizen' (thus C.'s claim, *Cat.* 3. 15, itself doubtful: Barlow 1994, 182–4), that would have been no more help, for depriving a person of his metaphorical *caput*—his *'life as a citizen', with its attendant rights—no more lay within the senate's power than depriving a person of his literal *caput* (= 'head').

call to mind...past fears This stirring of past fears seems to have no bearing on the case, beyond its relation to the patriotic character

C. has been creating for S.; but an argumentative link will emerge when C. contends that the Catilinarians' fearful work has simply been continued by his more recent enemies, against whom S. tried to defend him: see 42 **old forces** n. For the technique of appealing to the judges' imagination, esp. in emotionally charged ways, see esp. the evocation of Gabinius and Piso below: 17 **picture in your minds** n.

Letter of Cicero as Consul   The letter does not survive. Cf. *Planc.* 74, where C. directs that *Red. sen.* be read out in court (to show that his gratitude to Plancius, thanked at *Red. sen.* 35, is genuine); for magistrates' letters or the like adduced as evidence, see *Verr.* 2. 1. 83, 2. 3. 45, 92, 123, *Flac.* 20, 78.

Sestius' arrival ... tribunes of the plebs   C. summoned S. to return to Rome after the execution of the conspirators on 5 Dec. (**the senate ... had caught** n. above), which happened to coincide with the official end of S.'s *quaestorship (new quaestors entered office on 5 Dec.). S. arrived after Dec. 10, when the new tribunes entered office, and (apparently) before C. left the consulship on Dec. 29. On the hostility of the new tribunes Metellus Nepos and Calpurnius Bestia, see the following nn. and 72 **his colleague** n.

12. Marcus Cato ... defending the <common>wealth   C. anticipates 60–3 below, an encomium of Cato's actions before, during, and after his *tribunate. Here he has in mind Cato's *veto of Metellus Nepos' proposal to summon Pompey to take command against Catiline, a confrontation that led to a riot so violent it caused the senate to suspend Nepos from his tribunate: see 62 **temple was seized** n.; chronology and other considerations argue against Cato's belief that Nepos was Pompey's agent (Plut. *Cat. min.* 20. 2, Mitchell 1991, 71–2), but both here and in 62 C. treats the affair allusively lest he embarrass Pompey. Nepos made his attempt in Jan. 62, perhaps in the second week of the month (Shackleton Bailey on *Fam.* 2. 1–2(1–2)), and obviously before Catiline was defeated by Antonius' army; acc. to the chronology C. has in mind here, the episode marks the point after which S. went to rejoin Antonius, see below.

senate ... protect those who had guarded ... their own peril   'Those who had guarded the well-being of all' include chiefly C. himself: beyond affirming that the community was functioning properly thanks to Cato's action, C. probably refers to the senate's *decree, also apparently of Jan. 62, that 'all who had taken in hand the things done' against the Catilinarians should enjoy immunity from prosecution and that 'anyone who attempted to call them to account should be considered an enemy' (Cass. Dio 37. 42. 3); cf. 38 **I had done them** n.

Sestius sped off... caught up with Antonius   Since leaving Rome in the third week of Nov. 63 (9 **came with an army** n.), Antonius had been moving north into Etruria against Catiline, and neither C.'s account here nor any other source suggests that he had been eagerly forcing the march; it is not recorded whether—when S. caught up with him—Antonius asked his *quaestor where he had been and what he had been doing for (it appears) close to two months. In the event, after the praetor Metellus Celer moved from Picenum and Umbria (9 **Pisaurum** n.) to cut off Catiline's path to Gaul, Antonius' army met and defeated Catiline's forces near Pistoria, probably in the latter part of Jan. 62.

'the impartial god of war'   *communis Mars* (sim. Hom. *Il.* 18. 309 *xynos Enyalios*), placed in quotation marks because it is a cliché of sorts: e.g. *Verr.* 2. 5. 132, *Mil.* 56, *Phil.* 10. 20, *Fam.* 6. 4(244).1, Liv. 5. 12. 1 (and ten more times), Sen. *Dial.* 3. 12. 5, Serv. ad *Aen.* 12. 118; at *De or.* 3. 167 C. treats it, with 'Ceres' for 'grain' and 'Neptune' for 'sea', as a useful form of dignified metonymy. The thought is that once battle begins, anything can happen, the outcome being a matter of random chance (*casus*). The sentence as a whole does Antonius the small favour of treating him as a general with too little nerve, not too little loyalty—a George McClellan, not a Benedict Arnold: cf. next n.

Marcus Petreius   A soldier of more than 30 years' experience, a former praetor (*MRR* 2. 161), and in 63 one of Antonius' staff-officers (*legati*), Marcus Petreius (*RE* 3) plays much the same vigorous role in the accounts of Sallust (*BC* 59. 4–60. 7) and Cassius Dio (37. 39. 4–40. 1), who respectively ascribe Antonius' absence to gout and complicity in the conspiracy. Petreius joined Cato in opposing Caesar as consul in 59 (Cass. Dio 38. 3. 2) and remained an opponent until his death in north Africa, by suicide following the battle of Thapsus, in 46.

manliness   i.e. *virtus*: see the Glossary.

Apennines ... Italy's mountain pasturages and sheepfolds   Though
the textual testimony is divided—does C. refer to Italy's mountain
pasturages (*Italiae calles* PG) or its valleys (*Italiae valles* Sydow, after
ytalia et valeis V)?—the former (adopted here with Maslowski) is
certainly correct. The drovers' trails for transhumance in central and
southern Italy had been the site of widespread violence for a generation, not least during the slave uprising led by Spartacus. The
sheepfolds—lit. 'shepherds' stalls' (*pastorum stabula*)—would have
provided not just sheep for food and clothing but shepherds to press
into armed service: since these would mostly have been slaves,
C. alludes to the fear of servile uprising, which is elsewhere associated
from time to time with the Catilinarian conspiracy (e.g. 9 **Gaius
Marcellus** n.). Imagining Catiline in the role of predatory *brigand
or Sertorius-like guerrilla leader in the mountains of central Italy,
C. presents the picture of a formidable danger. By contrast, when in
Nov. 63 he had presented a similar sketch of the brigand lurking on
the 'wooded hills' (*Cat.* 2. 24), it was to assure the people that he was
a negligible force whom Roman might would soon eliminate.

13. his quaestorship in Macedonia   Strictly, his term as *quaestor
had ended on 5 Dec. 63, and he was *proquaestor (cf. *Fam.* 5. 6(4), of
Dec. 62, to 'Publius Sestius, the son of Lucius, pro q(uaestore)'), still
attached to Antonius, now the *proconsul governing Macedonia
(*MRR* 2. 175–6; the province had originally been allotted to C., who
ceded it to Antonius, see Allen 1952). In the same letter (§1) C.
expresses disbelief that S., previously eager to return to Rome, was
now just as eager to stay in his position; so far as we know he remained
with Antonius until the later returned to Rome late in 60. S.'s new
eagerness is prob. to be explained by a growing appreciation for the
opportunities to profit under a governor as corrupt as Antonius no
doubt was: hence C.'s vagueness in treating this period, and the
orotund haste (**drawing ... n.**) with which he puts it behind him.

uprightness ... in the duties of that office   On *uprightness (*integritas*) see the Glossary. When ascribed to an official, it chiefly conveys
that he did not try to enrich himself through extortion, and in that
respect it resembles the *temperate behaviour already praised in S.'s
service as a *military tribune (7).

I myself recently saw in Macedonia   During his exile, C. was at Thessalonica in Macedonia, under the protection of Gnaeus Plancius (*MRR* 2. 197), from 23 May 58 (*Att.* 3. 8(53)) until mid-to-late Nov. 58 (*Att.* 3. 22(67); *Fam.* 14. 1(8)), when he moved to Dyrrachium in anticipation of his enemy Piso's arrival in Macedonia as *proconsul. This is the only place in the speech where C. refers to some lived experience of his own away from Rome,

drawing... irresistibly   C. is laying it on a bit thick, and his imagery becomes uneven: the metaphor in the lemma (*absorbet*, marked as a consciously used metaphor by 'as it were', *quodam modo*) evokes the pull of a current or whirlpool that carries one along willy-nilly, whereas the metaphor of the main predicate denotes enthusiastic and purposeful navigation.

14–92. *An Account of the Events Relevant to the Charge (narratio)*

Most of the elements in the paragraph immediately following (14)— on Hortensius' speech, the passion C. feels because of his personal ties to S., and his intention to verbally requite his enemies—are repeated with minor modifications from the exordium (3–5 with nn.): the repetition is a form of punctuation, as C. pauses to gather himself for the onslaught that is to come. At this point in a conventional defence-speech, the advocate would give his version of the acts that provoked the charge, stressing the aspects favourable to his case, explaining, downplaying, or suppressing those that were not, and in general 'spinning' the tale as effectively as he could; and that is what C. does, though not in the conventional way. Rather than argue that specific acts S. allegedly performed did not fall under the description of *public violence detrimental to the *commonwealth, C.'s strategy has the more radical premise that no act S. (or, by implication, anyone else) performed to achieve his recall could be detrimental to the commonwealth: as the attack upon himself had amounted to an attack up the commonwealth, so his restoration represented the commonwealth's restoration; working to achieve both was the proper task of the patriot. The strategy thus requires the account that the following seventy-nine sections provide: C. passes from Clodius' transfer to the plebs in 59 and his heinous compact with the consuls of 58 (15–35), through his own response to the attack—at first uncertain but finally firm and *patriotic (36–50)—to the further crimes against the community committed after his departure (51–66); and the subsequent attempts to reverse the damage to C.— from the first stirrings in mid-to-late 58 (66–71) to the events during S.'s *tribunate in 57 (72–92)—will be portrayed as attempts to heal the commonwealth. Though S. himself will vanish from the account for long stretches at a time, that is only because C. is doing his best to serve S.'s interests; on the strategy see more fully Introd. §3.

14. for our youth If Madvig's generally accepted emendation (*iuventuti*) is correct (the MSS offer various forms of nonsense), Cicero anticipates a theme expressly introduced at 51 and developed at length in 96 ff.: viz., that the arguments made in a case like this are valuable as much for the lessons they teach the next generation as for the forensic purposes at hand. Though C.'s estimation of 'the youth' varies according to the argument he is making, he generally thinks they need to be kept in line: at *Dom.* 47 he claims to see in them only a generation of opportunistic cut-purses—a view consistent with the lesson he aims to teach them here—and at *Att.* 4. 2(74). 2 he hopes that the same speech, of which he was quite proud, will soon be made available to 'the youth' (on C.'s publication of his speeches for the edification of the young, and others, Stroh 1975, 50–2); more generally, and predictably, he grumbles about the younger generation's lust and profligacy (e.g. *Pis.* 82, *Att.* 1. 18(18). 2, 1. 19(19). 8, 2. 8(28). 1).

attack Directly upon his return C. stated his intention of using his best weapon—speech—to take vengeance on his enemies (*Red. pop.* 20); that intention would have been in any case obvious, for all three earlier speeches that survive from after his return (*Red. sen., Red. pop., Dom.*) include extended passages of exuberant invective, as refs. in the notes below will indicate. The sort of revenge he sought is expressed in plainest terms at *Pis.* 99: 'I was never out after your blood,... but I wanted to see you cast aside, scorned, despised by all, abandoned even by yourself in your despair, ever wary, quaking at the slightest sound, stripped of confidence, of speech, of freedom, of authority,... shivering, trembling, groveling before all. And I have seen it.'

freedom Though the *freedom (*libertas*: Glossary) of the *civil community as a whole is a common theme in the speech, only here does C. refer to his own *libertas*, in the limited sense of 'freedom to say what needs to be said for the purpose at hand' (cf. e.g. *Planc.* 33): contrast the end of both *Red. sen.* (36) and *Red. pop.* (25), where C. pointedly emphasizes that not only will he not retreat from his *libertas*—his political independence, broadly understood—in defending the *commonwealth, he will even increase it now he has returned (cf. *Dom.* 27). Those were not forensic speeches, however, and the more limited freedom C. asserts here is best explained by his more restricted role as advocate: for all the speech's apparent self-aggrandizement, the most important political role C. claims for himself is as a model of *loyalty to the commonwealth (49–50). On the muting of C.'s *libertas* soon after this trial, see Introd. §5.

I shall proceed with restraint In the event he shows very little, though he does stop short (e.g.) of conjuring up the sadistic fantasy of seeing Gabinius and Piso crucified (*Pis.* 42) or of accusing Vatinius of practicing child sacrifice and necromancy (*Vat.* 14), nor does he turn ghoulish as he does at *Mil.* 33 (on the indignities inflicted on Clodius' corpse); compare the disclaimer at *Cael.* 31–2 'I shall say nothing about (Clodia) save for the sake of warding off this charge.... Now I shall proceed with restraint and go no farther than my faithful handling of the case compels' (this is offered just after he has 'slipped' and called Clodius her 'husband', cf. App. 2). Personal attacks in forensic cases were conventional, esp. the prosecution's attack on the accused's private life and character and the advocate's more or less spirited response (for expression of the protocols, see e.g. *Mur.* 11, *Cael.* 7–8, *Tull.* 5). In this speech, however, C.'s fire is not directed at the prosecutor, whom he does not name and barely notices (cf. 77 **You charge** n.), and it is far more intense. On the expectations governing such attacks, see Craig 2004.

if some tacitly disapprove ..., if others worked to harm me ... The latter category, of former enemies now reconciled, is represented most conspicuously in the speech by Metellus Nepos, see 72 **his colleague** n. Given the picture C. later paints of all-but-unanimous enthusiasm attending his recall (107–8, 129–30), we might think the former category, of covert enemies who disapproved, a null set included only for formal balance with the category of overt enemies (Clodius, Gabinius, Piso). But C.'s phrasing even in that later depiction (130 'only one man was found to dissent *openly*') implies awareness that some were tacitly opposed; certainly, as C.'s political position changed after Pompey and Caesar met and renewed their working agreement at Luca, he came expressly to claim that some of the more radically conservative faction had shown their malice toward him all along (see esp. *Fam.* 1. 9(20). 10 ff., and 46 **some felt** n.).

nor will what I say offend ... have collided with him   The contrast between accidental collision (*incurrere*) and intentional attack (*invadere*) emerges from literal meaning of 'offend' (*offendere*), 'to strike against': 'offending' someone without provocation would typically make him a personal and political enemy (*inimicus*). Two months later he speaks more frankly of the 'war beyond placation' (*bellum inexpiabile*) he has declared against Gabinius and Piso *(Har. resp.* 4).

15–35. *The Events of 59–58: The Attack of Clodius, Gabinius, and Piso*

Having brought the narrative down to S.'s *tribunate of 57 (end of 13), C. resumes, after the brief pause (14), by stepping back to the events of 'the previous year', 58—or rather, of the year before ('that infamous year when ...'), because he must include Clodius' transfer to the plebs in 59 (we will not reach S.'s tribunate until 71). The specific events C. will recount in 15–35 are not many: after Caesar facilitated Clodius' transfer to the plebs and made his election as tribune possible (15–16), Clodius struck a bargain with the consuls of 58, arranging desirable provincial assignments for them if they would surrender the *commonwealth—that is, C. himself—to Clodius' will (24–5); when in response the public at large and the senate showed their support for C., esp. by taking on mourning (25–6), the consuls tried to suppress the demonstrations, one of them banishing an equestrian in the process, both of them ordering the senate to resume normal dress (27–9); they further connived at other of Clodius' measures intended to tyrannize the community (32–4, these last presented out of chronological sequence, see 33 **while the same consuls sat** n.). C.'s decision to devote *c.*4000 words (in the Latin text) to events summarized here in just over 100 is attributable, first, to the fact that the start of the narrative (15–25) is mostly not narrative at all, but the promised attack on the character of the three magistrates; second, to the fact that the events are not simply narrated but stated and then restated, amplified and generalized (thus e.g. the banishing of one equestrian, 29, becomes an attack on 'the whole equestrian order', 35), to make them seem monumental wrongs. The latter device thus does for events what invective does for individuals, making the worst features appear larger, more repulsive, or more terrifying. Both devices—extended passages of personal abuse (or, to the opposite effect, praise), and the amplification of events beyond their actual dimensions—are the basic tools used in the rest of the speech.

15–25. *The 'Pact' of Clodius, Gabinius, and Piso*

15. shipwreck   On the 'ship of state' in the speech see 7 **commonwealth was tossed** n. With this sentence C. begins the speech's key move, identifying the attack upon himself with an attack upon the *commonwealth (on the strategy see Introd. §3): his own misfortune is the commonwealth's foundering, restoring his own civic *well-being (end of sentence, cf. 1 n.) restores 'the well-being of us all', and 'everything Sestius later said, did, and intended' aimed only at that patriotic end. The strategy's gestures are pervasive (cf. following, 'the bow was bent... against the entire commonwealth') and become, if anything, ever more insistent as the speech proceeds: they will not ordinarily be noted hereafter.

There had already passed that infamous year when... a bow was bent   I follow Maslowski in adopting Madvig's small correction at the start of the sentence (*fuerat ille annus iam* (*tam* PGV)), taking *ille* here to denote special notoriety ('that infamous', cf. *OLD* s.v. 4c); also tempting is 'There had already passed that deadly year...', *fuerat ille annus iam* (Madvig) <*funestus*> (Grumme), on which Shackleton Bailey 1987, 277, builds *fu*<*unestus*> *erat ille annus iam tum*. For much the same thought cf. *Har. resp.* 45, where a flaming torch (*fax*) replaces the bow.

transfer... desperado   Publius Clodius (*RE* 48) Pulcher, who on 20 Jan. 56 had been elected curule aedile (App. 1): though in the course of the speech C. uses the epithet 'Clodian' for various entities (e.g. groups of thugs), he does not deign to name the man himself (in the six 'post-return' speeches narrowly defined, C. names Clodius freely only in the two concerning his house, where he could hardly avoid it, otherwise only in *Vat.* 33, 36). The form of the name Clodius evidently preferred (vs. 'Claudius') perhaps reflected the pronunciation of non-elite speakers whose political support he courted (see most recently Riggsby 2002*b*; against a political motive, Tatum 1999, 247–8), but it certainly reflected no formal change of name and had no connection with his transfer to the plebs. That transfer was required because Clodius belonged to a patrician branch of the Claudian clan (*gens Claudia*) and therefore could not be *tribune of the plebs. Though Clodius evidently aimed at the transfer at least as early as spring of 61 (*In Clod. et Cur.* frag. 14 Crawford, cf. *Att.* 1. 18(18). 4, Jan. 60; on arguments for placing Clodius' decision substantially earlier, Tatum 1999, 95–6), it was not achieved until March 59, by the procedure referred to in 16 (**one of the consuls** n.). With the attack on Clodius begun here, cf. esp. the venomous review of his 'career' at *Har. resp.* 42–6 (a negative counterpart to the review of S.'s early life and career in 6–14 above), and contrast C.'s subtly modulated treatment of Clodius when addressing Clodius' main constituency, the people, in *Red. pop.* (10, 13, 31, with Morstein-Marx 2004, 216); on Clodius' relations with C. more generally see next n. and Introd. §1.

bore a grudge   The rites of the Good Goddess (*Bona Dea*) were conducted 'for the well-being of the Roman people' (*pro salute populi Romani*: *Har. resp.* 12) in the home of a magistrate with *imperium*, and were forbidden to men. In Dec. 62 Clodius violated the rites by dressing as a woman and entering the house of Caesar (then praetor), whose wife, reportedly Clodius' lover, was leading the rites; he was revealed and expelled, then prosecuted for sacrilege (May 61) before a specially constituted court (*TLRR* no. 236). Though Clodius reportedly supported C. against Catiline in 63 (Plut. *Cic.* 29. 1), the two clashed publicly both before and after the trial, in which bribery allegedly bought Clodius a narrow acquittal; at the trial C. gave testimony contradicting Clodius' alibi; and in the trial's aftermath C. described Clodius as a seditious force on a par with Catiline and Lentulus Sura (*Att.* 1. 16(16). 8–10, July 61). The episode as a whole, if not the testimony in particular, sparked Clodius' hatred of C.: sources and refs. to modern discussion in *LUO* no. 29–30, *TLRR* no. 236, Tatum 1999, 62–86; differently Benner 1987, 39–40.

Gnaeus Pompeius   C.'s standard way of referring formally to the man who since 81 wished to be known as Gnaeus Pompeius (*RE* 31) Magnus, 'Pompey the Great'. Omission of the honourific cognomen implies no disrespect ('Gnaeus Pompeius' was the form of address used in the senate), and C. elsewhere uses all three names in formal contexts (e.g. the salutation of *Fam.* 5. 7(3)) and 'Magnus' alone when referring to Pompey more informally (e.g. *Att.* 1. 16(16). 11–12, *Mil.* 68). The style comprising praenomen + cognomen ('Gnaeus Magnus'), which C. customarily used when an aristocrat's cognomen was an established part of his nomenclature (cf. 87 **Titus Annius** n.), C. uses in addressing Pompey only when replying to letters in which Pompey uses the style himself (*Att.* 8. 11 (161) B, D)— where refusing to do so would be aggressively rude—and he rarely uses 'Magnus' in any context after 59 (Adams 1978, 160–1; cf. Dyck 2004*a*, 260–1 on *Leg.* 2. 6). C. first came to know Pompey in 89, when he served with him under his father, Pompeius Strabo, during the Social War (*Phil.* 12. 27), and their political ties became important in the 60s, when C. supported Pompey's extraordinary command against Mithradates in the face of optimate opposition. No political relationship was more enduring or more important to C., and none was more conflicted and ambivalent: for the evidence see esp. Johannemann 1935; on Pompey's role in C.'s exile, return, and subsequent marginalization, see Introd. §§1, 5. Because Pompey had since Sept. 57 held proconsular *imperium* as the specially appointed supervisor of Rome's grain supply, he must have been given special permission to enter the city (normally forbidden to holders of *imperium*), for he attended the trial to give a testimonial for S. (*Fam.* 1. 9(20). 7; as consul four years later Pompey passed legislation abolishing this sort of character reference, see 9 **written testimonial** n.). Accordingly, unlike Caesar, he could hear for himself what C. said about him, and the present passage is typical of the way C. handles the two men. Whereas every ref. to Caesar has at least an edge (in the instance just below, more than an edge: 16 **either (as I believe)** n.) that allows the reader to judge the man's behaviour unfavourably, virtually all refs. to Pompey have the warmth of Italian sunlight on their surface (for a possible exception: 69 **a plan** n.). Here Pompey appears as a loyal friend who did all he could to restrain the monster before succumbing himself, and that character is completely consistent with C.'s public statements about Pompey in the months following his return (see *Har. resp.* 45 for a similarly blameless account of Pompey's role in the transfer, and for more general encomia *Red. sen.* 5, 7, 29, 31, *Red. pop.* 16–18, *Dom.* 3, 27–31, 69; on C.'s treatment of Pompey in the 'post-return' speeches, cf. Riggsby 2002*a*, 176–7). Nothing hints at the cold-blooded betrayal seen in Pompey's behaviour by some contemporaries (see *QFr.* 2. 3(7). 3, C.'s embarrassment on this trial's eve when a tribune denounced Pompey's 'perfidy' toward C. on the senate floor), by the later tradition (Plut. *Pomp.* 46. 5, *Cic.* 31. 2–3, Cass. Dio 38. 15. 3–16. 1), and by C. himself at certain times (Introd. §1). Yet as C. was surely aware, most of his listeners knew that as augur Pompey had facilitated Clodius' transfer (**auspices** n., below).

despite the best efforts of many In the period leading up to C.'s exile these included Caesar (Plut. *Cic.* 30. 4) and Crassus (*Att.* 2. 22(42). 5, Aug.? 59: the text is corrupt but the sense seems probable).

every sort of pledge... if he became tribune In April 59, after the transfer, C. wrote to Atticus about agreements (*pacta*) made between Pompey and Clodius on this matter (*Att.* 2. 9(29). 1); the first two terms that C. uses here would normally imply written assurances (*cautio, foedus*; the last, *exsecratio*, implies that Clodius placed himself under a curse in the event of violation), but C. heaps up the terms merely for effect. The tribunician elections were held sometime in July or August. By July, as he saw danger looming, C. was saying 'Pompey shows great zeal on my behalf and at the same time assures me that (Clodius) will not make a peep about me; in saying this he does not deceive me but is himself deceived' (*Att.* 2. 19(39). 4, July 59; sim. 2. 20(40). 1, mid-July 59). Less than a month later he seems confirmed in his doubts: 'Clodius is plainly hostile to me. Pompey is certain that he will do nothing against me, but I believe that at my peril. I'm getting ready for a standoff' (*Att.* 2. 21(41). 6, late July 59); *Att.* 2. 22(42). 2 (Aug.? 59) relates a report from Pompey—whom by now C. seems not to believe—that he had 'dealt forcefully' with Clodius, stressing the disgrace he (Pompey) would suffer were

C. harmed because of the transfer he had allowed and exacting a solemn promise (*fides*) regarding the conduct of Clodius and his brother Appius. For more on Clodius' duplicity and Pompey's assurances see also *Att.* 2. 23(43). 3, 2. 24(44). 5 (both Aug.? 59), and *QFr.* 1. 2(2). 16 (late 59): the last mentions promises from both Pompey and Caesar that C. is not much inclined to trust. When in late July 54 C. remarks to Quintus that he is not making the mistake he once made in estimating the support he enjoys, adding as explanation that he has a firm grip on the favour (*gratia*) of both Pompey and Caesar (*QFr.* 2. 15(19). 2), he plainly has in mind the circumstances leading up to his exile, starting with the events described here in the text.

fear perils of his own   On Pompey's fear of a plot by Clodius to assassinate him, causing him to close himself up in his house in Aug. 58, see 69 below, esp. **a plan was formed** n.

16. beast   On the semantics of the term (*belua*) in C., see the Glossary. C. applies it to all his most formidable opponents, from Verres (*Verr.* 2. 5. 109) through the Catilinarians (*Sull.* 76), Clodius (beyond the present passage, *Har. resp.* 5, *Mil.* 85), Piso (*Red. sen.* 14, *Pis.* 1), and esp. Mark Antony (*Phil.* 3. 28 and often)—but not, even in his fiercest denunciations, to Caesar; cf. Opelt 1965, 143–4.

auspices...ways of our ancestors...sacrosanct legislation   The 'ways of our ancestors' (*mos maiorum*), the sum of traditional Roman custom, law, belief, and values, forbade any member of a patrician clan from becoming *tribune of the plebs. The other two terms distill the alternatives C. will express more fully at *Prov. cons.* 46: 'if (Clodius) was tribune of the plebs as a patrician, it was against the sacrosanct legislation; if he was *tribune of the plebs as a plebeian, it was against the auspices.' 'Sacrosanct legislation' (*leges sacratae*) refers to compacts sworn by members of the plebs early in the Republic stipulating that anyone who violated them would be 'accursed' (*sacer*) (cf. Altheim 1940, Bleicken 1975, 89–90, Paananen 1993, 17 ff.); because this 'sacrosanct legislation' had established the tribunate as a position to be held by and for members of the plebs, it would be violated if a patrician held the position. On the other hand, Clodius could have become a plebeian holder of the office only by violating the *auspices because the measure that secured his transfer was made void (in C.'s view) by the fact that Caesar's consular colleague, Bibulus, had announced that he was 'watching the heavens' for omens: C. raises the latter objection to the adoption at *Dom.* 39–40, and it was presumably to set such obstacles aside that Pompey lent his *authority as augur to the measure, a role to which C. twice alludes soon after the transfer (*Att.* 2. 9(29). 1, 2. 12(30). 1, cf. 2. 7(27). 2, and esp. 8. 3(153). 3). See further next n., and on 'watching the heavens' see the Glossary s. vv. auspices, obnuntiate.

one of the consuls ... in the curiate assembly   In this first and most overtly critical ref. to Gaius Julius (*RE* 131) Caesar, C. leaves him unnamed (when mentioning behaviour he deplores C. tends to suppress the name of a man with whom at least publicly he is on non-hostile terms, cf. 72 **his colleague** n.; the gesture is different from his complete avoidance of Clodius' name, cf. **transfer ... desperado** n. above). In March 56 Caesar was in Cisalpine Gaul, his mind divided between a revolt of the Veneti that had begun at winter's start (*BG* 3. 7–16) and the state of political affairs at Rome, but he no doubt received a full report; he met with Clodius' brother Appius in Ravenna at the time of this trial or right after (cf. *QFr.* 2. 5(9). 4) and would soon meet there with Crassus. On the motives ascribed to Caesar for his action here, next n.

The procedure followed was a special form of adoption called *adrogatio* (Watson 1967, 82–8), required when an adoptee who was already *sui iuris* (i.e. not subject to *patria potestas*, cf. 6 **With his father's sponsorship** n.) passed into another person's *potestas* as a result of the adoption; it could be sanctioned only by a law passed by the curiate assembly (*comitia curiata*), a *voting assembly of the people organized by the city's 30 'wards' (*curiae*). As Tatum (1999, 104) describes the maneuver: 'Caesar, as (*pontifex maximus*), summoned ... the thirty lictors who represented the *curiae* (the normal manner of convening this assembly in this period) and promulgated the (relevant proposal). ... The assembly then approved Clodius' adoption by P. Fonteius, a plebeian youth of some twenty years, who forthwith emancipated his new son (sc. from his *patria potestas*).' That the adoption was a charade is obvious; that it was strictly illegal is less clear. C. offers legal objections most fully at *Dom.* 34–42 (cf. Cass. Dio 39. 11. 1–2), on grounds ranging from the ages of

adoptive father and son to Caesar's failure to allow the proper length
of time to pass between *promulgation and vote (cf. 25 **public notice
was given** n.); for critique, see Tatum 1999, 104–7. At *Dom.* 40 and
Har. resp. 48 C. argues that Clodius' later attacks on Caesar's consular
legislation impugned the validity of his own transfer; but by *Prov.
cons.* 45 the view that Caesar's consular legislation was technically
invalid is ascribed only to Caesar's extreme *optimate foes.

either (as I believe)... ignorant and careless   C.'s articulation of the
alternatives leaves room to think each is valid (*vel... vel...*, implying
'either A or B or both'). Though he says he prefers the reason not
rooted in Caesar's own intention, and so the slightly less culpable
one, the gesture is undercut at the sentence's end: while 'ignorant'
(*ignarus*) might strictly be neutral (since no human can truly know
the future), 'careless' (*imprudens*) is certainly critical and probably
insulting, *practical intelligence (*prudentia*) being a virtue, its absence a vice. If C. took anything like this line when treating the
incident in Book 1 of the poem *On His Times*, he had good reason
to fret over Caesar's enigmatic reception of the book, as we see him
doing in late Aug. 54 (*QFr.* 2. 16(20). 5). A few months before this
speech, C. made plain his own understanding of Caesar's hostility
(again without naming him: *Dom.* 41): while speaking in defence of
his consular colleague, Gaius Antonius (8 n.), C. had 'made certain
complaints about (the state of) the commonwealth'; and after these
complaints had been reported to Caesar as criticisms, the assembly
was convened and Clodius' adoption put through within three hours
(cf. Suet. *Iul.* 20. 4, Cass. Dio 38. 10. 3–11. 2, 12. 1–2; C.'s explanation
is accepted by e.g. Gelzer 1969*b*, 124–5, Gruen 1974, 289, Wiseman
1994*b*, 372, Seager 2002, 91–2, doubted by e.g. Mitchell 1991,
114–18). Presumably that reason for the grudge is on C.'s mind
here, unstated; with this treatment of Caesar cf. *Vat.* 13–18, on
Vatinius' *tribunate in 59, where C. takes pains to distinguish Vatinius from Caesar as his target, all the while inviting the audience to
judge that Caesar had gone too far (see esp. *Vat.* 15, and cf. criticism
of Vatinius' legislation at *Vat.* 35–6). But after the meetings at Luca,
when C. refers to the matter again (*Prov. cons.* 41–2) and frames the
alternatives as he does here, the reason mooted for Caesar's possible
hostility is C.'s own refusal to accept Caesar's overtures (first noted in

Att. 2. 3(23). 3–4, Dec. 60) and the honours he offered (*Att.* 2. 4(24). 2, 2. 5(25). 1–2, 2. 18 (38). 3, 2. 19(39). 5; *Fam.* 14.3(9). 1; and cf. *Att.* 9. 2a(169). 1, of March 49). C. then goes on to exculpate Caesar, who had tried to 'save' him, and to place the onus entirely on Clodius, Piso, and Gabinius.

what sort of muscle . . . every unprecedented form of lust?   With the last phrase cf. *Pis.* 9 (also of Clodius) 'a person involved in wicked and unprecedented forms of illicit sex (*stuprum*)', and sim. *Cael.* 57 (on the household of his sister Clodia Metelli). The question's premise is the conventional belief that excessive sexual activity left a man enervated and, if not actually 'effeminate' (*mollis*), then something less than a fully vigorous man: see Rousselle 1983, 5–20, Brown 1988, 18–20, Edwards 1993, 85–6, and esp. Corbeill 1996, 115 (on this passage), noting the belief's origin in the idea that semen is derived from blood and concluding that this belief favours Koch's conjecture *exsanguis* ('bloodless'), adopted here, for the MSS' *insani* ('crazed'), retained by Maslowski. By contrast, the allegation that a man had been reduced to this state through excessive sexual activity with his *siblings* (whether male, female, or both) is certainly not conventional: I have made the translation blunter than the Latin (*fraternis flagitiis, sororiis stupris*, lit. 'shameful acts involving his brother(s), illicit acts of sexual penetration involving his sister(s)') to give full force to an insult that—even by the standards of ancient abuse—should take us aback. On the evidence for the insult, and its non-conventional character, see App. 2.

17. 'consuls'?   C. begins the invective that extends the attacks launched in similar terms at *Red. sen.* 10–18: according to the organizing conceit in both places, one of the consuls (Gabinius: 18, 20) proved to be as corrupt as everyone thought he was, whereas the other (Piso: 19–20, 21–4) proved to be a treacherous hypocrite. C. had not always been of this view: writing to his brother late in 59, before Gabinius and Piso entered office, he expected that they would be favourable to him (*QFr.* 1. 2(2). 16, cf. Cass. Dio 38. 15. 6), and his disappointment—esp. in Piso (20 **friend** n.)—surely increased his bitterness. On C.'s techniques of characterization here, May 1988, 92–6, 103–5, Klodt 2003, 49–50.

enemies   i.e. 'public enemies' (*hostes*), see the Glossary.

fasces and... other tokens The fasces were bundles of wooden rods, each nearly as tall as a man, bound together by red thongs and carried by attendants (*lictors*) who walked before magistrates with *imperium*. The fasces symbolized the power to compel obedience and to punish disobedience (*coercitio*: cf. 29 **banished** n.); outside the city each bundle's central rod was tipped with an axe, omitted within the city's boundaries to represent the citizens' right to appeal (*provocatio*: Lintott 1974). The consuls had twelve fasces, which they took turns controlling in alternate months as a token of their collegial relations (see Marshall 1984, 127–41, Schäfer 1989, 196–232). The other tokens included: the 'curule seat' (*sella curulis*: Schäfer 1989, 24–196), a folding ivory chair, like the fasces part of Rome's Etruscan heritage, used by *curule magistrates (censors, praetors, and curule aediles besides consuls), by *promagistrates governing provinces, and some others (e.g. Vestal Virgins); the *bordered toga (*toga praetexta*); and the purple military cloak (*paludamentum*) worn by magistrates and promagistrates with *imperium* in command of armies (cf. 71 **two vultures** n., with Wilson 1938, 100–4).

equestrian order See the Glossary. Anticipating his account of Lucius Lamia's banishment, which he will inflate into an assault on the entire order (28–30), C. for the first time mentions the category of the citizen body from which he had emerged as a *new man, and the mention takes the hierarchical form usual when C. frames a general thought about the *civil community, glancing first at the senate, then at the equestrians, and then at the rest of the population either not at all (as here) or in highly general terms ('all patriots', or the like: see 25, 30, 38, 52, 68, 87, 122, cf. 26). In this way he acknowledges that the senate and equestrians were distinct from the rest of population in wealth, influence, and community of interests, with the senate taking precedence in point of public honour; cf. Plin. *HN* 33. 34, 'from that time (Cicero's consulship) this became the third component of the commonwealth, "the equestrian order" being added to (the fixed phrase) "the senate and people of Rome".' C.'s narration of the events of 58 gives a large role to the equestrians and their support, though when in exile he included the timidity of (specifically) the *publicani* among 'the many factors that combined to throw (his) mind into confusion' when he decided to leave (*QFr.* 1. 4(4). 4, early Aug. 58).

if you do not yet wish   Intending to preface his account of the consuls' collusion with Clodius (25–34) by caricaturing their general manner and appearance (18–24), C. introduces and justifies the move with the conceit that the deeds are too awful, the memories too painful, for the judges to entertain them unprepared: conjuring up a mental picture of the two, who were still away in their provinces (cf. 71, 93–4), will allow the flood of memory to flow more freely.

branded the commonwealth   C.'s usually adopts the metaphor of 'branding' to convey something both abiding and deeply negative: an ingrained flaw (*Cat.* 1. 13), a negative feeling or emotional disposition (*Dom.* 92, *Har. resp.* 55), an injury to body or reputation (*Prov. cons.* 16, *Phil.* 1. 32, 13. 45), and esp., as here, a wrong done the *commonwealth (*Cat.* 2. 20, *Phil.* 2. 117, 14. 7, cf. *Fam.* 1. 9(20). 15). In this last use the metaphor conveys that the commonwealth is being treated like a slave (though slaves seem to have been tattooed more often than branded: Jones 1987), and in any case that it is being treated cruelly: the metaphor contributes to the imagery of the commonwealth as the 'body politic' subjected to sadistic abuse, 'battered' and in need of 'revival' (1 n.) or 'medicine' (43 n.), 'exposed and cut ... to pieces ... battered and bound' (24), 'manhandled ... battered beyond hope' (31), yet 'still breathing' (54, sim. 78, 81, 109, 135; but cf. 109 'commonwealth's funeral'), to be revived and restored to *well-being with C.'s restoration. On physical metaphors applied to the commonwealth, see Drexler 1957, 279–81, 1958, 3–4.

picture in your minds   C. claimed that his investigations in Sicily had enabled him to present his case against Verres so vividly that 'the judges seemed not to hear the things I described but to see and almost touch them' (*Scaur.* 26; Quintilian agreed, cf. esp. 8. 3. 64–5), and that is the effect he seeks here, to make the absent vividly present through appeals to the judges' imagination: see Dion. Hal. *Lys.* 7, Quint. 8. 3. 61–71 (on *evidentia = enargeia*), cf. Anon. *ad Herenn.* 4. 51 (*descriptio*) and 68 (*demonstratio*), Lausberg 1998, §§810–19, Dubel 1997, Webb 1997. For examples, see *Balb.* 47 (the judges are to picture Marius standing before them), *Flac.* 66

(the judges are to imagine the vices of various Asian nations just caricatured by C.), *Mil.* 79 (the judges are to imagine Clodius brought back to life); cf. also the similar device used to a similar end at 11 above, in the reading of C.'s consular letter to S., and the more distantly related technique of 'impersonation' (*prosopopoeia*) C. will use a few weeks later in 'summoning up' the spirit of Appius Claudius Caecus to berate his degenerate descendant Clodia (*Cael.* 33–4). On C.'s way of evoking vivid 'images of the world' in his orations more generally, Vasaly 1993 is excellent.

18. One of them   Aulus Gabinius (*RE* 10–11): grandson of a *trib-une of the plebs of 139 (called 'a filthy nobody' at *Leg.* 3. 35, cf. 103 **Lucius Cassius** n.) and son of a man who reached the praetorship (prob. 90), he began his career as a *military tribune under Sulla in 86 and became an adherent of Pompey, whose command against the pirates he made the centrepiece of his tribunician legislation in 67 and whom he served as *legate in the war against Mithradates in 66–63. After gaining the praetorship (prob. 61), he became consul for 58 in a power-sharing arrangement between Pompey and Caesar, whose father-in-law Piso (19 **The other one**) became his colleague (sources, *MRR* 2. 55, 78, 144–5, 156, 160, 164, 170, 179, 193–4, 3: 97–8; family relations, Badian 1959, Konrad 1984). On his actions in collusion with Clodius, against C., see passim below with nn. and Introd. §1; on the arrangement that brought him first Cilicia and then Syria as his province see 24 **their pick** n.; on C.'s treatment of his governorship, see 71 **lost the province** n. Though Gabinius turned against Clodius in spring 58 (*Pis.* 27, Cass. Dio 38. 30. 2, the latter linking the turn to Pompey's falling out with Clodius, cf. App. 1), it was too late to help C., who does not mention the turn in this speech, cf. 69 **the consuls** n. C. maintained his enmity and on his return attacked Gabinius at *Red. sen.* 10–13, in terms very similar to those used here, and more briefly at *Red. pop.* 11, where he accuses Gabi-nius of ingratitude despite C.'s having defended him on a 'capital' charge (*TLRR* no. 380; the case is otherwise unknown, its reality doubted by Gruen 1974, 527). A few months after S.'s trial C. was ecstatic when the senate paid Gabinius the all-but-unprecedented insult of refusing his request for a *supplicatio* for his operations in Syria (*QFr.* 2. 7(11). 1, *Prov. cons.* 14–16, cf. *Pis.* 45), and in midsummer he attacked Gabinius' governorship, urging his (and Piso's) supersession at the earliest possible moment. Gabinius, however, remained in Syria until 54, when he returned to Rome to face prosecution on charges of treason (*maiestas*)—of which he was acquitted, despite C.'s damaging testimony (*TLRR* no. 296, *LUO* no. 64)—and electoral corruption (*ambitus: TLRR* no. 304), a charge that was dropped after he was convicted, at the very end of 54 or start of 53, of extortion (*repetundae*) for taking bribes from Ptolemy XII (*TLRR* no. 303, Crawford ibid., Fantham 1975). That Pompey could coerce C. into defending Gabinius in this last case, only a few months after C. affirmed that he would not be reconciled with him 'if I retain any shred of independence' (*QFr.* 3. 1(21). 15), is eloquent testimony of C.'s ever worsening position after Luca (cf. Introd. §5). Having gone into exile upon his conviction, Gabinius was recalled by Caesar and fought during the civil war as his commander in Illyricum, where he died of disease in 47 (Hirt.(?) *BAlex.* 42–3; Cass. Dio 42. 11. 1–5). Whatever formal reconciliation Pompey might have compelled (cf. *Rab. Post.* 32), it did not change C.'s sentiments: in May 49 C. included Gabinius among his 'enemies' and listed the thought of having to sit with him in the senate as one of the 'indignities' impelling him to join Pompey (*Att.* 10. 8(199). 3).

perfumed ... and curled   In C.'s antithetical caricatures, Piso is the speciously austere libertine, Gabinius the openly primping effeminate, and their hair—the neglect affected by the one (19 **hair so unkempt** n.), the luxurious care expended by the other (perfumed oils, 'curling tongs')—is a prime point of contrast. C. describes Gabinius similarly at *Pis.* 25; the description matches that of the worst category of Catiline's adherents (*Cat.* 2. 22–3), a group with which C. otherwise associates Gabinius (see **old despoilers** n., below). On the semiotics of effeminate luxury vs. Roman *manliness, see Herter 1959, Edwards 1993, 63–97, Gleason 1995, Corbeill 1996, 128–73, and 2004, 118–23, Gunderson 2000. Like the closely related charges to follow, these were conventional: even C., improbable though it seems, was targeted (by Verres: Plut. *Cic.* 7. 5).

despising his accomplices in lust   The MSS' text, read here, could mean either 'despising those aware of (his) illicit sexual acts' or 'despising (his) accomplices in ...': I take it in the latter sense, with the phrase that follows as a gloss telling us who the 'accomplices' were. In either case, 'despising' (*despiciens*)—whether because they are despicable per se or, more likely, because he had now grown greater than they (cf. **bloated with conceit** n. below)—seems preferable to Shackleton Bailey's *respiciens*, adopted by Maslowski (as Shackleton Bailey 1985, 148, notes, C. 'does not elsewhere use the verb with the required nuance ("look back affectionately to")').

old despoilers of his oh-so-delicate boyhood   The noun *vexator* (lit. 'one who roughly handles / beats') seems unique to C. in classical Latin, and he uses it only here in a sexual sense, for the behaviour of what colloquial usage today calls 'rough trade'; the diminutive noun *aetatula* ('oh-so-delicate boyhood') conveys that he took up the profession at a tender age, 'to appear more marketable for sexual purposes' (*Schol. Bob.* 128. 4–5 St.) Though C. elsewhere associates Gabinius sexually with Catiline above all—calling the latter his 'lover' and 'husband' (*Red. sen.* 10, 12, cf. also *Pis.* 20), and calling him Catiline's 'sexual pet' and 'dancer' (*Dom.* 62, *Planc.* 87; for 'dancer' cf. also *Red. sen.* 13, *Dom.* 60, *Pis.* 18, 20, 22)—he also suggests that Gabinius spent his youth as a prostitute more generally, performing oral sex acts (*Red. sen.* 11, cf. *Dom.* 126). When such charges were made a few weeks later against Caelius, C. waved them off as 'trite abuse', implying that they were often levelled at any man who was not actually deformed (cf. *Cael.* 6–7, 29–30, with *Mur.* 13, *Flac.* 51, *Planc.* 30); C. made such charges about Clodius (*Har. resp.* 42, 59) and Mark Antony (*Phil.* 2. 3), Mark Antony made them about Octavian (implied by *Phil.* 3. 15), and others made them about Caesar (Suet. *Iul.* 2) and C. himself ((Sall.) *in Cic.* 2).

puffed up   A puzzle. Acc. to the MSS, he was *puteali et faeneratorum gregibus inflatus*, 'inflated / puffed up with respect to the Well-head (next n.) and the flocks of usurers' (= 'the flocks of usurers who hang about the Well-head', in a kind of hendiadys): i.e. he was puffed up with arrogance (a common sense of *inflatus*) directed at his former creditors. The thought would be consistent with the arrogance already ascribed to him vis-à-vis his former 'despoilers' (**despising** n. above), another group belonging to a discreditable past Gabinius was pleased to think he had put behind him; yet I know no convincing parallel for the grammar, and Shackleton Bailey's '<displaying

himself > in his pride' (1985, 148: *inflatus <se ostentans>*) is perhaps more nearly what C. wrote.

Well-Head The 'Well-head of Libo' (or 'of Scribonius': *puteal Libonis/puteal Scribonianum*, *NTDAR* 322 f., *LTUR* 4. 171–3, *MAR* 211–12) was a decorated marble cylinder, of the sort placed around well-heads, set up by a Scribonius Libo to mark a place struck by lightning and accordingly considered sacred. C. alludes to its use as a common meeting-place for parties in litigation: when a defendant posted a bond to guarantee his appearance in court, he would agree to meet the plaintiff at a given landmark and accompany him thence to their court-date (Cloud 2002); since it was near the urban praetor's tribunal, before which defaulting debtors were brought by creditors (*Red. sen.* 11, Hor. *Serm.* 2. 6. 32–9, *Epist.* 1. 19. 8–9, Ov. *Rem.* 561–2), the Well-Head served as one such landmark (cf. Cloud 2002, 245).

flock of usurers In Roman ethical tradition usury was no better than theft (for the elder Cato, interpreting Rome's most ancient law code, worse than theft: *Agr.* pr. 1–4). Though that tradition was not always observed by members of the Roman elite (most notoriously, Brutus), C.'s rhetoric acknowledges it here by applying to the discreditable usurers a collective noun, 'flocks' (*greges*), properly used of animals and used of humans only pejoratively (e.g. 42 **old forces** n., Opelt 1965, 133, 151).

seek the tribunate … on the column A charge made in similar but non-Homeric terms at *Red. sen.* 11. Here Gabinius' debt is, metaphorically, the Sicilian strait made perilous by the monster Scylla (the strait's other peril, the whirlpool Charybdis, is deprecated as a 'farfetched' metaphor by C.'s spokesman Lucius Crassus at *De or.* 3. 163 and is absent here); the *tribunate is a haven because legal action could not be brought against a magistrate in office; and the phrase 'become affixed (*adhaeresceret*) to the column' refers to the column of Maenius (*columna Maenia*), next to the Comitium at the foot of the *clivus Capitolinus*, where notices of auctions of bankrupts' goods were posted (cf. 124 below, *Clu.* 39, *NTDAR* 94–5, *LTUR* 1. 301–2, Cascione 1996). Since C.'s audience could prob. see both the column and the Well-Head of Libo as he spoke, we can imagine his gesturing to them, to make Gabinius' plight more vivid: on such use of Roman political space in C.'s oratory, see Vasaly 1993, and cf. Hölkeskamp 2001, Morstein-Marx 2004, 92–107; it seems unlikely that either C. or his audience would think of the tower erected in the Sicilian strait off Rhegium, as a dedication to Poseidon (thus a secondary allusion suggested by Holden 1889). On the stigma of debt see 97 **hobbled by embarrassments** n.

peddling himself to his henchmen With the senate and equestrians set aside, the *henchmen remain, the disreputable 'popular' elements (cf. 27, 38, 57, 59, 65, 127), here as the political base to which Gabinius 'peddled himself' by serving their interests as consul; we are to imagine that Gabinius made the statements ascribed to him— 'declaring… and affirming'—when he was already in office, cf. **charge of electoral bribery** n. The phrase suggests that as Gabinius had prostituted himself in his youth (above), he continued the pattern in a different sense as a public man (sim. *Har. resp.* 1, of Clodius).

expected to gain a province… whatever the senate's will in the matter Lit. 'even if the senate is unwilling' (*etiam invito senatu*). On the senate's role in normal procedures for assigning consular provinces vs. those followed in Gabinius' case, see 24 **their pick** n.

charge of electoral bribery Late in 59 Gaius Cato (tr. pl. 56) sought to bring the charge (*ambitus*) with ref. to the consular elections for 58 but could not get a hearing from 'the praetors' (*QFr.* 1. 2(2). 15, *TLRR* no. 248; we do not know which praetor presided over the *ambitus*-court that year). The calendar worked in Gabinius' favour, because he could not be prosecuted after entering office on 1 Jan. 58; see also **if he did not** n. below, on the charge brought in 54.

expected to gain a province C. anticipates the tribunician law through which Clodius arranged the desired provincial assignments for Gabinius and Piso, see 25 **the provinces, by name** n.

if he did not… retain his civic well-being At *Pis.* 12 C. says that Gabinius' colleague, Piso, in conversation with C. and his son-in-law, attributed much the same thoughts to Gabinius. By passing directly from his consulship to a provincial command, as he did (cf. 71),

Gabinius could again avoid prosecution for electoral bribery, because
*promagistrates too were exempt from prosecution during their
tenure; this understanding is preferable to the view that Gabinius
wished to avoid bankruptcy (cf. **seek the tribunate** n. above), esp.
because the charge of electoral corruption brought against him on his
return from Syria in 54 (*TLRR* no. 304) did grow out of his campaign
for the consulship. The term translated 'retain his civic well-being' is
incolumis, lit. 'not afflicted with catastrophe (*calamitas*)' and so 'safe,
unharmed': an *incolumis* person still had his civic *well-being (*salus*)
and had not forfeited his *life as a citizen (*caput*, see Glossary;
conviction under C.'s bribery law of 63 meant exile, Lintott 1990, 9).

19. The other one   Lucius Calpurnius (*RE* 90) Piso Caesoninus was
a grandson and great-grandson of the homonymous consuls of 112
and 148 (respectively), though his father rose no higher than *quaestor or, possibly, praetor (see *MRR* 3. 47, and ibid. 48 for 'L. Calpurnius Piso (98?)'; on the consuls Badian 1990, 399–400); on his
mother's family, see 21 **his mother's lineage** n.; on his cultivation
of Epicurus' philosophy, see 22–3 nn. and the evidence gathered and
discussed at Castner 1988, 16–23, Griffin 2001. Piso was elected
quaestor (70), curule aedile (64), praetor (61), and consul, all without defeat (*Pis.* 2 and *MRR* 3. 47); in 59 his candidacy for the
consulship was supported by Caesar, whose father-in-law he became
that year (Plut. *Caes.* 14. 5, *Pomp.* 47. 6, App. *BCiv.* 2. 14, Cass. Dio
38. 9. 1). Having had reason to regard Piso as a friend (20 n.), C. felt
especially betrayed, and that no doubt determined the character—
hypocrite—that C. creates for him in the speeches delivered after his
return to Rome. C. attacks Piso more sharply and copiously than he
does Gabinius: cf. esp. *Red. sen.* 13–17, where we find both the same
conceit as here—that Piso at first deceived all, save a few who knew
what he was 'really' like—and many of the same details (his unkempt
and forbidding appearance, his seeming austerity and hidden appetites, his ignorant zeal for Epicureanism, his mother's family:
nn. below); in *Red. sen.* 10 and *Dom.* 62, but not in this speech,
C. attempts to link him to the Catilinarians via his cousin Gaius
Cornelius Cethegus. Clodius' legislation gave Piso the governorship
of Macedonia (25 **the provinces, by name**, 71 **lost the province...**
nn.): by criticizing Piso's conduct as governor in July 56 (*Prov. cons.*

passim; cf. Steel 2001, 47–50, 181–9), C. tried to accelerate his supersession. When Piso returned to Rome in summer 55, he and C. clashed: C.'s side is preserved in *Against Piso*, on which see Nisbet 1961, Koster 1980, Marshall 1985 on Asc. 1–17 Cl., Corbeill 1996, 169–73; for a critique of Piso's consulship, see esp. *Pis.* 11–31, with 12–21 concentrating on C.'s travails. C. was never reconciled with Piso (*Fam.* 8. 12(98). 2, from Caelius in 50, implies continuing enmity, and cf. *Att.* 7. 13(136). 1 'I approve *even* Piso', for behaviour C. interpreted as anti-Caesarian in Jan. 49; C. does praise the stand Piso took against Mark Antony on 1 Aug. 44, *Phil.* 1. 10); Piso for his part resumed public life with no impairment after his governorship: there is no record of a prosecution (at *Pis.* 82 C. implies that Caesar deterred him from prosecuting Piso himself); after becoming censor in 50 he was a moderating influence on his colleague, Appius Claudius Pulcher, and tried to avoid the outbreak of war through mediation in 49 (*MRR* 2. 247–8). His daughter, Calpurnia, remained Caesar's wife until his murder; his son, Lucius Calpurnius (*RE* 99) Piso, was consul in 15 and enjoyed a remarkably successful career under both Augustus and Tiberius.

foul and fierce   In an alliterative series capturing Piso's appearance (*taeter… truculentus… terribilis* ~ 'foul… fierce… formidable'), C. chooses first an epithet suggesting actual visceral revulsion: for the general idea see esp. *Red. sen.* 13 'unrefined, unkempt (so also below), a peasant, scarcely human', and for other plays upon his appearance (besides his 'brow', n. below) cf. *Prov. cons.* 8, 12, *Pis.* 13.

old longbeards   C. derides Piso's 'hairy cheeks' (and bad teeth) at *Pis.* 1. The custom of daily shaving came late to Rome (acc. to the elder Pliny, drawing on Varro, with the younger Africanus: *HN* 7. 211) but was the norm in Cicero's day, as the veristic portrait busts of the late Republic show (bibliography in Hiesinger 1974, 820–5). For C., trim little beards mark fashionable young swells with dangerous political leanings (*Att.* 1. 14(14). 5, 1. 16(16). 11); he associates full beards with the virtuous times of old-fashioned ways (*Mur.* 26, *Cael.* 33, *Corn.* II frag. 4 Crawford, *Fin.* 4. 62), as the phrases that follow here in the text also suggest. When opposing the agrarian bill of the tribune Publius Servilius Rullus in 63 C. similarly depicted the man as unkempt, dressed in old clothers, with shaggy hair and a beard, for the same purpose, to suggest that the man's austerity was merely a hypocritical mask (*Leg. agr.* 2. 13).

plebeian purple (almost brown, really)   Like Cato (Plut. *Cat. min.* 6. 3, and cf. next n.), Piso shunned fine Tyrian or Tarentine purple, rich and vividly reddish, that was most fashionable and costly: cf. *Cael.* 77 and esp. Nepos frag. 27 Marshall, on the criticism Lentulus Spinther received for first using Tyrian purple on his magistrate's toga as aedile in 63; Wilson 1938, pl. i, shows different purple hues produced from the recipes in the *Papyrus Holmiensis* (Uppsala). Though this duller, cheaper variety is called 'plebeian' in something like the modern sense ('belonging to the usage of common folk'), Piso (like Cato) would ordinarily have shown his purple on the broad stripe (*latus clavus*) that senators were allowed to wear on their tunics, and in Piso's case, during his consulship, on the upper border of his toga.

hair so unkempt   Piso's hair was 'shaggy' (*horridus*) because it was not carefully cut and curled, and because, like Cato (Plut. *Cat. min.* 3. 6), he abstained from perfumed oils; hence the reference to the Seplasia following. In both respects he was the opposite of Gabinius (18 **perfumed** n.).

the Seplasia   Piso's appearance suggested a desire to demolish the square in Capua where perfumed oils were sold, a symptom of the corruption for which Capua was once known; sim. *Pis.* 24–5, including a contrast with Gabinius, whom the perfume sellers would recognize as one of their own.

duumvirate ... his image   The 'duumvirate' is the office held by the *duoviri* (lit. 'two men'), the chief magistrates of the colony founded at Capua in 59 (9 **'settlers'** n.), analogous to the consuls at Rome: Piso simultaneously held these offices in Rome and Capua in 58 (implied here, stated at *Red. sen.* 17); C. mocks Piso's holding the honour at *Dom.* 60 and *Pis.* 24 also. The mockery is not aimed at the magistracy of a 'provincial' town as such, for Roman dignitaries commonly received these honours: e.g. Pompey was Piso's colleague at Capua in 58 (*Red. sen.* 29, referring to the period in 58 when Pompey had taken to his house for fear of Clodius' attacks, see 69 **a plan** n.), and Milo held an analogous office at Lanuvium as *dictator* in 52 (*Mil.* 27).

Rather, C. mocks the thought that Piso would aim to use this minor honour to 'adorn' his memory for posterity ('image', *imago*, see the Glossary s.v. *wax mask).

lofty brow It was a commonplace, as it is today, that one could read expressions for clues to another's thoughts or internal traits, and correspondingly that expressions could be managed to suggest the presence of non-existent traits: see e.g. *Off*. 1. 146, *Fin.* 5. 47, and on the brow, Quint. 11. 3. 78–9; on the representation of character in extant late Republican portraits, Curtius 1931 and Winkes 1973; on the politics of facial expression, Corbeill 2004, 144–57; on the more systematic ancient science of physiognomy, Barton 1994, 95–131, Gleason 1995, 55–81. C. refers here specifically to Piso's imposing brow (*supercilium*), by which he was accustomed to convey *gravity and the 'fierce' and 'formidable' qualities already noted (drawing one's brows together to appear fiercer was a flaw, Quint. 11. 3. 160); C.'s other refs. suggest that Piso relied equally on moving his eyebrows expressively—raising one while lowering the other—and furrowing his forehead (*Red. sen.* 15–16; *Pis.* 12, 14, 20, 68, 70). If the effect suggested to some the mask of a stock figure from the comic stage, the angry old man (*senex iratus*: Hughes 1992, cf. Klodt 2003, 49–50), others would have thought of the 'powerful overhanging brow' that appears prominently in the many sculpted busts of Epicurus (Griffin 2001, 98).

seriousness See the Glossary.

20. Still C. introduces the supposed quotation with an adverb (*tamen*) marking a contrast with a previous statement to which the speaker responds, here left implied but disparaging of Gabinius ('Yes, granted, Gabinius is worthless. Still. . . .'). On the device of the imagined interlocutor (*sermocinatio*) see Anon. *ad Herenn.* 4. 55–6, 65, Quint. 9. 2. 31 (regarding it as a type of 'impersonation'/ *prosopopoeia*, cf. 17 **picture in your minds** n.), Lausberg 1998, §§820–5; C. uses the device again at 45, 47, 61, 77, 84, 110.

that slimy blot Lit. 'that blot and slime' (*labi illo et caeno*), a form of hendiadys, the two words again used together against Gabinius at 26 (cf. *Vat.* 25 'blot and bane'). C. uses each as a term of harsh abuse (orations only, never in the correspondence), the former of Verres (*Verr.* 1. 1. 2), Clodius (*Dom.* 2, 107, 133, *Har. resp.* 46), and Piso

(*Pis.* 3, 56), the latter of Sextus Cloelius (*Dom.* 47) and Piso (*Pis.* 13); Gabinius alone has the distinction of having both used against him simultaneously.

'pon my word   The obsolete English oath (*OED* s.v. 'word' 15a–b) suggests the archaic Latin oath that C. uses here, *me dius fidius* (or *medius fidius* or *mediusfidius*), calling on Dius Fidius—roughly, divinity of good faith (associated in antiquity with Gk. 'Zeus Pistios', with Jupiter, and with the mysterious Semo Sancus: see Latte 1967, 126–8, Radke 1987, 120–3, 289–91, *NTDAR* 347, *LTUR* 4. 263–4, *MAR* 103). It is a less common and more forceful asseveration than 'By Hercules!' (120); both are colloquial.

irresponsibility   i.e., *levitas*: see the Glossary.

friend and a relation by marriage   C.'s first son-in-law, Gaius Calpurnius Piso Frugi, belonged to another branch of the Calpurnii Pisones: the relation between the two branches, already distinct in the 2nd cent., is difficult to define (see Badian 1990, 399–400), but no more than a remote cousinage could have linked young Frugi and the consul. The consul's links with C. were still more slender, but C. nonetheless asserts the relationship, so that he can later point indignantly to its betrayal (54 below; sim. *Red. sen.* 15, *Red. pop.* 11). As for friendship, beyond the favourable if general expectations C. had of both consuls after their election in 59 (*QFr.* 1. 2(2). 16), he twice mentions friendly gestures that Piso made in his honour (*Red. sen.* 17, *Pis.* 11): he asked C. to serve as the 'guardian' (*custos*) of the votes of the *century that cast the first ballots at the election in which he was chosen consul; and at the first meeting of the senate at which he presided he gratified C.'s dignity by placing him third in the order in which senators would be asked their opinions. C. apparently had prima facie reason to expect Piso to counter the *irresponsible Gabinius; but early in his consulship, speaking with C. in his son-in-law's presence (*Pis.* 12), Piso allegedly said that 'each man had to look after his own interests', and that in the matter of the provinces he was only obliging his colleague as C. had obliged Antonius (8 **Gaius Antonius** n.).

tiller of so great a dominion   On the metaphor see 7 **commonwealth was tossed** n.; for the proper 'pilots', see 98.

a person...blinking...undone In depicting Gabinius' openly debauched lifestyle C. uses the brushstrokes already found at *Red. sen.* 13: 'Heavy with wine, sleep, and sexual dissipation... barely able to keep his eyes open... with weak and trembling voice... amid whoring and gluttony...'.

thanks to others' resources This might hint at the political support of Pompey and, through him, of Caesar and Crassus, but it primarily looks to the bribes needed to win the election, which in turn caused him to fear prosecution for electoral corruption, see 18 nn.

21. The other one... deceived many C. turns to develop the commonplace of vice hidden beneath a veneer of virtue, so that a charge of hypocrisy can be added to corruption: for the tactic recommended, see *Inv. rhet.* 2. 34, Anon. *ad Herenn.* 2. 5.

the very notability of his lineage... commended him C. takes a similar line at *Pis.* 1–2, where he compares his own electoral success as a *new man with that of Piso, who enjoyed the 'commendation of smoke-stained *ancestor masks', denoting descent in the male line from men who had been *curule magistrates (cf. 19 **duumvirate** n.). On *notability, see the Glossary: C. here calls it 'that charming little matchmaker' (a trans. adopted from Treggiari 2003, 141) because notable men enjoyed a great advantage in winning support for public office, above all the consulship (see Badian 1990).

it serves... their ancestors A man's concern with being, and being seen to be, worthy of his ancestors was among the most powerful motives in Roman public behaviour: see Treggiari 2003, and see the reflections ascribed below to Milo in a crisis (87 **example** n.). It is C.'s premise that *notable men's ancestors became notable themselves through acts of *manliness (*virtus*) benefiting the *commonwealth (next n.): if the notable men of today are to show themselves worthy of their ancestors, they must perform similar acts.

men who have earned the commonwealth's gratitude On the idiom, describing the behaviour of both personal friends and patriots, see 2 **thanking** n.

his name suggested... sober soundness C. refers not to the name Lucius Calpurnius Piso Caesoninus but to a name, Frugi ('virtuous, honest'), likely to be evoked by mention of any Piso: given first to the public man and historian Lucius Calpurnius Piso Frugi (cos. 133, *RE* 96) in recognition of his integrity (*TD* 3. 16, *Schol. Bob.* 96. 26–9 St., Marshall 1985, 85, on Asc. 2. 18–19 Cl.), it was thereafter adopted as part of the family's formal nomenclature by his descendants, including C.'s son-in-law (20 **friend** n.).

his mother's lineage   C. elsewhere asserts that Piso's maternal grandfather, Calventius, was an Insubrian Gaul and was moreover—a point nearly as damning in the eyes of C. and his contemporaries—a merchant and auctioneer (*Pis.* frag. xi, 62, cf. *Pis.* 34). Acc. to *Pis.* frag. ix–x, 14, 53, 67, Calventius had moved from his native Mediolanum (mod. Milan) and settled at Placentia (mod. Piacenza), on the S bank of the Po by the Trebia, where a Roman colony had been established in 218. C. repeatedly uses this relation to mock Piso (*Red. sen.* 13, *Prov. cons.* 7, *QFr.* 3. 1(21). 11), going so far as to suggest that Calventius had hailed from Transalpine Gaul (*Red. sen.* 15, sim. *Pis.* 53, cf. Asc. 4. 10–11 Cl.): see Nisbet 1961, 53, and (on status as auctioneer) Marshall 1985, 91–2. Wherever the line between fact and abusive invention lies in all this, the family is unlikely to have been radically more 'outlandish' than that of, say, Catullus, whose northern Italian milieu is brilliantly evoked by Wiseman 1985, 101–15, and 1987, 311–70; the slur could be deflected with mockery ('You would think that she came from Ephesus or Tralles!': *Phil.* 3. 15, discounting Antony's sneer at the origins of Octavian's mother). Maternal lineage could also be used as a positive model: 101 **your maternal grandfather's brother** n.

22. I never reckoned ... though I was long aware   I translate the text recommended by Shackleton Bailey 1987, 277 (against Maslowski and the vulgate), primarily a change in punctuation that makes the clauses expressly antithetical ('one the one hand ... , on the other hand ...').

recklessness   A more vicious counterpart of *irresponsibility, with which Piso is also taxed (next sentence): see the Glossary.

good for nothing and irresponsible   Having just denied that *this* Piso was *frugi*, 'sober and sound' (21 **his name suggested** n.), C. applies to him the antithetical epithet *nequam*, 'good for nothing', commonly used of the 'rascal slave', a stock character of Roman comedy; on *irresponsibility, see the Glossary.

mistaken judgement that people had formed of him Cf. *Red. sen.* 15 'To be sure, he in no way deceived *me*,... but he deceived you (viz., the senate) and the Roman people, not through the eloquent expression of public policy... but with his furrowed brow and austere expression', sim. *Prov. cons.* 8. (I depart from Maslowski, who follows Madvig, and join most editors in believing that an interpolation lurks in the transmitted text, 'et falsa opinione errore hominum ab adulescentia commendatum': I take *errore* to be a gloss on *falsa opinione* that later came to be incorporated in the text.)

the set of his expression ... masked his disgraceful behaviour C. treats Piso's partly hidden and wholly voluptuary way of life in *Pis.* 13, 66–72; the spokesman for Epicureanism in *De finibus*, Lucius Torquatus, is similarly criticized for concealing his 'hedonist' interior, publicly using the language of 'duty... worthy of (our) dominion (and) of the Roman people', because he recognizes that professing his beliefs would be thought disgraceful (2. 77). Given the common misunderstanding of Epicurean hedonism, which C.—who knew better—exploits against Piso (23 **those who ... praise pleasure** n.), the more sober-seeming an adherent of the sect was, the more easily could he be painted a hypocrite.

observant eyes ... see through it Curiosity about the life-styles of the noted was no doubt fed by the habits of the noted themselves (cf. the relation between modern 'celebrities' and various tabloids), who lived much of their lives on display, from the morning reception of friends and dependants at their homes (*salutatio*), through the promenade to the forum surrounded by their entourages (*deductio*) or the presentation of themselves to crowds at the theater and *games (cf. 105, 115 ff. below), to the continuity between 'public' and 'private' in the architecture of their houses (24 **his private quarters** n.). Living with an awareness of others being aware of them, they aimed at maximizing the creditable attention they received as honour and at minimizing the discreditable attention they experienced as shame: on the complementary relation of these forms of attention, see Barton 2001, 202–43, and Kaster 2005.

slothful and supine behaviour   Epicurus enjoined political quietism (Long and Sedley 1987, 1. 126 (D1) and 133 (Q5)) as most conducive to the sort of 'pleasure' properly sought as an end in itself (23 **those who . . . praise pleasure** n.). The aim was easily taken to be a form of solipsistic idleness inimical to the vigorous and *manly engagement with civic affairs that C., true to the values of Rome's political elite, regarded as life's proper end (1 nn., on the first sentence of this speech, and *Fin.* 2. 67–77): on the conflict of values, and the ways some Romans mediated the conflict in their own lives, see Minyard 1985, Fowler 1989, Griffin 1989, Sedley 1997. To the objection that Piso's career was not *prima facie* evidence of sloth—it matched C.'s own for offices held without electoral defeat—C. would reply that whereas he had had to toil at every stage, because he was a *new man, Piso's *notability had allowed him to coast: 'all the favours of the Roman people are bestowed on men of notable birth while they snooze' (*Verr.* 2. 5. 180).

23. this or that philosopher   C. declines to name them, to avoid a display of erudition before the jury (cf. 48 **the daughters of king Erechtheus** n.), especially of a sort he affects to despise.

he couldn't say their names   The Latin, *neque . . . nomina poterat dicere*, could mean that Piso was unable either 'to name them' (Gardner 1958*a*; sim. Holden 1889, Shackleton Bailey 1991*a*)—i.e. identify them—or 'to pronounce their names': either failure would betray ignorance, and each would be ludicrous, given that the Greek philosopher Philodemus was his intimate (*Pis.* 68–72, Asc. 16. 12–13 Cl.: see next n.). The latter failure would betray ignorance more profoundly and is perhaps favoured by the description of Piso at *Red. sen.* 14: 'When you met up with the fellow in the forum, you'd swear you couldn't tell whether you were talking to a person or a fence-post—no awareness, no zest, tongue-tied, slow, a subhuman piece of work, a Cappadocian (from the Roman point of view, an esp. dim sort of barbarian) just snatched from a gaggle of slaves on sale'; on Piso's alleged inarticulateness cf. also *Pis.* frag. iii, 1.

those who . . . praise pleasure and urge its pursuit   The followers of Epicurus (341–270): one noted Epicurean, Philodemus (*c.*110–*c.*40), was a member of Piso's household, and the so-called 'villa of the

papyri' in Herculaneum, where a number of Philodemus' works have
been recovered, is commonly ascribed to Piso's family. Epicureans
distinguished two kinds of 'pleasure' (*voluptas*, Gk. *hēdonē*), the
'kinetic' and the 'static' (or 'katastematic'), corresponding roughly
to the pleasure of eating (to satisfy a need) and the pleasure of being
contented with what one has eaten (and so being free from 'pain'),
respectively. Though Epicureanism no more held 'kinetic' pleasures
to be the final good than any other ancient philosophical school, it
expressly made one kind of 'static' pleasure—*ataraxia*, or *tranquillity, the state of being free from psychic disturbance (Gk. *tarachos*)—
the proper end of life, the thing to be pursued for its own sake and
not as a means to some other end (on the doctrine, concisely, Annas
1993, 188–200, Sharples 1996, 84–99, with the texts and discussion at
Long and Sedley 1987, 1. 112–25). Epicureanism was therefore a
'hedonist' doctrine in this limited sense; but its critics, conflating
the two forms of 'pleasure', often portrayed the doctrine as hedonist
in the modern sense, urging the pursuit of sensual pleasure. This
conflation was especially (but by no means only) common at Rome,
where the political quietism encouraged by the goal of tranquillity
put the doctrine at odds with the elite culture and its values (cf. 22
slothful n.). Here C. implies that the fault lay at least in part with
Piso, for failing to ask the sorts of questions that a would-be philosopher should ask (next sentence) and fastening instead on the
word 'pleasure', which he then misunderstood; and C. makes the
same point explicitly two years later at *Pis.* 42 ('Even those Greek
"voluptuaries" of yours affirm (that chance misfortune is not a true
evil): I wish only that you had listened to them in the proper spirit,
for then you would never have plunged up to your neck in such
outrageous behaviour...') and 69 (on Piso's resistance to the distinctions that Philodemus tried to draw). Yet soon after this speech
C. himself will casually efface those same distinctions, in attacking
Epicureanism at *Cael.* 41 (without ref. to Piso), just as he had already
grossly misrepresented Piso's teachers as 'arguing that ... every part
of the body at every moment ought to be experiencing some joyful
delight' (*Red. sen.* 14); and there is no mistaking the genuine contempt for the sect's quietism in the remarks that follow, which are
echoed elsewhere (esp. *Red. sen.* 14, *Pis.* 56–63, *Rep.* 1. 1). To a degree
C. is responding to the demands of advocacy: e.g. in 63, when

defending Murena when he was prosecuted by a Stoic (Cato), C. is no less pleased to lampoon some of the Stoics' behaviour and beliefs (*Mur.* 3, 60–6, 74–7). But in that case his target is the sect's excessive rigour or its members' gracelessness, not—as in the case of Epicureanism—the essential rottenness of its principles; near the end of his life C. will devote all of *Fin.* 2 to exposing that rottenness. On the development of C.'s anti-Epicureanism, see Maslowski 1974, Ferrary 2001; on the Republican elite and Greek philosophers, see the surveys of Jocelyn 1976–7, Rawson 1985, 282–97, Griffin 1994, 721–8.

<particle> A noun fell out of the text in the medieval MSS' common ancestor, and Halm's supplement (*partibus*), adopted by Maslowski, is as good as any other and better than some.

he used to say... the contrasting principles of others On Epicurean political quietism and its conflict with Roman *mores*, see 22 **slothful** n.; for a more just appreciation of Epicurean social thought than C. offers here, see Long 1986 and Annas 1993, 293–302, with the texts and discussion in Long and Sedley 1987, 1. 125–39. The very Roman-sounding catchwords that convey the 'contrasting principles'—'worthy standing', 'duty', 'public interest'—are just those that the duplicitous Epicurean at *Fin.* 2. 76 is said to mouth, to disguise his true inclinations. With the views here ascribed to Piso, compare *Pis.* 59–61, a (hilarious) lecture that C. gives him to speak to his son-in-law, Caesar, on the vanity of political ambition.

toil in the service of A slightly free version of *esse serviendum*, lit. 'ought to be a slave (*servus*) to...': even when the connotation of specifically servile behaviour is not intended or much felt, the verb *servire* always denotes the behaviour of one who puts himself entirely at another person's or thing's disposal. In this expression the good Roman's *worthy standing (dignitas)* is conceived as a superordinate entity virtually external to himself, like the 'commonwealth' and 'duty' in the following, parallel phrases; all three are thus contrasted with the idea of 'acting entirely for (one's) own sake' (*omnia sua causa facere*).

24. his private quarters The Roman elite's homes followed the plan of the *atrium*-house, which typically included a suite of spaces, extending from the street into the interior, that had the effect of bringing the outside in: an enclosed entryway (*vestibulum*) of some length, where (e.g.) friends and dependants would wait to extend the morning greeting (*salutatio*), leading to the rectangular *atrium*, its roof open to the sky, where families having the right to display the masks of distinguished ancestors would do so (on the masks, 19 **duumvirate** n.); and behind the atrium, on the same axis as the entryway, the *tablinum* ('tablet-room'), where a Roman of rank would (among other things) receive visitors. Looking from the street when the doors were open, a passer-by could see the master of the house seated in dignity, the entryway providing a kind of frame, and the ancestor-masks adding further to the effect in the middle ground: Livy 5. 41. 7–8 vividly evokes the majesty of the sight. These more public spaces in Piso's house (C. implies) made the same dignified impression as the expression on his face; behind both façades lay the corrupt reality. On the social organization of space in the Roman house, see Wallace-Hadrill 1994, Grahame 1997, and on C.'s treatment of 'public' and 'private', Treggiari 1998.

so smoky that it exuded the heavy odor <of gluttony> Maslowski marks the transmitted text as hopelessly corrupt; I adopt as a stopgap Nisbet's suggestion (1966, 336), *helluationis* ('of gluttony'), for the MSS' *sermonis*, 'of conversation' (so, independently, Shackleton Bailey 1987, 277–8; other suggestions have run along similar lines). But note that the house's smokiness figures in a different connection at *Pis.* 1 (of soot darkening the *ancestor masks in the *atrium*), and at *Pis.* 13 fumes associated with gluttony are mentioned with ref. to cheap eating establishments ('greasy-spoon', *popina*, and 'dive', *ganea*; cf. *Pis.* 18 'shadowy greasy-spoon', *tenebricosa popina*), not Piso's own house: deeper corruption might lurk here.

if you gave a sword With this extended analogy, or parable (Anon. *ad Herenn.* 4. 60–1 on *similitudo*; more briefly *Inv. rhet.* 1. 49, Quint. 5. 11. 23, 8. 3. 77, with Lausberg 1998, §§422–5), compare *Sex. Rosc.* 56–7 (analogy of accusers and watch-dogs) and esp. 45 **if I happened to be sailing** n.: C. uses the figure to move from invective, on the character of Piso and Gabinius, to narrative of their harmful actions, as he takes up the sequence of events that caused his departure.

openly made a pact C.'s chief grievance against Gabinius and Piso, to which he returns time and again in the speeches after his return (e.g. *Red. sen.* 10; *Red. pop.* 11, *Dom.* 23–4, *Har. resp.* 3–4, *Prov. cons.* 2, *Pis.* 56–7, cf. *Fam.* 1. 9(20). 12, *MRR* 2. 193–4). The pact both purchased the consuls' active support, about to be described (25–35, cf. also esp. *Dom.* 55), and restrained them from leading the senate in bringing its *authority to bear on Clodius, in the extreme case by suspending him from his magistracy, as it had suspended Metellus Nepos in 62 (12 **Marcus Cato** n.), or by passing the 'ultimate *decree of the senate', as it had against the *tribune Saturninus in 100 (37 n.): on the failure of leadership cf. C.'s statement that the senate '(had) no leaders but, in place of leaders, traitors or rather declared enemies' (35), and on the (quite limited) means at the consuls' disposal, see further 25 **all citizens** n.

their pick of the provinces   The procedures securing the 'pact' were irregular but not unprecedented. To minimize the play of personal influence in allotting consular provinces, the *lex Sempronia* of Gaius Gracchus (123 or 122: *MRR* 1. 514) had established that the provinces entrusted to consuls after their term should be set by senatorial decree before the consular elections, with the winners then drawing lots for the specific assignments; thus the provinces that Gabinius and Piso would ultimately take up in 57 should have been designated before they were elected in 59 (cf. the debate that occasioned *Prov. cons.* in July 56, concerning the provincial assignments for the consuls of 55 still to be elected). But there were recent exceptions to the rule: the consuls of 60 were assigned the provinces of Transalpine and Cisalpine Gaul by a *decree of the senate when they were already in office (*MRR* 2. 183); more to the point here, while consul in 67 Acilius Glabrio received Bithynia and Pontus thanks to a tribunician law passed by Gabinius himself (*MRR* 2. 143–4), then was superseded the following year when another tribunician law, the *lex Manilia*, reassigned the *provincia* to Pompey, along with Cilicia (the latter already held by Marcius Rex, cos. 68: *MRR* 2. 153–4); most recently, Caesar had received his 5-year command in Cisalpine Gaul and Illyricum while consul in 59 through another tribunician law, the *lex Vatinia* (*MRR* 2. 190). This last gave Clodius his model (so *Vat.* 36), not least in its provision of 5-year commands; the model would again be followed in 55, when the *lex Trebonia* gave the consuls Pompey and Crassus their 5-year commands in Spain and Syria.

We do not know what action the senate took in 59. Foreseeing the probable election of Pompey's protégé Gabinius and Caesar's father-in-law, Piso, the consul Bibulus had by edict postponed the elections from July to 18 October (*Att.* 2. 20(40). 6, 21(41). 5); he and his senatorial allies perhaps also delayed or manipulated the allotment of provinces (so in 60 the senate allotted inglorious *provinciae* within Italy to the consuls of 59 when it seemed inevitable that one of them would be Caesar, Suet. *Iul.* 19. 2). At *Dom.* 24 C. flatly says that Clodius' legislation 'rescinded' the senate's allotment; yet he nowhere says what that was, while remarks he attributes to Piso indicate that Gabinius had 'despaired' of getting anything from the senate before making the 'pact' with Clodius (*Pis.* 12; cf. also 18 above, the remark attributed to Gabinius: 'he expected to gain a province through (his supporters') efforts whatever the senate's will in the matter'). If C.'s statements are all true, the senate's allotment had included no provincial assigment for Gabinius, at least. On the initial assignment of Cilicia to Gabinius under this measure, see 53 **assignment of provinces** n.

an army and budget   The budget for raising and provisioning an army for a provincial command was usually set by senatorial decree once the consuls began their term (*Att.* 3. 24(69). 1–2, with Momm-sen 1887–8, 3. 1097–9); evidently in this case it was included in the tribunician legislation. Piso allegedly received 18,000,000 *sesterces* to outfit his army, then left the money at Rome to be lent out at interest (*Pis.* 86); some of the money budgeted to the two reportedly was transferred from funds that Caesar had earmarked in 59 for the purchase of public land (*Dom.* 23, and more generally on the funding *Red. sen.* 18, *Dom.* 55, *Har. resp.* 58, *Pis.* 28, 37, 57).

handed over the commonwealth … sealed with my blood   Less figuratively: the consuls connived at Clodius' legislation—the chief instrument of his 'assault' on the *commonwealth (see esp. 33, 55–6 below)—an element of which was aimed at C. (**25 brought ruin** n.). On the personification of the *res publica*, facilitating its identification with C., see **17 branded** n.: here the association between the 'battered' commonwealth and C. as 'bloody' sacrificial victim is esp. close. On the same topic see also *Red. sen.* 32 and *Red. pop.* 13: in the latter place C. again describes the consuls' pact as sealed (lit.

'solemnly sanctioned', *sanciri*) with his blood, sim. *Dom.* 23, *Pis.* 28; for the metaphor, drawn from the archaic practice of solemnizing a treaty (*foedus*, the word C. uses twice here) with a blood sacrifice, cf. also Livy. 23. 8. 1, Lucan 7. 351.

25. when the affair was exposed A thought not obviously consistent with the preceding statement that the consuls made the pact openly (*palam*). Perhaps C., accustomed as he was to describing the consuls as openly corrupt (Gabinius) and secretly vicious (Piso), unthinkingly attributed both traits to this pact.

public notice was given Any proposal (*rogatio*) on which the people as whole or (in this case) the plebs would vote had to be published (*promulgated, *promulgari*) both by being read aloud in an *assembly of the people and by being posted on whitened boards ('albums'). Because the vote could not be held until the proposal had been publicized on three market days (*nundinae*)—when the most people were in town and proposals received maximum exposure—at least seventeen to twenty-four days would pass between promulgation and vote; these proposals were prob. promulgated late in the intercalary month, between Feb. and March, in 58 (on the period of promulgation and the timing of these measures, see App. 1). They were preceded by four other proposals promulgated soon after Clodius entered office (10 Dec. 59) and passed on 4 Jan. 58: 33 **while the same consuls sat** n. and 55, with App. 1.

tribune's proposals These would be voted on in an *assembly of the plebs over which the tribune presided: when approved they were, strictly, not laws (*leges*)—which could be approved only by the entire *populus* meeting in a *voting assembly—but plebiscites (*plebiscita*); but these had had the same binding force as laws since 287 and were commonly referred to as *leges*.

brought ruin to me Of the two measures aimed at C. that Clodius brought to a vote, this first one did not mention C. by name but was drafted in general terms to address the treatment of a citizen's rights (*caput*: see 1 **lives as citizens** n.): on its scope and intention see 53 **assembly** n. From exile C. remarked with regret that its *promulgation threw him into a panic, causing him to put on mourning dress (see 1 n. and 26 **put on mourning dress** n.), when he might better have ignored it, or even welcomed it, as having no bearing on him (*Att.* 3. 15(60). 5, Aug. 58). The second proposal, aimed specifically at C. and declaring that he had been exiled, was promulgated as soon as he left the city: see 65 **proposal** n.

the provinces to the consuls, by name Because the *lex Sempronia* aimed to insure impartiality in assigning consular provinces (24 **their pick** n.), Cicero stresses the irregularity of awarding them 'by name': see esp. *Dom.* 24.

25–35. *Rome's reaction, the consuls' offensive*

25. you, gentlemen of the equestrian order One of C.'s prompting gestures (6 **as most of you recall** n.), meant to involve the judges in the narrative by 'reminding' the *equestrians among them (Introd. §2 and Glossary) of the dismay that they felt in common with other members of their order. On C.'s relations with the members of the order, as they had a bearing on his advocacy, see Berry 2003.

all Italy The unity of 'all Italy' in its regard for C., and hence for the *commonwealth, is a major motif in this speech (cf. 26, 32, 35–8, 72, 83, 87, 107, 128–9, 131, 145), as it is in all the speeches delivered after his return from exile (*Red. sen.* 24–6, 28–9, 39, *Red. pop.* 1, 10, 16, 18, *Dom.* 26, 57, 75, 82, 90, 132, 147, *Har. resp.* 5, cf. *Pis.* 3, 11, 23, 34, 51, 64). Here it supports two of C.'s chief, complementary theses: that the forces opposing C. and the commonwealth are isolated renegades (1 **domestic brigands** n.), and that the *Best Sort includes all who are not renegades (96 ff.).

all citizens . . . aid should be sought from the consuls Cf. Piso's reported assurance to C. that '(he) had no need to call upon the consuls for protection' (*Pis.* 12), early in 58 after Clodius' intentions were known. As the senate's leaders, the consuls guided discussion of matters of public concern, including the direction given to magistrates (cf. 137 **magistrates rely** n.), and they could shape opinion in response to perceived sedition, as C. had done in 63; but constitutionally the consuls by themselves could play only an indirect and limited role against a tribune. Using the *auspices to block tribunician legislation would have been unprecedented (33 **consuls sat and watched** n.), nor could they *veto it: Mommsen (1887–8, 1^3. 281–7) described the principle that any magistrate could veto the acts of any other magistrate who was his peer or inferior in rank, but McFayden (1942) showed that evidence of this principle in action is vanishingly rare, and there is no evidence at all that any but tribunes used the power to block legislation (cf. Mommsen 1887–8, 1³. 285–6)—a perceived weakness that C. apparently aimed to remedy several years later when drafting the laws of his ideal state (*Leg.* 3. 11 with Dyck 2004*a*, 474–6; cf. also 3. 27). In speaking of 'the public interest . . . critically at stake' (*summa res publica*) and of the consuls' power (*imperium*), C. perhaps alludes to the consuls' acting 'to see that the commonwealth suffer no harm', in a state of emergency declared by the so-called 'ultimate *decree of the senate' (*ultimum senatus consultum*: on the decree, see Lintott 1999*b*, 89–93); the thought had perhaps been encouraged at the time by some disingenuous remarks of Pompey (see *Pis.* 77, quoted at 41 **Crassus was saying** n.). But though the 'ultimate decree' had been used against one tribune, the 'seditious' Lucius Saturninus, in 100 (37 n.) and would be used against other tribunes (those defending Caesar's interests) again in Jan. 49, C. had no prospect of seeing it passed against Clodius, any more than he could expect the senate simply to suspend Clodius from his *tribunate, as they had suspended Metellus Nepos four years earlier (12 **Marcus Cato** n.). At most, the consuls might have done what C. praises Lentulus Marcellinus for doing a few weeks after this speech, viz., using procedural maneuvers to prevent 'pernicious' legislation from coming to a vote, esp. by manipulating the calendar: 'The consul is outstanding—Lentulus, I mean, not that his colleague gets in his way—really good, I've never seen one better: he's got rid of all the comitial days—even the Latin festival is being done over, and there's no lack of *supplicationes. . . .*' (*QFr.* 2. 5(9). 2; note C.'s remark, ibid. 3, that 'there was no one to veto' the same legislation). That even rather oblique consular action could prompt such extravagant praise is eloquent of the office's limitations in this area.

tornadoes bearing down on the commonwealth   The metaphor thus applied to persons is not common, but C. uses it similarly in addressing Clodius at *Dom.* 137: 'You—you storm-gust (*procella*) aimed at the fatherland, you tornado (*turbo*) and tempest (*tempestas*) destroying peace and tranquillity—you have made unclean with the very name of religion what you tore down and built up in the commonweath's foundering (*naufragium*),...when the Roman people were drowned, the senate capsized.' In the latter passage the metaphor complements the larger metaphor of the ship-of-state (cf. also *Pis.* 20, and 7 **commonwealth was tossed, 15 shipwreck** nn.); in the present passage the governing metaphor is rather of a structure teetering on the brink of collapse as the tornadoes approach. C. here prob. was inspired to personify the consuls as tornadoes (*turbines*) for the sake of the pun on *tribunus* ('the pair of them alone, apart from the frenzied tribune, were the tornadoes...', *illi soli essent praeter furiosum illum* tribunum *duo rei publicae* turbines).

refer the matter to the senate   Among the annually elected magistrates, praetors and tribunes could, like consuls, convene the senate, preside at the meeting, and 'refer to the senate'—put before it for formal discussion and vote—any matter touching the *public interest (on the procedures in general, Bonnefond-Coudry 1989, 452 ff.): C. mentions the consuls' obstructionism, not because the road to senatorial debate ran solely through their office (cf. 26, on Lucius Ninnius' action), but to stress their complicity with Clodius (cf. *Pis.* 29).

26. crowd of unbelievable size...   C. says 20,000 at *Red. pop.* 8, cf. Cass. Dio 38. 16. 2. Raising such crowds was often orchestrated: so in urging Atticus to do all he could to secure a measure for his recall, C. says 'if there is any hope of getting the thing done through the enthusiastic will of patriots, through influence, or by getting a great crowd together (*multitudine comparata*), make an effort to smash through at one go' (*Att.* 3. 23(68). 5, 29 Nov. 58). The Capitol was probably chosen in part to evoke the memory of the support marshaled there for C. during the Catilinarian crisis: see **28 the equestrians** n. and cf. **temple of Concord** n. just below.

put on mourning dress   In this they took their lead from C. himself, who assumed mourning when Clodius' bill was *promulgated, a move he later regretted (*Att.* 3. 15(60). 5, with **25 brought ruin** n.); see also *Red. sen.* 12, *Dom.* 99, Plut. *Cic.* 30. 4, 31. 1, App. *BCiv.* 2. 15 (implying that he judged the display distasteful); Cass. Dio 38. 14. 7

(38. 16. 3 ascribes the initiative to Lucius Ninnius, perhaps in confusion with his action in the senate, cf. n. below); on the custom in connection with 'capital' trials, see 1 **clad in mourning** n. Intended both to arouse pity for a person presumed to be suffering unjustly and to stir ill-will against the person responsible for the suffering, the custom was followed in a wide range of circumstances in the late Republic: see e.g. below 144 (**toga of manhood** n., on the son of the consular Lentulus Spinther); Plut. *Ti. Gracch.* 10. 6–7 (opponents of Tiberius Gracchus don mourning to protest his actions in 133), 13. 5 (Tiberius himself dons mourning and commends his wife and children to the people's care); Sall. *Hist.* 2 frag 47 (the consul Cotta, wearing mourning to speak as a suppliant before the people); Cic. *Verr.* 2. 2. 62, 2. 3. 6, 2. 4. 41, 2. 5. 128 (aggrieved suppliants from Sicily); *Fam.* 5. 1(1). 2 (Metellus Celer, when his brother, Nepos, was suspended from his *tribunate); *Att.* 3. 10(55). 2 (Quintus, for C. in exile); *Vat.* 30–2 (Vatinius, to signal disapproval of a *supplicatio*); Cass. Dio 37. 33. 3 (the population at large, when war with Catiline looms; cf. 37. 40. 2, normal dress resumed at Catiline's defeat); 37. 43. 3 (the senate, after riots involving the tribunes Nepos and Cato, see **62 temple was seized** n.); 39. 28. 1–4, 30. 3–4 (= Livy *Perioch.* 105, the senate, to protest *vetoes of the tribune Gaius Cato in 56); 39. 39. 2 (the consuls Pompey and Crassus, and their partisans, to protest tribunes' actions); Plut. *Pomp.* 59. 1 and *Caes.* 30. 3 (senate and people together, as civil war looms). For the custom retrojected to the early Republic, see e.g. Livy 2. 61. 5, 6. 16. 5; on its use as an instrument of 'popular justice', Lintott 1999*a*, 16–20.

temple of Concord … memory of my consulship Set at the foot of the Capitoline hill, looking out over the Rostra and the forum, this temple of Concord was built by Lucius Opimius, cos. 121, after crushing Gaius Gracchus' uprising in compliance with the senate's 'ultimate decree' (cf. 25 **aid should be sought**, 140 **his monument** nn.); see *NTDAR* 98–9, *LTUR* 1. 316–20, *MAR* 96–7. It thereafter often served as a site for meetings of the senate, as any temple could, including the critical meetings presided over by C. on 3–5 Dec. 63 (*Cat.* 3. 21, Sall. *Cat.* 46. 5, 49. 4, Plut. *Cic.* 19. 1).

the curly-headed consul Gabinius: cf. 18 above and **you prostrated yourselves** n. below.

the other consul ... was intentionally keeping to his house Having already remarked Piso's personal betrayal of him (20 **friend** n.), C. stresses here that Piso had of set purpose (*consulto*) absented himself from the first meeting of the senate at which he could have influenced Gabinius. Piso perhaps used the excuse of ill health (if *Pis.* 13 refers to this incident, cf. Cass. Dio 38. 16. 6, reporting that Piso 'was ill quite a lot'); if so, C. certainly did not believe him.

that slimy blot See 20 n., on the same abusive phrase.

lost entirely though he was plying his trade C. resumes his allegation that Gabinius had been both a prostitute and a bankrupt (18 nn.), here suggesting that Gabinius went broke despite the fact that he was selling himself for sexual use (the idiom *quaestum facere*, lit. 'to make (one's) livelihood', is associated esp. with prostitution). I adopt Halm's correction of the MSS' nonsense ($<$*to$>$ tum quamvis*, 'entirely though', for *tum qua* P[1], *tum* (*tu* V) *quasi* P[2]GHV); with the correction proposed by Paul (*tum cum*, 'then, when', accepted by Maslowski and Shackleton Bailey) C. instead suggests that Gabinius went bankrupt in the course of prostituting himself.

You came to the senate ... and all patriots with you For address to the equestrian judges, cf. 25 **you, gentlemen of the equestrian order** n. Acc. to Cass. Dio 38. 16. 2–4, Gabinius refused to admit the delegation of equestrians (apparently contradicted by C. in what follows here and *Red. sen.* 12), who were escorted by two consulars, Quintus Hortensius (3 n.) and Gaius Scribonius (*RE* 10) Curio (cos. 76). The latter could be taken to be a neutral voice, in so far as he had supported Clodius in the furor surrounding the Bona Dea scandal in 61; on the pamphlet C. had then written attacking them both, embarrassingly put into circulation during his exile when he needed Curio's help, *Att.* 3. 12(57). 2, 3. 15(60). 3, *FS* 227–63.

you prostrated yourselves at the feet of that utterly filthy pimp C. recycles abuse of Gabinius from *Red. sen.* 12, where he describes the same contemptuous response to the delegation and bestows very similar epithets, 'curly-headed' (*cincinnatus*, cf. just above) and 'utterly unchaste pimp' (*leno impudicissimus*). Refs. to grovelling at another's feet in supplication recur throughout the speech (54, 74, 145), and the practice, which has a close analogue in Greek culture

(Gould 1973), was so common as to have a quasi-ritualized character: e.g. in Feb. 61 Clodius threw himself at the feet of every senator in turn at a meeting attended by over 400 members (*Att.* 1. 14(14). 5; sim. *QFr.* 2. 6(10). 2 on the senator Fulvius Flaccus; cf. Asc. 28. 16 ff. Cl., a defendant and his supporters supplicating the judges about to render their verdict); the gesture could become stale with repetition, cf. 74 **Atilius' father-in-law** n. Like the assumption of mourning, the act aims to stir pity and thereby gain a request, when the person entreated is able to relieve your wretchedness (e.g. *Quinct.* 96–7, *Phil.* 2. 45, *Att.* 8. 9(188). 1, 10. 4(195). 3, *Lig.* 13 with *Fam.* 6. 14(228). 2); when that person is also held responsible for your wretchedness (very commonly, as here), the gesture also typically aims to arouse onlookers' pity and their indignation against the offender, to shame him into action (see e.g. Plut. *Pomp.* 3. 3, and cf. 27 **whom could you be said to entreat** n.). In all cases it is understood to be a voluntary act of self-humiliation. Actually to kick someone who thus abased himself before you was a mark of monstrous arrogance (Val. Max. 8. 1(absol.). 3); to fail to bid him rise, hardly better (*Att.* 10. 4(195). 3, on Pompey's treatment of C.).

Lucius Ninnius   Lucius Ninnius (*RE* 3) Quadratus, one of nine (later, eight) tribunes of 58 professedly loyal to C.: his attempts to block Clodius' first laws were outmanoeuvred (Cass. Dio 38. 14. 1, Asc. 7. 21–2 Cl., with Tatum 1999, 136–8); for his later actions in support of C. see 68 **Lucius Ninnius** n. He is not known to have held further office, but C. still refers to him as an intimate in 49 (*Att.* 10. 16(208). 4).

loyalty, largeness of spirit, and firm resolve   On the traits, see the Glossary. *Loyalty and *resolve recur at 139 below, again joined with *largeness of spirit and with *authority added: cf. 37, on the glory Metellus Numidicus gained by his resolve; 68, praising Ninnius again for loyalty and *manliness; 99, associating largeness of spirit and great resolve with 'ample intelligence'.

brought...a matter touching the public interest   As he had the right, as tribune, to do: see 25 **refer the matter to the senate** n. Note, however, that C.'s praise for Ninnius tends to obscure one of the act's implications: if the tribune could make this wholly symbolic gesture before the senate, while neither he nor any of the eight remaining tribunes on C.'s side dared use the veto or auspices (33 n.) to obstruct Clodius' legislation before the people, it is prob. because they saw that the legislation was far more popular than C. is able to admit. On the *de facto* limits constraining tribunician obstruction in this period see Morstein-Marx 2004, 124–8, with further refs.

a packed meeting of the senate   The phrase C. uses (*frequens senatus*: sim. 68, 72, 129 below) standardly denotes a well-attended meeting (e.g. *Mur.* 51, *Att.* 4. 1(73). 7, cf. *QFr.* 2. 1(5). 1 describing a meeting as *frequentior*, 'better attended', than expected just before the Saturnalia; for varying interpretations of the phrase, see Balsdon 1957, 19–20, Bonnefond-Coudry 1989, 425–35, with Ramsey 2001, 260–1, Ryan 1998, 36–41). A magistrate convening a meeting to take up an issue requiring a quorum (e.g. assignment of consular provinces) might specify in his edict that the meeting was to be *frequens*, but the issue here does not seem to fall in that category.

assume mourning dress   The senate collectively did so on several other occasions from the late 60s on (**put on mourning dress** n., above), though not to signal concern for one man's plight; the claim expressly stated at *Planc.* 87, that the gesture had never before been made as a matter of 'public policy' (*publicum consilium*: 27 n. just below) on one man's behalf, is implied in what C. says at the start of 28 below ('For what greater distinction...'). If that is so, it was a unique honour comparable to having a period of thanksgiving (*supplicatio) declared in his name as a civil magistrate (not a victorious general) for saving Rome from the Catilinarians (*Cat.* 3. 15, 4. 5, 20) and to the consuls' summoning all citizens in Italy on behalf of his recall in 57 (128 **consuls send letters** n.). It thus lends weight to C.'s argument that the attack on himself was tantamount to an attack on the community at large, justifying any means used by S. and others to repel it (see *Schol. Bob.* 128. 24–8 St. on this passage, and Introd. §3). On the present demonstration and the consuls' response, beyond the refs. at **put on mourning dress** n. above, see also *Red. sen.* 31, *Red. pop.* 8, *Dom.* 26, *Pis.* 17–18, Plut. *comp. Dem. et Cic.* 4. 1. On the kinds of mourning dress, 1 **clad in mourning** n.: senators would have put off the tunic with a purple stripe (*latus clavus*) that their rank entitled them to wear, and *curule magistrates would have put off the *bordered toga (*toga praetexta*) of office, cf. *Red. sen.* 12 'And when you (senators)... had as a body put on mourning..., *he* (Gabinius) mocked your squalor, smeared with perfumed oils as he was and wearing the *toga praetexta* that all the praetors and aediles had cast off'.

27. memory that posterity will have of me   C. looks to the future glory that will offset the misery he suffered and thus compensate his patriotism (cf. 47 **glory eternal** n.); he also anticipates the complementary role that posterity's memory will play in 47–50, where he explains that he chose not to die, despite his misery, in order to set an example for future generations (on the place of historical 'exemplarity' in the speech see 37 **Quintus Metellus** n.). Both views imply the understanding that any action sufficiently praiseworthy to win glory is also sufficiently edifying to serve posterity as a model.

a matter of public policy   In the structure of Republican government it was the senate's chief role to advise or (on C.'s view: 97, 137 nn.) to direct the magistrates, by 'consulting' or 'taking thought' (*consulere*) on matters touching the common interest through the medium of debate. The fruit of this consultation was commonly termed *consilium publicum*, 'public policy', the senate's judgement of what best served the common interest. As formalized in a motion that was approved by vote, fixed in writing, posted publicly, and stored in the treasury, this was known as 'the senate's considered view' (*senatus consultum*: Glossary s.v. 'decree'), a decision that— while lacking the binding force of legislation—was much more authoritative than mere 'advice' (cf. 32 **senate's authority** n.).

not as a formal gesture of entreaty but as an expression of genuine grief   For the contrast between formality and passion, cf. 10 **not a forced expression** n., on the Capuans' testimonial for S. Such assurances were no doubt often needed, and no doubt nearly as often disbelieved, just because semi-ritualized expressions of deep feeling were so common in public life and therefore apt to be regarded as formulaic or stale: cf. 26 **you prostrated yourselves** n.

whom could you entreat...   i.e. the one person who could grant the request was the one person plainly opposed to granting it. The ritual would then be directed not so much at gaining the request as at shaming the person who was its object (cf. 26 **you prostrated your-selves** n.)—though that person had already shown himself to be 'shameless'.

I leave to one side   An instance of *praeteritio* ('passing by'), a stock rhetorical device whereby a speaker addresses a subject while denying that he will address it (Lausberg 1998, §§882–6): see other examples at 54, 56, 109; contrast 13, where C. says that he will set aside S.'s *quaestorship in Macedonia and actually does so (sim. 52, 101).

all things human and divine   On the phrase see 1 n.

summoned... and exposed them to his henchmen's swords and stones   i.e., Clodius convened a *contio*, a non-voting *assembly of the people, and summoned these persons—either on the pretext of giving them a chance to address the crowd or under compulsion to explain their actions—all of which he was competent as tribune to do; he then used the setting to lay an ambush. Sim. *Dom.* 54, where the victims are 'those who spoke in favour of my well-being at a meeting of patriots', cf. Cass. Dio 38. 16. 5.

28. One consul   Gabinius, as the refs. to the senate meeting (which Piso did not attend) and creditors (cf. 18) immediately make clear. The translation marks the shift in thought—from the consuls to-gether as C.'s target to one consul in particular—more clearly than does the transmitted text, in which the preceding sentence is followed simply by the clause 'quite beside himself (he) flies from the senate' (*exanimatus evolat ex senatu*): some words of transition have perhaps been lost (Shackleton Bailey 1991*a*, 150 n. 33).

assembly of the people   A *contio*: see the Glossary. A non-voting assembly, the *contio* was the gathering at which legislative proposals (*rogationes*) were first read out, where magistrates presented their edicts or general views, praised friends, or traduced enemies, and where episodes of mob violence often were ignited. No institution in the late Republic was more important as a channel of communica-tion between mass and elite; for recent recognition of that import-ance, and debate on its implications, see esp. Hölkeskamp 1995, 25 ff., Pina Polo 1996, Laser 1997, 138–82, Millar 1998, Mouritsen 2001, Morstein-Marx 2004. Unless specifically termed a *voting assembly or *assembly of the plebs, any assembly mentioned in this speech can be assumed to be a *contio*.

a victorious Catiline   The speech is similarly described at *Red. sen.* 12, cf. also ibid. 32. Here C. first introduces the thought that Clodius and his associates not only were as wicked as the Catilinarians but were actively and sympathetically continuing their work: see esp. **42 old forces** n.

equestrians...when I was consul   A body of armed *equestrians had occupied the *clivus Capitolinus*, the path up the Capitoline hill from the forum, to protect the senate when it met in the nearby temple of Concord (26 n.) on 5 Dec. 63 to debate the fate of the captured conspirators: *Att.* 2. 1(21). 7 (describing Atticus as their 'leader'), *Phil.* 2. 16, Sall. *Cat.* 49. 4, cf. Plut. *Caes.* 8. 2. From C.'s point of view, the action expressed the patriotic concord of the *civil community's two leading orders; C.'s critics took it to be, if not an act of sedition *per se*, then the sort of occupation of a strategic public place vulnerable to a charge of 'public violence' (cf. Introd. §2).

he was referring, of course, to the conspirators   Some conspirators who escaped execution in Dec. 63 did not perish with Catiline but continued to live in exile: as C. went into exile himself, his letters recorded his fear of meeting some of these enemies in Greece (*Att.* 3. 8(53). 1), including Publius Autronius Paetus (*Att.* 3. 2(48), cf. 3. 7(52). 1). Convicted of electoral bribery and expelled from the senate in 66 (*TLRR* no. 200), Autronius had joined Catiline and went into exile in Epirus when convicted of *public violence in 62 for his part in the conspiracy, after C. refused to defend him and instead gave testimony against him (*TLRR* no. 229, *LUO* no. 24; on C.'s allegation that Autronius sent an assassin to kill him in Nov. 63, see Berry 1996, 169, on *Sull.* 18).

29. banished   Banishment (*relegatio*) differed from exile in having a fixed term (not specified in this case), in allowing one to live closer to Rome (**200 miles** n. below), and esp. in not entailing loss of one's *life as a citizen (*deminutio capitis*: 1 **lives as citizens** n.). C.'s account, of course, represents the action only as an unprecedented abridgement of a citizen's rights (he calls it *proscription at *Planc.* 87), a view still spiritedly maintained in one of his last extant letters

(*Fam.* 11. 16(434). 2, May–June 43). From Gabinius' point of view, the act no doubt represented the consul's use of sanctions to enforce his commands and maintain order (*coercitio*), the limits of which were not very closely defined (Greenidge 1901, 334, Nippel 1995, 5); at *Leg.* 3. 6 C. himself gives *coercitio* a prominent role. One wonders what sort of vigorous action lurks beneath C.'s euphemism, 'eager even to meet death on behalf of the commonwealth . . . he had dared make an entreaty': if Lamia tried to disrupt the assembly, the consul would have set his lictors upon him (**17 fasces** n.). From C.'s point of view the incident was clearly a signal token of his enemies' outrages, and he returns to it often in speeches from this period (though not in *Red. pop.*, before a less sympathetic audience): Lamia is mentioned by name at *Red. sen.* 12 and *Pis.* 64 (cf. *Fam.* 12. 29(433). 1, and 11. 16(434) above,), with more general refs. at *Red. sen.* 32, *Dom.* 55, *Pis.* 23, *Planc.* 87 (cf. Cass. Dio 38. 16. 4). In all the latter cases, as at 35 and 52 below, C. generalizes to make the action an attack on 'equestrians' (plural) or the whole *equestrian order.

Lucius Lamia   Lucius Aelius (*RE* 75) Lamia later began a senatorial career under Caesar the dictator, as aedile in 45, and was (prob.) praetor in 42 (refs. *MRR* 2. 307, 3. 4): if he was born *c*.82, as these posts suggest, he was in his mid-twenties at the time of this incident. C.'s relationship with the family, as he notes here, was then primarily through the father; at the time of this speech some members of the family were renting Quintus Cicero's house in 'The Keels' (*Carinae*), a fashionable section just ENE of the forum on the SW slope of the Esquiline (*QFr.* 2. 3(7). 7). We do not know how long the relegation lasted, but Lamia was certainly back in Rome, and hostile to Gabinius, in Feb. 54 (*QFr.* 2. 12(16). 2), and we have traces of his subsequent relations with C.: in mid-51 he was among those who helped C. sort out the sale of Milo's properties after Milo's departure for exile (*Att.* 5. 8(101). 2–3); in late 48, he helped negotiate C.'s return to Italy after the Pompeians' defeat at Pharsalus (*Att.* 11. 7(218). 2); though C. disapproved when Lamia joined in observing the anniversary of Munda after Caesar's murder (*Att.* 14. 14(368). 1), he supported his candidacy for the praetorship in 43 (*Fam.* 12. 29(433). 1, 11. 16(434). 2, 11. 17(435)); when C. was murdered in Dec. 43, Lamia perhaps saw to the mutilated body's burial (Davis

1958, on the evidence of *Anth. Lat.* 1.2. 608, 611, 614 Riese). The family prospered under the principate: a son was a *legate *pro praetore* of Augustus in Spain in 24 (*PIR*² A.199) and received two odes in Horace's first collection (1. 26, 3. 17: Nisbet and Hubbbard 1970, 301, Nisbet and Rudd 2004, 212), with honourific mention in a third (1. 36. 6–9); a grandson earned a consulship (3 CE), the urban prefecture (32 CE), and an obituary notice in Tacitus (*Ann.* 6. 27. 2). On the family, Treggiari 1973, 246–53; Syme 1986, 394–5.

200 miles … the city   By contrast, Clodius' second bill against C., imposing exile, specified 400 miles from Italy (*Att.* 3. 4(49): on a discrepancy in the sources, 65 **proposal** n. and App. 3).

so perverse a member … or rather an enemy …   With this 'self-correction' cf. *Red. sen.* 19 'a criminal member of the community, or rather a domestic enemy of the community' (of Clodius), and for the distinction (*civis* vs. *hostis*) see 11 **domestic enemies** n.

misfortune   One of Cicero's preferred euphemisms for his exile (*casus*, lit. 'fall': 51, 53, 60, 123, 140, 145, cf. 54), along with 'catastrophe' (*calamitas*: 32, 83, cf. 141, 142, 146) and 'disaster' (*clades*: 31): cf. 47 **exile** n. and Riggsby 2002a, 168.

a Roman citizen … expelled … without trial   Even before Catiline's conspiracy had been fully put down, some charged that C. had done just this, in 'expelling' its leader from the city (*Cat.* 2. 12, cf. 3. 3), and C. in turn charged that Clodius had done the same to him (e.g. *Dom.* 80, *Mil.* 26, 46 **proscription** n.). C. speaks of Lamia here but perhaps thinks of himself; when he comes to the law under which he was exiled, he uses a similar figure of speech: 65 'a proposal… made on the life and standing of a citizen—what sort of citizen is beside the point—', cf. *Dom.* 58.

30. Our allies and the Latins   The standard phrase (*socii et Latini*) denoting the non-Roman inhabitants of Italy: all these, by the time of the Punic Wars, were by treaty military 'allies' (*socii*) of Rome, though in practice subject to Rome; some, being natives of Latium ('Latins'), had from 338 on also enjoyed the 'right of Latium' (*ius Latii*), entitling them to intermarriage and trade with Romans and full citizenship if they settled in Rome. By the late Republic the *ius*

Latii was also extended to some communities in Italy beyond Latium, and in the provinces beyond Italy; through the *lex Iulia* (90) and the *lex Plautia Papiria* (89), prompted by the 'Social War' waged by the *socii* against Rome (91–87), virtually all Italy south of the Po gained Roman citizenship: Brunt 1971*a*, 84–90, Sherwin-White 1973, 96 ff., Galsterer 1976, Brunt 1988, 93–130, Gabba 1994.

as happened very rarely   In 126 the tribune Marcus Iunius Pennus passed a measure barring Italian non-citizens from Rome and expelling those present (opposed by Gaius Gracchus: *MRR* 1. 508, cf. esp. *Off.* 3. 47); in 122 the consul Gaius Fannius barred 'allies and friends' from the city by edict (in opposition to Gaius Gracchus: Plut. *C. Gracch.* 12. 1–2); the tribune Gaius Papius specifically excepted inhabitants of Italy (including, apparently, the region beyond the Po) from a measure expelling resident aliens in 65 (*MRR* 2. 158, esp. Cass. Dio 37. 9. 5). The *lex Licinia Mucia* of 95 is commonly cited in this connection, after *Schol. Bob.* 129. 10–12 St., but that law was aimed at Italians who were wrongly claiming citizen status and was not a blanket expulsion: see *Off.* 3. 47, Asc. 67. 20 ff. Cl. with Marshall 1985, 239, Badian 1973, 127–8, *MRR* 3. 118.

to their own household gods   C. specifies the *Lares*, 'protecting spirits of place . . . worshipped in various contexts: in the house, at the crossroads, in the city (as guardians of the state)'; the *Lares familiares* received 'offerings, sacrifices and prayers within the household' (Beard, North, and Price 1998, 2. 30–1). Though 'no mythological stories attached to them . . . (and) they (were not) defined as individual personalities' (ibid.), a Roman's *Lares familiares* (like his *penates*, following) were prob. more intimately tied to his day-to-day sense of personal well-being than the highly individualized gods of the Olympian pantheon: cf. *Leg.* 2. 42, where C. speaks with feeling of the destruction of his own *Lares familiares* at the time of his exile. See Wissowa 1912, 166–74, Latte 1967, 90–4.

away from their household gods   Here C. specifies the *penates*, the other form of divinity paid cult in every Roman household, by tradition brought by Aeneas from Troy: on the *penates* see Wissowa 1912, 161–6, Latte 1967, 89–90, *RE* 19 (1937), 449–51 (Weinstock); Dubourdieu 1989; and 45 **gods of our hearths** n.

individually and by name   Consular disciplinary action (*coercitio*) of the sort taken against Lamia by its nature tended to affect one or more specific individuals; the relevant question was whether it over-stepped the rather loosely defined limits of magisterial competence (29 **banished** n.). In this respect C.'s point is something of a red herring, engendered by the fact that he has been blending Lamia's experience with his own: for C. repeatedly claims that the second law Clodius brought against him, declaring that he had been exiled individually and by name, was a *privilegium* and therefore contrary to Roman legal tradition from the Twelve Tables on: see 65 **measure... to the disadvantage** n.

phantom likeness of courts and judges   With the image of a 'phantom likeness' (*imago iudiciorum aut simulacrum*) and the general tenor of the statement, cf. *Fam.* 10. 1(340). 1 (Sept. 44), on the state of Rome under Mark Antony: 'What hope can there be in a commonwealth... where neither senate nor people has any vigor, where there are neither laws nor courts nor the least phantom trace of a civil community' (*nec omnino simulacrum aliquod ac vestigium civitatis*).

rights and freedom of all citizens   A tautology, in so far as the *freedom of all citizens *qua* citizens—their political freedom—was nothing more or less than the rights (*iura*) they enjoyed acc. to Roman custom and statute: see Brunt 1988, 296–8 (esp. n. 37).

31. you are listening   One of C.'s periodic cues to the judges (6 **as most of you recall** n.), which here also punctuates the speech as he pauses between rounding off one outrage and beginning another. He uses the pause to make explicit ('It is, however, my aim to show...') the premise implicit in the defence all the while (Introd. §3): the last sentence of this section puts the point most plainly ('you and all patriots have judged that disaster of mine to be the most grievous wound to the commonwealth...').

someone among you might wonder at the purpose of so long a speech   'Indeed, he has already said a lot and is about to say a lot more: (this remark), therefore, seeks to mitigate criticism, so (his way of speaking) might be judged a defence tactic rather than garrulity' (*Schol. Bob.* 129. 17–19 St.).

battered beyond hope ... placing those terrible wounds before your eyes On the metaphors of physical abuse applied to the *commonwealth, see **17 branded** n.; on the aim and technique of vivid representation, 17 **picture in your minds** n.

If I shall seem ... please do forgive me The tone of formal courtesy is motivated by the need to speak about himself: on the point of etiquette that prompts the scruple, found also in C.'s more formal correspondence and his treatises, see Allen 1954, 126–7.

32. town ... colony ... prefecture I.e., every sort of community in Italy beyond Rome, irrespective of its history or form of governance: C. combines the three terms, to stress inclusiveness and unanimity, also at *Pis.* 41, *Phil.* 2. 58, 4. 7; note too (Q. Cic.) *Comm. pet.* 30. 'Towns' (*municipia*) were so called because—though originally independent of Rome—they were willing 'to accept duties' (*munia capere*), chiefly provision of military support, in return for a limited form of Roman citizenship for their inhabitants (*civitas sine suffragio*, lit. 'citizenship without the vote', a status that became obsolete in Italy after citizenship was generally extended to Italians south of the Po, 30 **Our allies** n.). 'Colonies' were communities founded, typically but not invariably in conquered territory, under the *auspices of leaders with *dominion sent out from Rome, and the structure of their government mimicked the mother city's. 'Prefectures' (*praefecturae*) were communities that had no local government of their own but were overseen by 'prefects' nominated by the urban praetor at Rome. For the latter two statuses see 9–10 nn. on Capua, which had at different times been a town, a prefecture, and (since 59) a colony.

corporation of public revenue-collection C. uses the term (*vectigal*) that originally denoted revenue derived from Rome's public properties (e.g. rents from land, profits from mines) but by this date covered all forms of public revenue, including transit-dues (*portoria*) and the 5 per cent tax on the value of manumitted slaves, with the exception of the direct tax (*tributum*) paid by the inhabitants of the subject-provinces beyond Italy (on the *tributum*, Nicolet 1976, esp. 79–86). Collection of these levies was contracted by *publicans (*publicani*), who raised the capital required by forming corporations (*societates*) largely controlled by members of the *equestrian order (senators were specifically barred from partnership in these corporations). Despite the slightly limiting term *vectigal*, the corporations C. has in mind had since 123 also been responsible for collecting the direct tax on land (*tributum soli*, also called the 'tithe', *decuma*) in the province of Asia; that arrangement was extended in 59, when Pompey's settlement of vast territories in the east made the *publicani* responsible for the *tributum* in those provinces too.

club i.e. *collegium*: see the Glossary. In 64 the senate by decree suppressed *collegia* that 'were deemed to be against the common interest' (Ascon. 7.9–10 Cl., with Linderski 1995, 165–203): if there were indeed *clubs to issue decrees in C.'s behalf, as he claims, in late Interkal./March 58 (on the date, App. 1), either they were of a politically acceptable sort not targeted by the senate's *decree, or the clubs quickly revived after Clodius passed his law permitting their re-emergence on 4 Jan. (*Pis.* 8–9 and App. 1, 34 **alleged purpose** n.).

passed a decree ... concerning my well-being Cf. the Capuan town council's decree passed as a testimonial for S., 10 n. Sim. *Dom.* 73 'for what deliberative body in all the world, great or small, did not express the most gratifying and handsome views on my accomplishments?', with *Dom.* 74–5, a more detailed catalog of the relevant bodies; cf. *Vat.* 8, *Pis.* 41, on decrees passed when he was already in exile.

the two consuls decreed ... their normal dress As an affront to the senate's *authority and ordinary human sentiment (both invoked just below), the act was an enormity C. often found it useful to recall: see *Red. sen.* 12 (quoted next n.); *Red. pop.* 13 (mentioning knights as well as senators), *Dom.* 55, *Pis.* 18, *Planc.* 87, cf. Plut. *Cic.* 31. 1, Cass. Dio 38. 16. 3. In the next sentence C. implies that, like Gabinius' relegation of Lucius Lamia (29 n.), the action was unprecedented, and indeed its constitutional basis is unclear: since no consular *vetoes of resolutions before the senate are known later than 95 (Bonnefond-Coudry 1989, 555–62), it seems a fortiori still more untoward for consuls to annul a resolution already adopted. If they offered a justification, it was prob. cast as a response to the senate's equally unprecedented display of mourning for an individual as a matter of 'public policy', see 26 **assume mourning dress** n. and *Red. sen.* 12 (next n.).

What tyrant ever forbade the distressed to grieve? Cf. *Pis.* 18, *Red. sen.* 12 (linking the action to Gabinius) 'He did...what no tyrant ever did: he issued an edict that, while saying nothing to keep you from groaning over your own woes in private, bade you not lament the fatherland's misfortunes in public', where the distinction between private and public behaviour perhaps reflects the wording of the edict (Shackleton Bailey 1991*a*, 11 n. 34).

Is it not enough, Piso...? Turning aside from addressing the judges to address an individual (*apostrophe*) was supposed to signal that high emotion had overcome the speaker and deflected him from his course (Lausberg 1998, §§762–76). Here the address to the absent Piso—fussily distinguishing him from his colleague ('to say nothing of Gabinius') so that his deceit can be paraded once again—is a flat gesture made for merely formal balance: having spent 28–30 belaboring Gabinius for an action that was entirely his own, C. now spends 32–3 belabouring Piso for an edict both consuls issued.

senate's authority Though the senate in the Republic was entrusted with the oversight of some matters by legislation (e.g. the allotment of consular provinces: see 24 **their pick** n.), it treated most matters that it treated either because no other institution existed to treat them in a structurally sensible way, or because the people willingly relied upon it to treat them, or because it had traditionally treated them (or could colorably claim that it had), or for some combination of these reasons (Lintott 1999*b*, 86–8, is clear and concise). These factors, together with the cumulative personal *authority of its members, gave the senate its institutional authority, the quality that made its decrees normative even though they lacked the force of law (on the legal value of senatorial decrees, Watson 1974, 21–30). The senate's authority—to which C. refers five more times in this speech (53, 75, 96, 98, 140, cf. 73, on Cotta's proposal) and scores of times elsewhere—was what allowed it to do nearly all that it did; and by doing all that it did, it could claim (properly, in C.'s eyes) to be the most authoritative institution in the community.

Did you also dare The MSS' *audeas* (subjunctive: 'would you dare') is retained by Maslowski, but Lambinus' *audebas* (indicative), favoured by Madvig, is preferable in point of sense (for he in fact did

dare) and syntax (with the imperf. subjunctive verbs *maererent...*
significarent following).

33. when their friends are in distress   For the practice 1 **clad in
mourning** n.

Will no one do the like for you?   That is, when Piso is prosecuted
upon returning from his governorship: C. elsewhere anticipates that
outcome for both consuls (52 **First of all** n., cf. 135 **this excellent
law** n.), though in Piso's case he was to be disappointed.

that lot you appointed to your staff   Clodius' law giving Piso and
Gabinius their provincial commands and funding (24 **their pick** n.)
also allowed them to name their own *legates, thus doubly offending
senatoral prerogative; cf. 66 below, where provinces, funding, and
legates are mentioned together. In this, C. charged (*Vat.* 35–6), Clodius had modeled his law on Vatinius' law of 59 (*MRR* 2. 190), which
had granted a sitting consul (Caesar) his provincial command, contrary to the *lex Sempronia*, and allowed him to name his own legates.
C.'s claim (*Vat.* 36) that the latter provision, in particular, was wholly
unprecedented implies that even when the people voted Pompey
his extraordinary command against the pirates via the *lex Gabinia*
in 67, his legates were appointed by a *decree of the senate; at least the
literal truth of the claim is corroborated by Cass. Dio 36. 37. 1 (on the
senate's 'unwilling' ratification; cf. also *Leg. Man.* 57–8, on resistance
to Pompey's request that Gabinius serve as his legate). Though
C. refers to the men dismissively, he speaks better of two of them at
Pis. 54, calling Lucius Valerius Flaccus—praetor 63, defended by
C. in 59—'most unworthy (viz. because of his decency) of being a
member of your staff' and referring to Quintus Marcius Crispus as his
'friend' (*familiaris*); at *Prov. cons.* 7 he praises another, Gaius Vergilius,
as a 'brave and blameless' man who checked some of Piso's crimes.

the calendar   Sim. *Pis.* 30 'Can any—I will not say human sentiment—but can any calendar tolerate (such men) as consuls?' On
Rome's official calendar (*fasti*) any given year was identified, not by
number, but by the names of that year's consuls.

that demon, that plague   The first term here, *furia*, is cognate with
the terms for 'frenzy' and 'frenzied' persons (*furor, furibundus,*

furiosus) C. often uses to stigmatize disruptions of the status quo, especially on the part of tribunes (see 20 'frenzied and reckless tribune of the plebs' with e.g. *Rab. Perd.* 22, *Mur.* 24, *Red. sen.* 12, *Dom.* 103, 123, *Vat.* 18, *Planc.* 86), and he commonly terms the result of such 'frenzy' a 'plague' on the community (*pestis*: e.g. *Dom.* 2, *Phil.* 2. 55, cf. 78 below; the 'frenzied tribune' and the 'plague' meet at *Phil.* 1. 22). But the term *furia* is more specific than 'frenzy' and more confined in C.'s usage: transferred from the 'Furies', the supernatural agents of retribution who properly dwell in the underworld, it is used by C. to denote no humans save the 'hellish' Clodius (39, *Dom.* 99, 102, *Har. resp.* 11, *Vat.* 33, 40, *Fam.* 1. 9(20). 15, *QFr.* 3. 1(21). 11, and cf. his 'hellish voice', *furialis vox*, or the like at 106, *Har. resp.* 39, *Planc.* 86), his *henchmen (109, 112, *Pis.* 26), the consuls Gabinius and Piso (*Har. resp.* 4, *Pis.* 8, 91), and the associates of Vatinius (*Vat.* 31, in a context concerned with a funeral).

assembly of the people in the circus Flaminius The circus Flaminius was a large plaza built by Gaius Flaminius (cens. 220) near the Tiber at the southern edge of the Campus Martius (*NTDAR* 83, *LTUR* 1. 269–72, *MAR* 86–7), just outside the city's sacred boundary (**pomerium*: *NTDAR* 293–6, *LTUR* 4. 96–105). It was known as a site of popular assemblies (**contiones*) convened by tribunes (Morstein-Marx 2004, 59–60, with Vanderbroeck 1987, App. B nos. 4, 29, 45, 46), its location outside the *pomerium* being esp. useful in this case for a reason C. suppresses in all refs. to the event: Clodius wished to question before the assembly not just the consuls (next n.) but also Caesar (Cass. Dio. 38. 17. 1–2, cf. Plut. *Cic.* 30. 4), then preparing to depart for his province and so vested with proconsular *imperium* that would lapse if he crossed the sacred boundary back into the city without special dispensation (cf. 15 **Gnaeus Pompeius** n.). Acc. to the chronological sequence that C. appears to be following (25–33), the *contio* was held in early March, between Clodius' *promulgation of his first law against C. and the vote; see further App. 1.

voiced their approval . . . against the commonwealth C. gives colorful accounts of Gabinius' appearance at *Red. sen.* 13 and of Piso's at *Red. sen.* 17, *Pis.* 14; for further important detail, Plut. *Cic.* 30. 4, Cass. Dio 38. 16. 6–17. 2. Calling each man before the assembly, Clodius asked his opinion (as the various reports have it) of C.'s consulate or of executing citizens not condemned at trial: the latter question, both more pointed and yet framed with reference to no specific person, suits the law of Clodius that, once *promulgated, caused C. to take on mourning (see 25 **brought ruin to me, 53 assembly...** nn.). Of Gabinius it is reported that he 'disapproved in the strongest terms' (*Red. sen.* 13), with criticism (Cass. Dio 38. 16. 6) of the senate, which passed the relevant decree in Dec. 63, and the equestrians, who guarded the Capitol while the senate debated (28 **the equestrians** n.); of Piso, that he claimed to be always 'merciful' (*Red. sen.* 17) and disapproved of 'cruelty' (*Pis.* 14, sim. Cass. Dio ibid.); of Caesar, that he thought the execution of the conspirators illegal, but that it was inappropriate for a law to be drafted now to govern past acts (Cass. Dio. 38. 17. 1–2; Plut. *Cic.* 30. 4 reports only the first part of Caesar's answer). Gabinius' reply, in C.'s report, was more plainly hostile to C. than Piso's equivocation or Caesar's superficially balanced statement; but though C. nowhere mentions the latter, there is reason to think that it still rankled in his heart (see 132 **a gentle person** n.).

while the same consuls sat ... the entire commonwealth was undone?   This segment is embedded in a problem concerning Clodius' legislation, and late Republican legislative and electoral procedure more generally, about which we know enough to surmise a fair amount but too little to establish much with certainty. The origin and scope of the two laws that Clodius' law is said to have abrogated—*lex Aelia* and *lex Fufia,* passed 'about 100 years ago' (*Pis.* 10)—remain controversial. It seems certain that both laws concerned the right of (certain) magistrates to impede (at least) legislative assemblies by *obnuntiation, that is, by reporting unfavourable omens to the presiding magistrate (see Glossary; for the view that these laws gave only tribunes the right to obnuntiate against each other, Weinrib 1970); and that the *lex Fufia* also imposed or reaffirmed certain calendrical restrictions on the holding of assemblies (see **bring a law ... on all days** n.; it was probably a law 'governing the right to put legislation to a vote and the proper time for doing so', as C. puts it in 56). The other texts bearing on the problem are 56 below, *Red. sen.* 11, *Har. resp.* 58, *Vat.* 18, 23 (with *Schol. Bob.* 148. 10–12 St.), *Prov. cons.* 45–6, *Pis.* 9–10 (with Asc. 8.12–9.2 Cl.),

Cass. Dio 38. 13. 5–6. The bibliography is extensive: Fezzi 1995 lists 60 items from the period 1861–1993, to which add *RE* Suppl. 10 (1965): 607 (C. Meier), Linderski 1995, 115–36 (= Linderski 1971), and the judicious survey of Tatum 1999, 125–33. Sumner 1963 made the greatest advance; see also esp. Astin 1964, Weinrib 1970, and Mitchell 1986; Williamson 2005, 382, gives a garbled account that echoes C.'s hyperbolic charges, without ref. to the previous scholarship.

To focus on Clodius' actions and C.'s presentation of them, we can claim to know the following as matters of fact:

1. The law in question was one of four that Clodius passed in the *assembly of the plebs on 4 Jan. 58 (*Pis.* 9), having *promulgated them all immediately or very soon after entering office on 10 Dec. 59 (the other three are mentioned together in 55 below, see nn., and cf. **34 alleged purpose** n.; on the probable time of promulgation, 10–15 Dec., see App. 1). By addressing the topic here, C. breaks the chronological sequence he has been following and returns—with no signal that he is doing so—to a time before the promulgation of the first law aimed at him (25 above).

2. C. speaks as though the four partial clauses he offers ('"Let the auspices…"', etc.) represent actual clauses in the law, but several plainly cannot be even responsible paraphrases: e.g. Clodius' law no more annulled the *auspices and the *veto, tout court, than his law on censorial review destroyed that magistracy, as C. claims it did (55); and since we know that the tribune Gaius Cato was prosecuted in 54 under the *Lex Fufia* (*Att.* 4. 16(89). 5), Clodius' law cannot have abrogated it (there is no evidence that Clodius' law was itself either 'temporary' or annulled, nor is there any other *lex Fufia* under which Cato could have been prosecuted: Sumner 1963, 339, Linderski 1995, 132–3). None of these 'clauses' can be taken at face value.

3. Taking C.'s statement here with his other remarks (esp. *Prov. cons.* 46), the most one can certainly say is that Clodius aimed to limit the religious obstructions that could be put in legislation's way, and that he perhaps aimed also to increase the number of days on which promulgated laws could be brought to a vote.

The following also seem at least probable conclusions to be drawn from the partial, partly conflicting, and generally tendentious accounts that C. gives us:

1. Clodius learned a lesson from Vatinius' legislation in 59, which three tribunes tried to block merely by announcing that they were 'watching the heavens' (*Vat.* 15–16): though the tactic failed, it left lingering doubts, or useful talking points, about the legislation's validity (indeed, later in 58 Clodius himself attacked the legitimacy of Vatinius' laws on this basis: *Dom.* 40, *Har. resp.* 48).

2. Clodius therefore aimed to limit the ability of magistrates in general, or tribunes specifically (Sumner 1963, Weinrib 1970, cf. **consuls sat and watched** n.), to raise such obstacles to legislation. This limitation either was absolute or—more likely, because the practice had arisen of merely announcing by messenger that one was 'watching the heavens'—required a proper form of obnuntiation: the report of an omen actually seen, made in person to an assembly's presiding magistrate (Mitchell 1986, Tatum 1999, 132, cf. Glossary s.v. auspices);

3. It is possible but—given Clodius' extensive legislative plans—hardly necessary to believe that the law was intended specifically to facilitate his attack on C. (so Cass. Dio 38. 13. 6, cf. Fezzi 1995, 328).

4. If any part of the law in fact increased the number of days on which legislative assemblies could be held, we cannot say how or why (see **bring a law... on all days** n.).

Given what we know and can reasonably infer, it is difficult to see the law as revolutionary in aim or effect; the likeliest limitation it placed on the reporting of omens is actually milder than the limitations decreed by the senate, with C.'s obvious approval, when the legislation for his return was being prepared in July 57 (129 **the senate decreed** n.). Were the law as alarming as C. paints it here, it would have been irresponsibly weak of him, when it was promulgated, to acquiesce in it in exchange for Clodius' promise not to attack him (Cass. Dio 38. 14. 1–3, a hostile source).

consuls sat and watched The striking regularity with which C. stresses the consuls' passivity vis-à-vis this law—saying that they 'sat and watched', 'sat in silence', 'sat and dozed' (*Red. Sen.* 11, *Pis.* 9, 10, cf. *Vat.* 18)—might suggest that he intends 'a rebuke for not having exercised *obnuntiatio* against it' (Astin 1964, 426 n. 1); and that thought would be consistent with C.'s other, more general statements that the *lex Aelia* and *lex Iulia* were bulwarks against the efforts of 'frenzied tribunes' (cf. *Red. sen.* 11, *Vat.* 18, *Har. resp.* 58). But though consuls could *obnuntiate against each other (as Bibulus did against Caesar in 59, cf. also Livy 22. 42. 8), it is very doubtful that they legally could do so against tribunes (Weinrib 1970, cf. 78 **If that praetor** n.), and there is in any case no evidence that they ever actually did so; on the limited range of actions that a consul could take against tribunes, see more generally 25 **all citizens** n. On the other hand, any of the nine other tribunes whose support C. claimed to have early in 58 (69 below) could have *vetoed the proposal, as Cato had vetoed Metellus Nepos in Jan. 62 (praised by C. in 62 below), or obnuntiated to block it—had it been as unpopular as C. wishes us to believe, cf. 26 **brought ... a matter** n.

auspices ... bring word of portents   Clodius' law did not annul either of these institutions, and later uses of auspices to obstruct *voting assemblies are known: see 78 below and the Glossary s.v. obnuntiate.

veto   Only tribunes used the magistrates' right of intercession that we commonly call *veto (25 **all citizens ... thought** n.), and even tribunes had come to prefer *obnuntiatio* as a means of obstruction. They might have been influenced in this by the example of Lucius Trebellius, who in 67 withdrew a veto when Gabinius (then tribune) threatened to depose him from office (Astin 1964, 442, Weinrib 1970, 414–16); but the case of Trebellius, in which the tribune's veto could be criticized for harming the interests of the plebs he was supposed to represent (cf. Badian 1989b), seems unlikely to have had such a generalized effect. The statement that Clodius ended the veto (cf. also *Prov. cons.* 46) is in any case absurd. If at all based on reality, it uses the term 'veto' very loosely, to mean 'block by *obnuntiatio*' (McDonald 1929, 178); but C. is more likely following out the logic of his own exaggeration: since the *lex Aelia* apparently affirmed both the veto and *obnuntiatio* as ways of blocking legislation, if Clodius' law had abrogated the *lex Aelia*, it would also have abrogated the veto (Sumner 1963, 342–3). In fact it did neither.

bring a law ... on all days   Cf. *Prov. cons.* 46, mentioning a similar effect of the law. The 'days when public business can be conducted' are the *dies fasti*, 'lawful days', of which there were two sorts: those on which criminal and civil trials could be held but *voting assemblies (*comitia*) could not, and those available for all forms of public business, including assemblies (i.e. *dies fasti et *comitiales*). We happen to know that the *lex Fufia* forbade the holding of legislative assemblies in the interval (at least 17–24 days: App. 1) between announcement of an election and the elective assembly (Sumner 1963, 340–1, 343), in effect making all days in that interval non-comitial: had Clodius' law voided that provision, it would be an easy stretch for C. to claim what he does here. But there is no reason to suppose that that was the only calendrical provision in the *lex Fufia*, and no reason to suppose that Clodius chose to target the one provision we happen to know (as was usual, his legislation was concentrated at the start of the year, months before the standard times for elections). Nor is it likely that Clodius' law reversed a rule—dating to the *lex Hortensia* (287) and presumptively reaffirmed by the *lex Fufia*—that market-days were *fasti* but not *comitiales*, thereby allowing assemblies to 'convene at precisely the time that Rome was most crowded by an influx of farmers from the countryside' (Weinrib 1970, 421): the change would not have served Clodius, whose following was mostly urban, not rural; and *Att.* 4. 3(75). 4 (Nov. 57) shows that market-days were still not comitial, at least for elective assemblies, after Clodius' law. If this is not another case of C. merely extending the logic of his hyperbole (by altering the rules of *obnuntiatio* Clodius 'abolished' the *lex Fufia* along with the *lex Aelia*; and if he abolished the *lex Fufia*, then he also …), Clodius' law may well have effected some change, but we do not know what it was.

34. a levy of slaves   For this 'levy' cf. *Dom.* 5, 54, 129, *Pis.* 23; *Pis.* 11 expressly places it, and the 'fortification' of the temple of Castor (below), in 'the days immediately following' the passage of Clodius' first laws on 4 Jan. 58, the period also implied here. Its association with the *clubs* (n. below, cf. also *Red. sen.* 33, *Pis.* 9) might partly account for the density of military language ('levy', *dilectus*; 'enlist', *conscribere*; 'form into squads', *decuriare*), for the 'clubs' themselves had a 'quasi-military organization' (Tatum 1999, 25–6). But the metaphors primarily suggest an outrageous parody of a proper military levy conducted in the consuls' presence ('while the same consuls looked on'); and with Spartacus' revolt still a fresh memory, mention of paramilitary slave-gangs was a reliable defamatory tactic, tending in C.'s rhetoric to link Clodius with Catiline (cf. 9 **Gaius Marcellus**, 47 **commonwealth...of slaves** nn., Favory 1978–9). It would help animate C.'s characterization of Clodius until the latter's death, and beyond: a few months before this speech, after Clodius' gangs attacked the site of C.'s house on the Palatine and burned Quintus' house nearby, C. claimed that Clodius was 'going from block to block openly offering slaves the hope of freedom for their services' (*Att.* 4. 3(75). 2, sim. ibid. 4); Clodius' use of slaves to terrorize the Megalesian *games a month after this trial is alleged at *Har. resp.* 23–6, 39, his intention (ended by his death) to enlist an army of slaves, at *Mil.* 76. C. will suggest below (53) that this 'levy' was meant to intimidate him and influenced his decision to leave Rome when he did.

Aurelian tribunal A structure mentioned only in this passage and three others referring to the same incident (*Red. pop.* 13, *Dom.* 54, *Pis.* 11), no doubt in the forum (so the ref. to the consuls, and cf. the temple of Castor, following), but otherwise of unknown location; sometimes associated or identified with the 'Aurelian steps' (*gradus Aurelii*), likewise known only from C. (*Clu.* 93, *Flac.* 66) and likewise of unknown location. Conjectures are summarized in *LTUR* 5. 86–7, cf. *NTDAR* 400–1.

alleged purpose of forming clubs Though suppressed by senatorial decree in 64 (32 **club** n.), old *clubs were revived, and creation of new ones was enabled, by one of Clodius' laws of 4 Jan. 58; the event was anticipated on 1 Jan. 58, when Clodius' lieutenant Sextus Cloelius led a celebration of the *games of the Crossroads (*Ludi Compitales*: Scullard 1981, 58–60), with which the clubs were associated, for the first time since their suppression (*Pis.* 9 with Asc. 8. 22–3 Cl., cf. 7. 9–11 and 75. 17 Cl. with Marshall 1985 ad locc.). At one point (apparently) before its passage, C. judged that the law would serve his interests, probably in the belief that he and his supporters could exploit the clubs as effectively as Clodius (for C.'s support by clubs, see 32 n.), but once in exile he changed that view (*Att.* 3. 15(60). 4). After his return he speaks of the measure only in grim terms, cf. 55 below, *Dom.* 129, and esp. *Red. sen.* 33; note, however, that when speaking before the people (*Red. pop.* 13), though he refers darkly to forces being 'enlisted' and formed into 'platoons' (cf. above), he mentions neither slaves nor clubs—perhaps because in the people's view Clodius had only 'restored the right of free association, which was supposed to go back to Numa and which the senate had abrogated ... by sheer usurpation of legislative power' (Brunt 1988, 331). The clubs were open to all social classes and categories, including slaves; but C. implies here ('alleged purpose', sim. *Red. sen.* 33 'under the pretence') that the institution of new clubs merely disguised the creation of paramilitary slave-gangs. On the clubs' suppression and restoration, and their place in Roman politics at this time, see Flambard 1977, Salerno 1984–5, Linderski 1995, 165–203, Lintott 1999*a*, 77–83, 193, Tatum 1999, 25–6, 117–19.

temple of Castor   Located in the SE corner of the forum (*NTDAR* 74–5, *LTUR* 1. 242–5, *MAR* 84–5) and fronted by a high tribunal, the temple of Castor was often a site of senate meetings, *voting assemblies (**comitia*: Mouritsen 2001, 21–5), and assemblies of the people (**contiones*: Taylor 1966, 28, Ulrich 1994, 101–3): it was a scene of violence in 62, when Cato opposed his fellow-tribune Metellus Nepos (62 **temple was seized** n.), and in 59, when Caesar's supporters attacked the consul Bibulus there in the furor over Caesar's agrarian legislation (*Vat.* 5, 21–3, Plut. *Pomp.* 48. 1, *Cat. min.* 33. 2, Cass. Dio 38. 6. 2–3); in 57 it was the site of the attack on S. that C. will elaborate in 79–80. Its conversion into a 'citadel' by Clodius is among C.'s more obsessive themes (see 85 below with *Dom.* 54, 110, *Pis.* 11, 23, sim. *Red. sen.* 32, *Dom.* 5, generalizing to 'temples', in C.'s manner), no doubt because seizure of a public building and stockpiling arms were *per se* subject to a charge of *vis* (cf. *Dig.* 48. 6. 1, Lintott 1999*a*, 109, Riggsby 1999, 83, Introd. §2). As for the reality underlying the charge, it may simply be that Clodius held assemblies there to rally support early in 58 (cf. Tatum 1999, 142–4; for the timing, *Pis.* 10–11); yet C.'s insistent ref. to the removal of steps (sim. *Red. sen.* 32, *Dom.* 54, *Pis.* 23) is a notably circumstantial detail. These were prob. not the lateral steps built into the tribunal's two ends, whose removal would cause permanent damage and strand occupiers 10–12 feet off the ground, but the temporary wooden steps regularly placed at the tribunal's front to facilitate assemblies and voting (Cerutti 1998): cf. *Att.* 1. 14(14). 5, Clodius' thugs impede voting by blocking the 'gangways' (*pontes*) attached to these wooden steps during voting. Since C. has been referring to events of Jan., it is perhaps relevant that 20 of the month's 29 days were *comitial, when voting assemblies could be held (cf. 74 **very few**, 75 **Quintus Fabricius** nn.).

35. With matters standing this way   The paragraph provides punctuation of the sort already seen in 14. Though C. interrupted the chronological sequence in 33–4 to assail actions Clodius took soon after 1 Jan. 58, we are to understand that we have returned to the circumstances C. faced in late Interkal. and early March, after Clodius *promulgated the first law aimed against him (25). Here, as C. gathers himself to talk about himself, he assembles in highly generalized form the details mentioned in 25–34, to depict a *civil community in collapse. For the move, cf. *Red. sen.* 4, 33, *Pis.* 26, and esp. *Red. pop.* 14: the latter offers an even longer catalogue—including events after his departure—to support a claim that he left Rome, not to save the *commonwealth (as he is about to argue, 36–50), but because the commonwealth was already lost (if the commonwealth no longer existed, he could not be an exile: cf. *Parad.* 4. 27).

I would have stood fast   The essential act of *manliness, displayed by one endowed with *resolve (*constantia*), *seriousness (*gravitas*), and *bravery (*fortitudo*) when he sees peril bearing down on the *commonwealth: see e.g. *Sull.* 25 (quoted in the Glossary s.v. freedom), and for 'standing fast' (*resistere*) associated with the traits just mentioned, *Att.* 2. 3 (23). 3, *Fam.* 5. 17 (23). 3, *QFr.* 1. 1 (1). 20, *Tusc.* 2. 33; and cf. esp. *Fam.* 14. 3 (9). 1, quoted at 36 **I grant** n.

36–50. *A Consular apologia*

Having focused, in 15–35, exclusively on others' bad acts that caused the circumstances just described, C. now gives an almost equally long account of his response, explaining why he chose neither resistance nor suicide and arguing that his decision to leave the city amounted to saving it a second time; for the same argument, more briefly, see *Red. sen.* 33–4, *Dom.* 96–9, *Vat.* 7. The *apologia*'s gross structure is comparable to *Prov. cons.* 18–25, a remarkable passage where C. explains his apparent shift in attitude toward Caesar: in both

places C. first acknowledges an apparent weakness in his position—
in this case, the feebleness of his withdrawal (36 **I grant** n.), in the
latter, the inconsistency of his stance—and then affirms that the
apparent weakness in fact manifests the most honourable strength
and patriotism. Both passages are 'typical of Cicero's penchant for
specious justification whenever he chose (expedience) over (honour)' (Mitchell 1991, 93–4, on letters written to Atticus in early 60,
justifying his growing political attachment to Pompey, see esp. 1.
20.(20). 2–3, 2. 1(21). 6).

36. eager as you are to hear   Cf. 31 **you are listening** n.

the crowd   C. often refers to the circle of listeners (*corona*, 'garland'),
gathered to witness the trial in the forum, as part of the audience that
the orator addresses and by implication as witnesses of the judges'
performance: see e.g. *Sex. Rosc.* 11, *Verr.* 1. 1. 4, *Flac.* 69 (contrast *Mil.*
1), with *De or.* 2. 338, *Brut.* 188, 192, 283, 289; cf. *Fam.* 8. 2(78). 1
(Caelius Rufus), on the uproar raised by spectators at a patently
corrupt verdict, and *Deiot.* 5–7, where C. claims to be disoriented by
the crowd's absence when arguing before Caesar as sole judge.

<the equestrian order>   A noun or phrase fell out at some point
before the Middle Ages: the only plausible alternatives are some form
of 'the equestrian order' (Kayser's *equestri ordine* is adopted here,
with e.g. Cousin 1965 and Shackleton Bailey 1991a, in line with the
refs. to the order in both 35 and 38), or a more generalized ref. to 'the
(Roman) people' (e.g., Peterson and Maslowski after Mommsen).

I grant...devoid of spirit and strategy   After his return C. often
defends himself, expressly or by implication, against charges of
cowardice (see *Red. sen.* 6, 33–4, *Red. pop.* 19, *Dom.* 5, 56, 63–4,
95–9, *Har. resp.* 45 and esp. 49, *Vat.* 6, *Planc.* 89), not without reason.
Even some of his supporters said that he had 'swerved a bit', a
euphemism for lacking *resolve (constantia)*: see 73, summarizing
remarks made by Lucius Cotta, a senior consular, on 1 Jan. 57. More
to the point, C. passed the same judgement on himself when in
exile: see esp. *Fam.* 14. 3(9). 1–2 (Nov. 58), in which he expresses
to his wife his grief and shame for failing his 'duty either to avoid the
peril..., or to stand fast against it (*resistere*, see 35 n.) with the

cunning and resources at my disposal, or to die bravely'. In what
follows C. is in part vigorously trying to improve on the self-image
that prompted this ashamed and remorseful judgement.

37. Quintus Metellus The first of the speech's historical *exempla*,
or 'paradigmatic cases', of the sort that the Romans (far more than
the Greeks: cf. Quint. 12. 2. 30) took to be the foundation of their
political and ethical thought, as models for action and standards of
evaluation. It was to set such an example (C. will claim) that he chose
exile over resistance or suicide (47–50), and he will invoke historical
exempla time and again in the speech's course (37–9, 48, 50, 101–2,
116, 127, 130, and esp. 140–3; cf. e.g. *Cael.* 39, *Prov. cons.* 20, *Balb.* 40,
Pis. 58, *Planc.* 60, *Mil.* 8); on *exempla* in Roman thought and
literature see esp. Litchfield 1914, Lind 1979, 11–15, David 1980,
Maslakov 1984, Mayer 1991, Robinson 1994*a*, Skidmore 1996,
Hölkeskamp 1996, Chaplin 2000, Stemmler 2000, Roller 2004.

Quintus Caecilius (*RE* 97) Metellus Numidicus (cos. 109, cens.
102) went into voluntary exile in 100 rather than swear not to impede
a tribunician law he believed to have been passed illegally (sim. 101),
only to be restored as a patriot in 98 (*MRR* 2. 5). For anyone wishing
to cast C.'s withdrawal as a principled political stance, Metellus was
an obvious model to adduce, and he evidently was so adduced by C.'s
partisans even before his return: see 130 below, on Publius Servilius'
speech in July 57. C. himself refers to Metellus repeatedly after his
return to support various arguments: see 101 below, *Red. sen.* 37–8,
Red. pop. 6, 9–11, *Dom.* 87, *Pis.* 20, *Planc.* 89, *Fam.* 1. 9(20). 16;
Velleius follows C.'s lead when he says that 'after Numidicus' exile
and return, no one's expulsion was ever more the cause of indignation (than C.'s) nor their return more the cause of joy' (2. 45. 3). Here
C.'s initial (rhetorical) question introduces a different tactic, as
C. goes on to stress important distinctions between the two: insofar
as C.'s support was more broad-based than Metellus', he had less
reason to withdraw, and more need to explain his withdrawal; insofar
as Metellus' act was a gesture of purely personal principle, made in
the face of a *fait accompli* and with no consequence for the public
good, it was unlike C.'s actions (in 63: 38 **The things . . . n.**) that had
preserved the *well-being of all; and insofar as Metellus had a better
class of opponent, he was more fortunate. Beyond giving C. another

opportunity to revile the consuls and Clodius (38–9), this last point moves us on to a new topic C. must address, the position of the triumvirs (39–41).

category of the citizenry i.e. a citizen 'order' (*ordo*): taken strictly (so generally in this speech), the word denotes a formally constituted subset of the citizenry, juridically defined not by their economic class but in terms of their civic relations to one another and to the *civil community as a whole; see esp. Cohen 1975, with Nicolet 1984. The judges at this trial represented three such categories, the senatorial order ('the most august category of the citizenry', *summus ordo*: cf. 87), the *equestrian order—whom C. has in mind here—and the *treasury tribunes; other 'orders' included the 'scribes' who assisted the various magistrates (cf. 133 **Sextus Cloelius** n.), the 'decurions' (*decuriones*) who served as town councillors in towns beyond Rome (cf. 9 **'settlers'** n.), and former slaves, who gained citizenship upon emancipation ('freedmen', *liberti*: cf. 97 **even freedmen** n.).

some notion of personal glory See *Dom.* 87, where C. says that Metellus gained more glory from his exile than from his other achievements, and *Planc.* 89, where C. (again contrasting his own case) says that Metellus was acting to maintain his personal principle (*perseverantia sententiae*) rather than the *commonwealth's *well-being (cf. *Att.* 2. 15(35). 2, similarly judging Bibulus' resistance to Caesar's legislation noble but pointless, an act that made plain his own principle, *iudicium*, with no gain for the commonwealth, and C.'s comments on Cato's avoiding such gestures, 61). Note, however, that neither of those judgements on Metellus, nor any of C.'s other comments on him, quite amounts to the present, rather ungenerous attribution of motive, where C. claims that personal glory was Metellus' actual *aim*, what 'he had had his eye on' (*ad suam... gloriam ... spectarat*) all along. The point is not softened when C. goes on to use the language of contracts ('stipulation', *condicio*) to suggest that Metellus' bartered away his love of homeland (*patriae caritas*) in return for glory: contrast 53, where C. says it was precisely his own *patriae caritas* that motivated his withdrawal. One wonders how this was received by Marcus Scaurus, the presiding praetor whose kinship with Metellus C. invokes in 101 (n.).

refusing...violence   The law, an agrarian measure passed in Marius' favour by Saturninus as tribune (the two are about to be named), included a clause compelling all magistrates and senators to swear not to impede it: see esp. Plut. *Marius* 29–30, App. *BCiv.* 1. 130–40, with *MRR* 1. 575–6; on the 'law not legally passed' (*lex non iure rogata*), for reasons including violence, see Heikkilä 1993, 121–3 (ref. to this law at 127 n. 49). Some Roman statutes include clauses exacting such oaths from current and future magistrates; the only extant parallel for an oath demanded of all senators is a law inscribed on a bronze tablet discovered near Bantia in S Italy (*tabula Bantina*), dating to the end of the 2nd cent. BCE and perhaps pertaining to Saturninus' legislation (but not the present law): see *RS* no. 7 (oath: lines 23 ff., trans. 1. 203–4, and cf. 1. 23 more generally), and 61 **sworn allegiance** n.

resolve   i.e. *constantia*: see the Glossary.

Gaius Marius   Not only seven times consul and one of Rome's greatest generals but also a fellow Arpinate and distant kinsman of C. (by marriage), Gaius Marius (*RE* 14, Suppl. 6 (1935), 1363–1425, cf. *MRR* 3. 139–40) is C.'s favourite historical *exemplum*, and the most ambiguous. On the one hand, he had (like C.) overcome the handicap of being a *new man to save Rome (cf. e.g. *Sull.* 23, *Red. pop.* 9, *Leg.* 2. 6), when Germanic tribes threatened Italy at the end of the 2nd cent.: C. developed this aspect of Marius in a brief epic poem written sometime in the 50s (an extract at *Div.* 1. 106). On the other hand, he sometimes allied himself with unsavoury 'popular' politicians (next n.) and in the end brought civil war to Rome in order to advance his personal standing. He figures in both guises in the speech, cf. 50 and 116; Carney 1960 reviews C.'s use of him as an *exemplum*.

his personal enemy   The enmity began in 109, when Marius served on Numidicus' staff in the war against Jugurtha in North Africa (Sall. *Iurg.* 63–5, Plut. *Mar.* 7–8, Epstein 1987, 36–7): after Numidicus refused Marius' request for a leave so that he could stand for the consulship, Marius schemed against him, winning the consulship for 107 and replacing Numidicus in Africa by vote of the people (*MRR* 1. 550).

Lucius Saturninus   Lucius Appuleius (*RE* 29, *MRR* 3. 20–3) Saturninus was *tribune of the plebs in 103 and again in 100, when he passed the law that Metellus resisted, providing land for veterans of Marius' German campaigns both beyond the Po and in Africa (a special sphere of Metellan influence): C.'s audience would think of Caesar's agrarian legislation of 59, put through with the tribune Vatinius's help and resisted by Caesar's colleague, Bibulus (cf. **some notion of personal glory** n.). After the Gracchi, Saturninus is C.'s favourite *exemplum* of the 'seditious' tribune: beyond the present comparison cf. 39, 101, 105, and e.g. *Cat.* 1. 4, 29, 4. 4, *Dom.* 82, *Har. resp.* 41, *Vat.* 23, *Mil.* 14, *Phil.* 8. 15. In 100, after a third victory in the tribunician elections, he turned to violence to manipulate the consular elections for 99: when the senate passed its 'ultimate decree' (25 **all citizens** n.), he was arrested by the consul Marius, who had turned against him, and was murdered by a mob.

at least personally if not politically temperate   i.e. unlike Clodius, who was neither. The word used to denote temperate behaviour here— *abstinenter*, cognate with *abstinentia* (7 **temperate behaviour** n., and Glossary)—looks less to the absence of personal vices (lechery, debauchery, etc.) than to the refusal to take bribes or lay hands on others' goods: for allegations of such crimes on Clodius' part see e.g. 39 (will-forgery), 56 (bribery) with nn.

either lose . . . or gain . . .   Loss would bring disgrace by showing that he lacked support. C. takes the liberty of casting Metellus' choice as essentially the same as his own; cf. *Red. sen.* 34, on his own options: 'had I been killed all by myself, it would have been a disgrace (*turpe*), but if I was killed with many others, it . . . would be deadly for the commonwealth.'

38. The things . . . on his own authority   That is, as consul in Nov.–Dec. 63, esp. in carrying out the execution of the chief conspirators after the senate meeting of 5 Dec. The glance back to 63 entails a characteristic glide in C.'s thought (cf. e.g. 47 **engaged in matters** n.). The comparison with Metellus began from their similar withdrawals, which had similar *proximate* causes, as principled responses to 'frenzied' tribunes; the main contrast between them was their different motives (personal principle and glory vs. the *public interest and glory). In this sentence, though that contrast is the same ('with a view not only to my glory as an individual but to the well-being of all citizens'), the basis of the comparison has shifted to the *root* cause of C.'s withdrawal, his actions as consul. On this he takes the line we have already seen him take, from which he never swerves: though the leadership (hence, the glory) was his, the *authority (hence, the responsibility) was the senate's: see **11 the senate** n., 53, 145 below, and sim. *Sull.* 21, *Red. sen.* 7, 32, *Dom.* 34, 94, *Pis.* 14, *Mil.* 8. C. was stressing the senate's responsibility already in Jan. 62, see *contra contionem Q. Metelli* frag. 9 Crawford, *Fam.* 5. 2(2). 8.

I had done them . . . and defend my action   C. denotes this 'provision' with the term (*condicio*) used just above to denote the 'stipulation' governing Metellus' 'exchange', drawing on the language of contracts in both places; but beyond the broadly contractualist premises of Roman Republicanism (1 **If anyone** n.), it is not clear what he can have in mind. In Jan. 62 'the senate gave immunity (*adeia*) to all who had administered those events and decreed that if anyone should later dare to call any of (those responsible) to account, he would be considered both a personal and a public enemy' (Cass. Dio 37. 42. 3), but what the senate did in Jan. 62 could not constitute a *condicio* for what C. had done a month earlier. In the *Catilinarians* his remarks run in a quite different direction: he asserts that he will not regret acting to protect the *commonwealth even should he later be threatened with death or the like (e.g. *Cat.* 4. 20), and he even promises that *he* will defend and take responsibility for the senate's decrees (4. 24). At *Prov. cons.* 3 C. refers to a 'public promise' (*fides publica*), a phrase that can denote a grant of immunity, apparently in the same connection; cf. also *Sull.* 26–7 (C. moots but rejects 'honourable retirement' as a 'reward' from senate and people for his services, instead saying that he will receive reward enough if only no peril overtakes him), *Dom.* 145 (an 'understanding', *condicio*, that C. claims to have reached with the *gods*, in connection with his 'self-sacrifice', *devotio*: cf. 45 **if I happened to be sailing** n.).

I . . . was locked in conflict . . . with hired thugs incited to plunder the city   Because C.'s opponents were more disgraceful, he could not fear that he would be reproached for their deaths (thus 39 'I had no worry that anyone would criticize . . .'); for the same reason, however, conflict with them was, if not humiliating *per se*, then less glorious. For the theme of unworthy opponents, see *Har. resp.* 40–2, where the *commonwealth itself faces the shameful foe.

perverse monsters ... consigned ... as chattel C.'s abusive metaphors bustle about in different directions (cf. 54 **they swooped in ... to drag off its spoils** n.). The 'monsters' are lit. 'portents of disaster' (*prodigia*), phenomena contrary to nature (e.g. a rain of meat, talking cows) that as signs of divine anger had to be reported to the consul, who would refer them to the senate and (usually) to the appropriate religious authorities for expiation (*Har. resp.* is prompted by such a portent; see esp. the *prodigia* culled from Livy by Julius Obsequens, with MacBain 1982, 82–106, Beard, North, and Price 1998, 1. 37–9, and cf. 53 **By the immortal gods** n.). C. uses this metaphor only of the consuls (*Vat.* 36, *Har. resp.* 4; of Piso at *Pis.* frag. 1) and Clodius (*Pis.* 9, *In Clod. et Curion.* frag. 21 Crawford), of Catiline (*Cat.* 2. 1, *Cael.* 12), and of Verres before them (*Verr.* 2. 2. 79, 2. 4. 47); cf. Lévy 1998. In the other metaphor C. applies the term (*addicere*) used when the praetor handed property over to a claimant, and in particular when a debtor was handed over to his creditor in a form of debt-bondage (survey: Ste. Croix 1981, 165–70), here regarded as the equivalent of slavery.

39. insult was intended ... from himself, as quaestor Saturninus was superseded in (prob.) 104 (*MRR* 3. 20–1), when a grain shortage (*Har. resp.* 43) allegedly caused his 'laziness and irresponsibility' to be noticed (Diod. 36. 12, cf. *Mur.* 18 on the position's reputation as 'annoyingly burdensome', *negotiosa et molesta*). Supervising the grain supply at Ostia, Rome's seaport, was an important sphere of *quaestorian responsibility: being relieved of the responsibility for cause would be a disgrace (*ignominia*, the term used here), comparable to a modern military officer's being relieved of a key command; if the disgrace was taken to be intentionally inflicted, as the prickly Roman sense of honour would tend to urge, it would be thought an insult (*iniuria*) worthy of anger and demanding satisfaction (see below). (Taking the phrase *per ignominiam* to denote the manner of the transfer—'the grain supply was transferred ignominiously'— Shackleton Bailey suggested 'growing incensed', *suscensebat*, for 'knowing', *sciebat* (1987, 278: 'Knew it? As if he could help knowing it! Read *suscensebat*.'). But the phrase can also denote the intended or purported effect of an act: cf. *Dom.* 65 'Sic M. Cato ... quasi per beneficium Cyprum relegatur', 'Thus Marcus Cato ... is banished to Cyprus as if a favour were intended/as if he were being done a favour.' The MSS' text is sound.)

Marcus Scaurus ... foremost man of the senate and the civil community Marcus Aemilius (*RE* 140) Scaurus, cos. 115, cens. 109, father of the praetor who presided at this trial (101 **your father** n.) and an acquaintance of C.'s paternal grandfather sufficiently intimate to reprove him for preferring life in Arpinum to a public career at Rome (*Leg.* 3. 36); at *Off.* 1. 76 C. mentions the admiration he had for Scaurus as a boy; for his 'political biography', see Bates 1986. Beyond superseding Saturninus in this affair he also moved the 'ultimate decree' of the senate that led to Saturninus' murder in 100 (37 **Lucius Saturninus** n.). Unlike the phrase 'foremost man of the *civil community' (*princeps civitatis*), an informal honourific that could be used of more than one man (cf. 84 **detain the foremost man** n.), the phrase 'foremost man of the senate' (*princeps senatus*) was the singular, formal title of the man whom the censors entered first when they enrolled the senatorial order's members: the title conferred great prestige and influence, since the 'foremost man' was the first to deliver his opinion on any issue under debate. Scaurus was the last great holder of the position before it was abolished by Sulla (*RE* Suppl. 6 (1935), 699–700 (O'Brien-Moore), Suolahti 1972, Bonnefond-Coudry 1989, 687–96).

sought satisfaction for his anger C. implies that Saturninus' sense of grievance (*dolor*) over this episode caused him to become a 'popular' agitator; so more plainly *Har. resp.* 43, differently Diod. 36. 12.

but with ... a brigand Some of these insults we have already met (male prostitute, cf. 18 **old despoilers** n.; incest, 16 **what sort of muscle** n. and App. 2; *brigandage, 1 **domestic brigands** n.); 'high-priest of debauchery' alludes to the Bona Dea affair; C. makes circumstantial charges that Clodius was a poisoner (*veneficus*) and will-forger (*testamentarius*) at *Dom.* 115 (sim. *Har. resp.* 30) and *Har. resp.* 42; with the ensemble, cf. esp. *Cat.* 2. 7 'In all Italy what poisoner, what gladiator, what brigand, what assassin, what parricide, what forger of wills, what cheat, what glutton, what wastrel, what adulterer, what woman of ill repute, what corruptor of the youth, what corrupted youth, what desperado can be found who would deny that he has been Catiline's intimate?' For comparison of Clodius with a pair of typically 'bad' examples (the Gracchi), to show that—bad though they were—Clodius was still worse, see *Har. resp.* 43–4.

If I defeated . . . by force of arms   Writing to his brother late in 59, C. said: 'if (Clodius) brings a charge against me, all Italy will gather in my support, so I'll come away with glory heaped on glory; but if he tries force, I expect that I'll be able to meet him with force, thanks to the eager support not just of friends but even of strangers: they're all volunteering themselves, their friends, dependants, freedmen, slaves, and their money too' (*QFr.* 1. 2(2). 16); cf. the options mentioned in the letter to Terentia from exile (*Fam.* 14. 3(9). 1), quoted at 36 **I grant** n., and his later claim that had he chosen to act he would not have lacked an army, only the generals (*Fam.* 1. 9(20). 13, referring esp. to Pompey's failure to support him).

our bravest patriots were demanding   The same claim is made, in similar terms, at *Red. sen.* 33. In later sources, Pompey (deceitfully) and Lucius Lucullus urge C. to remain in Rome (Cass. Dio 38. 15. 3, Plut. *Cic.* 31. 4, respectively, neither mentioning force: Dio's Pompey speaks of 'desertion', Plutarch's Lucullus gives hope of 'success'), whereas Hortensius and Cato raise the spectre of civil war to blunt C.'s readiness to resort to arms (Cass. Dio 38. 17. 4); acc. to Plut. *Cat. min.* 35. 1, Cato urged against force on similar grounds (see 46 **meet and undergo** n.).

I had no worry that anyone would criticize   C. made a similar point, employing heavy irony, concerning Catiline (*Cat.* 1. 5): 'If . . . I order that you be seized and killed, I will—no doubt—have to fear, not that all patriots will say I acted too late, but that someone will say I was too cruel'.

citizen-desperadoes . . . public enemies   On *desperadoes 2 n.; for 'homegrown' *public enemies, 11 **domestic enemies**. In 11 C. implies that the Catilinarians, having assumed the character of public enemies, could be killed with impunity; his point is the same here, and it further implies a defence of S.'s actions on the same grounds (*Schol. Bob.* 129. 22–3 St.).

the following considerations moved me   The balance of the paragraph strives to misdirect, as C. suppresses the triumvirs' actual indifference or hostility while yet explaining how their influence—as Clodius 'misrepresented' it—worked against him (cf. *Schol. Bob.* 129. 28–30 St.). A few touches nonetheless graze the truth, in asides (**to the extent possible** and esp. **who was not obliged to be estranged** nn.), and C. implies criticism a bit more openly in the next paragraph (**people … came to think** n.). Elsewhere in the 'post-return' speeches the three magnates are mentioned together only at *Har. resp.* 47, to much the same effect.

demon   On the epithet, 33 **that demon** n.

Gnaeus Pompeius   On Pompey and C., Introd. §1 and 15 **Gnaeus Pompeius** n.

to the extent possible   An odd phrase in context: if it does not refer to Clodius' attempts to make Pompey think C. plotted against him—not mentioned until 41 below—it must refer to the other triumvirs' efforts to keep him from supporting C., acknowledgement of which runs counter to C.'s surface argument.

Marcus Crassus   Marcus Licinius (*RE* 68) Crassus served under Sulla, becoming rich during the *proscriptions, and later put down the forces under Spartacus, though Pompey took the credit; he was twice Pompey's colleague as consul (70 and 55) and was censor in 65 (biographies: Marshall 1976, Ward 1977). Crassus and C. spoke on the same side in this case (3 **summed up the case** n., cf. 48 below), as they had in 63 and would again several months later in 56 (*TLRR* nos. 224 (Murena), 276 (Balbus)), but despite these and other dealings—both were mentors of Marcus Caelius Rufus (*Cael.* 9), C. bought Crassus' splendid house on the Palatine in 62 (*Fam.* 5. 6(4). 2, cf. Gell. 12. 12. 2–4, Berry 1996, 30–2) and enjoyed being praised by him in the senate in 61 (*Att.* 1. 14(14). 3–4)—they were never friends: in all C.'s correspondence there is not one truly warm ref. of the sort C. could at times manage even toward Caesar, and several that paint him an operator and a rogue (e.g. *Att.* 1. 16(16). 5, 4. 13(87). 2).

In the first 8 months of exile C. mentions him only once in the extant correspondence, mistrustfully (*Fam.* 14. 2(7). 2, cf. *Att.* 3. 23(68). 5, where both Crassus and Pompey are counted among the the factors 'holding things up'); in the post-return speeches he appears about one-third as often as Caesar, who appears one-third as often as Pompey (Riggsby 2002*a*, 173). A few weeks before this speech Pompey told C. that Crassus was funding Clodius (*QFr.* 2. 3(7). 4); there was an open break in 55, when Crassus enraged C. by calling him an 'exile' on the senate floor (Cass. Dio 39. 60. 1 with *Fam.* 1. 9(20). 20, where C. acknowledges the 'pent-up hostility' that the incident released). Caesar and Pompey urged their reconciliation; acc. to Plutarch, at least a superficial reconciliation was achieved by Crassus' son, whose literary interests attached him to C. (cf. *Fam.* 13. 16(316). 1) and who put on mourning during C.'s crisis in 58 (Plut. *Crass.* 13. 2–4, vague chronology; cf. Plut. *Cic.* 26. 1, 33. 5). For later relations, see C.'s disingenuous letter to Crassus, then governor of Syria (*Fam.* 5. 8(25), Jan. 54), and the account in *Fam.* 1. 9(20). 20. Father and son both died in the debacle at Carrhae in June 53 (*MRR* 2. 230).

Gaius Caesar   On Caesar and C., Introd. §1, 16 **one of the consuls** n., and next n.

who was not obliged to be estranged … through any fault of my own   Contrast with the preceding claims of friendship makes plain the statement's coolness: cf. 52, 71, *Dom.* 39, *Pis.* 79–82, *Planc.* 93. With the qualification implied in 'fault of my own' (*meo merito*) compare the similar qualification in 52 ('just cause'): both at least allow the reader to infer that Caesar in fact behaved in a hostile and unjust manner (sim. 71 'inclined to be well-disposed'); the edge was still more evident at *Red. sen.* 32, 'I do not say that he was my enemy, but I know that he was silent when he was said to be my enemy.' All refs. to Caesar in this speech convey at best a merely formal neutrality; yet there are no overtly hostile remarks of the sort C. says he made in interrogating Vatinius after this speech (reported in *Fam.* 1. 9(20). 7, not found in the extant *Vat.*). By the time of *Prov. cons.* the tone has of course changed: see Introd. §5.

declared by the same man … to be most hostile to my well-being Clodius could well have made such representations in some assembly (cf. *Dom.* 22: Clodius reads out in a **contio* a letter purportedly from Caesar, on Cato's commission to Cyprus); but C. suppresses the fact that Caesar himself appeared at one of Clodius' assemblies (33 **assembly of the people** n.).

40. one of them had a very large army in Italy   Caesar, preparing to depart for his provinces (cf. *Red. sen.* 32, *Dom.* 5, 131, *Har. resp.* 47, 33 **voiced their approval** n.); but the army was not 'in Italy', for Caesar's existing legions were in Gallia Narbonensis (mod. southern France) and Aquileia (not then administratively part of 'Italy'), and his further recruiting was done in Cisalpine Gaul (Caes. *BGall.* 1. 6–10).

holding no office   The Lat. term is *privatus*, specifically denoting someone who is not a magistrate (cf. our 'private citizen'): cf. *Red. sen.* 31 'Today I have decided that I must give thanks by name to the magistrates and to one of those who hold no office (*privati*) (viz., Pompey)....'

could...raise and command their own armies   Early in his career Pompey raised a private army in Picenum, where his father had built a following (Plut. *Pomp.* 6. 1–2), and six years after this speech, on the eve of civil war, he said that he needed but to stamp on the ground in any part of Italy for an army to spring up (ibid. 57. 5); Crassus' maxim held that no man should be considered rich who could not support an army from his personal wealth (*Off.* 1. 25, Plut. *Crass.* 2. 7). In late summer 59 C. remarked the effect on Clodius himself of the fear of the triumvirs' 'resources, force, armies' (*Att.* 2. 22(42). 1), and before this trial, in Feb., C. told Quintus of Pompey's intention to 'summon people from the fields', marshaling forces to meet Clodius, with a 'large band expected from Picenum and Gaul' (*QFr.* 2. 3(7). 4).

no trial before the people...no chance to argue my case   C. names the institutions of Roman due process: a 'trial before the people' (*iudicium populi*) was held in the tribal assembly (**comitia tributa*) if the penalty was a fine, in the **centuriate assembly (**comitia centuriata*) if a man's **life as a citizen was at stake; a 'contest covered by law' (*legitima contentio*) was a trial like S.'s, a prosecution brought under a specific law before one of the **standing courts of inquiry (*quaestiones* *perpetuae*) administered by the praetors; and in either case there would be an exchange of views (*disceptatio*: cf. *Off.* 1. 34, *disceptatio* as the distinctively human way of resolving disputes vs. the violence of beasts) and a chance for both sides to make a 'statement of the case' (*causae dictio*).

aimed so wickedly at men of the greatest distinction   i.e. Clodius' threats defamed the triumvirs by falsely ascribing to them attitudes that would be dishonourable, because unjustified, if the ascription were true; cf. 132 **slandered ... by asserting** n.

people ... came to think ... the absence of denial a kind of acknowledgement   In his first recorded ref. to the triumvirs' silence after his return, C. said (*Red. sen.* 33): 'In circumstances where the commonwealth was reckoned to comprise two factions, people thought one of them was calling for my punishment out of personal enmity, while the other was afraid to defend me because they sensed bloody murder looming. Moreover, those who seemed to call for my punishment increased the dread of conflict by offering no denials to allay mens' anxiety.' Though also cast in terms of what 'people thought', that version does not call the reckoning false or state that the triumvirs were being used (it is also preceded by a more sharply critical ref. to Caesar, quoted at 39 **who was not obliged to be estranged** n.). The present formulation less openly imputes bad motives to the triumvirs, though it surely implies a kind of carelessness: cf. 8 **at no point** n. (Gaius Antonius' failure in 63 'to remove (by denial) ... the general terror of us all'), 16 **either (as I believe)** n. (Caesar's 'ignorant or careless' behaviour in 59). The triumvirs' silence is still an issue at *Planc.* 86; C. very likely recalled what he had said of the senate's judgement of Catiline, 'their silence concerning you shouts out' (*Cat.* 1. 21 *de te ... cum tacent, clamant*).

all they had accomplished ... undermined by ... the foremost men   Esp. the ends achieved by Caesar's agrarian legislation, the ratification of Pompey's settlement of the East, and Caesar's extended Gallic command: early in 58 the praetors Lucius Domitius Ahenobarbus and Gaius Memmius launched several attacks on these measures and on the (now former) tribune Vatinius (sources: *MRR* 2. 194; Suet. *Iul.* 23. 1 puts at least some of these attacks before Caesar's departure for Gaul). The 'foremost men' are the hardened optimate opposition, including Caesar's former consular colleague, Bibulus, Quintus Hortensius, and Cato, the last soon removed by the commission to Cyprus (59–63 below).

41. Crassus was saying..., while Pompeius appealed...   In view of the emphasis just placed on their public silence, these are evidently private communications, like the presumably private acknowledgement of personal interest just mentioned ('they said their own dangers...'); the Latin leaves unclear whether Crassus offered this opinion to C. or to the consuls, but the parallel with Pompey's actions is prob. meant to suggest the latter. See next n.

though he held no magistracy... as a matter of the public interest   Pompey's reported statement in effect counters the claim ascribed to Clodius in 40 ('(Pompey and Crassus), though then holding no office, could if they wanted to raise and command their own armies'). *Pis.* 77 elaborates Pompey's role: 'Didn't Lucius Lentulus, then the praetor, come to you (Piso), didn't Quintus Sanga (a senator), the elder Lucius Torquatus (cos. 65), Marcus Lucullus (cos. 73)? All these and many others too had gone to (Pompey)..., to beseech and entreat him not to abandon my interests, intertwined as they were with the commonwealth's well-being; and he sent them back to you and your colleague, (with the request) that you *take up my cause as a matter of the public interest* and refer it to the senate (cf. 25 above), (adding) that he did not wish to engage an armed tribune of the plebs without public authority (cf. 27 above), but that he would take up arms if the consuls acted to defend the commonwealth in accordance with the senate's decree' (i.e. the senate's 'ultimate decree', see 25 **all citizens** n.). As Nisbet remarks (1961, 146): 'deliberately misleading (so *Sest.* 41); Pompey was simply trying to pass the responsibility'; see also 67 below. For the threat of arms cf. Plut. *Pomp.* 47. 4–5 (sim. *Caes.* 14. 3, Cass. Dio 38. 5. 4): brought before an *assembly of the people by Caesar as consul, Pompey promised to meet force with force if resistance was offered to Caesar's legislation.

warned by agents posted at my house   Cf. *Dom.* 28, 55 and *Pis.* 76, alleging in the latter two places that Gabinius and Piso were responsible.

the same suspicion ... of others again On the chronology C. is following (see App. 1), the campaign must be set in early 58, after Vettius' allegations that Cicero was involved in a plot on Pompey's life (132 **Vettius** n.) and before C.'s departure. At 133 below C. places Vatinius among the whisperers (**advised a person** n.), while Piso and Gabinius are implicated at *Pis.* 76; cf. also *Dom.* 28. Not a month before the present speech Pompey had told C. that another plot was being laid against him (*QFr.* 2. 3(7). 4); on Pompey's recurrent fear of assassination, perhaps at times alleged for political gain, Marshall 1987.

he certainly feared nothing from me But see *Dom.* 28: 'inflamed by so many criminal allegations put about by certain people, he was not sufficiently ready to promise what my circumstances demanded'.

set some mischief in motion and blame it on me Plausible (cf. 82, on Numerius Rufus) but misleading: Pompey was avoiding C. out of treachery and bad conscience (cf. Introd. 1, App. 1).

Caesar himself ... was at the city gates See 40 **one of them had a very large army** n.

brother of my enemy Gaius Claudius (*RE* 303) Pulcher, second of the three brothers: then a *legate of Caesar (not mentioned in Caes. *BG*), at the time of the trial a praetor. Prob. because he was away on the service mentioned here, he was less active than Appius in supporting his brother against C. (cf. 77 ff.); later in 56 he helped Clodius when Cicero tried to remove from the Capitol the tablet inscribed with the law declaring him exiled (Cass. Dio 39. 21. 1–2). After governing Asia in 55–53, he was convicted of extortion (*repetundae*) in 51 and went into exile rather than pay the assessed damages (*TLRR* no. 336).

42. So when I took all this in ... what was I to do? At the last pause of this sort, in 35, C. said 'With matters standing this way (summarizing 25–34), ... still, judges, I would have stood fast.... But other fears and other anxious suspicions had me in turmoil.' Having now explained how those fears arose from Clodius' use of the triumvirs' names, he paints a picture of the *civil community in collapse like that in 35, now drawing in detail developed since that sketch. He then

puts the question central to his *apologia*: 'What was I to do?' The pose
of stock-taking resembles the attitude struck at *Fam.* 1. 9(20). 10, in
the *apologia* for his actions in and after 56. When C. strikes this pose,
we should expect the sequel to be maximally creditable to himself,
perhaps thereby improving on other, more truthful versions.

(**and none of it was hidden**)   The parenthetical figure, litotes, neg-
ates one quality to stress by implication its opposite ('not hidden' =
'obvious', 'blatant'): so very similarly *Clu.* 45 and *Leg. agr.* 2. 9,
perhaps in imitation of Dem. *On the Crown* 19, cf. Weische 1972,
57 f.

establishing public policy   i.e. *consilium publicum*, the senate's 'taking thought' for the *public interest that should result in sound
'public policy': see 27 **a matter of public policy** n.

harangues   The term *contio* can denote the *assembly of the people
convened by a magistrate or the address that he delivers there; the
idiom used here, *contionem habere* (lit. 'to have a *contio*'), can mean
'hold an assembly of the people' or 'deliver a harangue'. C. uses the
idiom in both senses indifferently (where the two can be distinguished at all: 'hold an assembly', 104 below, *Mil.* 27, *Phil.* 14. 16,
Att. 10. 4(195). 8, *Fam.* 5. 2(2). 7; 'deliver a harangue', *Clu.* 77, *Leg.
agr.* 2. 1, *Brut.* 305, *Or.* 30, *Att.* 1. 14(14). 5, 7. 8(131). 5). Here the
latter sense seems more likely, esp. with the phrase 'against me'
(*contra me*).

old forces of conspiracy... under a new leader   C. first tied Clodius
to the 'flock' (*grex*) of Catilinarian sympathizers—but not as their
leader—in Feb. 61 (*Att.* 1. 14(14). 5); by mid-May of that year, after
his acquittal in the Bona Dea affair, C. attacked him in the senate as
the peer of Catiline and Lentulus Sura (*Att.* 1. 16(16). 8–10 with *LUO*
nos. 29–30, cf. *FS* 227 ff.); a year later he again compared Clodius
with the Catilinarians in the senate (*Att.* 2. 1(21). 5 with *LUO no.* 36).
But only in the 'post-return' speeches does he regularly portray
Clodius as Catiline reborn, a 'Catiline with luck' (*felix Catilina*, a
nickname allegedly given him by his *henchmen: *Dom.* 72), whose
attacks on C. merely awakened Catiline's dormant conspiracy under
new leadership (*Dom.* 63, cf. *Red. sen.* 32–3, *Red. pop.* 13, *Dom.* 13,
61, 58, 75, 92, *Har. resp.* 5, 42, *Pis.* 11, 15, 23, *Mil.* 37, *Att.* 4. 3(75). 3,

cf. 111 **defended the commonwealth** n.). But no good evidence links Clodius to Catiline, whom he prosecuted in 65 (*TLRR* no. 212), and no common traits link their politics, beyond 'a willingness to exploit popular discontents and a willingness to turn to violent methods' (Tatum 1999, 145, noting that these traits were not unique to the two men, see also Lintott 1967). C. in part chooses this line of attack for personal reasons: since opposing Catiline defined his consulship, his opposition to any subsequent enemy would tend in his mind to resemble the earlier pattern. But there was also good practical reason to press the comparison in this speech: the more Clodius could be assimilated to Catiline, the more S.'s efforts on C.'s behalf could be assimilated to his noble efforts as *quaestor against Catiline (6–13 introd. n.).

43. a man with no public office... with a tribune of the plebs? C. glances both at a possible charge of *public violence and at the tribune's sacrosanct status (sim. *Red. sen.* 33, cf. 5 **tribunate** n.). Taken with the qualification just below, 'especially if (the tribune's blood was) spilled with no public authority (*consilium publicum)*', C.'s scruple here matches the concerns ascribed to Pompey at *Pis.* 77 (quoted 41 **though he held no magistracy** n.): 'he did not wish to engage an armed *tribune of the plebs without public authority (*consilium publicum*), but... he would take up arms if the consuls acted to defend the commonwealth in accordance with the senate's decree.' C. again emphasizes his status as one 'holding no office' (*privatus*) at 47 (sim. e.g. *Dom.* 91).

medicine... stopped... a plague C. joins two recurrent metaphors—of the embodied *commonwealth (1 **commonwealth... battered,** 17 **branded** nn.) and political opponents as a plague (33 **that demon, that plague**)—to produce the metaphor of the 'body politic' ailing and needing a cure. On C.'s use of the metaphor see Fantham 1972, 128–9, and cf. 135 **apply a cure** n.

I would have to contend with... his 'avengers' Sim. *Dom.* 55, 91 *Pis.* 78, *Planc.* 88. The consuls, of course, would regard themselves as suppressing a form of outlawry no better than Catiline's; see next n.

44. we could not maintain the commonwealth An outcome so catastrophic (cf. 47 **commonwealth... of slaves** n.) was wildly unlikely;

insofar as it supposes that C. would have found wide support in raising an armed resistance (cf. **39 If I defeated** n.), even mooting such a cataclysm tends to contradict his view elsewhere that he was beset on all sides by enemies and ill-wishers (cf. **46 some failed to defend me** n.). Because none of the triumvirs would have supported C., the forces involved would not have divided the community as they did in the civil war of 49: C. would have been quickly crushed, and it would have been left to the victors to describe for posterity their triumph over armed insurrection. But C. is less concerned here with probability and consistency than with establishing his character as a patriot, to prepare for the climactic passage about to come, on his exemplary self-sacrifice (45–50).

the same moment   The synchronism, already mentioned in 25, is treated more elaborately in 53.

45. some … hero   Lit. 'a man brave (*fortis*) and of a fierce and large spirit (*acris animi magnique*)'. C. uses special emphasis and mild sarcasm to suggest that it is always easy to urge another to die: though he speaks occasionally of the person with a 'keen' or 'fierce spirit', *acer animus* (*Mil.* 29, *Fin.* 1. 57, *Tusc.* 1. 52), and often of the *large-spirited person, nowhere else does he combine both attributes to limn the sort of fire-breathing hero imagined here. From exile, however, he spoke of this same option, of 'falling bravely', as one of the honourable alternatives preferable to the course he chose (*Fam.* 14. 3(9). 1).

I call you to witness   The oath is a solemn gesture that C. reserves for a key moment in an argument (*Caecin.* 83) or one otherwise deserving of high emotion (*Mur.* 78, *Sull.* 86, *Mil.* 85, *Phil.* 13. 20); he repeats it in the last sentence of the speech, 147.

gods of our hearths and our ancestors   After invoking the father-land itself (*patria*, uniquely in the orations for this purpose, but cf. *Mil.* 103), C. invokes its household and ancestral gods (*penates patriique dei*), as he does, for similar purposes and with slight variations in phrasing, at *Sull.* 86, *Dom.* 144, *Har. resp.* 37. There were *penates familiares*, the gods worshipped in individual Roman households (see 95 below, and cf. 30 **household gods** nn., on *penates* and *Lares familiares*), and *penates publici*, the gods of communal

Roman cult; the latter were associated both with the temple of Vesta
(Tac. *Ann.* 15. 41. 1) in the SE corner of the forum, where sacred
objects brought from Troy by Aeneas were kept (*NTDAR* 412–13,
LTUR 5. 125–8, *MAR* 256), and with their own temple on the Velia,
the slight rise farther to the ESE, on the Sacred Way (*NTDAR* 289,
LTUR 4. 75–8, *MAR* 189–90). Whichever form of the *penates*
C. intends, we can suppose that 'Cicero...turned to the temple of
Vesta as he addressed the *penates* (if he did not, it would have been an
opportunity missed)' (Berry 1996, 306).

it was for the sake...   From here through 50, C. purports to give us
his thinking at the moment of decision, in a version we cannot
confirm or refute absent C.'s correspondence between late fall 59
(*QFr.* 1. 2(2)) and March 58 (*Att.* 3. 1(46)). When refs. to the
decision begin to appear in the correspondence, we find C. describing it as a product of mental 'disturbance' and a cause of shamed
regret (esp. *QFr.* 1. 4(4). 4, *Fam.* 14. 3(9). 1–3). The rationale here is
very much the advice of Plutarch's Cato, that C. 'not cause an
uprising and throw the city into armed conflict and bloodshed but
yield to the crisis and once again become the fatherland's saviour'
(*Cat. min.* 35. 1, cf. Cass. Dio 38. 17. 4 at 39 **our bravest patriots** n.).
More surprisingly, Plutarch represents it as the advice given in a
'gentle' vein by the consul Piso, that C. 'stand aside and yield to
Clodius' onrush, endure the change in circumstances, and once again
become the "saviour of the fatherland" when it was suffering woeful
sedition' (*Cic.* 31. 4, prob. based on *Pis.* 78, where a similar piece of
advice is presented as a sarcastic taunt on Piso's part: see 49 **one man
alone** n.).

if I happened to be on a voyage with some friends   C. develops
another parable (see 24 **if you gave a sword** n.), here based on a
common theme of the rhetorical schools: Anon. *ad Herenn.* 4. 57
'The man who, while voyaging, does not put his ship's safety before
his own merits contempt; no less despicable is the man who, when
the commonwealth is in crisis, gives thought only to his own well-
being' (going on to the *exemplum* of Publius Decius, see following).
In adapting the theme, C. makes the safety of fellow-passengers (not
the ship itself) the issue and fits it out with touches particularly
pertinent to the context: the implied depiction of Clodius and his

supporters as 'pirates' (cf. esp. *Dom*. 24, on the 'pirate-in-chief and his flock of freebooters' endangering the ship of state, sim. *Red. sen*. 11, on Gabinius), the details drawn from the circumstances of Interkal.-March 58 (46 **armed vessels** n.), and the distinctively Roman ritual of *devotio* (48 **the elder Publius Decius** n.; C. expressly refers to his act as a *devotio* at *Red. pop*. 1, developing the conceit at length, sim. *Dom*. 64, 145, cf. Graff 1963, 32–3, Dyck 2004*b*). The rhetorical theme and the dilemma C. develops are both kin of the casuistical problems—apparent conflicts between 'expedience' (*utilitas*) and 'honour' (*honestas*)—treated at *Off*. 3. 50 ff., from Hellenistic ethical writings. C. had used a similar parable, more briefly and to quite different effect, when venting his pique at the senatorial conservatives in April 59: 'I would rather have a rocky voyage with a bad pilot than steer a good course (myself) for such ungrateful passengers' (*Att*. 2. 9(29). 3).

hordes of pirates   As mention of slaves would raise the specter of Spartacus (9 **Gaius Marcellus**, 34 **a levy of slaves** nn.), mention of pirates would remind the audience of the Mediterranean corsairs fought a decade earlier by the forces under Pompey, and still not eradicated: see Siani-Davies 2001, 166 (on *Rab. Post*. 20), and on Rome's efforts against piracy Pohl 1993, 208–82, De Souza 1999, 97–178.

I would hurl myself into the depths   The choice of self-sacrifice, prompted by the friends' refusal to abandon him, is sleight of hand: the friends' stance places on the pirates' side the enemies to be catalogued in 46 (**some felt … some hurt** n.), implicitly including Caesar and his fellow-advocate Hortensius; suicide, treated here as creditable, is rejected in 47–50 as harmful to the *commonwealth. Drowning was generally not regarded as a suitably aristocratic form of self-killing: Grisé 1982, 94.

46. armed vessels … poised to attack   C. refers both to the general menace of the *desperadoes and to Clodius' threats (40–1) of Caesar's army and the armies Pompey and Crassus could raise.

proscription   At *Dom*. 43–5 and 48, C. equates punishment of a citizen without trial—what he repeatedly says he suffered—with the Sullan *proscriptions (cf. also 133 below, *Dom*. 58, *Pis*. 30), and that is surely what he intends here; his claim bears esp. on Clodius' second law against him, imposing the 'ban on fire and water' by name, see 65 nn. The effects of Sulla's proscriptions, the first use of the procedure, were still felt (male descendants of the proscribed were barred from public life until 49); C. was to die in Dec. 43 during the proscriptions begun by the second triumvirate.

some failed to defend me...   This longish catalogue is not fully consistent with the impresssion C. otherwise tries to convey, that only the corrupt consuls, Clodius, and his hirelings opposed him. With the categories here, cf. the categories of the *commonwealth's enemies at 99 below; for a shorter list used to a similar end, e.g. *Red. pop.* 13; for a longer, slightly different, and more particular list, *Red. pop.* 21.

some felt...some hurt   Those 'who thought (C.) stood in their way' included, in C.'s view, Caesar (16 **either (as I believe)** n.). C. often yokes the other two categories—the *invidi* (variously 'spiteful' or 'envious') and *inimici* ('personal enemies')—usually to assign responsibility for misfortune: e.g. as he was about to leave Italy (29 April 58), he wrote that he had fallen 'through the utterly criminal wrongs done me, not so much by *inimici* as by *invidi*' (*Att.* 3. 7(52). 2), and at 121 below he speaks of 'those hostile to my person (= *inimici*) and envious of my success (= *invidi*).' *Inimici*, 'personal enemies', believed you had wronged them and therefore felt obliged to wrong you in return (cf. 2 **thanking** n.): they are the people who 'wanted to avenge some hurt'. The *invidi* were hostile because you enjoyed some good they wanted for themselves ('envy') or resented your having ('spite' or 'malice'), or both (Kaster 2005, 86–103). C. believed that the conservative *notables harboured such feelings for him as a *new man (136 n. and e.g. *Verr.* 2. 5. 182, *Mur.* 17); though he need not be thinking of them here (cf. 138, on the *optimates themselves as targets of *inimici* and *invidi*), the notables' *invidia* was a theme well before his exile (e.g. *Att.* 1. 19(19). 6, 1. 20(20). 3, 2. 1(21). 7, all from the first half of 60). Whereas *inimici* were known as such and open in their hostility, the *invidi* disguised their feelings and even posed as friends: thus catching their victim off guard, they could do more harm than *inimici* (cf. *Att.* 3. 7(52). 2, quoted above). C. at times placed Quintus Hortensius (3 n.) in that category: see esp. *Att.* 3. 9(54). 2, referring to 'Hortensius and men of that ilk' and adding, 'Don't you see yet who worked to bring me down through their criminal treachery? ... I'm saying no more than you know: it was *invidi*, not *inimici*, who destroyed me' (cf. *QFr.* 1. 3(3). 8, *Fam.* 1. 9(20). 13, Shackleton Bailey on *Att.* 3. 8(53). 4). But though C. sometimes names names, he often leaves the impression that he has no particular people in mind (e.g. *Fam.* 14. 3(9). 2 '*inimici* are many, *invidi* almost universal'), and he is ready to invoke the same categories to explain others' woes (e.g. *Fam.* 1. 9(20). 2, on the *inimici* and *invidi* besetting Lentulus Spinther). This is simply how the world behaves, and these categories are a way of representing it.

meet and undergo... over everyone's head Similarly *Dom.* 63, 96 cf. 45 **if I happened to be sailing** n. (on the self-sacrifice of *devotio*) and 49 **protected** n.

47. 'The wicked would have been beaten.' Yes, but they were fellow-citizens. For the exchange with an imagined interlocutor (*sermocinatio*), cf. 20 **Still** n. For the scruple over the status of 'fellow-citizens', cf. *Dom.* 63 'But if I had wanted to meet force with force and have a fight to the finish, ... either I would have prevailed, with a huge toll of the wicked—but citizens still—or....' We are to understand that this scuple distinguishes C. from his enemies.

by resort to arms... The MSS lack this phrase, but the phrase 'without resort to arms' (*sine armis*) in the next clause wants the same pointed contrast found in 'consul' vs. 'person without public standing'; the phrase *at armis* (lit. 'but with arms'), first proposed by Heraeus, is preferable to other suggestions. At *Planc.* 86 a similar structure is used to spin the matter differently: 'Would it have been a great achievement for me to fight it out under arms with the remnants of (the Catilinarians), whom I had vanquished without arms when they were fresh and in their prime?'

commonwealth... of slaves C. makes a similar, hyperbolic prophecy at *Dom.* 92 (cf. ibid. 110): in both places he means that the 'gladiator' (Clodius: 55 below) and the slaves he allegedly marshaled (cf. 34, 53, 75, 81, 95) would have taken control for good. The idea is more clearly expressed at *Planc.* 87: 'We would have had to fight it out under arms...; and when slaves and their leaders had used these arms to slaughter the senate and (all) patriots, it would have been the end of the commonwealth.' Cf. *Fam.* 1. 9(20). 13, *Mil.* 36, and already *Cat* 2. 19 (the Catilinarians seek power to the community's ruin, for once gained it must pass to 'some fugitive slave or gladiator').

ought I have calmly met my death?   The phrase C. uses (*mortem oppetere*, lit. denoting active pursuit, 'to set (one's) course toward') can describe death met aggressively in conflict (e.g. 23 'face death on behalf of the fatherland', 29 'meet death on behalf of the commonwealth', 45 'met death in battle') or by one's own hand (e.g. *Verr.* 2. 3. 129, *Fin.* 3. 61). Since C. has already explained why he rejected armed resistance, and so the chance of falling in combat, he means now to explain why he rejected suicide: on the strategy of 47–50 as a whole, next n. In March 58 he did consider, and perhaps even prefer, suicide: when in flight he wrote that he hoped one day to thank Atticus for 'forcing' him to live (*Att.* 3. 3 (47)), while the letters from his first five months in exile repeatedly express a desire for death and regret at having missed the 'most honourable moment' of meeting it (see *Att.* 3. 7(52). 2, *Fam.* 14. 4(6). 1, 5, *Att.* 3. 9(54). 1, *QFr.* 1. 3(3). 1–2, 6, 1. 4(4). 4); one of the latest letters from exile still makes veiled reference to the possibility of suicide (*Fam.* 5. 4(10). 2, mid-Jan. 57, with Shackleton Bailey ad loc.).

On these earlier occasions and in this speech C.'s thinking owes more to Roman tradition than to Greek philosophy (Griffin 1986 lucidly surveys the latter). Though Stoic ethics, embraced with increasing warmth as C. aged, held that a 'well-reasoned exit from life' could be sought when circumstances warranted it, a Stoic sage would judge that C.'s circumstances did not meet the standard: the matters that occupy C. both in his correspondence and here (family, possessions, and esp. honour: see 48 below and *Att.* 3. 7(52). 2, *QFr.* 1. 4(4). 4) are all, in Stoic term, 'external goods' quite distinct from the only true good—virtue—identified with the wholly internal actions of a mind making choices in accord with right reason; loss of these external goods, and the resultant external evils (solitude, poverty, disgrace), should not prevent the mind from making right choices (C. addresses this issue esp. at *Fin.* 3. 60–1, cf. C.'s treatments of the important *exemplum* of Marcus Atilius Regulus cited at 127 n.; on C.'s treatment of suicide in the philosophical works more generally, Hill 2004,

31–71). As C. soon remarks, however, there was good Roman precedent for destroying oneself, either to benefit the community or to
escape the pain of disgrace: see the examples in 48 (where the elder
Crassus most closely matches C.'s case), the long catalog of exemplary
suicides at *Scaur.* 1–6 (where the elder Crassus stands first in the
fragmentary text), and the catalogue in Hooff 1990, 198–232. On his
return (*Red. sen.* 34) C. addresses the thought that he might have
committed suicide ('if I thought that perpetual misery lay before
me'), saying that he rejected it on prudential grounds (he foresaw his
restoration: cf. *Red. pop.* 14, *Dom.* 64). The stunningly self-aggrandiz-
ing argument developed below (49–50) appears first here and receives
an encore at *Planc.* 90. In 46 Cato's suicide again made the option a
matter for C.'s reflection, if only to consider why he did not choose it
himself (cf. *Fam.* 9. 18(191). 2, *Off.* 1. 112, and esp. *Fam.* 4. 13(225). 2,
with Griffin 1986, 196–7, Hill 2004, 64–71). When the time came three
and a half years later, he did meet death calmly (Plut. *Cic.* 48. 2–4).

did I do what I did to escape death? . . . In the following argument
C. moves nimbly from rejecting avoidance of death as a cowardly
motive (47–8) to embracing avoidance of death as a desirable *outcome*
beneficial to the community (49–50). In 47–8 the argument's main
device is the rhetorical question, eight of which (in the Latin) are
strung together in a remarkable series. (Because the translation re-
solves several of these into smaller units in a way more congenial to
English, it has eleven consecutive questions.) The effect is of a boxer
throwing a flurry of jabs, or a wrestler throwing sand in his opponent's eyes; in any case, we are to applaud the sentiments animating the
questions without considering the questions too closely. If we do, we
see that the literal answer to this first question is an uninteresting
'Of course not' (in leaving Rome after Clodius' first law was passed,
C. anticipated a prosecution in which the possible sentence was exile,
not death) and that two others—framing death 'as a gift offered up for
the sake of the fatherland' and 'faced on the commonwealth's behalf'—are otiose once he has rejected armed resistance to 'the wicked'
and is discussing only the disposition of his own life. But because C.'s
mind insistently shuttles between the events of 58 and those of 63
(next n.), he might well have been unaware of the lack of fit.

engaged in matters of such great moment ... Did I not foretell all this ...? C. seemingly refers to the 'matters' leading to his exile in 58, but his thought again recurs to Dec. 63 (cf. 38 **The things** n.): by speaking of prophecy he refers to statements like *Cat.* 4. 3 'if anything should befall me, I shall die with mind calm and composed' and esp. *Cat.* 4. 20 'But if at some point that rabble, *roused by some man's frenzied crime*, should overpower your worthy standing and the commonwealth's, I shall still never regret my actions and my policies'—a passage that foresees Clodius' actions so pointedly that some have thought it was added before C. published his consular speeches in 60.

exile The only place in the speech where C. uses the term (*exsilium*) even hypothetically of himself, preferring to speak of his 'misfortune' (29 n.) or 'departure' (49, 128) or of the period 'while I was away' (50): cf. Robinson 1994b and *Dom.* 72–92 (denying the appropriateness of the term). For the label hurled at him as an insult by Crassus in 55, see 39 **Marcus Crassus** n.; by Gabinius in 54, see *QFr.* 3. 2(22). 2.

mine by nature or by fortune C.'s children, about to be mentioned for the first time (49), were his 'by nature'; his various properties (cf. 54) are the 'gifts of fortune', as he puts it at *Dom.* 146.

Had I heard, seen, learned *nothing* ...? In philosophy and history, that is. The rest of the paragraph briefly develops a 'commonplace' (Lat. *locus communis*): in rhetorical theory this is not a 'platitude' or 'cliché', as in ordinary Eng. usage (though the passage suggests why the association arose), but a theme or topic (Gk. *topos* = Lat. *locus* = Eng. 'place') applicable not to one case or argument only but to a range of arguments, and in that sense common (Gk. *koinos* = Lat. *communis* = Eng. 'common') to them (cf. Lausberg 1998, §§1126–8). Here the 'topic' can be defined as 'choosing appropriate action given life's brevity'; cf. e.g. the commonplace on the development of human society at 91–2 below, on the vagaries of youth at *Cael.* 39–42, and on gratitude at *Planc.* 80–1.

glory eternal The proposition that *manly deeds on the *commonwealth's behalf would spread your fame, causing peers to judge you excellent and posterity to remember you respectfully, 'forever', supported Republicanism's contractualist ethic, providing the political elite with much of its motivation and consolation (1 **If anyone** n., cf. 143 **Accordingly** n.). C. often invokes the proposition in comparable terms: e.g. *Arch.* 28, *Balb.* 49, *Pis.* 7, 57–63, *Mil.* 82, 93–4, 96–7 (putting his own thoughts in Milo's mouth), *Fam.* 5. 12(22). 2, 9, and cf. 48 **standing** n. He less often qualifies it by stipulating that only the judgement of good (i.e. *patriotic) men matters (e.g. 139 below, *Tusc.* 3. 3–4) or by adding that good (i.e. patriotic) actions ought to be performed for their own sake, not to achieve another end (note esp. *Mil.* 96–7, with e.g. *Rep.* 1. 27, *Fam.* 15. 4(110). 13 (to Cato)). Only near the end of his life, in *Off.*—when the Republic's ruin made plain the cost of power-seeking disguised as glory-seeking—does he qualify it more fundamentally, by granting it a role only as a cooperative value tied to justice. See Sullivan 1941, Knoche 1967, Haury 1974, Lind 1979, 16–19, 57–8, Thomas 1994, and esp. Long 1995.

since death is a certainty... until nature makes its claim   The last phrase introduces a metaphor not present in the Lat. (lit. 'not held in reserve for nature'), to make the meaning plain. For the thought centring on the fatherland, cf. e.g. *Phil.* 10. 20, 12. 30, 14. 31, Anon. *ad Herenn.* 4. 55

the very wisest men have disagreed   The first view is Epicurean: because being ends entirely with death, the time of non-existence after death should be no more terrible for us than the like time before we were born. The second view is associated most prominently with Plato: the imperishable soul is imprisoned in the body and experiences true being only after it is freed from the body by death. For C.'s meditations on the immortality of the soul see esp. *Tusc.* 1. 26–81; for the commonplace opposition of the two views, cf. *Leg.* frag. lib. inc. 2 (Dyck 2004*a*, 558).

48. standing of which I was held worthy   i.e. his *dignitas*: the following remarks ('a consular with such a record of achievement') stress the elements of standing most in his mind here. For a member of the Roman elite, self-consciously gauging his actions by the canon of his *worthy standing should be a matter of reflex: cf. the thoughts attributed to Milo in similar circumstances at 87 below and Servius Sulpicius Rufus' exhortation to C., overwhelmed by grief at Tullia's death in 45 (*Fam.* 4. 5(248). 5). We can follow C. as he regards his *dignitas* in the run-up to the conflict with Clodius: writing in March 60, he says 'having once achieved an extraordinary and immortal glory (cf. above) from the great (events of 5 Dec. 63)..., I have not ceased to engage in the people's business with the same largeness of spirit and to maintain the *dignitas* then achieved and accepted' (*Att.* 1. 19(19). 6, cf. 1. 20(20). 2); as Clodius' threats loomed larger, in July 59, he could say 'the conflicts in prospect concern me only moderately, for I think that I can either face them with the utmost *dignitas* or dodge them with no great effort'—at the same time imagining Atticus' response, 'Enough with the old song about *dignitas*! Please: take thought for your well-being (*salus*)!' (*Att.* 2. 19(39). 1); and a month later, in the penultimate extant letter to Atticus before exile, he says, 'I'm absolutely sick of life, seeing every form of misery everywhere I look.... Still: I'm confident and calm(!), and I maintain both <my well-being and> my *dignitas* very carefully and honourably' (*Att.* 2. 24(44). 4).

consular   A former consul and therefore an elder statesmen of the senate, asked for his views early in any debate. When the consul Piso established the order of precedence in Jan. 58 he served C.'s *dignitas* by calling upon him third (*Red. sen.* 17, *Pis.* 11: the others are unknown, but on 1 Jan. 57 Lucius Cotta and Pompey apparently spoke first and second, cf. 73 below).

the daughters of king Erechtheus   Erechtheus saved Athens in a war with Eleusis by sacrificing one or more of his daughters, described in some versions of the myth as volunteers (Gantz 1993, 1. 242–3): *Schol. Bob.* 131. 13–16 St. and C. at *Tusc.* 1. 116 refer to such a version (cf. *Fin.* 5. 62), consistent with his description here and with the Roman *exempla* to follow, esp. the Decii; only here does C. apply an example from myth to himself (Sinkovich 1976, 189). Varro was prob. not C.'s source, despite *Schol. Bob.* 131. 16–17 St. (the work cited, *Antiquitates rerum humanarum* 2 was prob. written after 56: *RE* Suppl. 6 (1935), 1230 (H. Dahlmann)); in Euripides' *Erechtheus* the daughters not chosen for sacrifice vowed to join in death the one who was (frag. 360, 370 Kannicht), and C. perhaps knew this version, either directly or as mediated by Ennius' *Erechtheus*. Here and elsewhere C. qualifies such refs. ('I believe') to avoid parading his knowledge of Greek literary and philosophical culture: cf. *Sex. Rosc.* 46, *Verr.* 2. 4. 39, *Pis.* 69, *Scaur.* 4, and 23 **this or that philosopher** n., with Berry 2004, 302–3; contrast the tactic at *Mur.* 61, where C., touching on Stoic philosophy, flatters the judges as men conversant with the higher culture—though the manner of his exposition (as Berry ibid. remarks) shows that he assumes their ignorance.

Gaius Mucius With the Decii (next n.) and Regulus (127 n.), among the most often cited examples of patriotic self-sacrifice: when the Etruscan king Lars Porsenna tried to force Rome to restore the disgraced Tarquin the Proud to his throne, Gaius Mucius (*RE* 10) slipped into the enemy camp, intending to assassinate Porsenna; taken captive, he thrust his right hand into a fire and, as it burned, warned Porsenna that Rome had many other such men: 'Take a good look, so you know how cheap they hold their bodies when their sights are set on great glory' (so Livy's version: 2. 12–13. 5, with Ogilvie 1965, 262–3). Released by Porsenna, who was awed by his *courage, Mucius thereafter bore the honourific nickname Scaevola, 'Lefty'.

the elder Publius Decius, then some years later his son Two canonical tales of Roman heroism: leading his army against the Latins as consul in 340, Publius Decius (*RE* 15) Mus 'devoted' himself and the opposing army to the gods of the underworld i.e. voluntarily gave up his own life in return for his army's safety and victory (sources: *MRR* 1. 135, esp. Livy 8. 19–11. 1 with Oakley 1998, 477–86; on the ritual, Versnel 1976 and 1980); his son (*RE* 16) imitated him when, as consul in 295, he commanded an army against the Gauls (*MRR* 1. 177). The second story is sometimes thought a fiction spun from the first (or vice versa); in any case, C. returns to the edifying model at 143 below, sim. *Dom.* 64, *Rab. Post.* 2, *Phil.* 5. 48, and esp. the philosophical works: *Fin.* 5. 64, *Tusc.* 2. 59, *Parad.* 1. 12, *Sen.* 75, *Off.* 1. 61; *Fin.* 2. 61 and *Tusc.* 1. 89 seem to imply that a third Decius, in command against Pyrrhus in 279, followed his father and grandfather, but C.'s language is (perhaps intentionally) equivocal, and the awkward fact that the Romans lost the battle makes the story problematic in any case. Cf. 45 **if I happened to be on a voyage** n.

within living memory the father of Marcus Crassus Stressing that this *exemplum* is not drawn from 'ancient history', C. implies that the age of heroes is not past (cf. 101, distinguishing ancient and recent *exempla*). C. might emphasize continuity to disguise the *un*likeness of the other two examples (death chosen for the common good) and this example of suicide from more personal, honour-based motives: had C. chosen suicide in 58, it would have been for reasons more like Crassus' (cf. 47 **ought I have calmly met my death?** n.). The triumvir's father, Publius Licinius (*RE* 61) Crassus (cos. 97, cens. 89), died opposing Marius and Cinna in 87: C. casts him as a noble suicide, as at *De or.* 3. 10, *Scaur.* 1–3 (cf. Asc. 23–4 Cl., Marshall 1985, 140), *Scaur.* showing that the nobility lay in preferring death to the disgrace of 'falling into his enemy's hands', the fate implied here (at *Tusc.* 5. 55 Crassus is one of many *notables whom Cinna ordered decapitated—posthumously, if we suppose C. is consistent: cf. Rawson 1991, 554). In another version Marius' *legate Gaius Flavius Fimbria executes Crassus and the triumvir's older brother (Lucan 2. 125, Plut. *Crass.* 4. 1, 6. 3, sim. Flor. 2. 9. 14); for apparent attempts to harmonize the traditions, see Livy *Perioch.* 80 (Crassus kills himself after his son is killed by Fimbria's cavalry) and App. *BCiv.* 1. 72 (Crassus kills his son, anticipating their pursuers, who then kill him).

49. if my death had the effect ... the commonwealth would perish with me   The condition distributed between these two sentences presents C.'s premise, as he moves from rejecting the option of death to embracing the choice of life as a noble duty (47 **did I do what I did** n.). So far from being valid, however, the condition is the most brazen move in a speech not lacking for brass, there plainly being no reason to suppose that C.'s death would have had the posited effect. Cf. 1 **if anyone** n. for the tendentious use of conditional clauses to frame an issue.

Accordingly   The inferential particle (*igitur*) joining this sentence to the last could point either to the conclusion he drew at the time ('Following this line of reasoning, I acted to save....') or to the conclusion he thinks his present argument has secured ('On this line of reasoning, I can now be seen to have saved...'): he presumably means the latter, as the next clauses suggest.

my departure   On C.'s preference for some term other than 'exile', see 47 **exile** n. We have now reached *c.*18 March 58 in C.'s narrative: for the date see App. 1.

I protected ... from slaughter After the Catilinarians' suppression, Lucius Gellius (cos. 72, cens. 70) said in the senate that C. deserved the 'civic crown' (*corona civica*: *Pis.* 6), an oak-leaf garland awarded to a soldier who had saved a fellow-soldier in battle, slain the enemy, and held the contested ground (Polyb. 6. 39. 6–7, Plin. *HN* 16. 7–14, Gell. 5. 6. 11–15). Since C. is equating his actions in 63 and 58 (next n.), he means to connote that sort of merit, if he does not allude directly to Gellius' remark.

one man alone ... my grief C. develops the same thought still more elaborately at *Dom.* 76, and the motif 'I twice saved' (or the like) recurs at *Red. sen.* 36, *Red. pop.* 13, *Dom.* 99, *Pis.* 78 (a taunt attributed to Piso, replying to a delegation on C.'s behalf: '(He said) I could save the commonwealth again, if I withdrew'); cf. 43, 73 (Cotta's speech), Vell. 2. 45. 2.

never deny ... no grief In *Cat.* 4. 3 C. anticipates that acting against Catiline might one day cost him his brother, wife, children, and son-in-law; in this sentence and the following two he revives those sentiments and with them the burden of *Dom.* 97–8, 'Nor do I claim for myself the wisdom some desiderated when they said my spirit was too broken and battered. ...' C. implies that strong emotion of this sort is both natural ('I shall never deny that I am human': cf. esp. *Tusc.* 3. 12–13) and correlated with the value of his actions ('if I had been unmoved, what sort of favour...', a thought repeated below): radically opposed to the Stoic view of emotion that C. elaborates eleven years later in *Tusc.* 3–4 (Graver 2002), the statement perhaps alludes to criticism by the Stoic Cato, who advised him at the time of his withdrawal (cf. 39 **what our bravest patriots ...**, 45 **it was for the sake ... nn.**); alternatively, or additionally, it acknowledges non-sectarian criticism of the sort he experienced in 45, when his daughter's death enveloped him in a grief some thought unbecoming in a man of his stature (implied by e.g. *Att.* 12. 20(258). 1, 12. 28(267). 2). The letters to Atticus and his wife from the first months of exile, many of them blending paranoia, grief, shame, and despair, do more nearly suggest a man unhinged than any even of those after Tullia's death; Atticus, at least, urged C. to get a grip on himself, while reporting rumors that he was actually deranged (*Att.* 3. 13(59). 2).

brother C.'s younger brother, Quintus Tullius (*RE* 31) Cicero (praetor 62), had been governing Asia since 61 and was away from Rome during C.'s crisis: he left his province at the end of April 58, returning to Rome to work for his brother's restoration (68, 76, 145 below, *Red. sen.* 37, *Red. pop.* 5, 7–8, *Dom.* 59, cf. *QFr.* 1. 4(4). 5, *Att.* 3. 22(67). 1, 3. 26(71)) and to prepare to defend himself against an anticipated prosecution (*TLRR* no. 263, see esp. *Att.* 3. 8(53). 2–3, 3. 9(54). 1, *QFr.* 1. 3(3). 4, 1. 4(4). 2, 5, *Att.* 3. 17(62), 1, 3. 19(64). 3), which did not come about. After C.'s return, Quintus provided an important liaison first with Pompey, on whose staff he served in 57–56 (see esp. *Fam.* 1. 9(20). 9), and then with Caesar, whom he served similarly in 54–51, winning distinction in the Gallic Wars. After serving on C.'s staff in Cilicia, he joined the Pompeian side in the civil war and after Pharsalus received Caesar's pardon. Like C., Quintus and his homonymous son were murdered in the proscriptions of 43.

children ... wife Cicero had two children by his first wife, Terentia. The elder, Tullia (*RE* Tullius 60), was already married to Gaius Calpurnius Piso Frugi (54 n.) by 63 and after his premature death in 57 had two other marriages, to Furius (*RE* 54) Crassipes and Publius Cornelius (*RE* 141) Dolabella, both ending in divorce; she died in childbirth in Feb. 45, causing C. a grief matched only by that of his exile. His son, Marcus (*RE* 30), born in 65, was still a child at the time of this trial. Serving with Brutus and the 'liberators' away from Italy in 43–42, he was the only male member of the family to survive the *proscriptions; after benefiting from the amnesty of 39 he ultimately threw in his lot with his near contemporary, Octavian, whose colleague he was as suffect consul in 30. Terentia herself (*RE* Terentius 95), a wealthy and well-born woman (her uterine sister, Fabia, was a Vestal Virgin), remained in Rome while C. was away and played an important role in managing the family's interests (see *Fam.* 14. 1–4(8, 7, 9, 6)); in the 'post-return' speeches she and the children serve as pathetic tokens of C.'s suffering and his enemies' iniquity (54, 145, *Red. pop.* 8, *Dom.* 59, 96). She and C. were divorced in (prob.) 46, for reasons that are not quite clear.

what sort of favour ... held cheap The favour's value to the recipient is assumed to be directly proportional to its cost to the benefactor, which in turn is gauged by the intensity of his emotion: cf. **never deny** n. above.

50. I remember Marius' flight and exile of 88–87, about to be invoked, fell late in C.'s teens: he says he heard the story from Marius himself (*Red. pop.* 20), and he refers to it often (*Verr.* 2. 2. 110–11, 113, *Red. sen.* 38, *Red. pop.* 7, 10–11, 19–21, *Pis.* 43, *Planc.* 26, *Parad.* 2. 16, *Div.* 1. 106, 2. 140, *Fin.* 2. 105); for the narrative, Plut. *Mar.* 34–44 (a hostile account). C. uses the story to highlight his own unselfish behaviour (sim. *Red. sen.* 38): the *exemplum* thus serves the same function as the earlier case of Metellus Numidicus (37), C.'s rhetoric giving two great enemies a unity of purpose they did not otherwise enjoy.

godlike C. applies the epithet *divinus* to humans only metaphorically, to denote someone who is 'god*like*'—esp. as a benefactor whose excellence has enhanced some aspect of human life—not someone to whom divinity is ascribed (for the metaphorical sense in C. and elsewhere in Latin, *TLL* s.v. *divinus* 1624. 11–1625. 7, cf. Classen 1993). The epithet was later applied in that spirit to C. himself, with respect to his eloquence (e.g. by his admirer Quintilian: 1. 6. 18, 2. 16. 7, 4. 1. 70, 4. 3. 13, 11. 1. 62), and in his dialogue *On the Orator* C. has his characters use the epithet similarly (e.g. 1. 40); in his own voice, however, he applies it almost exclusively to political actors who have benefited the *commonwealth. Within that frame of reference he uses the epithet freely of his supporters (Milo at 85–6 below, where the phrase *divini hominis* makes the metaphorical sense plain, and *Har. resp.* 6; Milo and S. together at *Red. pop.* 15; Publius Lentulus at *Red. sen.* 28) and of relatively few others: Marius again at *Rab. perd.* 29 and *Prov. cons.* 32, Scipio Aemilianus (*Mur.* 75, *Arch.* 16), Pompey (*Leg. Man.* 10, *Phil.* 2. 39), Cato (*Fin.* 3. 6), and the 'godlike youth' Octavian (*Phil.* 4. 4, 5. 43). The metaphor is used less frequently in the correspondence, of Caesar's *generosity to himself and Quintus in 54 (*Fam.* 1. 9(20). 18) and of the 'favour' done the commonwealth by Caesar's murderers ten years later (*Fam.* 10. 28(364). 1, sim. *Att.* 14. 14(368). 3, *MBrut.* 23. 7).

sprung from the same roots as I ... Gaius Marius C. refers primarily to their common origin in Arpinum (37 **Gaius Marius** n.), though the town's three leading families—the Marii, the Tullii, and the Gratidii—also had kinship ties through intermarriage.

in deep old age   Vell. 2. 19. 2 puts his flight to Minturnae in 88 (below) 'after his sixth consulship (held in 100) and his 70th year', sim. Plut. *Mar.* 41. 4 ('over 70 years' in 87).

force of arms raised almost justly against him   The arms belonged to Sulla, elected consul for 88 with the command against Mithradates allotted to him, when Marius schemed with the tribune Sulpicius Rufus to have the plebs transfer the command to himself; Sulla then marched on Rome with six legions and took the city while Marius fled (sources: *MRR* 2. 40). C. acknowledges the highhandedness of Marius's maneuver in the epithet 'just' (*vim armorum prope iustorum*), qualified by 'almost' because Sulla's march on Rome was not unproblematic itself. (I prefer this reading to taking *arma iusta* as = *bellum iustum* = 'formal, regular warfare': 'a violent struggle which was almost a pitched battle' Gardner 1958*a*, 'the violence of what might almost be called regular warfare' Shackleton Bailey 1991*a*; for *bellum prope iustum* in the sense understood here, cf. *Prov. cons.* 4, quoted at 94 **peoples of Thrace** n., on the war waged by the Thracians provoked by Piso's extortion. The ambivalence of the phrase 'raised almost justly' is consistent with Marius' ambivalent standing as an *exemplum* here, while the aptness of specifying the 'regularity' of the warfare is less apparent: what was remembered of the occasion was not the violence or formality of Marius' resistance to Sulla, but its brevity and weakness: e.g. Plut. *Mar.* 35. 5, *Sull.* 9. 5–7.)

Minturnae   A town near the coast of Italy between Latium and Campania; for the episode see most elaborately Plut. *Mar.* 37–9. C. uses Marius' flight there, and the time spent hiding in the nearby marshes, for various exemplary purposes at *Red. pop.* 20, *Pis.* 43, *Planc.* 26.

the most desolate shores of Africa   Acc. to Vell. 2. 19. 4, he lived in a hovel on the site of Carthage's ruins; acc. to Plut. *Mar.* 40. 3–4, he visited the vicinity of Carthage but, barred from settling there by the Roman governor, moved on to Cercina (ibid. 7), one of the small islands SE of Carthage off the coast of mod. Tunisia.

boded no good for the commonwealth The MSS offer various forms of nonsense: my translation is based on Pantagathus' emendation, *fatum*, adopted by Maslowski and Gardner 1958*a* (*ad rei publicae fatum*, lit. 'to / for the commonwealth's doom', cf. *Dom.* 145 *in illo paene fato rei publicae*); other alternatives (Peterson's *interitum*, 'death, destruction'; Jacob's *casum*, 'fall, misfortune', adopted by Cousin 1965 and Shackleton Bailey 1991*a*) aim at much the same sense. The point is that the events C. has in mind—Marius' violent return to Rome with Cinna and the internecine war that followed—were disasters prompted by one man's desire to avenge his injured honour, in notable contrast to C.'s own behaviour. C. stresses different facets of the story according to his audience: at *Red. sen.* 38 Marius is said to have 'almost destroyed the entire senate on his return'; at *Red. pop.* 7 C. stresses the 'most unworthy misfortune' that Marius suffered in his exile. On C.'s tendency to place responsibility for the civil war forced by Marius' return more squarely on Cinna, see Carney 1960, 115–16.

the commonwealth had a crucial stake in my staying alive Lit. 'I was living at the commonwealth's hazard' (*periculo rei publicae vivebam*): the idiom conveys that C.'s life was critically important to the *commonwealth, hence its responsiblity (*OLD* s.v. *periculum* 4b)—not (of course) that his life posed a risk to the commonwealth—and resumes the identification of self-interest and public interest central to his strategy (Introd. §3).

commended...by the consuls The consuls are not Gabinius and Piso in 58 but, by anticipation, Lentulus and Nepos in 57: on this resolution of the senate see 116 **honour had been paid** n.

if that model is maintained, imperishable Sc. by gaining 'glory eternal' (47 n.), bestowing on C. the patriot's reward and causing the *commonwealth to benefit from those who imitate him, in the ideally complementary relationship of personal glory and communal *well-being.

51–2. *A Transition Back to the Narrative*

C. has finished defending his decision to withdraw (36–50) and moves to resume the events of 58 (53–66). Three quick strokes suffice: he draws a (somewhat misleading) contrast between external peace and domestic division, throwing all stress on the latter (51); he extends a major premise of his *apologia*—that he acted as he did in the domestic sphere to set an example for generations to come—by explicitly addressing the youth whom the example should edify and reassure (51); and he bases his reassurance, in part, on the claim that the monsters faced in 58 were of a sort never to be seen again (52). With the consuls and Clodius once again squarely in his sights, he briefly reminds his audience of their enormities: Clodius' threatening use of the triumvirs' names (cf. 39–41); the consuls' edict forbidding the senate to wear mourning (cf. 26–7); and Gabinius' relegation of Lucius Lamia (cf. 29–30).

51. long since   Though expressions for indeterminate time-periods are at least as elastic in Lat. as in Engl. ('recently', 'long ago', etc.), the phrase (*iam pridem*) is strained, given that the Mithradatic Wars had been ended only seven years earlier—just before the still-vividly-remembered conspiracy of Catiline—and that Caesar was at the moment waging war fiercely in Gaul (C. makes a similar observation at *Prov. cons.* 30–1, though he there naturally acknowledges Caesar's campaigns and the Gallic threat, esp. ibid. 34). C. downplays foreign concerns to make the domestic scene appear all the more formidable, thus reviving a tactic used against Catiline (*Cat.* 2. 11 'All regions abroad have been made peaceful on land and sea through the *virtus* of one man (sc. Pompey): a war at home remains, the treachery is within, the peril is penned up within, the enemy is within').

those whom we allow to live in settled circumstances   A euphemism for the nominally independent peoples reduced to client-status ('live in settled circumstances' = *pacatos esse*, 'to have been pacified') rather than being annexed as provinces: C. will soon deplore at length the treatment of one such client-king, Ptolemy of Cyprus (57–9); cf. also his apparent ref. to Piso's maltreatment of the free communities of mainland Greece (94 **ordered** n.).

virtually no one … wars won abroad   In contrast with C., whom the *reckless citizens about to be mentioned subjected to ill-will (*invidia*) for his domestic leadership. Cf. esp. *Cat.* 4. 21–2, contrasting military heroes and civilian leaders, with remarks on the honours they both deserve and the different risks they face; his point here is that the prophecy he made then—'I see that I have undertaken eternal war with citizen desperadoes'—has proved true. In the last 20 years of C.'s life the *invidia* risked and suffered for his acts as consul is a constant motif: see *Cat.* 1. 22, 28–29, 2. 3, 15, 3. 3, 28–29, *Sull.* 9, 33, *Dom.* 44, *Har. resp.* 61, *Pis.* 72, *Mil.* 82, *Phil.* 3. 18, *Leg.* 3. 26.

commonwealth must keep... a remedy... robbed by my death A difficult passage. The 'remedy' might be the 'ultimate *decree of the senate' (so Reid in Holden 1889 ad loc.), on which C. relied in 63 and which he perhaps hoped would be invoked in 58 (cf. 25 **all citizens...** n.); or Sestius (so Holden 1889 and Cousin 1965), who opposed the *reckless, worked for C.'s restoration, and now faced exile; or, perhaps most aptly, the example of selfless patriotism that C. himself set, which (he has been arguing) it was his chief aim to preserve. Only the last of these would the *commonwealth directly have lost by C.'s death (so C. claims in 49); how any would have been lost had his death deprived the senate and people of the ability to grieve is more obscure. We are prob. to understand that his death would have deprived the senate and people of the chance *to show their grief*—their painful longing for him—*by achieving his restoration*: thus when C. repeats his argument against suicide at *Planc.* 90, in terms that track this passage closely, he says that if he had died, 'the support available to future generations (*auxilia posteritatis*, cf. the 'remedy', *medicina*, here) would have been much less, for my death would have destroyed the example the senate and people set in restoring me.' This understanding is consistent with what precedes, and with the encouragement he is about to offer 'the youth'.

young men Cicero first speaks explicitly as elder statesman instructing the next generation: cf. 14 **for our youth** n. and esp. 96 ff.

52. First of all... if these get what is coming to them i.e. if they are prosecuted for maladministration on resigning their provinces: C. already (too optimistically) referred to this prospect for Piso in 33 (**Will no one** n., cf. 135); on the fates of the two see 18 **One of them** (on Gabinius), 19 **The other one** (on Piso) nn. For the sentence's general point, cf. the statement of Quintus Lutatius Catulus (cos. 78, cens. 65) that 'seldom (in Roman history) had one consul been wicked, never had both been wicked, save in the times of Cinna (sc. 87–84)' (*Red. sen.* 9, cf. *Dom.* 113); in 77 below C. invokes the bloody clash of Cinna and Octavius, colleagues in 87, as an iconically awful event.

just cause   See 39 **who was not obliged to be estranged** n., where this behaviour by Caesar is first mentioned, sim. 71 **if Caesar was inclined to be well-disposed** n.

other, much more serious things...set aside   Presumably these include Clodius' other bad acts that C. attacks in 55–66, thus not so much setting them aside as postponing them.

brief interval   Just short of 18 months intervened between his departure from Rome *c*.18 March 58 and his landing at Brundisium on 5 August 57 (Introd. §1 and App. 1).

53–66. *The Account of 58 Resumed: Other Acts of 'Criminal Frenzy'*

Reopening the dossier of Clodius' and, especially, the consuls' crimes, to show that 'the commonwealth was overcome', C. proceeds in a manner straightforward and efficient, relative to earlier segments. There is once again a chronological dislocation or confusion (cf. 33 **while the same consuls sat** n.), in so far as the account creates the impression that C. had already left Rome when Clodius passed all the legislation yet to be mentioned and decided on Cyprus' annexation (see nn. ad loc.); but that is just a side-effect of C.'s having placed his own case centre-stage, as his basic strategy demanded, and it has no substantive bearing on his argument. The segment comprises three main divisions: having mentioned already (25) the *promulgation of the first law against him, and the law on the consuls' provinces, C. comes to the vote and to his departure after its passage (53–4); he quickly surveys Clodius' other legislation, bearing on matters domestic (55) and foreign (56); and he expands on the annexation of Cyprus (57–9) that was mandated to Cato (60–1), whom he praises at length (61–3). He then rounds off the segment with a miscellaneous review and a renewed attack on the consuls (64–6). Almost lost in this last is notice of the second law Clodius passed against him, under which he declared, by name, to have been exiled (65).

53. my main thesis in this speech ... the consuls' crimes The most direct statement of C.'s premise throughout 18–71, viz., that the true villains of the year were the consuls: though Clodius is hardly absent from this segment, it is not until 72–92, after the consuls' departure for their provinces, that he takes stage-center. On the strategy determining this choice of emphasis, see Introd. §3.

because of that very dearness What C. said Metellus Numidicus traded away in exchange for personal glory (37 **some notion of personal glory** n.), using the same phrase (*patriae caritas*).

not only my fellow humans ... mourned Cf. the personification at 128 'for whom did the senate chamber ever yearn more, the forum mourn, whom did the very tribunals miss as much? ...', sim. *Pis.* 32 'the senate's grief ..., the equestrian order's yearning ..., the mourning drab of Italy ..., the senate chamber's year-long silence ..., the unbroken quiet of courts and forum.' Clodius mocked this sort of talk: *Dom.* 4 ' "Are *you* the one," he said, "whom the senate could not do without, for whom patriots grieved, the commonwealth yearned, whose restoration (we thought) restored the senate's authority ...?" ' In 52 C. returned the favour in a sardonic description of mourning for Clodius, crowned by evoking the grief of 'the very fields' (*Mil.* 20).

assembly was asked to approve my destruction The *assembly of the plebs, over which the tribune presided; on the measure's *promulgation, 25 **public notice was given** n. Though aimed at C., the measure was framed in general terms, 'concerning the *caput* (1 n.) of a citizen', imposing 'interdiction from fire and water' (i.e. status as an outlaw whom it was a crime to shelter) on anyone who put a Roman citizen to death save at the express will of the people (sources: *MRR* 2. 196, esp. Livy *Perioch.* 103, Vell. 2. 45. 1, sim. Cass. Dio 38. 14. 4–6). Thus reaffirming a principle of Roman legal thought already adumbrated in the Twelve Tables (65 **centuriate assembly** n.) and enacted in the *lex Sempronia* of 123 (*MRR* 1. 513), the law raised no point not already made against the conspirators' execution; its innovations lay in extending its force not only to magistrates but (acc. to Cass. Dio, ibid.) to the senate as the magistrates' 'advisers', and esp. in making its force retroactive, a point from which Caesar demured (33 **voiced their approval** n. and, on the law in general,

Tatum 1999, 153–6). Its passage *c*.18 March (App. 1) precipitated C.'s flight: he later claimed that it had no bearing on him (a dubious legal position: 11 **domestic enemies** n.), and that allowing it to panic him had been his first mistake (*Att.* 3. 15(60). 5). On the bill brought by Clodius after C. left, declaring that he had been exiled, see 65 **proposal** n.

assignment of provinces to Gabinius and Piso   See 24 **their pick** n.; C. stresses the measures' simultaneity also at 25 and 44, cf. *Red. sen.* 17–18, *Pis.* 21. By this law Piso received Macedonia (cf. *Att.* 3. 1(46)) and Gabinius Cilicia, changed later to to Syria (55 **instead of Cilicia** n.). The change is most plausibly explained by Badian (1965, 115–17): Gabinius first chose Cilicia when Cyprus' annexation (57–9 below) was already planned, expecting the potentially profitable task to fall to the governor of Cilicia, to which Cyprus would be attached; he then had to settle (how contentedly, we do not know) for the rich province of Syria, created by Pompey's disposition of the east, when Clodius chose to mandate the annexation to Cato. On Cato, 60–1 nn., and on the implied chronology, App. 1.

By the immortal gods . . . what prodigies   'Prodigies' (*monstra*, 'notices, warnings' < *monere*, 'to make aware'), one label for phenomena indicating that the city's gods ('who protect and preserve this city and its dominion') were displeased and that the *peace of the gods had been upset: see 38 **perverse monsters** n., where C. uses a like term (*prodigia*) metaphorically to describe the consuls; he now uses *monstra* to denote the bad acts in which they were complicit, part of his tactic of showing that his enemies had overturned 'all things divine and human' (1 n.).

defended the commonwealth on the authority of the senate   C.'s consistent description of his role, see 11 **the senate . . . had caught and crushed**, 38 **The things on his own authority** nn.

expelled from the city . . . without a hearing . . . with the slave population roused   Splendidly tendentious: C.'s own decision to depart forestalled an opportunity for a hearing. For the 'rousing' of slaves, see 34 **a levy of slaves** n.

passed despite the senate's having taken on the dress of mourning   C. means: in a properly functioning *civil community, the senate's *authority, expressed by this gesture, would have had the weight to discourage the law's passage, even if the senate had no formal power to block it.

54. <misfortune> A word was lost from the medieval MSS' ancestor: the noun supplied here (*casus*) appears already (probably by conjecture) in one medieval MS (H) and is the term C. uses most often in this speech to denote his exile (29 **misfortune** n.).

they swooped in … to drag off its spoils C. identifies himself with the *commonwealth (Introd. §3) in esp. vivid terms, while thought of the consuls again provokes him to mix his metaphors (cf. 38 **perverse monsters** n.). In the first, we are to think of them as vultures (so explicitly at 71, or perhaps as Furies (cf. 109 'demons roused to a frenzy swoop down … on the commonwealth's funeral', with 33 **that demon** n.; Aeschylus' Furies are blood-drinkers, e.g. *Eum.* 264–7); the second, the seizure of 'spoils' (*spolia*), evokes the activity of human warriors or—as we are prob. meant to think here—freebooters (*praedones*: e.g. *Dom.* 140).

I say nothing But at sufficient length to make the point: on the figure (*praeteritio*) see 27 **I leave to one side** n.

My wife was roughly treated Writing to Terentia in Oct. 58 (*Fam.* 14. 2(7). 2), C. laments that she was 'roughly treated' (*vexari*, as here) when she was taken from the atrium of Vesta (her half-sister, Fabia, was a Vestal) to the tabula Valeria (*NTDAR* 376, *LTUR* 5. 16) in the Comitium, where the tribunes met. Terentia prob. took refuge with Fabia when C.'s house on the Palatine was sacked on his departure (below), but C., writing more than six months later, seems to indicate that news of this summons, received from another correspondent, was then fresh; the reason she was summoned, presumably at Clodius' behest, is not known. C. describes the matter still more forcefully at *Dom.* 59 ('What violence had my wife done you all, that you treated her roughly, dragged her away, wounded her in every cruel way?'), cf. more generally *Cael.* 50, *Prov. cons.* 3, *Mil.* 87.

my children were sought out for slaughter What, if anything, lies behind this claim is unknown: C. makes the same charge, about young Marcus only, at *Dom.* 59; no letters from exile mention an attempt on the children.

my son-in-law—a Piso   Gaius Calpurnius (*RE* 93) Piso Frugi (*quaestor 58), Tullia's first husband, whose devotion to C.'s family and efforts to gain his recall—including his decision to remain in Rome to work on C.'s behalf rather than take up his posting as quaestor to Bithynia and Pontus (*Red. sen.* 38)—C. recalls with consistent warmth (cf. 7 **devotion** n., with *Red. pop.* 7). C.'s prayer that the gods allow him to enjoy his son-in-law's presence again (*Fam.* 14. 3(9). 3) was not answered, for Piso died before C.'s return (cf. 68 below), sometime between Dec. 58 and the end of May 57 (see App. 1).

repulsed ... consul Piso   *Red. sen.* 17 adds that Tullia performed this supplication with her husband. For C.'s use of the distant relation between the two Pisos, see 20 **friend** n.; on the ritualized gesture of supplication, 26 **you prostrated yourselves** n.

my property ..., my home on the Palatine   C. justifiably speaks in terms of 'plunder' (*diripere*, lit. 'sieze and disperse'): his property was not forfeit to the community until Clodius passed his second law, declaring that C. was exiled (65 below), and even then it was not free for the taking. He repeatedly laments the sacking of his prized house on the Palatine (paired with the pillaging of his Tusculan villa at *Red. sen.* 18, see also 93 below, *Dom.* 60, 62, 123, 113, *Pis.* 26, more generally *Dom.* 146, *Har. resp.* 4) and from exile says that its loss, and its potential restoration, mean more to him than anything (*Att.* 3. 20(65). 2, *Fam.* 14. 2(7). 3). Its restoration is the subject of the extant speech *Dom.* (secondarily, *Har. resp.*); from *Att.* 4. 2(74). 2–5 we learn that his villa at Formiae was also damaged.

the consuls feasted   Sim. *Dom.* 62, juxtaposing the consuls' celebration (cf. *Pis.* 22) with the firing of his house; at *Pis.* 26 he holds Piso responsible for the arson, 'practically putting the torches in the hands of Clodius' demons'.

55. the other plagues of that year ... dose of medicine, of every sort   On the metaphor see 43 **medicine ... stopped ... a plague** n. C. stresses 'medicine, *of every sort*' (*omnium remediorum*), to remind the judges that S. is on trial because he was willing to provide just that.

not only...put to a vote but also...posted as pending The distinction between measures voted and those only *promulgated perhaps alludes to a hobbling of Clodius' legislative plans after the break with Pompey in late spring 58: cf. 67 '(Pompey) blocked with his authority the measures still awaiting execution' and nn. But since all the measures mentioned in 55–65 were certainly voted, and since measures merely promulgated are mentioned again only in a context of generalized innuendo (66 'measures that were published...promises...plans... hopes ..plots...'), we cannot say just what C. has in mind.

laws were voted on The first three laws mentioned in what follows were all passed on 4 Jan. 58 (*Pis.* 9). The law changing Gabinius's provincial assignment was presumably *promulgated, and certainly voted, after passage of the law granting him Cilicia in the third week of March (53 **assignment of provinces** n.), and before Clodius' break with Pompey and Gabinius in the late spring (56 **Great Mother**, 58 **Gnaeus Pompeius saw him** nn.); if the change was motivated by the decision to send Cato to Cyprus (53 **assignment of provinces** n.), then both measures were prob. voted in April (see App. 1). Sources for these and all following measures: *MRR* 2. 196.

the review of the censors...eradicated The censors periodically reviewed the senatorial order's members (*lectio senatus*), expelling those deemed unfit on financial or moral grounds (cf. 101 **your maternal grandfather's brother** n.). Despite C.'s heat, this measure simply required that both censors agree on a senator's expulsion after he had been allowed to answer any charges: see *Har. resp.* 58, *Prov. cons.* 46, *Asc.* 8. 24–6 Cl., Cass. Dio 38. 13. 2, with Mommsen 1887–8, 2^3. 418 ff., Astin 1985, 187–8, Benner 1987, 51–2, Tatum 1999, 133–5 (stressing the innovation of combining the censors' *lectio*, previously a private affair, with formal hearings). This basic form of due process proved too time-consuming when the *lectio* was next attempted in 54 (*Att.* 4. 16(89). 8), and the law was abrogated in 52 (Cass. Dio 40. 57. 1).

clubs...contrary to the senate's decree On the measure, 34 **alleged purpose** n.; Caesar repealed the law (Suet. *Iul.* 42. 3), excepting Jewish synagogues (Joseph. *Ant.* 14. 216).

gladiator Clodius, whose use of gladiators, and so his characterization as one himself, is a motif of the 'post-return' speeches, e.g.

Dom. 48, *Pis.* 19; for gladiators as 'the lowest sort of person', see *Mil.* 92, cf. *Att.* 1. 16(16). 5, Opelt 1965, 136.

a fifth of the public income... lost lowering the price of grain by 6 $\frac{1}{3}$ **asses per measure**   A 'supremely popular' measure, Asconius says (8. 13–17 Cl., on *Pis.* 9), using the epithet *popularis* in the political sense—appealing to the masses—that C. discusses later in the speech: Asconius specifies the same price-cut (6 $\frac{1}{3}$ *asses* = just over 1$\frac{1}{2}$ *sesterces* per measure, at a time when grain cost *c.*4 *sesterces* per measure before transport, milling, and other costs), and he adds—as it is mildly surprising C. does not—that the cut meant the grain was available *gratis* (sim. Cass. Dio 38. 13. 1, *Schol. Bob.* 132. 28–9 St.). In the history of such subventions at Rome the most important milestones were these: 123, when Gaius Gracchus first made grain regularly available to citizens living in Rome at a reduced price (cf. 103 below, *MRR* 1. 515; at Liv. *Perioch.* 60 the corrupt number giving the price is emended to match the figure C. and Asc. give for 58); 78, when the consul Marcus Aemilius Lepidus restored the price-support, which Sulla had cancelled, with a limit of 5 measures (sc. per month) per recipient (*MRR* 2. 85; 5 measures/month perhaps met the basic caloric needs of an adult male, see Duncan-Jones 1982, 146–7); 73, when the consuls Terentius Varro Lucullus and Cassius Longinus passed a similar law (*MRR* 2. 109: Cic. *Verr.* 2. 3. 72 implies that 40,000 people received grain under this law; like Clodius' grain law, this measure was prob. underwritten by annexation of foreign territory, in this case Cyrene, cf. Badian 1965, 120); and 62, when Cato as tribune further extended the benefits to 'the poor and property-less masses' (Plut. *Cat. min.* 26. 1), a response to the unrest stirred by Catiline costing the treasury an additional 1,250 talents (= 30,000,000 *sesterces*: *MRR* 2. 175, Pelling 1989); if Clodius' measure made the grain available *gratis*, the price under Cato's law was 6$\frac{1}{3}$ *asses* per measure. C.'s statement that the law cost the treasury 20 per cent of the yearly public income is unlikely to be exact, but the burden must have been great: Cyprus' annexation (57–9 below) was prob. prompted by, or conceived in tandem with, this measure and certainly added a welcome revenue-stream. The grain shortage became critical soon after C.'s return, leading to Pompey's special command and further conflict with Clodius. On grain-distributions at Rome, see Brunt 1971a, 376–82, Nicolet 1980, 186 ff., Rickman 1980, 156–97, Marshall 1985, 97, Tatum 1999, 119–25.

instead of Cilicia... Syria... <thanks to a new> law   C. makes the same complaint at *Dom.* 23, adding that Cilicia was transferred to a (former) praetor (prob. Ampius Balbus: Shackleton Bailey on *Fam.* 3. 7(71). 5, *MRR* 3. 15). For the first law, and the reason for the change, see 53 **assignment of provinces** n. The bracketed words represent a conjecture that fills a gap where a negligent scribe omitted about nineteen letters in the medieval MSS' common ancestor: the required sense is clear, whatever the exact wording might have been (I follow Maslowski and other editors in adopting the supplement first suggested by Halm, 'rogata <lege potestas per nov>am legem').

56. the law   This is the fourth measure voted on 4 Jan. 58, already denounced in 33 above (**while the same consuls sat** n.). The ref. here to 'magistrates' powers' corresponds to the earlier charge—more specific but no less misleading—that Clodius' law did away with the *veto.

even foreign nations   Ground for indignation because dealings with foreign nations were traditionally the concern of the senate, which managed them by decree, not the *assembly of the plebs acting through plebiscite (thus the 'tribunician law' mentioned next). Note, however, that the annexation of Cyprus was also supported by a *decree of the senate, if the transmitted text of Vell. 2. 38. 6 is correct (*senatus consulto*, credited by Badian 1965, 117, and printed in Hellegouarc'h's Budé of 1982, *contra*, e.g. Oost 1955, 110 n. 13; Watt's Teubner of 1988 adopts Cuiacius' *p(lebis) s(cito)*). In any case, C.'s is the only voice ever heard in opposition to the move.

a tribunician law...   At *Dom.* 52–3 C. appears to say that the Byzantine exiles' restoration and Cyprus' annexation were voted 'in a single law' (*lege una*), in violation of the *lex Caecilia Didia* forbidding 'miscellaneous' bills dealing with substantively diverse matters in a single motion (*leges saturae*, cf. 135 below); but that passage is better taken to refer to the subsequent law mandating both matters to Cato (60 nn., see Badian 1965, 116). The affair of Brogitarus (next n.) was certainly treated in a separate law. C. generally links all three matters, as he does here, to stigmatize Clodius' corruption (exiles and Brogitarus together at *Dom.* 129 and *Har. resp.* 59, Brogitarus and Ptolemy together at *Har. resp.* 58 and *Mil.* 73); but the measures on the exiles and Cyprus had certainly been passed by late March 58 (see App. 1), while the issue of Brogitarus perhaps first emerged slightly later, after Clodius began to attack the interests of Pompey more directly, see next n., 67 **he blocked** n., and App. 1.

Great Mother...sold...to Brogitarus   The cult of the Great Mother goddess (Cybele) had its chief site at Pessinus in Phrygia; in 205–4, when an oracle in the Sibylline Books foretold victory in the Second Punic War if her cult was brought to Rome, an embassy was dispatched and her aniconic cult-object (a black stone generally taken to be a meteorite) was fetched, installed in a temple on the Palatine (*NTDAR* 242–3, *LTUR* 3. 206–8, *MAR* 163–4), and celebrated by the founding of the Megalesian *games (*MRR* 1. 304, Gruen 1990, 5–33). In his settlement of the East Pompey had made the tetrarch of Galatia, Deiotarus, high priest of the cult at Pessinus and gained for him recognition as 'king', confirmed by the senate during Caesar's consulship in 59 (Braund 1984, 57, Sullivan 1990, 164–5). Acc. to C., Deiotarus' son-in-law, Brogitarus, bribed Clodius to acquire the title 'king' (next n.) and the priesthood (refs. preceding n. and most fully *Har. resp.* 28–9); in early 55 Clodius was angling for a 'free legation' with the aim (C. infers) of collecting his bribes from Brogitarus or the Byzantine exiles (below) or both ('the affair is full of cash': *QFr.* 2. 8(13). 2). Clodius' measure was a blatant swipe at Pompey: taken with the affair of Tigranes (cf. 58 **Gnaeus Pompeius saw him** n.) it led to the rupture of their relations and sparked both Pompey's efforts on C.'s behalf (67 nn.) and longstanding strife between Clodius and Pompey. For judicious analysis of Clodius' motives, and his encouragement by 'patriots', see esp. Tatum 1999, 169–70.

bestowed the title 'king' on men   i.e. on Brogitarus (*Har. resp.* 29): C.'s way with plurals being what it is (cf. 'citizens not condemned' below), 'men' is meaningless. This is in fact the only known case in which the title was bestowed by the people rather than the senate.

condemned exiles were restored to Byzantium   By Cato, who in Plutarch's worshipful account 'reconciled the exiles and left Byzantium in harmony' (*Cat. min.* 36. 1): on the mission see more fully 60 **Marcus**

Cato n. We do not know the exiles' identity or their offence, but it was presumably a matter internal to the city: because Byzantium had been awarded status as a 'free and federated civil community' (*civitas libera et foederata*) after allying itself with Rome in a series of wars in the 2nd cent., this tampering with her domestic affairs was a gross breach of her autonomy, cf. 64 'free communities...wronged', 84 'use our legates to restore to free communities people convicted on charges that make their lives as citizens forfeit'.

citizens not condemned...exiled He means himself, not citizens of Byzantium.

57. King Ptolemy Illegitimate son of Ptolemy IX Soter, Ptolemy governed Cyprus, part of the kingdom of Egypt since the reign of Ptolemy I, while his brother Ptolemy XII Auletes (next nn.), also Soter's illegitimate son, ruled Egypt. Each gained his position in 80, on the death of their cousin Ptolemy XI Alexander II, whom Sulla installed on the Egyptian throne after Soter died in 81: the annexation could be justified by the fact that Ptolemy X Alexander I (Soter's brother, Alexander II's father) had bequeathed Egypt, including Cyprus, to Rome in 88; the annexation of Cyrene in 75–74, after Ptolemy Apion's bequest of 96, is analogous on several counts (cf. Badian 1965, 119–20). If Gabinius' initial choice of Cilicia as his province anticipated the annexation (53 **assignment of provinces** n.), then a *terminus ante quem* for the plan is late Interkal. 58, when the law granting the consuls their provinces was *promulgated (App. 1); if the annexation was planned in tandem with Clodius' grain law (55 **lowering the price of grain** n.), it was intended from the first days of his *tribunate, if not before. C. attacks the affair in similar terms at *Dom.* 20–2, 52; later sources deplore Ptolemy as vicious (Vell. 2. 45. 4), greedy (Val. Max. 9. 4. 1(ext.)), and 'ungrateful to his benefactors' (Strabo 14. 6. 6), and explain Clodius' hostility in similarly *ad hominem* terms, alleging that Clodius was requiting Ptolemy's earlier refusal to ransom him from pirates (Cass. Dio. 38. 30. 5, sim. App. *BCiv.* 2. 23). See more fully Badian 1965, Braund 1984, 134–5, Sullivan 1990, 236–7, Huss 2001, 684–6.

not yet himself received the title 'ally' 'Not yet' is clever, implying that the title would of course have been his in the fullness of time.

In 59 the senate granted Auletes the title 'ally and friend' (*socius et amicus*), amounting to acknowledgement as legitimate ruler, after he offered spectacular bribes (6,000 talents = 144,000,000 *sesterces*) to beneficiaries including Caesar and Pompey (Suet. *Iul.* 54. 3: Diod., who visited Egypt in this period, says that 6,000 talents was the king's yearly income, 17. 52. 6); the view of the Cypriot king as 'greedy', or 'ungrateful' (preceding n.) might have arisen in part from an unwillingness to pay similar bribes. Because he cannot claim that Ptolemy was similarly acknowledged, C. first argues by analogy with Auletes, then shifts to an a fortiori argument based on Rome's more clement treatment even of foreign kings who were openly hostile. Cf. 59 **ever our friend** n.

brother of a king   Soon after his recognition as 'ally and friend' (above) Auletes was expelled by his people for being too much the Romans' lapdog: the intrigue, bribery, and violence inspired by his quest to regain the throne with Rome's help significantly deformed the city's politics up to and after his restoration in 55 by Gabinius, then nearing the end of his governorship of Syria: Siani-Davies 2001, 1–38, is an excellent survey, with further refs.

enjoying to the full his father's ... kingdom   Ignoring (as he does throughout) the bequest of Alexander, C. alludes to the fact that Soter had governed Cyprus in 107–88, between his expulsion from the Egyptian throne and his return.

hired hands   C. has spoken of Clodius' 'hired *brigands' or the like before (2, 38, cf. 82), referring to the armed gangs that did his bidding; here he refers to people participating in a lawful public gathering, the *assembly of the plebs, where Clodius' measure on Cyprus was approved. In so doing C. anticipates a major theme of the speech's last third, where he will argue (on the one hand) that the categories 'popular' and 'optimate', though once opposed, have co-alesced in a single mass of *patriotic citizens, and (on the other hand) that this united mass is still beset by many enemies: these enemies (it follows) can only be those 'hired' to appear at Clodius' *contiones and *voting assemblies; see esp. 104–7, with 113–14, 126–7. C. no doubt has in mind the urban poor and small shopkeepers who responded when Clodius put out the word to 'close up the shops', for a demonstration or *contio*; for a survey of the social composition of the *Clodiani*, see Vanderbroeck 1987, 199–209, Tatum 1999, 114–16, and esp. 142–8.

put up for public auction In the two years Cato was in Cyprus (58–56) he realized 7,000 talents (168,000,000 *sesterces*) from the royal treasury and the auction of the kings' possessions; some calculations suggest that the island subsequently sent a like amount in yearly revenue to the treasury at Rome (Siani-Davies 2001, 17, 168).

restored their kingdoms... restoration of property wrongly taken C. introduces the theme to be developed in the next two paragraphs by referring to a doctrine central to Rome's interstate dealings: the 'restoration of property wrongly taken' was among the relatively few just grounds for war (cf. 94 **peoples of Thrace** n.), which could be declared only after a request was formally made and time for reparation was allowed; for C.'s view, esp. *Off.* 1. 36, invoking the ancient 'fetial law' of Rome (cf. Livy 1. 22, Beard, Price, and North 1998, 1. 26–7).

58. our ancestors... south of the Taurus Mountains Antiochus III of Syria (reign: 223–187) invaded Thrace in 197, arousing Roman fears for their interests in the area. When his invasion of Greece in 192 ended long and fruitless negotiations, he was met by Roman forces and defeated at Thermopylae (191), by Manius Acilius Glabrio (*MRR* 1. 352), and at Magnesia (190), by Lucius Cornelius Scipio Asiaticus (*MRR* 1. 356). Under the peace of Apamea (188: Gruen 1984, 2:639–43), he relinquished claims to territory N and W of the Taurus Mountains while retaining Pamphylia and Cilicia in SE Asia Minor and other lands reaching from Syria and Palestine through mod. Iran into central Asia.

took Asia Minor... giving it to Attalus Rather, to Eumenes II (reign: 197–58) of Pergamum, eldest son of Attalus I (reign: 241–197) and brother of Attalus II (reign: 158–38), who served his brother prominently in the Antiochene War. The territory ceded by Antiochus (preceding n.) was divided between Pergamum and Rhodes; the territory given to Pergamum passed in turn to Rome when Attalus III (reign: 138–33) bequeathed the city his kingdom.

over land and sea The phrase *terra marique*, a form of polar expression (cf. 1 **all things divine and human** n.), echoes the corresponding Gk. phrase (*kata gēn kai kata thalassan*) customary both in treaties of peace or alliance and in praise bestowed on Hellenistic kings as universal conquerors: on its pedigree, Momigliano 1942. Suited to panegyric or quasi-panegyric contexts like the present one, it recurs in the praise of Pompey to come (67 'who ended all wars on land and sea', cf. *Cat.* 2. 11, *Balb.* 16); its orotund character lends it more readily to public than private discourse (15 times in the speeches, only once—not without irony—in correspondence with Atticus, 9. 1(167). 3).

Recently waged . . . with . . . Tigranes Tigranes II of Armenia (reign: *c*.95–*c*.55), son-in-law and ally of Mithradates (next n.): when Rome foiled his attempt to seize Cappadocia in 92, he waged wars of expansion at the expense of the Parthians and Seleucids, then retook Cappadocia in 78–77 (thus 'injuring our allies' here) and established a royal city at Tigranocerta, between Armenia and Mesopotamia. Having forced Mithradates to flee to Tigranes in 72, Lucius Lucullus invaded Armenia and gained major victories in 69–68 (next nn.) before Pompey superseded him in 66. As C. here implies, Lucullus' recall left Tigranes with fight still in him, but much of that was spent quashing the rebellion of his homonymous son, who fled to Pompey; Tigranes II surrendered to Pompey in 66 (**Gnaeus Pompeius saw him** n.).

Mithradates Mithradates VI Eupator, king of Pontus (reign: *c*.120–66): after waging wars of expansion to the N and E, Mithradates clashed with Rome in the 90s while variously intriguing with his neighbour Nicomedes III of Bithynia and harassing the latter's successor, Nicomedes IV, a client of Rome; under provocation he declared war on Rome in 88, occupying the province of Asia and invading mainland Greece before Sulla and Fimbria repelled him. Sulla concluded the First Mithradatic War in 85 with the treaty of Dardanus, which allowed the king to retain Pontus (*MRR* 2. 58); the treaty's terms were violated by Lucius Licinius Murena, whose incursions provoked the brief Second Mithradatic War (83–82: *MRR* 2. 64). Low-grade hostilities continued until Nicomedes IV bequeathed his kingdom to Rome (76/75): perceiving a threat, Mithradates started the Third Mithradatic War by invading Bithynia (the date, 74 or 73, is disputed: *MRR* 2. 101, 106–8, 3. 121–2). After defeating Marcus Aurelius Cotta at Chalcedon in 73, he was defeated by Lucius Lucullus at Cyzicus and fled to his son-in-law, Tigranes, whom Lucullus defeated in two major battles (next n.). Mithradates returned to Pontus in 68, but Pompey, having superseded Lucullus, easily defeated both him and Tigranes in 66. Withdrawing still farther, to Panticapaeum on the Cimmerian Bosporus (N rim of the Black Sea), he allegedly was planning to invade Italy when a rebellion by his son, Pharnaces II, caused him to commit suicide in 63. Overviews and further bibliography: Rubinsohn 1993, Hind 1994, Sherwin-White 1994, 229–55.

<**Lucius**> **Lucullus**   Lucius Licinius (*RE* 104) Lucullus (cos. 74), loyal lieutenant of Sulla, was effective against Mithradates as *procon- sul (preceding n.) and delivered the 'blow' referred to here by defeating Tigranes at Tigranocerta in 69 and at Artaxata in 68 (*MRR* 2. 133, 139), stripping him of Syria, Phoenicia, Cilicia, Galatia, and Sophene. Mu- tinies in Lucullus' army—one of them led by his brother-in-law, Clodius—allowed Tigranes to recoup his losses; that fact, combined with political opposition at Rome, led to the transfer of Lucullus' command, in part to Manius Acilius Glabrio in 67 (*MRR* 2. 144, 146), and entirely to Pompey in 66 (*MRR* 2. 153, 155).

Gnaeus Pompeius saw him … bade him rule   For the tableau, depicting Pompey as the maker of kings, cf. esp. Plut. *Pomp.* 33. 3–4; cognate imagery, casting Pompey as 'king of kings' (that is, Agamemnon), was later used both by Pompey himself and by his critics (Plut. *Pomp.* 67. 3 and Champlin 2003, 297–305). Pompey allowed Tigranes to retain the throne of Armenia on condition that he pay a penalty of 6,000 talents (= 144,000,000 *sesterces*) and cede the provinces lost in the war with Lucullus (preceding n.). One of these, Sophene, was offered to Tigranes' rebel son to rule: when he rejected the offer, Pompey took him as a prisoner to Rome, led him in his triumph in 62, and held him as a hostage until Clodius—in one of the moves that alienated Pompey in the spring of 58 (cf. 56 **Great Mother** n.)—engineered his escape: Plut. *Pomp.* 33. 4–5, 45. 4, 48. 6, and on the young Tigranes, esp. Asc. 47. 12–26 Cl., with *Dom.* 66,

Mil. 18, 37, *Schol. Bob.* 118. 23–119. 3 St., Cass. Dio 38. 30. 1–2, and cf. 67 **Here at last** n.

59. **<This man, then,> made <war on us>**   The medieval MSS' common ancestor suffered both loss (cf. 55 **instead of Cilicia** n.) and interpolation, to judge from the text of P, which has a gap of about seventeen letters followed by the nearly synonymous verbs *tulit gessit*, one of which prob. stood as an interlinear gloss on the other before creeping into the text (the MSS GV do not mark the lacuna but have the same verbs). I translate Koch's *<is igitur qui bellum in>tulit*; the general sense is plain in any case.

ever our friend, ever our ally   Rounding off the theme, C. bestows on Ptolemy the title he did not gain from the senate: 57 **not yet himself received the title 'ally'** n. In 59 C. had remarked Ptolemy's usefulness as a check on pirates (*Flac.* 30).

no really serious suspicion   A notably qualified phrase (*nulla... suspicio durior*), perhaps acknowledging that Ptolemy's faults of character were well known (57 **King Ptolemy** n.).

'alive and aware' (as the saying goes)   Lit. 'alive and seeing' (*vivus et videns*): C. uses the phrase in his first extant speech, also with ref. to a man whose goods were on the block (*Quinct.* 50, with Kinsey 1971 ad loc., cf. Otto 1890, 377), sim. Ter. *Eun.* 73, Lucr. 3. 1046. In fact Ptolemy anticipated Cato's arrival by suicide (Vell. 2. 45. 4, Plut. *Cat. min.* 36. 1–2, Cass. Dio 39. 22. 2–3).

60. sought to blot the splendid distinction   Viz., by involving Cato in the tawdry affair just described: the statement raises the question, why did Clodius decide to involve Cato? It was certainly not because 'he had not even a hope of undoing Cicero were Cato still present' in Rome (Plut. *Cat. min.* 34. 2): on the most likely chronology, the decision followed passage of the first law on the consular provinces (53 **assignment of provinces** n. and App. 1) and thus of the first law aimed at C., *promulgated and passed at the same time; and the present passage shows that Cato was still in Rome after C.'s depart-ure, 'brawling' with the consuls, apparently while the bill moving his mandate was awaiting a vote (**a brawl** n.). Cato's mission is best separated from the attack on C.—who nowhere suggests a causal link—and regarded as 'a happy afterthought' to the plan to annex Cyprus (Badian 1965, 117): Clodius would be rid of a bothersome presence who was also the one man to be relied on scrupulously to convey the funds to the treasury.

Marcus Cato Though 11 years C.'s junior and barely midway in his career—he would hold no curule office but the praetorship of 54— Marcus Porcius (*RE* 20) Cato already had great *authority, in part inherited with the mantle of his great-grandfather, Cato the Censor (*RE* 10), but largely earned by his support (brave and vigorous, if blinkered and excessively stiff-necked) of the senate's primacy and a moral rigor underwritten by his serious commitment to Stoicism. In many of his public actions he and C. found themselves on the same side: as tribune-elect he played a crucial part in the senate's debate of 5 Dec. 63, strongly supporting the execution of the Catilinarian leaders held in custody (61 below); in Jan. 62 he opposed his fellow-tribune Metellus Nepos, who had humiliated C., in an incident to which C. has already alluded (12 n.) and to which he returns below (62 **temple was seized** n.); and in 59 he aggressively opposed Caesar's agrarian legislation (see esp. Plut. *Cat. min.* 31–3, and cf. 61 **sworn allegiance** n.). On other matters the two were divided: in Nov. 63 Cato prosecuted, and C. defended, the consul-elect Murena on a charge of electoral bribery (*TLRR* no. 224; on C.'s treatment of Cato in his defence speech, Craig 1986), and C. thought Cato sometimes out of touch with political reality (esp. *Att.* 2. 1(21). 8, sim. 1. 18(18). 7); for his part Cato later opposed C.'s argument that all Clodius' legislation was invalid, as passed by one not legally a tribune, on the ground that his own commission to Cyprus would be invalidated as well, and for a time C. broke off relations (Plut. *Cat. min.* 40, *Cic.* 34, sim. Cass. Dio 39. 22. 1); in 50 he enraged C. by voting—out of principle priggishly applied, or actual bad faith—against the *supplicatio* C. sought to honour his victories in Cilicia (esp. *Att.* 7. 2(125). 7, with Kaster 2005, 134–5). But C. did admire the man, prob. more than any other contemporary of the first rank: he excepted Cato from the company of erstwhile 'friends'—primarily other optimate leaders like Hortensius (3 n.)—who he thought betrayed him during his crisis (on Cato, *Att.* 3. 15(60). 2; for the charge, 46 **some felt** n., and for Cato's advice to C., Plut. *Cat. min.* 35. 1), and he wrote the lost *Cato,*

praising him after he killed himself rather than accept Caesar's clem-
ency in 46. Like this passage, that praise had a deeply political purpose
(it provoked a vicious retort from Caesar); in neither case need that
mean the praise was insincere. The eulogy inserted here in the defence
of S., like the eulogy of Milo at 85 ff., suggests the sort of thing
C. would have said about S. when eulogizing him in his defence of
Lucius Calpurnius Bestia on 11 Feb. (*QFr.* 2. 3(7). 6). Unlike Milo,
however, Cato did not hear himself praised, for he did not return from
Cyprus until later in 56. The praise primarily assimilates C.'s and
Cato's acts by claiming that each chose to forgo resistance—honourable for themselves, potentially harmful to others—when faced with
an opponent's 'lawless' actions. Secondarily, the encomium is a
gesture of political independence, for to praise so resoundingly in
Pompey's presence the man who had done most over the last six years
to impede Pompey's interests could not be a casual or neutral act.

manliness   On this quality and those it here embraces—*seriousness, *uprightness, *bravery, *large-spiritedness—see the Glossary;
for a similar enumeration of Cato's virtues, *Dom.* 23.

which remains calm … others' dirty doings   The calm demeanour
of *virtus* is appropriate to one, like Cato, aiming at Stoic wisdom,
which regarded human passions as 'diseases' of the mind (47 **ought
I have calmly met my death?** n.); but it is also appropriate to
Epicurean wisdom, which aimed at *tranquillity (23 **those who…
praise** n.), and is no less at home in non-sectarian discourse on *virtus*
(e.g. Enn. *Ann.* 562 Sk.) than talk of *virtus* as a source of illumination
(e.g. *Leg. Man.* 33, *Red. sen.* 5, *Phil.* 13. 44).

**Marcus Cato ought to be banished…—or so *those* men suppo-
sed**   Sim. *Dom.* 21, 65, cf. Vell. 2. 45. 4 (echoing C.'s diction)
'Publius Clodius…, under the cover of a most honourific title
(next n.)…, banished Marcus Cato….' Acc. to Plutarch, Clodius
offered the commission to Cato as an honour highly coveted (so it
might have been, by Gabinius: 53 **assignment of provinces** n.), then
replied to Cato's refusal: 'Very well, if you'll not take it as a favour,
you'll take the voyage as a punishment' (*Cat. min.* 34. 3; ibid. 34–9 on
Cato's conduct on the mission). The measure at issue here mandated
to Cato both the annexation of Cyprus and the restoration of the

Byzantine exiles (56–7 above, *MRR* 2. 198): on the annexation, Badian 1965 is fundamental; for the motives on both sides, see **sought to blot** n. above and '**Why then...?**' n. below. The plural 'those men' refers both to Clodius, who *promulgated the measure sometime after C.'s departure (see below and App. 1), and to the consuls, for reasons C. makes plain at the paragraph's end.

torn...the tongue...that had...spoken against extraordinary commands   Viz., by giving him his own extraordinary command, 'by name' (*nominatim*: cf. 62, *Dom.* 21) and outside the regular system of magistracies and *promagistracies; he was sent with the rank of *quaestor but with the command powers (*imperium*) of a praetor, an unusual but not unprecedented commission (*pro quaestore pro praetore*: Balsdon 1962, 135, Badian 1965, 110–11). In 62 he had opposed Metellus Nepos' proposal to transfer the command against Catiline to Pompey (62 **temple was seized** n.); in 59 he had opposed both the special commission instituted by Caesar's agrarian legislation and esp. Caesar's own 5-year command in Gaul, reportedly calling the latter a step toward 'tyranny' (Plut . *Cat. min.* 33. 1–3). Caesar surely had this last in mind when he wrote to Clodius to congratulate him 'because (he) had stripped (Cato) of the freedom to speak in future about extraordinary commands' (*Dom.* 22, alleging that Clodius read the letter in an *assembly, presumably the one mentioned here or one like it). For the brutal image, cf. *De or.* 3. 5.

They will soon, I hope, come to feel the abiding presence   i.e. on Cato's return from Cyprus.

brawl with the despicable consuls   The occasion—a public one, thus Piso's discomfiture—is otherwise unknown; the description does not show whether the setting was an altercation in the senate or (more likely) an *assembly of the people convened by the consuls and disrupted by Cato: cf. *Att.* 1. 14(14). 5, on the verbal 'bruising' Cato gave another consul Piso at an assembly in 61; sim. Plut. *Cat. min.* 33. 1. It certainly postdated C.'s departure, apparently after *promulgation and before passage of the law establishing his mandate, when he 'had given up hope that his personal authority could have any effect' in blocking the measure (on the chronology, App. 1).

'Why then did Cato obey the measure?'   i.e. why not model himself on Metellus Numidicus (cf. 37 n.), who looms over this passage, though unnamed? On the exchange with an imagined interlocutor (*sermocinatio*): **20 Still** n. The main reasons C. gives below— disobedience was fruitless (62), obedience would serve the common- wealth (63)—are possibly authentic. A further consideration is com- patible with those reasons, and with C.'s other statements here and elsewhere (cf. 63 **could he calmly remain** n.), though it is naturally absent from the later, reverent tradition surrounding Cato: as drafted, Clodius' law *de capite civis* touched not just a magistrate who put a citizen to death without trial but any senator on whose advice he acted (53 **assembly was asked** n.)—and as C. soon reminds us (61, 63), no senator's advice carried more weight on the critical occasion than Cato's: the mission to Cyprus and Byzantium would make him immune from prosecution during his tenure and take him far from Rome for the balance of Clodius' *tribunate. At *Dom.* 21 and 64 C. says that Clodius attacked Cato publicly for his role in Dec. 63 and that 'Cato would have been next' among his victims. Whatever the latter tells us of Clodius' intentions, Cato would have been neither foolish to be on guard nor inconsistent in concluding that he could better serve the commonwealth by placing himself out of harm's way.

61. sworn allegiance to other laws ... passed illegally   Caesar's agrarian law of early 59 included a clause requiring all senators to swear to uphold it (Plut. *Cat. min.* 32. 3, Dio 38. 1. 1–2; *Att.* 2. 18(38). 2 mentions a like requirement for candidates for office attached to Caesar's subsequent law distributing Campanian land): Plutarch's dramatic account invokes the example of Metellus Numidicus (cf. 37 **refusing** n.) and makes C. chiefly responsible for persuading Cato to take the oath (*Cat. min.* 32. 3–6, cf. App. *BCiv.* 2. 12 and next n.), which would have been sworn before an *assembly of the people (*contio*: Morstein-Marx 2004, 10 n. 48). On the view of Cato and others, the law was 'passed illegally' (*iniuste rogata = non iure rogata*) because it had been carried amidst violence and against the *auspices (sources: *MRR* 2. 187–8; on *lex non iure rogata*, Heikkilä 1993).

He does not expose ... derives no advantage   Cf. C.'s comments on Metellus Numidicus in 37 above; C. reportedly made this argument in persuading Cato to swear to uphold Caesar's agrarian legislation (Plut. *Cat. min.* 32. 4–5, with chronological confusion; sim. Cass. Dio 38. 7. 1–2, alleging the same considerations without mentioning C.).

tribune of the plebs-elect ... expressing an opinion The debate of 5 Dec. 63, in which Cato argued strongly that the conspirators in custody should be executed (cf. 63 'the whole senate and his opinion in particular'), took place five days before Cato began his *tribunate; on his role, esp. Sall. *Cat.* 50–5, Plut. *Cat. min.* 22–3 (purportedly based on Cato's preserved speech). On the danger to his life, cf. *Mur.* 82, delivered days before the debate, where C. (as advocate for the defence) warns Cato (as prosecutor) of those eager to kill him because of his views.

ill-will and ... danger upon his own head Some ill-will (*invidia*) attached to Cato at once, as it did to C. (see Introd. §1); danger to his 'head' (*caput*)—his *life as a citizen—was posed most clearly by Clodius' *lex de capite civis* in 58, cf. '**Why then ...?** n. above.

62. term as tribune Beyond the incident about to be mentioned, Cato as tribune passed a measure extending subsidized grain to more citizens—his one concession to 'popular' pressures (55 **a fifth of the public income** n.)—and collaborated with Lucius Marius, another tribune, in regulating requests for military triumphs (MRR 2. 174).

temple was seized by one of his colleagues The riotous incident took place at the temple of Castor (34 n.) in Jan. 62, when Cato kept his fellow tribune, Metellus Nepos (72 **his colleague** n.), from passing a measure transferring command in the war against Catiline to Pompey, then returning from the East; it is treated with great drama by Plutarch (*Cat. min.* 26. 2–28, sim. Cass. Dio 37. 43. 1–3), stressing Cato's *courage and moral *authority in the face of the 'foreigners, gladiators, and slaves' marshalled by Nepos, whose name C. here tactfully elides.

quelled people's shouts with his authority A figure of real *authority could overawe others by a word or a look: cf. Metellus Celer, blocking celebration of the forbidden *ludi Compitales* (32 **club** n.) by his *auctoritas* as the consul-designate in late Dec. 61 (*Pis.* 8), and Cato himself calming a 'turbulent assembly' with his authority in the aftermath of Clodius' murder in 52 (*Mil.* 58). The first simile of the *Aeneid* (1. 148–53) sets such a scene: 'as often when... there has arisen | civil unrest, the nameless mob rages out of control | and— there, now—the air is filled with torches, stones, the arms frenzy supplies; | just then, if someone catches their eye, a real man weighty with the devotion | he has earned, they fall silent and stand with ears pricked (to hear him speak)'.

whose gravity there is no need for me to describe now   C. means: further description might compel me to explain why entrusting a critical military command to our greatest living general, seated here before you, posed a danger to the commonwealth more worthily resisted than the seizure of a foreign kingdom I have deplored at length as wholly unprincipled.

kingdom ... confiscated ... measure ... brought forward   The law on the annexation (57–9) was *promulgated and passed sometime in Feb.–March; the law commissioning Cato 'by name' (*nominatim*) to confiscate the royal property (and restore the Byzantine exiles) was promulgated after the first law fixing the consular provinces (53) was passed in March, and it was voted in April (App. 1).

63. it was more expedient ... <be wasted> by others   The transmitted text (lit. '... more expedient that it be salvaged by himself than by others', *utilius esse per se conservari quam per alios*) is possibly correct (it is printed by e.g. Halm 1886 and Maslowski), though it requires placing virtually all stress on the adjective 'more expedient' (*utilius*: 'more expedient ... by himself than by others') and next to none on the verb 'be salvaged' (*conservari*). But C.'s (or Cato's) point is not that others—Gabinius, say—would merely be less efficient, but that they would embezzle more than they would salvage: most editors, accordingly, adopt some verb to contrast with *conservari*; I translate Zumpt's *dissipari*, 'be wasted'. It is in any case clear that C. is talking about 'salvaging' the revenues from Cyprus, not 'salvaging' the situation in some more general sense.

he had kept away ... previous year   In protest, during Caesar's consulship: though useful to C.'s argument, the point is unlikely to be literally true (Plut. makes no such claim, and *Cat. min.* 32. 1 seems to contradict it), but cf. Plut. *Caes.* 14. 8 ('of the other senators (i.e. other than Cato, subject of the preceding anecdote) very few used to go with (Caesar) into the senate, while the rest stayed away in disapproval') and Cass. Dio 38. 6. 6 (tribunes supporting Bibulus join him in boycotting public business). C.'s parenthetical comment following ('had he come') is perhaps faintly disapproving: cf. *Dom.* 8, 'I disagree with those who decide not to attend the senate in trying times, since they fail to see that this excessive rigour of theirs is wonderfully agreeable to those they wish to aggrieve.'

could he calmly remain … when … his opinion … condemned C. apparently means that in circumstances where *brigands reigned, Cato's departure from Rome to take up the commission was an act of principled revulsion, like his boycott of the senate. C. perhaps also brushes up against the thought, encouraged by the comparison with himself, that Cato's departure took him out of range of the *lex de capite civis*, cf. 60 'Why then … ?' n.

draught of grief … cup of anguish C. wants to claim pride of place as victim while granting all possible scope to Cato's sympathy and suffering (cf. *Dom.* 65, similarly coordinating their woes, in different terms), but the attempt turns on a contrast between two ideas too closely related to make the point completely clear, *luctus* ('grieving', incl. its outward signs) and *dolor animi* ('mental pain, anguish'): though C. uses the terms to express a contrast elsewhere (*Balb.* 61 'Others experienced anguish (*dolor*), I experienced grief (*luctus*) and mourning (*maeror*)'), they are naturally more often aligned than antithetical (32, on the assumption of mourning on his behalf, sim. *Pis.* 17, cf. 49 'my own pain and grieving', *Clu.* 168, *Phil.* 12. 25, *Att.* 3. 15(60). 2, *Fam.* 4. 6(249). 1, *De or.* 2. 193, *Tusc.* 3. 64). Presumably the point is that Cato's 'anguish', though (allegedly) as great as C.'s own, was to a degree eclipsed in others' eyes by the mission's speciously honourific character, whereas C.'s 'anguish' was accompanied by the outward signs of mourning and a disgrace that could not be concealed. There is further awkwardness in attributing such anguish to Cato at all, since it implies that he ascribed real value to external goods in a notably un-Stoic way (cf. 49 **never deny** n.). But C. was a man of ready sentiment who almost by reflex used his own feelings as the yardstick by which to measure others': cf. a letter written about the same time as this trial, consoling his champion Lentulus Spinther

(70 n.), then passing through a political rough patch, by recalling 'my own circumstances, whose reflection I see in yours: for though your worthy standing suffers less affliction than the onslaught borne by mine, the likeness is still so great that I hope you will forgive me if I do not find formidable (in your case) the sorts of things that you never found formidable (in mine)' (*Fam.* 1. 6(17). 2, cf. 1. 7(18). 2–3).

64. free communities   i.e. Byzantium: cf. 56 **condemned exiles** n.

kings . . . protection of that magistracy   Because the consuls were the chief ministers of the senate, which traditionally managed relations with foreign states: cf. 56 **even foreign nations** n.

(Come to that . . . complain?)   C. returns to the theme of the consuls' inaction in the face of Clodius' iniquity (cf. 33, 34). The sentences either side of this question relate directly to each other as elements of that theme, while the question itself is best regarded as an insult tossed off in an aside ('and yet . . .' = 'come to think of it'): its point is not that there was no one to listen (sc. because the senate was browbeaten, the people in Clodius' thrall: so Halm 1886, followed by Holden 1889 and Gardner 1958*a*), but that the consuls, universally regarded as despicable creatures, could command no attention and respect (*audire* = 'pay heed'). The contrast is with Cato: 60, 62.

the plebs' ill-will . . . (which was not in fact the case)   C.'s attempt parenthetically to falsify a point like this gives us license to think that it contains a fair amount of truth (see e.g. 16, 42, and for denial of the plebs' hostility, *Leg.* 3. 25): in this case we know that Clodius in fact inspired popular ill-will against C. (*inter alia*) for failing to acknowledge citizens' rights in executing the conspirators (53 **assembly was asked** n.), thereby seeming to annul a basic component of liberty, a citizen's protection against summary execution and other abuses of magisterial power (cf. 109 **'tyrant'** n.; Tatum 1999, 153–4 is clear and concise).

65. proposal . . . on the life and standing of a citizen . . . and his goods   Construing C.'s departure as an admission of guilt after passage of the law *de capite civis*, Clodius immediately *promulgated a law declaring that he had been exiled, by name (**measure . . . n.** below), for executing citizens without a trial and forging a *decree of the senate. A charge of falsification—of the record of senate proceedings, not a decree—had already been made against C. by Publius Sulla's prosecutor in 62 (*Sull.* 40–5 with Berry 1996 ad loc.); if the present charge referred to the 'ultimate *decree' on which C. had relied in carrying out the executions (cf. Gabba 1961, 92–3), then the charge—though surely a fiction—would have the specious effect of giving cover to the senate, which otherwise would have been liable under the law *de capite civis* (53 **assembly** n.). While in flight C. learned the law's provisions (*Att.* 3. 1(46), 3. 4(49)), which were revised between its initial promulgation and its enactment *c.*24 April (chronology: App. 1). As enacted it included a declaration that C. was an outlaw ('interdiction from fire and water') who could be killed on sight within 400 miles of Italy (*Att.* 3. 4(49), making plain that outlawry went into effect immediately on the law's passage, before C. could reach the 'safe' distance, and alluding to the danger faced by any who sheltered him; see further App. 3); confiscation of his property and its sale at auction (his house on the Palatine had already been plundered: 54); construction and dedication of a monument on part of the site his Palatine house had occupied (the 'shrine of Liberty' built by Clodius: *NTDAR* 234, *LTUR* 3. 188–9); and a clause forbidding the senate's discussion of his recall (cf. 69 **deterred by Clodius' law** n.) or legislation to that end (sources: *MRR* 2. 196, Rotondi 1912, 395–6; Moreau 1987 is fundamental, and his contribution at *RS* 2. 773–4, is concise and clear, as is Tatum 1999, 156–8; see also Stroh 2004, 317–21, and on the consecration of his house, Liou-Gille 1998, 53–9). C. attacks the law most fully in *Dom.*, aimed (successfully) at regaining his property on the Palatine. His property's confiscation was an esp. harsh blow, not only because of all it signified for C.'s status and identity (issues well surveyed by Tatum 1999, 159 ff.), but also because C. himself had joined Caesar in blocking confiscation of the conspirators' property when they were executed in Dec. 63 (Plut. *Cic.* 21. 4). The law was still posted on the Capitol, along with all of Clodius' other legislation, when C. was delivering this speech; only later in the year did he attempt forcibly to remove it (Cass. Dio 39. 21. 1).

Twelve Tables and the laws that it is a sacrilege to disobey The Twelve Tables were the earliest codification of Roman law, compiled (acc. to tradition) by a Board of Ten in 451–50: for text, translation, and commentary see *RS* no. 40. On 'sacrosanct legislation' (*leges sacratae*), 16 n.; C. stresses *leges sacratae* (so also *Dom.* 43) because these were instruments of the plebs, in whose assembly the offending law was passed.

measure…to the disadvantage of a specific individual   That this law was a **privilegium*, and hence illegal, is among the points on which C. insists most vehemently (see 73 below, *Dom.* 26, 43, 57–8, 110, *Prov. cons.* 45, *Pis.* 30; cf. *Att.* 3. 15(60). 5, *Rep.* 2. 54, 61, *Leg.* 3. 11 and esp. 3. 44). In so doing, he falls into imprecision or exaggeration: he tends to conflate this measure with the earlier, general *lex de capite civis* (53) and describe Clodius' measures as *privilegium* tout court (Gruen 1974, 245, cf. 73 **justice and the courts** n.); he too quickly finds his view of *privilegium* supported in the Twelve Tables (see *RS* 2. 698–700) and misinterprets another of that code's provisions (next n.); and he at times misleadingly suggests (e.g. *Dom.* 43, though not here) that passage of such a law concerning a person 'not condemned' (*indemnatus*) was against Roman legal tradition (defendants already standing trial who anticipated condemnation by going into voluntary exile had in the past been formally exiled by plebiscite: Tatum 1999, 157, citing Livy 25 4. 9, 26. 3. 12). But he rightly insists (*Dom.* 26) that he was 'not only not condemned but *not even accused*': that no charge had been brought against him at the time he left the city does lend force to his outrage at suffering something more like Sullan **proscription (46 n.) than a penalty sanctioned by decent Roman precedent. He was not alone in that view: see 73 below (Lucius Cotta), *Red. sen.* 29 (a speech delivered by Pompey at Capua later in 58).

centuriate assembly…an assembly…of the plebs   C. makes the same point at *Rep.* 2. 61 and ascribes it to Lucius Cotta at 73 below (recounting a speech of 1 Jan. 57) and *Leg.* 3. 45; he connects the point to the Twelve Tables via a clause cited at *Leg.* 3. 11 (cf. 3. 44): 'concerning the *caput* of a citizen, <unless> the gathering <is> the fullest possible, they are not to carry (a measure)' (9. 2 *de capite civis, <ni> maximus comitiatus <est>, ne ferunto*: text and trans. *RS* 2. 700–1, with Dyck 2004*a*, 478–9, on *Leg.* 3. 10). The citation is not on all fours with his case: the relevant phrase, *maximus comitiatus*, refers to the size of a competent assembly ('gathering... the fullest possible') but does not define which assembly was competent; C. (and, acc. to C., Cotta) evidently took the phrase to denote specifically the *comitia centuriata*, the *voting assembly organized by categories of the citizenry defined by wealth. This interpretation was prob. encouraged by two facts: the *comitia centuriata* did have *judicial* competence in capital cases (this association is plain in 73: 'where a person's life as a citizen is at stake, not only can no legislative measure be proposed but *no judicial decision* can be made *save in the centuriate assembly*'); and the *assembly of the plebs—the *concilium plebis*—could not, strictly, be 'the fullest possible gathering' because it comprised only part of the citizenry (hence the term *concilium*—used here, cf. *Dom.* 79, Gell. 15. 27. 4—not *comitia*, a voting assembly of the people as a whole).

66. measures that were published   C. glances back at the distinction with which he began this segment, between measures actually brought to a vote and those *promulgated but not voted (55 **not only... put to a vote** n.). The balance of the paragraph blends abuses already assailed with new charges both pointed (**people condemned** n.) and wild (**minting** n.).

public charge   Here the term *provincia* in its original sense, 'sphere of (public) activity' (7 **temperate behaviour** n.); the term recurs in its geographical sense below (**look to the senate** n.).

minting money or raking it in   One of the oddest charges in the speech, seemingly made for the sake of the play on the cognate Latin verbs *flare* and *conflare* (both lit. 'blow (on)' a fire, to set it blazing): *flare* is regularly used in connection with minting coinage (a fire was needed to melt the metal to be poured into dies); *conflare* commonly has the sense 'scheme' or 'concoct' (*OLD* s.v. 3–4) or 'rake together', 'assemble' (ibid. 7). The latter is doubtless meant here, hence Shackleton Bailey's 'raking it in', which I have adopted. It is not clear that C.'s ref. to 'minting' has a point beyond the jingle produced by the verbs: he might allude to the especially large issue of coinage in 58 (connected with Clodius' grain law by Tatum 1999, 121; more cautiously *RRC* 1. 87, 446–7, 2. 707), but it is obscure how that—or any other minting—could be called a 'plan' (*ratio*) of Clodius' own, since the directive would have been the senate's, and the issue of 58, like all coinage, was supervised by the curule aediles.

look to the senate for a province, a budget, a staff appointment On the abuses C. has in mind see 24 **pick of the provinces**, 33 **that lot you appointed to your staff** nn.

Return from exile...for people condemned for crimes of public violence Romans in exile because of their involvement in the Catilinarian conspiracy: late in 59 C. was implying that a Catilinarian 'fifth column' in Rome wished to restore those who had been 'cast out' (*Flac.* 96); linked here with Clodius' supposed ambition for a consulship (next n.), the thought resumes the charge that he was the neo-Catilinarian leader (see **42 old forces** n.).

'priest of the people'...for the consulship For the 'title' see also *Pis.* 89: 'of the people' (*popularis*) for his political inclinations; 'priest' (*sacerdos*) to direct attention back to the Bona Dea scandal (cf. 39 'high-priest of debauchery'). Ref. to Clodius' ambitions for the consulship implies that Clodius was already making long-range plans: under the system of eligibility then in force, he could not legally have held the consulship for another 8 years.

67–71. *The Balance of 58: The Tide Turns*

C. has been concerned since 15 with 'the shipwreck that the commonwealth suffered' in 58, devoting just over one-third of the speech to the events of roughly the first four months (cf. next n.). In the next five paragraphs—the first segment wholly treating matters C. could not have witnessed—he touches on the chief events of the following eight months, in fairly straightforward chronological order: the re-engagement of Pompey in opposition to Clodius (spring: 67); the frustrated senatorial decree of 1 June and his brother's return from Asia (68); the attempt on Pompey's life (August) and the *promulgation of a tribunician measure for C.'s return (October: 69); the emergence of the consul-elect Lentulus as C.'s champion in the senate (70), and S.'s mission to Caesar in Gaul (71). Among the notable matters left in silence: the reason for Pompey's changed stance (next n.); the reason for his brother's return (68 **left his governorship** n.); and the break between Gabinius and Clodius (69 **the consuls** n.).

67. Here at last Writing from Thessalonica on 29 May 58, C. acknowledged a conversation Atticus had had with Pompey several weeks earlier and added, 'I see no impending upheaval in public affairs as significant as you see, or as you allege in trying to console me' (3. 8(53). 3, referring in ibid. 4 to a letter he had written to Pompey). He was wrong. Atticus had communicated the first reverberations of the break between Pompey and Clodius after the latter's legislation on Brogitarus' behalf and esp. his tampering with Tigranes; see 56 **Great Mother...**, 58 **Gnaeus Pompeius saw him** nn. By suppressing mention of the break C. suggests that the scales simply if belatedly fell from Pompey's eyes (next n.), so that he saw his patriotic duty to defend C. and thereby the *commonwealth. Rather, 'Pompey saw in Cicero's restoration the stick with which he intended to beat Clodius' (Tatum 1999, 172).

reawakened his habit... slowed by some suspicion See 41 **warned by agents** n., on tales of C.'s alleged plots. Pompey's 'reawakening' is cast in similar terms at *Dom.* 25, where C. adopts the pose of one telling an uncomfortable truth about a friend; cf. also *Pis.* 27, Vell. 2. 45. 3.

citizens utterly steeped in crime... even slaves A rapid review of Pompey's opponents, touching on insurrections led by Sertorius in Spain and Marcus Aemilius Lepidus, cos. 78 (*MRR* 2. 85); his campaigns in Africa and the East; his special command against the pirates; and Spartacus' rebellion. At mention of the last, Crassus— seated on the advocates' bench, with Pompey's theft of credit for that campaign still in mind (Plut. *Plut.* 21. 2, cf. *Pomp.* 32. 7, *Crass.* 11. 7)— perhaps bit his tongue.

extended... to the ends of the earth For the comparison with Alexander here implied, and the geographical scope of Pompey's achievements, see *Prov. cons.* 31, App. *BMith.* 117 (on his triumph in 62), *Anth. Lat.* 1. 396–9 S.B., and Pompey himself quoted at Plin. *HN* 7. 99, cf. Gruen 1984, 285.

he blocked with his authority the measures still awaiting execution See 55 **not only... put to a vote** n.; it is not known what measures these were.

indignation at what had already been done His 'indignation' is evoked in similarly general terms at *Dom.* 25; his speech at Capua expressing indignation over the *privilegium* aimed at C. (cf. 65 **measure** n.) falls later in the year (*Red. sen.* 29, apparently after the assassination attempt of August), though he could have expressed the same opinion earlier.

68. Lucius Ninnius... on my behalf   On this tribune's earlier support see 26 **Lucius Ninnius** n.; for his role at this juncture see also *Red. sen.* 3, Cass. Dio 38. 30. 3–4 (where he acts as Pompey's agent); for his 'consecration' of Clodius' goods at some point in 58, after Clodius had 'consecrated' the consul Gabinius' goods, see *Dom.* 124–5 (Nisbet 1939, 210–12, cf. 69 **the consuls** n.). Though C. here heartily praises Ninnius' *loyalty and *courage, he had had occasion later in 58 to question his good sense; cf. 69 **published a bill for my return** n.

Some good-for-nothing named Ligus... interposed a veto   Aelius (*RE* 83) Ligus, a tribune C. had counted a supporter and whom he therefore treats with special contempt as a traitor: cf. *Dom.* 49, calling him *novicius*, 'a person newly enslaved' (sc. having sold himself to Clodius); the abuse at *Har. resp.* 5—'blockhead' (*stipes*) and 'stupid and docile beast' (*pecus ac belua*)—is inspired by the cognomen Ligus = 'the Ligurian', from the people of NW Italy whom Roman prejudice held to be rough and backward (*duri ac agrestes*: *Leg. agr.* 2. 95), cf. 69 **one... of the clan** n. His role is also mentioned at *Red. sen.* 3.

perk up   Lit. 'raise its eyes' (*erigere oculos*) sc. after being at death's door.

whoever had added to my grief... was condemned   A reprise of *Dom.* 49–50: 'those who came to court, whether as prosecutors or defendants, came out losers when (Clodius) interceded for them.... Whoever played the least part in that law (sc. on my exile), with gesture or utterance, by predation or vote, came away rejected and convicted wherever he went' (with Nisbet 1939 ad loc.); the ref. there ('gesture' and 'predation') to those who had bid on C.'s confiscated property is here folded into the general ref. to C.'s 'grief'. No trials matching C.'s allegation are known, but C., usually our chief source on such matters, was absent during the relevant period; at *Dom.* 49 C. says that Aelius Ligus brought an accusation concerning his brother's murder but dropped the case because he knew the charge was false (*TLRR* no. 253).

left his governorship ... with tears and lamentation   As in the case of Pompey (67 **Here at last** n.), C. lets the audience infer that the behaviour described was motivated solely by concern for his own position; but Quintus was returning from Asia dressed in mourning (*squalor*: cf. 1 n.) and plunged in grief at least in part because he expected to be prosecuted for extortion as governor (refs. at 49 **brother** n.; in the sequel the prosecution did not take place).

Discussion was held ... more freely   In a letter of 17 Aug. 58 C. acknowledged Atticus' report of a favourable debate held in the senate, presumably sometime in July (*Att.* 3. 15(60). 3).

not allowed to enjoy the reward for his devotion   Because he died before C.'s return: cf. 54 **my son-in-law** n., on an earlier supplication of the consul Piso.

senate kept refusing ... my restoration   Cf. *Pis.* 29 'Were you (Piso and Gabinius) consuls then, when the entire senate shouted you down no matter what item you started to address or move, showing that you would accomplish nothing if you did not first make a motion on my account?', sim. Plut. *Cic.* 33. 2. Presumably it was this position that moved Clodius to post in the senate doorway the clause in his law on C.'s exile forbidding the senate to discuss his recall (see *Att.* 3. 12(57). 1, dated 17 Jul. and so referring to events of June, with *Att.* 3. 15(60). 6, of 17 Aug.). Taking this still to be the senate's position in Dec., C. was miffed when other business was addressed (*Att.* 3. 24(69). 2); cf. also 74 below. For the procedural move, to force discussion of a given matter, cf. e.g. *Att.* 1. 14(14). 5; limited to the senate's own sessions, the move did not (*pace* Brunt 1981) entail a full and formal cessation of public business—in the courts and *voting assemblies, as well as the senate—as is shown by C.'s ref. to trials just preceding (**whoever** n.) and by the holding of elections on schedule (70). Such a *iustitium* did occur, but not until after the riot of 23 Jan. 57: see 71–92 n.

69. Success now seemed within our grasp   For an abbreviated version of this narrative (69–75) see *Red. sen.* 4–6.

the consuls   C. speaks as though Piso and Gabinius were still united in their attitude to Clodius (sim. 70 below), but their stances had differed since the late spring, when Gabinius split with Clodius, like his patron, Pompey: a series of confrontations led to the shattering of Gabinius' fasces by Clodius' thugs (in June: App. 1) and to Clodius' 'consecration' of Gabinius' goods to the tutelary god of the plebs, Ceres (thus provoking Ninnius' 'consecration' of Clodius' goods in turn, 68 **Lucius Ninnius** n.): see *Dom.* 66, 124, *Pis.* 27–8, Cass. Dio 38. 30. 2, Liou-Gille 1998, 52–3.

senators who then held no public office   i.e. *privati*, who could state their opinion only if called on by a magistrate empowered to convene the senate and bring a matter to discussion: 25 **refer the matter to the senate** n.

deterred by Clodius' law   On the law and this clause cf. 65 **proposal . . .**, 68 **senate kept refusing** nn.; for C.'s view that such clauses traditionally had no binding force, *Att.* 3. 23 (68). 2, 4. As C. makes plain, he thought the consuls were 'deterred' only by the 'bargain over the provincial assignments', and he makes their patent hypocrisy a recurrent theme: *Red. sen.* 4, *Dom.* 69–70, *Pis.* 29, cf. *Red. sen.* 8, *Red. pop.* 11.

a plan was formed . . . shut himself up in his house   The passive voice, 'a plan was formed' (*initur consilium*), at first seems to ascribe it to the agents most recently mentioned, the consuls; whether or not C. intended that implication, it is misleading. On Aug. 11—not long after Pompey let Atticus know that he favoured C.'s recall (*Att.* 3. 15(60). 1)—one of Clodius' slaves dropped a dagger in the vestibule of the temple of Castor, where the senate was to meet; taken with the weapon to the consul Gabinius, the slave said that Clodius had ordered him to kill Pompey: see *Red. sen.* 4–5, 29, *Dom.* 66–7, 110, 129, *Har. resp.* 48–9, 58 (cf. 6), *Pis.* 16, 28, 29, *Mil.* 18, 37, 73, Asc. 46. 17–47. 9 Cl. (giving the date), *Schol. Bob.* 171. 1–4, 172. 2–8 St., Plut. *Pomp.* 49. 2. On other real or alleged plots against P., see 41 **the same suspicion** n.; Caesar similarly shut himself up in his house and stayed away from the senate for the balance of the year when attacked by some equestrians after the meeting of 5 Dec. 63 (Suet. *Iul.* 14. 2), but that was a matter of a few weeks, not over four months. As the refs. preceding indicate, C. never tired of recalling this incident, often returning to it several times in the course of a single speech. Doing so of course served to rouse *invidia* against Clodius for outrageously striking at a great man. It also provided C. with an excuse: if even Pompey quailed, C. could hardly be blamed for yielding to Clodius' onslaught (so explicitly *Har. resp.* 49; for C.'s need to defend himself against charges of cowardice, 36 **I grant** n.). Yet we might also suspect (with Riggsby 2002*a*, 176–7) that at some level of his mind an abiding hostility over Pompey's abandonment moved C. to tell this story over and over again and thereby suggest Pompey's cowardice: the implicit comparison with the behaviour in 59 of the consul Bibulus (cf. *Vat.* 22)—no one's idea of a strong character—points in that direction; so too, more clearly, does the contrast with Milo, whose *manly stance vis-à-vis Clodius C. praises at 89 below, capping the praise with the question, 'Was he to cast off the cause he had taken on, *or just shut himself up in his house?*' More directly still, see *Dom.* 67, depicting Pompey as hiding from Clodius' forces even after they had spent their full fury on C. It is in any case striking that the incident looms so large in the 'post-return' speeches yet leaves not a trace in the letters from exile, despite C.'s concern to track Pompey's intentions in late summer and fall of 58 (Introd. §1).

Eight tribunes   That is, all the tribunes of 58 (*MRR* 2. 195–7) except Clodius and Aelius Ligus, whose defection C. is about to mention. C.'s critique of the bill (next n.) implies that Ninnius (26, 68 nn.) was the leader of the effort and prob. the draftsman.

promulgated a bill for my return   On 29 Oct. 58 (*Att.* 3. 23(68). 1): the bill could therefore have been voted any time after the required period of *promulgation ended on 16 Nov. (the three *nundinae* following the promulgation were 31 Oct., 8 Nov., and 16 Nov., see App. 1; 17–23 and 25–9 Nov. were all comitial days). Since C. would surely have used any attempt to obstruct it as further evidence of the opposition's 'crimes', we should infer that it was not brought to a vote, despite the endorsement by Lentulus that C. will stress below (70), perhaps because the *assemblies (*contiones*) held after its promulgation showed that it lacked sufficient popular support (on the failure of legislation in such circumstances, see Morstein-Marx 2004, 186–94; more sceptically Mouritsen 2001, 65–6). Sent a copy of the

bill, C. criticized it for restoring his citizenship and status in the
senate but not his property (ibid. 2); he also faulted a clause protecting the tribunes from sanctions that Clodius' law imposed on legislating for C.'s recall (ibid. 2–4): writing with a nearly paranoid
crankiness, C. even suspects 'some malice' in the drafting, alleging
that the clause was not needed by the incumbent tribunes, who were
not subject to any penalty in Clodius' law, and inferring that it was
intended to constrain the incoming tribunes in a way contrary to his
interests. On the proposal see Moreau 1989 and his remarks in *RS*
2. 775–6. The bill was distinct from one that S. drafted as tribune-
elect (which C. found even more wanting), no later than Sept., in
anticipation of his entry into office in December: see 72 **tribunes** n.
C. goes on to speak of Lentulus' backing just below (70); at *Red. sen.*
29 he says that the tribunes were encouraged by Pompey ('though he
was staying in his house out fear of bloodshed (viz., after the assassination attempt of 11 Aug.), he already asked the tribunes of (58) to
promulgate (a measure) for my well-being').

some whom I had taken to be friends proved otherwise   This is not
a ref. to Ligus, whom he is about to belabor directly, but a parenthetical remark inspired by mention of 'friends', briefly reviving the
'treachery of friends' motif seen elsewhere: see 46 **some felt** n.

one ... of the clan   A laboured slur on Aelius Ligus, warmed over
from *Clu.* 72 (similar conceit, different target). C. means that Aelius
adopted the cognomen Ligus to fake descent from Publius Aelius
Ligus, cos. 172, whose family was entitled to display the *wax mask
(*imago*: 19 **duumvirate** n.); but instead of linking him to that noble
clan (*genus*), people assumed he was a Ligurian, a member of a
barbarian tribe (*natio*: cf. 68 **Some good-for-nothing** n.).

70. magistrates for the next year had already been elected   C.
thinks esp. of the consular and praetorian elections held in the
*centuriate assembly, usually in mid-to-late July, some weeks after
the tribunician elections in which S. and Milo were chosen (on those
chosen with them, 72 **tribunes** n.). The elections were held on
schedule, and C. in Thessalonica knew by the first week of Aug.
that Lentulus (below) was to be consul (*QFr.* 1. 4(4). 5, cf. App. 1).
Lentulus' colleague, Quintus Caecilius Metellus Nepos, with whom

C. had a history of bad relations, does not enter the narrative until 72 below (**his colleague** n.); Clodius' brother Appius, among the praetors elected, makes his first appearance (by innuendo) at 77 (**patrician and praetorian** n.).

leader of the senate   Lentulus was 'leader' (*princeps*) because in this period the presiding magistrate customarily asked the consuls-designate for their opinion first in the interval between their election and entrance into office (cf. Sall. *Cat.* 50. 4 'then Decimus Iunius Silanus was asked his opinion first, because he was then consulelect'), and Lentulus had been returned ahead of Metellus Nepos in the election. After entering office on 1 Jan. 57, Lentulus will preside and, fixing a new order of precedence, ask Lucius Cotta (cos. 65, cens. 64) to give his opinion first (73).

Publius Lentulus   Publius Cornelius (*RE* 238, cf. *MRR* 3. 69) Lentulus (the nickname 'Spinther', given him because he resembled an actor of that name, is one he did not desire and C. never used in addressing or referring to him): at the time of this trial he was in Cilicia as governor. Younger by some six years (he was aedile 63, praetor 60, offices C. held in in 69 and 66), he and C. had been acquainted since boyhood (*Fam.* 1. 6(17). 2), and he emerged in 57 as C.'s chief champion, along with S., Milo, and (ultimately) Pompey; he evidently played an appropriately large and heroic role in C.'s poem on his exile and return, *On His Times* (*Fam.* 1. 9(20). 23), and he receives encomia in all the 'post-return' speeches, see *Red. sen.* 5, 8–9, 24–8 (cited by C. at *Fam.* 1. 9(20). 4), *Red. pop.* 11, 15, 18, *Dom.* 7, 9, 30, 70, *Har. resp.* 13, cf. *Pis.* 80, *Mil.* 39. From the outset C. anticipated his goodwill (*QFr.* 1. 4(4). 5, with ref. to Quintus' expected prosecution) and his utility as a link to Pompey, in whose pocket he was said to be (esp. *Att.* 3. 22(67). 2, cf. *Att.* 3. 23(68). 1; but *Att.* 3. 24(69). 1 shows C. unwilling to take anyone's support for granted). After his return C. was annoyed with Lentulus (and Nepos) for what he judged inadequate compensation for his properties (*Att.* 4. 2(74). 5, with *QFr.* 2. 2(6). 3; *Fam.* 1. 9(20). 5, written later to Lentulus, shifts the blame to others); but he continued to act appropriately toward a man to whom he professed to feel bound not just by the duty (*officium*) owed a friend but even by the devotion (*pietas*) owed a family member (*Fam.* 1. 1(12). 1, sim. *Fam.* 1. 4(14). 3, 1.

5a(15). 1, 1. 6(17). 2, 1. 8(19). 6, 1. 9(2). 1). It was to Lentulus that
C. offered, late in 54, a formal apologia for toeing the triumvirs' line
(*Fam.* 1. 9(20)).   -

he saw   It was plain at the time that C.'s case could not advance until
the new magistrates entered office; C. flatters Lentulus by ascribing
to him this unselfish preference for the other's good over his own
social credit.

71. Meanwhile, at about this time   November: see next n. and
App. 1.

Publius Sestius travelled to see Gaius Caesar   S. re-enters the story
for the first time since the beginning of 15 (the MSS include the
epithet *designatus* here, indicating that S. was still tribune-elect; but
since C. registers the same fact just below in a way integral to the
context, I join most editors in regarding the epithet here as interpol-
ated gloss). He had been in correspondence with C. at least from late
summer and through the fall of 58 (no letters are extant but see *QFr.*
1. 4(4). 2, 5, *Att.* 3. 17(62). 1, 3. 19(64). 2, 3. 20(65). 3); we do not
know on whose initiative he went to Cisalpine Gaul, where by this
time Caesar was making the governor's rounds of the towns, having
settled his army in winter quarters (*BG* 1. 54. 2–3). We do know that
C. himself was not in direct contact with Caesar: *Att.* 3. 15(60). 3 and
3. 18(63). 1 show him relying on third-hand information, including
(in the latter, from early Sept.) a report that Pompey was awaiting a
letter from Caesar before taking up C.'s cause; *Fam.* 1. 9(20). 9 (citing
Pompey) gives cause to think the letter arrived, but we do not know
when (cf. 74 **Gnaeus Pompeius** n.).

he thought that... bring the affair to a good end   The MSS transmit these words after the sentence 'Now I enter... as tribune-elect'
below: I adopt Peterson's transposition to this context, where they
both give an explanation for the journey at an appropriate point and
anticipate the phrase 'for the commonwealth's sake' below; both
sentences end with the same verb (*suscepit*), which perhaps encouraged the original displacement.

if Caesar was inclined to be well-disposed...   If Caesar had been
inclined to be well-disposed (*aequus*, lit. 'even, fair'), C. would not

leave the point in doubt but would turn it to S.'s credit: for the presentation of the alternatives, giving pro forma parenthetical endorsement to the one more favourable to Caesar while leaving room for us to choose the other, see 16 **either (as I believe)** n., cf. 39 **who was not obliged to be estranged**, 52 **just cause** nn.

punctiliousness and uprightness   C. has already praised S.'s *up-rightness (integritas)* in an official capacity early in his career (13); 'punctiliousness' (*sedulitas*) is one of several qualities, like 'diligence' (*diligentia*) and 'energetic application' (*industria*), proper to one who knows how to do his duty (*officium*), and C.'s earlier account showed S. to be such a man, esp. in his behaviour toward his father and two fathers-in-law (6–7).

71–92. *The Events of Early 57 and the Defense of Sestius*

We come to the time that prompted the charge against S., and an account that in a more conventional defence would directly follow the review of S.'s early career (6–13) and directly address the acts alleged in the charge. This account does not do the latter, for the same reason it does not do the former: since C.'s strategy demands that the story be about himself, and about the *commonwealth as it is tied to and reflected in his *well-being, we continue to follow the drama surrounding his recall. After noting the departure of Gabinius and Piso for their provinces (71), C. dwells on the *promulgation of (72) and abortive vote on (75–8) the new tribunes' measure for his recall, inserting between these events (in due chronological order) the parallel but distinct expressions of support in the senate's meeting of 1 Jan. (72–4). Then, to his account of the violence that disrupted the vote on the tribunes' bill, C. appends S.'s single act *qua* tribune actually treated in the speech: his attempt to halt by *obnuntiation an assembly convened by the consul Nepos, which led Clodius' thugs to attack him (79). There then follows the lone passage in which C. mounts a defence in a narrow sense: he uses the attack to reduce the charge against S. to absurdity (80–5), then— seizing (and twisting) an opening provided by the prosecution— develops a comparison with Milo that heaps praise on the latter in a way useful to S. (86–92). S.'s action and its violent sequel, which C. evidently had in mind from the moment S. was indicted

(79 **Sestius...lost consciousness** n.), could not have been the basis of the charge; rather it gave ground for refuting the charge, since it provided a reason to think that Sestius had acted in self-defence, and without criminal intent, in assembling an armed posse (see Introd. §2).

Stressing this one episode, while passing over in silence all of S.'s other acts as tribune, was also a form of misdirection, allowing C. to use an aspect of the case he could profitably exploit to eclipse other, perhaps less tractable aspects (cf. Gotoff 1986, 125). But his account is misleading in another, more profound sense; for C. omits a key fact that establishes the context of several events he describes, clarifies the actors' motives, and hints at interrelations that have not previously been discerned. The omission cannot be inadvertent: not only does it encourage misinterpretation of S.'s behaviour in ways congenial to C.'s strategy (79 **announced** n.), but it is fundamental to his (in any case) highly tendentious treatment of Milo (esp. 85 **not only no special court** n., 89 **one consul** nn.), whose portrayal as the soul of sober but frustrated constitutionality is both useful for this speech and helpful to Milo in light of the prosecution he was facing (95 **aedile** n.). It is a fact that C. mentions prominently in a parallel, more straightforward narrative at *Red. sen.* 6–8:

Indeed, in that month (Jan. 57) you were able to judge the difference between me and my enemies. *I* abandoned my own well-being to keep the commonwealth from being smeared with the gore of citizens' wounds on my account (cf. e.g. 45–6); *they* thought my return should be blocked, not by a vote of the Roman people, but by a river of blood (the riot of 23 Jan., see 75–8). *And so from then on you (senators) made no responses to citizens, to our allies, to foreign kings, juries made no declarations with their verdicts, nor the people with its ballots, nor (the senate) with its decrees; you saw the forum speechless, the senate house mute, the civil community silent and shattered.* (7) *And at that very time...you saw* people (Clodius' thugs) dashing about the whole city with swords and torches, magistrates' houses assailed, temples of the gods in flames, the fasces of an excellent man and most distinguished consul smashed, the most sanctified body of a supremely brave and excellent tribune of the plebs not violated by the touch of a hand but stabbed and drained. At that carnage some magistrates drew back a bit from my cause..., the rest (remained firm). (8) Publius Lentulus, the parent and divine protector of my life, fortune, fame, and repute, took the lead...

The passage in italics provides the fact suppressed in this speech: the riot of 23 Jan. was followed by a suspension of all public business, in the courts (a *iustitium* strictly so called), *voting assemblies, and senate. That the senate denied receptions to foreign embassies (thus 'allies' and 'foreign kings' above), in particular, shows that the move was made as a matter of public policy (*consilium publicum*, see 27 n.) and did not somehow follow from Clodius' 'controlling the streets' (Gelzer 1969*b*, 145, relying incautiously on *Sest.* 85): this was a more generalized form of the protest mounted by the senate after its decree in C.'s favour was *vetoed on 1 June 58 (68 **the senate kept refusing** n.), in this case prob. decreed in an edict by C.'s ally Lentulus with the senate's backing; the suspension certainly extended through Feb., the month the senate regularly devoted to receiving foreign embassies, and perhaps beyond (cf. Meyer 1919, 109 n. 3, Maslowski 1976, 30, Brunt 1981, 229–30, and App. 1; Mitchell 1991, 153 n. 29, and Tatum 1999, 307 n. 25, deny the *iustitium*, but without considering *Red. sen.* 6–8 or the structure of *Sest.* 71–92 as a whole). C. also refers to five events that people witnessed during the suspension ('at that very time...', cf. also *Red. pop.* 14), before the movement to secure C.'s return gathered steam under Lentulus' leadership, prob. in May (for the latter cf. 116–17, 120–3 with App. 1). The first two, despite C.'s plural ('magistrates'), refer to Clodius' attack on Milo's house (85 **another tribune** n.; the ref. to crowds 'with swords and torches' recurs at 85 and in the ref. to the same attack at *Red. pop.* 14, cf. 90 **fire and sword** n.); the last obviously refers to S. (the third and fourth prob. refer to the same riot at the temple of Castor, see 79 **announced** n.).

The suspension inspired by the riot of 23 Jan. thus provides the chronological framework for all the events C. addresses in 79–92. This framework is welcome in itself, since that segment's lack of clear chronological markers has yielded confusion (e.g. causing the attack on Milo's house mentioned below to be identified with a later attack, in Nov. 57: 85 **another tribune**, 95 **has assailed** nn.). More important, the suspension intelligibly explains all the behaviour of S. (79 **announced** n.), Milo, and Nepos (cf. 85 **not only no special court**, 89 **one consul** nn.) that C. is about to recount. This event is hardly the only relevant fact that C. suppresses in this speech, or the most important: Pompey's break with Clodius (67 **Here at last** n.) was far more consequential, for C.'s recall and Roman politics more generally, but C. says not a word about it (he could not acknowledge the break without being more candid about Pompey's earlier behaviour than served his ends). But perhaps precisely because the event concerned here is less consequential, the importance of its suppression for this segment of the speech has not been fully grasped.

71. journey before   The MSS read *primum iter*, 'first journey': but 'if the trip to Gaul... was Sestius' first journey in the public interest, what was the second? For *primum* read *prius* (before he took office as tribune)' (Shackleton Bailey 1987, 278).

two vultures clad in commanders' cloaks   Piso reappears as a vulture when setting off to his province at *Pis.* 38; for the metaphor, cf. 54 **they swooped in** n. On the ceremonial assumption of the scarlet commander's cloak (*paludamentum*: cf. sim. *Pis.* 31, and 17 **fasces** n.) in place of the civilian toga, see Marshall 1984, 121–3.

bad omens and people's curses   For the same point, *Pis.* 31, 33. The start of any journey was esp. fraught with omens for the outcome and vulnerable to divine ill-will invoked by human curses: the curses cast by the tribune Ateius Capito when Crassus departed for his ill-fated governorship of Syria were long remembered (*MRR* 2. 216). Inspired by Gabinius' embarrassed return from Syria in Sept. 54 (cf. Cass. Dio 39. 62. 1), C. imagined inserting in the council of the gods that concluded Book 2 of his poem *On His Times* a scene in which Apollo foretold 'the sort of return the two generals would have, the one having lost his army, the other having sold it' (*QFr.* 3. 1(21). 24): the appropriate point in the narrative would be the moment described here, a turning point before the splendid triumph of C.'s return (*QFr.* 2. 7(13). 1, written in Feb. 55, makes plain that the council of the gods was the climax of Book 2, which was long completed by the time C. contemplated the 'insertion', *embolium*; cf. Harrison 1990, 457, Courtney 1993, 173–4).

lost the province... units in Syria   The *proconsular shortcomings of Piso and Gabinius are remarked in 94 and 93 (respectively), where extortion is the focus. On Piso (*MRR* 2. 207, 210, 218), see *Prov. cons.* 4–8 (with the same hyperbole regarding the 'total loss' of an army, sim. *Pis.* 47, *Planc.* 86) and *Pis.* 37–40, 42–7, 83–94 (with Nisbet 1961, 172–80). Piso can hardly have governed Macedonia less well

than C.'s consular colleague, Antonius (8 n.), and the charge that the
province was 'lost' wildly overstates the effects of Thracian attacks
during his tenure. On Gabinius (*MRR* 2. 203, 210–11, 218), see *Prov.
cons.* 8–12 (ibid. 9 on the casualities mentioned here), *Pis.* 41, 48–50,
with Nisbet 1961, 188–92, Fantham 1975, 429–32, Siani-Davies 2001,
132–4, the last esp. on his role in restoring Ptolemy XII Auletes to the
Egyptian throne; in mid-May C. will have the chance to gloat over
the senate's refusing Gabinius' request for a *supplicatio* (*QFr.* 2. 6(8).
1, *Prov. cons.* 14–16, 25). When the senate fixed the consular provinces for 54, in the meeting (early July 56) at which C. delivered *Prov.
cons.*, Macedonia was made a praetorian province, and Piso was
superseded at the start of 55; Syria remained a consular province,
and Gabinius was left in place until the following year, when Crassus
succeeded him.

72. tribunes … publish a measure concerning my recall As early
as Aug. 58 C. said that his hopes rested with the tribunes-elect for 57,
esp. S. (*Att.* 3. 13(59). 1, *QFr.* 1. 4(4). 3); writing to Terentia on 29
Nov., he worried over their action's timing (*Fam.* 14. 3(9). 3 'now our
remaining hope lies with the new tribunes, and indeed in (their
acting within) the first few days'). C's narrative is most naturally
taken to imply that the tribunes *promulgated their bill between Dec.
10, when they entered office, and the senate's meeting of 1 Jan.
(below), while the schedule of *nundinae* in Jan. shows that it could
have been promulgated any time on or before 6 Jan. (75 **a day** n.); on
the question how the tribunes' action was coordinated with the
senate's, see 74 **unanimous support** n.; in any case, the bill would
have come to a vote on 23 Jan. but for the riot C. describes in 75–7.
Laws had been drafted well in advance by or for at least two tribunes-
elect, S. himself, whose bill C. criticized as inadequate in point of
dignity and security, and Titus Fadius, his former *quaestor, whose
bill he preferred (*Att.* 3. 20(65). 3, on S.'s draft, criticized also at *Att.*
3. 23(68). 4, where he approves the bill drafted for Fadius by Gaius
Visellius Varro, son of a jurist and a *iudex quaestionis* around this
time, *MRR* 2. 195); another tribune, Gaius Messius, 'at first (*initio*)
promulgated a bill for my well-being on his own (*separatim*)' (*Red.
sen.* 21)—an independent initiative preceding the joint measure at
issue here, which was proposed under Quintus Fabricius' name

(75 n.) with the subscription of (at least initially) all the other tribunes. After the defection of the two tribunes about to be attacked, eight remained on C.'s side (cf. *Red. sen.* 4, *Mil.* 39), of whom Milo and S. are thanked at length at *Red. sen.* 19–20, the remaining six more briefly but by name at *Red. sen.* 21–2: Gaius Cestilius, Marcus Cispius (76 n.), Titus Fadius (cf. above, and C.'s letter of consolation to him, on his conviction on a charge of electoral bribery, in 52: *Fam.* 5. 18(51)), Manius Curtius (whose father, Sextus Peducaeus, C. had served as quaestor in 75 (*MRR* 2. 98) and whose *loyalty C. recalled and repaid in 54, see *QFr.* 3. 1(21). 10), Gaius Messius (cf. above; his actions later in the year show him to be aligned with Pompey, *Att.* 4. 1(73). 7), and Quintus Fabricius (75 n.).

'Gracchus'... that field-mouse... nibble away at the common-wealth   Quintus Numerius (*RE* 5) Rufus, mocked also at 82 below (cf. 94, *Pis.* 35): the man's full name, with filiation and tribe, is given by *CIL* 1². 759 (Q. Numerius Q(uinti) f(ilius) Vel(ina) Rufus, cf. also 1². 2. 2513; Q. Numerius, Asc. 11. 18 Cl., *Schol. Bob.* 122. 30 St., Q. Numerius Rufus, *Schol. Bob.* 134. 27 St.); C. deigns to mention him by name only once (94). With the name 'Gracchus', transmitted by the MSS, the insult is woven together from two distinct strands. People (acc. to C.) sarcastically referred to him as another Gracchus, presumably because he adopted the 'popular' stance of the brothers whose reforms (the well-off thought) helped the poor by depleting the *commonwealth (see 103 below, and cf. *Att.* 4. 11(86). 2, where C. calls Clodius 'the people's Appuleia', a similar political sneer, referring to the tribune Appuleius Saturninus, blended with a sexual insult); the mockery derived from Numerius' patent inferiority to the great populists—he was what a Roman might call *Gracchus dimidiatus*, a 'half-pint Gracchus'. C. compounds that insult with the image of the *nitedula* (dimin. of *nitela*), a 'reddish field-mouse' (*mus agrestis robeus* DServ. on Verg. *G.* 1. 181), playing on the man's cognomen (Rufus = 'red(-haired)'). Mockery of his allegedly humble rural origins ('plucked from the thorn-bushes') is resumed at 82 (**mule-driver's cowl** n.) and is presumably based on his roots in Picenum, a region on Italy's Adriatic coast esp. identified with the *tribus Velina* (cf. Taylor 1960, 63 ff., 238); but we need not suppose he was any more 'rustic' than another member of that *tribus*, C.'s sleek protégé Marcus Caelius Rufus, from Interamnia Praetuttiorum near Picenum (ibid. 199–200). Skutsch's conjecture 'Brocchus' (for 'Gracchus'), referring to projecting front teeth (Varro *RR* 2. 7. 3, 2. 9. 4, Plin. *HN* 11. 169, cf. Eng. 'Bucky'), would make the insult all of a piece (adopted here and in 82 by Cousin 1965 and Shackleton Bailey 1991*a*), but at the cost of stepping on another joke at 82 (**killing their own Gracchus** n.); Skutsch (1943) withdrew the conjecture and defended 'Gracchus' along the lines offered here.

the famous Serranus   Acc. to an etymology known to C. and later writers, the nickname Serranus (as though < *serere*, 'sow, plant') was given to one of the Atilii who was found plowing his land when summoned to a command in the First Punic War (*Sex. Rosc.* 50, Val. Max. 4. 4. 5); if the story had any basis in fact, this would most likely be Gaius Atilius (*RE* 47) Regulus, cos. 257 and 250. But the etymology is almost certainly false (the original form of the name is prob. 'Sar(r)anus' = 'Tyrian', i.e. 'of Carthage': see *RE* 2 (1896): 2094–5 (Klebs)); when first found securely attested, in the second cent. BCE, the name is associated with a different branch of the family (the Atilii Serrani, see next n.), not the Atilii Reguli.

the one from … the Gavii of Gaul   Sextus Atilius (*RE* 70) Serranus: like S. he had been *quaestor in 63, when C. claims to have done him 'very important favours' (*Red. pop.* 12), and no doubt for that reason C. expected to find him an ally (*QFr.* 1. 4(4). 3, early Aug. 58, reading *Atilius* with Shackleton Bailey for the certainly corrupt *Gratidius*). Atilius continued to be hostile to C.'s interests after his return, threatening to *veto a favourable senatorial decree concerning C.'s house (*Att.* 4. 2(74). 4), and C. later implicated him in the profanation of sacred sites (*Har. resp.* 32); he was perhaps dead some time before late 54 (see Shackleton Bailey on *QFr.* 3. 26(26). 5). C. here alleges that he was an Atilius not by birth but by adoption: this was not a reproach per se, because adoption was commonly used by elite families to insure their continuity; C.'s mockery lies rather in the suggestion that the man's birth-family (the Gavii) was utterly obscure, perhaps even foreign (see further below). Were C.'s allegation true, the man's full name after adoption would be Sextus Atilius Serranus Gavianus, with his original clan-name (Gavius) transformed into an agnomen with the suffix -*anus*; in fact the name 'Gavianus' occurs only in 74 below, where it is surely meant insultingly (cf. C.'s use of the name 'Caesoninus Calventius' to mock Piso for his supposedly Gallic grandfather: *Red. sen.* 13, *Prov. cons.* 13, *Pis.* 14). The conceit of adoption, combined with the supposed etymology of the cognomen Serranus (preceding n.), prompts C. to elaborate an agricultural metaphor of 'grafting', much of which has been corrupted in transmission. Where the medieval MSS' common ancestor offered gibberish (apparently, *sed ex deserto gavio laeliore a calatis Gaviis in calatinos at illos insitus*), the translation here is based on an emended text—'sed ex deserto *Gavi Oleli rure* (Madvig), a *Galatis* (Mommsen) Gaviis in Calatinos *Atilios* (edd.) insitus'—adopted only as a plausible stop-gap (Cousin 1965 prints the same text): acc. to this text, the man's biological father was a Gavius Olelus (the cognomen is very doubtful: see Shackleton Bailey 1991b, 26), and the balance of the insult ascribes Gallic origins to the man, along the lines of the smear used against the consul Piso (21 **mother's lineage** n.: I take *Calatinos* to have a primarily geographical meaning, 'of Calatia' sc. in Campania, balancing in that respect *Galatis*; others treat it as a cognomen, 'the Atilii Calatini', as though referring to Aulus Atilius Calatinus (or Caiatinus: cos. 258 and 254), perhaps correctly).

removed his name ... entries in account books i.e. when the bill's text, along with its sponsors' names, had already been read out and posted by way of *promulgation, Serranus removed his name (*nomen*) from the text on the notice-board (*tabula*) after certain entries (*nomina*) had been made in interested persons' account books (*tabulas*): C.'s charge entails 'an untranslatable play with the double senses of *nomen* ("entry," of a sum due, and "name") and *tabula*(*e*) ("ledger" and "writing tablet"), implying that Serranus had been bribed to take his name off the list' (Shackleton Bailey 1991*a*, 171 n. 91).

The first of the year arrives The date on which the consuls began their tenure, with the 'senior consul' (*consul prior*, here Lentulus), who had been returned first at the election, presiding at the year's first meeting of the senate: for this meeting see also *Red. pop.* 11–12, *Pis.* 34.

delegations from all of Italy As there would be again for the successful initiative in July: see 129 and nn. The delegations must have been summoned by C.'s supporters, using their patronal and other ties to the towns: the speech Pompey made at Capua in the latter part of the year, denouncing Clodius' law as a *privilegium (Red. sen. 29), was prob. an example of such an effort.

his colleague   Quintus Caecilius (*RE* 96) Metellus Nepos (named at 101, 130) was both close kin to Clodius (*frater, Dom.* 7, *Att.* 4. 3(75). 4, *Fam.* 5. 3(11). 1: either 'cousin'= son of Clodius' mother's brother, or—less likely, *pace* Shackleton Bailey 1977—uterine brother) and an open enemy of C. since the end of 63, when as a tribune critical of the Catilinarians' execution he kept C. from addressing the people as he left office (*MRR* 2. 174: see esp. *Fam.* 5. 1–2(1–2), from and to Nepos' brother, Metellus Celer, with *LUO no.* 25, *FS* 215–26, and 129 **I alone** n.); barbs C. aimed at him (Plut. *Cic.* 26. 6–7) give the flavour of their relationship. In July 58 the prospect of his enemy's election as consul caused C. to despair (*Att.* 3. 12(57). 1), but Atticus interceded with Nepos and prepared the ground for the position adopted at this meeting: in a letter of 25 Oct. 58 Atticus told Cicero that Nepos had dropped his objection to the recall (*Att.* 3. 23(68). 1, cf. *Att.* 3.22(67). 2), and C. added a letter of his own (mentioned at *Fam.* 5. 4(10). 1, cf. *Att.* 3. 24(69). 2, 10 Dec. 58: Nepos 'was very decently setting aside his quarrel'). When Quintus reported Nepos' position at this meeting, C. wrote again, urging him not to support the enmity of others (i.e. Clodius) now that he had overcome his own enmity for the *commonwealth's sake (*Fam.* 5. 4(10). 2). On Nepos' behaviour, see also 79 **announced,** 130 **Quintus Metellus** nn.

conscript fathers   *Patres conscripti*, a traditional phrase for 'members of the senate': its origins were unknown even to the Romans of the late Republic, who derived it either from the enrollment (*conscribere*) of the heads of patrician households (*patres*) in the original senate or (as though *patres et conscripti*, 'fathers and conscripts') from the enrolment of new, plebeian 'conscripts' alongside patrician members after the establishment of the Republic (Fest. 304. 24–30 L.).

73. Lucius Cotta ... was called on to give his opinion first   In fixing the order of precedence in the senate—among his first honourific tasks as new consul—Lentulus gave pride of place to Lucius Aurelius (*RE* 102) Cotta, cos. 65, cens. 64 (his older brothers, Gaius and Marcus, had been consuls in 75 and 74); C. seems to indicate (74) that Lentulus, as Pompey's protégé, gave him the honour of speaking second. Cotta's speech of 1 Jan. 57 receives detailed notice, to similar effect, at *Dom.* 68; *Dom.* 84 adds more detail on the support he showed C., prob. in the same speech, corroborating the view C. is about to describe: 'Lucius Cotta, a former censor, said under oath in the senate that if he had been censor when I was absent, he would have read out my name as a senator in my proper place'—i.e. he would not have recognized as valid the law that stripped C. of his civil status.

a statement completely worthy of our commonwealth And completely in agreement with C.'s own views, see nn. following. But though some points are expressed in ways prob. owing more to C. than to Cotta (**justice and the courts** n.), we should not think that C. merely ventriloquizes the man; indeed, on the status of Clodius' law as a *privilegium (next n.), Cotta's standing as a respected jurist perhaps rather shaped or confirmed C.'s own view.

not only . . . save in the centuriate assembly For the legal issues, see 65 **centuriate assembly** n. and *Red. sen.* 11, *Dom.* 33–4, 47, 68; Cotta is cited for the same view at *Leg.* 3. 45.

justice and the courts had been uprooted i.e. he had been *proscribed, his *life as a citizen destroyed and his property confiscated without trial (65 **measure** n.). But while that claim could be made with some justice in ref. to Clodius' law declaring that he had been exiled, the immediate context concerns Clodius' first law, *de capite civis*, and C.'s panicky reaction to it (next n.): the statement thus conflates the measures in a way typical of C. (cf. 65 **measure** n.). That conflation, and the characteristic hyperbole with which it is expressed, show that at least this part of Cotta's speech is paraphrased in C.'s idiom; equally revealing is the claim that the courts were 'uprooted', which will play a large role, in a different sense, in the argument that C. makes concerning Milo at 85 ff. (cf. 85 **no special court**, 89 **courts were uprooted** nn.).

I had swerved a bit from my course and . . . escaped the storm-tossed seas An allusion to the view—that he betrayed a lack of *resolve in his withdrawal—which C. sought to counter earlier in the speech (36 **I grant** n.) and which he himself acknowledged in writing to Atticus (3. 13(59). 2, 5 Aug. 58: 'they saw that I swerved a little out of fear')

and esp. to Terentia (*Fam.* 14. 3(9). 1–2, Nov. 58). Cotta's point is put
a bit differently at *Dom.* 68 ('yielded to the storm').

I had rescued the commonwealth from perils no less great . . .   As
C. argues in 49 (**one man alone** n.).

was such . . . that . . . it could not have the force of law   i.e. the law
naming C. an exile was flawed not only as a *privilegium but also in
technical aspects of its drafting: C. himself argues this point at *Dom.*
43 ff. (basing himself on prior discussion in the senate), after making
the more fundamental argument (ibid. 34–42) that none of Clodius'
legislation was properly passed because his transfer to the plebs and
so his election as tribune were invalid.

recalled by the authority of the senate   Cotta's position (sim. *Dom.*
68) gives full scope to the senate's *authority, as expressed in its decrees,
while acknowledging that it did not have the same force as the people's
will expressed in proper legislation cf. 32 **senate's authority** n.

74. Gnaeus Pompeius was called upon for his opinion   Sim.
Dom. 69, where the concern for popular opinion expressed here
is attributed to the senate more generally. By the time of this
statement Pompey had received Quintus' pledge that C. would be
politically tractable if he returned (*Fam.* 1. 9(20). 9) and on the
strength of that pledge had made his own pledge to Caesar (ibid.
12, cf. 71 **Publius Sestius travelled** n.). Pompey had been working
for the recall behind the scenes and away from Rome before the
meeting of 1 Jan.—e.g. attacking Clodius' legislation at Capua (*Red.
sen.* 29), and prob. encouraging the tribune Messius to draft his bill
(72 **tribunes** n.)—but this is the first public act at Rome that
C. ascribes to him, and it differs notably from Cotta's in style as
much as in substance. Where Cotta is represented as forcefully
expressing direct opinions (with a touch of C.'s own hyperbole),
the great general leans heavily on euphemism, speaking of C.'s need
of *tranquillity (*otium*) free of 'harassment from "popular" quarters' (*popularis concitatio*)—as if C. required only a bit of peace and
quiet, not protection from being killed on sight—and describing
the Roman people's sovereign power to make its own laws as a
'beneficence' (*beneficium*) aptly 'joined to the senate's authority'
(*beneficium populi Romani* is a cliché for election to office—cf. 134

below, *Verr.* 2. 5. 163, 175, 180, *Leg, Man,* 69, *Clu.* 150, *Mur.* 2, 4, 86, 90, *Dom.* 98, *Phil.* 14. 25—but C. nowhere else applies it to legislation). Whether the brief turn owes more to Pompey's idiom or to C.'s, it is plump, grave, and complacent.

unanimous support had been expressed in a vote i.e. for a decree commending legislation, in line with Pompey's recommendation: thus the procedures followed in July-August, when the senate's *decree was followed by legislation in the *centuriate assembly, see 109

put before...the senate n. C. leaves unclear how the senate's vote was coordinated with *promulgation of the tribune's bill. Supposition that the latter promulgation occurred only after the senate had expressed its will (e.g. Lintott 1968, 192) is consistent with the fact that a bill brought to a vote on 23 Jan. could have been promulgated any time on or before 6 Jan. (75 **a day** n.), and it relieves us of having to imagine two uncoordinated pieces of legislation going forward toward the same end, one moved by the tribunes, the other emerging from the senate's debate. That supposition is inconsistent, however, with C.'s narrative, which plainly implies that the tribunes promulgated their bill before the senate's meeting of 1 Jan. (72 **tribunes** n.); note also that after Quintus sent him a copy of the motion on which the senate voted, C. told Atticus that he intended to await 'passage of the laws' (plural: *legum latio*), adding that should opposition arise, he would 'rely on the senate's authority'—i.e. adopt Cotta's position— and return home, even if it put his life in danger (*Att.* 3. 26(71)). In the event, the legislative question was made moot by the riot of 23 Jan. (75 ff.), and C. did not simply return home.

Atilius Gavianus See 72 **the one** n.

as you know C. reminds the senatorial judges of something they witnessed in the *curia*, the *equestrians and *treasury tribunes, of something they recall—in either case (we are to understand) memorable because scandalous.

he did not dare...be given the night The same procedural manoeuvre is the centerpiece of the parallel account at *Red. pop.* 12; Atilius used it again at the senate's meeting of 1 Oct. 57, on the subject of C.'s house, when his initial *veto met fierce opposition (*Att.* 4. 2(74). 4, cf. next n.).

Atilius' father-in-law...in supplication   Gnaeus Oppius Cornicinus (*Red. pop.* 12, *Att.* 4. 2(74). 4): though a senator, he is not
atttested as having held office. Ten months later Atilius repeated his
ploy, and Oppius his performance, prompting C.'s comment that
'Cornicinus went into his old act (*fabula*): he cast off his toga and
threw himself at his son-in-law's feet'; for the gesture, see 26 **you
prostrated yourselves** n.

the 'ponderer' had his fee doubled   Beyond blackguarding Atilius
further as a bribe-taker (cf. 72 **removed his name** n.), C. must imply
that Atilius *vetoed the decree the next day; cf. *Red. pop.* 12, 'His
"pondering" was spent, not in returning his fee, as some thought he
would, but—as became clear (i.e. from his veto)—in increasing it.'

very few on which the senate was permitted to meet   Because 20 of
January's 29 days were *comitial, and because the senate typically
did not meet on days when *voting assemblies could be held, January
meetings were infrequent: the eligible days were 1, 2, 5, 6, 9, 11,
13–15 Jan.

no business...my case   Cf. 68 **senate kept refusing** n.

75. a day..., 23 January   Since 22 Jan. 57 was itself nundinal, the
*promulgation could have taken place any time on or before 6 Jan. 57
(App. 1), but C.'s narrative implies that it was promulgated before the
senate's meeting of 1 Jan. The setting was the *assembly of the plebs,
the same body that had passed Clodius' laws (65 **assembly...of the
plebs** n.). Given that the tribune Atilius had already been willing to
use his *veto, and presumably could be relied on to obstruct either by
veto or by *obnuntiation if called on, it is unclear why the opposition
resorted to violence, beyond sheer intimidation (cf. also next n.). For
other accounts of the bloodshed see *Red. sen.* 6, 22, *Red. pop.* 14, *Mil.*
39, Plut. *Cic.* 33. 3, Cass. Dio 39. 7. 2 (placing the attack during the
vote, when Clodius saw that it was going badly: not consistent with
C.'s account, cf. 76 **Marcus Cispius** n., 77 fin.). Informed of the day's
events, C. replied—in the latest extant letter from exile—'I see that
I am utterly destroyed' (*Att.* 3. 27(72)).

Quintus Fabricius...occupied the sacred precinct   As *promulga-
tor of the measure (72 **tribunes** n.), Fabricius would preside at the

*assembly of the plebs and bring the measure to a vote. C. here designates the Rostra (*NTDAR* 334–5, *LTUR* 4. 212–14)—the platform between the Comitium (*NTDAR* 97–8, *LTUR* 1. 309–14) and the forum—with the term, *templum* ('sacred precinct'), proper to a place where 'transacting business with the people' (*agere cum populo*) was sanctioned by *auspices: for *templum* = Rostra, see *Verr.* 2. 3. 223, *Leg. Man.* 70, *Vat.* 18, 24, *Pis.* 21, *De or.* 2. 197, Livy 8. 14. 12; C. returns to the incident at 78 ('eject magistrates from a sacred precinct') and 84 ('dislodge tribunes of the plebs from the Rostra'), in the former again using *templum,* in the latter, Rostra. It has been inferred that Fabricius seized the spot to 'manipulate' the vote, or to block another tribune's *veto or *obnuntiation, or both (refs. Tatum 1999, 178); but occupying the Rostra was not necessary to achieve the former or sufficient to achieve the latter, unless Fabricius was also prepared to use physical restraint and thus violate a fellow-tribune's 'sacrosanct' status (16 **auspices** n.)—in which case occupying the Rostra was not necessary (for violence against a tribune seeking to veto a measure, *Vat.* 5, *De or.* 2. 197). Fabricius prob. acted as he did because he anticipated that the opposition would occupy the venue (sim. Vanderbroeck 1987, 245): cf. 34 **temple of Castor** n., on Clodius' forces' occupying the temple in Jan. 58. He erred in not anticipating the heightened level of violence; cf. the tribune Dolabella's supporters in 47, barricading themselves in the forum before a vote when they feared (correctly, in the event) that violence would be used to disrupt the assembly (Cass. Dio 42. 32. 3, cf. Plut. *Ant.* 9. 2).

Sestius ... spent the day quietly   But what was Milo doing? Though C. is silent, Milo must have been present, since he arrested some gladiators at or immediately after this riot (see 85).

many slaves   Predominantly (C. will imply) gladiators provided by Appius Claudius Pulcher, cf. 78 **support your ... aedileship** n.

76. Marcus Cispius ... entering the forum   Cf. 72 **tribunes** n. If he was just entering the forum, the voting prob. had not yet started. At *Red. sen.* 21 praises Cispius for putting community before personal grievance, after C. had incurred his family's enmity over a private lawsuit; C. defended him on a charge of electoral bribery, prob. in 56 (*Planc.* 56, cf. *TLRR* no. 279, *LUO* no. 57).

looking for my brother   Plutarch says that Quintus was escorted to the forum by Pompey (*Pomp.* 49. 3): a strong show of support, if true, and given Pompey's fear of assassination (41 **the same suspicion** n.), perhaps a sign that violence was not expected.

He for his part...the hope of my return   C. seems to feel the need to forestall thought that his brother's cowering was unimpressive: cf. *Dom.* 59 'What of my brother? When he had returned from his province not long after my departure, with the thought that life was not worth living if I was not restored, a sight of unbelievable and unprecedented grief and mourning that roused pity in all—how often did he slip from the swords in your hands!'

rostra, whither he had come to plead   On the site, 75 **Quintus Fabricius** n. Quintus would have spoken in an *assembly of the people (*contio*) preceding the vote: he presumably was invited by Fabricius, the presiding magistrate, for as a private citizen he could not otherwise address the people.

he hid...shielded him with their bodies   C.'s picture implies that Quintus was the sort of man to inspire such *loyalty in his current and former slaves, who chose not to run away; in Plut. *Cic.* 33. 3 Quintus survives by lying motionless among the dead.

77. You recall, judges,...surely (everyone thought)   C. blends a prompting gesture (6 **as most of you recall** n.) with a vivid evocation of the scene of carnage, meant to arouse emotion (cf. 17 **picture in your minds** n.), and a tendentious claim about the conclusions 'everyone' drew.

not private or plebeian but patrician and praetorian   i.e. pointing not to Clodius—a plebeian since his transfer and, since 10 Dec. 58, a person without public office (*privatus*)—but to the eldest of the brothers, Appius Claudius (*RE* 297) Pulcher, praetor in 57; like Clodius he is not named in the speech, cf. 78, 85. As consul C. had relied on him to record the statements of the conspirators before the senate in Dec. 63 (*Sull.* 42), but he of course supported his brother against C.; his continuing unfriendliness is revealed in C.'s letters (e.g. *QFr.* 2. 11(15), Jan. 54), though a 'reconciliation' had restored a civil public relationship by the time Appius entered his consulship in 54 (*QFr.* ibid., *Fam.* 1. 9(20). 4, *Scaur.* 31, adding, ibid. 32, that their mutual enmity never brought either one 'disgrace', *dedecus*); a member of the college of augurs, he dedicated a book on augury to C. after he became an augur too (*Fam.* 3. 4(67). 1). As late as 50 C. took pains to dispel rumors of continuing bad blood (*Fam.* 2. 13(93). 2; cf. *Fam.* 3. 1(64). 1, 5(68). 1–2, written earlier to Appius himself, to the same effect): by that time Appius was censor, and C. had succeeded him as governor of Cilicia (*Fam.* 3 preserves C.'s extant correspondence with him, concentrated in the period of C.'s governorship). He chose the Pompeian side in the civil war (one of his daughters was married to Pompey's son Gnaeus) and died in Greece in 48.

You charge... 'But yet...'   C. refers to the prosecutor for the first time: so far from casting himself as his opponents' friend, as he often does (Craig 1981, Siani-Davies 2001, 190), in this speech he does not even name them. The objection, 'But yet...?', is the prosecutor's (cf. 78): C. varies the figure that we have seen before—the exchange with an imaginary interlocutor (*sermocinatio*: 20 **Still** n.)—by ascribing the objection to a specific person.

that awful day when Cinna and Octavius clashed   When he refused to uphold Sulla's reforms, Lucius Cornelius Cinna was violently expelled from Rome by his colleague in the consulship of 87, Gnaeus Octavius (*MRR* 2. 46). At *Cat.* 3. 24 C. similarly evokes the 'heaps of corpses' produced that day, though he could as well have referred to the sequel: when Cinna gained Marius' support (50 **boded no good** n.) and seized control of the city by force, Octavius was slain, and Cinna and Marius took terrible vengeance on their enemies. Appius' father (cos. 79), an adherent of Sulla, was tangentially involved when the army he commanded went over to Cinna.

obstinacy or resolve   A vice (*pertinacia*) or a virtue (*constantia*), respectively: see the Glossary. Given the circumstance here described, C. is thinking primarily of *resolve displayed in principled opposition to a bad act.

the ignorant   With this epithet (lit. 'the inexperienced', *imperiti*: see the Glossary), C. implies a key element of senatorial ideology: the inexperienced know only what they *want* and so are easily seduced by unscrupulous ('popular') politicians; only those experienced in

public life (senators) truly know what is *needed* in any given circumstance and thus possess 'authority and . . . weighty wisdom' (137, of
the senate; cf. also 86 **practical intelligence, 104 excessive desires, 107
Gnaeus Pompeius** nn.). The point of view is epitomized in the words
reportedly uttered by the consul Publius Scipio Nasica when addressing the people: 'Citizens, please be quiet, for I understand better than
you what is good for the commonwealth' (Val. Max. 3. 7. 3). The
ability to distinguish needs from wants is deeply implicated in
*freedom (*libertas*), as it is seen from the senatorial point of view:
see *Sull.* 25 (quoted in the Glossary s.v. freedom).

no assembly . . . put to the vote   C. refers to the opposition's seizure
of the Comitium and senate house—thus, 'unrest stirred up at night'
(*concitata nocturna seditio*), cf. 75 'seized . . . in the dead of night'
(*multa de nocte . . . occupavissent*)—tendentiously, since by his own
account the violence did not start until Fabricius arrived to convene
the assembly and put his law to a vote.

78. Is it really likely that a Roman citizen, or any free person   He
alludes to the gladiators supplied by Appius Claudius Pulcher, cf.
support your . . . aedileship n. below and 85.

battening   The verb *saginare* connotes a rich diet meant to add
physical mass, esp. for athletes or gladiators and animals destined
for slaughter. C. prob. glances at the former here; in any case, the
word registers contempt.

that pestilentially desperate citizen   Clodius: for the metaphor of
'plague' or 'pestilence' (*pestis*, here *pestifer*, lit. 'plague-bearing'), see
31 **that demon** n.; on *desperadoes see the Glossary.

the prosecutor himself   Cf. 77 **You charge** n.

armed guard of massive proportions   Both Milo and S. maintained
armed guards (2 **hired brigands** n.), which played a part in the
charge against S. (cf. Introd. §2); C.'s general position is that S. did
not rely on his guard until after he had been attacked and nearly
killed, cf. 79.

not by appeal to auspices   i.e. by *obnuntiation, to abort the
convening of an assembly: see Glossary and next n.

If that praetor... had announced a sighting   Three problems attach
to the sentence. First, the medieval MSS all have a form of the non-
sensical *is pr qui*. Because the context concerns someone authorized to
watch the heavens for 'sought after' *auspices—a *curule magistrate or
tribune—and because the next sentence ('If one of Fabricius' fellow-
tribunes...') can be taken to imply that the person meant here was *not*
a tribune, the correction *is praetor qui*... ('that praetor who...') is
standardly adopted: the praetor in question would then be Clodius'
brother Appius, the only praetor of 57 hostile to C. That reading,
however, makes this passage anomalous, as the only text that even
hypothetically grants a curule magistrate the right to *obnuntiate
against a tribune (see the Glossary s.v. auspices). There is also a further
problem, whoever the magistrate is taken to be: the verb in the relative
clause (*dixerat*, indicative mood) means that the magistrate in question 'had (in fact) declared' (before the assembly convened) that he had
in fact watched the heavens (on the night of 22–23 Jan.)—but he had
not then announced a sighting. This is anomalous, if not perverse,
because a magistrate who watched for 'sought after' omens would
inevitably see one and, having seen it, announce it to the magistrate
whose assembly he wished to thwart; for otherwise he would not have
bothered to 'watch the heavens' (the convening magistrate, anticipating the announcement, might just abandon his intention before it was
made, but that is obviously not the case here).

The standard response to this cluster of problems, by implication
accepted in my translation, adopts the emendation *is praetor
qui*... and accepts the anomalies. An alternative (Sumner 1963,
353–4) accepts the emendation and the final anomaly but attacks
the second: on this view, when C. goes on to say that tribune's
*veto would have harmed the *commonwealth, 'but constitution-
ally' (*sed... iure*), he means to contrast that act with the praetor's,
which would have been both harmful (if not fatally) and *un*constitutional; but the sequence of thought from the preceding sentence
('the commonwealth's interests were undone... not by appeal to
auspices, not by a veto, not by ballots, but by violence, by the fist,
by the sword. *For* (*nam*) if...') shows that all the hypothetical
acts—obnuntiation no less than veto (or, for that matter, ballots)—are to be understood to be licit forms of opposition. A final

approach—not recently entertained, but one that I have come to find ever more tempting—is the more radical way of Madvig (1887, 366–8), who made the proposition fully hypothetical, and not at all anomalous, by reading 'si obnuntiasset Fabricio is [pr] qui [se] servasse<t> de caelo [dixerat] ...' (treating the stray *pr* as textual flotsam and positing that *se ... dixerat* was introduced to give *servasse* a construction once *servasset* lost its *–t*): 'if one who had watched the heavens for omens had announced a sighting to Fabricius.'

bear Shackleton Bailey's *gerere* (1979, 270), adopted by Maslowski, is the best solution for the MSS' barely intelligible *gemere* ('groan').

Would you ... would you ... and then ... accuse Though C. adopted the conceit of addressing the prosecutor just above, he now addresses Clodius as the force behind S.'s prosection, as he was openly Milo's prosecutor (1 **those who joined** n.): sim. *Vat.* 41, where C. makes the distinction explicit.

spring assassins from prison Since Rome's one prison (*carcer*: *NTDAR* 71–2, *LTUR* 1. 236–7, *MAR* 181) was not used for long-term detention of citizens, and slaves would not have been held there at all, C. presumably means to suggest that these were convicted criminals awaiting execution. C. similarly alleged that the 'seditious' tribune Saturninus (38 n.) had 'broken (?) open the prison', *Rab. perd.* 35.

brought in surreptitiously to grace the aedileship you planned Sarcasm: at the time of these events Clodius intended to stand in the elections for aedile later in 57, and by the time of this speech he had been elected (20 Jan. 56: App. 1) and was preparing to give the Megalesian *games in early April; but in the late Republic, no games given by aediles included gladiatorial contests (115–27 n.; if Clodius had given games as a candidate he would have violated C.'s own *lex Tullia*: cf. 133 n.). Cass. Dio 39. 6. 3–7. 2 says that Appius had acquired the gladiators for the funeral games of a kinsman, a common occasion for gladiatorial shows (124 **offering** n.), hence a plausible report, or a plausible pretext for the brothers.

eject magistrates from a sacred precinct   Referring to the man-
handling of Fabricius, C. again refers to the Rostra as *templum*,
'sacred precinct': 75 **Quintus Fabricius** n.

79. fortify himself…to conduct his magistracy safely   C.'s euphemism for S.'s decision—at the heart of the charge against him—to go
about with an armed gang: cf. 84 **'You hired henchmen'** n. and 90, with
Introd. §2; for the euphemism, cf. the description of Milo's measures
at 95 ('safeguards (used to) defend his household gods in private life
and the rights of a tribune and the auspices in the public sphere').

sacrosanct status of tribunes…laws it is a sacrilege to break   The
former (cf. 75–6 above, on Fabricius and Cispius) was established by
the latter: see 16 **auspices** n. The wounds S. suffered when this status
was violated are the focus whenever C. refers to the incident: cf. *Red.
sen.* 6–7, 30, *Red. pop.* 14, *QFr.* 2. 3(7). 6, *Mil.* 38.

he came into the temple of Castor   On the temple as a site of
assembly and, often, of upheaval, see 34 n.

announced to the consul   C. highlights S.'s lawful action, in contrast
with the thugs just described (indeed, in reporting an unfavourable
omen in person, he satisfied what was most likely a key provision of
Clodius' own law on *obnuntiation, 33 **while the same consuls sat** n.;
for one reason for this emphasis, see 86 **even you praise Milo** n.). In
so doing C. leaves much else in shadow. The consul was presumably
Nepos, not C.'s hero, Lentulus; and C. makes plain that this assembly
followed the riot of 23 Jan. ('not even from that point on…'). *Red.
sen.* 6–8 gives further clues (see 71–92 n.): after the riot, and at least
through Feb., C.'s supporters observed a suspension of all public
business, in courts, senate, and assemblies, to protest the tactics of
the *Clodiani* and force action on C.'s recall, and C. mentions five
outrages that took place during that suspension: 'people dashing
about the whole city with swords and torches, magistrates' houses
assailed, temples of the gods in flames, the fasces of an excellent man
and most distinguished consul smashed, the most sanctified body
of a…tribune of the plebs…stabbed and drained' (sim. *Red. pop.*
14). The first two certainly refer to an attack on Milo's house that
C. will soon mention (85 n.), the last to the riot C. is about to

describe; the third and fourth prob. refer to the same riot at the temple of Castor, where Nepos' fasces could have been smashed in the melee: the ref. to an 'excellent man and most distinguished consul' does not inevitably point to Lentulus—cf. 'Quintus Metellus, a most notable person and excellent man' just preceding (*Red. sen.* 5)—and if Nepos convened his assembly in Feb., when C. shows the suspension was being observed, the fasces that were shattered would have been his, for Feb. was his month to control the fasces; for the 'temples of the gods in flames', cf. 84.

It is certain, too, that the assembly S. attempted to halt was a legislative session of the *comitia tributa*: some in the mob attacked S. with chunks of wood torn from the barriers (*saepta*: n. below) set up to organize the people for a vote; and because the *comitia centuriata* (on all occasions) and elective assemblies of the *comitia tributa* met outside the *pomerium* in the campus Martius, only a legislative assembly of the *comitia tributa* would meet at the temple of Castor (the vestigial *comitia curiata* was not attended by the people at all, the consul presiding instead over a meeting of 30 lictors representing the city's 30 'wards', *curiae*). Thus it was the same form of assembly that Caesar convened two years earlier to act on his first agrarian law, when the temple of Castor was also a site of tumult (refs. at 34 **temple of Castor** n.). As for S.'s motives, which C. leaves entirely in the dark: he could have wished to forestall a vote because Nepos' measure was detrimental to C., or because it was in Clodius' favour, or for some other reason entirely. The first reason is commonly assumed (e.g. Gardner 1958*a*, 20, Maslowski 1976, 28), as C. might indeed have wished, since it would most directly serve his basic strategy of claiming that all S.'s acts were aimed at his recall—but it is actually the least likely of the three: though Nepos continued to support his kinsman in other ways during the year (89 **one consul** n.), he had dropped his resistance to C.'s recall months before 1 Jan. (72 **his colleague** n.), he actively supported it in July (130), and no source hints that he worked against it in the interval.

In fact, the entire incident appears in a different light when we know that it occurred during the suspension of public business following the riot of 23 Jan.; for that suggests S. was motivated by the bill's timing, not its content (cf. Tatum 1999, 179). Like the change to mourning dress (26 n.), the suspension of public business

aimed to arouse ill-will against the Clodian outrages as much as it
was aimed at C.'s recall (for the issue of ill-will, cf. 82): despite that
suspension Nepos convened the *comitia tributa* to vote on legislation,
prob. on the view that ceasing to oppose C.'s recall did not require him
to join in a gesture bringing *invidia* on his own kin; S., wishing to
enforce the suspension, sought to obstruct the vote—and the *Clodiani*,
seeing his gesture for what it was, attacked. S.'s act could thus be seen
as a step toward C.'s recall, though a step less direct than has been
assumed, and less direct than C. might wish to imply: cf. his treatment
of Pompey's 'reawakening' (67), which depends on suppressing Pompey's break with Clodius. In both cases, and no less that of Milo to
come, C. is economical with the truth: he says nothing that is exactly
false but gains his effect by withholding information that would reveal
the full import of what he does say. Relatedly, viewing S.'s action in
this light solves a central puzzle in this segment of the speech, C.'s
failure to say one word to explain S.'s motive: we can now see that
acknowledging his motive would wreck C.'s plan for showing Milo in
the most favourable light in 85–9, for that plan depends entirely on
suppressing the fact that public business had been suspended
(see 85 **not only no special court,** 86 **On this topic,** 89 **one consul** nn.).

barriers   The *saepta*, lit. 'fenced areas', set up to organize voters by
*tribe or *century, depending on the assembly: these *saepta* were
temporary pens set up in the forum; for magisterial elections they
were set up in the Campus Martius, where a monumental structure,
planned as early as 54, was completed by Augustus (*NTDAR* 340–1,
LTUR 4. 228–9, *MAR* 219, cf. Taylor 1966, 40–1, 47–8, 93–9, Ulrich
1994, 105, Mouritsen 2001, 26–30).

Sestius . . . lost consciousness and collapsed   Defending Lucius Cal-
purnius Bestia on 11 Feb. (*TLRR* no. 268, *LUO* no. 49), C. credited
Bestia with saving S.'s life as he lay wounded, then gave a eulogy of
S., who had been indicted the day before (*QFr.* 2. 3(7). 6).

80. Lentidius . . . Titius, the Sabine from Reate   The former is mentioned as a Clodian henchman also at *Dom.* 89, *Har. resp.* 59 (a 'dog'),
the latter at *Dom.* 21, both of uncertain status (cf. Benner 1987, 162,
164, Nippel 1995, 73–4, Tatum 1999, 146). Titius, whose identity is

glossed for the jury, perhaps was known to C. from his patronage of Reate (9 **sole patron** n.).

order commonly given to gladiators ... 'receive the sword'   The order to offer up his neck for the deathblow, given to a defeated gladiator whom the crowd or the giver of the *games declined to spare: cf. *Tusc.* 2. 41 'What gladiator of even middling rank ever groaned or changed his expression? ... What gladiator ... when ordered to "receive the sword", drew back his neck?', *Sex. Rosc.* 33, Ville 1981, 424–5. It might seem mildly jarring that S. is said to have behaved like a proper gladiator, given C.'s repeated stress on the links between gladiators, as violent slaves, and Clodius; but C. elsewhere invokes the gladiator's code of calmly facing death as a choiceworthy model, see esp. *Phil.* 3. 35 'Let us do what notable gladiators do ...' (shortly after referring insultingly to Mark Antony's brother, Lucius, as an ex-gladiator, ibid. 31).

Where is the crime here?   Of course there is none, and that is why C. dwells on it.

81. I ask you this question, judges   C. has put a question or request to the judges before (42) and will do so again (91, 119), thus involving them in his speech (cf. 6 **as most of you recall** n.); but this instance is different, as the questions aggressively place the judges on the scene and compel them to imagine choosing between a patriotic response ('would you have taken up arms ... ?') and cowardice ('would you still keep mum ... ?'). 'Still' (*etiam tum*) is esp. daring, in so far as it includes the judges among those cowed by the *Clodiani*; cf. 84 **you mourned in silence**.

to be free men living in a commmonwealth   Lit. 'to be free and have a *commonwealth' (*liberi esse et habere rem publicam*), where the state of *freedom is balanced by, and virtually equated with, the political condition that makes it possible, cf. 91 **possession** n. and the Glossary s.v. freedom.

82. sort to murder their own kin   i.e. *parricidae*, in the Roman view murderers of the most heinous sort, whose crime 'overturns all laws divine and human' (*Sex. Rosc.* 65, cf. 70): in the traditional punishment, the parricide was flogged, sewn up in a sack with a cock, snake, monkey, and dog, then thrown into the sea (*Dig.* 48. 9. 9. pr., adding that if no sea happened to be near, the parricide should be thrown to the beasts; Quintus Cicero apparently imposed the punishment while governing Asia, *QFr.* 1. 2(2). 5). The label was easily turned against those who would 'murder' the fatherland (*patria*), the common parent of all: cf. 111 below with, e.g. *Cat.* 1. 17 (the *patria* 'addresses' Catiline), 29, *Sull.* 6 (with Berry 1996, 144, ad loc.).

killing their own Gracchus   On the name, see 72 n.: alluding to the senatorial opposition's murders of Tiberius and Gaius Gracchus, C. jokes that this 'Gracchus' would have been done in by his own 'popular' associates; for the ploy of doing a murder in order to pin it on your opponents, cf. 41. The vignette that follows, with its elements of disguise and mistaken identity, shows the gift for farce that marks the bathhouse-scene C. develops a few weeks later in *Cael.* 61 ff.: here C. fittingly calls the agents *good-for-nothings (*homines nequam*), using what is virtually the fixed epithet of the 'rascal slave' who often sets the plot going in Roman comedy (cf. 22 **good for nothing** n.). The contrast in tone with the set-piece that follows, on the notional statue for S., is striking, as is the swift and smooth transition between them.

mule-driver's cowl he had worn when he first came to Rome to vote   C. mocks his rural origins in 72 (**that field-mouse** n.) and here caps the insult by alleging origins not just rural but disreputable, mule-drivers being among the humblest labourers, if not actually servile (C. cannot, however, mean that Numerius was a freedman, a status that would bar him entirely from public office). If the label was not chosen merely for its insult value (e.g. Juv. 8. 148 'the mule-driver consul', cf. Sen. *Epist.* 45. 7), it prob. indicates that Numerius had made money raising or contracting mules (cf. *Fam.* 10. 18(395). 3, Munatius Plancus' slur against 'that mule-driver Ventidius', cos. suff. 43, Plin. *HN* 7. 135, Gell. 15. 4. 3, with Syme *RP* 1:396) or in some other way thought inconsistent with senatorial standing (cf. Suet. *Vesp.* 4. 3).

Numerius ... Quintus ... his two first names   The MSS say 'Quintius' (= 'Quinctius'); but since the man was Quintus Numerius Rufus (refs. at 72 '**Gracchus**' n.), none of his erstwhile associates would have been looking to kill a 'Quintius' (or 'Quinctius'). C. jests in saying that he was saved by (lit.) 'the error of his double name' (*gemini nominis errore*): the point is that like someone today named 'Patrick Henry' or 'John Thomas', he could be said to have two first names, Quintus (Orelli's correction, adopted here), which was very common, and Numerius, which served both as a clan-name and as a (relatively rare) *praenomen* (that C. says *nominis*, not *praenominis*, does not matter, since *nomen* can be used of *praenomina*). Shackleton Bailey's solution (1979, 271), reading *Numerium* <*Quinctium*> ... *Quinctium* ('some were looking for "Numerius Quinctius" and others just for "Quinctius"'), takes C. to mean that Numerius' pursuers made a 'double error' involving his name ('The double error (*gemino* would be easier) must have lain in taking the name "Numerius" for a praenomen and, by consequence, the praenomen "Quintus" for a nomen "Quintius"'); but that is not what C. says, or means. To try to puzzle out how any sort of error would have saved the man's life is to worry a point that did not concern C. as he was tossing off a silly joke.

as it were, an agreeable crime Conscious of indulging in oxymoron—'agreeable' (or 'gratifying': *grato*) being a notion not usually associated with 'crime' (*scelere*)—C. qualifies the epithet by adding 'as it were' (*quodam*).

83. a statue ... as one who died for the commonwealth The notion is conventional, based on Republicanism's contractualist premises that held out a reward, even if posthumous, to those who 'had earned the commonwealth's gratitude': see just below and 2 **thanking** n., and cf. *Phil.* 9. 15–16, C.'s motion in the senate that a bronze statue be raised to Servius Sulpicius Rufus, for having been of 'great service to the *commonwealth' (*magnus usus rei publicae*). The expression here is awkward, relying on one counterfactual condition (S. did not die) pregnant with another (the senate did not have its proper place, the Roman people's majesty had not revived, at the time of S.'s near death—though presumably both were in better condition now that C.'s restoration had restored the commonwealth).

those ... statues ... set ... on the Rostra By *decree of the senate or act of the people (Lahusen 1983, 97 ff.). Honorific statues were planted so thickly on and around the Rostra that they nearly crowded out any other use and occasionally had to be removed: see esp. Plin. *HN* 34. 18–26, a remarkable 'tour' of the sites in the forum on which specific statues were set, with Lahusen 1983 (esp. 14–22, for Rostra and Forum), Flower 1996, 71–5, Sehlmeyer 1999 (esp. 178 ff. for the late Republic).

a man who had earned the commonwealth's gratitude   On the formula, see 2 **thanking** n.

the sacred auspices   See 33 and the Glossary s.v. auspices.

sanctified . . . sanctified . . . sanctified   C. adroitly sandwiches the 'sanctification' of the cause—his own—between the indubitably sacrosanct status of temple and magistrate.

84. 'You hired henchmen . . .' To do what?   S.'s resort to some form of armed support as tribune was the crux of the charge against him (Introd. §2): having referred to it euphemistically in 79 (**fortify himself** n.), C. speaks of it directly here for the first time; he will refer to it again, for the last time, in 90. At each point he does his best to deflect attention from the issue: in 79, by stressing S.'s straight-forwardly constitutional behaviour that provoked the assault; in 90, by twisting a comment by the prosecutor and turning it against him. Here, and on into 85, C. achieves the same end by retailing the crimes of Clodius and his faction, almost all fetched up, in no particular order, from indictments made earlier in the speech: compare 54 ('send citizens . . . , steal . . . , burn . . . , overturn . . .'), 75 ('dislodge tribunes . . .'), 24 and 53 ('sell . . . provinces'), 56 ('recognize . . . kings, use our legates . . .'), 69 ('detain the foremost man . . .': cf. also next n.), 34 ('forum . . . seized . . . , the temple of Castor occupied . . .'), 75 ('magistrates . . . driven from temples'), 76 ('others . . . forbidden to enter the forum'); C. nowhere else reports Clodius' 'lay(ing) siege to the senate', but cf. Plut. *Cic.* 31. 1; 'set(ting) the temples of the. . . gods on fire' prob. refers to the riot at the temple of Castor just recounted, cf. 79 **announced** n., with 95, *Red. sen.* 7, *Red. pop.* 14 (*pace* Halm 1886, followed by Holden 1889, it cannot refer to the temple of the Nymphs, an arson just prior to this trial: see 95 **aedile** n., App. 1). We meet no new and circumstantial outrage until the gladiators' arrest (85) provides a transition to Milo, a crucially useful foil.

detain the foremost man ... at sword-point   After the attempt of
11 Aug. 58 caused Pompey to take to his house (69 n.), a freedman
of Clodius, Damio, besieged the house later that month (Ascon.
46. 26–47. 9 Cl.). As already noted (39 **Marcus Scaurus** n), the phrase
princeps civitatis was an informal honourific (cf. *RE* 22.2 (1954),
1998–2056 (L. Wickert) and Wickert 1974, 12–15), and non-
exclusive: there could be several 'foremost men of the community'
(cf. 40, 97–8, 103–4, 108, 123: in C.'s usage the plural form generally
denotes a group comprising former consuls, cf. Hellegouarc'h 1963,
332–3). But C. here almost certainly means to call Pompey '*the*
foremost man', raising him above all others, if only for the rhetorically useful end of making the act more outrageous (cf. e.g. *Dom.* 66
'Gnaeus Pompeius ... in the judgement of all by far the leading man
of the civil community'). The usage would reverberate in the next
generation, when Augustus gained general recognition as *the*
princeps (for Pompey as 'the *princeps civitatis*', see the passages
gathered, with comment, by Miriam Griffin, *OCD*[3] 1246).

'But the time was not yet ripe ...'   The prosecutor prob. did make an
argument of this sort: C. gains nothing by introducing it (he continues
the same catalog of Clodian sins) and had no motive to confect
or distort it; it is in line with the contrast the prosecutor appears to
have drawn between Milo and S. (86 **even you praise Milo** n.).

you mourned in silence   'You' (plural), the judges (cf. 81 **I ask you**
n.), or the Roman audience more generally.

85. Men made desperate by need and recklessness   On the link
between *recklessness and 'need' (*egestas*) in Republican discourse,
Wirszubski 1961, 17–18.

<Some> magistrates..., others...   Acc. to the transmitted text
(*magistratus temples pellebantur, alii omnino aditu ac foro prohibe-
bantur*), 'magistrates were driven from sacred precincts, other (men/
people) were entirely forbidden to enter the forum', implying that the
latter were not magistrates. But since the only person kept from the
forum in C.'s account was also a magistrate—the Marcus Cispius,
mentioned immediately after the expulsion of the tribune Quintus
Fabricius from the 'sacred precinct' of the Rostra (75–6)—we should

read <*alii*> *magistratus...*, *alii...*, 'Some magistrates..., other (magistrates)...' An inattentive scribe could easily have skipped over *alii* after writing a sequence of letters with a similar appearance at the end of the preceding word (*perfereb*atis).

Gladiators from the praetor's entourage This refers to the riot of 23 Jan. (75–8), not the attack on S. (79): the two preceding details refer to the former (Fabricius driven from the Rostra = 'temple', 75; Cispius prevented from entering the forum, 76); only in the former are gladiators mentioned in connection with Appius as praetor (77); and the next clause refers to the same event ('citizens massacred at night', cf. 75 'a little before dawn... in the dead of night').

thrown into prison by Milo, then released by Serranus Both acting as tribunes, the one constitutionally empowered to intercede against the other: on Serranus, see 72 n., on Milo see following.

not only no special court of inquiry established... but existing venues... uprooted The remark comprises two tendentious moves. First, and less consequential, it misleadingly implies that the circumstances required or merited a special court of inquiry (*nova quaestio* = *quaestio extraordinaria*), of the sort set up to try Clodius for profaning the Bona Dea's rites (*TLRR* no. 236). The violent disruption of the assembly could have been prosecuted before the relevant *standing court under a charge of *public violence, which S. now faced, or a charge of *maiestas* (roughly, 'treason': in 65 C. defended Gaius Cornelius against that charge after he disrupted an assembly as tribune in 67, *TLRR* no. 209, *FS* 65 ff.); C. himself makes much the same point when protesting the special proceedings established to deal with Clodius' murder in 52 (*Mil.* 13–14, cf. *Phil.* 2. 22). Second, and more important, C. profits from suppressing all ref. to the suspension of public business—including the *iustitium* in the courts—that his own supporters had fostered after the riot of 23 Jan. (cf. 71–92 n.). Having omitted that detail, he can now treat the suspension as an outrageous 'uprooting' of the courts and cast Milo as a law-abiding patriot frustrated by his opponents' high-handed behaviour: see esp. 89 **one consul** n.; cf. C.'s suppression of Gabinius' break with Clodius (69 **the consuls** n.), which facilitates his consistent characterization of the consul.

another tribune of the plebs...had his house attacked   i.e. Milo:
this is the first of two attacks Clodius' gangs made on his house in 57,
the second coming on 12 Nov. (*Att.* 4. 3(75). 3, cf. 95 **has assailed** n.;
on the distinction, Meyer 1919, 110, Maslowski 1976). Cf. *Red. sen.* 7,
Red. pop. 14 (both with the detail of 'flame and sword', on which see
90 **fire and sword** n.).

godlike   On the force of the epithet see 50 n.

largeness of spirit, gravity, and loyalty   On the qualities—*magnitudo animi, gravitas, fides*—see 1, 6, 26 nn., respectively.

86. On this topic even you praise Milo   The topic (*locus*) is the one
he is about to elaborate (86–9), that Milo first responded to attack by
trying to bring Clodius to trial, only thereafter acquiring an armed
force; 'you' (sing.) = the prosecutor (cf. *Vat.* 40–2, Vatinius' alleged
praise in a different context). Scholars accept the literal truth of C.'s
remark too readily. It is easy to believe that the prosecutor drew a
comparison with Milo, prob. one of the reasons C. so strongly emphasizes S.'s use of constitutional means (79 **announced to the consul** n.).
But if the prosecutor was not a moron or actually engaged in collusion
(*praevaricatio*: Introd. §2), he can hardly have 'praised' Milo; the mere
fact that C. says he did need no more be taken at face value than his
statement, a few weeks later, that Caelius' prosecutors attacked him
for being the son of a Roman equestrian (*Cael.* 4). Had the prosecutor
said 'Even Milo, frenzied brigand though he is, tried lawful means
before turning despicably to force—how much worse the violence of
Sestius?' (cf. e.g. *Har. resp.* 43–4, comparing Clodius unfavourably
with the Gracchi), C. would have had all the warrant needed for his
gambit, which he will repeat in 87 and use in 90 to convict the
prosecutor of incoherence; for a still more violent distortion of an
opponent's remark, see 132 **slandered** n. The gambit is useful for the
defence of S., and for constructing a Milo—as C. proceeds to do—who
is praise*worthy,* not the violent, headstrong, and erratic character there
is reason to think he was. That C. had Milo's own trial in mind from
beginning to end (cf. 1 **those who joined**, 94 **these two men**, 144
Milo . . . nn.) fundamentally shaped his strategy in 85–9.

have we ever seen his like for immortal manliness   C. already
offered brief encomia of Milo at *Red. sen.* 19, 30, *Red. pop.* 15, sim.

Att. 4. 3(75). 5 (22 Nov. 57); cf. *Har. resp.* 6, where he compares Milo with the younger Africanus.

Seeking no other reward than the good opinion of patriots   The reward implied in the contractualist premises of Republicanism (1 n.): the 'good opinion of patriots' is what men like Clodius (*Dom.* 114) and Vatinius (114 n.) are said to despise, and what C. feared he had lost by leaving the Pompeians and returning to Italy in Dec. 48 (*Att.* 11. 7(218). 3). This 'good opinion', when published abroad and transmitted to posterity, produces 'the good *report* of patriots', equated with 'true glory' at 139 (n.). Conversely, being praised by 'worthless' men is equivalent to a form of blame, cf. 105 and *Vat.* 41 (Vatinius' praise of Milo).

what it is ever right for outstanding men to do ... and what they are constrained to do   To express the contrast C. uses two expressions that can each be translated by 'must': *oportere*, in the first, denotes acts that are ethically choiceworthy in any circumstance; *necesse*, in the second, describes acts that circumstances impose willy-nilly (cf. 'must of necessity' below), turned in this instance to honourable ends. Cf. sim. 89 and, for the alternatives facing Milo, *Red. sen.* 19; on the argument from necessity, and its relation to choiceworthy goals, *Inv. rhet.* 2. 172, 174–5; for a defence of Pompey similarly framed, *Leg.* 3. 26 with Dyck 2004 ad loc.; and for a survey of C.'s own views on the 'morality of political violence', Lintott 1999*a*, 54–65.

practical intelligence ... courage ... manliness   See the Glossary s. vv.

87. Milo ... affairs   C. implies that—unlike S., a quaestor before becoming tribune—Titus Annius (*RE* 67) Milo held no public office before the *tribunate of 57, and in fact no earlier office is attested for him. He would be praetor in 55 and continue to be Clodius' most vigorous opponent, until their retinues clashed at a chance meeting on the Appian Way on 18 Jan. 52, when Milo was returning from Lanuvium, his family's place of origin. The murder of the wounded Clodius, which Milo ordered, led to his prosecution; when C. managed only a weak defence, Milo anticipated conviction by going into exile at Massilia (cf. 7 n.). He was killed four years later after joining C.'s protégé Marcus Caelius Rufus in a hare-brained insurrection in Italy. C. exploited Milo's role in his recall in much the same terms when he defended him in 52 (*Mil.* 34–5); later sources tend to give most if not all credit for C.'s restoration to Milo, with no mention of S. (Vell. 2. 45. 3, App. *BCiv.* 2. 16, 20, Cass. Dio 39. 6. 2).

Titus Annius   In referring formally to a person whom he acknowledges as one of the social elite, C. generally uses the praenomen + cognomen when the man has three names ('Publius Lentulus', 'Marcus Scaurus'); that C. always refers to Titus Annius Milo as either 'Titus Annius' or (about seven time more often) just 'Milo'—never as 'Titus Milo'—is consistent with Milo's standing as a person of lesser rank (hence the praenomen + nomen) with whom C. wished to demonstrate a certain solidarity (hence the cognomen): on the pattern, Adams 1978, 154–5 (the refinements offered by Shackleton Bailey 1992, 5–6, do not seem to affect Adams' point in this case).

The cause was straightforward   The rest of the paragraph conveys no new or even specific acts on Milo's part: it allusively reintroduces the cast of characters on hand since 1 Jan.—Lentulus ('one of the consuls'), Nepos ('the other's sentiments'), Appius ('one of the praetors'), the dissident tribunes Serranus and Numerius ('two men had been bribed')—and sculpts a Milo poised in sober reflection (next n.) and united with the senate ('the most august segment'), to set the context for Clodius' attack on his house. In narrative terms, the start of 88 brings us back to where we were at the end of 85; Milo's behaviour thereafter, and one remark of C. (89 **or even thinking he would?** n.), suggest that he was perhaps acting with less poise than C. here grants him.

example set by brave patriots   Explained by the questions that follow, on which a patriot should reflect when engaged in public action. These combine consideration of the *public interest and of his own *worthy standing (*dignitas*: cf. 48 n., on C.'s reflections in his crisis), and consideration of his ancestors, who provide the foundation of that standing and are worthy objects of grateful devotion (*pietas*): see e.g. *Verr.* 1. 1. 51 (to the praetor presiding at Verres' trial) 'Reflect on the position that you occupy, what you owe the Roman people, what you owe your ancestors', *Flac.* 104 '(Even if the defendant is convicted) he will never regret that he looked out for your well-being...; he will always believe that (patriotic resolve) was what he owed the worthy standing of his family, his sense of devotion, and his fatherland'; cf. 130 **burst into tears** n. Though consciousness of one's ancestors was no doubt more intense the higher on the social pyramid one stood (cf. e.g. Publius Servilius' appeal to Metellus Nepos, recounted at 130), the present passage is not reliable evidence that Milo himself had senatorial forebears (*pace* Shackleton Bailey 1992, 15): any upright Roman—the character C. tries to construct for Milo here—would be concerned to 'make a proper return' to his ancestors, for that was the essence of *pietas*. Thus C., relying on that sentiment, bids an *assembly of the people as a whole (*contio*) to preserve through their own toil the *freedom gained through the 'sweat and blood of (their) ancestors' (*Leg. agr.* 2. 16)

88. He did not budge this man   With Milo's *resolve contrast C.'s 'swerve' remarked by Cotta in 73 (n.); at the end of 89 his *courage seems contrasted with the behaviour of another *notable (**just shut himself up** n.).

his anguish... break violence with violence   'Anguish' (*dolor animi*) is what Cato allegedly felt when ill-used by Clodius (63 n.), and close kin to the emotions C. claims to feel at the speech's start (3 **devotion...** n.); in Milo's case the anguish would embrace both anger at a personal affront and indignation at the violation of a social norm. It was assumed that both emotions would move you to respond vigorously, if you were not servile or womanish—hence ref. to Milo's 'innate spirit of *freedom' (*innata libertas*) and *manliness (cf. 138 **passively** n.).

war dance   Lit. 'doing the *tripudium*', the dance of the Salii (< *salire*, 'to leap'), a brotherhood associated with Mars at Rome (Livy 1. 20. 4, Porph. ad Hor. *Carm.* 1. 36. 11–12, Serv. ad Verg. *Aen.* 8. 285, 663, Plut. *Numa* 13. 4–5; cf. Livy 21. 42. 4, 23. 26. 9, 25. 17. 5, 38. 17. 5, Tac. *Ann.* 4. 47, *Hist.* 5. 17, applying the term to the war dances of other nations). The label is otherwise applied to joyful and/or religious dancing (Acc. *trag.* frag. 249–50 Ribb., Catull. 63. 25–6, Curt. Ruf. 7. 10. 4, Sen. *NQ* 7. 32. 3, Apul. *Met.* 7. 16, 8. 27, Porph. ad Hor. *Carm.* 3. 18. 15–16).

89. He came to the forum to lodge an accusation   C. refers to the *postulatio* (lit. 'demanding'), the stage at which a person intending to prosecute another first sought leave to do so from the relevant official. Milo intended to prosecute Clodius for *public violence (*vis*) under the law used against S. (*Red. sen.* 19, *Mil.* 35, cf. *Mil.* 38, 40, *Att.* 4. 3(75). 2, Plut. *Cic.* 33. 3, *TLRR* 261); trials on charges of *vis* were not assigned to a specific praetor for the year of his term, and we do not know which praetor Milo would have approached. It was certainly not Clodius' brother, Appius, who presided over the court for extortion (*MRR* 2. 200).

provoked by no personal enmity, with no reward in prospect   'Personal enmity' (*inimicitiae*) was to the Roman criminal courts what oil is to the internal combustion engine (cf. Epstein 1987, 96–100); successful prosecution on certain charges (but not *public violence) brought the prosecutor a material reward (thus e.g. the successful prosecution of Milo on a charge of campaign bribery in 52: *TLRR* no. 311, and more generally Alexander 1985). Neither enmity nor reward was dishonourable, but the disinterested service to the community C. paints was nobler, cf. 86 **Seeking no other reward** n.

or even thinking he would?   Of course not, since his allies were observing a suspension of public business: C. here virtually winks at his suppression of this fact (71–92 n.). The remark does hint, however, that Milo, having been powerfully provoked (88 **his anguish** n.), was something of a loose cannon, acting with less poise and less consultation of the 'most august category of the citizenry' than C. wants to suggest (87 **The cause was straightforward** n.): note esp. C.'s complaint a few weeks after this trial (*QFr.* 2. 5(9). 4) that Milo's 'imprudence' was responsible for an ill-timed prosecution of Clodius' supporter Sextus Cloelius (= *TLRR* no. 273).

the disgraceful miscarriage ... his earlier trial   For profaning the rites of the Bona Dea: see 15 **bore a grudge** n.

one consul, one praetor, one tribune of the plebs produced new and unprecedented edicts   Respectively, Nepos, Appius, and either Numerius or Serranus: the edicts probably based themselves, with nice irony, on the very *iustitium* that the anti-Clodian forces had instituted (see Meyer 1919, 111). Indeed, if S. had already acted to block Nepos' assembly on much the same grounds (79 **announced** n.), we can readily suppose that Nepos relished using those grounds to frustrate Milo ('Fine: if it's a suspension you lot want, it's a suspension you shall have'); nor would this be the last time in 57 that Nepos saved Clodius from prosecution by turning his enemies' tactics against them: see 95 **not been granted leave** n. Mitchell (1991, 153 n. 29) seeks the edicts' basis in 'the general right of higher magistrates to suspend the functions of (lesser magistrates)': perhaps not impossible in principle, where Nepos is concerned, though the explanation leaves unclear what role the praetor and tribune would have played. In any case, the reason Mitchell gives ('It can hardly have been a *iustitium*, or Cicero would surely have said so') ignores the fact that C. does say so, at *Red. sen.* 6 (71–92 n.); it just happens not to serve his purpose to say so here, or in 79–92 as a whole. Cf. his treatment of Clodius' turn against Pompey and Gabinius in spring 58: though stressed at *Dom.* 66, that milestone is wholly suppressed in this speech, at the cost of various gaps and distortions, because remarking it would not suit C.'s strategy (cf. 67 **Here at last,** 69 **the consuls** nn.).

the courts were uprooted   For the same misleading charge, see 85 **not only no special court** n.

offer his neck   Sc. for decapitation, the gesture of a fallen gladiator, a condemned criminal, or one otherwise completely subject to another's power: *Sex. Rosc.* 30, *Phil.* 5. 42, 12. 15, Sen. *Dial.* 3. 18. 3, cf. Vell. 2. 69. 2.

just shut himself up in his house   Like a certain great general seated in court? Cf. 69 **a plan** n.

Reckoning it equally disgraceful . . .   On this reckoning's psychology, **his anguish** n. above.

since he could not use legal measures . . . reason to fear peril from his violence   C. finishes the argument begun in 86: since Milo had been prevented from doing what was 'ever right' he would now do what he was 'constrained' to do; cf. 95 **safeguards** n.

90. How then can you accuse Sestius . . . for arranging the same sort of armed protection   C. caps his argument—the last devoted to the charge, though one-third of the speech remains—by resuming two earlier tendentious moves: the euphemism applied to S.'s armed force, as a means to 'fortify himself with supporters in order to conduct his magistracy safely' (79); and the conceit that the prosecutor 'praised' Milo (86 **On this topic** n.).

fire and sword   A formulaic detail in C.'s refs. to the attack on Milo's house (cf. 85, *Red. sen.* 7, *Red. pop.* 14), adapted from similar descriptions of Catiline's threat (e.g. *Cat.* 2. 1, 3. 1, *Mur.* 85, *Sull.* 83, *Flac.* 102, cf. *Cat.* 4. 18). C. was well aware of the mannerism, which others adopted: recounting Crassus' praise of his leadership against Catiline (*Att.* 1. 14(14). 3, Feb. 61), C. says 'Crassus wove together, with marvelous gravity, the whole theme (*locus*) that I'm wont to treat with varied colors in my speeches (you know my palette), on fire, on the sword. . . .'

91. who among us does not know...   Capping the argument that most nearly addresses the charge of *public violence, C. develops another commonplace (see 47 **Had I heard, seen, learned** n.), on the origins of social life, to stress the contrast between lawful procedure and violence; cf. *Clu.* 146–7, on the foundational importance of law, developed to similar effect. He takes as his jumping-off point another question to the judges, here not posed to them *qua* judges but including them cosily in the company of cultivated men who of course have pondered such matters ('who among us does not know...?'; cf. the flattery of the judges' culture at *Mur.* 61). The anthropology that C. uses might well have been familiar, for it was a commonplace in the modern Engl. sense too: about thirty years earlier C. himself had developed very much the same theme when introducing his youthful rhetorical work *On discovering arguments* (1. 2):

For there was a certain time when human beings wandered at random in the fields, like beasts, and sustained their lives with the provender of beasts, accomplishing nothing by reason but most things by physical force, cultivating no system of godly worship or human obligation: no one had grasped the utility of justice. Thus . . . desire, that blind and rash mistress over the mind, used physical force to sate itself. . . . And at that time a certain man, great and wise, recognized that the human mind had in it raw material well suited to great accomplishments, were someone able to draw it out and improve it through education: by a systematic application of thought (*quadam ratione*) he brought together into one place the people scattered in fields and hidden away in their sylvan lairs and ... made them mild and gentle where they had been wild and monstrous.

The young C. went on (1. 3) to claim that the great man who had this effect was the first practitioner of eloquence (cf. *De or.* 1. 33 'What other force (sc. than eloquence) could have gathered people into one place when they were scattered or drawn them away from living like beasts in the fields to the refined life of human beings in communities or, once those communities were established, draw up the codes and institutions of law?'). He thus exploited a commonplace's readiness to lend itself to the needs of a given context, a virtue from which the older C. profits, too, with few adjustments needed. The commonplace has kinship, further, with the Epicurean anthropology Lucretius develops, at about this time or slightly earlier, in Book 5 of *On Nature* cf. esp. 5. 925 ff. for humans living in the manner of beasts, 953 ff. for the lack of any conception of common interests or institutions, 1105 ff. for the effect of the 'great man'; cf. also Hor. *Serm.* 1. 3. 99 ff. (a picture of similarly brutish beginnings, minus the great man's intervention), Verg. *Aen.* 8. 314 ff. (the unsocialized state of Italy's inhabitants before Saturnus' arrival as law-giver), and on the background more generally Campbell 2003, esp. 159 ff. The natural state of humankind that the commonplace posits, before the 'great man' intervenes, more closely resembles a Hobbesian state of natural aggression and hostility than it does the 'natural tendency of human beings to, as it were, form herds' (*naturalis quaedam hominum quasi congregatio*) that C. stresses a few years later at the start of *Rep.* (1. 39, cf. *Leg.* 1. 33–5) and develops more fully, in the Stoicizing thesis of natural sociability, near the end of his life in *Off.* (see esp. 1. 11–12, 158, 2. 73, with Dyck 1997, 88–9; on the contrast see Schofield 1995, 70–1, and on C.'s approach to the history of communal life and the development of law see Cancelli 1971, Perelli 1972, Wood 1988, 120–42). C. glances at the latter conception only once here, introducing a minor incoherence in his development of the theme (92 **distinctively human qualities** n.).

either natural or civil law   The concept of natural law (*ius naturale*) was developed by the Stoics and is closely tied to their doctrine that justice is 'according to nature' (cf. 92 **distinctively human qualities** n.): it comprises the principles that should be recognized by all human beings as such, just because failing to do so would be as 'unnatural'—as contrary to our nature as human beings—as failing to distinguish 'hot and cold, bitter and sweet' (cf. *Rep.* 3. 13). Civil law (*ius civile*) is the body of principles that in fact are recognized by the members (*cives*) of a given *civil community (principles in fact recognized by all civil communities, yet without attaining the status of being 'natural', constitute the 'law of nations', *ius gentium*, which for obvious reasons was not easily or consistently distinguished from the *ius naturale*). On the categories in C.'s thought and antiquity more generally, see esp. Jolowicz and Nicholas 1972, 102–7, Striker 1987, Inwood 1987, Wood 1988, 70–8, Zetzel 1996, Coleman 2000, 280–4. Though the civil law by definition could not exist before the development of civil communities that C. will describe, the natural law was coeval with 'nature' itself; hence C. says, not 'before either natural or civil law existed', but before they were 'codified' (*descriptum*).

only the goods... to seize or retain Here and in the ref. to 'justice and mildness' in the next sentence C. only glancingly touches on the connection between property rights and justice that is otherwise central to his social thought: see esp. *Off.* 1. 25–6, 42–3, 50–4, 2. 72–85, 3. 19–21, with Wood 1988, 128 ff., Atkins 1990, Long 1995, 233–40, and cf. 143 **let us take thought** n.

manliness and practical intelligence Here *virtus* and *consilium*, the latter in effect = *prudentia*: see the Glossary.

possessions... which we call 'public' I slightly overtranslate *res*, as 'possessions and activities', to bring out both dimensions of the term in the phrase *res publica* (Glossary s.v. commonwealth); by glossing 'public' (*publicas*) as that which 'bears on the common advantage' (*ad communem utilitatem*), C. concisely stresses the communitarian bent of Republicanism, though at the cost of omitting another crucial aspect, its reliance upon a body of agreed-upon law: see *Rep.* 1. 39 'the *res publica* is the *res* of the people (*populus*)—but "the people" is not any and every human gathering, assembled any which way, but a gathering of some size brought into cooperative relation (*sociatus*) by agreeing on the law (*iuris consensus*) and sharing a community of interest (*utilitatis communio*)', cf. esp. Schofield 1995, with Coleman 2000, 276–9.

the human gatherings..., the assemblages of dwellings i.e. the *civitas* as the citizens (*cives*) taken collectively (Glossary s.v. civil community) vs. the *urbs* as the physical city, sim. Gk. *polis* vs. *astu*.

principles of divine and human law 'Divine law' is not law divinely established (e.g. the Decalogue) but law governing relations between humans and gods, esp. for the sake of the *peace of the gods; 'human law' is the law that governs relations among humans, esp. (in the setting C. has in mind) in the form of 'civil law', cf. above.

92. distinctively human qualities Lit. 'the quality of being human', *humanitas*. If the life proper to *humanitas* is to law as the 'monstrous' (*immanis*) way of life is to violence—the homology implied here—it should in principle be possible to map that correspondence onto the distinction drawn just above, between knowing 'justice and mildness' and being in a 'bestial state' (*ecferitas*): 'the quality of being human', the law, and 'justice and mildness' would then all occupy one side of the division, and 'justice and mildness' would by implication be essential—*natural*—traits of 'being human', as opposed to the 'monstrous' and 'bestial' violence on the other side. That state of affairs would be consistent with the Stoicizing view of human nature C. presents a few years later (91 **who among us** n.), in which humans are naturally sociable creatures in part because justice and mildness are indeed essential human traits (see e.g. *Rep.* 2. 27, *Leg.* 2. 36); but it is not consistent with the commonplace anthropology that C. learned at school, in which humans are bestial, with the advantage only of being naturally 'teachable'. C.'s appeal to *humanitas* thus introduces an incoherence in his development; given that he was not conducting a lesson in political philosophy but only seeking a fine-sounding closure for this segment of his speech, we should suppose that he did not care, and that his audience did not notice.

If we do not wish . . . the other With a major structural break in sight (93–6), C. turns back from the commonplace to the comparison of Milo and S.: he links commonplace and comparison by aligning the distinction just drawn, between law and violence, with the distinction he had used to justify Milo's actions, 'what it is ever right for outstanding men to do' vs. 'what they are constrained to do' (86 n.).

the courts   Which C. has repeatedly and misleadingly said were 'uprooted' by his enemies to foil Milo: see 85, 89.

Milo both saw it and took steps to avail himself of the law and ward off violence   i.e. prosecuting Clodius for *public violence was his preferred way of warding off that violence. Shackleton Bailey (1985, 149, 1991*a*, 180) emends to read 'Milo both saw and acted. He repelled force in order to make trial of law' (*Milo et vidit et fecit, <qui> ut ius experiretur, vim depelleret*); but that is not what C.'s Milo did.

nor indeed was there need for everyone to do the same thing   Hoping no one will ask 'Why?', C. quickly skates past a detail crucially distinguishing S.'s case from Milo's; the sidestep is well remarked by Craig 2001, 119–20.

93–96. *A Conclusion, and a Transition*

We come to another major punctuation mark (emphasized by the invocation of the gods, next n.), and the most important point of articulation in the speech's structure since 14. That we have reached at least a preliminary conclusion is made plain by 93–4, where C. looks back to the speech's first paragraph: the question 'How few men of such manliness will be found . . . ?' returns to the opening conceit—1 'If anyone . . . used to wonder why brave and large-spirited citizens could not be found . . .'—now making explicit the exchange of service for glory that was there only implied (1 **If anyone** n.); the rest of the paragraph plots the vigorous depredations of Clodius' *henchmen—including Piso and Gabinius, given one last turn under C.'s lash—and thus resumes the claim of the speech's second sentence, that 'the sort of people who did sharp and repeated violence to all things divine and human . . . dart about with an energized delight'.

The most important of these people, of course, is Clodius, whose introduction at the start of 95 as 'the aedile' prosecuting Milo shows that we have returned to the present day: whereas 84–5 catalogued Clodius' earlier crimes, the present catalogue brings us very much up to date (esp. 95 **has assailed** n.). The return to the present prepares for the survey of the current political scene that C. will provide in the last third of the speech: Clodius here mainly serves as a foil for Milo, the patriot who remains firm for the *commonwealth despite all threats; and Milo mainly serves to facilitate C.'s transition to that survey. Milo does this in two ways: he gives C. a reason to ask 'what will the younger generation think?', bringing to the fore the conceit of instructing the youth that has been in the background since 14 (**for our youth** n., cf. 51 **young men** n.) and making it the dominant theme of the rest of the speech (96 'an excellent lesson for the younger generation'); and because Milo's latest frustration in bringing Clodius to trial apparently inspired the prosecutor to sarcasm (96 '**breed of the Best Sort**' n.), it gives C. an opening to articulate the highly tendentious contrast of **populares* and **optimates* that follows.

93. O immortal gods   C. has sworn by the gods before (45, a solemn invocation; 53, a more informal 'by the immortal gods!', cf. 122); here he addresses them, dramatically and directly in the 2nd pers. plur., asking their aid in a form of prayer, a gesture he elsewhere uses only at *Phil.* 4. 9.

almost wrote 'The End'   Lit. 'were almost the fated end (*fata*) of the commonwealth': C. uses this metonymy only here (cf. Ov. *F.* 5. 389, Hercules and Achilles as the two *fata* of Troy), but compare *Prov. cons.* 2 'two monsters (*portenta*) of the commonwealth and almost (its) death (*funera*)', and 109 **catastrophe of the commonwealth** n.

The former daily drains immeasurable quantities of gold   Late in 54, in a humiliation crowning his political impotence, C. will be prevailed on to defend Gabinius against a charge of extortion (*TLRR* no. 303) for accepting bribes from Ptolemy XII Auletes. Gabinius' alleged mistreatment of the **publicani*, a prominent feature of C.'s other attacks on his governorship (e.g. *Prov. cons.* 10–11, *Pis.* 41, 48), is absent here.

declares war against peoples now quiescent   Sim. *Dom.* 23, 60, *Pis.* 50. Roman law, most recently Caesar's *lex Iulia* of 59, forbade governors from waging war or entering the province of an allied king without the senate's approval save in an emergency (*MRR* 2. 188 for the *lex Iulia*, 2:75 for Sulla's *lex Cornelia de maiestate*; on Gabinius, Siani-Davies 2001, 166–7).

the villa that ... he used to describe   As tribune in 67 (C. says) Gabinius regaled the people in **contio* with accounts of Lucius Lucullus' grand villa near Tusculum, no doubt claiming that it represented Lucullus' plunder of the East, as part of his campaign to arouse *invidia* against Lucullus and win support for the *lex Gabinia* that transferred Lucullus' command in Bithynia and Pontus to Manius Glabrio (*MRR* 2. 144); now C. seeks to arouse *invidia* against Gabinius in much the same way. Gabinius' villa in Tusculum (*Dom.* 124, *Pis.* 48) was allegedly graced by goods stolen from Cicero's nearby villa after his departure (*Dom.* 62, 124, 113).

from a painted representation   Gabinius brought a mural of the villa (*villa quam ... pictam ... explicabat*) to the **assemblies to use as a 'visual aid' in decrying its grandeur (correctly Pina Polo 1989, 289): cf. the tribune Labienus' using a portrait or bust (*imago*) of Saturninus to stir the crowd at a *contio* during the trial of Saturninus' alleged murderer (*Rab. Perd.* 25); the general Lucius Hostilius Mancinus' explicating a town-plan of Carthage set up in the forum for his fellow citizens' edification, to illustrate his role in the city's capture (Plin. *HN* 35. 23); and murals carried in triumphal processions to represent generals' exploits (Morstein-Marx 2004, 106 n. 174, with refs.).

94. peoples of Thrace and Dardania ... to harass and despoil   Thus one argument made later in 56 to urge Piso's supersession in his province: *Prov. cons.* 4 'Macedonia ... is being harassed by barbarians robbed of peace out of (Piso's) greed. ... Thus those nations that had given our distinguished commander a powerful amount of silver, so they might enjoy peace, ... have—in place of the peace they purchased—brought against us a war that is almost justified' (*bellum ... prope iustum*, cf. 50 **force of arms** n.: reclaiming property wrongfully taken was one of the criteria of a 'just war', cf. 57 **restored their kingdoms** n., but as a Roman C. cannot quite say that the 'barbarians' are fully justified); cf. *Pis.* 96. For Piso's maladminstration of Macedonia see *Pis.* 83–94, partly overlapping with and much extending the catalog here, with the appendix in Nisbet 1961, 172–80.

shared out ... the goods ... of creditors who were Roman citizens   Sim. *Pis.* 86 'Didn't you (Piso) ... actually surrender Fufidius, a most honourable Roman equestrian, to his debtors, making their creditor a debt-bondsman?' As Nisbet (1961) notes ad loc., this prob. means that Fufidius, like C. a native of Arpinum, had lent money to the locals at extortionate rates, and Piso had reduced the debt; cf. also *Dom.* 60. The 'outrage' lay not just in meddling with private financial arrangements but in doing down a Roman to the advantage of Greeks, a people whom C. held in low regard: on C.'s attitude, Vasaly 1993, 198 ff., Siani-Davies 2001, 196, Swain 2002, 136, all with further refs.; for the prejudice that contrasted contemporary Greeks with those of 'ancient Greece', *QFr.* 1. 1(1). 16, and on the contemporary Greeks' 'innate readiness to deceive' (*ingenia ad fallendum parata*), *QFr.* 1. 2(2). 4, sim. *Flac.* 9–12, *Scaur.* 4 (presumably speaking to the judges' prejudices). Cf. 110, 126, 141 below.

extorted huge sums from the people of Dyrrachium   The people of Dyrrachium allegedly bribed Piso, early in his governorship, to kill Plator of Orestis (*Pis.* 83, cf. *Pis.* 38, *Har. resp.* 35); but C. prob. refers to the transit-dues (*Prov. cons.* 5: *vectigal ac portorium*) that Piso reportedly extorted from Dyrrachium, where C. stayed in the latter part of his exile.

ordered . . . a fixed sum each year   These were the 'free communities' (*liberae civitates*) of mainland Greece (*Achaea*), protected against governors' meddling by the *lex Iulia* on extortion of 59: cf. *Dom.* 23 (referring to the law), *Prov. cons.* 5, 7, with Nisbet 1961, 172–3.

did not leave . . . adornment   Sim. *Prov. cons.* 6–7 (Byzantium), *Pis.* 85 (temple of Jupiter Urius).

these two men   He includes Milo, whose prosecution he is about to mention; on C.'s consciousness of Milo's trial shaping his portrait of Milo in 85–9, see 86 **On this topic** n.

Numerius, Serranus, Aelius   On Quintus Numerius Rufus, see 72 'Gracchus'. . . , 82 **Numerius** nn.; on Sextus Atilius Serranus, 72 **the one** n.; on Aelius Ligus, 68 **Some good-for-nothing** n.

95. aedile . . . date for the trial   On Clodius' prosecution of Milo, in adjournment at the time of this speech, see 1 **those who joined** n. The reference to the trial, and to Clodius as aedile—the office he assumed on 20 Jan. 56—shows that we have left the events of 58 and early 57, covered in 15–92, and are now concerned with events of the recent past and the present day: thus one of Clodius' crimes has virtually been ripped from the headlines (**assailed ... his enemies' homes** n.), and the frustrated prosecution of Clodius to which C. now refers is not the attempt blocked early in 57 (89) but the more recent attempt of Nov. 57–Jan. 56 (**not been granted leave** n.).

no wrong done him ... the younger generation   i.e. as a true patriot, Milo must act for the *commonwealth even if the basic contract of Republicanism (1 **If anyone** n.) is not honoured: cf. *Rep.* 1. 8–9, *Mil.* 82–3, and esp. the extravagant sentiments put in Milo's mouth at *Mil.* 93–4, 96; for the thought cast in the form found here ('X will never regret ...'), see *Leg. agr.* 2. 26, *Cat.* 4. 20, *Flac.* 104, *Att.* 13. 28(299). 2, *Fam.* 9. 5(179). 2 (sim. *Fam.* 7. 3(183). 1–2), *Div.* 1. 27; cf. Cic. *Fam.* 10. 23(414). 1 (Plancus), Livy 28. 39. 1 (sim. 10. 45. 5). The 'younger generation'—a dubious lot (14 **for our youth** n.) not yet tested and taught by experience—cannot be assumed to have equally firm principles.

has assailed ... his enemies' homes   A clutch of recent crimes: 'public monuments' and 'enemies' homes' refer to an attack of 3 Nov. 57 on workers rebuilding Catulus' portico and Cicero's home on the Palatine (Clodius had engrossed both for his own home and his 'shrine of Liberty') and on Quintus Cicero's home on the Esquiline (*Att.* 4. 3(75). 2), and another attack, of 12 Nov. 57, on Milo's house (*Att.* 4. 3(75). 3: this is the second attack on Milo's house, cf. 85 **another tribune** n.); 'temples' is prob. our earliest ref. to the burning of the temple of the Nymphs (*NTDAR* 269, *LTUR* 3. 350–1, *MAR* 182) in late Feb./early March, roughly contemporary with this trial (otherwise first noted at *Cael.* 78, ascribed to Clodius' henchman Sex. Cloelius: see Tatum 1999, 211–12).

during his tribunate emptied the prison into the forum   Because C. is now talking about Clodius' more recent crimes, he says 'during his tribunate' (*in tribunatu*) in this case, attaching it to this act only: the charge is similar to 78 'Would you spring assassins from prison ... ?', though it should not (if C. is being precise) refer to that occasion, the riot of 23 Jan. 57, when Clodius was no longer tribune.

safeguards so that he could defend . . . the auspices   Acc. to C.'s account in 86–9, this is the armed force Milo adopted after he was prevented from prosecuting Clodius early in 57; with C.'s phrasing here cf. the euphemistic description of S.'s efforts to 'fortify himself with supporters in order to conduct his magistracy safely' (79); for the 'household gods' (here, *penates*), see 30 nn. Ref. to the *auspices shows that C. is thinking specifically of Milo's success in blocking by *obnuntiation the aedilician elections of Nov. 57, in which Clodius was a candidate (*Att.* 4. 3(75). 4–5, a letter which also describes Milo's 'safeguards' in action, ibid. 3); see also next n.

was not granted leave . . . to accuse   As the context shows, this is not the prosecution foiled in the first half of 57, when edicts of Nepos et al. turned the suspension of public business against Milo (89 **one consul** n.); rather, C. refers to Milo's second attempt (*TLRR* no. 262), begun in late Nov. but foiled when Nepos once again hoisted his enemy on his own petard. After Clodius' gangs attacked Milo's house and Milo used the *auspices to block the aedilician elections (preceding nn.), he again tried to prosecute Clodius, before the *voting assembly could be held and Clodius' election protect him from prosecution during his term. But Nepos blocked prosecution on the ground that a jury could not be chosen before new *quaestors were elected, while quaestors could not be elected before the aediles were elected—and of course the aediles had not been elected because Milo had blocked the assembly (*Att.* 4. 3(75). 5, Milo's intention to prosecute in late Nov.; Cass. Dio 39. 7. 4, Nepos' manoeuvre, evidently after 4 Dec., when the quaestors of 57 went out of office; see Meyer 1919, 109 n. 3, Maslowksi 1976, Brunt 1981, 230, Tatum 1999, 197–8). Details of the sequel are spotty; we know that when the senate met after 10 Dec., before the Saturnalia began, the consul-designate Marcellinus proposed a way to circumvent Nepos' road-block, but the meeting broke up in tumult before a vote could be taken (*QFr.* 2. 1(5). 2–3: C. predicted that the matter would be unresolved until Jan.). Whatever happened when the matter was (or was not) resumed, the elections were held on 20 Jan. 56, Clodius' victory saved him from prosecution for the rest of the year, and it was left for Nepos—later in 56, when Clodius turned against him—to tell C. he now regretted having 'saved (Clodius) twice' (*Fam.* 5. 3(11). 2).

by the senate's authority   Two things can be said with certainty
about this ref. to the senate's *auctoritas*: it has no link at all with
the edicts mentioned in 89 (though a link has often been made); and it
alludes to an element in Milo's frustration that inspired the prosecutor to use the phrase 'breed of the Best Sort' (next n.). We do not know
whether the senate frustrated the prosecution by refusing to circumvent Nepos' roadblock (preceding n.) or by insisting that the elections
be held or in some other way; we cannot even say that the senate acted,
beyond debating the matter sufficiently for a 'sense of the house' to
emerge (cf. Mitchell 1991, 162, *contra* Gruen 1974, 296). Much the
same can be said about certain *sententiae* deplored by C. in a letter
written at the end of 54 and often cited in connection with the present
passage (*Fam.* 1. 9(20). 15): '(Clodius) got off scot-free thanks to the
sententiae of those who—when a tribune of the plebs wished to
punish (him) through a judgement rendered by patriots—stripped
from the commonwealth what would have been a brilliant precedent
for punishing sedition.' C. must refer to a prosecution attempted late
in 57 (by the time the *sententiae* in question were voiced, the senate
had decreed 'unprecedented honours' for Caesar, a *supplicatio* of 15
days voted after the campaign season ended in 57, when Caesar had
settled his legions in winter quarters, *Fam.* ibid. and Caes. *BGall.*
2. 35. 4); if the tribune in question was Milo, it must point to a time
before 9 Dec., when Milo left office (thus also before the senate
meeting described in *QFr.* 2. 1(5), preceding n.). If C. refers to a
known event, it must be the meeting of 14 Nov. 57, when three
senators—Nepos, Appius, and a 'good friend' of Atticus (almost
certainly Hortensius)—used the opportunity of stating their *sententiae* to filibuster a discussion of Clodius' prosecution (*Att.* 4. 3(75). 3,
also mentioning S.'s anger at the tactics).

96. No doubt this is the point of the question   Ref. to 'the senate's
authority' in the preceding sentence makes clear that the prosecutor
exploited Milo's frustration by the senate, or at any rate its failure to
help: e.g. 'You claim that Clodius' violence justified Sestius' resort to
an armed gang, yet how terrible could that violence be when the
breed of the Best Sort itself blocked Milo's prosecution?' At *Arch.* 12
C. uses a similar question to develop a theme supporting one element
in his defence, although in that case—because the prosecutor had not

been so obliging as actually to ask the question—C. must put it in his mouth ('You *will* ask me, Grattius...'; on the theme's role in the defence, Berry 2004). That famous excursus on literature and its exponents bulks even larger in the economy of its speech (*Arch.* 12–30: nineteen of the speech's thirty-two paragraphs) than the following discussion does in this.

'breed of the Best Sort'...the phrase you used.   Cf. 132 'So you have the answer to your question, who are the "Best Sort". They are not a "breed", as you put it...', again addressing the prosecutor, where C. makes plain that the sting lay in the term 'breed' (*natio*: 'tribe' might be preferable but would risk confusion with the division of the Roman people called *tribus*, 'tribe'). On the derivation and connotation of the term *Best Sort = optimates, see the Glossary. The choice of *natio* was prob. inspired by the ethnic associations of the suffix (*-as, -ates*) used to form the term *optimates*, both *natio* and suffix suggesting a status acquired by birth, not achievement (C. opposes that notion in 137: **the members... n.**); the noun stings because it is mostly used to denote *foreign* tribes. In a few months C. will turn the jibe against Clodius, when certain omens are interpreted by the soothsayers (*haruspices*) as warning 'Beware the worse people' (*deteriores*): 'indeed, there is a great breed (*natio*) of them, but still the leader and chief of them all is this man here' (*Har. resp.* 57). Yet by the end of 54, in his dejection at the treachery of senatorial conservatives, he refers to 'those who used to be called "the best sort"' (*Fam.* 1. 9(20). 17).

I shall say a few words   For the formula marking a departure from a main line of argument already begun or anticipated, see *Cat.* 4. 20, *Mur.* 2 (both, it happens, signaling C.'s intention to talk about himself).

not be inconsistent with...the case of Publius Sestius itself   C. echoes the promise made at the end of the exordium (5), 'to omit nothing that is pertinent to your inquiry, to the defendant, and to the public interest', using it to bind what follows to the body of the speech. Having set a modest standard of success—lit. 'will not draw back from' = 'will not be inconsistent with', and in that broad sense 'pertinent'—he more than meets it: see next n.

96–135. *Optimates, Populares, and the Political Condition of Rome*

On the function of this segment see Introd. §4. Simply to summarize its movement here: C. begins by identifying two sorts of statesmen (96), the *Best Sort (*optimates) and *men of the people (*populares), who represent, respectively, the polity's aristocratic–oligarchic and popular–democratic elements implied by the phrase *senatus populusque Romanus*. But C. no sooner introduces the distinction than he collapses it, in a baldly tendentious definition of the Best Sort so broad as to include all save those whom he elsewhere calls *desperadoes (97, cf. Glossary s.v.): the distinction that moments before 'always' existed exists no more. Instead—after remarking the goals, values, and qualities of the Best Sort thus understood (98–100) and noting examples for emulation (101–3)—C. describes a new alignment (104–6): on the one hand, the desperadoes who, though neither few nor weak (cf. 99 'The commonwealth is assailed with greater forces than it is defended'), have no legitimate role in the *civil community; and the Best Sort as C. has defined them, who constitute the civil community properly so called and accordingly can be identified both with the truly 'popular' and with 'the best'. At this point, the 'lesson for the younger generation' emerges, a lesson in political action—Out with the desperadoes!—that is fundamentally optimistic: 'our civil community is in a state where—if you could get rid of the hired *henchmen—there would be unanimous agreement on matters of the public interest' (106). To confirm the cause for optimism C. devotes the rest of the lesson to proving that 'the best' are 'the popular', surveying expressions of popular favour in *contiones (106–8), *voting assemblies (108–14, including an attack on the witness Gellius), and theatrical *games (*ludi*) and gladiatorial shows (115–27), before capping the excursus by defending himself (127–31) and the Best Sort (132).[2]

---

[2] The excursus, strictly regarded, ends at 132, when C. turns back to the prosecutor: 'So you have the answer to your question, who are the *Best Sort'. The attack on Vatinius (a foretaste of the interrogation that would follow the next day: Introd. §2) then intervenes before the exhortation to the young begins the *peroratio.*

96–105. *The Popular and Best Sort Defined, and Redefined*

96. there have always been two sorts of people   Riggsby (2002*a*,
183) well notes C.'s tendency in the 'post-return' speeches to present
this distinction only to collapse it: cf. *Red. sen.* 20, *Dom.* 77, 89, *Prov.
cons.* 41. Despite the adverb 'always', C. elsewhere (like Roman
commentators more generally) usually treats 'popular' politicians
in the sense meant here as a phenomenon dating from the 130s:
see e.g. the individuals mentioned at 101 and 103, and cf. esp. *Rep.*
1. 31, on the tribunate of Tiberius Gracchus that 'split a unified
people into two factions'; for an exception, see *Leg.* 3. 20 (Gaius
Flaminius, tr. pl. 232, cos. 223, cens. 220, cos. II 217).

'men of the people'   See the Glossary.

**97. grandest categories of the citizenry, to whom the senate chamber
lies open**   'Grandest' (*maximi*) refers to stature ('principal orders' in
Shackleton Bailey's trans.), not size ('largest', 'very large') as Halm 1886
proposed (followed by Holden 1889, Gardner 1958*a*, Cousin 1965), in
the mistaken belief that expression of *dignitas* would require *summi
ordines* (for which cf. *Rep.* 2. 69); but the 'largest' or 'very large' orders
were the poorest—what C. calls the *infimi*, 'lowest', ibid.—and even at
his most tendentious C. would not claim that the *curia* lay open to
them. C. refers primarily to the orders represented by the judges: the
senators, to whom 'the senate chamber lies open' (*patet curia*) in a
literal sense (only senators and those introduced by them were allowed
to enter), and equestrians broadly so called (both members of the
*equestrian order and the *treasury tribunes, cf. Glossary s.v. 'treasury
tribune'), who had the financial and social capital to embark, as C. had,
on the public career leading to senatorial status. C. is thinking in
expressly hierarchical terms, as the succeeding *categories show, and
so acknowledges as a matter of fact what he later slightly obscures as
a matter of ideology (137 **the members** n.).

Roman citizens   At this time, virtually all free residents of Italy S of
the Po: cf. 30 **Our allies** n.

even freedmen   In the context of ancient slavery only the Romans
freed ('manumitted') many of their slaves, during the masters'

lifetimes or in their wills, and made a Roman citizen's freed slave a citizen in turn (on manumission see Hopkins 1978, 133–71; on freedmen in the Republic, Treggiari 1969). Yet though they were citizens, they were distinguished by various obligations (to their former masters) and limitations (e.g. ineligibility for public office); though some grew wealthy, their social status was always ambiguous. That C. here includes freedmen among the **optimates* shows that he is stretching the definition almost to the breaking point. At *Cat.* 4. 15–16, where he is similarly keen to depict universal consensus, C. praises (in order of descending rank) the zeal of the equestrians, the *treasury tribunes, the 'scribes' (cf. 133 **Sextus Cloelius** n.), and all 'freeborn men' (*ingenui*), then adds freedmen—and goes on to include even slaves (at least those whose treatment allows them to be content with their lot).

hobbled by embarrassments in their domestic affairs   The definition of non-**optimates* identifies them with the *desperadoes whose crowning trait is insolvency caused by crushing debt (cf. 99, those whose 'finances are in a shambles'), a very great evil in Roman eyes, for several reasons. As a product of uncontrolled appetites (the typical assumption), it marks a moral failure, and its vicious effect is multiplied by threatening the debtor's family, among the worst of all sins. In a public man it raises the suspicion that he will profit illegally from positions of trust (cf. 18, on Gabinius, and *FS* 265 ff., C.'s defence of Milo in the senate against Clodius' attack on his indebtedness in 53). When widespread, insolvency foments agitation for the cancellation of debt (Catiline's aims included *novae tabulae*, 'new accounts', *Cat.* 2. 18, Sall. *Cat.* 21. 2): since from a creditor's perspective cancellation of debt was theft, and since protection of property was (in C.'s view) among the foremost aims of civil life (cf. 91 **only the goods** n.), insolvency threatened civil life at its roots. Cf. 99 **validity** n., and on debt in the late Republic, Frederiksen 1966.

98. pilots of the commonwealth   On the metaphor of the ship of state, 7 **commonwealth was tossed** n.; cf. the inept piloting of Gabinius, drunk and agog, at 20. The metaphor is repeated with emphasis at 99.

flourishing   The *beati*, those understood most inclusively to enjoy the choiceworthy condition of being both psychologically 'happy'/ 'content' and materially 'well off'/'prosperous': a life lived in this condition (*vita beata*) corresponded to Gk. *eudaimonia* ('happiness', 'flourishing', 'the best human life') that was highest good of the 'eudaimonist' schools of Greek philosophy (Aristotelian, Stoic, Epicurean). The flourishing C. thinks of here is purely material, as the epithet looks back to those who are 'not hobbled by embarrassments in their domestic affairs' but have 'their domestic affairs in good order'. C. never pretended that he was other than a supporter of the moneyed classes: cf. *Att.* 1. 19(19). 4 (March 60, referring to his position on an agrarian law), 'I... am trying to strengthen private citizens' claims on their holdings; for that's my "army", as you know—the propertied'.

tranquillity joined with worthy standing   In effect, the status quo, of persons and the community alike, as it is maintained in *otium* and expressed in *dignitas*. By *tranquillity C. means both domestic tranquillity, the condition of the *commonwealth as a whole invoked at the start of the speech (5), and the personal condition stressed in the next sentence (for the distinction cf. the Glossary s.v.): for the *patriot, the personal and communal conditions are hardly distinguishable. In a state of domestic tranquillity there is no upheaval, hence no significant change, which could result only from what C. would likely call 'sedition' (cf. Wirszubski 1954, 4); in that state each person can retain or augment his *worthy standing by engaging in the accepted forms of behaviour that rest on the 'bases or components' enumerated below. In so far as it connotes such essentially complacent social and political goals, the phrase can be regarded as a slogan of the senatorial conservatives: for further refs. see Introd. §4 at nn. 70, 72.

it is not fitting... either... or...   In both deprecated categories the *otium* and *dignitas* at issue are primarily the individual's: the first category includes those so immersed in public striving that they lack peace of mind (cf. Lucr. 5. 1120–35) or cultivation (by implication Marius, *Arch.* 19); the second category includes those who embrace the philosophical quietism C. attacks at 23 above, or who 'bury themselves in books' (*Arch.* 12) and dwell in the 'shady leisure' of learning (e.g. *Balb.* 15), or—especially—who withdraw from public life to the comfort provided by their wealth, to contemplate their fishponds (so the *piscinarii* like Lucius Lucullus whom C. derides, *Att.* 1. 19(19). 6, 20(20). 3; cf. 100, those who 'want... to maintain their tranquillity even absent worthy standing', and more generally 138).

Yet in both categories *otium* can also be understood in the communal sense: the first clause then decries the pursuit of individual *dignitas* at the expense of 'domestic tranquillity' (Caesar's position at the start of the civil war in 49, see *BCiv.* 1. 7. 7, cf. 1. 4. 4, 1. 9. 2, 1. 32. 4, 3. 91. 2); the second clause would warn against valuing domestic *tranquillity so highly as to become an appeaser, avoiding the *manly resistance to bad behaviour that *dignitas* demands. Three and a half months later C. will vary the present theme to state a lesson learned from hard experience, in justifying his defection from the *optimates* to support Caesar: 'we must give thought neither to safety bereft of worthy standing, nor to worthy standing without safety' (*Fam.* 1. 7(18). 10, to Lentulus, sim. ibid. 7–8, *Att.* 4. 5(80). 2–3). Within a year he told Lentulus that they could look at most for tranquillity, because the system (*ratio*) of public life had changed: *Fam.* 1. 8(19). 4 'we should hope for *otium*.... As for a brave and firm senator's proper role as ex-consul (*dignitas consularis*)—there's no reason to give it a thought'.

the following bases or components   Most of these components have been mentioned several times over in the speech or are otherwise obvious goods of the *civil community, for which a *patriot should be willing to sacrifice. Brunt remarks that *freedom (*libertas*) is notably absent, perhaps 'because of the more distinctly popular nuance of the term..., especially as the freedom (C.) prized himself was inherent in the (senate's authority), whose maintenance is for him the most vital of all these principles' (1988, 331).

validity of one's word   i.e. *fides*. This could refer to financial 'credit', an extension of the basic sense of *trustworthiness: cf. *Off.* 2. 84 'The commonwealth is held together by no bond stronger than *fides*, which cannot exist if the payment of loans is to be treated as optional' (where C. has just condemned the cancellation of debt, cf. 97 **hobbled** n.). But given the stress on law and trials just before, the term more likely denotes scrupulous honesty.

99. largeness of spirit, ample intelligence, and great resolve   See the Glossary s.vv. largeness of spirit, resolve; the term translated as 'intelligence' is *ingenium*, the talent or natural capacity with which each person is born.

a great mass of men who...or who...or who... The traits
oppose those of the *Best Sort (97), 'who do no harm, are not wicked
or rabid in their nature, and are not hobbled by embarrassments in
their domestic affairs', and partly overlap the categories of C.'s enemies in March 58 (46). With the last category cf. the Catilinarians in
63 who 'because they see that all is lost, would rather perish together
with all than by themselves' (*Cat.* 4. 14).

the commonwealth is tossed by turbulent seas   Cf. 98 **pilots of the
commonwealth** n.

100. this path is...rough or steep   C. perhaps anticipates the first
of his quotations from tragedy (102) by adapting a half-remembered
line on the return from the Underworld: 'I am here, returned—but
barely—from Acheron by a path high and steep | through caverns
where rough rocks hang' (*TD* 1. 37, from an unknown tragedy).

**The commonwealth is assailed with greater forces than it is
defended**   C. must walk a fine line: his strategy requires that the
*desperadoes be an isolated remnant opposed by all the *Best Sort, in
the broad sense of the term (cf. 96–143 n. and 106); yet he cannot make
their threat seem negligible. He therefore stresses the danger but finds
its main cause in the patriots themselves, their hesitation and torpor, in
short, their lack of *manliness. The shaming gesture refers back to the
speech's first words, on the 'brave and large-spirited citizens (who
cannot) be found...to put themselves and their well-being boldly on
the line'; worthy examples of the desiderated manliness follow.

101. only those abide   The following *exempla* evoke the traits elsewhere praised in the speech, esp. *resolve, *bravery, and *largeness of
spirit.

your father, Marcus Scaurus   C. addresses the presiding praetor,
Marcus Aemilius (*RE* 141) Scaurus, whose family on both sides
provided examples C. has already invoked: 39 **Marcus Scaurus** n.
on his father, 37 **Quintus Metellus** n. on his mother's uncle; their
éclat represented the family's recent renaissance, cf. *Mur.* 16, citing
the elder Scaurus as a *notable who refurbished an old family's glory
that had been dimmed for generations. After governing Sardinia in

55, Scaurus was prosecuted for extortion in 54 (*TLRR* no. 295) and successfully defended by C. (and five others, including Clodius) in the extant speech *pro Scauro* (C. figuratively 'conjures up' the elder Scaurus' shade at *Scaur.* 45–6). When C. failed to counter a charge of bribery, after the hugely corrupt consular elections of 54 (*TLRR* no. 319, cf. no. 300, *LUO* no. 66), Scaurus went into exile. C. addresses him again below, in connection with his aedileship of 58 (116 **I ask you** n.).

troublemakers from Gaius Gracchus to Quintus Varius   i.e. from the *tribunates of Gaius Sempronius (*RE* 47) Gracchus in 123–22 to the tribunate of Quintus Varius (*RE* 1) Severus 'Hibrida' in 90, just before Scaurus' death in 89. He was prosecuted under Varius' law on 'treason' (*maiestas*) for having provoked Rome's allies to war (*TLRR* no. 100) and used his *auctoritas* to resist the charge (Ascon. 22. 8–20 Cl., sim. but garbled Val. Max. 3. 7. 8); he is not known for resisting Gracchus, in whose tribunates he was still a junior senator (prob. aedile in 122, *MRR* 1. 517), though a late source refers to his support of Gracchus' murderer, Lucius Opimius, cos. 121 (*De vir. ill.* 72.9; on Opimius, 140 n.). C. mainly intends to establish Scaurus as an 'anti-popular' figure over the span of his career.

your maternal grandfather's brother, Quintus Metellus   Though one's family strictly so called (*gens*) was traced through the male line, maternal descent was useful for both praise (as here) and blame (21 **his mother's lineage** n.). Scaurus' mother was Caecilia (*RE* Caecilius 134) Metella, daughter of Lucius Caecilius (*RE* 91) Metellus Delmaticus (cos. 119) and niece of Metellus Numidicus, whose acts are at issue here; marrying Sulla soon after the elder Scaurus' death, she bore him a boy and girl, the latter of whom Milo married in 55 (*Att.* 4. 13(87). 1). C. has already compared the last of the incidents mentioned here, Numidicus' refusal to swear to uphold Saturninus' law, with his own case: see 37 **Quintus Metellus** and **refusing...** nn. The other two date to his censorship in 102 (*MRR* 1. 567): the first concerns the censorial mark (*nota*) he placed by the names of Saturninus (cf. 37 n.) and Servilius Glaucia (cf. *MRR* 3. 196) on the senate roll, with the aim of expelling them from the senate (his colleague and kinsman, Metellus Caprarius, did not agree, cf. 55 **review of the censors** n.); the second concerns Lucius Equitius, whose claim to be Tiberius Gracchus' son

Numidicus rejected, thereby refusing to 'graft' him onto the *gens Sempronia* (see Val. Max. 9. 7. 1–2, cf. 9. 15. 1; for the metaphor of 'grafting' used in a related sense, 72 **the one** n.).

leave aside ancient examples . . . avoid naming any of the living The singular quantity and quality of their ancient *exempla* is a Roman article of faith, cf. Livy 1. pr. 11, Plin. *HN* 7. 116, Quint. 12. 2. 30. C. avoids naming the living, not because it would be improper, but because he would stir *invidia* by naming some but not all exemplary contemporaries: cf. (in a similar connection) 108 'I do not name them at this point in my speech, lest my remarks seem ungrateful, if I say too little about any individual, or endless, if I say enough about them all', *Rep.* 1. 1.

Quintus Catulus Quintus Lutatius (*RE* 8) Catulus, cos. 78, cens. 65, an adherent of Sulla, whose memory he honoured and whose rigidly pro-senatorial measures he supported (in the end, vainly) against reform, hence the nature of the praise offered here; his defeat by the much younger Caesar in the election for *pontifex maximus* in 63 (*MRR* 2. 171) marked the waning of his influence. He suits C.'s needs here on several counts: he was fairly recently dead (late 61/early 60); his name was a byword for optimate leadership (cf. *Att.* 1. 20(20). 3, of May 60: 'since Catulus' death I have maintained the optimate path without guard or companion'); he was, like C., a symbol of Clodian oppression, because the portico his homonymous father (cos. 102) built on the Palatine from spoils won against the Cimbri was destroyed by Clodius at the same time that he razed Cicero's neighbouring house (*Dom.* 102, 114, 137, cf. *Cael.* 78); and he had had the discernment to declare C. 'father of the fatherland' (*pater patriae*) for his actions against the Catilinarians (see 121, *Dom.* 132, *Pis.* 6).

fear of peril's tempest or hope of honour's breeze Two clichés nicely paired. A 'tempest' or 'storm' (*tempestas*) can evoke both disturbances in the *civil community (e.g., *Clu.* 88, 96, *Mur.* 36, 81, *Sull.* 40. 59, *Red. sen.* 38; combined with the nautical metaphor, *Caec.* 88, *Mur.* 4) and the 'storms of ill-will' (*tempestates invidiae*) of the sort C. means here, which bear down on a patriot because of his *manly but unpopular action (*Clu.* 94, *Cat.* 1. 22, 2. 15, *Dom.* 68, the last referring to the 'storm' to which C. yielded in departing from Rome). The contrasting figure of a 'breeze' (*aura*) connotes a fair wind at one's back, esp. when joined with 'honour' (i.e. office); C. prob. has in mind what he will call 'popularity's breeze' a few months later (*Har. resp.* 43 *popularis aura*), the 'breeze' of the people's favour (sim. *Clu.* 130, Hor. *Carm.* 3. 2. 20 *arbitrio popularis aurae*, Verg. *Aen.* 6. 816 *nimium gaudens popularibus auris*, Livy 3. 33. 7, 22. 26. 4, 29. 37. 17, 30. 45. 6, 42. 30. 5). By implication that breeze is fickle, like the *irresponsible (*levis*) people (cf. Quint. 11. 1. 45, contrasting *aura popularis* with *gravitas senatoria*), and is closely related to the *popularis gloria* contemned at *Tusc.* 3. 3–4, in contrast to 'true glory' (for which see 139 **the good report of patriots** n.). The figure more clearly suits the old contrast between *popular and *optimate (cf. 96) than the coming argument that men of the Best Sort are the truly popular.

102. godlike and deathless   Cf. 50 **godlike** and 47 **glory eternal** nn.

many snares are set for patriots   The four lines quoted here are all from the *Atreus* (*trag.* 214–16, 203 Ribb., respectively) by the poet Accius (170–*c.*86): his plays were mostly based on Greek tales, though C. quotes from one of his dramas on a Roman theme (*fabula praetexta*) at 123; like all tragedies written in Latin before Seneca, they do not survive. Quintilian notes C.'s fondness for quoting or referring to verse (1. 8. 11, making clear that other orators did the same): the quotations are found beginning early in his forensic career (cf. *Sex. Rosc.* 46–7), primarily as an adornment (as here; cf. *De or.* 2. 257) and by no means in all his speeches; his use of Ennius' *Medea* and Caecilius' comedy in defending Caelius a few weeks later (*Cael.* 18, 37–8) is exceptional in being integrated more closely in his argument, and of a piece with the speech's theatricality, inspired by the coincidence of the trial with the Megalesian *games that had stage productions at their center (see Geffcken 1995, Klodt 2003, 82–97, Leigh 2004). C.'s next tragic quotations (121–3) are in a different vein, offered as evidence of audiences' and actors' taking the verses, in performance, to comment on C. and his plight.

what wicked citizens pluck from another context   Spoken by Atreus (preceding n.), the line is similarly quoted in deprecation of tyranny at *Phil.* 1. 34, *Off.* 1. 97, and by Seneca at *Dial.* 3. 20. 4, *Clem.* 1. 12. 4, 2. 2. 2; the emperor Tiberius offered a variation on it (Suet. *Tib.* 59. 2

'Let them hate me, so long as they assent (*probent*)'), whereas Caligula allegedly quoted it in earnest (Suet. *Cal.* 30. 1). On the line's political use at Rome, Champlin 2003, 306–8.

the younger generation   At *Planc.* 59 C. quotes the first two lines above, saying that it is advice he gives his son.

103. the people's advantage Strictly, 'the people's advantage' (*populi commodum*) should be as one with the *commonwealth (*res publica =* *res populi =* 'the people's interests'): they can be at odds only if the *populus* is understood not as the collective body of all citizens but in a factional sense, identified (as here) with 'the masses' (*multitudo*), a bloc with interests distinct from the elite's, esp. the senate's. On 'the people's advantage' in factional rhetoric of the late Republic, Hellegouarc'h 1963, 556–7, Brunt 1988, 346–9, Morstein-Marx 2004, 222–3.

Lucius Cassius ... concerning the secret ballot As tribune in 137, Lucius Cassius Longinus Ravilla (cos. 127, cens. 125) passed a measure introducing the secret ballot in all trials before the people except in cases of *perduellio* (acting as an enemy of the state, a charge largely replaced by *maiestas*, 'treason', in C.'s time; *MRR* 1. 485); the secret ballot had been introduced in elections two years earlier by the tribune Aulus Gabinius (*MRR* 1. 482), the grandfather of C.'s enemy, the consul of 58. The secret ballot endangered 'the well-being of the Best Sort' (*salus optimatium*) less in being used against them (e.g. in trials where their *salus*—their standing as citizens—was at stake) than in limiting their *auctoritas by shielding less powerful men's votes from their inspection: see the critique put in Quintus Cicero's mouth at *Leg.* 3. 33–9 (esp. 34–5), with Yakobson 1995, Dyck 2004, 523–5.

Tiberius Gracchus moved his agrarian law In 367 the tribunes Gaius Licinius Stolo and Lucius Sextius Sextinus passed a measure limiting individual tenancy (*possessio*) of public land (*ager publicus,* acquired mainly through conquest in Italy) to 500 *iugera* (*MRR* 1. 114, cf. 1. 108–9; *c.*1.5 *iugera =* 1 acre); Tiberius Gracchus' law of 133 (*MRR* 1. 493, Lintott 1992, 44–9) reaffirmed those limits, allowing an additional 250 *iugera* per son for up to two sons, and redistributed to the landless any land thus reclaimed in heritable but not alienable tenancies of 30 *iugera* each, on which they would pay a modest rent (*vectigal*) to the treasury. In saying that 'the rich (*locupletes*, a term esp. denoting landed wealth) were dislodged from their long-time holdings (*possessiones*)', C. elides what Gracchus' measure implied, that the rich had over time engrossed tenancies far in excess of the legal limits.

Gaius Gracchus moved his grain law See 55 **a fifth of the public income** n.

generously provided sustenance free of toil... The objection could be adapted to any measure intended to relieve the plebs: see e.g. the peroration of C.'s second speech against Servilius Rullus' agrarian law of 63, *Leg. agr.* 2. 102–3 (a *contio); cf. his calling the 'wretched and hungry refuse of the plebs' (*misera ac ieiuna plebecula*) 'a leech on the treasury' (*hirudo aerari*: *Att.* 1. 16(16). 11), and his condemnation of Gaius Gracchus' grain dole as a 'large handout' (*magna largitio*) that 'drained the treasury' (*Off.* 2. 72, cf. 55 **a fifth of the public income** n.).

104. excessive desires... policy The opposition between *cupiditas* (a 'desire' that is always intense and usually excessive), identified with the *populus* in the factional sense of the term (**the people's advantage** n.), and *consilium* of the 'foremost men' (a product of 'taking thought', *consulere*, identified with the *consilium publicum* achieved in senatorial debate, cf. 27 **a matter of public policy** n.) alludes to the ability to distinguish needs from wants on which the senate partly based its dominance of public affairs, cf. 77 **the ignorant** n.

there is no cause for the people to dissent from the elite and the leading men To begin collapsing the distinction between *populares and *optimates, a move critical to his argument, C. reworks a theme sounded already in 51, where he contrasts the peace enjoyed abroad with an internal threat posed by an isolated group of *desperadoes.

largesse Here and on into 105 C. bases his argument on a distinction between *largiri*—the ill-regulated dispensing of a good to an individual or group (thus the Gracchan laws, from the elite's point of view), often with some *quid pro quo* implied—and *conducere*, paying someone expressly to perform a specific service. Both terms are pejorative (with 'largesse' contrast *generosity), the former tending to stigmatize esp. the giver, the latter (because no person with *dignitas* would work for pay) the recipient. For C.'s precepts on properly regulated largesse, see *Off.* 2. 54–64.

assemblies of the people crowded with their hired henchmen　Cf. 57 **hired hands** n.

105. hiring them with wages was unnecessary　C.'s point is perhaps not transparent, in so far as he seems at first sight to mean that earlier 'popular' leaders, who implicitly bribed the mob with 'largesse', were operating in a more straightforward or less discreditable way than the current leaders, who expressly pay their *henchmen a 'wage'. With the comparison, implying that even Saturninus is preferable, cf. the comparison at 37–8 ('Saturninus . . . was at least personally if not politically temperate . . . ').

if ever any of them was applauded, he had to fear that he had done something wrong　Sim. *Har. resp.* 50–2 (on Clodius' praise of Pompey), cf. *Vat.* 29, 41, *Pis.* 72, *Phil.* 2. 18; for the premise, *Tusc.* 3. 4 '*fama popularis*, which bestows praise for the most part on bad acts and bad habits, rashly and without judgement'; Halm 1886 cites the Athenian general Phocion (Plut. *Apophth.* 188A = *Phocion* 8. 3), who on finding his view well-received by the people turned to his friends and said, 'I didn't misspeak without noticing, did I?' For such applause as the opposite of 'glory', cf. 86 **Seeking no other reward** n., and 115 **Let's stipulate** n.

106–27. *A New Dispensation*

After developing a position based in part on redefining the *Best Sort, C. now asserts that the former division between 'popular' politicians and those of the Best Sort has been replaced by a state of affairs in which a certain number of *desperadoes and their hired henchman are distinct from, and opposed by, all others, who stand together under the newly expanded rubric of the Best Sort; the move both marginalizes the opposition and dilutes the significance of being an optimate in the traditional sense. C. does not explain the new dispensation's cause, though an explanation is at least invited by his earlier remarks on the people and their leaders (next n.). Instead, he sets about providing empirical evidence of the new alignment from the people's behaviour in *contiones (106–8), in *voting assemblies (108–14), and at the *games (115–27).

106. our civil community... agreement on matters of the public interest In light of C.'s premises (96 with 104 **excessive desires** nn.), this state of affairs should imply either that the *populus* (= *multitudo*) has somehow gained a more responsible understanding of needs vs. wants, or that its most clamant wants have been met, or that it is more willing to follow the lead of the *Best Sort (in the conventional sense of that phrase), or some combination of these; but C. does not explain. Nothing he says here or elsewhere suggests that he believed the first alternative. The third, which perhaps is implied by the last sentence of 105, is in any case integral to his often-stated belief that the *civil community is best served by the 'harmony of the orders' (*concordia ordinum*), produced when the community's several components all play their proper roles—the senate, esp., by leading, the people by following—in a state of liberty secured by their equality before the law (on C.'s view of *concordia* see Introd. §4 at n. 72). In this period C. esp. stresses the theme of consensus and *concordia* at *Har. resp.* 40–55, 60–3, where his view (see esp. 55, 60) is a good deal less upbeat than the one offered here, as indeed is the view expressed at the outset of this speech (1 **If anyone** n.). C. attempts the same sense of consensus, and isolation of the wicked, at the start of his failed defence of Milo (*Mil.* 3); more generally, the basic, recurrent thought—that 'I' stand with all good men while my foes, though perhaps powerful, are isolated—is inextricably embedded in his conception of Republican political life.

if you get rid of... The clause (*si...removeris*) can be taken to mean 'apart from' (Gardner 1958a, sim. Holden 1889, 'setting aside'), as if C. were simply bracketing the henchman in his analysis. But C.'s point is not merely analytical, it is politically prescriptive: cf. 'If we eliminate...' (Shackleton Bailey).

three places... touching <the commonwealth> Cf. *Vat.* 10 'There are two occasions on which we see the judgement our fellow-citizens have formed of us: on one occasion, our honour (*honos* = office) is at

stake (in elections), on the other, our well-being (in trials).' The
medieval MSS' ancestor seems to have read either *de r p iudicium*
(V) or *de p r iudicium* (PG): C. must have written *de re publica
iudicium* ('judgement concerning the commonwealth'); some editors, after Mommsen, judge that *re publica* (often abbreviated *r p* in
MSS) should be read instead of, not in addition to, *populi Romani*
(often abbreviated *p r* in MSS), 'the Roman people's'.

**assemblies where they are addressed by a magistrate, in their voting
assemblies** On the different forms of assembly C. mentions here,
*contio and *comitia, see the Glossary s.vv. assembly of the people
and voting assembly. C. pointedly omits, and will later disparagingly
dismiss (109 **scarcely five people** n.), the *assembly of the plebs,
which had passed Clodius' laws: that it was not an assembly of the
populus as a whole (*comitia*) makes it irrelevant to his argument as he
frames it, though framing his argument to omit a chief centre of
contemporary political activity is plainly tendentious.

To take the first of these After dismissing all *contiones convened
by Clodius as gatherings of hired henchman, C. bases his argument
on a contrast between one *contio* convened by his ally Lentulus (107)
and one addressed (but not convened) by Clodius (108).

**107. Publius Lentulus likewise convened an assembly to talk about
me** Lentulus convened this *contio c.9 July 57, the day after the
senate's *decree described in 129–31: the relation is obscured because
C. is distributing the relevant events among the different forms of
assembly; the sequence is more simply narrated at *Red. sen.* 26–8 (cf.
App. 1). The meeting's size and character are similarly stressed at *Red.
sen.* 26, *Red. pop.* 17, *Dom.* 75, *Pis.* 34.

**it seemed nothing so 'popular' had ever reached the Roman people's
ears** The first of the moves by which C. claims the label *popularis*
for the *Best Sort: cf. already *Red. sen.* 20 (speaking of S.) 'he
commended the senate's cause to the masses (*multitudo*) with such
earnest care that it seemed nothing was as "popular" as (the senate's)
name'; for 'the ancestors' (*maiores*) as *populares 'by no deceptive
fiction but truly and wisely', *Dom.* 77 (sim. 80).

Gnaeus Pompeius... \<presented\> himself as a suppliant   Pompey
appeared first among the 'foremost men of the community' (*principes
civitatis*)—former consuls and praetors—whom Lentulus, the *contio*'s
convener, invited to speak (108 just below, *Red. sen.* 26, *Red. pop.* 16,
Pis. 34). Pompey's speech is described in more detail at *Red. sen.* 29 and
esp. *Red. pop.* 16: 'First he instructed you (sc. the *populus*) that the
commonwealth had been saved by my policies (cf. 129 **I alone** n.), he
yoked my cause together with that of the general well-being (sc. thereby
anticipating C.'s premise in this speech: Introd. §3), and he urged you to
defend the senate's authority, the civil regime (*status civitatis*, cf. 1 n.),
and the fortunes of a citizen who had earned your gratitude (cf. 2 n.);
then, in rounding off the argument he asserted that you were being
petitioned by the senate, by the equestrian order, and by all Italy; and in
conclusion he not only petitioned you for my well-being but even
implored you.' The speech's first part is described rather differently for
the senate's benefit (*Red. sen.* 26 'he commended my cause to those of
*practical intelligence and gave a thorough lesson to the *ignorant'), but
the final contrast between petitioning (*rogare*) and imploring (*obse-
crare*) is described in similar terms whenever C. refers to the speech: cf.
Red. sen. 29 '(he) not only exhorted but even implored (*obsecrari*) the
Roman people on my behalf as though on behalf of a brother or parent'
(sim. 31 'he implored the Roman people as a suppliant'), *Har. resp.* 46
'he roused ... the Roman people ... not only with his *auctoritas* but also
with his entreaties (*preces*)', *Pis.* 80 'in assemblies of the people he
presented himself not only as a defender of my well-being but even as
a supplicant on my behalf (*supplex pro me*).' The present passage, which
contrasts acting as an *auctor*—i.e. putting the moral weight of one's
auctoritas behind a request—and acting as a suppliant (*supplex*: cf. also
Har. resp. 46, just quoted), suggests why C. so stresses this point. In a
request based on *auctoritas* the petitioner occupies the superior position
and expects to gain his aim just because the other party is disposed to
grant it; in supplication, the hierarchical positions are reversed, as the
petitioner presents himself as the dependent party (cf. 26 **you prostrated yourselves** n.). For one of Pompey's *dignitas* to present himself
thus to the *populus* was a self-humbling gesture made only for a very
close connection (cf. *Red. sen.* 29 'as though for a brother or parent'),
implying great emotional involvement (cf. Sall. *Hist.* 2 frag 47, the

consul Gaius Cotta assumes mourning dress to speak as a suppliant
before the people in a *contio* on the occasion of a grain shortage).

108. I do not name them   Cf. 101 **leave aside ancient examples** n.

a real assembly... Campus Martius   Any *contio was, as a matter of
ideology, an assembly of the people as a whole, what C. here calls 'the
real people' (*verus populus*): those who happened to be present just
were the *populus* for the purpose at hand; that is why e.g. proposed
legislation was *promulgated at *contiones*. But because C. has already
said (106) that every *contio* convened by Clodius was no assembly of
the people at all, but an 'assembly of desperadoes', this 'real assembly'
cannot be a *contio* that Clodius convened (e.g. not the *contio* held in
the Circus Flaminius on the Campus Martius in 58, 33 **assembly of
the people** n.), but one convened by another magistrate at which
Clodius was allowed to speak: *Dom.* 89–90, where C. develops a
similar contrast, shows that this was the *contio* held on 4 Aug. 57,
just before the vote for C.'s recall (cf. Pina Polo 1989, 301 no. 308).

**a gross miscarriage that he was alive and breathing, let alone speak-
ing**   Cf. *Red. pop.* 10 'that enemy... was alive in so far as he was still
breathing, though in fact he had been entirely consigned to the realm
of the dead.'

109. scarcely five people... not all of those in their proper tribe   In
effect C. acknowledges that his survey, as he has framed it (cf. 106
assemblies n.), excludes the *assembly of the plebs (*concilium plebis*),
and he justifies excluding it through hyperbole, alleging procedural
irregularities and thin attendance: read literally, his remark means
that measures binding the entire *civil community—like the one
about to be mentioned, declaring that he had been exiled—were
commonly passed in ill-sorted assemblies of no more than 175
persons (the tendentious character of these remarks seems too often
to have been ignored, cf. the refs. at Yakobson 1995, 434 n. 32; they are
still taken at face value, imprudently, at Mouritsen 2001, 23–4, 33–4).
Hyperbole aside, C. does not explain why the *comitia tributa, also
organized by tribes and implicitly included in his survey of *comitia*,
was exempt from the same objections: intent as he is on contrasting
Clodius' legislation with the law of the **comitia centuriata* that

restored him, he simply ignores the most common venue of consular legislation, including his own; cf. **people of all degrees of honour** n., below, where he clearly intends to contrast only the *concilium plebis* and the *comitia centuriata*, though the *comitia tributa* likewise included 'people of all degrees of honour'.

'tyrant' responsible for 'the theft of freedom'   The label and charge distil the view that by executing the conspirators without trial, against the *lex Sempronia* of 123 (*MRR* 1. 513), C. ignored a key element of *freedom, which guaranteed all citizens their rights under law, including the right not to be deprived of one's *life as a citizen without the people's authorization. C. anticipated the charge at *Cat.* 2. 14, nor did he have to wait long: on 29 Dec. 63 Metellus Nepos refused to allow him to address the people on that ground (cf. 129 **I alone** n.), and the charge of wielding 'royal' power (*regnum*) or being a 'king' (*rex*) was cast at him at the trial of Publius Sulla in 62 (esp. *Sull.* 21, with ibid. 8, 87, 93 for C.'s plea that he had been severe but not cruel; cf. Plut. *Cic.* 22. 2–3, charges of *dunasteia* = unconstitutional *potentia* made the same year) and on the senate floor in May 61 (*Att.* 1. 16(16). 10); it chiefly inspired Clodius to use part of the site of C.'s home on the Palatine for a shrine to Freedom (*aedes Libertatis*: *Leg.* 2. 42 and Tatum 1999, 162–6, 187–93). The charge reverberates in the post-return speeches (cf. *Dom.* 75, 94, *Vat.* 23), and C. still alludes to it in Aug. 45, contrasting it with his 'slavery' under Caesar (*Fam.* 7. 24(260). 1).

catastrophe of the commonwealth   Lit. 'collapse of the commonwealth' (*ruina rei publicae*), a metonymy denoting the person by the effect he produces: cf. *Prov. cons.* 13, on Piso and Gabinius as 'our allies'' plagues (*pestes*), our soldiers' disasters (*clades*), the publicans' catastrophes (*ruinae*), the provinces' devastations (*vastitates*), our dominion's stains (*maculae*)', and 93 **almost wrote 'The End'** n.

Is there anyone who will admit . . . put to the vote?   The law declaring C. had been exiled (65 **proposal** n.). He makes the same point at *Dom.* 79–80: finding no respectable person to cast the first vote (usually an honour), Clodius relied on a nonentity named Fidulius. C.'s political point, about the measure's lack of support, is related to the legal point he knew from the Twelve Tables, 'Concerning the *caput* of a citizen, <unless> the gathering <is> the fullest possible, they are not to carry (a measure)' (9. 2, trans. *RS* 2:701): 65 **centuriate assembly** n.

put before ... the senate   In accordance with the senate's decree of early July (see 129–31), the measure was voted on 4 Aug. 57 by the *comitia centuriata*, where the wealthy exercised disproportionate power; the procedure was that recommended by Pompey at the senate's meeting of 1 Jan. (see 74), when the tribune Atilius Serranus blocked action. The vote is similarly described in terms stressing consensus and unanimity at *Red. sen.* 27–8, *Dom.* 90, *Pis.* 35–6. The centuriate assembly's involvement was highly unusual, for that body had rarely been used for legislation, beyond declarations of war or confirmation of the censors' powers, since the time of the Second Punic War.

people of all degrees of honour ...   C.'s description is literally true: whereas all citizens were included in the *comitia centuriata*, members of patrician clans were excluded from the *assembly of the plebs, which therefore could not be an *assembly of the people as a whole (106 **assemblies** n.). But implications of democratic consensus are undercut by the *comitia centuriata*'s organization and procedures, which gave a wealthy man's ballot far more weight than that of a poor man, who often found that the decision had been made before it came his turn to vote.

demons roused to a frenzy swoop down   On 'demons' (*furiae*), see 33 **that demon** n., cf. 54 **they swooped in** n.

the commonwealth's funeral   A common metaphor (cf. *Red. sen.* 18, *Dom.* 98, *Pis.* 21), following from the *commonwealth's having been 'battered', 'bound', 'bled', and 'branded' (17 **branded** n., on C.'s physicalizing metaphors), but less logically linked to C.'s premise that his resoration revived the commonwealth. Some optimate leaders, who encouraged Clodius when he usefully (in their eyes) turned against Pompey, resisted C.'s argument that all Clodius' legislation was invalid because his transfer to the plebs was illegitimate: as C. puts it, they thought the commonwealth had received 'a properly declared funeral' (*Dom.* 42 'funus ... iure indictum', sim. *Prov. cons.* 45).

110. Gellius   This attack, at least as vicious as those aimed at Piso and Gabinius, seems to emerge from nowhere, though the turn was prob. less striking for those in court who knew that the man was to appear as a witness against S. (*Vat.* 4, where he is called 'the little nursemaid of all troublemakers'): the savagery, if not the formal awkwardness, is consistent with C.'s claim to be 'carried away by... hatred' (111). On the rough treatment of anticipated witnesses see Schmitz 1985 (on this speech, pp. 100–11).

Gellius' stepfather was Lucius Marcius (*RE* 75) Philippus, cos. 91 and cens. 86, and his uterine brother was Lucius Marcius (*RE* 76) Philippus, consul in 56 (the 'excellent consul' referred to here). As a praetor in 62 (*MRR* 2. 173, 180), the latter could not have been born after 102: the *terminus ante quem* for Gellius' birth is 103, if his mother was divorced and soon remarried, or 104, if his mother was widowed (more likely: see below) and waited the statutory ten months before remarrying; if Gellius' mother was not much older than the elder Philippus (born *c*.137), the *terminus post* quem for Gellius birth is *c*.120. A birthdate *c*.120–105 is consistent with the fact that Gellius's nephew had recently left prepubescent children at his death (111 **guardians** n.); since C. speaks of Gellius as 'withering away' (*consenescebat*), we can suppose that he was older than C., who had turned 50 on 3 Jan.

Gellius' paternal lineage is uncertain. After Münzer (*RE* 7.1 (1910), 991–2), Gellius was commonly identified as a younger brother of Lucius Gellius (*RE* 17, cos. 72, cens. 70); but that man reached the consulship late—a praetor already in 94, he was more nearly a contemporary of the elder Lucius Marcius Philippus, born *c*.137— and was thus prob. a full generation older than the man attacked here. Alternatively, Wiseman (1974, 119–29) identified him as a younger son of the consul of 72 and censor of 70, and uncle of the Lucius Gellius (*RE* 18) Publicola who would be cos. 36. But that identification, too, is highly unlikely: it is very difficult to believe, as a matter of protocol, that C. would so viciously slander the son, or any close male relative, of a man who had staunchly supported him both in 63 (49 **I protected** n.) and in the prelude to his recall (*Red. pop.* 17); more important, C. repeatedly stresses that Gellius squandered his patrimony (*paterna res, patrimonium*), beginning in his youth ('passing from his coarse and filthy youth, in which he had reduced his patrimony...')—but no son of Gellius cos. 72 and cens. 70 would yet have control of his *patrimonium* to squander, for that Gellius did not die until several years after this speech (still in the senate in 55, *Pis.* 6, he was evidently recently deceased *c.*52, when C. wrote *Leg.* 1. 53).

It seems best to separate the man entirely from the family of the consular Gellius (thus E. Badian's suggestion, too quickly dismissed at Wiseman 1974, 126 n. 32; cf. Evans 1983): Gellius was born before 105 to an equestrian or undistinguished senator who died by 104, perhaps in the wars against the German tribes who from 113 on inflicted a series of bloody defeats on Roman armies, culminating in the disaster at Arausio, precisely in 105; his widow then married the elder Philippus—himself something of a self-made man, from a family that had been in obscurity for several generations—in whose household Gellius was raised; he came of an age to control his patrimony in the 90s or 80s and was prob. somewhat older than C. (thus too old to be Catullus' Gellius, whose mother was clearly not a woman of very advanced years, cf. App. 2). Little else is known about him: in Nov. 57 C. referred to him in terms implying he was barely a step above a slave (*Att.* 4. 3(75). 2, cf. below on his marriage); later in 56 he includes him among the henchmen who play the 'dogs' to Clodius' monstrous 'Scylla' (*Har. resp.* 59). (I am grateful to John D. Morgan for discussing the issues involved in this note.)

his brother... excellent consul   Lucius Marcius Philippus, cos. 56: in Dec. 57 he supported his fellow consul-designate, Lentulus Marcellinus, in trying to clear procedural obstacles to Clodius' prosecution (*QFr.* 2. 1(5). 2, cf. 95 **not been granted leave** n.).

equestrian order... squandered its trappings   *Ornamenta* ('trappings') are not primarily 'ornaments', in the sense of the Engl. cognate, but are the material means supporting a given task or status (thus *ornare* lit. = 'to equip, outfit', *ornamentum* = 'equipment, armament'), in this case approaching the sense 'wherewithal'; we are clearly to suppose that the main 'trappings' Gellius squandered were the 400,000 *sesterces* required for equestrian status. Equestrian 'trappings' of a more purely ornamental sort included a gold ring and a tunic with a narrow purple stripe, similar to the senator's tunic with a broad purple stripe.

'Yes, for the fellow's devoted to the Roman people.' Oh yes... For
the exchange with an imagined interlocutor (*sermocinatio*), 20 **Still**
n.; as at 47 and 77, C. feigns agreement, here using sarcasm to suggest
that Gellius would more appropriately have shown his devotion by
following the model set by his senatorial stepfather. The tactic would
risk offending equestrians among the judges if C. seemed to imply
that choosing to remain an equestrian was *per se* a form of shirking;
but he has already made plain that Gellius was not a worthy equestrian, either.

most substantial offices of Lucius Philippus For his identity, see
Gellius n. above. Philippus began as a 'popular' tribune (C. refers to
his 'pernicious' proposal of an agrarian law, *Off.* 2. 73). As cos. 91 he
was at first aligned with the tribune Livius Drusus (*MRR* 2. 20, cf.
2. 21–2) but turned against him; as censor in 86 he supported the
government of Cinna, enrolled the first Italians enfranchised by
the Social War, and refused to acknowledge the senatorial status of
his uncle Appius Claudius Pulcher, father of Clodius and a Sullan
partisan in exile (*MRR* 2. 54); but he threw in his lot with Sulla
when he took Rome in 82. C. had heard him speak (*Brut.* 326, cf.
230) and admired his ability (*De or.* 2. 316, 3. 4, *Brut.* 166, 173, 186),
not least his wit (*De or.* 2. 245, 249).

**so far from being 'a man of the people'... all by himself... in
gluttony... coarse and filthy youth** The point of the first phrase
is concentrated in 'all by himself' (*solus*): Gellius did not give a hoot
for the *populus* but selfishly indulged his vices. That these happen to
combine the vices of Piso (as glutton: 24 **so smoky** n.) and Gabinius
(as sexual profligate: 18 **old despoilers** n.) suggests the conventional
nature of the charges; cf. also next nn.

from a fortune... to a pittance worthy of philosophers I follow
Maslowski and most editors in reading *reculam* (dimin. of *res*, 'a bit
of property', 'a pittance') for the MSS *regulam* ('rule, canon'): C.
alludes to philosophers' proverbial austerity and their injunction to
shun worldly goods. A 'layman' (*idiota*) is one who has not learned
such wisdom: meant ironically here, it is put in Piso's mouth at *Pis.*
62, 65, to mock his philosophical affectations.

proper Greekling of leisure... devoted himself to literary studies
Literary studies (*studium litterarum*) are not blameworthy unless so
pursued as to exclude devotion to the *public interest (98 **it is not
fitting** n.): we should infer that Gellius' devotion was of that sort
from the epithets *Graeculum... atque otiosum*, the latter implying
cultivation of a merely personal 'leisure' (cf. Glossary s.v. *tranquillity), the former (dimin. of *Graecus*, 'little Greek, Greekling') being
the standard term of contempt for contemporary Greeks (cf. 94
shared out... the goods n.) and their Roman imitators; it recurs at
126 below ('petty Greeks') and is used (e.g.) to characterize the Epicurean philosophers with whom Piso associated (*Red. sen.* 14, *Pis.* 70).

of a sudden   i.e. Gellius' literary pursuits were the product of a mere
fad or whim, and bound therefore to be inferior; contrast C.'s comments on his own philosophical studies at *Nat. D.* 1. 6.

readers who spoke pure Attic   Madvig's *sane Attici* is by far the best
solution for the MSS' nonsense (*sane attae* or the like): wealthy
Romans commonly used slaves trained to read literary texts with
attention to rhythm, sound, and meaning (Balogh 1926, Starr
1990–1), and *anagnostae* (C. uses the Gk. term) skilled in reading
Attic Greek, the dialect regarded as the standard of purity and
correctness, would fetch a premium price: Hor. *Epist.* 2. 2. 3 ff.
supposes that even a less accomplished slave, with a mere 'tincture'
of Greek letters, would fetch 8,000 *sesterces*, roughly equivalent to the
price of 2,000 measures of grain, enough to sustain an adult male for
up to thirty years. The detail caps the portrait of Gellius-as-profl-
igate, since the expense in his case went for naught.

***any* civil unrest... *Any* troublemaker**   i.e. *seditio* and *seditiosus*:
C. repeats for emphasis the term that he will use in characterizing
him at *Vat.* 4, 'the little nursemaid of all troublemakers' (*nutricula
seditiosorum omnium*).

sturdy patriot... attacked in the coarsest terms   C. anticipates
Gellius' testimony against S., then proceeds to the coarsest element
of his own attack.

seen to be cultivating the plebs   Lit. 'seen to be a *plebicola*' (< *plebem
colere*, 'to cultivate the plebs'), an epithet never used as a compliment,

cf. *Leg. agr.* 2. 84 *plebicola tribunus*, Livy 3. 33. 7, 3. 68. 10, 5. 16. 5. If Gellius was unrelated to the consular Gellius (above n.), C. fortuitously chose an epithet resembling the cognomen, Publicola (< *populum colere*, 'to cultivate the people'), of Lucius Gellius (*RE* 18) Publicola, grandson or adoptive son of the consular and himself cos. 36 (on the proper assignment of the cognomen, see Badian 1988, 8 n. 11). Alternatively, C. means to suggest that his target 'want(ed) to be a real Gellius (Publicola) by acting the *plebicola*' (Badian cited at Wiseman 1974, 126 n. 32): not impossible, but if (as Badian showed) the cognomen was borne only by the younger Lucius Gellius, still in his 'teens at the time of this trial, such an allusion would not likely have had much force.

married a woman who was once a slave   As C. attacked Piso through his 'mother's lineage' (21 n.), so he attacks Gellius through that of his wife, allegedly a freedwoman: marriage between a freedwoman and an equestrian was not illegal, but it would have been disgraceful (cf. Treggiari 1991, 64).

111. parricides' feasts and celebrations   For 'parricides' = 'traitors', cf. 82 **sort to murder their own kin** n.; for their 'feasts' 54 **the consuls feasted** n.

revenge when he kissed my enemies with that mouth of his   Assumed to be repulsive because sexual profligacy made him a fellator, a common implication of the sort of 'coarse and filthy' youth (*impurus... et petulans*) imputed to Gellius above (cf. 18 **old despoilers** n.); C. also delights in attributing such a mouth to Sextus Cloelius (133 n.), allegedly a devotee of cunnilingus.

defended the commonwealth against you and your cronies   The familiar charge that Clodius and his allies are the faction of Catiline in different guise: **42 old forces** n.

Postumius   Not identifiable: presumably of a plebeian family (the only patrician Postumii in the late Republic were Postumii Albini), but of some standing if the man's assignment of familial honours (next n.) was a matter of note.

guardians for his children   i.e. *tutores*, responsible for supervising the well-being of children orphaned before adolescence and esp. for preserving the integrity of their inheritance (Watson 1967, 102 ff., Saller 1994, 181–203, Rawson 2003, 71–3): we are to understand that this fiduciary responsibility esp. disqualified the wastrel Gellius and motivated his nephew's slight. Since a guardian's identity was normally revealed when the father's will was read, Postumius must have died young, with prepubescent children. C. stresses the large number of guardians named, to magnify Gellius' humiliation (he uses the verb *notare* appropriate to censorial condemnation): Postumius either had named some guardians *honoris causa* or had named a different guardian for each of a numerous brood, or both.

112. Firmidius, Titius   For Titius, see 80 **Titius, the Sabine**; Firmidius is otherwise unknown.

the one who actually brought the motion   Viz., Clodius.

restoring, not just me but the commonwealth   An esp. emphatic statement of the speech's premise: Introd. §3.

113. assemblies in which magistrates are elected   Consuls and praetors were chosen in the **comitia centuriata*, *military tribunes, *quaestors, and curule aediles in the *comitia tributa, *tribunes and plebeian aediles in the *concilium plebis*; C.'s survey touches on the first and third of these. With C.'s argument here contrast e.g. *Planc.* 7–9, denigrating the people's ability to recognize merit in the candidates for whom they vote, and cf. *Har. resp.* 56.

recently a cadre of tribunes   C. selects the tribunes of 59 because enough time had passed for several to seek further office (of the known tribunes of 58, only Clodius had been a candidate, successfully), and because C. can highlight Vatinius' defeat (114 **The other one** n.). He discusses the same cadre, to much the same effect, at *Vat.* 16. Two of the other five members are known: Quintus Caecilius (*RE* 99) Metellus Pius Scipio Nasica, a member of the college of pontiffs who had ruled on C.'s house (*Dom.* 123, *Har. resp.* 12) and whom C. had defended on a charge of electoral bribery in 60 (*TLRR* no. 238, *LUO* no. 34), had been elected curule aedile in 57 and would be elected to a praetorship for 55 (his memorial *games for his adoptive father in 57 are part of C.'s survey below, 124); Gaius Cosconius

(*RE* 5), a judge in this trial and plebeian aedile in 57 (*Vat.* 16), was prob. praetor in 54 (*MRR* 2. 233 n. 1, 3. 77). These two are omitted not because they had been politically 'unsound' as tribunes but because they had not take the strongly anti-Caesarian line of the three about to be named.

Gnaeus Domitius   Gnaeus Domitius (*RE* 43) Calvinus, pr. 56 presiding at the *standing court on electoral corruption (*MRR* 2. 208), cos. 53: with the two about to be named he joined Caesar's colleague, Bibulus, in trying to use the *auspices to block Caesar's and Vatinius' legislation in 59 (*Vat.* 16, Cass. Dio 38. 6. 1, *Schol. Bob.* 146. 24–5 St.).

Quintus Ancharius   Quintus Ancharius (*RE* 3), son of a praetor and pr. 56: cf. preceding n. He superseded Piso in Macedonia in 55 (*Pis.* 89, *MRR* 2. 218).

Gaius Fannius   Gaius Fannius (*RE* 9), like his tribunician colleague Metellus Scipio a member of the college of pontiffs (*Har. resp.* 12), apparently had not yet stood for further office (C. does not seem to be concealing a loss) and might not have fulfilled C.'s prophecy (*MRR* 3. 90).

114. One of them   Gaius Alfius (*RE* 7) Flavus' 'popular' credentials are validated at *Vat.* 38, where Caesar is quoted as regretting his defeat in the praetorian elections for 56 (Broughton 1991, 35). In view of C.'s praise for his 'sound' views and forbearance from legislating, it is not clear what those credentials meant in practice, beyond a general alignment with Caesar, while C.'s oblique comments effectively obscure the reasons for his defeat: both the praise and the indirectness are perhaps due to residual goodwill for Alfius' aid in 63 (*Scaur.* 104). He was either praetor or *quaesitor* (a non-elective presiding officer, often of aedilician standing) in 54, when he presided at the trials of Gnaeus Plancius for electoral misconduct (*TLRR* no. 293, cf. *MRR* 2. 222, 227 n. 3) and Gabinius for treason (*maiestas*: *TLRR* no. 296): C. praised him in court as 'a most serious and righteous person' on the former occasion (*Planc.* 43) and out of court as 'serious and firm' on the latter (*QFr.* 3. 3(23). 3).

The other one   Publius Vatinius (*RE* 2), Caesar's chief supporter among the tribunes of 59, by whose law Caesar gained his 5-year command in Cisalpine Gaul and Illyricum (*MRR* 2. 190): C. attacks him more generally at 132–5 and esp. in the *interrogatio* conducted the day after this speech, preserved as the *Against Vatinius* (Introd. §2).

he thought . . . all to be worthless Vatinius allegedly ignored reports of adverse omens in passing his laws: 'the consul' is Caesar's colleague, Bibulus, and his colleagues are the men named in 113 (**Gnaeus Domitius** n.); on the *lex Aelia* supposedly ignored by Vatinius before being 'overturned' by Clodius' legislation, see 33 **while the same consuls sat** n. C. attacks this aspect of Vatinius' *tribunate at 135 below, *Vat.* 5, 15–8, 23, 36–7, *Har. resp.* 56.

the good report of patriots Cf. 86 **Seeking no other reward** n.

stood for the aedileship In the elections for 56 (Broughton 1991, 43): acc. to *Vat.* 38, in commenting on the fortunes of various candidates Caesar dismissed Vatinius as someone who should not mind doing without further honours (i.e. offices), having sold his services as a tribune at a high price. C. is rubbing salt in a wound still fresh (cf. 134 **their recent beneficence** n.), for the elections had been delayed until 20 Jan., less than two months before this trial. In similarly delayed elections Vatinius would be elected praetor for 55 (*MRR* 2. 216).

did not even carry his own tribe and . . . lost the Palatine tribe Plebeian aediles were elected in the *assembly of the plebs (*concilium plebis*) organized by *tribes. Vatinius lost not only his own tribe (*tribus Sergia*: *Vat.* 36), humiliating in itself, but also the Palatine tribe, Clodius' base (the point is made explicit at *Dom.* 49). Cf. *Har. resp.* 56, quoted at 135 **shifted his . . . aedileship** n.

the people itself is, so to speak, not now 'popular' For the paradox cf. C.'s ill-judged remark of July 59, 'Nothing now is so popular as hatred for the "popular" sort' (*Att.* 2. 20(40). 4).

115–27. C. comes to the last element in his survey, the behaviour of crowds at public *games (*ludi*) and shows: on the political interpretation of the *ludi* surveyed, Vanderbroeck 1987, 77–81, *contra* Tatum 1990*a*; on political demonstrations at the theatre, Nicolet 1980, 363–73, Edwards 1993, 110–19, Stärk 2000; on the 'theatricality' of Roman political culture, see esp. Bartsch 1994 (pp. 72–4 on this section); on C.'s rhetorical use of the performances here surveyed, see Leach 2000 and briefly Klodt 2003, 62–4. Because the evidence might be thought less reliable than that provided by formal assemblies—a point C. addresses immediately following—and because the shows' frivolous character (cf. 119) is less obviously suited to a lawcourt's decorum than the proceedings of the Roman people in assembly, C. twice makes a show of begging the judges' indulgence (**your alert attention** n.). Though C. provides few signposts, the survey is in fact chronological: after commenting on the reliability of the evidence (115), he moves from games given in 58 by Marcus Scaurus (116) to games given by the consul Lentulus in May/June 57 (116–18); then after pausing for further comment on the appropriateness of his survey (119), he resumes his remarks on Lentulus' games (120–3) before concluding with the reception given Sestius at gladiatorial shows in (apparently) July 57 (124–6). Of the games themselves C. was not very patient, esp. when they ran to excess: see *Fam.* 7. 1(24) on Pompey's great games in 55 (esp. ibid. 3 on the so-called 'beast hunts').

115. your alert attention ... speak in a more informal way   Wishing his audience to be alert and receptive, C. tells them they are (cf. 6 **as most of you recall** n. and 31 above; for more direct requests that the judges attend, cf. *Sex. Rosc.* 10, *Clu.* 8, 66, 89). The 'informality' (*remissius genus dicendi*) requiring indulgence concerns the content of what he is about to say, not its style, a point of decorum made explicit at 119, where C. similarly excuses 'this unaccustomed way of speaking': cf. esp. *Arch.* 18, where he remarks the judges' careful attention (*diligenter attenditis*) and kind disposition (*benignitas*) while developing another excursus (on literary pursuits) that might be thought unsuited to the occasion; cf. also *Dom.* 32 'your kindness in listening so attentively carried me along as I spoke', at the end of an excursus (an extended defence of himself against certain allegations by Clodius).

Demonstrations of favour ... it is easy to see ... what the upright mass of people is doing   C. tries (not wholly successfully) to coordinate two thoughts: one he has stressed himself, that *contiones convened by his enemies tend to be corrupt (106); the other is likely to be on the judges' minds, that a crowd at a show is not an obviously more reliable index. His point is not that crowds at *contiones* and *comitia* are more corrupt than those at *ludi*, but that buying favour in the latter is more likely to be noticed and therefore less effective, presumably because the gathering's size and nature makes buying a large segment of it more difficult. He resumes the thought, and presses it strongly, when he punctuates his survey at 119 ('the true and uncorrupted judgement of the people as a whole . . .').

the sorts of men . . . who receive the most applause   For C's report of his own reception at *games and gladiator shows, see *Att.* 1. 16(16). 11, *QFr.* 2. 15(19). 2, *Att.* 4. 15(90). 6 (where C. affects embarrassment at reporting a 'silly' matter, cf. next n.), and cf. e.g. *Att.* 2. 19(39). 3 (on the cold reception for Caesar and Pompey vs. the warmth shown Curio), *QFr.* 3. 1(21) 14 (on applause for Milo in 54), *Att.* 14. 2(356). 1 (on demonstrations for Caesar's murderers in April 44). Evidence of such demonstrations in the late Republic— mostly those remarked by C., just noted—is gathered at Vanderbroeck 1987, Appendix B (nos. 20, 35–6, 53, 54, 76, 77, 90).

Let's stipulate that it is a trivial phenomenon . . .   An over-packed sentence, in which C. asserts two propositions that do not comfortably stand together: on the one hand, crowd response cannot be as trivial (*levis*) as common opinion holds, for it favours the best people; on the other hand, the people who regard it as least trivial are those who are themselves most trivial (*levis* = *irresponsible). The more important thought is the latter, where C. contrasts the indifference of *serious men (who, by implication, seek 'true glory' = good report of patriots': 139 n.) with the dependence of 'trivial' men on mere 'popularity' (next n.): we are to understand that the forthcoming survey promises more horror for the latter than comfort for the serious (cf. 105 **if ever any of them was applauded** n.).

as they themselves say   A distancing formula, treating the phrase 'people's favour' (*favor populi*) as a partisan slogan or modish coinage: Quintilian remarks, 'Cicero believes *favor* . . . is (a) new (usage)' (8. 3. 34), citing a letter (now lost) in which C. holds the word at arm's length ('I shall summon affection and—so to speak (*ut hoc verbo utar*)—favour to advise me'); C. otherwise uses *favor* only with ref. to the theatre, *Q.Rosc.* 29, and politics, *Leg.* 2. 11, the latter with pejorative force. The phrase *favor populi* is not attested elsewhere in Republican Latin but starts to appear a generation later, in both prose (Livy 4. 24. 7 and 6 more times, Vell. 2. 91. 3, Val. Max. 3. 8. 3, Sen. *Dial.* 3. 18. 2, 10. 8. 5, Suet. *Iul.* 11. 1, Tac. *Ann.* 14. 13, *Dig.* 48. 14. 1. 1, 48. 19. 31. pr.) and poetry (Ov. *F.* 4. 867, *Epist.* 3. 4. 29, Sen. *HF* 169, cf. Lucan 1. 178, 10. 417). When Livy traces the elder Scipio Africanus' cognomen (30. 45. 6) to either 'the soldiers' favour' (*militaris favor*) or 'the people's "breeze"' (*popularis aura*: for the latter cf. 101 **fear of peril's tempest** n.), he locates the semantic field where *favor* resided— in C.'s view, an undesirable neighbourhood.

hissing Crowds expressed disapproval with a sibilant whistling like the crowd noises at European football matches: the high-pitched quality is made clear by a metaphor—the shepherd's pipe, *pastoricia fistula*—C. uses to denote the reception he was pleased *not* to receive at *games in 61, *Att.* 1. 16(16). 1. Beyond several of the letters cited just above (**the sorts of men** n.), see e.g. *Pis.* 65, *Att.* 2. 21(41). 1, *Fam.* 8. 2(78). 1 (Caelius), Plut. *Cic.* 13. 3.

116. I ask you above all, Scaurus One imagines Marcus Scaurus, the presiding praetor, giving a small start as C. suddenly lurches from his laboured preamble to address him for the second time in less than fifteen minutes (101 **your father** n.). As curule aedile in 58, Scaurus went heavily into debt (Ascon. 18. 9–11 Cl.) to give *games that were remembered for generations, not least for the display of exotic beasts and other marvels and for the splendour of the temporary stage-set (*MRR* 2. 195, see esp. Plin. *HN* 36. 113–15). Of the games that included theatrical productions, the *ludi Megalenses* (April) and *ludi Romani* (Sept.) were given by the curule aediles.

an actor and a feature on the bill An insult: though C. speaks respectfully below of the tragic actor Aesopus (120 **supreme craftsman** n.), as he does elsewhere of other individuals (esp. Quintus Roscius, whose skills he admired and whom he defended in a civil suit, *Q.Rosc.*), the profession overall was viewed as disgraceful, its practitioners treated as *infames* (persons of no reputable standing) subject to legal liabilities (Greenidge 1894, 154 ff.; on actors in late Republican society, Edwards 1993, 98–134).

his sister's special numbers   Lit. 'his sister's *embolia*', a Greek term that can denote a musical interlude between a play's acts or any sort of episodic insertion in a literary whole: C. uses the term of an episode he contemplated inserting in his poem *On His Times* (*QFr.* 3. 1(21). 24, cf. 71 **bad omens** n.). But in this period C. cannot mention Clodius and Clodia together without alluding to their alleged incest (cf. 16 **what sort of muscle** n. and App. 2): Shackleton Bailey is surely right to say that 'there is doubtless an indecent double meaning' here (1991*a*, 191 n. 130, adding, 'but I do not know what it is'); a literal sense of *embolium*, 'insertion', suggests what it might be.

admitted...dressed as a harp-girl   Clodius' cross-dressing in the Bona Dea scandal is vividly evoked at *Har. resp.* 44; see also *Att.* 1. 12(12). 3, 1. 13(13). 3, *In Clod. et Cur.* frag. 21–3 (= *LUO* 242–3), *Dom.* 139, *Har. resp.* 4, 37, 56 ff., *Planc.* 86, *Mil.* 55, Plut. *Caes.* 10. 1–3, *Cic.* 28. 1–3.

Once and once only...   On Clodius' reception, 117–18.

honour had been paid to manliness in the temple of Virtus   By saying that honour (*honos*) had been paid to *manliness (virtus) C. alludes to the full name of 'the temple of Honos and Virtus' built by Gaius Marius from the spoils taken against the Teutones and Cimbri in 102–101, prob. on the Velia (*MRR* 1. 570–1, *NTDAR* 190, *LTUR* 3. 33–5, *MAR* 139). C.'s pun conveys the point made more directly in 128 (cf. also 50 above) and in C.'s other refs. to the occasion: the senate met in the temple—doubtless to acknowledge the common origin of C. and Marius, mentioned here—and passed a decree directing the consuls to send letters (1) to enjoin foreign kings and allies and Roman governors and their staffs to insure C.'s safety, (2) to thank *civil communities that had sheltered C., and (3) 'to call together (from the towns of Italy)...all who desired the common-wealth's safety'; see 128, with *Dom.* 85, *Planc.* 78 (also mentioning 'Marius' monument'), *Pis.* 34, cf. *Div.* 1. 59, 2. 136 ff., sim. Plut. *Cic.* 33. 4, App. *BCiv.* 2. 15. As C. says in 128, this was an honourific gesture never before made on behalf of an individual (**commend any citizen** n.), and the letters to the towns had their effect: when the senate convened in July to endorse the law to restore C., crowds of great size had gathered in the city (129, esp. **those who had gathered** n., with 124–6). The meeting cannot be dated precisely; on its probable date, between mid-May and mid-June, see App. 1.

the monument of Gaius Marius, who saved this dominion of ours Marius has figured as an ambiguous *exemplum* (cf. 37–8 and esp. 50), but here C. can straightforwardly refer to Marius' turning his weapons on a foreign enemy.

Marius' fellow townsman Cf. 37 **Gaius Marius** n., and *Planc.* 20, on the eagerness with which natives of Arpinum claimed the connection and traded anecdotes about Marius, and C. himself.

117. unanimous applause arose … when … members returned … to watch the games Since there were at this time no permanent theaters in Rome (cf. 126 **temporary seating** n.), the consul Lentulus—responsible for both convening the senate's session in the temple and giving these games (next n.)—presumably arranged for a temporary theatre to be set up not far from the temple: the main landmarks of Rome's political center would also have been nearby, facilitating the *coup de théâtre* to which C. alludes in 121 (**gesturing** n.).

the consul who was himself giving the games Viz., Lentulus; on the *games, see above and App. 1. At *Off.* 2. 57 (cf. Val. Max. 2. 4. 6) C. recalls the magnificent games Lentulus gave as curule aedile in 63.

holding out their upturned hands A prayerful gesture—the hands held apart, the palms facing out and up (cf. Gell. 15. 5. 3)—used by one making a vow (Quint. 11. 3. 100) or a supplication (Lucr. 5. 1200, Verg. *Aen.* 3. 263 with DServ. at *Aen.* 4. 205, German. *Arat.* 68), appropriate here because *supplicatio* comprised not only entreaty but also thanksgiving: thus the *supplications decreed for military victories and, exceptionally, for C.'s saving the city from the Catilinarians (cf. e.g. *Cat.* 3. 15, 4. 5).

118. already a candidate Though Clodius was not elected aedile until 20 Jan. 56, because the elections were delayed, he could have announced his candidacy by any date to which these *games can plausibly be assigned (116 **honour had been paid** n.). The troupe's gesture was notable not only for its visibility (cf. 120–3, on Aesopus) but also because it was against their interest: if elected aedile, Clodius would be a source of patronage for future games.

a comedy in Roman dress   A *fabula togata*: unlike the extant plays of Plautus and Terence, which adapt scripts of Greek New Comedy for plays performed in Greek dress (*fabulae palliatae*, named after the *pallium*, a Greek cloak), this comedy was performed in Roman dress on Roman or Italian themes; the genre survives only in fragments (on its social milieu, Rawson 1991, 479–81). This play's author, Afranius (frag. 304–5 Ribb.), was one of the genre's most productive exponents, active in the second half of the 2nd cent. BCE.

I believe   The phrase is chosen not to avoid a show of learning (cf. 48 **the daughters** n.) but to create an impression of plausible uncertainty regarding a detail he could not know from his own experience.

used to pack . . . choruses of orchestrated abuse   C. refers to the **contiones* Clodius held as tribune, dismissed as corrupt at 106 for reasons related to these comments; he could as easily have had in mind the raucous chorus Clodius led a month earlier during a session of Milo's trial before the people, to embarrass Pompey (*QFr.* 2. 3(7). 2).

driven from the orchestra by the chorus's abuse   As C. goes on to imply, Clodius' discomfort was not unique. At the *ludi Apollinares* in July 59 tragic verses had been similarly used against Pompey: 'you'd think one of Pompey's enemies had written them for the occasion', C. reported (*Att.* 2. 19(39). 3). Abuse of this sort skirted the principle that a person defamed by name from the stage could sue (Watson 1965, 250–1); the abused in any case usually preferred to appear to disdain the abuse as beneath contempt.

the people as a body   The phrase *populus* (*Romanus*) *universus* has not appeared in the speech before, but C. uses it here, and eight more times down through 125, to characterize these demonstrations: it conveys not just a unanimous judgement (which could result from all individuals coming independently to the same conclusion) but the sense that it was made by the people acting as a single body with one mind (cf. Instinsky 1967 on *consensus universorum*).

119. I beg you ... this unaccustomed way of speaking ... the task of teaching As a form of punctuation, the paragraph provides a momentary pause glancing back at points already raised: the judges' attentiveness (115 **your alert attention** n.); C.'s awareness of speaking in a way that might seem unsuited to the circumstances and the participants' *dignitas* ('I know ... what all these demand': on the rhetorical doctrine of decorum see Hariman 2001; with 'this unaccustomed way of speaking' here cf. 115 'speak in a more informal way'); and the aim of providing a lesson to 'the youth' (95–6). As a gesture of reassurance—if the audience is growing restless—the paragraph communicates C.'s sensitivity to their concerns. He then resumes his account of the same *games (120–3), shifting the focus from the crowd's spontaneous responses to the responses evoked by an actor's use of lines from a tragic script; this focus was signaled at the end of 118 ('all poetic tags ... given pertinent expression by the actor').

As C.'s account makes clear, his supporter Lentulus, the giver of the games, had been no less careful in selecting the theatrical bill than he was in selecting the sight of the senate meeting: as the latter stressed the connections between C. and the great Marius (116 **honour had been paid** n.), so the plays that were mounted—Accius' *Eurysaces*, recalling the pitiable expulsion of Telamon, father of Ajax, from his home (120 **the foremost poet's talent** n.), and the same poet's *Brutus* (123 n.), invoking the memory of Servius Tullius, a good king treacherously murdered—gave ample scope to highlight C.'s plight and prompt the demonstrations of support he is about to describe.

120. senate's decree passed in the temple of Virtus C. reminds us that he is speaking of the same occasion and the same *decree introduced in 116–17 ('when news of the senate's decree was learned ...').

supreme craftsman Aesopus (named at 123), a freedman (his son, Marcus Clodius Aesopus, used the *nomen gentilicium*, but he did not, cf. *RE* Clodius 16) and the most famous tragic actor of his day in Rome, much admired by Cicero, who had taken him as a model of delivery in his youth (Plut. *Cic.* 5. 3) and later befriended him: in 59, when one of Aesopus' slaves ran off to Ephesus, C. interceded with

Quintus, then governor of Asia, to have him returned (*QFr.* 1. 2(2). 14). By 57 he was near the end of his career: coming out of retirement two years later to perform at the *games inaugurating Pompey's new theater, he struck C. as being over the hill (*Fam.* 7. 1(24). 2).

by Hercules!   A common oath, less solemn than *me dius fidius* (20 **'pon my word** n.), used by men (Gell. 11. 6).

He gave expression ... through his grief   At *De or.* 2. 193–4 the notion that actors, and the poets who wrote the scripts, must experience the emotions they represent, if the representation is to convince, is used to support the view that orators must feel anguish, indignation, and the like in order to arouse them in the audience; a decade later, when endorsing the Stoic view of common human passions as diseases of the mind, C. takes exactly the opposite view (*TD* 4. 55 'You don't suppose, do you, that either Aesopus acted or Accius wrote in a state of anger (*iratus*)?'). Here he means that Aesopus' emotional performance was not 'acting' at all: he was expressing a grief for C. and the *commonwealth as spontaneously and authentically felt as the anguish that C. says he feels for S. (3 **devotion** n.).

the foremost poet's talent   Identification of the poet depends on the sort of performance we take C. to describe in 120–2. On the interpretation broadly accepted since Ribbeck, C. refers to Accius, whom he will name at 123 (cf. 102 **many snares** n.), and he describes Aesopus' performances of a single play, Accius' *Eurysaces*, on the son of the warrior Ajax (the play is identified at *Schol. Bob.* 136. 30 St.). On this interpretation the first two frags. quoted, in 120 (= frag. 357–8, 359–60 Ribb.), and the last one quoted, in 122 (= frag. 365–6 Ribb.), refer to the expulsion of Telamon, father of Ajax and grandfather of Eurysaces, from his *patria* (cf. *Tusc.* 3. 39). The fragments quoted in 121, by contrast, involve virtuoso improvisation by Aesopus as he responded to the emotion of the moment: here the first two fragments, taken together, produce a continuous trochaic line ('gréatest friend amídst the greatest wár, endowed with gréatest talent'), the first half also from the *Eurysaces*, the second half devised on the spot by the actor ('in the spirit of friendship he added...': ancient actors did not always feel bound by the poets' scripts); the remaining lines ('Oh father... All this I saw in flames!') were inserted by Aesopus from Ennius' *Andromacha* (frag. 87, 92 Ribb., quoted by C. also at *De or.* 3. 102, 217, *Tusc.* 3. 44–5), evoking the fall of Troy (the first line runs 'Oh father, oh fatherland, oh house of Priam!') and corroborating C.'s equation of his own fall with the *common-wealth's.

H. D. Jocelyn, however, judged it 'ludicrous' to think that 'even the most patriotic of actors put (all the verses) into the mouth of (a single) personage' (1967, 241): he instead assigned only the verses quoted in 122 to the *Eurysaces* ('Oh ungrateful... You leave him...') and assigned all those in 120–1 to a separate performance, of Ennius' *Andromacha*, in which Aesopus played the roles of both Ulysses ('The one who... when the going... greatest friend...') and, later in the play, Andromacha ('oh father...'): on this interpretation, 'the fore-most poet' is Ennius. But Jocelyn's objection is very weak: the traditional view is 'ludicrous' only if Aesopus is taken to have aimed at a verisimilar representation of a single character, which C.'s description of this *coup de théâtre* gives no reason to suppose. His solution, positing two separate plays in which Aesopus played three separate roles, is more awkward than the supposed difficulty it aims to remove.

Everyone called for a reprise In the midst of the performance, the audience demanded that he repeat the line over and over: cf. *Att.* 2. 19(39). 3 'At the *ludi Apollinares* the tragic actor Diphilus attacked Pompey outrageously: "To our misery are you great"—he was forced to repeat it countless times'.

121. Quintus Catulus See 101 n.

had called 'father of the fatherland' i.e. *pater patriae* (less com-monly, *parens patriae*), honouring C. after Catiline was suppressed. C. says that Catulus and others in the senate called him that (*nomi-narant*, sim. *Pis.* 6, mentioning only Catulus, cf. *Att.* 9. 10(177). 3 'non nulli... urbis parentem... esse dixerunt'), but he nowhere claims that it was a title bestowed by senatorial decree or that he was the first to be so called—significant silences, in view of C.'s general eagerness to note singular honours (cf. e.g. 129 below): in fact, C. himself had used the phrase of Marius earlier in 63 (*Rab. Perd.* 27; for the phrase used in connection with C., see also Plut. *Cic.* 23. 3, Juv. 8. 243–4; App. *BCiv.* 2. 7 improbably ascribes it to a vote or acclamation of the people on Cato's proposal). The elder Pliny, who does say that C. was the first so honoured (*NH* 7. 117), prob. took it to be a title conferred by the senate, as it was in his day: it had been decreed for Caesar after the battle of Munda (Livy *Perioch.* 116, Suet. *Iul.* 76. 1, 85. 1, Flor. 2. 13, 34, cf. *Phil.* 2. 31, 13. 23, 25, *Off.* 3. 83) and for Augustus in 2 BCE (Aug. *RG* 6, Suet. *Aug.* 58. 1–2, cf. Vell. 2. 123); Tiberius refused to accept it (Suet. *Tib.* 26. 2, 50. 3, 67. 2, Tac. *Ann.* 1. 72, 2. 87), but it was later a regular fixture of imperial titulature, so that it could simply be said 'The princeps is the *pater patriae*' (*Dig.* 48. 22. 18. 1).

gesturing toward my early good fortune, then whirling round to say In this *coup de théâtre* Aesopus prob. 'gestur(ed) (*demonstrare*) toward (C.'s) early good fortune'—that is, pointed to the north rim of the Palatine, where C.'s house had been plundered and burnt in March 58—then turned toward the audience to exclaim, 'All this I saw in flames!'; cf. the ref. to 'his home set afire and razed to the ground', just preceding, and Aesopus' gestures to the audience mentioned in 122 just below. On the temporary theatre's location, 117 **unanimous applause** n.

those hostile to my person and envious of my success For the two categories, personal enemies (*inimici*) and those moved by malice or envy (*invidi*), see 46 **some felt** n.

122. What a performance then followed! Matched by the current performance, as C. makes manifest what he himself did not see: on the goal of vividness (*enargeia*) see 17 **picture in your minds** n.

he was often accustomed freely to criticize and indict In his character as a true patriot and statesman: C. is thinking less of specific positions Catulus adopted than of the general freedom of speech displayed by such a man, who speaks to the common interest whether it offends this faction or that, 'stating his views freely in the senate, taking thought for what the people need, not what they want, yielding to no one, resisting many' (*Sull.* 25). For the equation of *libertas* specifically with freedom of speech, cf. *Sex. Rosc.* 9, *Planc.* 33, *De or.* 3. 4, Brunt 1988, 314–16.

Though that was not quite true ... But still ... Once again (cf. e.g. 63 **draught of grief,** 115 **Let's stipulate** nn.), C. tries to have it both ways, applying the verse to himself to cap the picture of his victimization, while trying to exculpate the *populus* that voted to restore him.

put up with it! The verb chosen (*patimini*) implies not just tolerance but a passivity and lack of gumption that is the opposite of *manly (cf. Kaster 2002).

123. pleading ... stopped by tears Cf. 3 **devotion ...,** 120 **He gave expression** nn.

were the Roman people truly free As Catulus had been: cf. 122 **he was often accustomed** n.

the 'Brutus' This play, also by Accius, was a drama on a Roman historical theme (*fabula praetexta*: frag. 40 Ribb.), which evidently was performed later in the same *games; on the genre, of which only exiguous fragments survive, Zorzetti 1980, Flower 1995, Wiseman 1998, 1 ff., Manuwald 2001 and the special issue of *Symbolae Osloenses*, 77 (2002). The play's protagonist was Lucius Brutus, in Roman tradition the leader in expelling Tarquin the Proud and establishing the Republic; Tullius was Servius Tullius, Rome's sixth king, murdered when his daughter and Tarquin schemed to replace him. C.'s account of his reign at *Rep.* 2. 37–40 stresses 'freedom ... for the citizens' less than Servius' creation of the timocratic system of *centuriae* that insured that 'the ballots were controlled by the rich, not the masses, ... lest the most numerous be the most powerful' (ibid. 39).

encores Cf. 120 **Everyone called for a reprise** n.

what those desperadoes accused us of destroying See 109 **a 'tyrant'** n., cf. 125 **lord it over the laws** n.

124. made its verdict plain most importantly As will become clear, C. says this both because much of the 'verdict' was expressed with ref. to S.—a clear point of contact between his argument in the excursus and his argument in S.'s defence—and because the demonstration occurred at roughly the same time as the senate session leading to the *promulgation of the law for his return (on the chronology 125 **the populace** n.).

Scipio ... offering ... Metellus Quintus Caecilius Metellus Pius Scipio Nasica, tribune in 59 (113 **recently a cadre** n.), was born Publius Cornelius Scipio Nasica, a member of a *notable family, and was later adopted by Quintus Caecilius (*RE* 98) Metellus Pius, cos. 80 and son of the Metellus Numidicus who has figured as an *exemplum* several times in the speech (37 **Quintus Metellus**, 101 **your maternal grand-father's brother** nn.). Pius had died perhaps as much as five years earlier, but it was not unusual to give memorial *games well after the honourand's death (Berry 1996, 242, on *Sull.* 54). Gladiatorial shows were known in Etruria and farther south in Italy (the place of origin is contested) before being introduced to Rome in 264 as an accompaniment to funeral rites. In the absence of a permanent venue (the first stone amphitheatre was built in Rome in 29) temporary arenas were commonly set up in the forum, as clearly in this case: cf. **Maenius' column** n. just below.

the masses take special pleasure But not C.: cf. *Att.* 2. 1(21). 1 (June 60) 'Your slave crossed my path on 1 June as I was going to Antium and eagerly leaving behind Marcus Metellus' gladiators.' He does not elaborate, but perhaps his reasons were the same as Seneca's (*Epist.* 7, on his revulsion).

as you all know Another 'prompting' gesture (cf. 6 **as most of you recall** n.), implying that S.'s epiphany was so vividly memorable that the judges could of course recollect it on their own.

Maenius' column On this landmark, next to the Comitium, 18 **seek the tribunate** n. above. We are to imagine that S. first came into view by the column, near the foot of the *clivus Capitolinus* (cf. next n.), to the sound of gathering cheers, then walked toward the expanse of the forum that opened up to the S and E, where the sites had been set up for the gladiatorial games.

vantage points as far away as the Capitol ... barriers The *games themselves were held in the forum, but spectators climbed the Capitoline to look down on the venues from a height. The 'barriers' here are not the *saepta* set up for voting (79 n.) but lattice-work railings (*cancelli*) used to mark off temporary arenas for the contests.

125. lord it over the laws   Lit. 'lords of the laws' (*legum domini*), cf. 127 'lords of these assemblies'. In both places C. uses the term properly used of a slave's master, *dominus*: to be *dominus* over the laws, which guaranteed the citizens' *freedom, is to be a specifically Roman sort of tyrant. Cf. 109 a **'tyrant'** n., on the charges made against C.

Do the wicked citizens have in their pockets some other 'people'...?   The phrase C. uses, *peculiaris populus*, alludes to the *peculium*, the fund that a slave or a son still in his father's power (6 **With his father's sponsorship** n.) was allowed to accumulate and manage while still legally incapable of owning property; what was *peculiare* could be used as one's own. The phrase is of a piece with C. allegations that the 'wicked' found support only from those they paid: the latter could thus be said to be 'in their pockets' in the same sense that we might speak of a corrupt politician being 'in the pocket' of this or that special interest.

the populace...in those very days   These crowds gathered in response to the letters sent to the towns of Italy, calling out all patriots, after the senate's *decree in the temple of Honos and Virtus described above (116–17, with 116 **honour had been paid** n.): their presence in July, to support the senate's action leading to the *promulgation of the law for C.'s recall (129 below), exacerbated the grain shortage that prompted rioting at the *ludi Apollinares* (6–13 July) 'because of the high cost of grain' (Ascon. 48. 20–2 Cl., cf. Vanderbroeck 1987, 247, App. 1).

126. that praetor   Clodius' brother, Appius Claudius Pulcher: see 77 **not private or plebeian** n.

putting the question...in the way of petty Greeks   The customary form of putting a question (*rogatio*) before a *voting assembly (*comitia*) was '(I ask) whether you wish, whether you order, Quirites, that.... This, then, as I have spoken, so I ask you, Quirites': Gell. 5. 19. 9, Mommsen 1887–8, 3. 391 n. 1, *RS* 1:10–11. But Appius—

appearing before a *contio*, not a *comitia*—spoke in the demagogic manner of a 'Greekling' (cf. 110 **proper Greekling** n.) indulging in the 'license' of Greek assemblies, which (the Romans thought) confounded the properly distinct stages of discussion and voting, the functions of the *contio* and *comitia* respectively: for orderly Roman procedure contrasted with the disorderly way of Greeks, see *Flac.* 15–17, with Morstein-Marx 2004, 36–7. C. himself, however, was not above prompting or playing off the responses of a *contio* just as he suggests Appius did: see esp. *Phil.* 4. 6–7 '. . . unless perchance, Quirites, you judge Mark Antony a consul, not a public enemy. (Pause for crowd reaction) Just as I thought, Quirites: you make your judgement plain' (my thanks to Peter White for drawing this passage to my attention); cf. also *Leg. Man.* 37, *Leg. agr.* 2. 49, 3. 2, 10, *Phil.* 4. 3, 5.

his father . . . grandfather . . . great-grandfather An example of what Treggiari calls 'C.'s infuriating (sc. to his opponents) habit of annexing another man's kin and using them against him' (2003, 153), a habit consistent with his general judgement that the *notables of his day had fallen away from the standards of their ancestors. Cf. the more innocent example of the habit in 101 (on Marcus Scaurus' kin), and 130 below, on Publius Servilius' use of Metelli against Metellus Nepos, showing that the habit was not C.'s alone. Appius' father was Appius Claudius (*RE* 296) Pulcher, cos. 79, praised at *Dom.* 83–4; his grandfather was Appius Claudius (*RE* 295) Pulcher, cos. 143 and cens. 136, used as an example against Clodius at *In Clod. et Cur.* frag. 23 Crawford (unless *nepos* there = 'descendant' and the ref. is to Appius Claudius Caecus, cens. 312); his great-grandfather, Gaius Claudius (*RE* 300) Pulcher, was cos. 177 and cens. 169. At *Cael.* 22 C. improves on this passage, invoking five generations of consular Claudii to reprove Clodia, and indeed the family offered unique scope for the purpose, providing a consul (or equivalent) in twelve consecutive generations (Appius would be cos. 54: see the stemma at *RE* 3 (1899), 2665–6 (F. Münzer)).

temporary seating Lit. 'planks' (*tabulae*), set up for spectators to sit on and removed once the occasion was past. Rome had no permanent setting for dramatic productions until Pompey's theater was completed in 55, and no permanent amphitheatre suitable for gladiatorial contests until the reign of Augustus.

Mother, I call on you!   A fragment from the tragedy *Iliona* by
Pacuvius (*c*.220–130), quoted by C. more fully at *Tusc*. 1. 106
(= frag. 197–9 Ribb.), 'Mother, I call on you!...Arise and bury
your son, before the birds and beasts (devour my unburied corpse).'
At the start of the Trojan War Polydorus, prince of Troy, was sent to
live with his sister Iliona, wife of the Thracian king Polymestor:
to insure his safety, Iliona raised him as though he were her own
son, Deïpylus, while treating the latter as her brother. Polymestor,
bribed by the Greeks to kill Polydorus, killed Deïpylus instead (Hyg.
Fab. 109. 1–3). Iliona hears the call in a dream-vision of her dead
son (*Lucull*. 88, Hor. *Serm*. 2. 3. 60–2): we are to understand that
Appius, emerging from beneath the planks, looked like a shade
rising from Hades.

'the Appian way'   Not among C.'s best jokes, but not his worst,
alluding to the great road from Rome to Capua (cf. 9 n.) begun by
Appius' ancestor Appius Claudius (*RE* 91) Caecus as censor in 312.
Quintilian (6. 3. 4, cited by Holden 1889) says that C. 'ascribed to
others the more frigid witticisms he directed against Verres...so...it
would be more readily believed they were just common gossip, not
his own devising'.

horses   Two sorts of combatants required horses: the mounted
fighters (*equites*, not to be confused with members of the 'equestrian'
order), who fought a duel at the start of a set of *games (Ville 1981,
395), and those who fought from Celtic war-chariots (*essedae*): C.
means that even these brute participants, who could not know what
the hissing signified (115 n.), were shaken by the sheer racket.

127. Do you see, then, how great a difference there is...   C. signals,
a bit perfunctorily, that his survey is at an end by returning to the
distinction with which he began in 106–8, between the 'true' Roman
people (cf. 108 **a real assembly** n.) and Clodius' assemblies of hired
*henchmen.

127–35. *A Conclusion, of Sorts*

We reach the structurally oddest point in the speech, and perhaps in any
of C.'s extant speeches. To appreciate the oddity, consider that C. could

have moved from the rhetorical question just posed ('Do you see that the lords of these assemblies ...?') to the first sentence of 132—'So you have the answer to your question, who are the "Best Sort"'—which obviously looks back to the start of the excursus and 'the question that you addressed to me, ... when you asked what our "breed of the Best Sort" is' (96). After thus rounding off the excursus C. could have moved straight to the exhortation offered in 136–43 ('But to bring my speech to a close, ... I shall ... stir ... and urge ...'), giving his 'lesson for the younger generation' (96) a resounding conclusion.

C. makes neither of those moves. The capstone seemingly laid by the first sentence of 132 is instead succeeded by the fierce attack on Publius Vatinius, who was to testify against S.: 132–5 thus parallel 110–11, the attack on another hostile witness, Gellius. The invective is ungainly, operating at a level of almost pedantic detail (esp. 134–5) and going on at notable length, though C. does work to link it with what precedes by claiming that the defamatory word 'breed', from which all of 96–143 depends, is a usage esp. favoured by Vatinius, who is then revealed as S.'s 'chief attacker' (the phrase refers specifically to Vatinius' role as hostile witness; C. has previously said that Clodius, not Vatinius, was behind S.'s prosecution, 78 **Would you ... would you** n.). Yet laboured as that transition is, it is a seamless marvel compared with this segment's clumsy start, as C. rounds on the prosecutor to rebut an attack ('Do *you* try to use against me the name of Marcus Atilius Regulus ...?'), with no preparation and no attempt to link the move with what goes before. The rebuttal gives C. the opportunity to include an account of the actions leading to his return to Italy and to Rome, a part of the story C. could scarcely have borne to omit (cf. Introd. §4). The truly odd point is that the account given in 129–31 could easily have been harmonized with the argument of 106–27 if Cicero had simply presented that account as the crowning example of the popularity the *Best Sort enjoyed. That he instead chose to achieve his end via an abrupt reply to a prosecutorial taunt perhaps suggests that the taunt had got under his skin, as something that simply had to be answered, even at the cost of formal awkwardness.

127. Do *you* try to use against me ... gangs of armed gladiators Albinovanus presumably said e.g. 'You claim to be a patriot, after violently forcing a return from an exile that expressed the Roman people's will? How different the great Regulus: though his capture while fighting in Rome's defence reduced him to servile status, he accepted that condition rather than violate his *fides* to gain a return!' (cf. next n.). By acknowledging the taunt C. most nearly reveals something he has worked to obscure, viz., the actual ground of the charge against S., of having assembled, and prob. used, an armed gang with the intent of forcing through C.'s return (cf. Introd. §2 and 2 **hired brigands** n.).

Marcus Atilius Regulus Marcus Atilius (*RE* 51) Regulus, cos. 267, cos. suff. 256, was defeated and captured in Africa in 255, during the First Punic War. As indicated in the preceding n., he had the legal standing of a slave while a captive, with his citizen-status and its attendant rights suspended; had he returned permanently to Rome, he would have resumed his *life as a citizen as though he had never lost it. Acc. to the patriotic legend known to C. and much elaborated in later generations, the Carthaginians sent Regulus to Rome to negotiate an exchange of prisoners, having first exacted his promise to return if the exchange was not made: instead of choosing either to remain in Rome, in violation of his promise, or to arrange terms favourable to Carthage, Regulus advised the senate not to negotiate, then returned to Carthage, where he was tortured and executed. He thus came to serve as a central *exemplum* of Roman *trustworthiness, and his torture was often elaborated, esp. by Stoicizing writers, to illustrate the theme that the wise man is happy even on the rack: see esp. *Parad.* 2. 16, *Fin.* 5. 82 ff., *Off.* 3. 97–115, Hor. *Carm.* 3. 5, Sen. *Dial.* 1. 3. 9 ff., Gell. 7. 4, Aug. *CD* 5. 18, with Mix 1970, Gaillard 1972.

who instead of remaining ... his dispatch to the senate The medieval MSS' text is defective (*redire ... Carthaginem ... quam sine iis captivis a quibus ad senatum missus erat Romae manere maluerit*: he 'preferred ... to return ... to Carthage rather than remain in Rome without the captives by whom he had been sent to the senate'—but acc. to the tradition he had not been sent by the captives, cf. preceding n.). The translated text reflects Shackleton Bailey's transposition of the conjunction *quam* (so also Cousin 1965) and adoption of the preposition *de* (for *a*, after Ursinus: '*redire ... Carthaginem ... [quam] sine iis captivis* (i.e. the Carthaginians) *de quibus ad senatum missus erat <quam> Romae manere maluerit*').

128. worry lest some reckon...a hunger for glory   C. has already
made very much that reckoning regarding Quintus Metellus' voluntary
exile (37 **some notion of personal glory** n.). For the idea that—absent
the harm done the *commonwealth—his 'misfortune' could be
thought desirable, given the luster it added to his name, see *Pis.* 32;
on C.'s preference for euphemism—here 'departure' (*exisse*)—cf. 47
exile n.

For did the senate ever...   For the measures summarized in this
and the next three sentences, decreed by the senate as it met in the
temple of Honos and Virtus in May/June 57, see 50 and 116 **honour
had been paid** n. Now thinking chronologically, C. moves next to the
events of July (129–30)—the senate's *decree backing a law for his
recall to be passed in the *comitia centuriata*—and Aug.–Sept.
(131)—his return to Italy and to Rome—omitting mention only of
the law's passage on 4 Aug.

provincial governors with the power of command   Including, most
relevantly, Piso, whose arrival in Macedonia late in 58 C. had feared.

quaestors and legates   i.e. the members of the governor's council
(*consilium*), responsible for advising him and for executing his commands; on the offices, see the Glossary.

consuls send letters...who desired the commonwealth's safety   Thus
Red. sen. 24: 'For what grander outcome...could I have enjoyed than
the one...you decreed: that everyone from all Italy who desired the
commonwealth's safety convene to restore and defend me alone...?
Using the formula that a consul had used only three times in Rome's
history—and then only to those who could hear the sound of his voice,
on behalf of the commonwealth as a whole—the senate roused...all
Italy to defend the well-being of one man'; sim. *Dom.* 73, *Pis.* 34 (cf. 76).
The formula in question is the appeal to 'all who desire the commonwealth's safety' (*omnes qui rem publicam salvam vellent*), in effect
declaring a state of emergency (cf. Serv. at Verg. *Aen.* 7. 614, 8. 1).
C. elsewhere specifies three occasions on which the formula was invo-
ked: by Scipio Nasica Serapio, in the assault he led on Tiberius
Gracchus in 133 (*TD* 4. 51, cf. Val. Max. 3. 2. 17); by the consuls
Gaius Marius and Lucius Valerius Flaccus, in their action against
Saturninus and Glaucia in 100 (*Rab. Perd.* 20, cf. 34); and by the consul

Gaius Calpurnius Piso, to thwart the tribune Gaius Cornelius in 67 (*Cornel.* I frag. 45 Crawford = Asc. 75. 20 ff. Cl.). The next sentence makes plain the weight C. attaches to this equation of the *common-wealth's *well-being with his own, a point once more relevant to his defence of S. (Introd. §3). The singular honour implied by the equa-tion, and by the effort to extend the message to all Italy (not just 'those who could hear the sound of (the consul's) voice', cf. above), parallels the senate's singular act of taking on mourning for his sake, 26 **assume mourning dress** n.

the senate chamber... grief and mourning On the personification, 53 **not only my fellow humans** n. C. repeated the figure the next day: *Vat.* 8 'the forum was—to say the least—plunged in gloom from yearning, the senate chamber was mute, in short all eager engage-ment with the liberal arts fell silent'.

129. Why bring to mind those... decrees of the senate touching my case C. turns to the meetings that directly prepared his recall. The present passage, read with the slightly fuller account at *Red. sen.* 25–7 (cf. also *Red. pop.* 10), makes plain that there were two meetings of the senate, on successive days, and that a *contio* (referred to already at 107–8 above) was also held on the second day (thus *Dom.* 27): that the *contio*—attended by 'all Italy' (*Dom.* 27, sim. 107 above) in response to the consuls' letters (116 **honour had been paid** n.)— preceded the senate meeting on the second day is implied by *Dom.* 27 and confirmed by the statement below that the senate at its second session acted 'at the urging of the Roman people itself and of those who had gathered from the townships of Italy' i.e. as they made their views plain in the *contio*. In these sessions the senate voted at least two decrees (at least three, if the measures mentioned in 129 were moved separately). The first, about to be described, was key, for the senate all but unanimously adopted Pompey's *sententia* that C. was the savior of the fatherland and as such should be restored to the fatherland; at the *contio* this view was urged upon the people and, very likely, the law to that effect was *promulgated. These meetings were certainly held before 10 July; there is reason to think that the senate's first session was held on 8 July, the *contio* and second session on 9 July, when the crowds gathered for the *ludi Apollinares* (6–13 July) would have increased attendance at the *contio*: see App. 1.

temple of Jupiter Best and Greatest   This massive, ancient temple, on the southern (lower) crest of the Capitoline hill, housed a central shrine (*cella*) of Jupiter with flanking shrines of Queen Juno (*Iuno Regina*) and Minerva; it had been rebuilt within the last generation, after a fire levelled the archaic temple in 83 (*NTDAR* 221–4, *LTUR* 3. 148–53, *MAR* 155–6). A place where the interpenetration of Roman religion, politics, and power was esp. visible, the temple was the site of the consuls' inauguration every 1 Jan. and the terminus of Roman generals' triumphal processions; it was a common site of senate sessions (Bonnefond-Coudry 1989, 85 ff.), and C. had dedicated a statuette of Minerva in the goddess's shrine there on the eve of his departure for exile (Plut. *Cic.* 31. 5, Cass. Dio 38. 17. 5).

hero who...celebrated...the three regions of the world   Pompey triumphed from Africa in 79, after defeating the renegade Gnaeus Domitius Ahenobarbus and the Numidian Iarbas; from Spain at the end of 71, after defeating Sertorius; and from Asia and the Aegean in September 61, after defeating Mithradates and the pirates. As Plutarch remarks, others had celebrated three triumphs, but never from three different continents, so that 'he seemed by his three triumphs to have subjugated the inhabited world' (*Pomp.* 45. 5): thus *Balb.* 16 '(Pompey's) three triumphs testify to the fact that the whole world is in the grip of our dominion', *Pis.* 29 'with his three triumphs (Pompey) had united all the territories of all people', cf. Cass. Dio 37. 21. 2.

a prepared statement   Lentulus called on Pompey first for his opinion (*Dom.* 30). That he read a prepared statement conveys the matter's gravity: thus C. says that his own *Red. sen.* 'was spoken from a prepared statement because of the magnitude of the occasion' (*Planc.* 74), cf. *Att.* 4. 3(75). 3, *Fam.* 10. 13(389). 1, *Phil.* 10. 5, *De or.* 1. 152.

I alone had saved the fatherland   On 29 Dec. 63 Metellus Nepos, as *tribune of the plebs, prevented C. from addressing the people after taking the oath that every outgoing consul swore, to the effect that he had done nothing against the law during his term; C. then substituted an oath that he had alone had saved the *commonwealth (*Fam.* 5. 2(2). 6–7, *Pis.* 6, sim. *Sull.* 33–4, *Rep.* 1. 7, Plut. *Cic.* 23. 1–2, Cass. Dio 37. 38. 1–2). The claim was a variation on a theme expressed at *Cat.* 4. 21: whereas many a great general—not least Pompey—had gone forth to extend Rome's *dominion, C. alone had insured that the great general would have a Rome to which to return (cf. Plut. *Cic.* 22. 4). Expressing such thoughts frosted the reception Pompey first gave C.'s account of his achievements (*Schol. Bob.* 167. 23–9 St., *Sull.* 67, the latter implying that C.'s letter had circulated publicly; cf. also *Fam.* 5. 7(3). 3, *Att.* 1. 14(14). 3, and Introd. §1). Yet by March 60, when it suited his turn, Pompey was ready to acknowledge C.'s claim in something like its present form (*Att.* 1. 19(19). 7, sim. *Att.* 2. 1(21). 6, June 60; cf. *Leg.* 2. 6, ascribing to Pompey the view that Arpinum had produced two saviors of Rome, *Phil.* 2. 12, where Pompey caps the catalog of great men who approved C.'s consulship, *Off.* 1. 78). The statement ascribed to Pompey here is characterized similarly at *Red. sen.* 29 (cf. *Red. pop.* 16, on Pompey's appearance at the *contio the next day, with *Prov. cons.* 43, *Mil.* 39, 73). That he 'alone' was responsible is among the notes C. strikes most insistently, both in his own voice (*Prov. cons.* 23, *Pis.* 21) and esp. in reporting the view of others (*Red. pop.* 5, 17, *Dom.* 73, 122, 132, *Har. resp.* 58, *Prov. cons.* 45, *Pis.* 23, 34). Memory of the claim did not die: on 20 Dec. 44 C. heard the acclamation that he had 'again saved the commonwealth' (*Phil.* 6. 2).

packed meeting of the senate   417 members attended, including all magistrates, *Red. sen.* 26, cf. *Red. pop.* 15. On the phrase *frequens senatus*, 26 **a packed meeting** n.

single enemy of the people   Clodius: making the same point at *Dom.* 26, C. says that 'there was a lone dissenter, the man who had reckoned that by his law (viz., declaring that C. had been exiled) the conspirators ought to be called forth even from the dead.' C. elsewhere says that Appius Pulcher, as praetor, and two tribunes (Atilius Serranus and Numerius Rufus, cf. 72) were the only magistrates not to join in promulgating the law for C.'s recall (*Pis.* 35, adding that it was something 'not to be required' of Appius, *non fuit postulandum*; cf. *Fam.* 1. 9(20). 16), as they were the only magistrates not to join in inviting him to address the people after his return, in the *contio that survives as *Red. pop.* (*Att.* 4. 1(73). 7, cf. App. 1). The present passage implies that they did not vote against him in this meeting.

very fact … entrusted to the public records   i.e. it was remarked when the decree was written up after the session, both for transmission to the treasury archives (*aerarium*) and for public posting on a bronze inscription.

at the urging   Presumably as the sentiments were conveyed, or were interpreted as being conveyed, at the *contio* that preceded this second session, see **Why bring to mind** n., above.

those who had gathered from the townships of Italy   In response to the letters sent by the consuls after the meeting in the temple of Honos and Virtus, see 116.

the senate decreed   For the decree see also *Red. sen.* 27, *Dom.* 73; the similar but not identical language in each case suggests that C. para- phrases the original without reproducing it. Since only magistrates could 'watch the heavens' in the sense relevant here, to observe and announce adverse omens for the purpose of blocking a *voting assem- bly (Glossary s.v. auspices), the decree set the senate's *auctoritas* against the formal power (*potestas*) legally entrusted to magistrates by the *populus*. It was in this respect a more radical measure than Clodius' law, on any plausible reading of the latter, despite C.'s fierce attack in 33; perhaps in part for that reason C. stresses as strongly as he does that the senate was responding to the direct will of the people (cf. Balsdon 1957, 16). Note, however, that the senate had passed a similar decree, temporarily suspending *obnuntiation, in 61 (*Att.* 1. 16(16). 13, Sumner 1963, 341–2); and Gellius notes (13. 15) that when the consuls issued edicts summoning the *comitia centuriata* (the assembly that passed the law for C.'s recall), they customarily stipulated that 'no lesser magistrate was to watch the heavens'.

seeking to overturn the commonwealth   For C.'s *well-being equated with the *commonwealth's, *Red. sen.* 36, *Dom.* 17, and passim in this speech. The equation here is not C.'s but the senate's; at *Pis.* 35, where C. says the motion was Pompey's, his language makes the legal point yet more ominously plain: 'if anyone blocked my return, he would be reckoned a public enemy (*in hostium numero*)'—the category of those with no rights as citizens, to which even the conspirators executed on 5 Dec. 63 had not been formally assigned (cf. 11 **domestic enemies** n., and for such decrees Mommsen 1887–8, 1³. 283 n. 3).

the first five days on which action could be taken The law was passed on 4 Aug., the fourth *comitial day on which a vote could have been taken after the period of *promulgation: see App. 1.

I was to return ... rank and standing restored Sim. *Red. sen.* 27. The clause seems to imply concern that an attempt would be made to disrupt the *comitia*, perhaps by violence: it establishes as the senate's fall-back position the view argued by Lucius Cotta on 1 Jan. 57 (73 above), that because the law exiling C. had not been valid, his restoration required no law, only the senate's *authority.

the same people be asked to reconvene when the matter was taken up again i.e. for the vote, after the period of *promulgation; cf. *Red. sen.* 27, *Pis.* 34.

130. such a competitive pitch ... on my behalf C. resumes and underlines a key point of the last paragraph: in response to the consular summons sent at the senate's direction, people had not only gathered from all Italy but had actually urged the senate to extend its efforts, hence the further decrees passed in the session held after the *contio.

only one man was found to dissent openly Clodius, see 129 **single enemy of the people** n. 'Openly' implies that some kept their opposition quiet, cf. 14 **if some tacitly disapprove** n.

Quintus Metellus For the background, see 72 **his colleague** n. After Nepos declared at the meeting of 1 Jan. 57 that he would set aside his enmity for the *commonwealth's sake, C. wrote to acknowledge the gesture (*Fam.* 5. 4(10). 2), which he frequently cites as a prime example of patriotism trumping personal feelings: *Red. sen.* 9, *Dom.* 7, 9, *Pis.* 35; for Nepos' behaviour and the speech of Servilius described here, *Red. sen.* 25, *Red. pop.* 10, 15, *Dom.* 70, and esp. *Prov. cons.* 22, where Nepos provides the climactic case in a long string of examples of men who have put aside personal enmity for the common good. Cf. also *Off.* 1. 87, citing Nepos' ancestor Quintus Metellus Macedonicus (cos. 143) and the younger Scipio Africanus as exemplifying 'disagreement without bitterness' in addressing the commonwealth's needs.

made a motion for my well-being C. uses the verb (*referre*) proper to putting a motion before the house; at *Red. sen.* 26 C. says, more specifically and perhaps more accurately, that Metellus added his name to the motion to restore C.'s *worthy standing (*adscriptor dignitatis meae*).

<**the senate**> The medieval MSS are defective (*excitatus summa cum auctoritate P. Servili quadam gravitate dicendi*): editors are divided on whether C. attributes both *authority and *gravity to Servilius (thus Manutius' correction, *cum summa auctoritate P. Servili,* <*tum incredibili*> *quadam gravitate dicendi*, printed e.g. by Peterson and, with minor modification, Cousin 1965) or authority to the senate, gravity of speech to Servilius (thus A. Klotz's correction, *cum summa auctoritate* <*senatus, tum*> *P. Servili* <*incredibili*> *quadam gravitate dicendi*, printed by e.g. Maslowski). C.'s ref. to the scene at *Red. sen.* 25 favours the former (*P. Servilius . . . et auctoritatis et orationis suae divina quadam gravitate . . .*); but C.'s stress here on the near unanimity of the senate, combined with his ref. to the scene at *Prov. cons.* 22 (*permotus cum auctoritate vestra* (viz., the senate's) *tum illius P. Servili incredibili gravitate dicendi*) inclines me toward the latter correction, which also provides better formal balance.

Publius Servilius Publius Servilius (*RE* 93) Vatia, cos. 79, gained the additional, honourific cognomen Isauricus for victories over the Isauri in Anatolia as *proconsul of Cilicia in 78–74; already in his 70s at the time of this speech (he had been praetor no later than 90), he became censor in 55. The dramatic intervention C. depicts (cf. *Red. sen.* 25, *Prov. cons.* 22) belongs to the senate's first meeting on the question in July (129 **Why bring to mind** n.), and Servilius supported C. at the *contio that followed the next day (*Red. pop.* 17). He was among the pontiffs who heard argument on C.'s house on 29 Sept. 57 (*Dom.* 43, 123, 132) and is shown gravely rebuking Clodius on another occasion at *Har. resp.* 2. On the kinship ties involved in the present transaction see next n.

summoned . . . from beyond the grave Sim. *Red. sen.* 25, Servilius' tactic showing that C. was not the only speaker at Rome who would use a man's ancestors against him to gain a point, cf. 126 **his father . . .** n.; for the gesture cf. C.'s 'summoning' of Appius Claudius

Caecus' shade to scold Clodia at *Cael.* 33–4. But in appealing to Nepos' ancestors Servilius also appeals to his own (thus 'his kinsman', cf. *Red. sen.* 25), for one of his mother's brothers, Q. Caecilius (*RE* 82) Metellus Balearicus (cos. 123, cens. 120), was Nepos' grandfather.

the calamity... of the great Metellus Numidicus   On Numidicus see 37 n.; C. speaks of his ambivalent 'calamity' (*casus*) similarly at *Red. sen.* 25: 'all thought (his) departure from the fatherland honourable (*honestus*), yet grievous (*luctuosus*)'.

burst into tears   At the senate's meeting of 1 Jan. 57, Nepos stated that he would not hinder C.'s recall, a position he had adopted privately more than two months earlier still (72 **his colleague** n.). But forbearing from harming an enemy is different from declaring yourself reconciled with him (below), esp. if the reconciliation is prompted by heartfelt appeal to what you owe your family (87 **example set** n.). To suppose Metellus' emotion eccentric or extreme would be to mistake an important element of Roman culture.

truly godlike gravity... of the great days of yore   Servilius embodies the traits found in S.'s father and first father-in-law (6 **very serious men** n.) and misleadingly affected by the consul Piso (19 and nn.).

declared himself reconciled with me, as a gift freely given   Since each party to a feud commonly thought himself the one wronged, each would expect to receive some form of 'satisfaction' before a reconciliation could occur (cf. *QFr.* 3. 4(24). 2–3, *Att.* 4. 18(92). 1, on the possibility of reconciling with Gabinius). These conflicting expectations naturally tended to raise an obstacle, in this case swept aside by Nepos' gesture, a 'gift freely given' (*beneficium*) to (it is implied) a deserving recipient.

131. his own brother   Quintus Caecilius (86) Metellus Celer, cos. 60, was sent as praetor in late Oct. 63 to raise an army in Picenum and the *ager Gallicus* after Catiline had taken the field under arms (9 **Pisaurum** n.); he later cut off Catiline's route to Gaul, keeping him in Italy. He died unexpectedly in 59, and at *Cael.* 59–60 C. will suggest that he was poisoned by his wife, Clodia, the eldest of Clodius' sisters. Though there C. stresses the solidarity he enjoyed with Celer, as he does here, their personal and political relations had been mixed: C.'s confrontation with Metellus Nepos in Dec. 63–Jan. 62 (72 **his colleague** n.) provoked an indignant letter from Celer (*Fam.* 5. 1(1)); and as an opponent of Pompey, Celer tried to thwart the general's interests at time when C. was more inclined to favour them.

As for my return   *Att.* 4. 1(73). 4–7 gives an account of C.'s return, parallel in many details with what follows, and of his first week's activities; the return's splendour (with variations in detail) is evoked also at *Dom.* 75, cf. *Red. sen.* 38, *Red. pop.* 18, *Pis.* 51–2, Plut. *Cic.* 33. 5. C. omits here the vote of 4 Aug. in the **comitia centuriata*, referred to in 108–9 and celebrated at *Red. sen.* 27–8, *Dom.* 90, cf. *Mil.* 38.

arrival ... the fifth of August   C. sailed from Dyrrachium on 4 Aug., the day of the vote, and reached Brundisium on 5 Aug. (*Att.* 4. 1(73). 4), evidently having received prior notice of the date and some assurance of the outcome (cf. **daughter...** n. below); he received written confirmation from Quintus only several days later when he was already at Brundisium (ibid.). The sail cannot have been leisurely: Dyrrachium is about 80 nautical miles (150 km) from Brundisium, as the crow flies, and with favourable winds '(a ship) could log roughly between $4\frac{1}{2}$ and 6 knots' (Casson 1971, 285). At least in early August C. was not likely to have faced the scirocco, which in the southern Adriatic blows most frequently in autumn and late winter.

gave birth to my arrival and return   C. speaks of the 'birthday of my return' at *Att.* 3. 20(65). 1 (Oct. 58: *diem ... natalem reditus mei*) and applies the metaphor to the day of the vote at Rome (4 Aug.) at *Red. sen.* 27: with the text translated here (Maslowski, after Baiter), C. applies the metaphor both to his return and to the three anniversaries about to be noted; with a different text plausibly suggested by Shackleton Bailey (1987, 279), *natalis* applies to only to the latter three. The point about the multiple coincidences remains the same in either case.

daughter ... Brundisium ... <temple of Well-being>   *Att.* 4. 1(73). 4, noting the same coincidences, allows the last detail to be restored here, where the MSS are defective. Tullia was born in 79 or 78 (D-G 6:614); a Latin colony was founded at Brundisium in 244 (Vell. 1. 14. 8); the temple of Salus on the Quirinal was vowed by Gaius Iunius

Bubulcus as cos. 311 and dedicated during his dictatorship in 302 (Livy
9. 43. 5, 10. 1. 9, *NTDAR* 341–2, *LTUR* 4. 229–30, *MAR* 219–20,
Winkler 1995, 16–35). The synchronism with the restoration of C.'s
civic *well-being was presumably intended by his allies, esp. Lentulus
(cf. esp. *Red. sen.* 27), and co-ordinated with C. in advance.

the Laenii . . had given me refuge   C. describes his stay with this
family during his flight, 17–29 April 58, at *Planc.* 97, cf. esp. *Fam.*
14. 4(6). 2 (29 April 58), with *Fam.* 13. 63(137). 1, *Att.* 5. 20(113).
8, 5. 21(114). 4, 10, 6. 1(115). 6, 6. 3(117). 5. If the law declaring that
C. had been exiled was passed on 24 April (App. 1), he was formally
an outlaw, 'interdicted from fire and water', during the last five days
of his stay in Brundisium: because anyone sheltering such a person
was liable to be punished (cf. 65 **proposal** n., and the concern
C. registers about an earlier host after the law had been promulgated,
Att. 3. 4(49)), the Laenii took a risk, and C. was grateful.

the length of the route … offering congratulations   Brundisium
was *c.*585 km from Rome, the length of the *via Appia*, usually 7–10
days' travel; that C. entered Rome on 5 Sept., one month after
landing at Brundisium, suggests his progress was stately, with frequent stops. The gathering of delegations from the Italian towns
hints at his allies' orchestration of events and recalls Pompey's reception on his return to Italy from the East in 62 (Plut. *Pomp.* 43. 3,
cf. ibid. 57. 2). From the quasi-triumphal grandeur sketched here
C. omits the detail of being conveyed 'by caparisoned horses and a
gilded chariot' *(Red. sen.* 28).

the city gate   The *porta Capena* (*Att.* 4. 1(73). 5) in the ancient
'Servian Wall' (by tradition built by king Servius Tullius in the 6th
cent., but mostly of 4th cent. construction), in the city's SE quadrant,
through which the *via Appia* entered the city.

climbed to the Capitol   Presumably to make an offering at the
temple of Jupiter Best and Greatest, where he had dedicated a small
statue of Minerva in that goddess's shrine on the eve of his departure
in March 58 (cf. 129 **temple of Jupiter** n.): the climb thus brought
him full circle.

returned home   Sim. *Dom.* 76. This is not the home on the Palatine
purchased from Crassus in 62 and destroyed by Clodius, but his

father's house in 'the Keels' (*Carinae*), on the Esquiline, which C. had inherited and then given to his brother when he bought the Palatine residence (Plut. *Cic.* 8. 3). By Feb. 56, when C. had regained the Palatine property, the house was being rented by some of the Lamiae (*QFr.* 2. 3(7). 7; for the Lamiae, 29 n.).

132. the person . . . chiefly attacked   With the view ascribed here to S. (sim. *Vat.* 2), referring to Vatinius' testimony, cf. C.'s ref. to 'Vatinius, by whom (S.) was being openly assailed', when reporting the verdict to Quintus (*QFr.* 2. 4(8). 1). The abuse that follows is more vehement even than the attack on Gellius (110–11), who like Vatinius testified against S., yet it gives only a foretaste of the invective C. was to heap on Vatinius in the next day's interrogation (Introd. §2). Despite these attacks, the two were reconciled through Pompey's mediation in 54 (*Fam.* 1. 9(20). 19, Plut. *Cic.* 26. 1), when C. defended Vatinius on a charge of electoral corruption (*TLRR* no. 292); that defence moved Lentulus to ask C. to explain his seemingly inconstant political behaviour, which in turn prompted C.'s lengthy *apologia* (*Fam.* 1. 9(20). 1–22), singling out his interrogation of Vatinius, along with his actions in respect of Caesar's agrarian legislation, as proofs of his political independence after his return (ibid. 7–8). The reconciliation's authenticity is borne out by Vatinius' attempt to help C. in 48, when he was ignominiously stalled in Brundisium awaiting Caesar's permission to return to Rome (*Att.* 11. 5(216). 4), and by the tenor of their brief extant correspondence from 45–44 (*Fam.* 5. 9–11(255–9)).

a gentle person to whom bloodshed is alien   Since Caesar's legions had been slaughtering Gauls by the myriad for two years, one might suspect irony, but C. is thinking only of Roman blood, and the irony lies elsewhere: C. alludes to Caesar's opposing the conspirators' execution on 5 Dec. 63 (*Cat.* 4. 7, Sall. *Cat.* 51) and to his restatement of that position in the *contio held by Clodius in the circus Flaminius in March 58; see 33 **voiced their approval** n.

slandered . . . by asserting   If Vatinius said that Caesar would not rest easy as long as the 'breed' existed, C. could pretend that it implied Caesar himself was not of the *Best Sort, in the broad sense sketched above, and hence that he was a *desperado. The comment would further slander Caesar in so far as it implied an intention to wipe out the 'breed' in order to ease his anxiety; C. gives a similar spin to a statement by Clodius about the triumvirs at 40 above.

Vettius the informer   Sometime before the consular elections were held in Oct. 59, perhaps in Aug., Lucius Vettius, an equestrian who had served C. as an informant in 63, told the younger Gaius Scribonius Curio that he (Vettius) was planning to assassinate Pompey. Curio told his father (cos. 76), who told Pompey, who brought Vettius before the senate: there Vettius accused (among others) Bibulus and the younger Curio himself, as leader of a segment of 'the youth' opposed to Pompey. By the next day, when Vettius was brought before a *contio, first by Caesar (as consul) and then by Vatinius (as tribune), he had revised his accusation to include a number of *optimates (see next n.) and C.'s son-in-law, Piso; he also coyly referred to C. Before more could be learned, Vettius was strangled in prison, the truth of the matter as unclear at his death as it is now: the chief sources are *Att.* 2. 24(44). 2–4, *Vat.* 24–6, Plut. *Luc.* 42. 7–8, App. *BCiv.* 2. 12, Cass. Dio 38. 9. 2–4. C. believed that Caesar was responsible (*Att.* 2. 24(44). 2); more recently suspicion has fallen on Clodius (Seager 2002, 98–9, *contra* Tatum 1999, 111–12) or Pompey himself (e.g. Marshall 1987, 121–4), though it is more prudent to suspend judgement (e.g. Pocock 1926, 183–5, Gruen 1974, 95–6, Tatum ibid.). It seems clear that the affair at least strained relations between C. and Pompey, and so perhaps deepened the isolation that resulted in C.'s exile; it doubtless made it easier to arouse Pompey's suspicions of C. early in 58, alleged at 41 above as a reason for Pompey's lack of support.

men of the highest distinction   Those named at *Vat.* 24–6 include Bibulus, Lucius Lucullus, the younger and elder Curio, Domitius Ahenobarbus, Lentulus Niger, Aemilius Paullus, Cicero's son-in-law Piso, and Marcus Laterensis (on whose connection with C. see *Planc.* 73, 86); a shorter but overlapping list already at *Att.* 2. 24(44). 3 (adding Gaius Fannius), where C. notes that Vettius referred to him, unmistakably, as 'the eloquent ex-consul, the current consul's neighbor' (Caesar, as *pontifex maximus*, had an official residence not far from C.'s house on the Palatine).

earned my gratitude   So with sim. irony at *Vat.* 26: 'why then should I complain? In fact I ought to thank you for thinking I should not be set apart from this company of utterly gallant citizens'.

133. daily spun some fiction about me for his audiences   As tribune, that is, in *contiones.

advised a person ... to ... keep an eye on me   Cf. at 41 **the same suspicion** n., on the whispering campaign intended to separate Pompey from C. early in 58.

my enemy   Clodius.

Sextus Cloelius   Among Clodius' more prominent *henchmen, Sextus Cloelius (*RE* Clodius 12; on the correct form of his name, Shackleton Bailey 1960) is more than once cast by C. as a man of servile origin (*Pis.* 8, *Att.* 2. 12(30). 2); whatever the truth of that, we know that he attained the status of 'scribe' (*scriba*: Asc. 33. 6 Cl.), one of several categories of magistrates' salaried assistants (*apparitores*), whose ranks included ambitious men of free birth (on *apparitores* in general and *scribae* in particular see Purcell 1983, Badian 1989*a*; Damon 1992 is the best discussion of Cloelius' standing and career). He participated in several notable events associated with Clodius' *tribunate, presiding over the not-yet-licit celebration of the *ludi Compitales* at the start of Jan. 58 (*Pis.* 8, Asc. 7. 16–21 Cl., with 32 **club** n.), engineering the young Tigranes' escape (Ascon. 47. 20–1 Cl. with 58 **Gnaeus Pompeius saw him** n.), supervising the distribution of the dole under Clodius' grain law (*Dom.* 47–8 with 55 **a fifth of the public income** n.), and drafting Clodius' legislation (alluded to here, stressed at *Dom.* 47–8, 50, 83, 129, cf. *Mil.* 33). Prosecuted unsuccessfully by Milo soon after this trial (*QFr.* 2. 5(9). 4, late March, *Cael.* 78, *TLRR* no. 273, charge uncertain), he was condemned on a charge of *vis* and exiled in 52 (Alexander, ibid. no. 315), having provoked a riot by bringing the body of the murdered Clodius into the senate chamber; he was restored by Antony, allegedly on Caesar's warrant, in 44 (*Att.* 14. 13(367). 6, 13a(367a). 2, 13b(367b). 3).

Beyond the matter of his social origin, C. exercises his contempt by making cunnilingus his distinctive vice (*Dom.* 25–6, 47, 83, *Cael.* 78, *Har. resp.* 11, *Pis.* 8, with Corbeill 1996, 112–24), as he makes incest the distinctive vice of his leader, Clodius (App. 2): C. prob. has that association in mind here when he says that Cloelius is 'in every way worthy of his closest friends'.

proscription On this view of (esp.) Clodius' second law, 46 **proscription**, 65 **measure** nn.

the latter was the board The most important contribution to sorting out the MSS' nonsense (*toambuam essese scriptorem esse* P, *tabulam esse se* (*se esse* V) *scriptorem* GV) was Halm's correction (*tabulam, sese scriptorem esse*), refined independently by Castorina (cf. Reggiani 1991) and Maslowski to produce the text translated here (*tabulam eum, sese scriptorem esse*). Whether one thinks of *proscription—with the names of the outlawed inscribed on publicly posted boards—or of the actual law declaring that C. had been exiled—with its text inscribed on publicly posted boards during its *promulgation—C.'s point is the same: Cloelius articulated Clodius' wishes as his 'draftsman' (above), Vatinius carried them out as his tool.

that law of mine The *lex Calpurnia* of 67 punished electoral corruption (*ambitus*) with expulsion from the senate, debarment from office, and a fine (Cass. Dio 36. 38. 1); the *lex Tullia* C. passed as consul added ten years' banishment. In Nov. 63 Lucius Murena, as consul-designate, was charged under the law and defended by C. in the extant speech (*TLRR* no. 224); S. was accused under the same law at the same time that he was charged with *vis* (*TLRR* no. 270, with Introd. §2). The clause mentioned here (more fully, *Vat.* 37) aimed to prevent candidates, and men who intended to be candidates in the foreseeable future, from using *games to curry the electorate's favour.

134. I suppose Before this sentence the MSS transmit four words (*iste nimia gloriae cupiditate*) that anticipate the characterization of Vatinius two lines further on ('fairly on fire with a lust for glory': *homo flagrans cupiditate gloriae*): rather than follow Halm 1886 (with e.g. Maslowski) in attempting to read the four words as an independent thought (*est e<nim> nimia gloriae cupiditate*) I follow Madvig (with e.g. Cousin 1965) in deleting them as an interpolation.

himself the fairest   C. both alludes to Vatinius' ugliness (135 **scrofula n.**) and implies that he would be at home in a troupe of gladiators i.e. slaves and condemned criminals.

their recent beneficence toward him   'The beneficence of the Roman people' (*beneficium populi Romani*) is a cliché for election to a magistracy (74 **Gnaeus Pompeius n.**): C. applies it sarcastically to Vatinius' recent defeat in the aedilician elections (114 **stood for the aedileship n.**).

but when … going to lead?   C. speaks with tongue in cheek: breaking the law was bad enough ('everyone would agree that it was culpable'), but breaking it only to mount a tawdry show on the cheap—*that* is truly deplorable! In C.'s *jeu d'esprit*, Vatinius' gladiators are not costly specimens selected and trained for their roles but the inmates of 'workhouses' (*ergastula*) where slaves good only for brute labour were kept: Vatinius (we may infer) bought these for next to nothing, then randomly assigned them roles as 'Samnite' (a heavily armed fighter with vizored helmet, short sword, large shield: *RE* II 1 (1920), 2132 (Hug)) or 'challenger' (*provocator*, of uncertain armament: Ville 1981, 307, 405).

135. He has two pleas to offer in defence   Elaborating (or belabouring) his point, C. scornfully imagines Vatinius' taking refuge in the letter of the law: according to the first plea, the fighters that Vatinius presented were not 'gladiators' strictly so called (next n.); according to the second, Vatinius presented only one gladiator, not the 'gladiators' (plural) forbidden by the law—a possibility that gives C. scope for further ridicule.

beast-fighters   As the name implies (*bestiarii*), these were pitted not against other humans but against wild beasts in 'hunts' (*venationes*), a euphemism for displays in which large numbers of exotic animals were gathered in a confined space and slaughtered (cf. Sen. *Epist.* 7. 4); at a later date the slaughter was varied by the practice of exposing condemned criminals to the beasts.

shifted his … aedileship   i.e. the money he would have spent on the aedileship, had he been elected: cf. *Har. resp.* 56 'those who were readying gladiatorial games contrary to the laws were rejected (viz., at the polls) by friends and strangers alike, by neighbors and fellow-tribesmen, by men of the town and men of the countryside', with 114 **did not even carry** n., on Vatinius' rejection by the voters of his own tribe.

One Lion 'Lion' was the name of a gladiator: the pun, which ties together Vatinius' two supposed pleas, was included by C.'s freedman Tiro in his anthology of C.'s witticisms (*Schol. Bob.* 140. 12–17 St.; on the anthology, in three books, Quint. 6. 3. 5, cf. Macrob. *Sat.* 2. 1. 12).

he's in the habit of summoning the tribunes of the plebs When accused in 58 under the *lex Licinia Iunia* (next n.), Vatinius appealed to Clodius' tribunician protection (*auxilium*), and the trial was disrupted by violence: see *Vat.* 33–4 with *TLRR* no. 255.

lex Caecilia Didia and lex Licinia Iunia Passed by the consuls of 98 and 62, respectively, the laws regulated legislative procedures (*MRR* 2. 4, 173, with Lintott 1999*a*, 140–5): the first is known to have established *promulgation of three market days before a bill could be brought to a vote (*promulgatio trinum nundinum*, cf. App. 1) and to have prohibited 'miscellaneous' legislation (*leges saturae*) treating two or more unrelated matters in a single bill; the second law, incorporating and extending the other's provisions, required that copies of proposed laws be deposited in the treasury, to prevent tampering after promulgation. Vatinius was accused under the *lex Licinia Iunia* in 58; in April 59 C. was alleging that both laws had been violated (*Att.* 2. 9(29). 1) by legislation then in process, using language ('the wickedness of *those* people', *improbitas istorum*) no doubt intended to embrace both Caesar and Vatinius. Given that C. speaks of the violations only in the most general terms, and that each law surely comprised more clauses than those we happen to know, we cannot say what form Vatinius' alleged violations took; for argument that the allegations arose out of the legislation confirming Pompey's settlement of the East, see Pocock 1926, 169–75, Seager 2002, 88.

law on extortion moved by Gaius Caesar The *lex Iulia de repetundis* establishing guidelines for provincial governors (*MRR* 2. 188) remained in force, with occasional modification, into the Principate.

As Caesar's *legate in Gaul (perhaps by 58, certainly in 57: *MRR* 2. 199, 205), Vatinius would have been in a position to engage in extortionate behaviour, thus 'showing his contempt' for the law; alternatively, or additionally, C. refers to Vatinius' peculations as tribune (*Vat.* 29), some of them involving transactions with foreign rulers.

his own law The *lex Vatinia* that gave Caesar his 5-year command in Cisalpine Gaul and Illyricum: see *MRR* 2. 190 with 24 **their pick** n.

they say that there are others who would annul Caesar's consular acts C. glances at and—with 'they say that there are others'— doubly distances himself from the controversy regarding Caesar's distribution of Campanian land: the tribune Publius Rutilius Lupus had raised the matter in the senate in Dec. 57 (*QFr.* 2. 1(5). 1), and on 5 April C. will propose that the senate schedule a discussion for 15 May (*Fam.* 1. 9(20). 8). The meetings at Luca will intervene, and C. will not attend the discussion: see Introd. §5.

this excellent law is disregarded ... by Caesar's father-in-law Piso, cos. 58: for C.'s anticipation that his governorship of Macedonia would result in prosecution on his return to Rome, see 52 **First of all** n.

a part of the body that is healthy In the prosecutor's appeal the 'part' would be S., whose conviction would 'excise' him from the *civil community; but C. prob. also thinks of himself, 'excised' by the 'butchery' of Clodius' legislation.

apply a cure to the commonwealth On the metaphor, see 43 **medicine ... stopped ... a plague** n. The present passage demonstrates that 'when his adversaries adopted the cliché, Cicero could turn it to his own account' (Fantham 1972, 128–9).

scrofula Vatinius suffered from *struma* ('scrofula'), a tuberculous infection of the lymphatic glands, to which C. here alludes in a form of synechdoche, allowing the swelling to stand for the man whose removal would heal the community: for his mockery of Vatinius' deformity, cf. *Att.* 2. 9(29). 2, *Vat.* 4, 10, 39, Plut. *Cic.* 9. 3 (an anecdote dating to 66), 26. 2, with Corbeill 1996, 46–56.

136–47. *Conclusion (peroratio): Exhoration and Commiseration*

'Many a restive audience has taken heart at the utterance of the blessed word "finally"' (Winterbottom 2004, 217). Saying 'to make certain that I finish speaking before you finish listening so attentively, I shall conclude...', C. signals 'the beginning of the end' (the heading under which Winterbottom's remark aptly appears): he looks back to his promise—now fulfilled—to teach a 'lesson to the younger generation' (96) and delivers a compound conclusion (*peroratio*), first using that 'lesson' to exhort the youth (136–43), then making the appeal for pity (144–7) that suitably caps the defence of S.'s *life as a citizen.

stir...notables to imitate...ancestors   Cf. 21 **it serves...their ancestors** n.

new men   On the term, see the Glossary. For a *new man like C., it was an article of faith that his upward mobility was proof of personal *manliness and a capacity for 'vigorous activity' (*industria*) that benefited the community: see e.g. *Verr.* 2. 4. 81 (cf. 2. 5. 180), *Leg. agr.* 2. 3, *Mur.* 15–17, *Sull.* 24, *Balb.* 18–19, *Pis.* 2, *Planc.* 17–18, with Wiseman 1971, 107–16. A new man's earned success, we are to understand, is the one 'novelty' that appropriately has a place in the apparently permanent and unchanging ancestral regime C. is about to describe in 137.

137. they had not been able to endure the power of kings   Acc. to tradition, kingly power had been endured for nearly two and a half centuries (753–509) by the time Tarquin the Proud was expelled; at *Rep.* 1. 62. 3 Scipio is made to say that the Romans, unaccustomed to *freedom, abused it after Tarquin's expulsion (cf. 2. 53 ff., Sall. *Hist.* 1. 29), and Livy advances the related point that under the kings the Romans had been unready for liberty (2. 1. 3–6).

the senate...ever to be at the head   The rest of the paragraph epitomizes C.'s view of the most desirable civil regime, elaborated in *Rep.*, 'which marries a fundamental recognition of popular sovereignty with an unshakeable and deepseated commitment to

aristocracy (instantiated, specifically, in the senate) as the best prac-
ticable system of government' (Schofield 1995, 77, cf. Mitchell 1991,
52–3); see also *Leg.* 3. 27–8.

the members . . . chosen from the people as a whole   With C.'s
statement compare the cliché that 'in the United States any child
can grow up to be President': in each case the generalization is false
on its face if applied randomly to any given member of the community; but as Brunt remarks, with ref. to this passage, 'we must beware
of supposing that an ideal which had very limited effect is of no
importance at all' (1988, 338). Men from senatorial families plainly
had an advantage in gaining senatorial careers themselves (cf. 97
loftiest categories n.), and among men of non-senatorial background
the wealthy enjoyed obvious advantages over those who were not. Yet
C.'s comment is nonetheless true as a matter of principle, and in
practice the senatorial *order was 'highly permeable to outsiders, to
an extent probably unparalleled in post-feudal European aristocra-
cies' (Hopkins and Burton 1983, 108).

**magistrates rely upon the senate's authority and . . . weighty wis-
dom**   C. says 'ministers, as it were', to mark a metaphor drawn from
the household, where *ministri* were servants; cf. *Planc.* 62, where
C. uses a related metaphor to describe the magistrates as 'the
commonwealth's stewards (*vilici*)'; in a large household both *ministri*
and *vilici* were typically slaves. In fact, the magistrates were the
'ministers' of the *populus* as a whole, exercising certain powers (*potes-
tates*) that the *populus* temporarily entrusted to them; C.'s language
simply caps the senate-centered view he has been elaborating.

supported by the splendid estate of the orders next in rank   The
remark acknowledges the dignity of the equestrians and *treasury
tribunes among the judges and is in line with C.'s habit, when
surveying the political community, of mentioning the senate first,
the equestrians second, followed by the people at large (e.g. 17, 25,
30, 35, 38, 52, 87, 122).

138. people who do what a man can do to protect   Lit. 'who
defend . . . in accordance with their role as men (*pro virili parte*)',
thus displaying their *manliness (*virtus*) by consistently following

its imperatives. C. again appeals to *virtus* just below, in a comparison that makes plain the alternative to manly behaviour.

guarantors i.e. *auctores*, people whose advice and support is especially sought because they possess *auctoritas: since these leaders of the *Best Sort are understood here, acc. to C.'s usual conception of good political order, to be the leaders of the senate, whatever personal *auctoritas* the 'guarantors' possess is massively supported by the corporate *auctoritas* of the senate (32 **senate's authority** n.).

manly behaviour... sleep and banquets and self-indulgence Approaching a climax in his exhortation of the youth, C. implicitly reintroduces the hedonism of Gabinius and Piso, initially attacked (18 ff.) as vices patent in the former, hidden in the latter, now for contrast with proper *manliness.

139. the good report of patriots—the only thing that can truly be called glory Cf. the muse Calliope's injunction to C. in Book 3 of the poem *On His Consulate*: 'Make greater your fame and patriots' praise' (*auge famam laudesque bonorum*: *Att.* 2. 3(23). 4 = frag. 11. 3 Courtney). Quoting it to Atticus, C. remarks that the thought is among the book's 'aristocratic' touches, with good reason: insisting on 'patriots' praise' or 'the good report of patriots' (*bona fama bonorum*), as here, distinguishes 'true' glory from competing conceptions not tied either to the right people's praise (cf. *Tusc.* 3. 3–4 on *laus bonorum* vs. *fama popularis*, sim. 5. 104) or to the performance of acts that benefit the *commonwealth. Cf. 86 **Seeking no other reward** n., and contrast 101 'honour's fickle breeze'. Regrettably, C.'s late work *On Glory* is lost; on his efforts in other writings near the end of his life to define true glory (*Phil.* 5. 49–50, *Off.* 2. 43, cf. *Phil.* 1. 29, 33) in terms of behaviour that is co-operative and therefore just, Long 1995, esp. 229–33.

sometimes, even the powerful In referring to *potentes*—those with personal power (*potentia*) not sanctioned by the community, unlike the power (*potestas*) entrusted to magistrates by the people—C. permits himself a glancing hit at the triumvirs.

blinded the ignorant with largesse Cf. 77 **the ignorant** n.

our kind of people... irresponsible and reckless and wicked and harmful 'Our kind of people' (*nostri homines*) are the *Best Sort, *optimates* in the conventional sense, just as the *irresponsible, those who 'have . . . whipped up the people to unrest or blinded the ignorant with largesse', are *populares* in the conventional sense: nearing the end of his 'lesson', C. has dropped the conceit that the old categories are no longer valid (104 ff.) and reinstated the clear distinctions he usually draws (cf. Wirszubski 1961, 18).

140. And lest any come to fear   The concern C. addresses in 140–3 reappears, both in general terms and in points of detail, in *Rep.* 1. 4–6, where the risks of civic engagement and the price paid by eminent men bolster the arguments advanced by some (esp. Epicurean quietists), but refuted by C.

Lucius Opimius   As consul in 121, Lucius Opimius (*RE* 4) relied on the 'ultimate *decree of the senate' (25 **all citizens** n.) to use force in putting down the protests led by Gaius Gracchus and Marcus Fulvius Flaccus, killing them and many of their followers (*MRR* 1. 520). As the first consul to rely on the 'ultimate decree' in this way, Opimius set a precedent to which C. appealed in dealing with the Catilinarians (*Cat.* 1. 4, and cf. next n.); the tribune Publius Decius prosecuted him in 120 for putting citizens to death without trial (*MRR* 1. 523, *TLRR* no. 27)—the 'blaze of ill-will' to which C. refers just below— and his acquittal set another precedent on which C. must have thought he could rely. Note that though he had adapted the case to suit his use at *Dom.* 91, and would do so again (*Planc.* 88, cf. *Cat.* 1. 3, *Rep.* 1. 6, *Brut.* 213, *TD.* 4. 51, *Off.* 1. 109, Binot 2001, 193), C. here conspicuously omits mention of Scipio Nasica Serapio, who so aroused popular anger by unleashing a mob against Tiberius Gracchus in 133 that he was forced to withdraw from the city (a mission to annex Asia provided a fig-leaf), dying thereafter in Pergamum (*MRR* 1. 494, 499).

come to a most unworthy end   See **an unfair trial** n., below.

his monument   After suppressing Gaius Gracchus, Opimius built the temple of Concord (26 n.) with the adjoining basilica Opimia (*NTDAR* 54, 98–9, *LTUR* 1. 183): Opimius' temple was the site of the senate's session of 5 Dec. 63, as his use of the 'ultimate decree' provided the precedent for C.'s actions against the Catilinarians following that meeting.

Dyrrachium   Where Cicero spent the latter part of his own exile, from mid-Nov. 58 until 4 Aug. 57: 'One can imagine Cicero's feelings when he ... saw Opimius' tomb' (Nisbet 1961, 167).

an unfair trial   Opimius was tried in 109 under the *lex Mamilia* (*MRR* 1. 546), a 'popular' measure that set up a special court of inquiry for accusations against *notables suspected of aiding or receiving bribes from Jugurtha (*TLRR* no. 53); C. refers to his condemnation in a sim. context at *Rep.* 1. 5. Acc. to Sall. *Iug.* 40. 4, the man chosen to preside over Opimius' trial was Marcus Aemilius Scaurus, cos. 115 and father of the Scaurus presiding at S.'s trial (39 **Marcus Scaurus** n.). If that is correct, C. is perhaps a bit tactless in calling the earlier trial 'unfair', though there is some reason to think that Sallust confused two different Marci Scauri (cf. *MRR* 3. 10, *TLRR* no. 52 n. 2).

all the other men ... given a new lease on life by the people itself   At *Dom.* 86 C. makes the same point by citing the trial, exile, and restoration of Kaeso Quinctius, Marcus Furius Camillus, and Gaius Servilius Ahala (on Quinctius and Camillus, *MRR* 1. 37 (461 BCE), 1. 93 (391 BCE)); the trial and exile of Ahala for killing Spurius Maelius (next n.) are mentioned elsewhere only at Val. Max. 5. 3. 2g (Livy knows only a failed move to confiscate Ahala's property, 4. 21. 3–4), and C. himself speaks only of Ahala's *offensio* ('unpopularity') in a later catalogue of statesmen whose actions brought them afoul of the people (*Rep.* 1. 6): Scipio Nasica and Publius Laenas, who incurred ill-will for the murder of Tiberius Gracchus (*MRR* 1. 494, cf. *Red. sen.* 38); Camillus and Ahala again (cf. the more general catalog of Roman heroes at 143 just below); and three men—Opimius, Metellus Numidicus, and Marius—who have already figured in this speech as *exempla*.

practically to a man ... their immediate death or disgraceful exile   C. alludes esp. to the Gracchi and Saturninus, already passed in review at 101; he perhaps also has in mind figures from the more distant past, Spurius Maelius (*RE* 2, *MRR* 1. 56, slain in 439 by

Servilius Ahala, who will be mentioned in 143) and Marcus Manlius (*RE* 51) Capitolinus (see esp. Livy 6. 14 ff.), whose alleged aspirations to tyranny were sometimes taken in the late Republic to have had populist coloration.

141. a Greek race very different from ... our serious ways   C. sometimes distinguishes contemporary Greeks (viewed as perfidious and grasping) from the 'classical' Greeks (viewed as paragons of culture), but he will generalize to include the latter in his political condemnations when it suits his argument, as it does here; on his attitude toward the Greeks, see 94 **shared out ... the goods** n. and next n.

all who did so were expelled from the civil community   C. refers to the 5th cent. Athenian institution of ostracism, under which one citizen each year could be compelled by vote of his fellow citizens to leave the city for ten years: in so far as the ostracized person did not lose his citizenship or property and suffered no disabilities on his return, the condition more nearly resembles relegation than exile under the Roman system (cf. 29 **banished** n.). By presenting the practice simply as evidence of the people's 'rashness' (*temeritas*) or 'irresponsible wrath' (below) victimizing wise and principled members of the political elite (sim. *Rep.* 1. 5, again citing Themistocles and Miltiades, cf. *Flac.* 16), C. at best grossly simplifies an institution that owed its character more to competition within the elite than to tensions between the elite and the people more generally: see Forsdyke 2005. His choice of examples was no doubt influenced by Plato's *Gorgias*, where Themistocles and Miltiades (along with Cimon) are adduced as leaders who failed to make the people 'better' and so were punished at their hands (esp. 516D5 ff., cf. 503C1 ff.).

Themistocles   The Athenian statesman and military man (*c.*524–459: Davies 1971, 211–20) most responsible for developing Athenian naval power in the first decades of the 5th cent., Themistocles shaped the strategy that allowed Athens and its allies to defeat the Persians at the battle of Salamis in 480: C. thinks of that victory in calling Themistocles the 'saviour of his fatherland'. Ostracized near the end of the following decade and—after a series of intrigues—condemned to death *in absentia* by the Athenians, Themistocles entered the service of the Persian king Artaxerxes; acc. to the tradition known to C. (cf. Thuc. 1. 138, Nep. *Them.* 10. 4, Plut. *Them.* 31. 5), he died by suicide (cited at *Scaur.* 3 as the exception proving the rule that Greeks, being better at words than at deeds, do not courageously destroy themselves as often as Romans). As the precedent of Miltiades' fall (next n.) is here said not to have deterred Themistocles, so at *Tusc.* 4. 44 the precedent of Miltiades' glory is said to have spurred him on.

Miltiades   Born to a dominant aristocratic family of Athens (Davies 1971, 293–312) and active as statesman and general in the second half of the 6th cent. and first decade of the 5th cent., Miltiades was credited with the plan to meet the Persians at Marathon in 490. The 'catastrophe' C. refers to resulted from a trial, not ostracism, when Miltiades followed up the victory at Marathon with a failed expedition against Paros: acc. to tradition (not known to Herodotus), he died in prison from wounds suffered at Paros before he could pay the fine levied in his conviction (Nep. *Milt.* 7. 6, *Cim.* 1, Plut. *Cim.* 4. 7, cf. *Rep.* 1. 5).

Aristides   Contemporary and rival of Themistocles (Davies 1971, 48–53): acc. to the schematic and prob. anachronistic view common in the sources, Aristides' famously 'righteous' or 'just' character provided an 'aristocratic' counterweight to Themistocles' cunning and 'democratic' leanings. He was ostracized in 483/82, prob. as a result of his rivalry with Themistocles (for a balanced account, Rhodes 1981, 280–1, on Arist. *Ath. Pol.* 22.7). At *Tusc.* 5. 105 ('Was not Aristides . . . driven from his fatherland just because he was extraordinarily just?') C. echoes the tradition that some voted maliciously to ostracize him just because they found his reputation for justice annoying or overbearing (Nep. *Arist.* 1. 3–4, Plut. *Arist.* 7. 5–6).

whom there is no need to name   C. must allude at least to Pericles, who figures with Themistocles and Miltiades in the passages from Pl. *Gorg.* cited above (**all who did** n.): he speaks of Pericles' pitting himself against the Athenians' wishes (*voluntas*), if not their anger, at *De or.* 3. 138. C. was prob. aware that Demosthenes too had withdrawn into exile (cf. Plut. *Comp. Dem. et Cic.* 4, App. *BCiv.* 2. 15), though none of his references to Demosthenes mentions that fact.

people's irresponsible wrath   Lit. 'the people's wrath (*iracundia*) and irresponsibility (*levitas*)': like the people's favour (101 **fear of peril's tempest** n., on 'honour's breeze'), the people's wrath is fickle, a transient symptom of the abiding bad judgement inherent in *levitas*; for C.'s critique of *popularis levitas*, Wirszubski (1961, 19 n. 49) compares *Cat.* 4. 9, *Phil.* 5. 59, 7. 4, *Att.* 2. 1(32). 6, sim. *Amic.* 95, *Brut.* 103.

so glorious a place to stand . . . appear trivial by comparison   Contrast the different 'place to stand', and different view, granted the younger Africanus in the *Dream of Scipio*, written four years later when C. himself had effectively withdrawn from the pursuits praised here: looking down on the earth from a vantage point among the stars, Scipio is made to say, 'Earth itself now seemed so small to me that I was pained by the shortcomings of our dominion, which touches only a little speck of it' (*Rep.* 6. 16).

<more desirable>   I translate's Maslowski's text, which adopts Schuetz's *optabilius* in place of the MSS' nonsense (one or another form of *ñ aliud*): the comparative degree of virtually any adjective denoting a preference would be acceptable.

142. Hannibal . . . celebrated, even though an enemy, in our literature and traditions   Hannibal's flight in 195, which brought him to Antiochus the Great's court (58 n.), was caused by the Carthaginian elite's in-fighting and intrigue, not his fellow-citizens' ingratitude and injustice, as C. implies here (sim. Nep. *Hann.* 1. 2). Hannibal, who had a place in Roman 'literature and tradition' from an early date (Books 7–9 of Ennius' *Annals* treated the Second Punic War), was usually represented as the incarnation of treachery, cruelty, and greed. Yet the Romans did not stint in recognizing his capacities as a general, perhaps aware that in granting these capacities they magnified their victory; in that regard it could be said that he was 'celebrated' in Roman tradition in something other than the merely neutral sense of 'named frequently' and hence 'made well-known' (cf. *OLD* s.v. *celebro* 7). In his own writings, when not citing Hannibal's hateful qualities (e.g. *Amic.* 28, *Off.* 1. 38), C. generally uses his name as a byword for 'great enemy general' (e.g. *Prov. cons.* 4, *Phil.* 5. 25,

13. 25, *De or.* 1. 211, *Att.* 7. 11(134). 1); Nepos, writing not quite a generation later, begins his life of Hannibal by stating that he 'was as superior to all other generals in *practical intelligence (*prudentia*)* as the Roman people are to all nations in bravery' (1. 1). The elder Pliny remarked that three statues of Hannibal could be seen within the city walls (*NH* 34. 32).

143. Accordingly In his lesson's climactic paragraph, C. invokes an honour roll of Roman patriots (next n.), formulates the principles they embodied in six hortatory clauses ('Let us....'), and holds out to those who act on these principles the reward—immortal glory— promised by the contractualist premises of Roman Republicanism, implicit since the speech's first paragraph (1 **If anyone** n.) and repeated at key points in the interval (cf. 47 **eternal glory** n., 93–6 n.).

exemplars C. offers an unusually full catalogue of Roman heroes, using the plural form of each name in the manner of such catalogues (lit. 'Brutuses, Camilluses, Ahalas...', cf. e.g. *Cael.* 39, *Balb.* 40, *Pis.* 58): in two cases these can be regarded as true plurals—the Decii, father and son, have already been mentioned in the speech (46 n.), and plural 'Scipiones' could not help but bring to mind at least the elder and the younger Africanus, conquerors of Carthage—but the plurals mostly serve as generic labels—'*men like* Brutus, etc.'—and imply that the man named in each case is the best known among many other Romans who have embodied the same virtues. Beyond the Decii and Scipios, the great historical personages and the acts with which they were most prominently associated include: Lucius Iunius (*RE* 46a, Suppl 5) Brutus, credited with expelling the last of Rome's kings and establishing the Republic (*MRR* 1. 1–2); Marcus Furius (*RE* 44) Camillus, regarded as Rome's 'second founder' for reclaiming the city after it was sacked by the Gauls in 390 (*MRR* 1. 95); Gaius Servilius (*RE* 32) Ahala, who in 439 killed Spurius Maelius when he was suspected of aiming at tyranny (*MRR* 1. 56); Manius Curius (*RE* 9) Dentatus—three times cons., cens. 272, and conqueror of Pyrrhus—and Gaius Fabricius (*RE* 9) Luscinus, cos. 278 and cens. 275, contemporaries and *new men who were paragons of old-fashioned austerity and integrity; and Quintus Fabius (*RE* 116) Maximus Verrucosus, five times consul and cens. 230, whose strategy of evasion and attrition wore Hannibal down and earned him the name Cunctator ('the Delayer'). To the traditional roll-call of great patriots C. adds 'men like Lentulus and Aemilius', to honour his benefactor, the consul of 58, and the presiding praetor, whose father he has named in honorific terms (39 n.); for the ploy cf. *Balb.* 40 'men like the Scipios, Brutus, Horatius, Cassius, Metellus, and this man here before us, Gnaeus Pompeius.'

whom I at any rate set among the company of the immortal gods The tradition that Romulus had been taken up among the gods at his death prob. went back to the 3rd cent. and was certainly known to C. and his contemporaries (*Rep.* 1. 25. 4, *Tusc.* 1. 28, cf. Livy 1. 16, Jocelyn 1989, Classen 1998, cf. Classen 1993; Romulus' identification with the god Quirinus is first attested at *Rep.* 2. 20. 3, *Leg.* 1. 3, and ascribed to 'some people' at *Nat. D.* 2. 62); so too a similar tradition regarding the earlier 'founder', Aeneas (Livy 1. 2. 6). But belief that great mortals might enjoy actual apotheosis, while familiar from Greek thought (see below on Hercules), was not at this time naturalized at Rome: unlike e.g. the deified emperors of a later date, Romulus was not paid cult. By saying 'I at any rate' (*equidem*) C. acknowledges that his view stands outside the mainstream, and indeed he pulls back from it a bit at the paragraph's end (**let us be equally confident** n.). Yet it is a position he substantially reinstates in *Rep.*, esp. in the *Dream of Scipio* that concludes Book 6: 'But so that you may be all the more eager, Africanus, to protect the commonwealth, know this: for all those who have saved, aided, or increased the fatherland there is a specific place set aside in the sky where they may enjoy eternity in blessedness...' (*Rep.* 6. 13. 1, tr. Zetzel), cf. 1. 12. 4.

let us take thought for the interests of patriots The 'interests' meant are material: C. refers to the political community's core function, maintaining justice and thereby securing private property, see refs. at 91 **only the goods** n. and the objection to Tiberius Gracchus' reforms at 103: 'the commonwealth would be stripped of its defenders if the rich were dislodged from their long-time holdings'.

bodies...are mortal, their minds' movements...are eternal For the strong distinction between ephemeral body (*corpus*) and eternal 'mind' or 'soul' (*animus*) cf. C.'s remarks on suicide at 47 (**since death is a certainty** n.), implicitly contrasting the metaphysical dualism of Plato with the materialism of Epicurus. The value ascribed to eternal glory, however, placed here on the same footing as the mind's movements, owes far more to traditional Roman values than to any philosophical school.

the most sanctified Hercules The ascent of Hercules (Gk. Heracles), mortal son of a human mother (Alcmene) and divine father (Zeus), to the realm of the gods after his death is among the most ancient elements of his legend; ethicizing interpretations known to C. linked the apotheosis to his role as benefactor of humanity, rewarded for performing his famous labors and thereby ridding the world of various scourges (*ND* 2. 62, *Off.* 3. 25, cf. *Fin.* 3. 66). C. invokes Hercules here with extraordinary emphasis, not only in applying to him the epithet 'most sanctified' (*sanctissimus*) but in speaking of a 'belief raised to the status of holy principle', the only place in classical Latin where the verb *consecrare* ('to consecrate') is applied to the noun *opinio*, denoting merely human judgement.

let us be equally confident C. makes a strong claim for the glory enjoyed by patriots before turning to the final appeal for pity (next n.); but by implicitly acknowledging that even the greatest Roman patriots did not achieve the apotheosis of a Hercules, he moderates the position taken at the start of the paragraph (**whom I at any rate** n.).

those who... preserved it For the distinction between those who have augmented the *commonwealth by conquest abroad and those who have preserved it by political action at home, see esp. *Cat.* 4. 21, insisting that the latter category—including C. himself above all—is as worthy of honour as the former; cf. also *Att.* 1. 19(19). 6 (the 'extraordinary and immortal glory' C. achieved by his actions of 5 Dec. 63) and the panegyric of Caesar at *Rab. Post.* 42–3.

144–7. *A Final Appeal for Pity*

By affecting to be brought up short ('my speech is checked...': sim. *Sull.* 92), C. signals the start of the speech's brief final movement, the stirring of pity (*miseratio*), at which he was unequalled: for C.'s

estimate of his own ability see *Or.* 130, and for the handbook
doctrine see *Inv. rhet.* 1. 106–9, Anon. *ad Herenn.* 2. 50, Quint. 6. 1.
21–35, and Lausberg 1998, §439. In accordance with that doctrine,
C. keeps the appeal short, first drawing attention to the grief of S.'s
supporters (144), then taking the burden of their grief upon himself:
because he—that is, his own unmerited suffering, which prompted
S.'s support—is its cause (145), C. pledges that he will share the
catastrophe S. would suffer by being convicted (146). If C. was not
confident of the verdict when vowing to join S. in exile, the tactic
would seem a rather bold move; but see 146 nn.

144. I see his son... with tears in his eyes   The young man has
been mentioned twice in the speech, glancingly in 6 (**this boy here** n.)
and more directly in 10 (**Lucius Sestius** n.), where he is asked to read
the Capuans' decree in his 'boyish voice'. The latter detail accords
with the fact noted here: Lucius still wears the *bordered toga (toga
praetexta)* and has not assumed the plain white toga of manhood
(*toga virilis*) that a father bestowed in a coming-of-age ceremony,
usually when the child was about 15. As the description of young
Lentulus just below confirms, a child not old enough to assume the
toga virilis was also not old enough to take on mourning dress in a
setting such as this. For the defendant's child as a source of pity, cf.
e.g. *Flac.* 106.

Milo   Milo's presence in mourning was noted at the very beginning
of the speech (1 **those who joined** n.); at his own trial in 52 he refused
to appeal for pity (*Mil.* 92, 105) or to don mourning (Plut. *Cic.* 35. 4),
on the ground that in killing Clodius he had only acted in the right.
Maslowski and some other editors read '<T.> Milo' here, introducing by conjecture the pattern (praenomen + cognomen) that
C. generally prefers when referring formally to a member of the
elite who has three names; but Milo was not a member of the elite
where this naming convention was concerned, see 87 **Titus Annius** n.

Publius Lentulus   Publius Cornelius (*RE* 239) Lentulus Spinther,
the son of C.'s champion: in the following clauses ('toga of manhood... bordered toga... toga of mourning...') C. alludes to the
fact that during his father's consulship in 57 young Lentulus had

both been given the plain white *toga virilis* (cf. above) and been elected an augur (*MRR* 2. 207), thus becoming one the few adults to wear the *bordered *toga praetexta.* The augurate, which C. himself longed for but would not receive until 53 (3 **Quintus Hortensius** n.), had required the young man's adoption by one of the Manlii Torquati (Cass. Dio 39. 17. 1), because only one member of a Roman *gens* could be an augur at any given time, and Sulla's son, Faustus Cornelius Sulla, already 'represented' the *gens Cornelia*: not unlike Clodius' transfer to the plebs, the procedure violated the spirit of the law, if not its letter; C. continues to refer to the young man by his birth-name. Though young Lentulus attended the trial as a representative of his father, who was in Cilicia, his mourning dress had less to do with S.'s circumstances than with his father's (next n.).

a most unjust proposal   In early Feb. the tribune Gaius Porcius Cato *promulgated a bill to deprive the elder Lentulus of his *proconsular province, Cilicia (*MRR* 2. 209), and his son put on mourning (*QFr.* 2. 3(7). 1, *Fam.* 1. 5a(15). 2). A few weeks after this speech C. will report that the consul Lentulus Marcellinus succeeded in using procedural manoeuvring to keep 'pernicious' legislation, including Cato's bill, from coming to a vote (*QFr.* 2. 5(9). 3).

145. What … crime?   Referring to the actions of Dec. 63, see at 38. This and the following sentence are repeated in the peroration of *Mil.* (103), where again (but in vain) C. identifies his client with himself and defines himself by his triumph over the Catilinarians; for sim. twin identification cf. *Flac.* 4–5.

your instructions   Referring to the judges of senatorial rank, and to the 'senate's ultimate decree' instructing the consuls to see that the *commonwealth suffer no harm (25 **all citizens** n.).

I have paid enough of a penalty   With the following list of outrages cf. esp. 54.

my affairs have been scattered, my children have been harassed   Acc. to the MSS, C. says 'my affairs have been thrown into a turmoil, my children have been scattered' (*fortunae vexatae, dissipati liberi*). But since C.'s children are elsewhere said to have been harshly treated or threatened (54, *Dom.* 59), but not separated, Shackleton Bailey (1985, 149) suggested that the participles were reversed in transmission, and that C. wrote *fortunae dissipatae, vexati liberi,* the version adopted here (cf. *Att.* 4. 1(73). 3 *re...familiari...dissipata,* referring to the same financial distress, and *Fam.* 4. 13(225). 2 *fortunas dissipari,* referring to the sim. distress of others).

146. revisit that same misfortune...those who defended me and saved me   Cf. the slightly different tack at *Mil.* 103 'Do not, I beseech you, allow my return to distress me more than my very departure! For how can I reckon myself restored, if I am torn from the embrace of those who restored me?'; with the last clause, cf. 'no misfortune will ever tear me from...' below.

Could I live in this city...have been driven from it   Milo's conviction will show that the literal answer to this question is 'yes'. On that occasion C.'s identification with his client, at least as expressed in the extant version of his speech, will take a different form: *Mil.* 99 'Judges, you will never cause me such burning pain—though what pain could be as great (sc. as your vote to convict Milo)?—...that I would forget how highly you have always valued me.'

this child here   Lucius Sestius, see 144.

foreign nations...thanked on my account   See 116 **honour had been paid** n. and 128.

147. whose own sacred precincts received me on my arrival   This should include at least the shrines of Jupiter, Juno, and Minerva on the Capitoline, cf. 131 **climbed to the Capitol** n.

I call the gods to witness   For the oath, cf. 45 **I call you to witness** n.

if you desired my restoration   As C. began with a condition (1 **If anyone** n.), so he closes with a condition, a pattern found only at *Cael.* and (after a fashion) *Prov. cons.* among the extant speeches.

CICERONIAN CHRONOLOGY,
58–56 BCE

This appendix has two aims: to present in summary form and chronological order the chief events in C.'s career from the time just before his exile (starting 1 Jan. 58) until the delivery of *Prov. cons.* (July 56) testified to his political capitulation; and to gather in one place the often interconnected arguments on chronological questions, instead of scattering them through the commentary.[1]

The table below is based on two important chronological premises, beyond the relatively small number of dates that we can claim to know absolutely:

(a) On the 'promulgation of three *nundinae*' (*promulgatio trinum nundinum*, the latter two words being genitive plural), entailing an interval between a law's promulgation and a vote: I take it that the regulation chiefly aimed, not to prescribe a fixed minimum number of days (17: Kubitschek 1928, 134, Brind'Amour 1983, 87–96; or 24: Mommsen 1887–8, 3. 376 n. 1, Grimal 1967, 20), but to insure that a given proposal would receive maximum exposure by being publicized on at least three successive market days, *nundinae* (Lintott 1965 and 1968). On this view, the minimum interval between promulgation and vote ranged from 17 to 24 days.[2]

(b) Because the Roman civil calendar comprised 355 days before Caesar's reforms in 46, it inevitably fell out of alignment with the solar calendar. Under the Republic the Romans addressed this misalignment by periodically

---

[1] The survey of 58 and 57 (through C.'s return to Rome) in Grimal 1967 is problematic or mistaken in too many premises or conclusions to be reliable; esp. unfortunate is its insistence on a fixed minimum of 24 days for the promulgation of laws, the least likely of the three main alternatives (see following in text). The tabulation for 58–56 in Marinone 2004, 104–25, is more reliable and offers extensive bibliography, though generally not extensive argument.

[2] Since the *nundinae* occurred every 8 days (on modern reckoning), the interval would be at least 17 days if promulgation occurred on a nundinal day, at least 24 if promulgation occurred on the day after a nundinal day. In either case, the nominal 'minimum' must often have been exceeded, because the vote could not be held before the first comitial day after the third *nundinae* (see e.g. n. 8 in the table below); of course this is also true if one believes in a fixed minimal interval of 17 or 24 days.

inserting an 'intercalary month' of 27 days after 23 or 24 Feb. Our knowledge of two dates makes it very likely that either 58 or 57 included an intercalary month: 18 Oct. 59, the date to which Bibulus by edict postponed the consular elections in that year (*Att.* 2. 20(40). 6: *comitia Bibulus... in a. d. XV Kal. Nov. distulit*); and 21 Nov. 57, which was nundinal (*Att.* 4. 3(75). 4: *a. d. X Kal.* (viz., *Dec.*) *nundinae*). The latter date necessarily implies that—absent intercalation in 58 or 57—18 Oct. 59 was also nundinal, in which case no elections could have been scheduled, because elective assemblies could not meet on *nundinae.*[3] If, however, either 58 or 57 was intercalary, 18 Oct. 59 was not nundinal, and elections faced no obstacle; Brind'Amour 1983, 49–51, adduces considerations that cumulatively point away from 57 and toward 58 (Grimal 1967, 12–13, similarly posits an intercalary month in 58, after the astronomer Le Verrier). In an intercalary year, the extra month of 27 days was inserted after either 23 Feb. or 24 Feb. to produce a net increase of 22 or 23 days in the year (on the procedure, Michels 1967, 160–1).[4] There is some slight reason to think an increase of 23 days more likely (cf. Lintott 1968, 192), and that option is reflected in the calendar for 58 at the end of this appendix.

It follows that some significant activity leading to C.'s withdrawal from Rome in March 58 must have fallen in the intercalary month (not Feb.). In general, however, the presence or absence of the intercalary month does not profoundly alter our understanding of the relevant chronology: the reckoning of *nundinae* is affected only before March 58, and many events can be dated only relatively in any case.

In the table below an en-dash (−) between two dates signifies inclusiveness ('Feb.–April' = 'February through April'); a virgule signifies indeterminacy ('Feb./April' = 'sometime in February, March, or April'). For economy's sake, I cite in the column marked 'evidence' not all texts attesting a given event but only those that contribute most directly to establishing its date.

[3] Lintott 1968, 192. Absent intercalation, the period 19 Oct. 59 through 21 Nov. 57 = 744 days, or exactly 93 nundinal intervals (744 ÷ 8 = 93): 18 Oct. 59 would therefore have been nundinal. I assume that in so deliberate an act Bibulus would not have made the gross error of scheduling elections for a non-comitial day.

[4] With 355 days in the standard pre-Julian year, and 28 days in Feb., insertion of an intercalary month after 23 Feb.—effectively shortening that month by 5 days—produced a year of 377 days (= 355 + 27 − 5); inserting the intercalary month after 24 Feb. produced a year of 378 days (= 355 + 27 − 4).

Date	Event	
58 BCE		
4 Jan.	Clodius passes laws on grain dole, censorship, *collegia*, and auspices.	*Pis.* 8–9[1]
Jan./Mar.	Two praetors attack Caesar's legislation of 59.	Suet. *Iul.* 23. 1[2]
Feb./Mar.	Clodius promulgates and passes laws on annexation of Cyprus and restoration of exiled citizens of Byzantium.	*Sest.* 56–7[3]
20/27 Interkal.	Clodius promulgates laws *de capite civis* and on consular provinces.	*Sest.* 25–6[4]
soon after	Demonstrations and assumption of mourning by people, rebuffed by Gabinius; C. and his son-in-law call upon Piso; the senate assumes mourning and is rebuked by consular edict; Clodius holds a *contio* in the Circus Flaminius at which the consuls and Caesar appear.	*Red. sen.* 12–13, *Sest.* 25–7, 32–3, *Pis.* 11–14[5]

(*Cont.*)

[1] 'When the Compitalia had coincided with 1 Jan., you allowed Sex. Cloelius to produce the games (= *ludi Compitales*)…Accordingly, when these foundations had been laid for your consulship, three days later you looked on silently (as Clodius passed his laws)' ('cum in Kalendas Ianuarias compitaliorum dies incidisset, Sex. Cloelium…ludos facere…passus es. Ergo his fundamentis positis consulatus tui, triduo post, inspectante et tacente te…'). With most scholars I take it that when C. speaks of 'these foundations' he means to refer loosely to 'the events on and around 1 Jan., with 1 Jan., the day Piso entered the consulship, serving as the main benchmark: the third day after would be 4 Jan., a comital day. Taking C. to be speaking more precisely, Michels 1967, 205, argued that that interval should be measured not from the Kalends but from the celebration of the *ludi*, which extended for 1 or more days *after* the Compitalia; and since 5–6 Jan. were not comital, 7 Jan. would be the day on which the legislation was passed. In either case, the laws would have been promulgated between 10 Dec. and 15 Dec. Nr. 59: Clodius entered office on the 10th, and (with intercalation of 23 days in 58) the *nundinae* fell on 15, 22, and 29 Dec.; 4 Jan. would then have been the first comital day after the third *nundinae* following promulgation. On the laws: 33 **while the same consuls sat, 55 laws were voted nn.**

[2] On these attacks by Lucius Ahenobarbus and Gaius Memmius see 40 **all they accomplished** n.; Suetonius places at least some of the attacks before Caesar's departure for Gaul, but they cannot be dated more closely.

[3] On the substance of these two laws and other sources for them, see nn. at *Sest.* 56–7; C.'s account in *Sest.* creates the impression that they were passed after his departure, but that is an incidental artifact of his strategy in the speech, see the headnote to 53–66. A probable *term. post quem* is provided by their absence from *Pis.* 8–11, C.'s most careful account of the 'crimes' that Clodius committed in Jan. 58 with the consuls' support; a *term. ante quem* is provided by the separate bill (thus *Sest.* 62) mandating both tasks to Cato, prob. not promulgated before the latter part of March, see n. 10 below.

[4] C. stresses that the two laws were promulgated (*Sest.* 25) and passed (*Sest.* 54) simultaneously. If the laws were passed in the third week of March (n. 7 below), they were promulgated in the period 20–7 Interkal.: Clodius is unlikely to have waited longer than the minimum prescribed by the *promulgatio trinum nundinum*, and the third *nundinae* before their passage was 27 Interkal.

[5] On the demonstrations, assumption of mourning, consular edict, and *contio*, see the nn. in *Sest.* 25–7, 32–3; the sequence of these events given here is that found in *Red. sen.* and *Sest.* (so also Cass. Dio 38. 16. 2–17. 3), where they are presented as immediately following the promulgation of the law *de capite civis*. C.'s visit to Piso, mentioned only at *Pis.* 12–13, should be tied closely to the initial demonstrations: those demonstrations were

Date	Event	Evidence
1st half Mar.(?).	Pompey fails to aid C.	Cass. Dio 38. 17. 3[6]
18–19(?) Mar.	Laws passed *de capite civis* and on consular provinces; C. leaves Rome.	*Sest.* 53–47
c.20 Mar.	Clodius promulgates law declaring that C. had been exiled, by name.	*Sest.* 65[8]

rebuffed by Gabinius while Piso 'was keeping to his house' (*Sest.* 26), and C. and his son-in-law called on Piso at his house, where they found him wearing his slippers (*Pis.* 13), i.e., dressed as one 'keeping to his house'. In any case, all these events evidently followed in quick succession, for C. says that Piso appeared at Clodius' *contio* in the Circus Flaminius 'about two days' after C. called upon him (*Pis.* 14). Note that *Pis.* 17–18 appears to place the consuls' edict directing the senators to put off mourning dress *after the contio* (*Pis.* 14); given the testimony of *Red. sen.* and *Sest.*, we should infer that in *Pis.* C. momentarily let loose the chronological thread as he launched into an extended denunciation of Piso as a neo-Catilinarian (*Pis.* 15–16).

[6] Describing Pompey's disingenuous failure to help C. in very general terms ('offering various excuses and arranging frequent absences from the city . . .'), Cassius Dio 38. 17. 3 places it after the *contio* in the Circus Flaminius: more circumstantial versions of the episode—which depict Pompey as equivocating with a delegation of senior senators (*Pis.* 77) and refusing to heed C.'s son-in-law or even meet with C. himself while ensconced in his retreat in the Alban Hills near Tusculum (Plut. *Cic.* 31. 2)—do suggest a context close to the vote on Clodius' law, when C. and his supporters were more desperate; cf. *QFr.* 1. 4(4). 4 (Aug. 58), where C. counts Pompey's 'sudden defection' among the factors that conspired to throw him into confusion and despair at this stage, and *Att.* 10. 4(195). 3 (April 49), referring to a time when C. threw himself at Pompey's feet, only to be rebuffed (Pompey would not even ask him to rise) with the claim that he could do nothing against Caesar's wishes, a scene that can belong only to this period. This same context should be associated with the story C. tells several times, with minor variations, alleging that Pompey avoided C. because had been warned of a plot against his life: 41 **the same suspicion** n. and esp. *Dom.* 28.

[7] The sparse data allow no certainty but most probably point, as Shackleton Bailey argued (*CLA* 2:227, reviewing earlier discussion), to the third week of March: C. 'tore himself away' from Rome on 'the very day' the law *de capite civis* passed (*Sest.* 53); Caesar waited to leave for Gaul until the law was passed (Plut. *Caes.* 14. 9) but then forced his journey to reach the Rhône in 8 days (reckoned inclusively: ibid. 17. 4), in order to arrive before 28 March, the date the Helvetii had appointed to assemble at the river (Caes. *BG.* 1. 6. 4–7. 3). 18, 20, and 21 March were comitial days: if the measures passed on the 18th, Caesar could have reached the Rhône with several days' margin, and Cicero could have dedicated his image of Minerva on the Capitoline (Plut. *Cic.* 31. 5, Cass. Dio 38. 17. 5, cf. *Leg.* 2. 42, *Fam.* 3. 1(64). 1, 12. 25(373). 1 (Plancus)) on the eve of the goddess's festal day (19 March), before being escorted from the city by his friends around midnight (Plut. *Cic.* 31. 5).

[8] Absent this law, C. would have been free to return to Rome whenever he chose: Clodius must have taken care to promulgate it almost immediately after C. left; indeed, C.'s first letter to Atticus on the way into exile, written when he can have been no great time or distance from the city, shows that the had seen a copy of the bill (*Att.* 3. 1(46): tentatively dated to 22 March by Shackleton Bailey, on the present chronology it could be dated a day or two earlier). Since the bill was certainly promulgated by 24 March (*nundinae*), the *promulgatio trinum nundinum* would have been achieved by 9 April; but it happens that after 4 April the earliest comitial day is the 24th, the probable date of passage. See next n.; the law is similarly dated by Rotondi 1912, 395.

Date	Event	Source
24/26(?) Mar.	Clodius revises the law declaring that C. had been exiled.	*Att.* 3. 2, 4(48–9)[9]
late Mar./late Apr.	Clodius promulgates and passes laws changing Gabinius' province from Cilicia to Syria and mandating to Cato the annexation of Cyprus and restoration of the Byzantine exiles.	*Sest.* 53–5, 60, 62[10]
not before 24 Apr.	Law declaring that C. had been exiled passed.	*Sest.* 65[11]
17–29 Apr.	C. stays in Brundisium before departing for Greece.	*Att.* 3. 7(52)
late Apr.	Quintus leaves Asia, to return to an expected prosecution in Rome.	*Att.* 3. 9(54). 1
by mid-May	Clodius passes law on the priesthood of the Great Mother and arranges escape of the younger Tigranes, provoking Pompey to oppose him.	*Dom.* 66, *Att.* 3. 8(53). 3[12]

(Cont.)

[9] After promulgating his bill Clodius made a revision chiefly affecting the distance from Italy C. was required to live (65 **proposal** n., App. 3): writing from Nares Lucanae, about 300 km from Rome on the border between Campania and Lucania, C. knew that a *correctio* was expected but had not yet (so far as he was aware) been made (*Att.* 3. 2(48)): by the time he wrote from Vibo (or *en route* to Thurii from Vibo) in Bruttium, about 300 km. farther south, he had received a copy of the revised bill (*Att.* 3. 4(49)). In his discussion of C.'s movements on his way out of Italy (*Att.* 2. 228–32), Shackleton Bailey dates the two letters, respectively, to 27 March (reading *VI K(al). Apr.* for *VI Id. Apr.*, the latter an impossibly late date) and 3 April (a plausible estimate). If this is more or less correct (it is preferable to the discussion of Grimal 1967, 68 ff.), then revision of the law should be put sometime in the period 24–6 March: any earlier, and a courier travelling ±75 km / day (about average) would have been able to reach C. at Nares Lucanae by the 27th; any later, and the same courier would have been hard pressed to reach him at or near Vibo by the 3rd. C.'s reference to a 'revised proposal' (*rogatio correcta: Att.* 3. 2(48)) evidently implies that the proposal could be revised without having to be promulgated anew (presumably with a copy of the revised *rogatio* deposited in the treasury to satisfy the *lex Licinia Iunia*, 135 n.); but even were the bill promulgated again in its revised form after 24 March, three *nundinae* (1, 9, 17 April) would have intervened before the first available comitial day, 24 April (see preceding n.).

[10] Promulgation of the law changing Gabinius' assignment presumes passage of the first law establishing that assignment, thus after 18 March on the present chronology. The change itself was most probably conditioned by Clodius' decision to entrust the annexation of Cyprus to Cato, a task that would otherwise have fallen to Gabinius as governor of Cilicia, to which Cyprus was to be tied administratively (53 **assignment of provinces** n., and Badian 1965, 115–17): the bill for Cato's mandate would thus have been promulgated after 18 March also. Note further that *Sest.* 60 shows Cato still at Rome and verbally 'brawling' with the consuls after C.'s departure (60 n., cf. also 63 **could he calmly remain** n.): the 'brawl' most likely occurred between the bill's promulgation and its passage, when (acc. to C.) Cato 'had given up hope that his personal authority could have any effect' in blocking it. Similarly, Caesar's letter congratulating Clodius on his clever stroke was prob. read out by Clodius in a *contio* (*Dom.* 22, cf. 60 **torn** n.) after the bill's promulgation: since Caesar was already in Gaul, his letter could hardly have been received before April (cf. n. 7). Any bill promulgated after 16 March could not be voted on before 24 April (see n. 8 above); given sailing conditions in the Mediterranean, a date in spring for Cato's departure is in any case more likely than one substantially earlier.

[11] See nn. 8, 9 above.

[12] For Clodius' attacks on Pompey's interests, prob. encouraged by the *optimates*, see 56 **Great Mother** (the priesthood of the Great Mother at Pessinus), 58 **Gnaeus Pompeius** (the escape of the younger Tigranes). At least in the case of Tigranes, Clodius waited until C. was gone into exile and

Date	Event	Evidence
23 May	C. reaches Thessalonica, where he remains until mid-Nov.	*Att.* 3. 8(53)
1 June	Senate passes decree in C.'s interest, vetoed by Aelius Ligus, tr. pl.	*Sest.* 68
June	Gabinius' fasces shattered by Clodius' thugs.	*Dom.* 66, *Pis.* 28[13]
June	Quintus reaches Rome.	*Sest.* 68, *QFr.* 1. 3(3)[14]
14 or 18(?) Jul.	Lentulus and Metellus Nepos elected consuls for 57.	*QFr.* 1. 4(4). 5[15]
late Jul.	Favorable debate on C.'s interests in the senate; Clodius posts in the senate doorway the clause in his law forbidding discussion of C.'s recall.	*Att.* 3. 15(60). 3, 6
before 11 Aug.	Clodius begins publicly to attack Caesar's consular legislation.	*Har. resp.* 11[16]
11 Aug.	An assassination attempt on Pompey is discovered; Pompey withdraws from public activity in Rome for rest of 58.	Ascon. 46. 17–47. 9 Cl.[17]
11 Aug./Oct.	Pompey, at Capua, attacks Clodius' law on C.'s exile.	*Red. sen.* 29[18]

Cato to Cyprus (*Dom.* 66), the latter event most likely dating to late April (n. 10 above). By mid-May (the date inferred from C.'s response of 29 May, *Att.* 3. 8(53). 3) Atticus was able to report a conversation with Pompey that gave the first intimations of the change in his position.

[13] Gabinius broke with Clodius after Pompey did (*Dom.* 66, and cf. 69 **the consuls** n.); since his *fasces* could be smashed only when he held them, in an even-numbered month, and since April would be too early, they must have been smashed in June.

[14] Quintus had left Asia in late April (above) and traveled to Rome without making a detour to see his brother (*QFr.* 1. 3(3). 4); in C.'s narrative in *Sest.* 68 Quintus' return is treated almost immediately after the senate's decree of 1 June, and when writing *QFr.* 1. 3(3) from Thessalonica on 13 June C. plainly expected it would find his brother in Rome.

[15] When not delayed, elections in the centuriate assembly were held in or just after mid-July, and this year they were evidently held on schedule: C. could write to Atticus on 5 August 'the elections have been held' (*comitia habita sunt*: *Att.* 3. 13(59). 1) and remark to his brother, prob. about the same time, that Lentulus had been elected (1. 4(4). 5); when on 17 July he wrote that 'my enemy will be consul-designate' (*Att.* 3. 12(57). 1), he was anticipating Nepos' election, not reporting it. 14 and 18 July were both comitial, and would allow enough time for the news to reach C. in Thessalonica by 5 Aug. (the 16th, usually also comitial, was in 58 nundinal).

[16] Grimal 1967, 114–16, correctly takes the passage to establish a *term. ante quem*; cf. Tatum 1999, 173–4.

[17] Ascon. 46. 17–47. 9 Cl. gives the date; on the other sources for the episode, 69 a plan was formed n. A freedman of Clodius besieged Pompey's house later in the month (Ascon. 46. 26–47. 9 Cl.).

[18] *Red. sen.* 29 synchronizes Pompey's speech with the withdrawal just noted and with his encouragement of the measure the tribunes promulgated on 29 Oct.

Date	Event	Evidence
by mid–late Sept.	Anticipating his entry into the tribunate on 10 Dec., Sestius drafts a bill for C.'s recall; C. finds it wanting.	*Att.* 3. 20(65). 3[19]
by 25 Oct.	Metellus Nepos tells Atticus he will not object to C.'s recall.	*Att.* 2. 23(68).1
29 Oct.	All the tribunes of 58 save Clodius and Aelius Ligus promulgate a bill for C.'s recall.	*Att.* 3. 23(68.1)[20]
Nov.	Sestius travels to intercede with Caesar in Cisalpine Gaul.	*Sest.* 71[21]
mid-Nov.	Anticipating Piso's arrival in Macedonia (cf. *Sest.* 71), C. moves from Thessalonica to Dyrrachium.	*Att.* 3. 22(67), *Fam.* 14. 1(8)
10/29 Dec.	Tribunes of 57 promulgate a measure for C.'s recall.	*Sest.* 72[22]
Dec. 58/May 57	C.'s son-in-law, Gaius Piso, dies.	*Fam.* 14. 3(9). 3, *Sest.* 68[23]
57 BCE		
1 Jan.	Senate meets, Catulus and Pompey speak in support of C.	*Sest.* 73–4
23 Jan.	Assembly held to vote on the tribunes' measure disrupted by violence.	*Sest.* 75
Feb.–Mar.	General suspension of public business (*iustitium*); Sestius attacked while 'obnuntiating' to block an assembly convened by Metellus Nepos; Milo's house attacked, his attempt to prosecute Clodius blocked by Nepos and others.	*Sest.* 79, 85, 89[24]

(*Cont.*)

[19] The letter criticizing the draft (cf. **72 tribunes** n.) is dated 5 Oct.; with allowance made for the time of transit from Rome to Thessalonica, Sestius cannot have drafted the bill later than the middle third of Sept.

[20] The letter to Atticus gives the date; for C.'s critique, 69 **promulgated a bill** n. It did not come to a vote.

[21] C. reports the incident after promulgation of the tribunes' bill, 29 Oct., before S. entered office on 10 Dec.; by Nov. the army would be in winter quarters (*BG* 1. 54. 2–3) and Caesar would be reachable in Cisalpine Gaul.

[22] C.'s narrative in *Sest.* 72–3 shows that the measure was promulgated after the tribunes entered office on 10 Dec. and before the senate's meeting of 1 Jan. (against the view that it was promulgated after the senate's meeting, see **73 unanimous support** n.). Given that it was brought to a vote on 23 Jan. (preceded by *nundinae* on 6, 14, and 22 Jan.), we might suspect that it was promulgated on 28 or 29 Dec., just before the senate's meeting; had it been promulgated on or before 27 Dec. (another *nundinae*) it could have been brought to a vote any time in the period 16–21 Jan., all the days then being comitial.

[23] The letter to Terentia, dated 29 Nov. 58, shows that Piso was (so far as C. knew) still alive, but he died before C.'s return (*Sest.* 68). Since Tullia was betrothed to Furius Crassipes on 4 April 56 (below), and since widows were expected to wait at least 10 months before contracting a new marriage (Treggiari 1991, 493), Piso is unlikely to have died later than May 57.

[24] On the context—a *iustitium* after the riot of 23 Jan., implied by C.'s account at *Red. sen.* 6–8 but suppressed in *Sest.*—see 71–92 n. *Red. sen.* 6 shows that the suspension affected the public business of at least Feb. (the senate's reception of foreign embassies); the manoeuvering implied by

Date	Event	Evidence
mid-May/mid-June	Senate passes first decree in support of C.'s recall.	Sest. 116, 128[25]

these events is unlikely to have lasted beyond March, given senators' habit of leaving Rome for their country houses after the *ludi Megalenses* at the start of April. On the symmetry between Sestius' action and the frustration of Milo, see 89 **one consul** n.

[25] The meeting at which the senate passed this decree, held in the temple of Honos and Virtus, coincided with theatrical games (exploited rhetorically by C. in *Sest.* 117–18. 120–3). Grimal 1967, 127–8, identified the games as the *ludi Florales* of 1–3 May, because those were *ludi scaenici* held at a time when C.'s ally Lentulus held the fasces (accepted by e.g. Cousin 1965, 206 n. 2, Seager 1969, 310, Vanderbroeck 1987, 246, Bonnefond-Coudry 1989, 46 n. 7, Tatum 1999, 181); but the *ludi Florales* were aedilician games (C. had given them in 69), whereas the *ludi* that coincided with this meeting were given by a consul (viz., Lentulus: *Sest.* 117); Bernstein 1998, 60, tried to salvage Grimal's dating by supposing Lentulus presided as consul at games given by an aedile, but C. clearly states that the consul himself was giving the games, *ipse qui ludos faciebat consul adsedit*, using the phrase (*ludos facere*) that regularly denotes the act of giving—i.e. paying for—games, whether as part of the regular festal calendar—e.g. *Verr.* 2. 5. 36, *Har. resp. 26, Phil.* 10. 7, *Brut.* 78—or as extraordinary games, e.g. *Fam.* 11. 28(349). 6. The *ludi Apollinares* (6–13 July), given by the praetor Caecilius Rufus, are ruled out for the same reason (*pace* Gardner 1958a, 194 n., and by implication Wiseman 1994b, 388); they would also produce much too late a date in any case (see below). These, then, were extraordinary games (cf. Mommsen 1887–8, 2³. 137 n. 4, *RE* 5.2 (1905), 1969 (E. Pollack), Shackleton Bailey 1991a, 191 n. 133). That status is consistent *prima facie* with the scholiast's claim that they were '*ludi* of Honos and Virtus, which were being celebrated to honor the memory of Gaius Marius . . .' (*Schol. Bob.* 136. 4–7 St, followed by Mitchell 1991, 154–5, who places them in May). But the scholiast is generally confused in this section of the speech (as 136. 23–7 St. shows, he failed to grasp that 116–18 and 120–3 all deal with the same occasion): his confusion might prompt suspicion that his identification is only a specious guess based on the context, and the suspicion tends to be confirmed by the fact that the festal day of Honos was 17 July; a comitial day when the senate would not have met, and in any case far too late for the preliminary decrees at issue (the law for the C.'s recall must already have been promulgated by 17 July: next n.). We are left to posit a date prob. between mid-May and mid-June: this would allow enough time before the mass gatherings of July (129 **Why bring to mind** n., cf. next n.) for the necessary planning and travel of those minded to attend, yet be sufficiently close to the date for the summons to be fresh; and it would be consistent with C.'s statement that the senate passed the relevant decree 'long before' (*Dom.* 85 *multo ante*) the law for his recall was voted on 4 Aug. Between the Ides and end of May there were five non-comitial days when the senate might have met, the 16th and 21st–24th: Stein 1930, 32 n. 179, favoured a date in the latter interval, not unreasonable in itself, though the evidence he cites gives no support (*CIL* 1² (pars prior) p. 319 = *Inscr. Ital.* 13. 2, pp. 247, 462: the 4th cent. CE calendar of Filocalus identifies 29 May as the festal day of Honos and Virtus, but that dating is valid only from the reign of Augustus); between the Kalends and Ides of June only two days (3–4) were comitial and so unavailable for meetings. Lentulus did not have the fasces in June, but he did not need them either to convene the senate or give extraordinary games.

Date	Event	Evidence
8–9(?) Jul.	Senate decrees support for law recalling C., further support expressed in a *contio* and a second meeting of senate.	*Red. Sen.* 25–7, *Dom.* 14–15, 27, *Sest.* 107, 125, 129[26]
4 Aug.	Law for C.'s restoration voted in *comitia centuriata*.	*Att.* 4. 1(73). 4
5 Aug.	C. lands at Brundisium.	*Att.* 4. 1(73). 4, *Sest.* 131
4 Sept.	C. re-enters Rome on the first day of the *ludi Romani*.	*Att.* 4. 1(73). 5
5 Sept.	C. delivers speech of thanks in the senate (= *Red. sen.*).	*Att.* 4. 1(73). 5
7 Sept.	C. proposes special *imperium* for Pompey to oversee grain supply, addresses the people in a *contio* (= *Red. pop*).	*Att.* 4. 1(73). 6[27]

(*Cont.*)

[26] The senate met on two successive days, with a *contio* held before the second meeting; at the first meeting the senate approved by decree a law for C.'s recall, which was very likely promulgated at the *contio* the following day: see 129 **Why bring to mind** n. That the meetings fell during the *ludi Apollinares* (6–13 July), certainly by 8–9 July and prob. not before, can be inferred from the following data. On the one hand, because the vote for C.'s recall was held on 4 Aug. (the fourth comitial day after the *nundinae* on 29 July), the law must have been promulgated on or before the *nundinae* of 13 July; and because 10–12 July are all comital the senate would prob. not have met on two successive days any later than 8–9 July. On the other hand, C. twice says that the senate's decree in its first meeting was immediately greeted by a sharp and unexpected drop in the high price of grain (*Dom.* 14 'subito illo ipso die carissimam annonam necopinata vilitas consecuta est', sim. *Red. pop.* 18): this is consistent with the report that the *ludi Apollinares* saw rioting over the high price of grain (Ascon. 48. 20–2 Cl.), no doubt aggravated by crowds that had gathered for the *ludi* themselves and in response to the letters the consuls had sent to the towns of Italy (116 **honor had been paid** n.). If the price had dropped before the start of the *ludi*, the riot presumably would not have occurred; if the crowds wasted no time in expressing their unhappiness by rioting at the start of the *ludi*, the unexpected drop in price a day or two later could have seemed the 'miracle' that C. represents it as being (*Dom.* 15 'There were those who thought— and I agree—that the immortal gods approved my return by this expression of their divine power . . .', sim. *Red. pop.* 18).

[27] The date is secured by the phrase 'in two days' (*eo biduo*), relative to the date 5 Sept. just mentioned; that the senate met on both 7 and 8 Sept.— comitial days when the senate would not ordinarily meet—makes plain the spirit of emergency that the shortage inspired, cf. *Att.* 4. 1(73). 6. 'since the price of grain was very high . . . (and) since the senate was meeting to discuss the grain supply throughout those days (*per eos dies*) . . .' From C.'s statement at *Att.* 4. 1. (73). 6—'When the decree (sc. concerning Pompey's *imperium*) was read out, I addressed them at the invitation of all the magistrates present except one praetor and two tribunes'—it is commonly assumed that C.'s speech on this occasion concerned the grain supply (e.g. *LUO* no. 40–1, with further refs. at Marinone 2004, 112, 495, and add Nicholson 1992, 126–8): that C. delivered *Red. pop.* not on this occasion but right after he addressed the senate two days earlier is often inferred, with support sought in the very compressed account at Cass. Dio 39. 9. 1 (cf. *Schol. Bob.* 110. 4–7 St.). This seems mistaken. That C.'s name was applauded when the

Date	Event	Evidence
8 Sept.	Senate accedes to all Pompey's conditions; C. named the first of his legates.	*Att.* 4. 1(73). 7
c.10 Sept.	C. claims to have regained all his former prestige in the courts, authority in the senate, and influence with 'patriots'.	ibid. 3
29 Sept.	C. delivers speech on his house before the college of pontiffs.	*Att.* 4. 2(74). 2[28]
1–2 Oct.	On pontiffs' recommendation, and after some obstruction, senate decrees that C.'s house is clear of religious sanction.	*Att.* 4. 2(74). 3–5, *Har. resp.* 13
3 Nov.	Clodius' thugs attack the site of C.'s house and burn Q. Cicero's house.	*Att.* 4. 3(75). 2
11–12 Nov.	Clodius' thugs assail C. on the *via sacra* and attack Milo's house the next day.	*Att.* 4. 3(75). 3
14 Nov.	Senate debates Clodius' behavior, with a view to launching a prosecution; Clodius follows with a *contio* C. calls 'utterly crazy'.	*Att.* 4. 3(75). 3–4
19–22 Nov.	Milo maneuvers to obstruct elections for curule aedileship in which Clodius was a candidate, intending to prosecute him.	*Att.* 4. 3(75). 4–5
after 4 Dec.	Metellus Nepos blocks Milo's prosecution of Clodius.	Cass. Dio 39. 7. 4[29]
10/15 Dec.	C. attacks Clodius in senatorial debate aimed at facilitating his prosecution; Publius Lupus, tr. pl, raises question of the Campanian land at the same meeting	*QFr.* 2. 1(5). 1–3[30]
56 BCE		
mid-Jan.	C. represents interests of his ally Lentulus in a series of senate debates on the restoration of Ptolemy XII.	*Fam.* 1. 1(12), 2(13), 4(14)

decree concerning the grain supply was read need imply nothing about the substance of his speech; that 'all the magistrates present save one praetor (Ap. Claudius) and two tribunes (Numerius and Atilius)' invited C. to speak, that the latter three, who had also refused to endorse the law for his recall (*Pis.* 35), made a point of dissenting on this occasion too—clearly to register disapproval of his return—and that C. took care to report these details to Atticus, combine to suggest that all the participants viewed the occasion as having a symbolic importance it would have lacked had C. addressed the people in assembly two days earlier—an address (the common view requires us to suppose) that C. did not bother to mention in the same letter.

[28] *Att.* 4. 1(73). 7, written not long after 8 Sept., implies that the pontiffs had already had the matter under consideration before C.'s return; cf. also *Har. resp.* 12 and Stroh 2004, 321–2.

[29] The manoeuvre (on which see 95 **not been granted leave** n.) relied on the fact that the quaestors of 57 had already left office, on 4 Dec.

[30] The debate was held after the tribunes for 56 had entered office (10 Dec.) and just before the Saturnalia.

Date	Event	Evidence
20 Jan.	Clodius elected curule aedile for 56.	QFr. 2. 2(6). 2[31]
2 Feb.	Supported by Pompey, Milo faces charges brought by Clodius before the people; trial adjourned to 7 Feb.	QFr. 2. 3(7). 1
2/6 Feb.	Gaius Cato, tr. pl., promulgates a bill to relieve C.'s ally Lentulus of the governorship of Cilicia.	QFr. 2. 3(7). 1
7 Feb.	Session of Milo's trial adjourned amid near riot.	QFr. 2. 3(7). 2, Fam. 1. 5b(16). 1[32]
8–9 Feb.	Meeting to discuss the foregoing disturbances, senate decrees them to be 'against the public interest'.	QFr. 2. 3(7). 3
10 Feb.	Sestius charged de ambitu by Gnaeus Nerius and de vi by Marcus Tullius	ibid. 5
11 Feb.	Defending Bestia, C. takes opportunity to lay grounds of his defense of Sestius.	ibid. 6
Feb./Mar.	Temple of the Nymphs, repository of census records, burned; Clodius suspected.	Cael. 78[33]
14 Mar.	Sextius unanimously acquitted.	QFr. 2. 4(8). 1
late Mar.	Sextus Cloelius, prosecuted by Milo, is acquitted.	Cael. 78[34]
before 1 Apr.	Publius Asicius acquitted of murdering Dio of Alexandria, C. defending.	Cael. 23–4
3–4 Apr.	Trial of Marcus Caelius Rufus, held during the Megalesian Games.	Cael. 1[35]
4 Apr.	Tullia betrothed to Furius Crassipes.	QFr. 2. 6(10). 1
5 Apr.	Senate votes Pompey funds for supervision of grain supply; Cicero proposes discussion of the Campanian land at a meeting to be held 15 May.	ibid.[36]

(*Cont.*)

[31] The letter, dated 17 Jan., gives the date of the election and anticipates Clodius' victory; his election is confirmed by e.g. *Sest.* 95.

[32] It has been thought that 2, 7, and 17 Feb. were the dates of the three preliminary meetings customary in a *iudicium populi*, and that 7 May (*QFr.* 2. 6(10). 4) was to be the day on which the verdict was announced and ratified by a vote of the people (see e.g. Lintott 1974, 64). But because the meeting of 7 Feb. was disrupted before its business had formally concluded (as C.'s description makes clear), it perhaps did not count as one of the three preliminary meetings; in any case, no voting assembly of the people could be convened on 7 May, which was not a comitial day.

[33] *Cael.* 78 is the earliest mention of the arson, unless C. alludes to it at *Sest.* 95 (**has assailed** n.).

[34] C. refers to the acquittal (*Cael.* 78) as having occurred 'within the past few days' (*paucis his diebus*).

[35] The lost letter to Quintus referred to at *QFr.* 2. 6(10). 1, apparently written late on 4 Apr. or before the senate's meeting on 5 Apr., presumably contained the news of Caelius' trial.

[36] The letter to Quintus mentions only the debate on the funding for Pompey; his own proposal at that meeting on Campanian land (a question already introduced in Dec. 57 by the tribune Lupus, see above), is not mentioned until *Fam.* 1. 9(20). 8, written two and a half years later.

Date	Event	Evidence
8 Apr.	On eve of leaving Rome, C. meets with Pompey.	ibid. 3
11/17 Apr.	Heading for Sardinia and Africa, Pompey first goes north to meet Caesar at Luca.	ibid.[37]
not before c.20 Apr.	Pompey tells Quintus that C. must stop opposing Caesar, sends similar message to C. via Lucius Vibullius Rufus.	Fam. 1. 9(20). 9–10[38]
8 Apr./c.8 May	Clodius attacks Cicero in a contio.	Har. resp. 8[39]
8 or 9 or 14 May	C. delivers speech On the Responses of the Haruspices in senate, following an altercation with Clodius the previous day.	Har. resp. 1, 2, 22, QFr. 2. 6(10). 3[40]
15–16 May	Senate discusses Caesar's distribution of Campanian land; Cicero, finding himself in a tight spot over the issue, is absent.	QFr. 2. 7(11). 1–2
late May/mid-Jun.	On C.'s motion, senate grants Caesar 10 legates and salary for army.	Prov. cons. 28[41]

[37] None of the main sources for the meeting (Fam. 1. 9(20). 9, Plut. Caes. 21. 2–4, Pomp. 51. 3, Cat. min. 41. 1, Crass. 14. 5–6, Suet. Jul. 24. 1, Appian BCiv. 2. 17) helps to date it; but since C. states that Pompey intended to leave Rome on 11 April (QFr. 2. 6(10). 3), and since it was 5–6 days' journey (c. 360 km, as the crow flies) from Rome to Luca, the meeting cannot have been held before 17 April (cf. e.g. Holmes 1923, 2. 292–5).

[38] The meeting with Quintus is placed 'within a few days' (paucis…diebus) of Pompey's departure from Luca, though we do not know how long he stayed there.

[39] The term. post quem is Cicero's departure from Rome early on 9 April (above); the term. ante quem is the date of Har. resp. (next n.).

[40] The speech was delivered to the senate after the Megalesian Games (Har. resp. 22), which ended 9 April; since on 9 April C. was on his way out of Rome and did not intend to return before May 6 (QFr. 2. 6(10). 3), we have a fairly firm term. post quem; since C. mentions Gabinius in the speech (Har. resp. 2) without gloating over the disgrace he suffered when the senate refused his request for a supplicatio on 15 May (next n.), we have a term. ante quem, albeit somewhat less firm (Har. resp. 1): since in the period between 6 and 15 May the 10th and 12th were comitial (the 14th, normally comitial, was nundinal in 56), the only dates on which the senate was likely to meet on consecutive days were 7–8 or 8–9 or 13–14 May.

[41] The session can be dated only relatively, before the speech On the consular provinces, in which C. says (28) that the senate acted on these matters 'recently' (nuper) and at his urging (his role is stressed also at Balb. 61, suppressed at Fam. 1. 7(18). 10, to Lentulus), presumably after the sessions of 15–16 May from which he stayed away. 21–24 May are the only non-comitial days remaining in that month, hence the only days in May when the senate was likely to meet (preferred by Stein 1930, 41, who dates Prov. cons. to June); if Prov. cons. belongs to July (next n.), then any non-comitial day in June (1–2, 5–15) is also possible. Since the measures C. supported on this occasion are among those he described as 'monstrous' in March (QFr. 2. 5(9). 3), his speech of support was as much a 'palinode' as Prov. cons. itself (for the term, Att. 4. 5(80). 1) and seems to mesh with the rest of the evidence more easily: see next n.

Date	Event	Evidence
1/9 Jul.	Cicero delivers speech *On the Consular Provinces*.	*Prov. cons.* 15[42]

[42] The *term. ante quem* is the anticipated consular election for 55, before which the assignment of provinces had to be made; the election would normally be held in or just after mid-July, though in the event it was delayed until the fall. At *Prov. cons.* 15, C. anticipates that 'within a few days' (*paucis diebus*) couriers will bring to Gabinius in Syria the shaming news that the senate denied his request for a *supplicatio* at its meeting of 15 May (cf. *QFr.* 2. 7(11). 1, Stein 1930, 41 n. 220, Gardner 1958b, 532): since C. would know that a courier needed ca. 6 weeks to cover the distance from Rome to Antioch, his remark should have been made early in July (a courier traveling ±75 km/day would in 28 days cover 2,100 km, just shy of the shortest distance by air between the two cities, 2140 km, but of course the distance by land and sea was substantially longer; for data on travel-speeds, see Friedländer 1907, 1:280–7). He certainly would not have spoken as though the journey took less than a month (15 May–15 June); and since 16–29 June are all comitial days, when the senate would not ordinarily meet, and 1–9 July are all non-comitial, a date in early July seems secure. If this dating is correct, the speech, which was a form of public humiliation for C., was delivered almost exactly a year after the meetings of senate and people that led to his recall, see above at n. 26.

When dating to late June the sequence *Att.* 4. 4a, 8, 5, 12(78–81), in the third of which C. speaks shamefacedly of his 'palinode', Shackleton Bailey placed the *Prov. cons.* in late May or June (*Att.* 2. 233–4) and identified it as the 'palinode'. But if *Prov. cons.* belongs to early July, either it cannot be identified with C.'s 'palinode', or the letters' dating should be reconsidered (for alternatives that have been proposed, see Marinone 2004, 122–4); on balance the identification of the 'palinode' and *Prov. cons.* is more likely mistaken, cf. preceding n. Cf. also *Fam.* 1. 7(18). 10–11, which presupposes the end of the debate on the provinces and is dated by Shackleton Bailey to July 56 ('June or July' in the Loeb edition of 2001) because C. acknowledges Lentulus' congratulations on Tullia's betrothal, which occurred on 4 April: even if C. wrote to Lentulus instantly and was instantly answered, not much less than twelve weeks could have passed.

Calendar 58 BCE[a]

Jan.	Feb.	Interkal.	Mar.	Apr.	Mai.	Jun.	Quint.	Sext.	Sept.	Oct.	Nov.	Dec.
1 F	1 N	1	1 NP	1 F	1 F	1 N	1 N	1 F	1 F	1 N	1 F	1 N
2 F	2 N	2	2 F	2 F	2 F	2 F	2 N	2 F	2 F	2 F	2 F	2 N
3 C	3 N	3	3 C	3 C	3 C	3 C	3 N	3 C	3 C	3 C	3 C	3 N
4 C	4 N	4	4 C	4 C	4 (C)	4 C	4 N	4 C	4 (C)	4 C	4 C	4 C
5 NO F	5 NO N	5 NO	5 C	5 NO N	5 C	5 NO N	5 NP	5 NO F	5 NO F	5 C	5 NO F	5 NO F
6 F	6 N	6	6 C	6 N	6 C	6 N	6 N	6 F	6 F	6 C	6 F	6 F
7 C	7 N	7	7 NO F	7 N	7 NO F	7 N	7 NO N	7 C	7 C	7 NO F	7 C	7 C
8 (C)	8 N	8	8 F	8 N	8 F	8 N	8 N	8 C	8 C	8 F	8 (C)	8 C
9 NP	9 N	9	9 C	9 N	9 C	9 N	9 N	9 C	9 C	9 C	9 C	9 C
10 C	10 N	10	10 C	10 N	10 C	10 N	10 C	10 C	10 C	10 C	10 C	10 C
11 NP	11 N	11	11 C	11 N	11 N	11 N	11 C	11 C	11 C	11 NP	11 NP	11 NP
12 C	12 N	12	12 C	12 N	12 (C)	12 N	12 C	12 C	12 F	12 C	12 C	12 EN
13 ID NP	13 ID NP	13 ID	13 EN	13 ID NP	13 NP	13 ID NP	13 C	13 ID NP	13 ID NP	13 NP	13 ID NP	13 ID NP
14 EN	14 N	14	14 NP	14 N	14 C	14 N	14 C	14 F	14 F	14 EN	14 F	14 F
15 NP	15 NP	15	15 ID NP	15 NP	15 ID N	15 F	15 ID NP	15 C	15 F	15 ID NP	15 C	15 NP
16 (C)	16 EN	16	16 F	16 N	16 F	16 C	16 (C)	16 C	16 C	16 F	16 (C)	16 C
17 (C)	17 NP	17	17 NP	17 NP	17 C	17 C	17 F	17 NP	17 C	17 C	17 C	17 NP
18 C	18 C	18	18 C	18 N	18 C	18 C	18 C	18 C	18 C	18 C	18 C	18 C
19 C	19 (C)	19	19 NP	19 NP	19 C	19 C	19 NP	19 F	19 C	19 NP	19 C	19 NP
20 C	20 (C)	20	20 C	20 N	20 (C)	20 C	20 C	20 C	20 (C)	20 C	20 C	20 C
21 C	21 F	21	21 C	21 NP	21 NP	21 (C)	21 NP	21 NP	21 C	21 C	21 C	21 NP
22 C	22 C	22	22 F	22 N	22 C	22 C	22 C	22 EN	22 C	22 C	22 C	22 C
23 C	23 NP	23	23 NP	23 F	23 NP	23 C	23 NP	23 NP	23 C	23 (C)	23 C	23 NP
24 (C)	24 N	24	24 F	24 C	24 F	24 C	24 (C)	24 C	24 C	24 C	24 (C)	24 C
25 (C)		25	25 C	25 NP	25 C	25 C	25 NP	25 NP	25 C	25 C	25 C	25 C
26 C		26	26 C	26 C	26 C	26 C	26 N	26 C	26 C	26 C	26 C	26 C
27 C		27	27 C	27 C	27 C	27 C	27 C	27 NP	27 C	27 C	27 C	27 (C)
28 C			28 C	28 C	28 (C)	28 (C)	28 C	28 C	28 (C)	28 C	28 C	28 C
29 C			29 C	29 C	29 (C)	29 (C)	29 C	29 C	29 C	29 C	29 C	29 C
			30 C		30 C		30 C			30 C		
			31 C		31 C		31 C			31 (C)		

[a] On the intercalation posited for 58, see the introduction above. Shaded dates are *nundinae*; NO = Nonae. ID = Ides, F = *dies fastus*, C = *dies comitialis* ((C)) = a comitial day rendered *fastus* but non-comitial by falling on *nundinae*), N = *dies nefastus*, EN = *dies endotercisus* (a day 'split' between F and C, with morning and afternoon having different functions), NP = (day of religious observance); on the significance of the days, see Michels 1967, 31 ff, Rüpke 1995, 245 ff. The senate ordinarily could meet on all days but C

Calendar 57 BCE

Jan.	Feb.	Mar.	Apr.	Mai.	Jun.	Quint.	Sext.	Sept.	Oct.	Nov.	Dec.
1 F	1 N	1 NP	1 F	1 F	1 N	1 N	1 F	1 F	1 N	1 F	1 N
2 F	2 N	2 F	2 F	2 F	2 F	2 N	2 F	2 F	2 F	2 F	2 N
3 C	3 N	3 C	3 C	3 C	3 C	3 N	3 C	3 C	3 C	3 C	3 N
4 C	4 N	4 C	4 C	4 C	4 C	4 N	4 C	4 C	4 (C)	4 C	4 C
5 NO F	5 NO N	5 (C)	5 NO N	5 C	5 NO N	5 NP	5 NO F	5 NO F	5 C	5 NO F	5 NO F
6 F	6 N	6 C	6 N	6 C	6 N	6 N	6 F	6 F	6 C	6 F	6 F
7 C	7 N	7 NO F	7 N	7 NO F	7 N	7 NO N	7 C	7 C	7 NO F	7 C	7 C
8 C	8 N	8 F	8 N	8 F	8 N	8 N	8 C	8 C	8 F	8 C	8 (C)
9 NP	9 N	9 C	9 N	9 N	9 N	9 N	9 C	9 (C)	9 C	9 C	9 C
10 C	10 N	10 C	10 N	10 C	10 N	10 C	10 C	10 C	10 C	10 C	10 C
11 NP	11 N	11 C	11 N	11 N	11 N	11 C	11 C	11 C	11 NP	11 C	11 NP
12 C	12 N	12 C	12 N	12 C	12 N	12 C	12 C	12 F	12 (C)	12 C	12 EN
13 ID NP	13 ID NP	13 EN	13 ID NP	13 NP	13 ID NP	13 (C)	13 ID NP	13 ID NP	13 NP	13 ID NP	13 ID NP
14 EN	14 N	14 NP	14 N	14 C	14 N	14 C	14 F	14 F	14 EN	14 F	14 F
15 NP	15 NP	15 ID NP	15 NP	15 ID N	15 F	15 ID NP	15 C	15 F	15 ID NP	15 C	15 NP
16 C	16 EN	16 F	16 N	16 F	16 C	16 C	16 C	16 C	16 F	16 C	16 (C)
17 C	17 NP	17 NP	17 N	17 (C)	17 C	17 F	17 NP	17 (C)	17 C	17 C	17 NP
18 C	18 C	18 C	18 N	18 C	18 (C)	18 C	18 C	18 C	18 C	18 C	18 C
19 C	19 C	19 NP	19 NP	19 C	19 C	19 NP	19 F	19 C	19 NP	19 C	19 NP
20 C	20 C	20 C	20 C	20 C	20 C	20 C	20 C	20 C	20 (C)	20 C	20 C
21 C	21 F	21 (C)	21 NP	21 NP	21 C	21 NP	21 NP	21 C	21 C	21 (C)	21 NP
22 (C)	22 C	22 F	22 N	22 F	22 C	22 C	22 EN	22 C	22 C	22 C	22 C
23 C	23 NP	23 NP	23 F	23 NP	23 C	23 NP	23 NP	23 C	23 C	23 C	23 NP
24 C	24 N	24 F	24 C	24 F	24 C	24 C	24 C	24 C	24 C	24 C	24 (C)
25 C	25 (C)	25 C	25 NP	25 (C)	25 C	25 NP	25 NP	25 (C)	25 C	25 C	25 C
26 C	26 EN	26 C	26 C	26 C	26 (C)	26 N	26 C	26 C	26 C	26 C	26 C
27 C	27 NP	27 C	27 C	27 C	27 C	27 C	27 NP	27 C	27 C	27 C	27 C
28 C	28 C	28 C	28 C	28 C	28 C	28 C	28 C	28 C	28 (C)	28 C	28 C
29 C		29 (C)	29 C	29 C	29 C	29 (C)	29 C	29 C	29 C	29 (C)	29 C
		30 C		30 C		30 C			30 C		
		31 C		31 C		31 C			31 C		

Calendar 56 BCE

Day	Jan.	Feb.	Mar.	Apr.	Mai.	Jun.	Quint.	Sext.	Sept.	Oct.	Nov.	Dec.
1	F	N	NP	F	F	N	N	F	F	N	F	N
2	N	N	F	F	F	F	N	F	F	F	F	N
3	(C)	N	C	(C)	C	C	N	(C)	C	C	C	N
4	C	N	C	C	C	C	N	C	C	C	C	C
5	NO F	NO N	C	NO N	C	NO N	NP	NO F	NO F	C	NO F	NO F
6	F	N	C	N	(C)	N	N	F	F	C	F	F
7	C	N	NO F	N	NO F	N	NO N	C	C	NO F	C	C
8	C	N	F	N	F	N	N	C	C	F	C	C
9	NP	N	C	N	N	N	N	C	C	(C)	C	C
10	C	N	(C)	N	C	N	(C)	C	C	C	(C)	C
11	NP	N	C	N	N	N	C	(C)	C	NP	NP	NP
12	C	N	C	N	C	N	C	C	F	C	C	EN
13	ID NP	ID NP	EN	ID NP	NP	ID NP	C	ID NP	ID NP	NP	ID NP	ID NP
14	EN	N	NP	N	(C)	N	C	F	F	EN	F	F
15	NP	NP	ID NP	NP	ID N	F	ID NP	C	F	ID NP	C	NP
16	C	EN	F	N	F	C	C	C	C	F	C	C
17	C	NP	NP	N	C	C	F	NP	C	(C)	C	NP
18	C	C	(C)	N	C	C	(C)	C	C	C	(C)	C
19	(C)	C	NP	NP	C	C	NP	F	C	NP	C	NP
20	C	C	C	N	C	C	C	C	C	C	C	C
21	C	F	C	NP	NP	C	NP	NP	C	C	C	NP
22	C	(C)	F	N	F	C	C	EN	(C)	C	C	C
23	C	NP	NP	F	NP	(C)	NP	NP	C	C	C	NP
24	C	N	F	C	F	C	C	C	C	C	C	C
25	C	C	C	NP	C	C	NP	NP	C	(C)	C	C
26	C	EN	(C)	C	C	C	N	C	C	C	(C)	C
27	(C)	NP	C	(C)	C	C	C	NP	C	C	C	C
28	C	C	C	C	C	C	C	C	C	C	C	C
29	C		C	C	C	C	C	C	C	C	C	(C)
30			C		(C)		C			C		
31			C		C		C			C		

APPENDIX 2
CLODIUS' 'INCEST'

On many occasions, and with varying degrees of explicitness, C. alleges that Clodius had incestuous relations with various siblings; these allegations are generally regarded as the kind of smear belonging to invective's conventional arsenal (see e.g. Nisbet 1961 on *Pis.* 28, Lenaghan 1969 on *Har. resp.* 9, and further below). The evidence shows, however, that the allegations about Clodius follow a clear pattern (cf. esp. Wiseman 1969, 52–5) and were certainly not conventional.

On the one hand, there are the relatively few but precise allegations of incest with his youngest sister, who was at one time the wife of Lucius Lucullus, cos. 74 (Clodia Luculli). These allegations evidently first surfaced at the time of the Bona Dea affair in 61, when Lucullus tortured his (by-then former) wife's slaves for the evidence, and the sources place the relations no later than the early 60s. Plut. *Cic.* 29. 3–4 is the chief text, specifying the time before Lucullus divorced her, on returning to Rome from the East in 66 (cf. *Luc.* 34. 1, *Caes.* 10. 5; presumably also Cass. Dio 37. 46. 2, where ref. to sex with an unspecified sister is paired with Clodius' fomenting mutiny under Lucullus, also alleged at Plut. *Luc.* 34. 2–5). For his part, C. speaks at *Mil.* 73 of Clodius' relations with Clodia Luculli, which is in turn consistent with *Har. resp.* 42, referring to an incestuous affair in Clodius' youth, before he began his public career *c.*68; in this speech, too, the ref. to Clodius as 'the adulterer of his own sister', sandwiched between his youthful service as a male prostitute and the Bona Dea scandal (39), must look to Clodia Luculli.

On the other hand, there are the more numerous, and equally precise, allegations that Clodius had relations with Clodia the wife of Metellus Celer (Clodia Metelli), who was older than he (*Cael.* 36).[1] All these allegations refer

---

[1] If Shackleton Bailey 1977 correctly describes the kinship ties of Clodius and his siblings with Metellus Celer and Metellus Nepos, Clodia Metelli was Clodius' half-sister (the relations would still be incestuous, and therefore both illicit and shameful, Watson 1967, 36–7, Robinson 1995, 54–7, Hickson-Hahn 1998, 2–3). But that argument is otherwise doubtful, while C.'s refs. to Clodia Luculli as Clodius' *soror germana* (*Mil.* 73) and to Clodius as the *frater germanus* of Clodia Metelli (*Cael.* 38) mean either that he intentionally spoke in such a way as to obscure any difference in the degrees of kinship among them or that he was unaware of any difference (had a difference existed, he would surely have known); his repeated implication that Clodia was to Clodius as Hera was to Zeus (see following in text) suggests that he thought of them as

to the period after the Bona Dea affair: they first appear in mid-60, when C. implies an incestuous relationship with Clodia Metelli in a public exchange with Clodius (*Att.* 2. 1(21). 5: he anticipates that Atticus will think the remark 'not very consular', which should imply that the slur had not yet become a habit); from April 59, in correspondence with Atticus, he refers to Clodia Metelli as 'Ox-Eyes'/*Boōpis*, the Homeric epithet for Hera, the sister and wife of Zeus (*Att.* 2. 9(29). 1, and four more times), and the same conceit is echoed at *Dom.* 92 (cf. also *Har. resp.* 38–9); most notorious are the repeated allegations soon after the present speech, in *Cael.* 32, 36, 38, 78 (cf. Livy *Perioch.* 103, on the Bona Dea affair, stating that 'Clodius entered the sacred space where no man can lawfully go and had illicit sexual relations with the wife of Metellus the pontiff', where Clodius' alleged adultery with the wife of Caesar the *pontifex maximus*, specific to the Bona Dea affair, is conflated with recollection of Clodia Metelli). We can therefore safely infer that the few references to an unspecified sister in this period—e.g. the 'utterly obscene verses . . . chanted against Clodius and Clodia' by Milo's partisans in street demonstrations about a month before this trial (*QFr.* 2. 3(7). 2)—also concern Clodia Metelli (see also 116 in this speech, *Dom.* 25, *Pis.* 28, cf. Vell. 2. 45. 1).

Thus, two clearly different sisters at two clearly distinct stages of Clodius' life, leaving only a handful of other refs. best regarded as epiphenomena emerging from the core allegations. The remaining sister—Clodia Tertia, wife of Marcius Rex (cos. 68)—is never mentioned by herself and is implicated only in C.'s general ref. to 'three sisters' at *Fam.* 1. 9(20). 15 (late 54) and, by name along with the other two, at Plut. *Cic.* 29. 3–4 (cf. the ref. to unspecified 'sisters' at *Har. resp.* 9 and 59, at the beginning and end of a speech in which C. alludes separately to Clodius' relations with both Clodia Luculli and Clodia Metelli). Relations with a brother are alleged only at *Sest.* 16 (**what sort of muscle** n.) and *Dom.* 26 (*fratricida, sororicida*, 'brother-smiter, sister-smiter', playing on a sexual sense of the verb *caedere*, 'smite (esp. with a weapon)', cf. Catull. 56. 7 and Adams 1982, 145–6). *Schol. Bob.* 127. 26–7 St., on *Sest.* 16, names Appius, no doubt a guess but prob. correct: he is an important secondary target in the speech; the third brother, Gaius, is referred to only in passing (41 **brother of my enemy** n.) and not accused of acting against C.

As already noted, the common view has it that such allegations are merely 'conventional' elements of invective (beyond the refs. above, see e.g. Tatum 1993, 34 'Incest was by no means an uncommon slur in the late republic', and 1999, 42 'The smear was not an uncommon one in the late republic', both times citing only (Sall.) *In Cic.* 2 and Cass. Dio 46. 18. 6,

---

'full' siblings. (My thanks to John D. Morgan for a productive and often spirited discussion of the term *germanus* and related issues.)

alleging incest between C. and Tullia; sim. Skinner 1982, 204 'In the political arena, incest can readily be attributed to members of the ruling elite', citing only Rankin 1976, 120, where no Roman evidence is given). This view is surely encouraged by some familiar poems of Catullus, both 79 (on Clodius, if 'Lesbia' = Clodia Metelli, and 'Lesbius pulcher' = Clodius Pulcher, as often assumed) and the series on the 'familial' relations of one Gellius (74, 88, 90–1, and esp. 89, implying incest practised to the point of enfeeblement, cf. 16 **what sort of muscle** n.; the attacks on Gellius are usually taken to be linked, via poem 91, to the poet's love for Lesbia; see also poem 78, an aunt and nephew, and 111, an uncle and niece). But the contrast with a truly conventional sexual slur—say, that of having been a male prostitute in one's youth (see 18 **old despoilers** n.)—could not be more striking. For all the savage things C. says about his enemies, he makes this charge about no one else.[2] Further, in all the texts produced by or referring to Republican literature and culture, the only other allegation of sibling-incest I know lurks at Plut. *Cat. min.* 54. 1–2 (Cato's relations with his half-sister Servilia, attacked in Caesar's *Anticato*). It seems likely that Catullus was directly inspired by talk surrounding Clodius (e.g. Skinner 1982, 205, Tatum 1993, 39), producing poems that provided models for Martial (12. 20, a couplet on sibling incest, see also 2. 4, 4. 16, with Hickson-Hahn 1998, 25–9). It seems much more than likely that accusing a man of sibling-incest, even in the hard-nosed discourse of Republican politics, was nearly as taboo as the act itself, an annihilating gesture made only against a deeply hated enemy.

  None of this, of course, implies that the allegations about Clodius were true. The evidence produced by Lucullus, who plainly hated the man, was hardly above suspicion, and false allegations could then simply have been transferred to Clodia Metelli during Clodius' later, greater prominence. Nor was sibling-incest the only sexual innuendo C. made about Clodius: beyond allegations of adultery with Caesar's wife, see e.g. *Dom.* 36, implying that Fonteius, his 'adoptive father', was really his sexual pet; *Dom.* 118, 134, 139, alleging an affair with his mother-in-law; *Sest.* 39 and *Har. resp.* 42, 59, on his youthful service of 'rich idlers' and, later, of pirates and barbarians; *Att.* 4. 11(86). 2, calling him 'the people's Appuleia' (referring to the tribune Appuleius Saturninus: 37 n.), a slam at both his politics and his sexuality (cf. 116 **admitted to a gathering of women** n.). But for C. sibling-incest was Clodius' defining vice, as cunnilingus was Sextus Cloelius' (133 n.); on the relation between the two in C.'s invective, Corbeill 1996, 112–24.

---

[2] In Attic oratory accusations of incest seem to occur only at Lys. 14. 28 and 41, on the son of Alcibiades; cf. also Antisthenes in Athen. *Deipn.* 5. 63, on Alcibiades himself. My thanks to Michael Gagarin for his help on this point.

APPENDIX 3

THE GEOGRAPHIC TERMS OF CICERO'S EXILE

Clodius' law declaring that C. had been exiled, in its revised form (*Att.* 3. 4(49)), allowed C. 'to live at a distance beyond 400 (Roman) miles' (= 367.4 statute miles = 591 km), that is, twice the distance specified in the relegation of Lucius Lamia (29). I assume with most that the distance transmitted in C.'s letter is correct, while Plut. *Cic.* 32. 1 and Cass. Dio 38. 17. 7 are incorrect in saying 500 miles.[1]

But 400 miles from where? Plutarch says Italy, which appears to agree with C.'s explaining why he will not go to Athens: 'my enemies (Catilininarians who had escaped: cf. 29 **he was referring** n.) are there ... and I'm afraid they'll take the line that that town too is not far enough away from Italy' (*Att.* 3. 7(52). 1). Yet both Dyrrachium and Thessalonica are much closer than 400 Roman miles to the nearest point in Italy; but each would satisfy the statute (Dyrrachium, just barely) if the benchmark was Rome. Should we take it that C. mispoke in *Att.* 3. 7(52), and that the distance was to be measured from Rome, as we might expect (cf. again the relegation of Lucius Lamia, 29)?

Probably not. We should instead take it that when C. says 'my enemies are (in Athens) ... and I'm afraid they'll take the line that that town too is not far enough away from Italy', it is the enemies' presence that matters at least as much as the town's location, and probably more. In C.'s circumstances, the presence of people inclined to make trouble posed the greatest danger. At Athens, there were certainly such people, and if they wished to cause trouble, they would in fact have been strictly correct, for Athens is only *c.*340 Roman miles from the nearest spot of Italian soil (conversely, had Rome been fixed as the benchmark, not even C.'s worst enemies could have contended that Athens—almost twice the stipulated distance away—was too close).[2] The advantage of Thessalonica (until the arrival of Lucius Piso in late 58)

---

[1] Marinone 2004, 105 n. 5, suggests that in specifying 400 miles C. was speaking without precise knowledge; but his remarks in *Att.* 3. 4(49) are based on the revised copy of the law that had come into his hands.

[2] Cf. C.'s statement that he could not stay on Malta (*Att.* 3. 4(49)): like Sicily, of which it was administratively part, Malta was a good deal less than 400 Roman miles from Italy; but unlike Sicily, it was a good deal more than 400 miles from Rome.

and of Dyrrachium lay not in their legality, but above all in the absence of enemies and the presence of friends (cf. *Fam.* 14. 1(8). 3, on the shelter provided by Gnaeus Plancius in Thessalonica, and the fear caused by Piso's expected arrival).[3]

---

[3] In *Fam.* 14. 1(8). 3 C. notes that Dyrrachium was 'dutifully disposed' toward him (*in me officiosa*), and another advantage besides: it was a 'free community' (*libera civitas*), which, while not immune to a governor's meddling, was in the normal course more able to resist it (cf. 56 **condemned exiles** n.).

THE TEXT

The translation is based on T. Maslowski's excellent Teubner edition of 1986. I have tabulated below the handful of places where I depart from it, and I briefly explain my decisions in the notes ad locc.

Teubner text	Translated text
6. *gravissimae antiquitatis viris* N, edd.	*gravissimis antiqu<ae sever>itatis viris* Weidner
7. *suis studiis et officiis* Maslowski	*assiduisque officiis* Mommsen
8. *bonis omnibus* Hertz	*vobis omnibus* P²BH
16. *insani* codd.	*exsanguis* Koch
18. *respiciens* Shackleton Bailey	*despiciens* codd.
22. *putavi. nequam esse hominem* edd.	*putavi, nequam esse* [*hominem*] Shackleton Bailey
22. *falsa opinione errore* codd.	*falsa opinione* [*errore*] edd.
23. *sermonis* codd. (†*sermonis*† Maslowski)	*helluationis* Nisbet
26. *tum cum* Paul	*<to>tum quamvis* Halm
32. *audeas* codd.	*audebas* Lambinus
36. *<populi Romani animo>* Maslowski	*<equestri ordine>* Kayser
59. (lacuna XVII litterarum) *tulit gessit* P (*tulit gessit* GV, *lac. omissa*))	*<is igitur qui bellum in>tulit* Koch
63. *per se conservari quam per alios* codd.	*per se conservari quam per alios* <*dissipari*> Zumpt
71. *pertinere et . . . non abhorrere* post *rei publicae causa suscepit* codd.	post *pro mea salute suscepit* transp. Peterson
71. *primum iter* codd.	*prius iter* Shackleton Bailey
72. *Gavi Oleli horto* Maslowski	*Gavi Oleli rure* Madvig
72. *a calatis Gaviis* codd.	*a Galatis Gaviis* Mommsen
82. *Quintium* codd.	*Quintum* Orelli
85. *magistratus* codd.	*<alii> magistratus* Kaster
134. *est e<nim> nimia gloriaeq cupiditate* Jeep	del. Madvig
144. *<T.> Milo* Heine	*Milo* codd.
145. *fortunae vexatae, dissipati liberii* codd.	*fortunae dissipatae, vexati liberi* Shackleton Bailey

GLOSSARY

This glossary comprises the terms for Roman political institutions and political–ethical values that recur in the speech, where they are translated as consistently as English idiom allows (e.g. *dignitas* always = 'worthy standing'). The terms included in the glossary are marked by an asterisk at their first appearance in any given note in the commentary.

ancestor mask See 'wax mask'.

assembly of the people (*contio*) A non-voting assembly (< *co-ventio, 'coming together') of the Roman *populus*: in Republican ideology, any given *contio* represented the citizen body in its entirety, irrespective of the number or character of persons actually present. Such assemblies, several of which might be held in one day, could be convened only by elected magistrates (and on some occasions priests) and be addressed only by the convener and the persons he allowed or compelled to speak. Cf. esp. 28 **assembly** n., and contrast s.vv. 'voting assembly' and 'assembly of the plebs'.

assembly of the plebs (*concilium plebis*) A voting assembly comprising only members of plebeian clans (*gentes*) organized by 'tribes' (see below in this Glossary), presided over by the tribune of the plebs and competent to hear certain criminal charges, elect tribunes and plebeian aediles, and pass plebiscites (*plebiscita*) having the force of law. Cf. 'assembly of the people' and 'voting assembly' (the latter comprises another form of tribal assembly, the *comitia tributa*: on the distinction, Lintott 1999*b*, 53–5).

auspices (*auspicia* < *avis specere*, 'to watch birds') Signs seen in the behavior of birds and other animals (including the feeding habits of special chickens) or in celestial phenomena (esp. thunder and lightning) and understood to mean that the gods favoured or opposed undertaking a given action at a given time: by legend responsible for determining that Romulus would take precedence over Remus (Enn. *Ann.* 72–91 Sk.), they were central to life in Rome and other areas of Italy; Linderski 1986 is fundamental. The authoritative interpreters of auspices were fifteen senators belonging to the college of augurs; the public auspices—relevant to (e.g.) military campaigns and elective or legislative assemblies—were administered by the magistrates. Auspices were of two kinds: those that 'presented themselves' to an observer spontaneously (*auspicia oblativa*), without being sought; and those that were 'sought after' (*auspicia impetrativa*).

The former could be observed by anyone and, once observed, had to be reported to the relevant magistrate. Only curule magistrates and tribunes had the right to 'seek after' auspices (cf. *Phil.* 2. 81 with Linderski 1995, 450): a magistrate exercising this right announced that he was 'watching the heavens' (*servare de caelo*, lit. 'to watch (for a something) from heaven') and reported any unfavourable sign he saw to the magistrate intending to preside over an assembly, in the practice known as 'obnuntiation' (see s.v.).

authority (*auctoritas*) The quality of an individual (cf. 62 **quelled** n.) or institution (cf. 32. **senate's authority** n.) that causes others to pay respect and give heed. See Fuerst 1934, Heinze 1960, 43–58, Balsdon 1960, Galinsky 1996, 10–41.

beast Of the two Latin terms that can appropriately be translated as 'beast', *bestia* and *belua*, C. never uses the former as a term of abuse to denote a human being, and when he uses it to express a comparison with certain humans' behaviour (e.g. *Sex. Rosc.* 56, *Clu.* 41), it is to establish a benchmark of low brutishness, not ferocity (a 'beast of the field' or a 'beast of burden', not a 'ravening beast'). By contrast, *belua* is regularly used as a term of political abuse; like 'brigand' and 'public enemy', it places the person so called beyond community, fellow-feeling, and social obligations, by segregating him from humanity and associating him with the uncanny and monstrous (Cossarini 1981, May 1996).

Best Sort, optimates (sing. *optimas* is rarely used) The label *optimates* is formed by adding the suffix *-as* (*-ates*), denoting membership in a category (esp. ethnic or geographic: e.g. *Antiates* = 'people of Antium', cf. Plaut. *Poen.* 994 'What sort (*quoiates*) are you or from what town?'), to the root *optim-* (superl. of *bonus*, 'good'), which like Gk. *aristos* (> 'aristocracy') commonly has socio-political connotations when used of persons: in this period the label denotes the senate's leaders (e.g. *Cat.* 1. 7, *Flac.* 54), esp. as conservative defenders of senatorial primacy against both 'popular' leaders from the Gracchi on and individuals of exceptional achievement and influence like Pompey (see *RE* 18.1 (1939): 773–98 (H. Strasburger), Brunt 1988, 470–88).

bordered toga (*toga praetexta*) The all-white toga was the distinctive dress of the adult male Roman citizen (*toga virilis*); a form of the toga with a purple border was reserved for freeborn boys who had not yet assumed the *toga virilis* (cf. 6 **this boy here** n.), for augurs (cf. 144 **Publius Lentulus** n.), and for curule magistrates (cf. 17 **fasces**, 26 **assume mourning dress** nn.).

bravery (brave), courage (*fortitudo, fortis*) Term of commendation applied esp. to men who participate in Rome's public life: the brave citizen is one who faces the danger he sees bearing down on him whether on military campaign or in domestic affairs; see *Part. or.* 77 with e.g. *Inv. rhet.* 2. 163, Lind 1992, 21–4, and the description of Cato at the end of §61; cf. 'largeness of spirit', 'manliness', 'serious'.

brigand, brigandage (*latro, latrocinium*) Originally a term for a mercenary fighter (*OLD* s.v. *latro* 1)—a sense it occasionally retains in C.'s usage (cf. 2 **hired brigands** n.)—*latro* more often denotes one who uses violence, beyond the civil community's laws, for merely personal ends: a bandit or outlaw. On the term see Jal 1963, 67–70, Favory 1976, Habinek 1998, 69–87, Riggsby 2002*a*, 169–70; on ancient brigandage more generally, Shaw 1984.

century (*centuria*) One of the 193 units into which the Roman people was divided on (primarily) the basis of wealth. In the late Republic the 'centuries' were most important in providing the basic structure of the *comitia centuriata* ('voting assembly organized by centuries'), which elected praetors, consuls, and censors and (rarely) voted on laws: the eighteen 'centuries' comprising the 'equestrian order' (see s.v.) voted first, followed in descending order of wealth by the remaining 'centuries'. Because each century voted as a unit, and because voting stopped as soon as a majority was achieved, the vote was usually halted before the last and most numerous 'century', comprising those with little or no property (*capite censi*, lit. 'appraised (by the censors) at the value of their life'), had the chance to vote.

civil community (*civitas*) Any collection of 'citizens' (*cives*)—persons with the rights and responsibilities stipulated by a given community's laws—was a 'civil community' (though the term *civitas* most literally denotes 'the quality of being a *civis*'—' citizenship'—C. happens to use that sense only once in the more than forty references to *civitas* in this speech, see 1 **role in the community** n.). In principle, all free persons were members of some civil community—at Rome or elsewhere—unless they had forfeited their 'lives as citizens' by some bad act, or unless their community had lost its autonomy (cf. 9 **Capua** n.). Though *civitas* often functions as an apparent synonym of *res publica* ('commonwealth'), the former looks more to the collection of persons, the latter more to their collective interests and the transactions that protect and enhance them: C. can hold that a *res publica* ceases to be a *res publica* when tyranny, oligarchy, or mob rule undermines its agreed-upon laws and the common interests of all (cf. *Rep.* 3. 43–5 with 5. 1 = Aug. *CD* 2. 21 and Schofield 1995, 74), but it would not thereby cease to be a *civitas*.

club (*collegium*) An organization having a religious basis and serving as a mutual aid society (e.g. by providing burials for its members) in a culture that lacked most modern social services; its membership was determined by city-district or trade. Even when organized by trade, the clubs lacked the expressly economic aims of modern guilds or trade unions, but in the late Republic they were available to be mobilized for public demonstrations (see esp. 34 **alleged purpose**).

comitia centuriata, comitia tributa See 'voting assembly' (*comitia* is not to be confused with the Comitium, the ancient meeting place of the people between the senate house (*curia*) and Rostra in the Forum).

comitial day (*dies comitialis*) A day on which a 'voting assembly' (*comitia*) could be convened, for an election or to act on proposed legislation or to confirm a verdict in a trial before the people. Of the 355 days in the pre-Julian calendar's year, 196 were regularly marked as comitial, distributed unevenly among the months, from a low of six and seven in Feb. and April to a high of twenty-three in November.

contio See 'assembly of the people'.

commonwealth, public interest (*res publica*) Lit. 'thing belonging to the people' (cf. 91 **possessions ... n.** and *Rep.* 1. 39), the *res publica* comprises: the goods and property—the material *wealth*—that the people (*populus*) holds in *common* as members of the civil community (*civitas*); all transactions concerning that 'thing' ('the people's business'); and the collective interests of the people more generally. When C. refers to the structure of customs, laws, and institutions through which those interests are secured—the polity or constitution—he speaks of the 'set-up of the commonwealth' (*status rei publicae*: e.g. *Leg. agr.* 1. 26, 3. 4, *Cat.* 1. 3, *Red. sen.* 16, *Har. resp.* 60, *Rep.* 1. 42, 68, *Leg.* 1. 15), much as he speaks of the 'set-up of the civil community' (*status civitatis*: cf. 1 **civil regime** n.). Wherever English usage tolerates, *res publica* is translated as 'commonwealth', otherwise, 'the public interest'; in 14, 'engage in politics' renders the idiom *rem publicam capessere*, lit. 'to take up / take in hand the public interest'. See also 'civil community'.

consistency See 'resolve'.

curule magistrate A censor, consul, praetor, or curule aedile, so called from the *sella curulis*, a folding ivory chair of Etruscan origin (cf. 17 **fasces** n.), that was one of the emblems of their office.

decree of the senate (*senatus consultum*) An expression of the senate's 'considered view' (*consultum* < *consulere*, 'to take thought (for)'), achieved by debate and vote on a motion, which was thereafter formally drafted, publicly posted, and stored in the treasury (*aerarium*). A decree of the senate did not have the binding force of a law passed in a 'voting assembly' of the people or of a *plebiscitum* passed in the 'assembly of the plebs'. But the authority of the senate (32 n.) was such that any of its decrees would be paid heed: indeed, a proponent of senatorial government like C. would take the people's willingness to pay such heed as a sufficient sign that the civil community was functioning properly. On the 'ultimate decree of the senate', which in effect declared a state of emergency, see 25 **all citizens** n.

desperadoes (*perditi*) People who are lit. 'ruined' (Hellegouarc'h 1963, 532–4)—having lost their resources, typically through wantonness, profligacy, and the like—and so are driven to desperate measures.

dominion (*imperium*) The warrant to give a command (*imperare*), on campaign or under law, and the power to compel obedience; in this period it was vested in consuls, praetors, persons governing provinces in place of consuls and praetors (proconsuls, propraetors), and individuals with special commissions (e.g. the commission Pompey received in Sept. 57 to regulate the grain supply: see 15 **Gnaeus Pompeius** n.). See also 1 **dominion's** n.

equestrian order (*ordo equestris*) Originally Rome's cavalry (*equites* = 'horsemen'), enrolled by the censors in the eighteen 'centuries' of citizens provided with the 'public horse' (*equus publicus*, paid for and maintained by public funds); but any essential connection between those centuries and cavalry service was largely effaced by the end of the 2nd cent. BCE, after which enrollment in the order's 18 centuries depended largely on free birth and wealth (at least 400,000 sesterces) derived from land, finance, and commerce; in particular, the equestrian order provided many of the influential 'tax-farmers' (*publicani*: see 32 **society of tax-farmers** n.) who collected the empire's taxes on a contract basis. See Henderson 1963, Nicolet 1974 (esp. 285–386), Badian 1983, Brunt 1988, 144–93, and for C.'s relations with the equestrians, Bleicken 1995, Berry 2003.

freedom (*libertas*) Most importantly, the counter-term to slavery (*servitus*), signifying that a person was both *free from* the domination of another's will and *free to* choose his own projects and commitments. At the same time, certainly under the Republic, this 'freedom from' and 'freedom to' were tied closely to 'freedom in': freedom as a person was the precondition for, and was protected by, membership in a 'civil community', which gave one's projects and commitments much of their positive content and united the individual with others whose rights were guaranteed and regulated by the same laws (for 'liberty and law' as a recurrent pair see *Verr.* 2. 5. 160, *Clu.* 146, 155, *Leg. Agr.* 2. 102, *Red. sen.* 34, *Mil.* 77, *Phil.* 8. 8, *Off.* 2. 24, 3. 83, with e.g. Cato orat. frag. 252, Caes. *BGall.* 7. 77. 14, Livy 24. 26. 8, 26. 32. 2; cf. also 30 **rights and freedom** n.). Republican freedom was in this respect the state of being, not a wholly autonomous self, but an engaged citizen embedded in a network of civic relations: that is why C. at one point in this speech virtually equates 'being free' with 'having a commonwealth' (81 **to be free men** n.), and why the 'freedom that we share' (1) was the opposite both of the slave's oppression and of his atomization (cf. *Balb.* 24 'we very often see slaves who have earned the commonwealth's gratitude publicly given the gift of *libertas*, that is to say, *civitas*'). For a one-sentence summary of Republican freedom—from a senatorial perspective, and with an overlay of Stoicizing sensibility—see *Sull.* 25: 'so to live as to be a slave to no man, nor indeed to any overpowering desire, to despise all strong appetites, to need neither gold nor silver nor any other material thing, to state one's views freely in the senate, to take thought for what the people need, not what they want, to yield to no one, to resist many.' The freedom of speech included in that summary is the only form of freedom C. claims for himself in this oration: 14 **the freedom** n. On the concept of *libertas* at Rome see esp. Wirszubski 1950, Brunt 1988, 281–350, and for its reflection in subsequent tradition, Berlin 1958, Pettit 1997, Skinner 1998.

games, shows (*ludi*) Public spectacles of several kinds were mounted both by private individuals on special occasions (e.g. to honor a kinsman, 124, cf. also 116 **honor had been paid** n.) and by magistrates at some of the Roman calendar's religious festivals (praetors gave the *ludi Apollinares* in honor of Apollo, aediles gave the rest—the *ludi Romani, ludi plebeii*, and those at the festivals honoring Ceres, the Great Mother, and Flora—with different festivals assigned to curule and plebeian aediles). The fare included gladiatorial contests—in the Republic, only at privately sponsored games—chariot races (*ludi circenses*, ignored by C. in this speech), and dramatic productions (*ludi scaenici*). On the *ludi* and theatrical shows see Balsdon 1969, 244–67, 270–4, Nicolet 1976, 361–73, Rawson 1991, 468–87, Gruen, 1993, 183–222, Bernstein 1998; on gladiatorial shows, Balsdon 1969, 288–301, Ville 1981, Wiedemann 1992.

generosity (*liberalitas*) Lit. 'the quality characteristic of a free man', the term denoted an inclination to give rather than take (thus the opposite of greed, *avaritia*) both properly calibrated and without expectation of *quid pro quo* (thus the opposite of largess or bribery, *largitio*), a virtue that complemented being 'large-spirited': in C.'s later, Stoicizing analysis of appropriate actions, the (unnamed) cardinal virtue that supports human social life comprises justice (*iustitia*)—'the avoidance of acts that undermine the community'—and generosity—'the performance of acts that bind the community together' (Dyck 1996, 106; on generosity, *liberalitas*, see esp. *Off.* 1. 42–60, 2. 52–64 with Dyck's comm.).

good for nothing (*nequam*) As a term of abuse, the antonym of *frugi* (sober, sound), esp. used of slaves stereotypically viewed as shiftless rascals: cf. 82 **killing their own Gracchus** n.

gravity See 'seriousness'.

henchmen, hired hands (*operae*) From the noun *opera*—lit. 'effort (devoted to a given task or goal)', and by extension the person who provides the effort ('labourer', 'helper')—one of C.'s favoured terms for the supporters of his opponents, esp. Clodius (see also 'brigand' and 'desperado'): the term (used in the plural only) embraces both ruffians paid to commit political violence and the ordinary citizens allegedly bribed to attend Clodius' *contiones* and vote for his measures; for the distinction, important in the last third of the speech, see 57 **hired hands** n.

ignorant, the (*imperiti*) Lit. 'the inexperienced', an epithet standardly applied to the non-political classes, who just because they are non-political lack the experience that would allow them to have *practical intelligence, the distinguishing trait of the senate: being 'ignorant', they cannot properly distinguish their own wants from the commonwealth's needs, cf. 77 **the ignorant** n. This tendentious view of the masses' grasp of policy, however, need not imply actual ignorance of history and politics: on the 'civic knowledge' of the urban population see Morstein-Marx 2004, 68–118.

irresponsibility (**irresponsible**) (*levitas, levis*). Lit. 'lightness', both literally and ethically the opposite of *gravitas* ('weightiness', see below s.v. 'seriousness'): a form of moral weakness that issues in frivolous, futile, and inconstant behaviour because the 'irresponsible' lack the qualities proper to the 'serious', esp. 'consistency', 'trustworthiness', and balanced 'moderation'. Cf. 'recklessness'.

iustitium Strictly defined, a suspension of activity in the courts (<*ius sistere*, 'to make justice stand still'), esp. in the face of public emergency or calamity; more generally a suspension of all public business, including meetings of the senate and voting assemblies, of the sort that followed the riot of 23 Jan. 57 in the Forum (see 71–92 n.).

largeness of spirit (**large-spirited**) (*magnitudo animi, magnus animus*) Lat. *animus* is a term for consciousness embracing both cognition (perception, judgement, belief, etc.) and affect (feeling, desire, etc.): people with a 'large spirit' possess the ample cognitive and affective resources that enable them to see what is truly important (in this speech, the commonwealth's well-being) and stir them to act accordingly, esp. by avoiding behavior that is pusillanimous, petty, and selfish; 'largeness of spirit' is accordingly a precondition for 'bravery' (*fortitudo*) and a key component of 'manliness' (*virtus*). For C.'s view of 'largeness of spirit', *magnitudo animi*, see esp. *Off.* 1. 61–92, with Dyck 1996 ad loc., cf. Knoche 1935, Lind 1979, 19–22.

legate (*legatus*) A members of the provincial governor's official staff: legates, who served as the governor's seconds-in-command with the army (cf. 'military tribune') and as members of his advisory council (*consilium*), were traditionally senators either appointed by the senate in consultation with the governor or approved by the senate on the governor's nomination; see in general Schleussner 1978, 101 ff., Thomasson 1991.

life as a citizen (*caput*) One's *caput*, lit. 'head', was in a political sense the totality of one's civic rights, which would be lost through condemnation on a 'capital' charge of the sort S. faced.

loyalty, trustworthiness (*fides*) Fundamentally, the disposition to stand by one's commitments; as such, inseparable from 'resolve' (for the pairing of two, see *Quinct*. 5, *Leg. Man*. 69, *Flac*. 36, *Vat*. 41, *Deiot*. 8, 16, *Phil*. 9. 10, 12. 30, *Fam*. 11. 27(348). 6, 11. 29(335). 2; cf. *Parad*. 2. 16 and *Fin*. 2. 46, on the hero Regulus, on whom see 129). 'Loyalty' and 'resolve' together are among the chief tokens of 'seriousness', which is in turn central to Roman 'manliness'. On *fides* see Fraenkel 1916, Heinze 1960, 59–81, Freyburger 1986, Lind 1989, 5–13, and cf. 98 **validity of one's word** n.

manliness (**manly**) (*virtus*) Lit. 'the state of being a real man' (cf. Gk. *andreia*), a normative term denoting the cluster of traits that an adult male citizen ought to possess (slaves and women standardly were excluded from possessing *virtus* in this sense). This cluster had at its core physical strength, the capacity for vigorous activity, and 'courage' (a common translation) and was associated with several other traditionally valued traits—e.g. 'bravery', 'largeness of spirit', 'seriousness'—that enabled resolved and energetic behaviour of the sort desiderated in the speech's first sentence: *virtus* in this sense—which it has throughout the speech—was predominantly a public, civic quality (cf. its association with 'practical intelligence', itself a key political virtue, in 77). Over time, and in part under the influence of Greek ethical discourse on moral excellence (*aretē*), the cluster of traits labelled *virtus* became broader, less exclusively oriented toward public action, and even less exclusively gendered (though when used of women it was still often used with a self-conscious sense of paradox): it thereby came more closely to resemble our notions of 'virtue' (see esp. McDonnell 2003, with further refs.). What shifted in this process was not, essentially, the meaning of the lexical item *virtus* (say, from 'courage' to 'virtue') but the meaning of the concept 'being a real man': for this concept, 'manliness' is the preferred rendering throughout the speech, including places that might suggest differences between C.'s notions of manliness and our own.

men of the people, *populares* Save when C. wishes to present himself as a *popularis consul* when addressing the people (see *Leg. agr.* 2. 6 ff.), the term *popularis* in his language usually at least hints at the label 'demogogue', the leader who wins influence by promising to give the *populus* what it wants rather than what it needs and who thus further corrupts a body lacking the experience and foresight to understand its needs (77 **the ignorant,** 104 **excessive desires** nn., and this Glossary s.v. 'practical intelligence'). On C.'s use of *popularis,* Seager 1972, Achard 1981, 194–7, and on the category more generally, Tatum 1999, 1–11.

military tribune Six military tribunes (*tribuni militum*), subordinate to the commander with dominion (*imperium*), were attached to each legion in the Roman army and served as the troops' immediate commanding officers, seeing to discipline and the life of the camp. In the Republican army there were only four standing legions, two attached to each consul, other legions being levied to meet specific needs (e.g. when the praetors Pompeius Rufus and Metellus Celer were sent against the Catilinarians in 63, each was specifically authorized to raise the army needed: Sall. *Cat.* 30. 5). Because the 24 tribunes assigned to these consular legions were elected by the tribal assembly (*comitia tributa*), the position counted as a magistracy (military tribunes in legions raised ad hoc were appointed by the commanders). On the military tribunes of the Republic, see Suolahti 1955.

new man (*homo novus*) The first member of a family (usually equestrian, as in C.'s case) to gain senatorial rank: on the category see Wiseman 1971, and on the term Shackleton Bailey 1986, 258–60.

notability (notable) (*nobilitas, nobilis*) The Engl. term 'notability' is the preferred rendering of *nobilitas* both because it has no connotations of ethical standing (unlike 'nobility') and because it more directly conveys the essential idea of the Latin, that of simply 'being known': in Roman public life the 'notables' were the known quantities, with 'known' broadly taken to imply not empirical knowledge gained by observing a man's actions but provisionally reliable inference from his ancestor's achievements. By the late Republic the epithet 'notable' (*nobilis*) seems to be used exclusively of men who were descended directly in the male line from at least one consul (Gelzer 1969*a*, Shackleton Bailey 1986; for argument that the term was applied to descendants of 'curule magistrates' more generally, Brunt 1982).

obnuntiate, obnuntiation (*obnuntiare, obnuntiatio*) The act of announcing the sighting of an unfavourable omen to a magistrate intending to preside at a 'voting assembly' or 'assembly of the plebs', with the intent of preventing the assembly from being held (*obnuntiare* = 'to report against', reflecting the act's essentially obstructive character). The announcement had to be made before the assembly began and could be made only by a magistrate with the authority to 'watch the heavens' for 'sought-after' omens (see s.v. 'auspices', with 33 **while the same consuls** n., and Libero 1992, 56–64). C.'s claim that merely announcing an intention to 'watch the heavens' was sufficient per se to block an assembly (e.g. *Dom.* 40) is certainly false as a matter of law, though the announcement was no doubt often effective de facto: because the person making the announcement would surely succeed in 'seeing' the sign he was looking for, the convening magistrate would be discouraged from going to the trouble, but only *viva voce* report of signs actually seen was a valid form of *obnuntiatio*; for an esp. vivid episode see *Att.* 4. 3(75). 3–5, on Milo's efforts as tribune to block the aedilician elections in Nov. 57. Which magistrates could legally 'obnuntiate' against which others and in what circumstances remains to a degree controversial (33 nn.), but there is no evidence of a 'curule magistrate' ever actually using the practice against a tribune, and only one apparent instance of such an action considered even hypothetically (78 **If that praetor...** n.).

obstinacy (*pertinacia*) A form of stubbornness (*Cael.* 77, *Balb.* 62, *Lig.* 17–18, *Luc.* 65, *Fin.* 2. 9) arising from lack of moderation (*Verr.* 2. 1. 134, *Planc.* 94, cf. *Fam.* 4. 7(230). 3), esp. in the desire to prevail (*Acad.* 1. 44, *Fin.* 1. 27, *Tusc.* 2. 5, *Off.* 1. 64): it is the vice that shadows the virtue of 'resolve'.

optimates See 'Best Sort'.

patriotic (*bonus*). The epithet, lit. 'the good (man/men)', is used throughout the speech, and by C. more generally, in the strongly politicized sense implied in the speech's first sentence, where the one 'given to thinking of himself instead of the commonwealth' is as clearly the opposite of the 'good'—the one given to thinking of the commonwealth instead of himself—as the 'fearful' man is the opposite of the 'brave'. For the thought cf. e.g. 93 and *Har. resp.* 60, and on 'the good' = 'the patriotic' vs. 'the reckless' = 'the seditious' see Wirszubski 1954.

peace of the gods (*pax deorum*) The balanced relations between the gods and the human community on which Rome's well-being depended: briefly, Linderski 1995, 610–14.

pomerium The religiously defined city-boundary of Rome.

populares See 'men of the people'.

practical intelligence (*prudentia* < *providere*, 'to see in advance') The product of native wit enriched by learning and experience in public affairs, and a key political virtue in C.'s lexicon (cf. Achard 1981, 399–402, Mitchell 1991, 16 ff.): it is what the first founders of human social life possessed, along with 'manliness' (91 n.); it is what 'the ignorant' (= 'inexperienced') by definition lack, being therefore unqualified for political leadership (77 n.); and it is what Caesar showed he lacked in facilitating Clodius' transfer to the plebs (16 n.).

privilegium A law drafted in such a way that it concerns a specific person or case, not a general category of persons or acts (cf. Berger 1953, 651): C. thought, with some justice, that the law declaring that he had been exiled, by name, was a *privilegium* and as such contrary to Roman legal tradition (65 **measure** n.).

promagistrate (specif., **proconsul, propraetor, proquaestor**) As the territory that Rome controlled beyond Italy increased and the demands of provincial governance exceeded the supply of magistrates in office, the system of promagistracies was developed, under which persons (typically, former magistrates) were sent out on provincial commands 'in place of' (*pro*) a magistrate of corresponding rank (thus a 'proconsul' served 'in place of' a consul, and so on).

promulgation, public notice (*promulgare*) The public reading and posting of any proposed piece of legislation: the proposal had to receive this publicity on at least three successive market days (*nundinae*) before an assembly could be convened for a vote (see 25 **public notice** n., App. 1).

proscription, proscribe (*proscriptio, proscribere*) Since the time of Sulla the term referred to depriving a person of citizenship's protections, and thereby punishing him with the disabilities of exile (including outlaw status and loss of property), without trial (see the material gathered in Hinard 1985); the term literally denotes the public posting of the names of the persons thus punished.

public enemy (*hostis*) An enemy of the civil community as a whole, as opposed to *inimicus*, a personal enemy; with 'brigand' and 'beast', among C.'s most commonly used terms of political invective, cf. Jal 1963, 11 **domestic enemies** n.

public interest See 'commonwealth'.

public violence (*vis*) The crime of which S. was accused, constituted by the use of violence 'against the public interest': see the Introd. §2.

publicans (*publicani*) Private persons, esp. but not exclusively of the equestrian order, who contracted to collect the commonwealth's various public revenues, paying a fixed sum for the right to collect a given levy: see 32 **corporation** n., and on *publicani* and the organization of their corporations (*societates*), see *RE* Suppl. 11 (1968), 1184–1208 (G. Ürögdi), Badian 1983, Nicolet 2000.

quaestor After the reforms of Sulla in 81, 20 of these hands-on administrators were elected each year and assigned by lot to a given sphere of duty: two were assigned to administer the treasury (*aerarium*: for the work of these 'urban quaestors' in managing public transactions and records see esp. Plut. *Cat. min.* 16–18), others were put in charge of the water supply, the grain supply at Ostia (cf. 39 **insult was intended** n.), and other concerns in Italy, while the rest, like S., assisted the consuls or the promagistrates serving abroad (briefly, Lintott 1999*b*, 133–7). The minimum age was 30, and the quaestors became members of the senate ex-officio.

recklessness (reckless) (*audacia, audax*) Though in the military sphere the trait could be spoken of approvingly, as 'boldness' or 'daring', in the same breath as 'bravery' and 'manliness' (e.g. Caes. *BGall.* 2. 26. 2, *BCiv.* 3. 26. 1, Livy 2. 10. 5–6, 2. 31. 6, 5. 16. 10, 25. 38. 11, 18), it consistently serves C. as the byword for the expression of individual will by those who pursue their own advantages in the civil sphere while ignoring the just claims of others and of the community (e.g. *Sex. Rosc.* 96, 118, *Verr.* 2. 1. 1, 6, 36, 142, 2. 2. 134, 2. 3. 65, 83, 166, 169, 2. 4. 44, 84, 2. 5. 62, 106, *Caecin.* 1, 2, *Clu.* 26–7, *Flac.* 35, *Dom.* 116, 133, *Pis.* 66, *Phil.* 2. 4, 19, 3. 18, 6. 7). On its use in late Republican politics, see Wirszubki 1961, with Weische 1966, 28–33, 66–70, Achard 1981, 247–8.

resolve, consistency (*constantia*) The trait entailed in persistent adherence to a position once that position has been thoughtfully adopted: see Hellegouarc'h 1963, 283–5, Weische 1966, 38–52, Lind 1989, 20–3, Linderski 1995, 294; on its close connection to *fides*, see 'loyalty'.

seriousness (serious), gravity (*gravitas, gravis*) Lit. 'weightiness', one of the core characteristics of a mature Roman man, which anchored him in his world and caused him to be consistent, trustworthy, and well-balanced, hence the opposite of 'irresponsible'; on the 'serious man' (*vir gravis*), see Weische 1966, 38–52, Hiltbrunner 1967, Lind 1979, 34–8, Achard 1981, 392–9, Mitchell 1991, 31–2.

standing court (*quaestio perpetua*) A court of inquiry (*quaestio*), typically presided over by a praetor, devoted to hearing accusations brought under one of several categories of crimes: these included the standing court on electoral corruption (*de ambitu*), the standing court on provincial extortion (*de rebus repetundis*), and the standing court before which S. was tried, on public violence (*de vi*).

supplicatio An expression of thanks to the gods, entailing offerings and suspension of normal public business for a specified number of days: because it was decreed by the senate in (typically) a victorious general's name, it bestowed honor on the human agent and was often the prelude to a formal triumph. A *supplicatio* was also decreed, uniquely, in C.'s honor as a civilian magistrate when the Catilinarian conspiracy was uncovered and suppressed.

temperance (temperate) (*abstinentia, abstinens*) A virtue linked to self-control and moderation (*continentia, modestia*: cf. *Off.* 2. 78, *Att.* 5. 9(102). 1) attributed to S. as an official (7), in whom 'temperance' means forbearance from using his position to do others harm (cf. *Verr.* 1. 1. 34, *Planc.* 64, *Att.* 5. 16(109). 3) or, esp., to enrich himself and those under him (opp. greed, *avaritia*: *Verr.* 2. 4. 46, 48, *QFr.* 1. 1(1). 32, *Att.* 5. 17(110). 2, 5. 18(111). 2).

tranquillity (*otium*) When used of a personal state of being, *otium* commonly denotes 'leisure'; when it refers to a condition of the commonwealth in which all citizens share, it denotes what the US Constitution's first chapter calls 'domestic tranquillity' (cf. Wirszubski 1954, 6). The latter form of *otium* was an unequivocal good for all save 'desperadoes', whereas the former was at best ambiguous: though it provided the occasionally necessary respite from busy-ness (*negotium*, 'not-*otium*') and the setting in which true cultivation was possible, it always threatened to turn into—or be interpreted by your enemies as—sloth, a slough of funk and enervation (see e.g. *Att.* 2. 6(26). 1, 2. 14(34). 1), the opposite of the energetic engagement in public affairs proper to the 'patriot' endowed with 'manliness'; see in general André 1966, Burck 1967. When C. attempts to mollify a ruffled Atticus by suggesting that his non-political friend's honorable tranquillity (*honestum otium*) stands on an equal footing with his own eagerness for honours (i.e. offices, *honorum studium*: *Att.* 1. 17(17). 5), it is telling that the claim can be made even speciously plausible only by gracing *otium* with the epithet 'honourable' (*honestum*, to balance *honorum*), while 'eagerness' (*studium*, implying energetic activity) is contrasted with 'tranquillity' (*otium*, implying the opposite).

treasury tribunes (*tribuni aerarii*) After senators and equestrians, the third order of the Roman *populus*, comprising men who matched the equestrians in wealth but were not enrolled in the 18 equestrian centuries of the *comitia centuriata*. At *Font.* 36, *Clu.* 121, *Flac.* 4, 96, *Planc.* 41, and *Rab. Post.* 14, C. apparently refers to equestrians and *tribuni aerarii* on the panel as simply 'equestrians': on the ground for distinguishing between them see Henderson 1963, 63–4, Nicolet 1974, 598–613, Wiseman 1987, 61–73, Brunt 1988, 210–11. The label *tribuni aerarii* was vestigial in the late Republic, the members of the order having no connection with the treasury.

tribe (*tribus*) One of the thirty-five units (4 urban, 31 rural) into which the *populus* was distributed. The distribution was originally based on a family's place of residence but had become more complex by the late Republic, when enfranchisement of virtually all Italians south of the Po (mostly distributed among the rural tribes) and an increasing number of freedmen (concentrated in the urban tribes irrespective of residence) produced a much larger and more geographically diverse *populus*. Each tribe's vote counted as a unit, determined by majority vote in the tribe; concentrating freedmen in the four urban tribes thus gave less weight to any individual's vote in those tribes.

tribune of the plebs, tribunate (*tribunus plebis, tribunatus*) The office emerged in the 5th cent. BCE to protect the plebs' interests and gradually acquired a range of powers (limited to the city of Rome proper) and formal status as a magistracy (without *imperium*) entailing membership in the senate; ten tribunes, who themselves had to be members of the plebs, were elected each year. Though Sulla had abrogated the tribunes' standing as magistrates and severely limited their powers, both standing and powers were fully restored by 70: these powers included the authority to convene the senate, to call and address an 'assembly of the people', to bring before the plebs legislation for their action (the *plebiscita*: 25 **tribune's proposals** n.) or certain kinds of criminal charge, and to veto proposed legislation, decrees of the senate, and acts of other magistrates (see 33, 68, 74 nn.). Because their physical persons were protected by 'sacrosanct legislation' (16 **auspices**... n.), a person who harmed a tribune was subject to religious sanction as one 'cursed' (*sacer*). The tribunate's importance in the late Republic, in its own right and in specific tribunes' alliances with men like Pompey and Caesar, cannot be overstated: for recent discussion see Brunt 1971*b*, Gruen 1974, 23–8, 180–9, Thommen 1989, Drummond 1989, Wiseman 1994*a*, 329–38, 1994*b*, 368–81.

trustworthiness See 'loyalty'.

uprightness (*integritas*) The term lit. denotes ethical 'wholeness', meaning that one's character has not been diminished by the loss of any desirable qualities or spoiled by the addition of any undesirable qualities: it is a virtue cognate with, but less inwardly oriented than, the modern virtue of 'integrity', see Kaster 2005, 134–48.

veto (*intercedere, intercessio*) The intervention by a magistrate to block the act of another magistrate, a decree of the senate, or a piece of legislation being brought to a vote: the question which magistrates had the right to veto which other magistrates is debated (see 25 **all citizens**... **thought**... n.), but in late Republican practice the veto was normally exercised only by tribunes of the plebs.

voting assembly (*comitia*) An assembly of the *populus* as a whole (not just the plebs, cf. 'assembly of the plebs') convened by a praetor or (usually) consul for the purpose of voting on laws (*leges*), on verdicts in certain kinds of trial (*iudicia populi*, trials before the people), or on the election of magistrates.

A voting assembly could be organized by 'centuries' (*comitia centuriata*, which elected the higher magistrates) or 'tribes' (*comitia tributa*, which elected military tribunes, quaestors, and curule aediles); a third form of voting assembly, the *comitia curiata* (organized by the city's 'wards', *curiae*), had only vestigial functions in the late Republic, which did not entail a meeting of the *populus* (see 16 **one of the consuls** n.). The different forms and functions of the *comitia* (and 'assembly of the plebs') are summarized in tabular form in Taylor 1966 (opp. p. 5) and Brennan 2004, 61–2.

wax mask, ancestor mask (*imago*) The image that descendants of a man who had held a curule magistracy were entitled to display in the atrium of their house, with an accompanying list of the man's distinctions: see Flower 1996, esp. 32–59, 185–222.

well-being (*salus*) The term denotes first of all physical health and well-being; by an extension very commonly used, it also denotes one's health or well-being as a citizen (see 'life as a citizen'). On his return from exile C. regained his well-being in the latter sense: cf. 4 'all who toiled on behalf of my well-being'. On *salus* as political concept and (as Salus) the object of civic cult in the Republic, see Winkler 1995, 16–35.

worthy standing (*dignitas*) An attribute signifying that a person enjoys a certain *standing* in the community—comprising both objective status (e.g. as a magistrate vs. a private citizen, a free man vs. a slave) and the respect, authority, etc., others are willing subjectively to grant him—and that he is regarded as *worthy* of this standing. Derived from the adjective *dignus* ('worthy'), *dignitas* most literally denotes 'worthiness'; as the etymological relation between *dignus* (< **dec-+-nus*) and *decus* ('appropriate or fitting appearance') suggests, this worthiness is conceived as a quality visible to an audience that judges the fit between person and standing. On *dignitas*, see Wegehaupt 1932, Hellegouarc'h 1963, 388–415, Lind 1979, 22–9, Piscitelli Carpino 1979, Mitchell 1991, 47–62, Thome 2000, 117–34.

The following 'reverse glossary' lists the Latin terms for political institutions or social values that recur in the speech with the standard translation used for each in this book:

abstinentia (*abstinens*): temperance (temperate)
auctoritas: authority
audacia (*audax*): recklessness (reckless)
auspicia: auspices
belua: beast
bonus, boni: patriot(s)

caput: life as a citizen
centuria: century
civitas: civil community
collegium: club
colonus: settler
comitia centuriata: centuriate assembly
comitia curiata: curiate assembly

comitia tributa: tribal assembly

comitia: voting assembly

concilium plebis (tributum): assembly of the plebs (organized by tribes)

constantia: resolve, consistency

contio: assembly of the people

decurio: town councilor

dies comitialis: comitial day

dignitas: worthy standing

fides: loyalty, trustworthiness

fortitudo (fortis): bravery (brave)

gravitas (gravis): seriousness, gravity (serious)

homo novus: new man

honos: office

hostis: public enemy

imago: wax mask, ancestor mask

imperiti: ignorant, the

imperium: dominion

inimicus: personal enemy

integritas: uprightness

intercedere, intercessio: veto

iudex (iudices): judge(s)

iustitium: suspension of public business

latro, latrocinium: brigand, brigandage

legatus: legate

levitas (levis): irresponsibility (irresponsible)

lex sacrata: sacrosanct legislation

liberalitas: generosity

libertas: freedom

ludi: games, shows

magnitudo animi (magnus animus): largeness of spirit (large-spirited)

moderatio: restraint

nequam: good for nothing

nobilitas (nobilis): notability (notable)

obnuntiare (obnuntiatio): obnuntiate (obnuntiation)

officium: (sense of) duty, dutiful behaviour

operae: henchmen, hired hands

optimates: Best Sort, men of the

ordo equestris: equestrian order

ordo: category of the citizenry

otium: tranquillity

patria: fatherland

pax deorum: peace of the gods

perditi: desperadoes

pertinacia: obstinacy

pietas: devotion

pomerium: the religiously defined city-boundary of Rome

populares: men of the people

promulgare, promulgatio: promulgation, public notice

proscriptio, proscribere: proscription, proscribe

prudentia: practical intelligence

publicani: publicans

pudor: shame

quaestio perpetua: standing court

quaestor (quaestura): quaestor(ship)

res publica: commonwealth, public interest

salus: well-being

sedulitas: punctiliousness

senatus consultum: decree of the senate

severus: strict

supplicatio: thanksgiving

toga praetexta: bordered toga

tribuni aerarii: treasury tribunes

tribunus militaris: military tribune

tribunus plebis, tribunatus: tribune of the plebs, tribunate

tribus: tribe (*tribus*)

virtus: manliness (manly)

vis: public violence

PERSONS[1]

Accius, Lucius 123 (120–2)
Aelius **Lamia, Lucius** 2
Aelius Ligus 68, 94[2]
Aemilius **Scaurus, Marcus** (father) 39, 101 (143)
Aemilius **Scaurus, Marcus** (son) 116 (101)
Aesopus 123 (120–2)
Ahala, *see* Servilius Ahala
Albania (wife of Sestius, 6)
Albanius, Gaius 6
Albinovanus, Publius (78 (accusator), 87, 96, 127, 135)
Alfius Flavus, Gaius (114)
Ancharius, Quintus 113
Annius Milo, Titus 85–7, 90, 92, 144 (88–9, 91, 94)[3]
Antiochus the Great 58
Antonius Hybrida, **Gaius** 8–9, 12
Appuleius **Saturninus, Lucius** 37, 39, 101, 105
Aristides 141
Atilius Gavianus Serranus, Sextus 72, 74, 85, 94 (87, 89)[4]
Atilius Regulus, Marcus 127

Atilius **Serranus**, Gaius 72
Attalus 58
Aurelius **Cotta, Lucius** 73–4
Brogitarus 56
Brutus, *see* Iunius Brutus
Caecilius Metellus Celer, Quintus (131)
Caecilius **Metellus** Nepos, **Quintus** 130 (72, 79, 87, 89)
Caecilius **Metellus** Numidicus, **Quintus** 37, 101, 130[5]
Caecilius **Metellus** Pius, Quintus 124
Caesar, *see* Iulius Caesar
Calpurnius **Piso** Caesoninus, Lucius 32–3, 53–4, 60, 70, 93–4 (17, 19–26, 29, 34–6, 38, 42–4, 52–5, 63–6, 68–9, 71, 111, 135)
Calpurnius **Piso** Frugi, Gaius 54, 68
Camillus, *see* Furius Camillus
Cassius, Lucius 103
Catilina, *see* Sergius Catilina
Cato, *see* Porcius Cato
Catulus, *see* Lutatius Catulus

---

[1] A person's full nomenclature is given where known; the name(s) in bold indicate the form of the name used by Cicero. Numbers denote the sections in the speech where the person is named, numbers in parentheses places where the person is referred to but not named; in a few instances (most notably, P. Clodius Pulcher) the person is referred to only and never named.

[2] 'Ligus iste nescio qui' at 68, 'Aelius' at 94.

[3] 'Milo' at 85–7, 90, 92, 95, 144; 'T. Annius' at 87.

[4] 'Atilius Gavianus Serranus' implied at 72, 'Atilius Gavianus' at 74, 'Serranus' at 85, 94.

[5] 'Quintus Metellus' at 37, 101, 'Metellus Numidicus' at 130 (where Metellus Nepos is also mentioned).

⁶ 'Quintus Numerius Gracchus' implied at 82, 'Numerius' at 94, 'Gracchus' at 72.

Maps

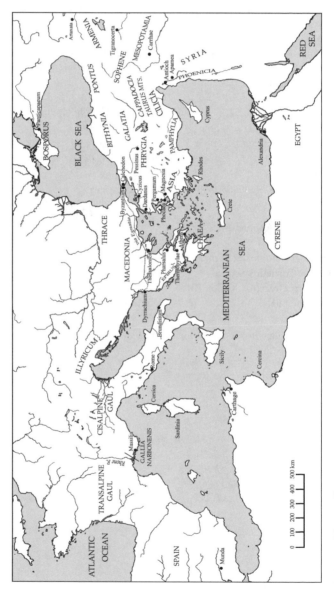

MAP 1. The Mediterranean

MAP 2. Italy

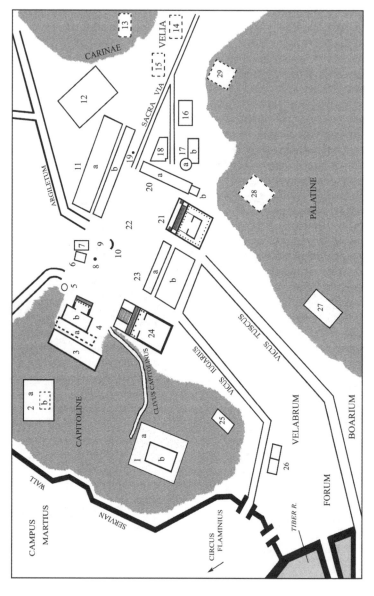

Map 3. Plan of Rome: The Political Centre c.56 BCE

The sketch-map represents the larger structures present in the centre of the city at the time of Sestius' trial: e.g. the basilica Sempronia (19b) is still in place, before being torn down to make way for the larger basilica Iulia *c.*54, and the atrium of Vesta (17) is oriented as it was during the Republic. Broken lines indicate structures whose location is uncertain; those mentioned in the text or commentary are noted by an asterisk (*) following the name.

1. a. Capitolium*, b. Temple of Iuppiter Optimus Maximus*
2. a. *arx* (citadel), b. Temple of Iuno Moneta (?)
3. Tabularium (record depository)
4. a. Basilica Opimia (?)*, b. Temple of Concordia*
5. *carcer Tullianum* (prison)*
6. Basilica Porcia
7. Curia Hostilia (senate house)*
8. *columna Maenia*
9. Comitium*
10. Rostra*
11. a. Basilica Fulvia/Paulli,[1] b. *tabernae novae* (shops)
12. Macellum (market)
13. Temple of Tellus (?)
14. Temple of Honos and Virtus (?)*
15. Temple of the Penates (?)*
16. *domus publica* (house of the *pontifex maximus*)
17. a. Temple of Vesta*, b. Atrium of Vesta (dwelling of the Vestal Virgins)*
18. Regia
19. Well-Head of Libo (?)*
20. a. Basilica Aemilia, b. *lacus Iuturnae* (sacred pool)
21. Temple of Castor*
20. Forum*
23. a. *tabernae veteres* (shops), b. Basilica Sempronia
24. Temple of Saturn and *aerarium* (treasury)*
25. Temple of Fides
26. Temples of Fortuna and Mater Matuta*
27. Temple of the Magna Mater*
28. Site of Cicero's house and the portico of Catulus on which Clodius built his shrine of Libertas (?)*
29. Temple of Iuppiter Stator (?)

---

[1] On the basilica Fulvia/Paulli and basilica Aemilia, see *LTUR* 1. 167–68, 173–5, Wisemen 1998, 106 ff.

REFERENCES

ACHARD, G. 1981. *Pratique rhétorique et idéoligie politique dans les discours 'optimates' de Cicéron*. Leiden: E. J. Brill.

ADAMS, J. N. 1978. Conventions of Naming in Cicero. *Classical Quarterly* 28: 145–66.

—— 1982. *The Latin Sexual Vocabulary*. Baltimore: The Johns Hopkins University Press.

ADOMEIT, K. 1980. 'Rechts' und 'links' bei Cicero. In M. von Harder and G. Thilman (eds.), *De iustitia et iure. Festgabe für Ulrich von Lübtow zum 80 Geburtstag*. Berlin: Duncker and Humblot, 81–91.

ALEXANDER, M. C. 1985. *Praemia* in the *Quaestiones* of the Late Republic. *Classical Philology* 80: 20–32.

—— 2002. *The Case for the Prosecution in the Ciceronian Era*. Ann Arbor, Mich.: University of Michigan Press.

ALLEN, W., Jr. 1952. Cicero's Provincial Governorship in 63 B.C. *Transactions of the American Philological Association* 83: 233–41.

—— 1954. Cicero's Conceit. *Transactions of the American Philological Association* 85: 121–44.

ALTHEIM, F. 1940. *Lex Sacrata: Die Anfänge der plebeischen Organisation*. Albae Vigiliae, 1. Amsterdam: Pantheon.

ANDRÉ, JEAN-MARIE. 1966. *L'otium dans la vie morale et intellectuelle romaine, des origines à l'époque augustéenne*. Paris: Presses universitaires de France.

ANNAS, J. 1993. *The Morality of Happiness*. Oxford: Oxford University Press.

ASTIN, A. E. 1964. *Leges Aelia et Fufia. Latomus* 23: 421–45.

—— 1985. Censorships in the Late Republic. *Historia* 34: 175–90.

ATKINS, E. M. 1990. '*Domina et regina virtutum*': Justice and *societas* in *de Officiis*. *Phronesis* 35: 258–89.

AXER, J. 1989. Tribunal-Stage-Arena: Modelling of the Communication Situation in M. Tullius Cicero's Judicial Speeches. *Rhetorica* 7: 299–311.

BADIAN, E. 1959. The Early Career of A. Gabinius (cos. 58 B.C.). *Philologus* 103: 87–99.

—— 1965. M. Porcius Cato and the Annexation and Early Administration of Cyprus. *Journal of Roman Studies* 55: 110–21.

—— 1973. Marius' Villas: The Testimony of the Slave and the Knave. *Journal of Roman Studies* 63: 121–32.

—— 1983. *Publicans and Sinners: Private Enterprise in the Service of the Roman Republic.* 2nd edn. Ithaca, NY: Cornell University Press.

—— 1984*a*. *Foreign Clientelae (264–70 B.C.).* Oxford: Oxford University Press.

—— 1984*b*. Notes on a New List of Roman Senators. *Zeitschrift für Papyrologie und Epigraphik* 55: 101–13.

—— 1988. The Clever and the Wise. *Bulletin of the Institute of Classical Studies.* Supplement 51. London: Institute of Classical Studies, 6–12.

—— 1989*a*. The *scribae* of the Roman Republic. *Klio* 71: 582–603.

—— 1989*b*. The Case of the Cowardly Tribune. *Ancient History Bulletin* 3: 78–84.

—— 1990. The Consuls, 179–49 B.C. *Chiron* 20: 317–413.

BALOGH, J. 1926. *Voces Paginarum*: Beiträge zur Geschichte des lauten Lesens und Schreibens. *Philologus* 82: 84–109, 202–40.

BALSDON, J. P. V. D. 1957. Roman History, 58–56 B.C.: Three Ciceronian Problems. *Journal of Roman Studies* 47: 15–20.

—— 1960. *Auctoritas, Dignitas, Otium. Classical Quarterly* 10: 43–50.

—— 1962. Roman History, 65–50 B.C.: Five Problems. *Journal of Roman Studies* 52: 134–441.

—— 1969. *Life and Leisure in Ancient Rome.* New York: McGraw-Hill.

BARLOW, J. 1994. Cicero's Sacrilege in 63 B.C. In C. Deroux (ed.), *Studies in Latin Literature and Roman History,* vol. 7. Collection Latomus v. 227. Brussels, 180–9.

BARTON, C. 2001. *Roman Honor.* Berkeley, Calif: University of California Press.

BARTON, T. S. 1994. *Power and Knowledge: Astrology, Physiognomics, and Medicine under the Roman Empire.* Ann Arbor, Mich.: University of Michigan Press.

BARTSCH, S. 1994. *Actors in the Audience.* Cambridge, Mass.: Harvard University Press.

BATES, R. L. 1986. *Rex in senatu*: A Political Biography of M. Aemilius Scaurus. *Proceedings of the American Philosophical Society* 130: 251–88.

BEARD, M., J. NORTH, and S. PRICE. 1998. *Religions of Rome.* 2 vols. Cambridge: Cambridge University Press.

BELL, A. J. E. 2004. *Spectacular Power in the Greek and Roman City.* Oxford: Oxford University Press.

BENNER, H. 1987. *Die Politik des P. Clodius Pulcher.* Historia Einzelschriften, 50. Wiesbaden.

BERGER, A. 1953. *Encyclopedic Dictionary of Roman Law.* Transactions of the American Philosophical Society, ns, vol. 43, pt. 2. Philadelphia.

BERLIN, I. 1958. *Two Concepts of Liberty: An Inaugural Lecture Delivered before the University of Oxford, on 31 October 1958.* Oxford: Clarendon Press.

BERNSTEIN, F. 1998. *Ludi publici: Untersuchungen zur Entstehung und Entwicklung der öffentlichen Spiele im republikanischen Rom.* Stuttgart: F. Steiner.

BERRY, D. H. 1996. *Cicero: Pro P. Sulla oratio.* Cambridge Classical Texts and Commentaries, 30. Cambridge: Cambridge University Press.

—— 2003. *Equester ordo tuus est*: Did Cicero Win His Cases Because of His Support for the *Equites? Classical Quarterly* 53: 222–34.

—— 2004. Literature and Persuasion in Cicero's *pro Archia.* In J. Powell and J. Patterson (eds.), *Cicero the Advocate.* Oxford: Oxford University Press. 291–311.

BINOT, C. 2001. Le rôle de Scipion Nasica Sérapion dans la crise gracquienne, une relecture. *Pallas* 57: 185–203.

BLEICKEN, J. 1975. *Lex publica: Gesetz und Recht in der römischen Republik.* Berlin: Walter de Gruyter.

—— 1995. *Cicero und die Ritter.* Abhandlungen der Akademie der Wissenschaften in Göttingen, Philologisch-Historische Klasse 3. Folge, Nr. 213. Göttingen: Vandenhoeck and Ruprecht.

BONNEFOND-COUDRY, M. 1989. *Le Sénat de la République romaine: De la guerre d'Hannibal à Auguste: pratiques délibératives et prise de décision.* Bibliothèque des Ecoles françaises d'Athènes et de Rome, fasc. 273e. Paris: Ecole française de Rome.

BOYANCÉ, P. 1941. *Cum Dignitate Otium. Revue des Études Anciennes* 43: 172–91.

BRAUND, D. 1984. *Rome and the Friendly King: The Character of the Client Kingship.* London: St Martin's Press.

BRENNAN, T. C. 2004. Power and Process under the Republican 'Constitution'. In H. I. Flower (ed.), *The Cambridge Companion to the Roman Republic.* Cambridge: Cambridge University Press, 31–65.

BRIND'AMOUR, P. 1983. *Le Calendrier romain.* Ottawa: Éditions de l'Université d'Ottawa.

BROUGHTON, T. R. S. 1991. *Candidates Defeated in Roman Elections: Some Ancient Roman 'Also-Rans'.* Transactions of the American Philosophical Society, 81.4. Philadelphia: American Philosophical Society.

BROUWER, H. H. J. 1989. *Bona Dea: The Sources and a Description of the Cult.* Etudes préliminaires aux religions orientales dans l'Empire romain, vol. 110. Leiden: E. J. Brill.

BROWN, P. 1988. *The Body and Society: Men, Women, and Sexual Renunciation in Early Christianity.* New York: Columbia University Press.

BRUNT, P. A. 1966. The Roman Mob. *Past and Present* 35: 3–27.

—— 1971*a*. *Italian Manpower 225 B.C.–A.D. 14*. Oxford: Oxford University Press.

—— 1971*b*. *Social Conflicts in the Roman Republic*. Oxford: Oxford University Press.

—— 1981. *Iudicia sublata* (58–57 B.C.). *Liverpool Classical Monthly* 6: 227–31.

—— 1982. *Nobilitas* and *Novitas*. *Journal of Roman Studies* 72: 1–18.

—— 1988. *The Fall of the Roman Republic and Related Essays*. Oxford: Oxford University Press.

BURCK, E. 1967. Vom Sinn des *Otium* im alten Rom. In H. Oppermann (ed.), *Römische Wertbegriffe*. Wege der Forschung 34. Darmstadt: Wissenschaftliche Buchgesellschaft, 503–15.

BURCKHARDT, L. A. 1988. *Politische Strategien der Optimaten in der Späten Römischen Republik*. Historia Einzelschriften 57. Stuttgart: F. Steiner.

CAMPBELL, G. 2003. *Lucretius on Creation and Evolution: A Commentary on 'De Rerum Natura' Book Five, Lines 772–1104*. Oxford: Oxford University Press.

CANCELLI, F. 1971. Sull'origine del diritto romano secondo un motivo ricorrente in scrittori ellenistico-romani e Cicerone, De re publica 5, 3. *Studia et Documenta Historiae et iuris* 37: 328–37.

CARNEY, T. F. 1960. Cicero's Picture of Marius. *Wiener Studien* 73: 83–122.

CASCIONE, C. 1996. *Bonorum proscriptio apud Columnam Maeniam*. *Labeo* 42: 444–55.

CASSON, L. 1971. *Ships and Seamanship in the Ancient World*. Princeton: Princeton University Press.

CASTNER, C. J. 1988. *Prosopography of Roman Epicureans, from the Second Century B.C. to the Second Century A.D.* Studien zur klassichen Philologie, 34. Frankfurt am Main.

CERUTTI, S. M. 1998. P. Clodius and the Stairs of the Temple of Castor. *Latomus* 57: 292–305.

CHAMPLIN, E. J. 2003. Agamemnon at Rome: Roman Dynasts and Greek Heroes. In D. Braund and C. Gill (eds.), *Myth, History and Culture in Republican Rome: Studies in Honour of T. P. Wiseman*. Exeter, 295–319.

CHAPLIN, J. D. 2000. *Livy's Exemplary History*. Oxford: Oxford University Press.

CHRISTES, J. 1988. *Cum dignitate otium* (Cic. *Sest*. 98): eine Nachbereitung. *Gymnasium* 95: 303–15.

CLASSEN, C. J. 1993. Gottmenschentum in der römischen Republik. In H. Bernsdorf, M. Vielberg, et al. (eds.), *Die Welt der Römer*. Berlin: Walter de Gruyter, 12–38.

—— 1998. Romulus in der römischen Republik. *Zur Literatur und Gesellschaft der Römer*. Stuttgart: F. Steiner, 21–54.

CLOUD, D. 2002. The Pompeian Tablets and Some Literary Texts. In P. McKechnie (eds.), *Thinking Like a Lawyer: Essays on Legal History and General History for John Crook on His Eightieth Birthday.* Mnemosyne Suppl. 231. Leiden: E. J. Brill.

COHEN, B. 1975. La notion d'*ordo* dans la Rome antique. *Bulletin de l'Association Guillaume Budé*, 259–82.

COLEMAN, J. 2000. *A History of Political Thought*, vol. 1: *From Ancient Greece to Early Christianity.* Oxford: Oxford University Press.

CORBEILL, A. 1996. *Controlling Laughter: Political Humor in the Late Roman Republic.* Princeton: Princeton University Press.

—— 2002. Ciceronian Invective. In J. May (ed.), *Brill's Companion to Cicero: Oratory and Rhetoric.* Leiden: E. J. Brill, 197–217.

—— 2004. *Nature Embodied.* Princeton: Princeton University Press.

COSSARINI, A. 1981. *Bestia* e *belua* in Cicerone. *Giornale filologico ferrarese* 4: 123–34.

COURTNEY, E. 1993. *The Fragmentary Latin Poets.* Oxford: Oxford University Press.

COUSIN, J. 1965. *Cicero: Discours*, vol. 14: *Pour Sestius, Contre Vatinius.* Paris: Les Belles Lettres.

CRAIG, C. 1981. The Accusator as *Amicus*: An Original Roman Tactic of Argumentation. *Transactions of the American Philological Association* 111: 31–7.

—— 1986. Cato's Stoicism and the Understanding of Cicero's Speech for Murena. *Transactions of the American Philological Association* 116: 229–39.

—— 2001. Shifting Charge and Shifty Argument in Cicero's Speech for Sestius. In C. Wooten (ed.), *The Orator in Action and Theory in Greece and Rome.* Mnemosyne Suppl. 225. Leiden: E. J. Brill, 111–22.

—— 2004. Audience Expectations, Invective, and Proof. *Cicero the Advocate.* Ed. J. Powell and J. Paterson. Oxford: Oxford University Press. 187–214

CURTIUS, L. 1931. Physiognomik des römischen Porträts. *Die Antike* 7: 226–54.

D'ARMS, J. H. 1981. *Commerce and Social Standing in Ancient Rome.* Cambridge, Mass.: Harvard University Press.

D'ISANTO, G. 1993. *Capua romana.* Rome: Edizioni Quasar.

DALFEN, J. 2000. Ciceros '*cum dignitate otium*': einiges zur (nicht unproblematischen) Freizeitkultur grosser Römer. In E. Sigot (ed.), *Otium - Negotium: Beiträge des Interdisziplinären Symposions der Sodalitas zum Thema Zeit, Carnuntum, 28.–30.–8. 1998.* Vienna: Ed. Praesens, 169–87.

DAMON, C. 1992. Sex. Cloelius, Scriba. *Harvard Studies in Classical Philology* 94: 227–50.

DAVID, J.-M. 1980. *Maiorum exempla sequi*: L'exemplum historique dans les discours judiciaires de Cicéron. *Mélanges d'Archéologie et d'Histoire de l'École française de Rome* 92: 67–86.

—— 1992. *Le patronat judiciaire au dernier siècle de la République romaine*. Rome: École française de Rome.

DAVIES, J. K. 1971. *Athenian Propertied Families 600–300 B.C.* Oxford: Oxford University Press.

DAVIS, H. H. 1958. Cicero's Burial. *Phoenix* 12: 174–7.

DENIAUX, E. 1993. *Clientèles et pouvoir à l'époque de Cicéron*. Rome: École française de Rome.

DE SOUZA, P. 1999. *Piracy in the Graeco-Roman World*. Cambridge: Cambridge University Press.

DREXLER, H. 1957, 1958. *Res publica*. *Maia* 9: 247–81 and 10: 3–37.

DRUMMOND, A. 1989. Rome in the Fifth Century, II: The Citizen Community. *Cambridge Ancient History*, vol. 7.2, 2nd edn. Cambridge: Cambridge University Press, 212–25.

—— 1995. *Law, Politics and Power: Sallust and the Execution of the Catilinarian Conspirators*. Hermes Einzelschriften, 93. Stuttgart: F. Steiner.

DUBEL, S. 1997. *Ekphrasis* et *enargeia*. In C. Lévy and L. Pernot (eds.), *Dire l'évidence*. Paris: L'Harmattan, 249–64.

DUBOURDIEU, A. 1989. *Les origines et le développement du culte des pénates à Rome*. Collection de l'Ecole française de Rome, 118. Rome: Ecole française de Rome.

DUNCAN-JONES, R. P. 1982. *The Economy of the Roman Empire: Quantitative Studies*. 2nd edn. Cambridge: Cambridge University Press.

DYCK, A. R. 1997. *A Commentary on Cicero, De Officiis*. Ann Arbor, Mich.: University of Michigan Press.

—— 2004a. *A Commentary on Cicero, De Legibus*. Ann Arbor, Mich.: University of Michigan Press.

—— 2004b. Cicero's *Devotio*: The Roles of *Dux* and Scape-Goat in His *Post Reditum* Rhetoric. *Harvard Studies in Classical Philology* 102: 299–314.

EDWARDS, C. 1993. *The Politics of Immorality in Ancient Rome*. Cambridge: Cambridge University Press.

EPSTEIN, D. F. 1987. *Personal Enmity in Roman Politics, 218–43 B.C.* London: Croom Helm.

EVANS, R. J. 1983. The Gellius of Cicero's *Pro Sestio*. *Liverpool Classical Monthly* 8: 124–6.

FANTHAM, E. 1972. *Comparative Studies in Republican Latin Imagery*. Toronto: University of Toronto Press.

—— 1975. The Trials of Gabinius in 54 B.C. *Historia* 24: 425–43.

Favory, F. 1976. Classes dangereuses et crise de l'État dans le discours cicéronien d'après les écrits de Cicéron de 57 à 52. *Texte, politique, idéologie: Cicéron.* Annales littéraires de l'Université de Besançon, 187. Besançon: Université de Besançon, 109–233.

—— 1978–9. Clodius et le péril servile, fonction du thème servile dans le discours polémique cicéronien. *Index: Quaderni Camerti di studi romanistici* 8: 173–205.

Ferrary, J.-L. 2001. Réponse à Miriam Griffin. In C. Auvray-Assayas and D. Delattre (eds.), *Les polémiques philosophiques à Rome à la fin de la République: Cicéron et Philodème de Gadara.* Paris: Éditions Rue d'Ulm, 101–5.

Fezzi, L. 1995. *Lex clodia de iure et tempore legum rogandarum. Studi classici et orientali* 45: 298–328.

Flaig, E. 2003. *Ritualisierte Politik. Zeichen, Gesten und Herrschaft im Alten Rom.* Historische Semantik Band 1. Göttingen: Vandenhoeck & Ruprecht.

Flambard, J. M. 1977. Clodius, les collèges, la plèbe et les esclaves. Recherches sur la politique populaire au millieu du I siècle. *Mélanges d'Archéologie et d'Histoire de l'École française de Rome* 89: 115–56.

Flower, H. I. 1995. *Fabulae Praetextae*: When Were Plays On Contemporary Subjects Performed in Rome? *Classical Quarterly* 45: 170–90.

—— 1996. *Ancestor Masks and Aristocratic Power in Roman Culture.* Oxford: Oxford University Press.

—— 2004. Spectacle and Political Culture in the Roman Republic. In H. I. Flower (ed.), *The Cambridge Companion to the Roman Republic.* Cambridge: Cambridge University Press, 322–43.

Forsdyke, S. 2005. *Exile, Ostracism, and Athenian Democracy: The Politics of Expulsion in Ancient Greece.* Princeton: Princeton University Press.

Fowler, D. 1989. Lucretius and Politics. In M. Griffin and J. Barnes (eds.), *Philosophia Togata.* Oxford: Oxford University Press, 120–50.

Fraenkel, E. 1916. Zur Geschichte des Wortes '*fides*'. *Rheinisches Museum* 71: 187–99.

Frederiksen, M. 1966. Caesar, Cicero, and the Problem of Debt. *Journal of Roman Studies* 56: 128–41.

—— 1984. *Campania.* Ed. with additions by Nicholas Purcell. British School at Rome. London: British School at Rome.

Freyburger, G. 1986. *Fides: Étude sémantique et religieuse depuis les origines jusqu'à l'époque augustéene.* Paris: Les Belles Lettres.

Friedländer, L. 1907. *Roman Life and Manners under the Early Empire.* Trans. L. A. Magnus. 4 vols. London. Routledge and Kegan Paul.

Fuerst, F. 1934. *Die Bedeutung der* auctoritas *im privaten und öffentlichen Leben der römischen Republik.* Diss. Marburg.

FUHRMANN, M. 1960. *Cum dignitate otium. Gymnasium* 67: 481–500.

GABBA, E. 1961. Cicerone e la falsificazione dei senatoconsulti. *Studi classici e orientali* 10: 89–96.

—— 1994. Rome and Italy: The Social War. *Cambridge Ancient History.* vol. 9, 2nd edn. Cambridge: Cambridge University Press, 104–28.

GAILLARD, J. 1972. Regulus selon Cicéron: autopsie d'un mythe. *Revue des études latines* 50: 46–9.

GALINSKY, K. 1996. *Augustan Culture.* Princeton: Princeton University Press.

GALSTERER, H. 1976. *Herrschaft und Verwaltung im republikanischen Italien: Die Beziehungen Roms zu d. italischen Gemeinden vom Latinerfrieden 338 v. Chr. bis zum Bundesgenossenkrieg 91 v. Chr.* Münchener Beiträge zur Papyrusforschung und antiken Rechtsgeschichte, 68. Munich: Beck.

GANTZ, T. 1993. *Early Greek Myth: A Guide to Literary and Artistic Sources.* Baltimore: The Johns Hopkins University Press.

GARDNER, R. (ed.). 1958*a*. *Cicero. Orations: Pro Sestio, In Vatinium.* Loeb Classical Library 309. Cambridge, MA: Harvard University Press.

—— (ed.). 1958*b*. *Cicero. Pro Caelio, De Provinciis Consularibus, De Balbo.* Loeb Classical Library 447. Cambridge, Mass: Harvard University Press.

GEFFCKEN, K. A. 1995. *Comedy in the Pro Caelio: with an appendix on the In Clodium et Curionem.* Wauconda, Ill: Bolchazy and Carducci.

GELZER, M. 1968. *Caesar: Politician and Statesman.* Cambridge, Mass: Harvard University Press.

—— 1969*a*. *The Roman Nobility.* Trans. R. Seager. Oxford: Basil Blackwell.

—— 1969*b*. *Cicero: Ein biographischer Versuch.* Wiesbaden: F. Steiner.

GLEASON, M. 1995. *Making Men: Sophists and Self-Presentation in Ancient Rome.* Princeton: Princeton University Press.

GOTOFF, H. C. 1986. Cicero's Analysis of the Prosecution Speeches in the *Pro Caelio*: An Exercise in Practical Criticism. *Classical Philology* 81: 122–32.

GOULD, J. 1973. Hiketeia. *Journal of Hellenic Studies* 93: 74–103.

GRAFF, J. 1963. *Ciceros Selbstauffassung.* Heidelberg: C. Winter.

GRAHAME, M. 1997. Public and Private in the Roman House: The Spatial Order of the Casa del Fauno. In R. Laurence and A. Wallace-Hadrill (eds.), *Domestic Space in the Roman World: Pompeii and Beyond.* Journal of Roman Archaeology. Supplementary series, no. 22. Portsmouth, RI: Journal of Roman Archaeology, 137–64.

GRAVER, M. 2002. *Cicero on the Emotions: Tusculan Disputations 3 and 4.* Chicago: University of Chicago Press.

GREENIDGE, A. H. J. 1894. *Infamia: Its Place in Roman Public and Private law.* Oxford: Oxford University Press.

—— 1901. *The Legal Procedure of Cicero's Time.* New York: H. Frowde.

GRIFFIN, M. 1986. Philosophy, Cato, and Roman Suicide. *Greece and Rome* 33: 65–77, 192–202.

—— 1989. Philosophy, Politics, and Politicians. In M. Griffin and J. Barnes (eds.), *Philosophia Togata*. Oxford: Oxford University Press, 1–37.

—— 1994. The Intellectual Developments of the Ciceronian Age. *Cambridge Ancient History*. vol. 9, 2nd edn. Cambridge: Cambridge University Press, 689–728.

—— 2001. Piso, Cicero, and Their Audience. In C. Auvray-Assayas and D. Delattre (eds.), *Les Polémiques philosophiques à Rome à la fin de la République: Cicéron et Philodème de Gadara*. Paris: Éditions Rue d'Ulm, 85–99.

GRILLI, A. 1994. Sul 'crollo' della repubblica in Pro Sestio 2,5. *Paideia* 49: 34–6.

GRIMAL, P. 1967. *Études de chronologie cicéronienne (années 58 et 57 av. J.-C.)*. Paris: Les Belles Lettres.

GRISÉ, Y. 1982. *Le suicide dans la Rome antique*. Montreal: Bellarmin.

GRUEN, E. 1974. *The Last Generation of the Roman Republic*. Berkeley, Calif.: University of California Press.

—— 1984. *The Hellenistic World and the Coming of Rome*. 2 vols. Berkeley, Calif.: University of California Press.

—— 1990. *Studies in Greek Culture and Roman Policy*. Leiden: E. J. Brill.

GUNDERSON, E. 2000. *Staging Masculinity: The Rhetoric of Performance in the Roman World*. Ann Arbor, Mich.: University of Michigan Press.

HABICHT, C. 1990. *Cicero the Politician*. Baltimore: The Johns Hopkins University Press.

HABINEK, T. N. 1998. *The Politics of Latin Literature*. Princeton: Princeton University Press.

HALM, K. 1886. *Cicero: Ausgewählte Reden*, vol. 4: *Die Rede für Publius Sestius*. 6., verb. aufl., besorgt von G. Laubman. Berlin: Weidmannsche Buchhandlung.

HARIMAN, R. 2001. *Decorum. Encyclopedia of Rhetoric*. New York: Oxford University Press, 199–209.

HARRIS, W. V. 1971. *Rome in Etruria and Umbria*. Oxford: Oxford University Press.

HARRISON, S. J. 1990. Cicero's '*De temporibus suis*': The Evidence. *Hermes* 118: 455–63.

HAURY, A. 1974. Cicéron et la gloire: Une pédagogie de la vertu. *Mélanges de philosophie, de littérature et d'histoire ancienne offerts à Pierre Boyancé*. Paris: École française de Rome, 401–17.

HEIKKILÄ, K. 1993. '*Lex non iure rogata*': The Senate and the Annulment of Laws in the Late Republic. *Senatus Populusque Romanus: Studies in Roman*

Republican Legislation. Acta Instituti Romani Finnlandiae 13. Helsinki: [s.n.], 117–42.

HEINZE, R. 1960. *Vom Geist des Römertums.* 3rd edn. Stuttgart: B. G. Teubner.

HELLEGOUARC'H, J. 1963. *Le vocabulaire latin des relations et des partis politiques sous la république.* Publications de la Faculté des lettres et sciences humaines de l'Université de Lille, 11. Paris: Les Belles Lettres.

—— (ed.). 1982. *Velleius Paterculus: Histoire romaine.* Paris: Belles Lettres.

HENDERSON, M. I. 1963. The Establishment of the *Equester Ordo. Journal of Roman Studies* 53: 61–72.

HERTER, H. 1959. *Effeminatus. Reallexikon für Antike und Christentum.* 4. 620–50.

HESKEL, J. 1994. Cicero as Evidence for Attitudes to Dress in the Late Republic. In J. L. Sebesta and L. Bonfante (eds.), *The World of Roman Costume.* Madison, Wis.: University of Wisconsin Press, 133–45.

HICKSON-HAHN, F. 1998. What's So Funny? Laughter and Incest in Invective Humor. *Syllecta Classica* 9: 1–36.

HIESINGER, U. W. 1973. Portraiture in the Roman Republic. *Aufstieg und Niedergang der römischen Welt* 1.4: 805–25 (1.4a: 159–71 for plates).

HILL, T. 2004. *Ambitiosa mors: Suicide and Self in Roman Thought and Literature.* Studies in Classics, 10. New York: Routledge.

HILTBRUNNER, O. 1967. *Vir gravis.* In H. Oppermann (ed.), *Römische Wertbegriffe.* Wege der Forschung 34. Darmstadt: Wissenschaftliche Buchgesellschaft, 402–19.

HINARD, F. 1980. *Paternus inimicus.* Sur une expression de Cicéron. *Mélanges de littérature et d'épigraphie latines, d'histoire ancienne et d'archéologie. Hommages à la mémoire de Pierre Wuilleumier.* Paris: Les Belles Lettres, 197–210.

—— 1985. Les proscriptions de la Rome républicaine. *Collection de l'École française de Rome,* 83. Rome: École française de Rome.

HIND, J. G. F. 1994. Mithridates. *Cambridge Ancient History.* vol. 9, 2nd edn. Cambridge: Cambridge University Press, 129–64.

HOLDEN, H. A. (ed.). 1889. *M. Tulli Ciceronis pro Publio Sestio Oratio ad Iudices.* 3rd edn., with Supplements by J. S. Reid. London: Macmillan and Co.

HÖLKESKAMP, K.-J. 1995. *Oratoris Maxima Scaena:* Reden vor dem Volk in der politischen Kultur der Republik. In M. Jehne (ed.), *Demokratie in Rom? Die Rolle des Volkes in der Politik der römischen Republik.* Historia. Einzelschriften, 96. Stuttgart: F. Steiner, 11–49.

—— 1996. *Exempla und mos maiorum:* Überlegungen zum kollektiven Gedächtnis der Nobilität. In H.-J. Gehrke and A. Möller (eds.),

Vergangenheit und Lebenswelt. Soziale Kommunikation, Traditionsbildung und historisches Bewußtsein. Tübingen: Narr, 301–38.

HÖLKESKAMP, K.-J. 2001. Capitol, Comitium und Forum: Öffentliche Raümesakrale Topographie und Errinerungs-landschaften der römischen Republik. In S. Faller (ed.), *Studien zu antiken Identitäten.* Würzburg: Ergon Verlag, 97–132.

HOLMES, T. RICE. 1923. *The Roman Republic and the Founder of Empire.* 3 vols. Oxford: Oxford University Press.

HOOFF, A. J. L. VAN. 1990. *From Autothanasia to Suicide.* London: Routledge.

HOPKINS, K. 1978. *Conquerors and Slaves.* Cambridge: Cambridge University Press.

—— and G. BURTON. 1983. Political Succession in the Late Republic. *Death and Renewal.* Cambridge: Cambridge University Press, 31–119.

HÜBNER, H. 1875. *Ephemeris Epigraphica* 2: 41.

HUGHES, J. J. 1992. Piso's Eyebrows. *Mnemosyne* 45: 234–7.

HUSS, W. 2001. *Ägypten in hellenistischer Zeit, 332–30 v. Chr.* Munich: Beck.

INSTINSKY, H. U. 1967. *Consensus universorum.* In H. Oppermann (ed.), *Römische Wertbegriffe.* Wege der Forschung 34. Darmstadt: Wissenschaftliche Buchgesellschaft, 209–28.

INWOOD, B. 1987. Commentary on Striker. In J. J. Cleary (ed.), *Proceedings of the Boston Area Colloquium in Ancient Philosophy,* vol. 2. Lanham, Md.: University Press of America, 95–101.

JAL, P. 1963. *Hostis (publicus)* dans la littérature latine de la fin de la République. *Revue des études anciennes* 65: 53–79.

JOCELYN, H. D. 1967. *The Tragedies of Ennius.* Cambridge: Cambridge University Press.

—— 1976–7. The Ruling Class of the Roman Republic and Greek Philosphers. *Bulletin of the Rylands Library* 59: 323–66.

—— 1989. Romulus and the *di genitales* (Ennius, *Annales* 110–111 Skutsch). In *Studies in Latin Literature and Its Tradition in Honour of C. O. Brink.* Cambridge Philolological Society Supplements. Cambridge: Cambridge University Press, 39–65.

JOHANNEMANN, R. 1935. *Cicero und Pompeius in ihren wechselseitigen Beziehungen bis zum Jahre 51 vor Christi Geburt.* Inaugural-Dissertation, Münster.

JONES, A. H. M. 1972. *Criminal Courts of the Roman Republic and Principate.* Oxford: Basil Blackwell.

JONES, C. P. 1987. Stigma. Tattooing and Branding in Graeco-Roman Antiquity. *Journal of Roman Studies* 77: 139–55.

References   449

KASTER, R. A. 1995. *Suetonius: De Grammaticis et Rhetoribus*. Oxford: Oxford University Press.

—— 2002. The Taxonomy of Patience, or When is *Patientia* not a Virtue? *Classical Philology* 97: 131–42.

—— 2005. *Emotion, Restraint, and Community in Ancient Rome*. Oxford: Oxford University Press.

KELLY, GORDON. 2006. *A History of Exile in the Roman Republic*. Cambridge: Cambridge University Press.

KINSEY, T. E. (ed.). 1971. *Pro Quinctio oratio*. Sydney: Sydney University Press.

KLODT, C. 2003. Prozessparteien und politische Gegner als *dramatis personae*. In B.-J. Schröder and J.-P. Schröder (eds.), *Studium Declamatorium: Untersuchungen zu Schulübungen und Prunkreden von der Antike bis zur Neuzeit*. Munich: K.G. Sauer, 35–106.

KNOCHE, U. 1935. *Magnitudo Animi*. Philologus Supplementband 27. 3. Leipzig: Dieterich'sche Verlagsbuchhandlung.

—— 1967. Die römische Ruhmesgedanke. In H. Opperman (ed.), *Römische Wertbegriffe*. Wege der Forschung, 34. Darmstadt: Wissenschaftliche Buchgesellschaft, 420–45.

KONRAD, C. F. 1984. A Note on the Stemma of the Gabinii Capitones. *Klio* 66: 151–6.

KOSTER, S. 1980. *Die Invektive in der griechischen und römischen Literatur*. Beiträge zur klassichen Philologie, 99. Meisenheim an Glan: Hain, 210–81.

KROSTKENKO, B. A. 2004. Binary Phrases and the Middle Style as Social Code: *Rhetorica ad Herennium* 4. 13 and 4. 16. *Harvard Studies in Classical Philology* 102: 237–74.

KUBITSCHEK, W. 1928. *Grundriß der antiken Zeitrechnung*. Handbuch der Altertumswissenschaft, I.7. Munich: Beck.

LACEY, W. K. 1962. Cicero, *Pro Sestio* 96–143. *Classical Quarterly* 12: 67–71.

—— 1986. *Patria Potestas*. In B. Rawson (ed.), *The Family in Ancient Rome*. Ithaca, NY: Cornell University Press, 121–44.

LAHUSEN, G. 1983. *Untersuchungen zur Ehrenstatue in Rom: Literarische und epigraphische Zeugnisse*. Rome: G. Bretschneider.

LASER, G. 1997. *Populo et scaenae serviendum est: Die Bedeutung der städtischen Masse in der späten römischen Republik*. Bochumer Altertumswissenschaftliches Colloquium 29. Trier: Wissenschaftlicher Verlag Trier.

LATTE, K. 1967. *Römische Religionsgeschichte*. Handbuch der Altertumswissenschaft, 5.4. Munich: Beck.

LAUSBERG, H. 1998. *Handbook of Literary Rhetoric*. Foreword G. A. Kennedy; trans. M. T. Bliss, A. Jansen, D. E. Orton; ed. D. E. Orton and R. D. Anderson. Leiden: E. J. Brill.

LEACH, E. W. 2000. The *Spectacula* of Cicero's *Pro Sestio*: Patronage, Production, and Performance. In S. K. Dickison and J. P. Hallett (eds.), *Rome and Her Monuments: Essays on the City and Literature of Rome in Honor of Katherine A. Geffcken.* Wauconda, Ill.: Bolchazy and Carducci, 369–97.

LEIGH, M. 2004. The *Pro Caelio* and Comedy. *Classical Philology* 99: 300–35.

LENAGHAN, J. O. 1969. *A Commentary on Cicero's Oration 'De Haruspicum Responso'.* Studies in Classical Literature, 5. The Hague: Mouton.

LÉVY, C. 1998. Rhétorique et philosophie: la monstruosité politique chez Cicéron. *Revue des etudes latines* 76: 139–57.

LIBERO, L. de. 1992. *Obstruktion: Politische Praktiken im Senat und in der Volksversammlung der ausgehenden römischen Republik (70–49 v. Ch.).* Hermes Einzelschriften 59. Stuttgart: F. Steiner.

LITCHFIELD, H. W. 1914. National *Exempla Virtutis* in Roman Literature. *Harvard Studies in Classical Philology* 25: 1–25.

LIEGLE, J. 1967. Pietas. In H. Oppermann (ed.), *Römische Wertbegriffe.* Wege der Forschung 34. Darmstadt: Wissenschaftliche Buchgesellschaft, 229–73.

LIND, L. R. 1979. The Tradition of Roman Moral Conservatism. *Latomus* 164:7–58.

—— 1986. The Idea of the Republic and the Foundations of Roman Political Liberty. In C. Deroux (ed.), *Studies in Latin Literature and Roman History,* vol. 4. Collection Latomus, 180. Brussels: Latomus, 44–108.

—— 1989. The Idea of the Republic and the Foundations of Roman Morality. In C. Deroux (ed.), *Studies in Latin Literature and Roman History,* vol. 5. Collection Latomus, 196. Brussells: Latomus, 5–34.

—— 1992. The Idea of the Republic and the Foundations of Roman Morality (second part). In C. Deroux (ed.), *Studies in Latin Literature and Roman History,* vol. 6. Collection Latomus, 206. Brussells: Latomus, 5–40.

LINDERSKI, J. 1971. Three Trials in 54 B.C.: Sufenas, Cato, Procilius and Cicero, *Ad Atticum* 4.15.4. *Studi in onore di Edoardo Volterra,* vol. 2. Milan: A. Giuffrè, 281–302.

—— 1986. The Augural Law. *Aufstieg und Niedergang der römischen Welt* II. 16. 3. 2146–312.

—— 1995. *Roman Questions.* Stuttgart: F. Steiner.

LINTOTT, A. W. 1965. *Trinundinum. Classical Quarterly* 15: 281–5.

—— 1967. P. Clodius—Felix Catilina? *Greece and Rome* 14: 157–69.

—— 1968. *Nundinae* and the Chronology of the Late Roman Republic. *Classical Quarterly* 18: 189–94.

—— 1974. *Provocatio*: From the Struggle of the Orders to the Principate. *Aufstieg und Niedergang der römischen Welt* 1. 2. Berlin, 226–67.

—— 1990. Electorial Bribery in the Roman Republic. *Journal of Roman Studies* 80: 1–16.

—— 1992. *Judicial Reform and Land Reform in the Roman Republic.* Oxford: Oxford University Press.

—— 1999*a. Violence in Republican Rome.* 2nd edn. Oxford: Oxford University Press.

—— 1999*b. The Constitution of the Roman Republic.* Oxford: Oxford University Press.

—— 2004. Legal Procedure in Cicero's Time. In J. Powell and J. Paterson (eds.), *Cicero the Advocate.* Oxford: Oxford University Press, 96–116.

LIOU-GILLE, B. 1998. La consecration du Champ de Mars et la consecration du domine de Cicéron. *Museum Helveticum* 55: 37–59.

LOMAS, K. 2004. A Volscian Mafia? Cicero and His Italian Clients. In J. Powell and J. Paterson (eds.), *Cicero the Advocate.* Oxford: Oxford University Press, 61–78.

LONG, A. A. 1986. Pleasure and Social Utility: The Virtues of Being Epicurean. In H. Flashar and O. Gigon (eds.), *Aspects de la philosophie hellénistique.* Entretiens sur l'antiquité classique, 32. Geneva: Vandoeuvres, 283–324.

LONG, A. A. 1995. Cicero's Politics in *De Officiis.* In A. Laks (ed.), *Justice and Generosity: Studies in Hellenistic Social and Political Philosophy.* Cambridge: Cambridge University Press, 213–40.

—— and D. SEDLEY (eds.). 1987. *The Hellenistic Philosophers.* 2 vols. Cambridge: Cambridge University Press.

LÜBTOW, U. VON. 1984–5. Cicero's Rede für Publius Sestius. In V. Giuffrè (ed.), *Sodalitas: Scritti in onore di Antonio Guarino,* vol. 1. Naples: Jovene, 177–201.

MACBAIN, B. 1982. *Prodigy and Expiation: A Study in Religion and Politics in Republican Rome.* Collection Latomus, 177. Brussels: Latomus.

MCDONALD, W. F. 1929. Clodius and the '*lex Aelia Fufia*'. *Journal of Roman Studies*: 19: 164–79.

MCDONNELL, M. 2003. Roman Men and Greek Virtue. In R. M. Rosen and I. Sluiter (eds.), *Andreia: Studies in Manliness and Courage in Classical Antiquity.* Mnemosyne Suppl. 238. Leiden: E. J. Brill, 235–61.

MCFAYDEN, D. 1942. A Constitutional Doctrine Re-examined. *Studies in Honor of Frederick W. Shipley.* Washington University Studies (NS), Language and Literature 14. St Louis: [s.n.], 1–15.

MACK, D. 1937. *Senatsreden und Volksreden bei Cicero.* Kieler Arbeiten zur klassischen Philologie, 2. Würzburg: K. Triltsch.

MACKENDRICK, P. 1995. *The Speeches of Cicero: Context, Law, and Rhetoric.* London: Duckworth.

MADVIG, J. N. 1887. *Opuscula Academica.* Copenhagen: Librari Gyldendaliana.

MANACORDA, D. 1978. The *Ager Cosanus* and the Production of the Amphorae of Sestius. New Evidence and a Reassessment. *Journal of Roman Studies* 68: 122–31.

MANNING, C. E. 1985. *Liberalitas*—the Decline and Rehabilitation of a Virtue. *Greece and Rome* 32: 73–83.

MANUWALD, G. 2001. *Fabulae praetextae: Spuren einer literarischen Gattung der Römer.* Zetemata, 108. Munich: Beck.

MARINONE, N. 2004. *Cronologia ciceroniana.* 2nd edn. E. Malaspina. Collana di studi ciceroniani. Bologna: Patròn Editore.

MARSHALL, A. J. 1984. Symbols and Showmanship in Roman Public Life: The Fasces. *Phoenix* 38: 120–41.

MARSHALL, B. A. 1976. *Crassus: A Political Biography.* Amsterdam: A.M. Hakkert.

—— 1985. *A Historical Commentary on Asconius.* Columbia, Mo.: University of Missouri Press.

—— 1987. Pompeius' Fear of Assassination. *Chiron* 17: 119–33.

MASLAKOV, G. 1984. Valerius Maximus and Roman Historiography: A Study of the *Exempla* Tradition. *Aufstieg und Niedergang der römischen Welt* 2. 32. 1. 437–96.

MASLOWSKI, T. 1974. The Chronology of Cicero's anti-Epicureanism. *Eos* 62: 55–78.

—— 1976. *Domus Milonis oppugnata. Eos* 64: 23–30.

MAY, J. 1980. The Image of the Ship of State in Cicero's Pro Sestio. *Maia* NS 3: 259–64.

—— 1981 The Rhetoric of Advocacy and Patron-Client Identification: Variation on a Theme. *American Journal of Philology* 102: 308–15.

—— 1988. *Trials of Character: The Eloquence of Ciceronian Ethos.* Chapel Hill, NC: University of North Carolina Press.

—— 1996. Cicero and the Beasts. *Syllecta Classica* 7: 143–53.

—— (ed). 2002. *Brill's Companion to Cicero: Oratory and Rhetoric.* Leiden: E. J. Brill.

MAYER, R. 1991. Roman Historical *Exempla* in Seneca. *Sénèque et la prose latine.* Entretiens sur l'antquité classique, 36. Geneva: Vandoeuvres, 141–69, 170–6.

MEYER, E. 1919. *Caesars Monarchie und das Principat des Pompeius.* 2nd edn. Stuttgart: Cotta.

MICHELS, A. 1967. *The Calendar of the Roman Republic.* Princeton: Princeton University Press.

MILLAR, F. 1998. *The Crowd in Rome in the Late Republic.* Jerome Lectures 22. Ann Arbor, Mich.: University of Michigan Press.

MINYARD, J. D. 1985. *Lucretius and the Late Republic: An Essay in Roman Intellectual History.* Mnemosyne Suppl. 90. Leiden: E. J. Brill.

MITCHELL, T. N. 1969. Cicero before Luca (September 57–April 56 B.C.). *Transactions of the American Philological Association* 100: 295–320.

—— 1979. *Cicero: The Ascending Years.* New Haven, Conn.: Yale University Press.

—— 1986. The *Leges Clodiae* and *obnuntiatio. Classical Quarterly* 36: 172–6.

—— 1991. *Cicero: The Senior Statesman.* New Haven, Conn: Yale University Press.

MIX, E. R. 1970. *Marcus Atilius Regulus: Exemplum Historicum.* Studies in Classical Literature, 10. The Hague: Mouton.

MOMIGLIANO, A. 1942. 'Terra marique'. *Journal of Roman Studies* 32: 53–64.

MOMMSEN, T. 1887–8. *Römisches Staatsrecht.* Handbuch der römischen Alterthümer, 1–3 Bd. Leipzig: S. Hirzel.

—— 1899. *Römisches Strafrecht.* Systematisches handbuch der deutschen Rechtswissenschaft, Abt. 1. Leipzig: Duncker und Humblot.

MOREAU, P. 1982. *Clodiana religio: Un process politique en 61 av. J. C.* Paris: Les Belles Lettres.

—— 1987. La *Lex Clodia* sur le bannissement de Cicéron. *Athenaeum* 75: 465–92.

—— 1989. La *rogatio* des huit tribuns de 58 av. J.C. et les clauses de *sanctio* réglementant l'abrogation des loi. *Athenaeum* 67: 151–78.

MORSTEIN-MARX, R. 2004. *Mass Oratory and Political Power in the Late Roman Republic.* Cambridge: Cambridge University Press.

MOURITSEN, H. 2001. *Plebs and Politics in the Late Roman Republic.* Cambridge: Cambridge University Press.

NICHOLSON, J. 1992. *Cicero's Return from Exile: The Orations Post reditum.* Lang Classical Studies, 4. New York: Peter Lang.

NICOLET, C. 1974. *L'Ordre équestre à l'époque républicaine (312–43 av. J.-C.).* 2 vols. Paris: E. de Boccard.

—— 1976. *Tributum: Recherches sur la fiscalité directe sous la republique romaine.* Antiquitas, Reihe 1, 24. Bonn: Habelt.

—— 1980. *The World of the Citizen in Republican Rome.* London: Batsford Academic and Educational.

—— (ed.). 1984. *Des ordres à Rome.* Publications de la Sorbonne: Série Histoire ancienne e médiévale, 13. Paris: Publications de la Sorbonne.

—— 2000. Deux remarques sur l'organisation des sociétés de publicains à la fin de la République romaine. *Censeurs et publicains: économie et fiscalité dans la Rome antique.* Paris: Fayard, 297–319.

NIPPEL, W. 1995. *Public Order in Ancient Rome.* Key Themes in Ancient History. Cambridge: Cambridge University Press.

NISBET, R. G. 1939. *M. Tulli Ciceronis De domo sua ad pontifices oratio.* Oxford: Oxford University Press.

NISBET, R. G. M. 1961. *Cicero: In L. Calpurnium Pisonem Oratio.* Oxford: Oxford University Press.

—— 1966. Review of Cousin 1965. *Classical Review* 16: 335–7.

—— and M. HUBBARD. 1970. *A Commentary on Horace Odes Book 1.* Oxford: Oxford University Press.

—— and N. RUDD. 2004. *A Commentary on Horace Odes Book 3.* Oxford: Oxford University Press.

NOWAK, K.-J. 1973. *Der Einsatz privater Garden in der späten römischen Republik.* Munich: Nowak.

OAKLEY, S. P. 1998. *A Commentary on Livy, Books VI-X,* vol. 2: *Books VII-VIII.* Oxford: Clarendon Press.

OGILVIE, R. M. (ed.). 1965. *A Commentary on Livy, Books 1–5.* Oxford: Clarendon Press.

OOST, S. I. 1955. Cato Uticensis and the Annexation of Cyprus. *Classical Philology* 50: 98–112.

OPELT, I. 1965. *Die lateinischen Schimpfwörter und verwandte sprachliche Erscheinungen.* Heidelberg: C. Winter.

OTTO, A. 1890. *Die Sprichwörter und sprichwörtlichen Redensarten der Römer.* Leipzig: B. G. Teubner.

PAANANEN, U. 1993. Legislation in the *comitia centuriata. Senatus Populusque Romanus: Studies in Roman Republican Legislation.* Acta Instituti Romani Finnlandiae 13. Helsinki: [s.n.], 9–73.

PATERSON, J. 2004. Self-Reference in Cicero's Forensic Speeches. In J. Powell and J. Paterson (eds.), *Cicero the Advocate.* Oxford: Oxford University Press, 79–95.

PELLING, C. 1989. Rowland and Cullens on Corn-Doles. *Liverpool Classical Monthly* 14: 117–19.

PERELLI, L. 1972. La definizione e l'origine dello stato nel pensiero di Cicerone. *Atti della Accademia delle Scienze di Torino.* 2, Classe di Scienze Morali, Storiche e Filologiche, 106: 281–309.

PETTIT, P. 1997. *Republicanism: A Theory of Freedom and Government.* Oxford: Oxford University Press.

PINA POLO, F. 1989. *Las contiones civiles y militares en Roma.* Zaragoza: Departamento de Ciencias de la Antiguedad, Universidad de Zaragoza.

—— 1996. *Contra Arma Verbis: Der Redner vor dem Volk in der späten römischen Republik.* Heidelberger Althistorische Beiträge und Epigraphische Studien, 22. Stuttgart: F. Steiner.

PISCITELLI CARCOPINO, T. 1979. *Dignitas* in Cicerone: Tra semantica e semiologia. *Bollettino di studi latini* 9: 253–67.

POCOCK, L. G. 1926. *A Commentary on Cicero 'In Vatinium'.* London: University of London Press.

POHL, H. 1993. *Die römische Politik und die Piratie im östlichen Mittelmeer vom 3. bis zum 1. Jh. v. Chr.* Untersuchungen zur antiken Literatur und Geschichte, 42. Berlin: Walter de Gruyter.

POWELL, J., and J. PATERSON (eds.). 2004. *Cicero the Advocate.* Oxford: Oxford University Press.

PURCELL, N. 1983. The *Apparitores*: A Study in Social Mobility. *Proceedings of the British School in Rome* 51: 125–73.

RADKE, G. 1987. *Zur Entwicklung der Gottesvorstellung und der Gottesverehrung in Rom.* Darmstadt: Wissenschaftliche Buchgesellschaft.

RAMSEY, J. T. 2001. Did Mark Antony Contemplate an Alliance with His Political Enemies? *Classical Philology* 96: 253–68.

RANKIN, H. D. 1976. Catullus and Incest. *Eranos* 74: 113–21.

RAWSON, B. 2003. *Children and Childhood in Roman Italy.* Oxford: Oxford University Press.

RAWSON, E. 1975. *Cicero: A Portrait.* Ithaca, NY: Cornell University Press.

—— 1985. *Intellectual Life in the Late Roman Republic.* Baltimore, MD: The Johns Hopkins University Press.

—— 1991. Theatrical Life in Republican Rome and Italy. *Roman Culture and Society.* Oxford: Oxford University Press, 468–87.

REGGIANI, R. 1991. Dare a Cesare . . : nota a Cic. Sest. 133. *Paideia* 46: 44–5.

REYNOLDS, J. 1982. *Aphrodisias and Rome.* Journal of Roman Studies monographs no. 1. London: Roman Society.

RHODES, P. J. 1981. *A Commentary on the Aristotelian 'Athenaion Politeia'.* Oxford: Oxford University Press.

RICHARDSON, J. S. 1991. *Imperium Romanum*: Empire and the Language of Power. *Journal of Roman Studies* 81: 1–9.

RICHARDSON, L. 2001. *Sestius noster.* In N. W. Goldman (ed.), *New Light from Ancient Cosa: Classical Mediterranean Studies in Honor of Cleo Rickman Fitch.* Bern and Frankfurt am Main: Peter Lang, 49–55.

RICKMAN, G. 1980. *The Corn Supply of Ancient Rome.* Oxford: Oxford University Press.

RIEMER, U. 2001. *Das Caesarbild Ciceros.* Schriftenreihe Studien zur Geschichtsforschung des Altertums, Bd. 8; Studien zur Geschichtsforschung des Altertums, Bd. 8. Hamburg: Kovac.

RIGGSBY, A. 1999. *Crime and Community in Ciceronian Rome.* Austin, Tex: University of Texas Press.

—— 2002*a*. The *Post Reditum* Speeches. In J. May (ed.), *Brill's Companion to Cicero: Oratory and Rhetoric.* Leiden: E. J. Brill, 159–95.

—— 2002*b*. Clodius / Claudius. *Historia* 51: 117–23.

RIGGSBY, A. 2004. The Rhetoric of Character in the Roman Courts. In J. Powell and J. Paterson (eds.), *Cicero the Advocate*. Oxford: Oxford University Press, 165–85.

ROBINSON, A. W. 1994*a*. Cicero's Use of the Gracchi in Two Speeches before the People. *Atene e Roma* 39 (2–3): 71–6.

—— 1994*b*. Cicero's References to His Banishment. *Classical World* 87: 475–80.

ROBINSON, O. F. 1995. *The Criminal Law of Ancient Rome*. Baltimore: Johns Hopkins University Press.

ROLLER, M. 2004. Exemplarity in Roman Culture: The Cases of Horatius Cocles and Cloelia. *Classical Philology* 99: 1–56.

ROTONDI, G. 1912. *Leges Publicae Populi Romani*. Milan: Società editrice libraria.

ROUSSELLE, A. 1983. *Porneia: On Desire and the Body in Antiquity*. Oxford: Basil Blackwell.

RUBINSOHN, W. Z. 1993. Mithridates VI Eupator Dionysos and Rome's Conquest of the Hellenistic East. *Mediterranean Historical Review* 8: 5–54.

RÜPKE, J. 1995. *Kalender und Öffentlichkeit: Die Geschichte der Repräsentation und religiösen Qualifikation von Zeit in Rom*. Religionsgeschichtliche Versuche und Vorarbeiten, 40. Berlin: Walter de Gruyter.

RYAN, F. X. 1998. *Rank and Participation in the Republican Senate*. Stuttgart: F. Steiner.

SALERNO, F. 1984–5. *Collegia adversus rem publicam?* In V. Giuffrè (ed.), *Sodalitas: Scritti in onore di Antonio Guarino*, vol. 2. Naples: Jovene, 615–31.

SALLER, R. P. 1986. *Patria potestas* and the Stereotype of the Roman Family. *Continuity and Change* 1:7–22.

—— 1994. *Patriarchy, Property and Death in the Roman Family*. Cambridge: Cambridge University Press.

SCHÄFER, T. 1989. *Imperii insignia, sella curulis und fasces: Zur Repräsentation römischer Magistrate*. Mitteilungen des Deutschen Archaeologischen Instituts, Roemische Abteilung, 29. Mainz: P. von Zaben.

SCHLEUSSNER, B. 1978. *Die Legaten der römischen Republik*. Vestigia, 26. Munich: Beck.

SCHMITZ, D. 1985. *Zeugen des Prozeßgegners in Gerichtsreden Ciceros*. Prismata, 1. Frankfurt-am-Main: Peter Lang.

SCHOFIELD, M. 1995. Cicero's Definition of *Res Publica*. In J. G. F. Powell (ed.), *Cicero the Philosopher*. Oxford: Oxford University Press, 63–83.

SCULLARD, H. H. 1981. *Festivals and Ceremonies of the Roman Republic*. London: Thames and Hudson.

SEAGER, R. 1969. Rev. of Grimal 1967. *Journal of Roman Studies* 59: 309–10.

—— 1972. Cicero and the Word *popularis*. *Classical Quarterly* 22: 328–38.

—— 2002. *Pompey: A Political Biography*. 2nd edn. Berkeley, Calif.: University of California Press.

SEDLEY, D. 1997. The Ethics of Brutus and Cassius. *Journal of Roman Studies* 87: 41–53.

SEHLMEYER, M. 1999. *Stadtrömische Ehrenstatuen der republikanischen Zeit: Historizität und Kontext von Symbolen nobilitären Standesbewusstseins*. Historia. Einzelschriften, 130. Stuttgart: F. Steiner.

SHACKLETON. BAILEY, D. R. 1960. Sex. Clodius—Sex. Cloelius. *Classical Quarterly* 10: 41–2.

—— 1977. Brothers or Cousins? *American Journal of Ancient History* 2: 148–50.

—— 1979. On Cicero's Speeches. *Harvard Studies in Classical Phiology*. 83: 237–85.

—— 1985. More on Cicero's Speeches (*Post reditum*). *Harvard Studies in Classical Philology* 89: 141–51.

—— 1986. *Nobiles* and *Novi* Reconsidered. *American Journal of Philology* 107: 255–60.

—— 1987. On Cicero's Speeches (*Post Reditum*). *Transactions of the American Philological Association* 117: 271–80.

—— 1989. Albanius or Albinius? A Palinode Resung. *Harvard Studies in Classical Philology* 92: 213–14.

—— 1991a. *Cicero, Back from Exile: Six Speeches on His Return*. American Philological Association Classical Resources Series, 4. Atlanta: Scholars Press.

—— 1991b. *Two Studies in Roman Nomenclature*. American Philological Association Monographs. Chico, Calif.

—— 1992. *Onomasticon to Cicero's Speeches*. 2nd edn. Stuttgart: B. G. Teubner.

SHARPLES, R. W. 1996. *Stoics, Epicureans, and Sceptics: An Introduction to Hellenistic Philosophy*. London: Routledge.

SHERWIN-WHITE, A. N. 1973. *The Roman Citizenship*. 2nd edn. Oxford: Oxford University Press.

SHERWIN-WHITE, A.N. 1994. Lucullus, Pompey, and the East. *Cambridge Ancient History*. Vol. 9, 2nd edn. Cambridge: Cambridge University Press, 229–73.

SIANI-DAVIES, M. 2001. *Cicero's Speech 'Pro Rabirio Postumo'.* Clarendon Ancient History Series. Oxford: Oxford University Press.

SINKOVICH, K. A. 1976. Mythological Comparisons in Cicero. *Rivista di studi classici* 24: 187–9.

SKIDMORE, C. 1996. *Practical Ethics for Roman Gentlemen: The Work of Valerius Maximus*. Exeter: University of Exeter Press.

458 *References*

SKINNER, M. 1982. Pretty Lesbius. *Transactions of the American Philological Association* 112: 197–208.

SKINNER, Q. 1998. *Liberty before Liberalism.* Cambridge: Cambridge University Press.

SKUTSCH, O. 1943. Cicero, *Pro Sestio* 72 Again (Continued). *Classical Review* 57: 67.

STÄRK, E. 2000. Politische Anspielungen in der römischen Tragödie und der Einfluß der Schauspieler. In G. Manuwald (ed.), *Identität und Alterität in der frührömischen Tragödie.* Würzburg: Egon, 123–33.

STARR, R. J. 1990–1. Reading Aloud: *Lectores* and Roman Reading. *Classical Journal* 86: 337–43.

STE. CROIX, G. E. M. DE. 1981. *The Class Struggle in the Ancient World.* Ithaca, NY: Cornell University Press.

STEEL, C. 2001. *Cicero, Rhetoric, and Empire.* Oxford: Oxford University Press.

—— 2005. *Reading Cicero: Genre and Performance in Late Republican Rome.* London: Duckworth.

STEIN, P. 1930. *Die Senatssitzungen der Ciceronischen Zeit (68–43).* Münster: Westfälische Vereinsdruckerei.

STEMMLER, M. 2000. *Auctoritas exempli:* Zur Wechselwirkung von kanonisierten Vergangenheitsbildern und gesellschaftlicher Gegenwart in der spätrepublikanischen Rhetorik. In B. Linke and M. Stemmler (eds.), *Mos maiorum: Untersuchungen zu den Formen der Identitätsstiftung und Stabilisierung in der Römischen Republik.* Historia. Einzelschriften, 141. Stuttgart: F. Steiner, 141–205.

STRIKER, G. 1987. Origins of the Concept of Natural Law. In J. J. Cleary (ed.), *Proceedings of the Boston Area Colloquium in Ancient Philosophy,* vol. 2. Lanham, MD: University Press of America, 79–84.

STROH, W. 1975. *Taxis und Taktik: Die advokatische Dispositionskunst in Ciceros Gerichtsreden.* Stuttgart: B. G. Teubner.

—— 2004. *De Domo Sua:* Legal Problem and Structure. In J. Powell and J. Paterson (eds.), *Cicero the Advocate.* Oxford: Oxford University Press, 313–70.

SULLIVAN, F. A. 1941. Cicero and Glory. *Transactions of the American Philological Association* 72: 382–91.

SULLIVAN, R. D. 1990. *Near Eastern Royalty and Rome, 100–30 B.C.* Phoenix Supplementary volume 24. Toronto: University of Toronto Press.

SUMNER, G. V. 1963. *Lex Aelia, Lex Fufia. American Journal of Philology* 84: 337–58.

SUOLAHTI, J. 1955. *Junior Officers of the Roman Army in the Republican Period.* Annales Academiae Scientiarum Fennica 97. Helsinki: Suomalainen Tiedeakatemia.

SUOLAHTI, J. 1972. *Princeps Senatus. Arctos* 7: 207–18.

SWAIN, S. 2002. Bilingualism in Cicero? The Evidence of Code-Switching. In J. N. Adams, M. Janse, and S. Swain (eds.), *Bilingualism in Ancient Society: Language Contact and the Written Word.* Oxford: Oxford University Press, 128–67.

SYME, R. 1986. *The Augustan Aristocracy.* Oxford: Oxford University Press.

TAKAHATA, T. 1999. Politik—Philosophie—Rhetorik in *cum dignitate otium* Ciceros. *Classical Studies* 16: 60–97.

TATUM, W. J. 1990a. Another Look at the Spectators at the Roman Games. *Ancient History Bulletin* 4 (5): 104–7.

—— 1990b. Publius Clodius Pulcher and Tarracina. *Zeitschrift für Papyrologie und Epigraphik* 83: 299–304.

—— 1993. Catullus 79: Personal Invective or Political Discourse. *Papers of the Leeds International Latin Seminar* 7: 31–45.

—— 1999. *The Patrician Tribune: Publius Clodius Pulcher.* Chapel Hill, NC: University of North Carolina Press.

TAYLOR, L. R. 1960. *The Voting Districts of the Roman Republic.* Rome: American Academy.

—— 1966. *Roman Voting Assemblies from the Hannibalic War to the Dictatorship of Caesar.* Ann Arbor, Mich.: University of Michigan Press.

THOMAS, J.-F. 1994. Un groupe sémantique: *gloria, laus, decus.* In C. Moussy (ed.), *Les problèmes de la synonomie en latin.* Paris: Presses de l'Université de Paris-Sorbonne, 91–100.

THOMASSON, B. E. 1991. *Legatus: Beiträge zur römischen Verwaltungsgeschichte.* Acta Instituti Romani Regni Sueciae, ser. 8°, 18. Stockholm: Svenska institutet i Rom.

THOME, G. 2000. *Zentrale Wertvorstellungen der Römer II.* Auxilia. Bamberg: C. C. Buchners Verlag, 117–34.

THOMMEN, L. 1989. *Das Volkstribunat der späten römischen Republik.* Historia Einzelschriften 59. Wiesbaden: F. Steiner.

TREGGIARI, S. 1969. *Roman Freedmen during the Late Republic.* Oxford: Oxford University Press.

—— 1973. Cicero, Horace, and Mutual Friends: Lamiae and Varrones Murenae. *Phoenix* 27: 245–61.

—— 1991. *Roman Marriage: Iusti Coniuges from the Time of Cicero to the Time of Ulpian.* Oxford: Oxford University Press.

—— 1998. Home and Forum: Cicero between 'Public' and 'Private'. *Transactions of the American Philological Association* 128: 1–23.

—— 2002. *Roman Social History.* London: Routledge.

—— 2003. Ancestral Virtues and Vices: Cicero on Nature, Nurture, and Presentation. In D. Braund and C. Gill (eds.), *Myth, History and Culture in Republican Rome: Studies in Honour of T. P. Wiseman*. Exeter: University of Exeter Press, 139–64.

ULRICH, R. B. 1994. *The Roman Orator and the Sacred Stage: The Roman Templum Rostratum*. Collection Latomus 222. Brussels: Latomus.

UNGERN-STERNBERG, J. VON. 1970. *Untersuchungen zum spätrepublikanischen Notstandsrecht. Senatusconsultum ultimum und hostis-Erklärung.* Vestigia, Band 11. Munich: Beck.

VANDERBROECK, P. J. J. 1987. *Popular Leadership and Collective Behavior in the Late Roman Republic (ca. 80–50 B.C.)*. Dutch Monographs on Ancient History and Archaeology, 3. Amsterdam: J. C. Gieben.

VASALY, A. 1993. *Representations: Images of the World in Ciceronian Oratory.* Berkeley, Calif.: University of California Press.

VERSNEL, H. 1976. Two Types of Roman *devotio. Mnemosyne* 29: 365–410.

—— 1980. Self-sacrifice, Compensation and the Anonymous Gods. *Le sacrifice dans l'antiquité*. Entretiens Hardt, 27. Geneva: Vandoeuvres, 135–94.

VILLE, G. 1981. *La gladiature en Occident des origines à la mort de Domitien.* Rome: École française de Rome.

WALLACE-HADRILL, A. 1994. *Houses and Society in Pompeii and Herculaneum.* Princeton: Princeton University Press.

WARD, A. M. 1977. *Marcus Crassus and the Late Roman Republic.* Columbia, Mo.: University of Missouri Press.

WATSON, A. 1965. *The Law of Obligations in the Late Roman Republic.* Oxford: Oxford University Press.

—— 1967. *The Law of Persons in the Late Roman Republic.* Oxford: Oxford University Press.

—— 1974. *Law Making In the Later Roman Republic.* Oxford: Oxford University Press.

WATT, W. S. (ed.). 1988. *Vellei Paterculi historiarum ad M. Vinicium consulem libri duo.* Leipzig: B. G. Teubner.

WEBB, RUTH. 1997. Imagination and the Arousal of the Emotions in Greco-Roman Rhetoric. In S. M. Braund and C. Gill (eds.), *The Passions in Roman Thought and Literature.* Cambridge: Cambridge University Press. 112–27.

WEGEHAUPT, H. 1932. Die Bedeutung und Anwendung von *dignitas* in den Schriften der republikanischen Zeit. Diss. Breslau.

WEINRIB, E. 1970. *Obnuntiatio*: Two Problems. *Zeitschrift der Savigny-Stiftung für Rechtsgeschichte. Romanistische Abteilung* 87: 396–425.

WEISCHE, A. 1966. *Studien zur politischen Sprache der römischen Republik.* Münster: Aschendorff.

—— 1970. Philosophie grecque et politique romaine dans la partie finale du *Pro Sestio. Bulletin de l'Association Guillaume Budé*, 483–8.

—— 1972. *Ciceros Nachahmung der attischen Redner*. Bibliothek der klassischen Altertumswissenschaft, 45. Heidelberg: C. Winter.

WICKERT, L. 1974. Neue Forschungen zum Principat. *Aufstieg und Niedergang der römischen Welt*. 2. 1. Berlin, 3–76.

WIEDEMANN, T. 1992. *Emperors and Gladiators*. London: Routledge.

WILL, E. L. 1979. The Sestius Amphoras. A Reappraisal. *Journal of Field Archaeology* 6: 339–50.

WILLIAMSON, C. 2005. *The Laws of the Roman People: Public Law in the Expansion and Decline of the Roman Republic*. Ann Arbor, Mich.: University of Michigan Press.

WILSON, L. M. 1938. *The Clothing of the Ancient Romans*. Baltimore: The Johns Hopkins University Press.

WINKES, R. 1973. Probleme der Charakterinterpretation römischer Porträts. *Aufstieg und Niedergang der römischen Welt* 1. 4. Berlin, 899–926.

WINKLER, L. 1995. *Salus: Vom Staatskult zur politischen Idee*. Archäologie und Geschichte, 4. Heidelberg: Verlag Archäologie und Geschichte.

WINTERBOTTOM, M. 2004. Perorations. In J. Powell and J. Paterson (eds.), *Cicero the Advocate*. Oxford: Oxford University Press. 215–30.

WIRSZUBSKI, C. 1950. *Libertas as a Political Idea at Rome during the Late Republic and Early Principate*. Cambridge: Cambridge University Press.

—— 1954. Cicero's *cum Dignitate Otium*: A Reconsideration. *Journal of Roman Studies* 44: 1–13.

—— 1961. *Audaces*: A Study in Political Phraseology. *Journal of Roman Studies* 51: 12–22.

WISEMAN, T. P. 1969. *Catullan Questions*. Leicester: Leicester University Press.

—— 1971. *New Men in the Roman Senate, 139 B.C.–14 A.D.* Oxford: Oxford University Press.

—— 1974. Who Was Gellius? *Cinna the Poet and Other Roman Essays*. Leicester: Leicester University Press. 119–29.

—— 1985. *Catullus and His World: A Reappraisal*. Cambridge: Cambridge University Press.

—— 1987. *Roman Studies: Literary and Historical*. Liverpool: F. Cairns.

—— 1994a. The Senate and the *populares*, 69–60 B.C.. *Cambridge Ancient History*. vol. 9, 2nd edn. Cambridge: Cambridge University Press, 327–67.

—— 1994b. Caesar, Pompey and Rome, 59–50 B.C. *Cambridge Ancient History*. vol. 9, 2nd edn. Cambridge: Cambridge University Press, 368–423.

—— 1998. *Roman Drama and Roman History*. Exeter: University of Exeter Press.

462   *References*

WISEMAN, T. P. 2002. Roman History and the Ideological Vacuum. In T. P. Wiseman (ed.), *Classics in Progress: Essays on Ancient Greece and Rome.* Oxford: Oxford University Press, 285–310.

WISSE, J. 1989. *Ethos and Pathos from Aristotle to Cicero.* Amsterdam: Hakkert.

WISSOWA, G. 1912. *Religion und Kultus der Römer.* 2. Aufl. Handbuch der klassischen Altertumswissenschaft, 5. 4. Munich: C. H. Beck.

WOOD, N. 1988. *Cicero's Social and Political Thought.* Berkeley, Calif.: University of California Press.

WOOTEN, C. (ed.). 2001. *The Orator in Action and Theory in Greece and Rome.* Mnemosyne Suppl., 225. Leiden: E. J. Brill.

YAKOBSON, A. 1995. Secret Ballot and Its Effects in the Late Roman Republic. *Hermes* 123: 426–42.

ZETZEL, J. E. G. 1996. Natural Law and Poetic Justice: A Carneadean Debate in Cicero and Virgil. *Classical Philology* 91: 297–319.

ZORZETTI, N. 1980. *La pretesta e il teatro latino arcaico.* Naples: Liguori.

INDEX

This index refers, by page-number, to the Introduction, Commentary, Appendixes, and Glossary; for individuals named or referred to in the text of the speech itself, see the list of Persons, where reference is by section-number. Men and women who participated in Roman public life are listed here by clan-name (*nomen gentilicium*), with the *RE* number (where available) given in parentheses.

as leader of 'pirates', 221

as 'public enemy', 365

assails Milo early in 57, 275, 292

assails Milo late in 57, 11, 301,
315

attacked by Cicero as 'new
Catiline', 4, 26, 110

attempted assassination of
Pompey, 149, 268–9

breaks with Pompey and
Gabinius, 13, 246, 251, 265,
268, 275, 300, 306, 397

candidate for aedileship, 349

censorship allegedly annulled by,
195, 243

compared with Catiline, 4, 16,
146, 184, 199, 217–18, 341,
396 n. 5

consecrates goods of Gabinius,
266

conspires with consuls of 58,
12–13, 145–75 passim, 239,
255

contio convened by, 183

contio of, in circus Flaminius,
193–4, 372, 395–6

dedicates shrine of Liberty, 261,
315, 335

destroys Cicero's house, 112

drives Cicero into exile, 3–4, 6–9
and *passim*

elected aedile, 11, 403

funded by Crassus in 56, 212

goods of, consecrated by Lucius
Ninnius, 266

instigates Sestius' prosection, 11,
291

insulted as 'actor', 347

invective against, 145–52

joined by Cicero in defense of
Scaurus, 118

legislation of, 8–9, 112, 112, 172,
174–5, 188, 192, 194–7,
199–201, 222, 238–64
passim, 395

makes 'pact' with consuls for
provincial assignment,
171–3

mocked as cross-dresser, 348

motive of, for mandating Cyprus'
annexation to Cato, 252–3

murdered by Milo, 302

not named by Cicero, 145–6

offenses against human and
divine institutions of, 112

plebeian status sought by, 4 n. 7,
6–7

political use of clubs by, 199–200

profanes Bona Dea rites, 3–4,
112, 146–7, 179, 209, 264,
305, 349, 409–10

prosecutes Milo, 11, 314, 403

prosecutions of, attempted by
Milo in 57, 31, 301–6,
315–17

protects Vatinius, as tribune,
377

right of veto allegedly annulled
by, 195, 197

seeks tribunate of the plebs, 6–7

speaks at *contio* before vote for
Cicero's recall, 334

still threatens Cicero after his
return, 11, 199, 315, 402

supplicates senate, 180

supports Cicero in 63, 146

transfer to the plebs of, 6–7,
145–52

aided by Pompey, 6, 13, 148,
150

trial of, for sacrilege, 4

turns against Metellus Nepos, 316